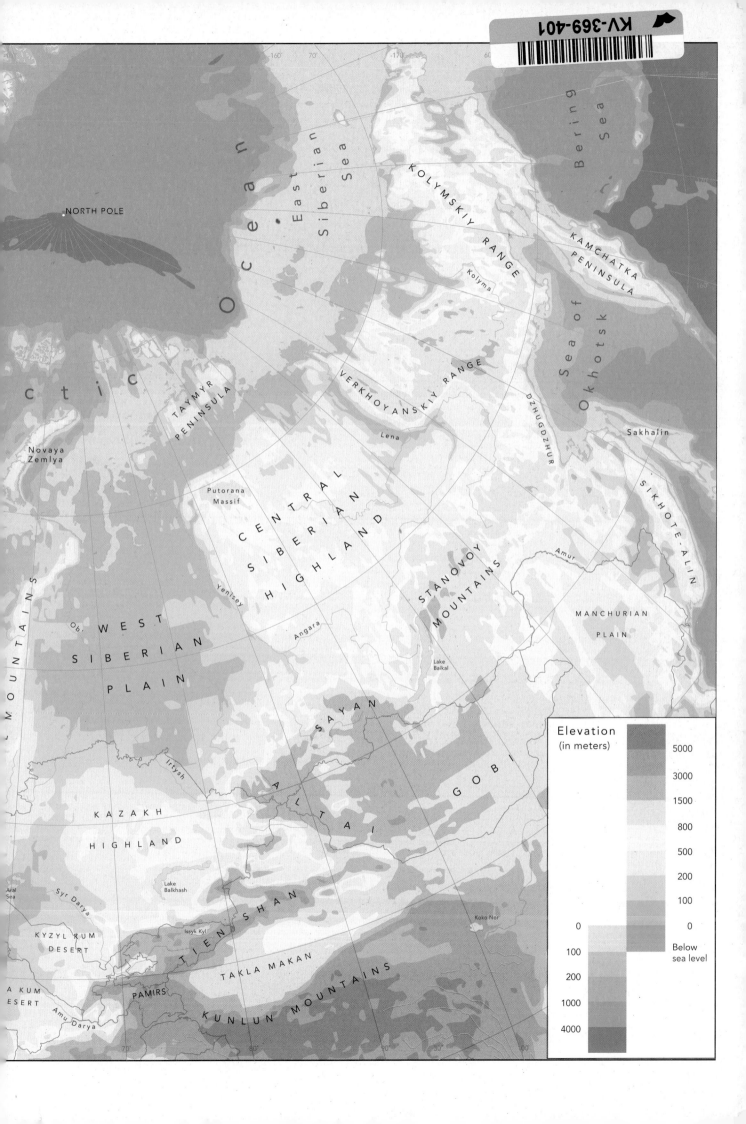

NORTH POLE

O c e a n

East
Siberian
Sea

KOLYMSKIY RANGE

Kolyma

Bering
Sea

KAMCHATKA
PENINSULA

c t i c

Sea
of
Okhotsk

TAYMYR
PENINSULA

VERKHOYANSKIY RANGE

DZHUGDZHUR

Sakhalin

Novaya
Zemlya

Lena

Putorana
Massif

C E N T R A L

S I B E R I A N

H I G H L A N D

STANOVOY
MOUNTAINS

Amur

SIKHOTE-ALIN

M O U N T A I N S

Ob

W E S T

S I B E R I A N

P L A I N

Yenisey

Angara

Lake
Baikal

MANCHURIAN
PLAIN

S A Y A N

Irtysh

A L T A I

G O B I

KAZAKH

HIGHLAND

Aral
Sea

Syr Darya

Lake
Balkhash

Issyk Kyl

Koko Nor

KYZYL KUM
DESERT

T I E N   S H A N

A KUM
ESERT

PAMIRS

TAKLA MAKAN

Amu Darya

K U N L U N   M O U N T A I N S

Elevation (in meters)	
	5000
	3000
	1500
	800
	500
	200
	100
0	0
100	Below sea level
200	
1000	
4000	

Europe's environment:
the third assessment

European Environment Agency

Cover: Painting by Judit Szècsi and Anita Guti, 13 years old, Atalanos Iskola, Szeged,
Hungary. Awarded first prize by Royal Award Foundation in European environment illustration
contest, 2002.
Layout: Folkmann Design A/S

Legal notice

A great deal of information on the European Union is available on the Internet. It can be
accessed through the Europa server (http://europa.eu.int).

Cataloguing data can be found at the end of this publication.

Luxembourg: Office for Official Publications of the European Communities, 2003

ISBN 92-9167-574-1

Environmental production
This publication is printed according to the highest environmental standards.
Printed in Denmark by Scanprint A/S
Environment certificate: ISO 14001
Quality certificate: ISO 9001: 2000
EMAS registered: Licence no. DK- S-000015
Approved for printing with the Nordic Swan environmental label, licence no. 541 055
Printed on recycled and chlorine-free bleached paper

European Environment Agency
Kongens Nytorv 6
DK-1050 Copenhagen K
Denmark
Tel: (45) 33 36 71 00
Fax: (45) 33 36 71 99
E-mail: eea@eea.eu.int
http://www.eea.eu.int

Contents

Foreword

This is the third assessment of the state of the environment at the pan-European level prepared by the European Environment Agency in support of the UN-ECE Environment for Europe process, with the help of the UN-ECE ad hoc working group on environmental monitoring. It follows earlier reports published in 1995 and 1998 for the same purpose. The second report made clear that the policy measures that had been taken up to the mid-1990s had not yet produced a significant improvement in the state of the environment overall. This, the third assessment, shows that most progress on environmental improvement continues to come from 'end-of-pipe' measures, actions under well-established international conventions and legislation, or as a result of economic recession and restructuring.

We know from the past that these gains will be lost again if economic growth continues to be based on traditional, environmentally damaging activities, still prevalent, rather than on more sustainable, eco-efficient options. This is a particular risk for the EU accession countries and countries in eastern Europe, Caucasus and central Asia to which large amounts of manufacturing industry have been transferred from western Europe and elsewhere in the world.

In this context, moving towards more sustainable approaches seems to be more aspiration than reality in many parts of Europe. Progress has been made on developing policy frameworks for sectoral integration (e.g. EU strategies being developed under the Cardiff process since 1998) and for sustainable development (e.g. the action plan from the Johannesburg world summit on sustainable development in 2002). There has been less progress on implementation and substantial barriers to real progress remain, both political and financial.

The EU sustainable development strategy is a step in the right direction but needs more operational action by the relatively well-off Member States to remain environmentally credible. The accession countries face the major challenge of managing with limited resources, and against competing economic, social and environmental priorities, the transitions to EU membership, sectoral integration and sustainable development all at the same time. The EECCA countries have a much lower GDP per capita than elsewhere in Europe, but arguably greater and competing calls on limited resources, yet have relatively limited access to capital markets for finance to improve social and environmental welfare.

Better coordination and use of existing funding sources and mechanisms available at the European level would help overcome some of these problems but what is most lacking is a decision-making framework that takes proper account of the competing but often complementary economic, social and environmental considerations. The various initiatives on European regional energy co-operation are a good example of such a framework in action. Account is taken of overall welfare considerations when making decisions (e.g. the role of renewable sources, issues of fuel poverty, and not just of economic considerations (e.g. increased energy supply from fossil fuels to meet increasing demand).

In such a framework though, trade-offs are just one side of the coin; the time dimension is also important. The timespan of five years between the second and third assessments is a short one for gauging progress. The time perspectives are much longer between early warnings of a problem, its scientific identification, political recognition and action, and resulting environmental improvements, as demonstrated by the development of air quality and acidification in Europe, substantially related to sulphur emissions, and the success story to date of pan-European cooperation.

Early warnings were available into the 1950s (London smog) and 1960s (acidification of Scandinavian lakes and rivers); initial international recognition was reached at the Stockholm UN environment conference in 1972; major policy initiatives were adopted in 1979 (Convention on long-range transboundary air pollution) and 1980 (first EU air quality directive); and action under Convention protocols and EU directives took effect during the

1980s and 1990s. The latest projections available indicate that there should be a return to sustainable air quality concentrations for sulphur dioxide and deposition rates for sulphur after about 2012, 40 years after initial recognition of the issue and over 100 years after sulphur emissions first exceeded sustainable rates across the pan-European space.

Many of the other environmental issues reviewed in this report are more complex and will require recognition and action by a wider range of players than was necessary for sulphur emissions. Examples include climate change, biodiversity loss, and soil degradation. The start of the Kyoto Protocol target period for limiting greenhouse gas emissions is now five years away and additional measures, not yet agreed, will be necessary to reach the targets in many countries; the target date for (significantly) halting biodiversity loss is only seven years away and there is no agreement yet on how to measure and monitor biodiversity loss; and strategies to prevent soil degradation have yet to be agreed. New approaches such as the precautionary principle and the EU's proposal on impact assessment should be considered further to help reduce the lead times between early warnings, scientific and policy action and resulting improvements.

Both the integrative nature of the above problems and the implementation of approaches like the precautionary principle, have major implications for the design and content of the monitoring and assessments systems that are needed to track progress and to indicate where more attention is required. In the face of increasing demands for information by policy makers, including issues involving much scientific uncertainty, and decreasing resources for monitoring in member states, some new thinking is required. For example, a better balance needs to be struck between efforts put into producing information through traditional approaches to monitoring and assessment and more recent ones. Examples of these relatively new approaches in the pan-European context include tissue-based monitoring of health impacts, the identification of biomarkers as the basis for considering wider impacts, the use of upstream proxy indicators for assessing downstream environmental impacts and, wider use of explorative and quantitative based scenarios tools. The EEA is fully ready to engage in processes that involve such new thinking.

Finally I would like to recognise the substantial progress in cooperation and provision of relevant data and information for this report, particularly (but not only) from the EU candidate countries and EECCA countries. There is a long way still to go and many gaps and inconsistencies remain in the information presented in this report. However we are making progress with countries and international programmes in the development of an increasingly focussed, streamlined and shared European environmental information system. On behalf of the European Environment Agency, I look forward to developing this vision, to monitoring progress in policies, action and outcomes and hence to supporting the environmental programme for Europe, in whatever form it continues after the Kiev Ministerial Conference.

I trust that this report will contribute to both the understanding of where we are in the sequence from early warning to resolution of the various prominent environmental problems facing Europe and to the decision-making required to restore and maintain environmental quality and achieve sustainable development

Gordon McInnes
Interim Executive Director
European Environment Agency

Acknowledgements

The report was written with the collaboration of a large number of individuals. This list serves to acknowledge their work. However, the responsibility for the assessment rests with the European Environment Agency (EEA). The editors apologise for the involuntary omission of any individual who contributed to the report.

National contact points and other national contributors

Albania:
Narin Panariti
Armenia:
Gennadi Kojoyan, Tamara Hovhannissian
Austria:
Bettina Götz, Johannes Mayer
Azerbaijan:
Gilinjkhan Hajiyev
Belarus:
Svetlana P. Utochkina
Belgium:
Eddie Muylle, Lore van Eylen, Marleen van Steertegem, Jan Voet
Bosnia-Herzegovina:
Mladen Rudez, Mehmed Cero
Bulgaria:
Krassimira Avranova, Svetlana Zhekova
Croatia:
Monica Trsic, Ivana Mijatovic
Cyprus:
Christina Pantazi, Antonis Antoniou
Czech Republic:
Erich Lippert, Klara Quasnitzova, Josef Sejak
Denmark:
Torben Moth Iversen, Bjarne Norup
Estonia:
Ott Roots, Leo Saare
Finland:
Pertti Heinonen, Tapani Säynätkari
Former Yugoslav Republic of Macedonia:
Darko Blinkov, Svetlana Gjorgjeva
France:
Philippe Crouzet, Thierry Pontille
Georgia:
Nino Sharashidze
Germany:
Barbara Clark, Christoph Schlüter
Greece:
Mata Aravantinou
Hungary:
Elemer Szabo, Pál Bozo
Iceland:
Ólafur Pétursson

Ireland:
Larry Stapleton
Italy:
Laura Migliorini, Claudio Maricchiolo
Kazakhstan:
Sapar Bazarbayev
Kyrgyzstan:
Omor Rustembekov
Latvia:
Ilze Kirstuka
Liechtenstein:
Hermann Schmuck
Lithuania:
Juozas Molis, Liutauras Stoskus
Luxembourg:
Eric De Brabanter
Malta:
Louis Vella
Moldova, Republic of:
Petru Cocirță
Monaco:
Wilfrid Deri
Netherlands:
Jan van der Plas, Pieter van der Most, Roel Thomas
Norway:
Oystein Nesje, Johnny Auestad
Poland:
Lucyna Dygas-Ciolkowska
Portugal:
Maria Leonor Gomes
Romania:
Silviu Stoica, Cornel Florea Gabrian, Dalia Maier
Russian Federation:
Olga A. Novosselova, Yuri S. Tsaturov, Valery Chelyukanov, Alexandr A. Chekhovtsov
Serbia and Montenegro:
Irena Mitrovic
Slovak Republic:
Vladimir Benko
Slovenia:
Anita Pirc-Velkavrh, Irena Rejec Brancelj
Spain:
Fransisco Cadarso, Juan Martínez Sánchez
Sweden:
Y. W. Brodin, Bernt Röndell
Switzerland:
Jean-Michel Gardaz, Nicolas Perritaz
Tajikistan:
Taginisso Nassirova
Turkey:
Irem Sesenoglu, Cumali Yüksek
Turkmenistan:
Irina Atamuradova

Ukraine:
Oleh Velychko
United Kingdom:
Stan Speller
Uzbekistan:
Nariman Umarov

European Commission contacts
Contact point: Hans Stielstra (Directorate-General (DG) Environment)

Contributions received from Commission services (DG Enterprise, DG Energy and Transport, DG External Relations, DG Fisheries, DG Environment)

Contributors by chapter

Chapter 1 Introduction
Coordination and authors:
Ronan Uhel, Peter Bosch, Jock Martin (EEA)

Chapter 2.0 Material flows
Coordination:
Pawel Kazmierczyk (EEA)
Authors:
Stephan Moll, Stefan Bringezu (Wuppertal Institute)

Chapter 2.1 Energy
Coordination:
Ian Smith, Aphrodite Mourelatou (EEA)
Author:
George Marsh (AEA Technology, United Kingdom)

Chapter 2.2 Industry
Coordination:
Ronan Uhel (EEA)
Author:
Sander de Bruyn (CE Solutions for environment, economy and technology, Netherlands)

Chapter 2.3 Agriculture
Coordination:
Jan-Erik Petersen, Peder Gabrielsen (EEA)
Authors:
Simon Turner, Harriet Bennett (ADAS Consulting Ltd, United Kingdom)

Chapter 2.4 Forestry
Coordination
Tor-Björn Larsson (EEA)
Authors:
Mercedes Rois Díaz, Andreas Schuck (European Forest Institute, Finland)

Chapter 2.5   Fisheries and aquaculture
Coordination:
Anita Künitzer (EEA)
Authors:
Crick Carleton, John Hambrey, Tristan Southall, Katharine Winnard (Nautilus Consultants Ltd, United Kingdom)

Chapter 2.6 Transport
Coordination:
Ann Dom, Wouter de Ridder (EEA)
Authors:
Jos M. W. Dings, Max Smith (CE Solutions for environment, economy and technology, Netherlands)

Chapter 2.7 Tourism
Coordination:
Ronan Uhel (EEA)
Author:
Aurélie Pelletreau (EEA)

Chapter 3 Climate change
Coordination:
André Jol (EEA)
Authors:
Lambert Schneider (Oeko-Institute, Germany), Jelle van Minnen ((RIVM (National Institute of Public Health and the Environment), Netherlands), Tinus Pulles (TNO (Netherlands Organisation for Applied Scientific Research), Netherlands)

Chapter 4 Stratospheric ozone depletion
Coordination:
Roel van Aalst (EEA)
Author:
Guus Velders (RIVM, Netherlands)

Chapter 5 Air pollution
Coordination:
Andreas Barkman, Roel van Aalst (EEA)
Authors:
Kevin Barret, Frank de Leeuw, Detlef van Vuuren, Janusz Cofala, Hans Eerens (European Topic Centre on Air and Climate Change (ETC/ACC))

Chapter 6 Chemicals
Coordination:
David Gee, Ingvar Andersson (EEA)
Authors:
Keith A. Brown, Martin L. Adams (AEA Technology, United Kingdom)

Chapter 7 Waste generation and management
Coordination:
Dimitrios Tsotsos (EEA)
Author:
Jens Brodersen with support of Despo Fatta, Fotis Kourmoussis, Brian Meaney, Stephan Moll, Maria Gabriella Simeone, Mette Skovgaard, Matti Viisimaa, Thomas Weissenbach (European Topic Centre on Waste and Material Flows (ETC/WMF), Denmark), contribution from Morten Sickel (Arctic Monitoring and Assessment Programme (AMAP))

Chapter 8 Water
Coordination:
Anita Künitzer, Peter Kristensen (EEA)

Authors:
Steve Nixon, Zoe Trent, Concha Lallana
(European Topic Centre on Water (ETC/
WTR))

Chapter 9 Soil degradation
Coordination:
Anna Rita Gentile (EEA)
Author:
Timo Tarvainen, Marrtha Wepner, Martin
Schamann, Banko Gebhard, Jaume Fons
Esteve (European Topic Centre on Terres-
trial Environment (ETC/TE))

Chapter 10 Technological and natural hazards
Coordination:
Ronan Uhel, David Stanners (EEA)
Author:
Glenn Pettitt (Environmental Resources
Management (ERM), United Kingdom),
contribution from Morten Sickel (AMAP)

Chapter 11 Biological diversity
Coordination:
Tor-Björn Larsson, Ulla Pinborg (EEA)
Author:
Dominique Richard (European Topic Centre
on Nature Protection and Biodiversity
(ETC/NPB))

Chapter 12 Environment and human health
Coordination:
Ronan Uhel, David Gee (EEA)
Authors:
Ingvar Andersson (EEA), Bent H. Fenger in
cooperation with World Health Organization
(WHO) staff, contribution from Morten
Sickel (AMAP)

Chapter 13 Progress in managing the environment
Cooordination:
Hans Vos, Ronan Uhel (EEA)
Authors:
Alan Bond (University of Wales, United
Kingdom); R. Andreas Kraemer, Aneke Klasing
(Ecologic, Denmark); Frans Oosterhuis
(Institute for Environmental Studies (IVM),
Netherlands); Elisabeth Wilson (Oxford
Brookes University, United Kingdom);
Françoise Breton (ETC/TE); contributions
from Malcolm Ferguson (Institute for Euro-
pean Environmental Policy (IEEP), United
Kingdom), Mirjam Schomaker

Chapter 14 Information gaps and needs
Coordination:
Ronan Uhel (EEA)
Author:
Nicolas Perritaz, with contributions from
coordinators of chapters (EEA) and Ljiljana
Stancic (Aarhus convention secretariat)

Annex 1 Country comparative tables
Peter Bosch, Nicolas Perritaz (EEA); Rosella

Soldi (Progress Consulting) and David
Simoens (EEA)

Annex 2 Multilateral environment agreements
Ronan Uhel (EEA); Rosella Soldi (Progress
Consulting)

Annex 3 International comparisons
Ronan Uhel (EEA); Rosella Soldi (Progress
Consulting)

Data collection and processing

EEA: Nicolas Perritaz (EEA) and Rosella
Soldi (Progress Consulting)

ETC/NPB: Grégoire Lois, Gabriela Augusto,
Ward Hagemeijer, Romain Julliard

ETC/WTR: Steve Nixon

ETC/ACC: Kevin Barret

ETC/TE: Jaume Fons Esteve, Françoise Breton

ETC/WMF: Jens Brodersen

International data: Eurostat, Food and
Agriculture Organization of the United
Nations (FAO), International Energy Agency
(IEA), World Trade Organization (WTO),
World Bank, UN Statistics Division, Organisa-
tion for Economic Co-operation and Devel-
opment (OECD)

With support on EEA 2002 questionnaire for
non-EEA member countries from:
- Adam Elbæk Jørgensen, Albina Shuyska,
  Irina Chernakova (COWI A/S, Denmark)
- Nickolai Denisov, Ieva Rucevska, (UNEP/
  GRID-Arendal)
- Andrew Farmer (IEEP, United Kingdom)

Maps: design and production
Coordination:
Andrus Meiner (EEA)
Production:
Mette Lund (EEA)

Graphs: design and production
Coordination:
Nicolas Perritaz, Charlotta Colliander
Golding (EEA) and Rosella Soldi (Progress
Consulting)
Production:
Folkmann Design

Coordinating and editing

Ronan Uhel, Andrus Meiner, Peter Bosch
(EEA), Peter Saunders (Consultant) with
support from: Alexei Kostin, Angela
Sochirca, Nicolas Perritaz, Anne-Dorthe
Hansen, Charlotta Colliander Golding,
Charlotte Islev (EEA)

1. Introduction

1.1. The third pan-European state of the environment report

This report, prepared by the European Environment Agency (EEA) for the environment ministers' conference in Kiev in May 2003, is the third pan-European state of the environment report in the context of the Environmental Programme for Europe, under the auspices of the United Nations Economic Commission for Europe (UNECE). The main aim of the report is to provide an overview of progress in the Environmental Programme for Europe. Unlike the previous reports, it covers Europe, the whole of the Russian Federation, and the Caucasian and central Asian countries, in other words the full geographical area of the 'Environment for Europe' political process.

This third assessment also differs in scope from the previous reports by taking a more integrated approach, both on environmental issues (e.g. environment and health, or combining inland and marine waters) and on the inclusion of environmental concerns in sectoral policies, reflecting policy developments in these areas. Indicator-based data were used to provide a picture of the environmental changes which are occurring in the main regions of Europe, highlighting those associated with the transition to market economies. The information on trends, although incomplete, clearly shows the areas where achievement of environmental targets is likely to present the greatest future challenge.

The development of state of the environment reports, including indicators, in support of the Environment for Europe process shows a simultaneous improvement in coordinating and harmonising the provision of information for policy-making at the pan-European level. The intention with this third report was to develop it as a fully fledged indicator-based assessment. However, limitations of data availability and comparability still pose problems for the development and use of indicators. Chapter 14 on information gaps and needs and Annex 1 country tables address these. A flexible approach was therefore adopted to enable coverage of all the relevant issues across the whole of the area studied.

The Kiev ministerial conference follows on from the World Summit on Sustainable Development in Johannesburg in 2002. Although the current report focuses on the environmental aspect of sustainable development, it still tries to make connections from the other issues regarding sustainable development to their implementation in Europe. The main focus of the report is, however, to analyse past and current progress in the Environment for Europe process. Hence the reader can find in this report:

- Eight chapters on developments in sectors such as agriculture and transport which assess progress in implementing the ministerial intentions of improving the integration of environmental concerns into sectoral policies.
- Ten chapters on environmental issues, which focus on the implementation of the international conventions. These chapters answer the general question of progress since the ministers first met in Dobris castle.
- A final assessment chapter on the successes and challenges in the implementation of specific instruments suggested at the various ministerial meetings.
- A chapter on information gaps and needs.
- Annexes giving statistics by country which could not be shown in the aggregated indicators in the report and providing international comparisons.

1.2. Key policy developments

Since the first ministerial conference 'Environment for Europe', held in Dobris castle in 1991, there has been much progress in pan-European cooperation to protect the environment. A large number of international conventions have been ratified, a process to continue at the Kiev conference where legislation on environmental impact assessment, civil liability and pollution registers is on the agenda. Annex 2 gives the state of play of signing and ratification of multilateral environmental agreements by countries.

In western Europe, the main policy lines are being set out by the European Union (EU) which is developing an interlinked set of policies. These are the sixth environment action programme (6EAP) encompassing the period up to 2010, the Cardiff process for the integration of the environment into other policies and the EU sustainable development strategy. These policies will provide the frame for detailed strategies and actions to enhance sustainable development within the EU, including the external dimensions of those policies.

In central Europe, accession to the EU dominates the agenda in many countries. The requirements of adjusting national legislation to EU requirements, and the large implied investments, raise issues of timing and provide an opportunity to prioritise other (environmental) measures that enhance sustainable development.

In the 12 countries of eastern Europe, the Caucasus and central Asia (EECCA), environmental problems are often on a different scale from those in western Europe, while the financial situation is much worse. Cooperation between countries is less developed, although a start has been made in developing a common sustainable development strategy for the Kiev conference.

The report shows developments in each of these three regions against the policy background sketched above. Furthermore, the outcomes of the Johannesburg summit show that there are common links connecting countries and issues. Management of basic resources such as energy and water requires an effort in the whole of Europe, as does the approach to managing the risks of producing and using more and more chemicals. Trade and environment issues vis-à-vis the rest of the world are also of common concern, along with sustainable production and consumption patterns.

Although much of what will happen over the next 30 years will be the result of policy decisions and actions taken during recent decades, new decision-making also has a vital role to play in shaping the future. Given the uncertainties in extrapolating current trends, today's decision-makers can only get a clearer picture of what tomorrow might bring by exploring different future scenarios. In this way, they can assess the likely impacts of their decisions and determine more accurately what they can do to create a more desirable future. Scenarios do not predict, rather they paint pictures of possible futures;

they can be used to explore what might happen if basic assumptions are changed (see UNEP *Global environment outlook* 3, 2002: http://www.unep.org/geo/geo3/). However, due to limitations of time and resources, this report does not contain an outlook section covering possible future trends.

1.3. Towards a more integrated monitoring and reporting process

One of the most important achievements of the 1998 Aarhus ministerial conference was the adoption of the convention on access to information, public participation in decision-making and access to justice in environmental matters (the Aarhus convention). Through seeking to guarantee public rights to information, participation and access to justice in the environmental sphere, its goal is to contribute to the protection of the right of every person of this and future generations to live in an environment adequate for his or her health and well-being. Among its obligations, the convention requires all signatories to make available their environmental information to the public and includes an obligation to produce a comprehensive overview of the state of the environment every four years. This aspect of the Aarhus convention will form the legal background for improving and strengthening capacities for national environmental monitoring and reporting (for details, see Chapter 14, Box 14.2). This report and eventual follow-up studies may become a catalyst for improved information and data flows at the national and the pan-European levels.

The need for more coordinated cooperation in this area was emphasised at a conference on environmental monitoring organised by the Russian Federation in Moscow in January 2001. All countries decided, in order to ensure their contribution to information gathering at the European level, to create the UNECE ad hoc working group on environmental monitoring (WGEM). Taking into account the positive experience of the Agency's European environment information and observation network (Eionet), WGEM was given the mandate to investigate possible improvements in monitoring, data exchange and reporting especially in the EECCA countries. To help carry out this task, the working group decided to take the production of the Kiev report as the main test case in order to come up with concrete and documented recommendations for monitoring and reporting in European countries to be addressed by the Kiev ministerial conference.

WGEM has fulfilled the indispensable function of guiding the data collection for the Kiev report in countries that are not members of the EEA. WGEM discussed the guidelines for data collection and the draft questionnaires, and its members functioned as national contact points (NCPs) during the data collection exercise. Support to the countries for data collection was part of EU CARDS (regional environment reconstruction programme for the Balkans) funding for the Balkan countries (Albania and Serbia and Montenegro not included) and EU Tacis (technical assistance programme for countries in transition) funding for the EECCA countries.

During this data collection phase, the NCPs had to cope with working with other institutes holding the data in their countries, which in some cases revealed practical difficulties in access to information. Due to the absence of bilateral funding in general, a number of in-depth discussions on detailed monitoring of waste, chemicals and air pollution could not be finished before the conference, but will continue until the end of 2003. Specific funding is now in place from the European Commission to build network and information capacities in EECCA countries and provides a stepping stone towards a more stable infrastructure for long-term building on the achievements of the Kiev report. The lessons from EIONET developments over the past decade or so show that many years of concentrated effort and funding will be needed to ensure sustainable improvements in the provision of environmental information at the pan-European level.

Providing the basis for a phase of 'learning from lessons', the report marks the start of a period of renewed cooperation in environmental monitoring and reporting in Europe. From the start, WGEM involved itself in articulating the contents of the report to make it relevant to policies and to include the proper analyses. Subsequently, WGEM involved itself in the necessary data flows and information processing. Such an activity is important for establishing an effective bridge between a responsive monitoring system and a relevant reporting process in support of policy-making. The

need to harmonise these processes at the pan-European level appears to be increasing.

During 2002 and 2003, the 13 accession countries to the EU joined the EEA as full members. In December 2002, the Council of the European Union decided to approve the accession of 10 of these countries to the EU as from 1 May 2004. The Russian Federation, Belarus, Ukraine, and somewhat later the Republic of Moldova, will be at the eastern border of the enlarged EU. After the accession of Turkey, for which no date has yet been set, the Caucasian countries would also be bordering the EU. Cooperation between the EU and the Balkan countries is well under way, with many reconstruction projects being implemented for recovering from the damage of war.

Knowledge of developments in the whole of the European continent will thus be increasingly necessary for supporting policy processes with environmental information. For the future, a higher level of investment is needed in streamlining monitoring and providing a basic environmental monitoring infrastructure (measuring equipment, data processing and exchange facilities, and publishing) particularly in EECCA. On the international level, continuation of a framework for cooperation between countries, as has been provided by WGEM to the present report, will be necessary, so as to improve the information base for regular indicator-based assessments. Those elements are documented in the official UNECE-WGEM paper 'Lessons learned from the third assessment data collection' for discussion at the Kiev conference (see also Chapter 14 on information gaps and needs).

To this end, the European Commission entrusted the EEA with the Tacis-funded project mentioned above, aimed at strengthening environmental information and observation capacity in the 12 countries of eastern Europe, the Caucasus and central Asia. The long-term objective of the project, up to and beyond the Kiev conference, is to help integrate EECCA environmental information and management systems into the mainstream of European practice, and thus help countries to create sound conditions for economic transition.

One short-term objective of the project is to strengthen environmental information and observation capacity and networks in order to provide good, reliable and relevant information on the state of the environment in EECCA as a basis for improved policy-making and public awareness. Another short-term objective is to enhance cooperation between existing environmental networks.

The project is expected to provide results beyond the Kiev conference in order to ensure a good follow-up. For that purpose, the key objectives of the project are:

- to support the preparation of the third assessment report as an urgent action;
- to strengthen the network of NCPs involved in the preparation of the third assessment report and start to build networks of national specialised institutes in EECCA extending the existing networks in western and central Europe;
- to support and extend the activities of WGEM in providing results for the Kiev conference and to support post-Kiev follow-up activities;
- to carry out general supporting activities for all the above tasks.

1.4. Presentation of the indicators

The assessments in this report are based on indicators that cover the most important aspects of the socio-economic and environmental framework (driving forces, pressures, state of the environment, impacts and societal responses, the so-called DPSIR assessment framework including eco-efficiency indicators). Analysis of the indicators can be found in detailed fact

sheets on the EEA's web site. The indicators presented in this report illustrate the most important trends in each policy domain. To the extent feasible, 'smiley faces' indicate progress, or lack of it, for key indicators.

The smiley faces in the boxes next to key indicators aim to give a concise assessment of the indicator:

 positive trend, moving towards qualitative objectives or quantified targets;

 some positive development, but either insufficient to reach qualitative objectives or quantified targets, or mixed trends within the indicator;

 unfavourable trend.

Unless explicitly stated, the assessment is based on the entire period covered by the report.

Within the DPSIR framework, indicators are presented in a standard format. Firstly, at an international level, totals are shown for the main regions of Europe. This is particularly relevant where there are international agreements on actions to tackle continental or global problems (e.g. greenhouse gas emissions). Secondly, where possible and relevant, subregional and national breakdowns are provided to highlight the differences between regions and countries.

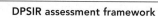

DPSIR assessment framework   Figure 1.1.

Source: EEA

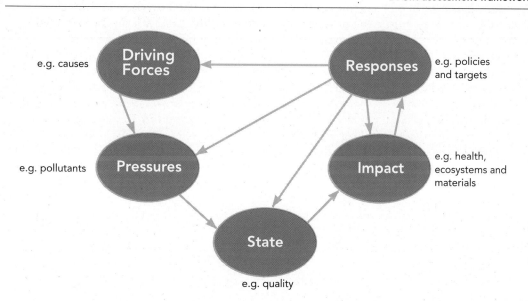

Box 1.1. Country groupings used in this report

Compared with the earlier reports, geographical coverage has expanded to cover the whole of the Russian Federation, Caucasus and central Asia. In any report of this type with such a huge geographical scope, it is necessary to group countries together and draw generalised conclusions. For practical reasons the groups used are based on established political groupings rather than environmental considerations, and there can be large variations in environmental performance within the groups and substantial overlaps between

them. Where possible this has been highlighted in the report.

Even though the geographical scope now includes large areas of Asia, 'Europe' is still used to denote the total area studied reflecting the framework within which the report has been developed.

The main and most-used grouping divides Europe in three parts:

Western Europe (WE)	Austria, Belgium, Denmark, Finland, France, Germany, Greece, Ireland, Italy, Luxembourg, the Netherlands, Portugal, Spain, Sweden, United Kingdom (EU-15); Iceland, Liechtenstein, Norway, Switzerland (EFTA); including the small states Andorra, Monaco, San Marino
Central and eastern Europe (CEE)	Albania, Bosnia-Herzegovina, Bulgaria, Czech Republic, Croatia, Estonia, the Former Yugoslav Republic of Macedonia, Hungary, Latvia, Lithuania, Poland, Romania, Serbia and Montenegro, Slovak Republic, Slovenia, Cyprus, Malta and Turkey
Twelve countries of eastern Europe, the Caucasus and central Asia (EECCA)	Armenia, Azerbaijan, Belarus, Georgia, Republic of Moldova, Russian Federation, Ukraine, Kazakhstan, Kyrgyzstan, Tajikistan, Turkmenistan and Uzbekistan

In some cases it is relevant to divide central and eastern Europe in two and make a regional subdivision in EECCA:

Western Europe	As above
EU accession countries (AC-13)	Bulgaria, Czech Republic, Estonia, Hungary, Latvia, Lithuania, Poland, Romania, Slovak Republic, Slovenia, Cyprus, Malta and Turkey
Russian Federation and the western EECCA	Belarus, Republic of Moldova, Russian Federation, Ukraine
Balkan countries	Albania, Bosnia-Herzegovina, Croatia, the Former Yugoslav Republic of Macedonia, Serbia and Montenegro
Caucasian countries	Armenia, Azerbaijan, Georgia
Central Asian countries	Kazakhstan, Kyrgyzstan, Tajikistan, Turkmenistan, Uzbekistan

2. 0. Material flows

The challenge for sustainable economic development is to increase the economic welfare and well-being of society while, at the same time, reducing resource requirements to a level consistent with the natural carrying capacity of ecosystems. Production and consumption by human societies have always been linked with the use of natural resources, which, in turn, can often have negative environmental effects.

All countries in the pan-European region face this challenge of sustainable management of resources, and there has been only limited progress in reaching a significantly higher efficiency of resource use and achieving a shift towards the wider use of renewable energy and material resources. Several major trends with respect to current resource consumption by European countries show that:

- *A stabilisation of the level of resource use has been achieved in several western, and central and eastern European countries.*
- *Despite this relative decoupling of resource use from economic growth, in absolute terms, material use still remains at unsustainably high levels with regard to both its volume and its structure.*
- *Central and eastern European countries will face difficulties in curbing growth in the use of resources whilst striving to reach western European levels of economic welfare.*
- *Western European economies increasingly import their raw materials, thereby shifting the associated environmental burden to other regions. A similar trend can be observed in most central and eastern European countries. The countries of eastern Europe, the Caucasus and central Asia are one of the main exporters of raw materials to the European Union.*

2.0.1. Introduction

2.0.1.1. Towards a sustainable use of material-based resources

Most changes in the natural environment are brought about by human activities and by the resulting flows of material. The cycle of this 'industrial metabolism' starts with the extraction of raw materials, then includes material and energy use for production and consumption, continues with recycling, and ends up with final disposal. Continuously high levels of material use have environmental implications as all this material must be extracted, transported, transformed and eventually disposed of, leading to environmental impacts at each stage.

Material flows form the 'bridge' between human activities and environmental impacts (Bringezu, 2002). These can vary greatly from local physico-chemical changes (e.g. acidification) through the effects of excessive nutrients (e.g. eutrophication) and mechanical destruction (e.g. excavation), to more structural effects (e.g. landscape change or habitat disruption). Many of the environmental problems presented in this report are directly or indirectly linked to the material throughput of the economy, for example air emissions as discussed in Chapter 3 and Chapter 5 as well as water abstraction presented in Chapter 8.

There is continuing discussion and debate on how to manage this industrial metabolism in a sustainable way, and even about what is a sustainable level of resource use. So far, robust scientific criteria to determine sustainable levels have only been developed for a limited number of material flows associated with well-known environmental problems (e.g. in the area of climate change, air pollution and hazardous substances). Due to the complexity and limited knowledge of the environmental impacts associated with this industrial metabolism, it does not seem feasible to scientifically determine sustainable levels for all human-induced material flows. However, some general principles — based on the concept of sustainable development and the precautionary principle — have been presented (see e.g. OECD, 2001). They include the following:

- the use of renewable resources should not exceed their long-term rates of natural regeneration;
- non-renewable resources should be used efficiently and their use limited to levels which can be offset by substitution by renewable resources;
- releases of hazardous or polluting substances to the environment should not exceed its assimilative capacity;
- irreversible adverse effects of human activities on ecosystems and on biogeochemical and hydrological cycles should be avoided.

Box 2.0.1. Monitoring the metabolism of the economy: what goes in must come out!

The economy takes in raw materials — from the domestic environment and imports from foreign countries — for further processing, manufacturing, production and consumption. Some materials, such as construction minerals, are stored in buildings and infrastructures for many years. At the end of their useful life, products become waste and may be recycled or finally disposed of in landfills or incineration plants. Hence, the size of the resource input also determines the amounts of subsequent waste and emissions.

Since any resource input will sooner or later become an output, it is possible to account for resource flows in terms of a summary balance. Figure 2.0.1 summarises the main flows involved, and introduces some of the terms used in the balance sheet.

The Statistical Office of the European Communities has developed economy-wide material flow accounts (Eurostat, 2001a), a methodology to provide aggregate descriptions of the total material throughput of economies (excluding water and air). The summary indicators derived from these accounts provide a physical description of a national economy, complementing the greater detail offered by other common indicators (e.g. energy use, waste generation, air emissions). In economic terms, the summary indicators show the dependency on physical resources and the efficiency with which they are used by national economies (Eurostat, 2002). In environmental terms, material input indicators can be used as a proxy for the environmental pressures associated with resource extraction, subsequent material transformation and final disposal of material residuals back to the environment.

Total material requirement (TMR) aggregates all material inputs required by a national economy on a whole life-cycle basis. TMR includes both the direct use of resources (e.g. tonnes of coal used), and the indirect flows associated with domestic

extraction (tonnes of topsoil removed to produce construction minerals) and those indirect flows related to the production of imported goods ('hidden flows', for example tonnes of topsoil removed in a foreign country to extract the imported minerals). In economic terms, TMR is a measure of the physical basis of the economy or the total primary resource requirements of all production activities of a national economy. In environmental terms, it is a proxy for potential environmental pressures associated with resource extraction. Since all these material inputs will sooner or later be transformed to material outputs (i.e. emissions, waste), TMR is also a proxy for potential future environmental pressures to the domestic as well as foreign environment on a whole life-cycle basis.

Direct material input (DMI) measures the input of materials that are directly used in the economy, that is, used domestic extraction and physical imports. Unlike TMR, it does not include hidden flows. DMI has been used as a substitute for TMR because data on TMR are more difficult and time-consuming to compile, and hence less readily available than DMI data. Although the DMI indicator may, theoretically, send a wrong signal if a country is decreasing its domestic resource extraction while increasing imports of raw materials, empirical analyses show that there is a correlation between DMI and TMR (see EEA, 2000).

Direct material consumption (DMC) accounts for all materials used by a country and is defined as all materials directly entering the national economy (used domestic extraction plus imports), minus the materials that are exported. In economic terms, DMC reflects consumption by the residents of a national economy. It is also the MFA indicator most closely related to GDP (Eurostat, 2001a). In environmental terms, DMC is a proxy for the potential environmental pressures associated with the disposal of residual materials to the domestic environment.

| Figure 2.0.1. | Economy-wide material balance scheme without water and air |

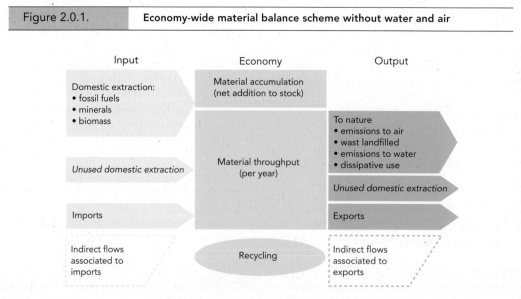

Notes: TMR = domestic extraction (fossil fuels, minerals, biomass) + unused domestic extraction + imports + indirect flows associated with imports; DMI = domestic extraction (fossil fuels, minerals, biomass) + imports; DMC = DMI minus exports.
Source: Eurostat, 2001a

2.0.1.2. Analysing the flows of materials

Material flow accounting (MFA) has been developed as a tool for systematically describing and monitoring industrial metabolism. The underlying principle of MFA is to account for all materials entering and leaving the economic system, based on a mass-balancing approach. MFA can be used to derive indicators on the metabolic performance of national economies, for instance resource inputs, and the efficiency of resource use (Eurostat, 2001a) (see Box 2.0.1).

The basic premise of MFA-based analysis is that the amount of resource flow into the economy determines the amount of all outputs to the environment including wastes and emissions (see Box 2.0.2.). Thus, a reduction in resource inputs will automatically also reduce the outputs — including emissions and waste — thereby lowering pressure on the environment.

So far, economy-wide MFA statistics have been established in only a few European countries. The data presented in this chapter are of a preliminary nature, and are based on several studies. Practically no MFA data are available for eastern Europe, the Caucasus and central Asia (EECCA).

2.0.2. Trends in material flows

2.0.2.1. Progress in decoupling

Recent analysis carried out for the EU Member States and accession countries has shown signs of decoupling materials use from economic growth (Figure 2.0.2.). The productivity of materials and energy has been increasing, and economic added value has been generated with less use of natural resources. This is a positive signal. At the same time, however, material use, in absolute terms, has been high and constant — or even on the increase — in many European countries.

Although direct materials productivity (the ratio between the GDP (gross domestic product) and DMI of a country) in the EU

> The productivity of materials and energy has been increasing in many European countries. However, material use, in absolute terms, has been high and constant — or even on the increase.

Box 2.0.2. What problems arise from the physical growth of the economy?

In the EU, physical stocks are increasing by about 10 tonnes/capita every year. This results mainly from the construction of new buildings and infrastructure, but also includes accumulation of consumer durables such as furniture, vehicles and household appliances (Bringezu and Schütz, 2001). Such a rapid physical expansion is a reason for concern, and has two major implications.

First, the generation of waste can be expected to rise significantly. This applies in particular to the construction sector. For instance in Germany, the annual amount of construction and demolition waste is expected to double over the next 15–20 years due to the age and composition of the current building stock and infrastructure (Öko-Institut, 1998).

Second the net growth of built-up areas is taking place at the expense of natural productive land (Bringezu, 2002). Such a trend cannot continue indefinitely without jeopardizing renewable materials and energy supply as well as natural habitats and biodiversity.

and accession countries has been on the increase over the past decade, DMI has remained fairly constant. This indicates that the environmental burden associated with the use of resources is also likely to have remained constant. Especially worrying signs are the intensive use and high rate of depletion of non-renewable resources, which is not in line with the principle of sustainability. The use of non-renewables is

Decoupling of resource use from GDP by country groupings – EU (a) and accession countries (b)   Figure 2.0.2.

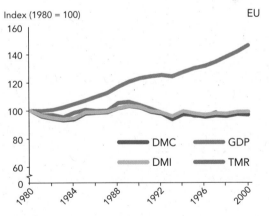

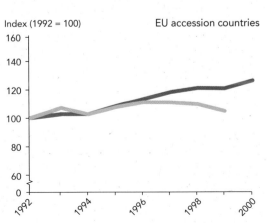

Note: See Box 2.0.1 for definitions

Sources: DMI, DMC for EU: Eurostat, 2002; TMR EU: Eurostat, 2001b; DMI accession countries: Wuppertal Institute, 2002; GDP: World Bank and Eurostat, 2003

associated with irreversible changes of landscape and climate, while their continuously high rates of extraction bring about a growing cumulative change in the environment.

2.0.2.2. National variations in resource productivity

When comparing the level of economic prosperity with material use across countries, it is evident that certain countries have been able to achieve high economic welfare with relatively low material inputs. In general, mining and heavy industry require large amounts of material throughput. For example, Italy and the United Kingdom have very different consumption and production patterns from Norway and Finland, which require very high amounts of material input to achieve their high levels of economic welfare. The underlying reason is that the production patterns of Norway and Finland are largely based on the use of natural resources (oil and timber).

In contrast, economies such as Italy and the United Kingdom seem to base their economic welfare to a larger extent on services combined with a lower consumption of fossil fuels and minerals. As a general rule, service-intensive economies tend to be less resource-demanding. On the other hand, some countries with a strong manufacturing sector — such as Germany — have managed to increase their resource efficiency. Two other countries with a high resource productivity are Austria and France, both having a strong agricultural sector and high GDP.

Policy-makers in central and eastern European (CEE) countries and EECCA may want to ask themselves a question while examining Figure 2.0.3: what path will their countries follow as they increase their GDP? Will they be able reach higher GDP per capita while maintaining or even decreasing resource use? Or will their growth be accompanied by significant increase in DMI, for instance through increased reliance on exports of natural resources and minerals?

For the accession countries, achieving the EU's level of economic prosperity will require a significant increase in resource productivity. As shown in Table 2.0.1, the direct materials productivity of the accession countries currently stands at 230 euro/tonne, or only 20 % of that of the EU.

In EECCA, extraction of natural resources and exports of raw materials (in particular fossil fuels, metals and biomass) are still the main pillars of economic development. However, the resource productivity (or added value) of this form of resource use tends to be rather low. For the domestic economy, exporting raw materials generates far less economic added value than does processing raw materials into more valuable final goods.

2.0.2.3. Scale and composition of materials use

Continuously high levels and the composition of resource use reflect unsustainable consumption and production patterns. The material flows into the EU

Figure 2.0.3.	Direct material input per capita versus GDP per capita by countries, 1999/2000

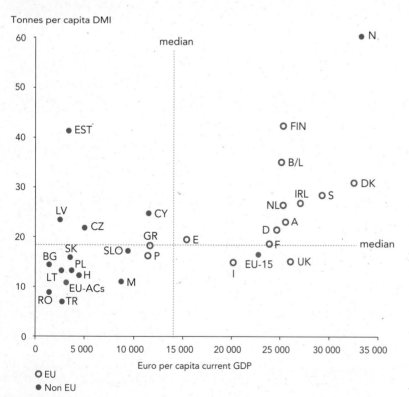

Tonnes per capita DMI

Euro per capita current GDP

○ EU
● Non EU

Note: Using DMC (not available for accession countries, however) instead of DMI as the indicator would yield a somewhat different picture, since countries with a high share of exports tend to appear less favourably on the current graph.

Sources: GDP in current prices: Eurostat, 2003; DMI: Eurostat, 2002 and Wuppertal Institute, 2002 (accession countries, Norway)

> Central and eastern European countries will find it difficult to avoid moving towards unsustainably high levels of direct material input.

economy — measured as DMI — have remained nearly constant since 1980, fluctuating around approximately 16.5 tonnes/capita per year. The DMC (i.e. DMI minus exports) of the EU has been slightly lower, at some 15.7 tonnes/capita, although for some countries with large amounts of exports, e.g. the Netherlands, Belgium and Norway, the difference has been much higher. The TMR of the EU, which also accounts for the hidden flows, has been fluctuating around 51.8 tonnes/capita.

The DMI of the accession countries — with data available only since 1992 — has been increasing slightly throughout the 1990s, finally reaching some 11.5 tonnes/capita per year. This is about one third smaller than that of the EU, and the difference can be attributed to the significantly lower use of minerals (2.8 tonnes/capita in the accession countries compared with 8.2 tonnes/capita in the EU). The economies of the EU countries seem to require much more mineral resources such as industrial minerals, building minerals and metals which are associated with a large amount of hidden flows (Figure 2.0.4.).

Comprehensive material input indicators are not available for EECCA. Given the limited availability of data, meaningful comparisons can only be made for fossil fuels. Although fossil fuel extraction in EECCA fell during the first half of the 1990s, the extraction rate has now reached 5 tonnes/capita per year. This is high compared with the rest of Europe (about 1.9 tonnes/capita in the EU and the Balkan countries and 2.4 tonnes/capita in the accession countries). As well as the disruption and physical changes to the landscape that result from mining operations, environmental problems associated with such extraordinarily high extraction rates include risks of accidental leakages of gas, spills of oil from pipelines and other related environmental contamination. On the other hand, some argue that despite the environmental consequences, exports of fossil fuels and natural gas are contributing to economic stability in EECCA.

In the EU, the share of non-renewable resources (minerals and fossil fuels) in DMI and DMC has been practically constant over the period 1980–2000, at about 75 %. In the accession countries, the share of non-renewable resources in DMI is lower, at about 60 % and slowly decreasing. Apparently, EU economies require

Direct materials productivity of European countries, 1999 (EUR/tonne)		Table 2.0.1.	
Austria	1 103	Norway	489
Belgium/Luxembourg	692	Bulgaria	78
Denmark	956	Cyprus	419
Finland	535	Czech Republic	185
France	1 203	Estonia	57
Germany	1 129	Hungary	329
Greece	582	Latvia	73
Ireland	729	Lithuania	109
Italy	1 078	Malta	697
Netherlands	892	Poland	238
Portugal	582	Romania	129
Spain	709	Slovak Republic	204
Sweden	936	Slovenia	500
United Kingdom	1 085	Turkey	328
EU	1 156	Accession countries	230

Notes: Direct materials productivity = GDP in constant prices. DMC, which is in general more suited to being related to GDP, is not available for the accession countries. DMI (unlike GDP) includes imports, hence artificially lowering the resource productivities of the smaller economies which are more open to foreign trade.

Sources: DMI: Eurostat, 2002 and Wuppertal Institute, 2002 (13 accession countries plus Norway); GDP: Eurostat

Composition of direct material input for EU and accession countries, 1999	Figure 2.0.4.

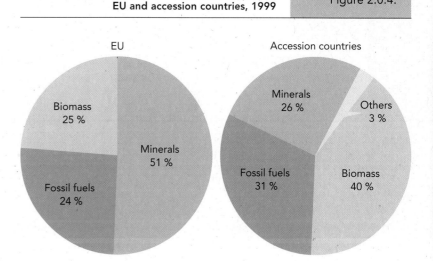

EU

Biomass 25 %
Minerals 51 %
Fossil fuels 24 %

Accession countries

Minerals 26 %
Others 3 %
Fossil fuels 31 %
Biomass 40 %

Sources: Eurostat, 2002 and Wuppertal Institute, 2002 (accession countries)

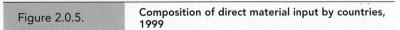

Figure 2.0.5. | Composition of direct material input by countries, 1999

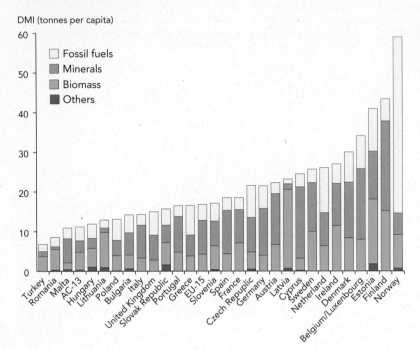

DMI (tonnes per capita)

- Fossil fuels
- Minerals
- Biomass
- Others

Sources: Eurostat, 2002 (EU), Wuppertal, 2002 (accession countries, Norway)

Figure 2.0.6. | Comparison of direct material input and direct material consumption — EU, 1999

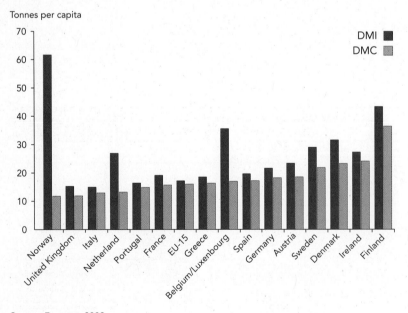

Tonnes per capita

DMI ■
DMC ▨

Source: Eurostat, 2002

significantly more mineral resources such as metals, industrial minerals and building minerals. Metal resources in particular are associated with a high amount of hidden flows. Fossil fuels — the main cause of climate change problems — are a major component of DMI in both accession countries and the EU, respectively accounting for 31 % and 24 % of the total.

The size and composition of material inputs vary between countries, and depend on the economic base and the size of the country, its consumption and production patterns, and its population density (Figure 2.0.5.). Smaller economies tend to have a higher DMI or DMC. For instance, in Finland and Ireland, this is due to relatively large domestic extractions of biomass. In the case of Estonia, it is high because of the use of oil shale as the primary energy source, and in Denmark, Cyprus and Finland because of the domestic extraction of large amounts of minerals.

The significant difference between DMI and DMC in the Netherlands and Belgium/ Luxembourg is due to the 'Rotterdam-effect' (Antwerp and Rotterdam harbours, with their large shipping/export volumes). In Norway, the difference is due to the high exports of fossil fuels, mainly to western European countries (Figure 2.0.6.).

2.0.2.4. Imports on the increase

As a result of increasing external trade and growing imports of natural resources, the resource base of most western European and CEE economies is increasingly shifting abroad. Decreasing domestic extraction and increasing imports of raw materials may be beneficial to the state of the environment of the importing country, and will probably decrease its DMI. At the same time, however, environmental pressures associated with the extraction of resources are moved to other regions of the world.

For the EU, the amount of imported goods has been increasing steadily since the mid-1980s, reaching about 3.8 tonnes/capita in 2000. If one takes into account the indirect hidden flows associated with those imports (e.g. total materials such as metal ores, energy carriers or chemical compounds required to produce an imported good), the increase is even more significant: from around 15 tonnes/capita in the mid-1980s to some 20 tonnes/capita in 1997 (Figure 2.0.7.). On the other hand, both domestic extraction and the associated unused hidden

🙁 Increasing imports of resources are resulting in shifting the environmental burden from the consuming to the exporting countries. Imports currently constitute almost 40 % of the total material requirement of the EU, and they grew particularly rapidly during the 1990s.

flows have been decreasing slightly. It is worth noting that imports currently constitute almost 40 % of the TMR of the EU (around 50 tonnes/capita), and these imports grew particularly rapidly during the 1990s.

In the accession countries, the amount of imported goods is much lower than in the EU, but the trend has been similar. Imports of goods increased by almost 30 %, from 1.5 tonnes/capita in 1992 to 1.9 in 1999. This situation was probably caused by the closure of uncompetitive domestic extraction industries, combined with increasing integration of the accession countries into the global economy. The trend for increasing imports is likely to continue into the near future.

The increase in imports into the EU is primarily related to fossil fuels and minerals. The increasing import of minerals is an issue of concern because the 'ecological rucksacks' (life-cycle-based resource requirements per tonne of imported final goods) of certain industrial minerals and metals can be extremely high. For example, the ecological rucksack of imported copper is about 150 tonnes per tonne of imported product, that for tin is 6 450 tonnes/tonne, while for precious metals it can even reach 59 000 tonnes/tonne (Bringezu, 2002).

Increasing imports of fossil fuels result in a growing dependency on foreign suppliers. As consumption of fossil fuels contributes to global warming, and at the same time these non-renewable resources will become increasingly scarce in the future, the countries which depend heavily on imports contribute to environmental problems and open themselves to potential economic risks and energy supply security problems.

In contrast, the countries of EECCA are typically exporters of mineral resources and fossil fuels. Those with the highest extraction of fossil fuels are the Russian Federation (1 100 million tonnes/year), Ukraine (105

Increasing foreign and decreasing domestic proportion of total material requirement over time, EU   Figure 2.0.7.

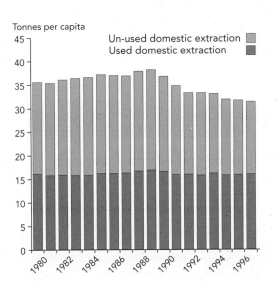

Sources: Eurostat and Wuppertal Institute

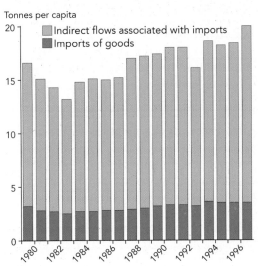

EU imports from eastern Europe, the Caucasus and central Asia, 1992–2000   Figure 2.0.8.

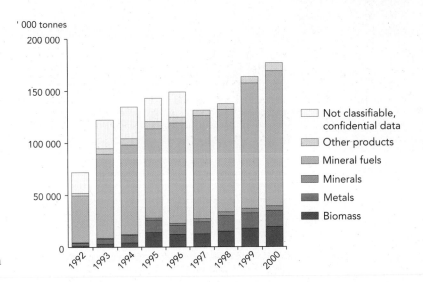

Source: Eurostat COMEXT

million tonnes), Kazakhstan (98 million tonnes) and Uzbekistan (64 million tonnes). On average, about one third of fossil fuels extracted in EECCA are exported, although Kazakhstan, for example, exports almost half of its domestic extraction.

The EU is increasingly importing from EECCA. Currently, about 12 % of the EU's 'physical' imports (i.e. imports measured in tonnes and not in currency) originate from EECCA, particularly as regards fossil fuels and metals (Figure 2.0.8.). This share doubled during the 1990s. Such imports can to some extent be correlated with the environmental problems associated with the extraction of natural resources in EECCA. On the other hand, however, the EU has reduced its domestic extraction and thereby pressures on the domestic environment. It can also be argued that there is a net environmental advantage in shifting to imported resources if the environmental efficiency of extraction is higher in the exporting country than it would be in the importing country.

2.0.3. Policy developments

The issue of consumption and production patterns was addressed for the first time as a policy matter during the United Nations Summit on Environment and Development in Rio in 1992. It was recognised that current patterns, particularly those in the developed economies, were unsustainable and had to be changed. One promising approach was to increase the resource efficiency of economic activities and processes, i.e. to produce greater welfare with less associated use of resources (see Box 2.0.3.).

The importance of the issue was confirmed 10 years later, in August 2002, during the World Summit on Sustainable Development in Johannesburg. It was decided to establish a 10-year framework programme to 'accelerate the shift towards sustainable consumption and production to promote social and economic development within the carrying capacity of ecosystems. This is approached by addressing, where appropriate, de-linking economic growth and environmental degradation, through improving efficiency and sustainability in the use of resources and production processes, and reducing resource degradation, pollution and waste' (UN, 2002). This emphasis may give new impetus to work on consumption and production patterns, as practical achievements in this area in the 1990s have been on a limited scale.

In the EU, the issue of resource use has also been put on the political agenda. The EU's strategy for sustainable development (European Commission, 2001b) emphasised the strategic objective of breaking the link between economic growth, the use of resources and the generation of waste.

Furthermore, the recently adopted sixth environment action programme (6EAP) (European Commission, 2001a; 2002) identified 'sustainable use of natural resources and management of waste' as one of the priority areas. The specific objectives for this area are:

- to ensure that the consumption of renewable and non-renewable resources does not exceed the carrying capacity of the environment;
- to achieve a decoupling of resource use from economic growth, through significantly improved resource efficiency, dematerialisation of the economy and waste prevention.

As part of the work plan, the European Commission is developing a thematic strategy on the sustainable use of natural resources. Through analysis, data collection and evaluation, the goal is to identify priority areas for policy intervention, and to propose the best mix of policy instruments to address the issues identified.

Box 2.0.3. Can absolute reduction of resource use be achieved?

To date, material use per capita has always increased as a result of economic growth. However, there are a few examples of absolute dematerialization, in terms of a decrease in the TMR of the economy.

In the first example, the TMR of the United States declined as a result of a successful programme to reduce erosion in agriculture. In the United States, erosion is a significant factor in agricultural production, and one that contributes strongly to TMR (25 % in 1975, and 15 % in 1994). In 1985, the US government introduced a special programme to pay farmers not to use arable land highly susceptible to erosion. As a result, TMR declined from 99 tonnes equivalent/capita in 1975 to 85 tonnes equivalent/capita in 1994 (Adriaanse et al., 1997).

The second example is more representative of the situation of transition countries. After the reunification of Germany in 1990, the TMR of the country declined significantly, from 88 tonnes equivalent/capita in 1991 to 77 tonnes equivalent/capita in 1997. This resulted from the widespread closures in the former East German lignite mining industries, which were no longer competitive when state subsidies were withdrawn.

In both cases, an absolute decline of TMR resulted from deliberate policy measures, either targeted at a specific resource use, or as a result of changes in the policy framework and economic incentives.

Meanwhile, in the countries of CEE and EECCA, questions of sustainable use of resources and changing consumption and production patterns are only beginning to gain prominence on the environmental policy agenda. Frequently, many of these countries seem more concerned with the problems arising from the restructuring of their economies. However, it is worth underlining that economic restructuring also offers a unique opportunity to establish more sustainable consumption and production patterns.

2.0.4. References

Adriaanse, A. *et al.*, 1997. *Resource flows — the material basis of industrial economies.* World Resources Institute, Wuppertal Institute, Netherlands Ministry of Housing, Spatial Planning, and Environment, Japan's National Institute for Environmental Studies. World Resources Institute Report. Washington, DC.

Bringezu, S. and Schütz, H., 2001. *Material use indicators for the European Union, 1980–1997.* Eurostat Working Paper 2/2001/B/2. Eurostat, Luxembourg.

Bringezu, S., 2002. *Towards sustainable resource management in the European Union.* Wuppertal Paper 121. Wuppertal Institute, Wuppertal.

EEA, 2000. *Total material requirement of the European Union.* Technical report No 55. EEA, Copenhagen.

European Commission, 2001a. *'Environment 2010: Our future, our choice' — the sixth environment action programme.* COM (2001) 31 final. 24.1.2001. Brussels. http://europa. eu.int/comm/environment/newprg/ index.htm

European Commission, 2001b. *A sustainable Europe for a better world: A European Union strategy for sustainable development.* Commission's proposal to the Gothenburg European Council. COM (2001)264 final. 15.5.2001 Brussels. http://europa.eu.int/ comm/environment/eussd/index.htm

European Commission, 2002. *Sixth environment action programme.* Official Journal L242. 10.09.2002.

Eurostat, 2001a. *Economy-wide material flow accounts and derived indicators — a methodological guide.* Methods and nomenclature series. Eurostat, Luxembourg.

Eurostat, 2001b. *Material use indicators for the European Union, 1980–1997.* Prepared by S. Bringezu and H. Schütz. Eurostat Working Paper 2/2001/B/2. Eurostat, Luxembourg.

Eurostat, 2002. *Material use in the European Union 1980–2000:* Indicators and analysis. Working paper and studies series. Eurostat, Luxembourg.

Eurostat, 2003. New Cronos online database. http://europa.eu.int/comm/eurostat/

OECD, 2001. *OECD environmental strategy for the first decade of the 21st century.* OECD, Paris.

Öko-Institut, 1998. *Bauen und Wohnen — Bedürfnisse und Stoffströme.* Commissioned by Federal Environmental Agency, Berlin.

UN, 2002. *United Nations Conference on Environment and Development, UNCED, 1992, Agenda 21. Plan of implementation of the World Summit on Sustainable Development.* Revised version as of 20 September 2002. http:// www.johannesburgsummit.org/

Wuppertal Institute, 2002. 'DMI of 13 EU accession countries and Norway 1992–1999'. Unpublished study. Wuppertal Institute.

2.1. Energy

Energy use contributes to a range of environmental pressures and is the major source of greenhouse and acid gas emissions in Europe. Options for reducing environmental pressures include using less-polluting energy sources, using energy more efficiently, and using less of the energy-consuming services such as transport, space heating and manufactured products.

Total energy consumption in Europe fell over the review period (1992–1999). This was due in part to increased energy efficiency across the region, but mainly to reduced consumption in eastern Europe, the Caucasus and central Asia (EECCA), linked to economic difficulties and restructuring.

Energy use continues to be dominated by fossil fuels, but the proportion of both total energy and electricity supplied from renewable sources increased in all three regions between 1992 and 1999. Fastest growth occurred in western Europe due to successful support programmes in a number of countries, but its share remains small. Output also increased in central and eastern European (CEE) countries, while the decline in the 12 countries of EECCA was less than for other energy sources.

Energy efficiency improved, but in western Europe this was not enough to prevent further growth in total energy consumption. Energy efficiency in the CEE countries also improved as a result of a combination of positive measures and economic restructuring. There has been little improvement in EECCA. In these latter two regions energy consumption per unit of gross domestic product remains considerably higher than in western Europe, indicating a substantial potential for further efficiency improvements.

Overall, energy-related greenhouse gas emissions fell substantially, mainly as a result of economic difficulties and restructuring that led to reduced energy use in CEE and EECCA. This improvement may be lost as these economies recover, unless stronger action is taken to improve energy efficiency and switch to low-carbon energy sources.

Energy-related acid gas emissions decreased substantially, helping put all three regions on track to achieve their 2010 emission targets.

Nuclear power, which does not emit greenhouse gases, raises concerns over safety and the long-term management of radioactive wastes.

2.1.1. Introduction

Energy is vital to social and economic well-being. It provides personal comfort and mobility, and is essential to most industrial and commercial activities. Although emissions of pollutants have fallen, today's energy production and consumption practices place considerable pressures on the environment, including contributing to climate change, damaging natural ecosystems, agriculture and the built environment, and adversely affecting human health.

The main determinant of these pressures is the source of the energy. Generally, coal use exerts the greatest pressures because of the high levels of greenhouse gas, acid gas (unless end-of-pipe clean-up or advanced technology is used) and particulate emissions associated with its use. Coal use also produces considerable solid and liquid pollution as a result of its extraction and the disposal of ash. Oil typically exerts less pressure on the environment than coal because of its lower carbon content and reduced solid waste combustion products. Natural gas is the cleanest of the fossil fuels because of its even lower carbon content and lower propensity to cause acid emissions. Nonetheless, natural gas is still a major source of carbon dioxide emissions, and natural gas production facilities and pipelines leak methane, a potent greenhouse gas. Nuclear and renewable energy sources exert the least pressure in terms of greenhouse gas emissions and air pollution. With nuclear sources, however, there is a risk of radioactive releases in the event of an accident, and highly radioactive wastes are accumulating for which no generally acceptable disposal route has yet been established. Renewable energy resources offer the cleanest source of energy, but they can have some adverse impacts on the environment such as loss of natural amenities, loss of habitat, visual intrusion and noise.

Certain European countries and the European Union (EU) have adopted policies to reduce the environmental pressures associated with energy. These include support for energy-saving measures, increased efficiency measures in energy conversion and consumption, switching to less-polluting fuels, removal of subsidies that favour more-polluting fuels, and the promotion of renewable energy sources and price structures that are more representative of the full cost to society of the energy being used.

But environmental pressures are not the only factors that affect international and national energy policies, which are also concerned with security of supply, competitive energy prices, market liberalisation, social factors and job creation (EEA, 2002). In some cases these concerns move in harmony with the environment, for example increased energy efficiency is beneficial to most, if not all, energy policy goals. But there are also conflicts. For example concerns over job creation and security of supply may prompt financial support for indigenous energy production, acting as a disincentive to energy saving through lower prices, and preventing the import of cleaner alternatives. Energy prices may also be kept low to support economic recovery and reduce social impacts. Market liberalisation, which can help attract international investment to modernise energy systems, can deliver lower energy costs in the long run, which, in the absence of appropriate policies to internalise the external costs of energy and improve energy demand management, may lead to reduced energy prices and even increased energy consumption.

2.1.2. Consumption and sources of energy

2.1.2.1. Total energy consumption
Total energy consumption fell by 7.5 % in Europe between 1992 and 1999 (Figure 2.1.1). This was mainly the result of reduced energy consumption in eastern Europe, the Caucasus and central Asia (EECCA), attributed to economic decline rather than increased energy efficiency. Energy consumption in central and eastern Europe (CEE) also fell due to a combination of economic restructuring and the implementation of energy efficiency measures. Turkey, a major energy consumer within the CEE region, increased its energy consumption substantially over the period as a result of high economic growth and only limited measures to improve energy efficiency. Energy consumption in western Europe (WE) increased, roughly in line with economic growth, a trend that is expected to be followed by CEE and EECCA as the countries in these regions complete their transition to market-based economies. To minimise the environmental impacts associated with

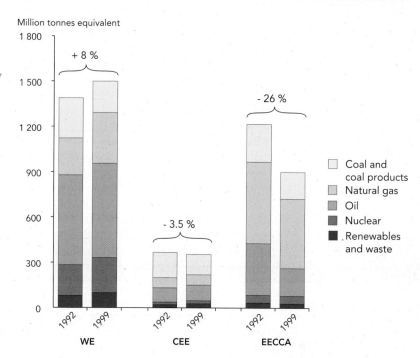

| Total energy consumption in Europe, 1992–1999 | Figure 2.1.1. |

Million tonnes equivalent

Notes: Total energy consumption is also known as total primary energy supply or gross inland energy consumption. It is a measure of the energy inputs to an economy and can be calculated by adding total indigenous energy production, energy imports minus exports and net withdrawals from existing stocks. Waste includes wood wastes, other biodegradable solid wastes, and industrial and municipal wastes which contain both biodegradable and non-biodegradable components. Only biodegradable waste is considered to be a renewable energy source.

Source: IEA, 2001

energy use in Europe, a substantial switch to less-polluting energy sources and large improvements in energy efficiency is needed (see Section 2.1.3).

> Total energy consumption fell in Europe but the environmental impacts of energy use seem destined to increase unless fossil fuels become less dominant and large improvements in energy efficiency are made.

2.1.2.2. Sources of energy
There have been overall reductions in coal and oil consumption with a growth in natural gas use. The reduction in coal use in CEE and EECCA is linked to the reduction of government support and the closure of a number of uneconomic mines. However, there is a risk of renewed growth in coal consumption if the Russian Federation turns to coal for electricity production to free up more natural gas and oil for export (European Commission, 2002). In WE the reduction in coal use is mainly the result of one-off fuel switching in favour of natural gas. European oil consumption fell entirely as a

result of reduced consumption in EECCA. Oil consumption increased in the countries of WE and CEE, mainly as a result of growth in transport demand, particularly road transport.

Nuclear power production increased in CEE and WE, and to a much lesser extent in EECCA. This trend is not expected to continue as nuclear plants start to be decommissioned throughout Europe and few new plants are in preparation. This is expected to result in a further growth in combustion-related emissions in the long term, including carbon dioxide, if the shortfall in capacity is replaced by fossil-fuelled plant. This highlights the importance of policies and measures to stimulate the development and deployment of renewable energy sources (see Box 2.1.1), i.e. the general problem of phasing out nuclear with timely and non-emitting replacements.

Overall, the proportion of renewable energy sources in total energy consumption increased slightly. Total renewable energy consumption (both electricity and heat) increased by 15 % between 1992 and 1999, increasing its share of total energy consumption from 4.5 to 5.6 %. Electricity production from renewable sources increased by 15 %, thus bringing its share of total production

from 18 to 20 % (see Figure 2.1.2). In WE this growth was supported by a range of policy interventions, mainly aimed at stimulating the growth of new renewable technologies for electricity production. In CEE most growth came from an expansion of biomass/waste combustion and hydropower, but this does not appear to be linked to any coordinated policy initiatives. Renewable energy production decreased in EECCA due to a decrease in production from combustible renewable sources and hydropower. However, due to falling overall energy consumption, the proportion of renewable energy sources in total energy consumption actually increased.

Renewable electricity production continues to be dominated by hydropower in all regions, and it accounts for about 90 % of production in CEE and EECCA. This source is unlikely to increase in WE since the majority of the most suitable sites have already been exploited and because damage to the environment through loss of land and the resultant destruction of natural habitats and ecosystems impedes further development. There are still a number of exploitable sites in CEE and EECCA. The use of 'new renewable' sources such as wind and solar remains small for countries outside WE. Western Europe made some headway in wind power increasing its share to 2.4 % of total renewable electricity production in 1999. This growth was greatly helped by the 'feed-in' arrangement implemented during that period by Denmark, Germany and Spain, according to which the utilities were obliged to purchase electricity from renewable electricity producers at a fixed, commercially favourable price. The share of electricity production from wind for EECCA and CEE was below 0.1 % of total renewable electricity production in 1999. Solar electricity production is reported only in WE, where it represented just 0.01 % of total renewable electricity production in 1999, with Germany and Spain driving its growth with the help of feed-in arrangements and state financial support (EEA, 2001).

2.1.3. Energy efficiency

One way to reduce the environmental pressures of energy use is to reduce the demand for energy-consuming services or to deliver these services with more efficient devices. The importance of using energy efficiently is recognised in a number of policy agreements and measures including

| Figure 2.1.2. | Contribution of renewable energy sources and waste to total energy consumption and electricity production, Europe 1992–1997 |

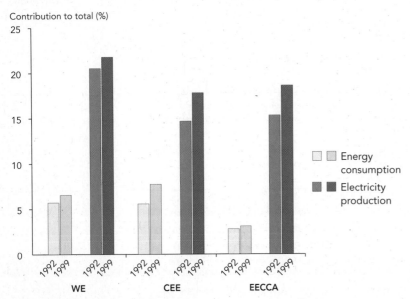

Notes: Waste includes wood wastes, other biodegradable solid wastes and industrial and municipal wastes which contain both biodegradable and non-biodegradable components. Only biodegradable waste is considered to be a renewable energy source.

Source: IEA, 2001

Box 2.1.1. Renewable energies: success stories

Renewable energy sources are seen as an increasingly important option for reducing the pressures placed on the environment by energy production and consumption, and can contribute to the security of energy supply by replacing imported fossil fuels.

The European Energy Agency (EEA) has found that the extent to which renewable energy technologies are successfully deployed depends on the cumulative benefits of a series of supportive measures. While no single factor has been identified as being of overwhelming significance, there are certain essential components which, when combined, allow the successful exploitation of renewable energy sources.

- **Political support**. Countries which showed a rapid expansion of renewable energy during the 1990s are most commonly those with long-established policies in support of renewable energy in general or of a particular renewable energy.
- **Legislative support**. Producers of electricity from renewable sources need access to electricity networks to be able to distribute the electricity produced. This requires the establishment of transparent and reasonable charging structures so that they can operate successfully within the electricity supply system. The 'feed-in law system' has given a great impetus to developments in electricity produced from renewable sources, in particular wind energy. This system combines commercially favourable guaranteed feed-in tariffs with an obligation on utilities to purchase renewable electricity at these tariffs.
- **Fiscal support**. Taxation is increasingly being used as a mechanism to reward the environmental benefits of renewable energy compared with energy generated from fossil sources.
- **Financial support**. The capital costs of renewable energy projects, which are often high, can be a significant barrier to development, especially for newer technologies. Subsidies or favourable loans for renewable energy developments are common where the successful market penetration of renewable technologies occurs.
- **Administrative support**. Successful replication of renewable energy projects can be achieved on a wide scale only where there is active support for renewable energy at the level at which individual projects are brought forward for approval. In most cases this is the local or regional level. Administrative support at the national level is also important.

- **Technological development**. The development of renewable energy technologies requires support at all stages - research, demonstration and implementation - to help achieve strong and competitive indigenous industry capabilities in renewable energy.
- **Information, education and training**. Activities that raise awareness of the benefits of renewable energy among the general public are a vital component of national, regional and local renewable energy support programmes. Energy agencies at local or regional level are one of the most successful initiatives to help raise public awareness of the benefits of renewable energy and increase public acceptance of new renewable energy developments.

Case study: Biomass district heating in Austria

District heating is very common in Austria, and the use of biomass as a fuel increased by more than 60 % in five years as a result of a series of supportive measures.

Austria has few indigenous fossil fuel resources, and so its energy policy addresses a number of security of supply issues including stimulating the use of renewable energy sources. The government and, in particular, the regions provide active political support for biomass energy and several regions have biomass-related targets.

In addition, Austrian energy taxes favour renewable energy schemes, and financial support for biomass installations, particularly for district heating schemes, is provided at both national and regional level. Local and regional authorities support the use of biomass as a fuel resource and, in some cases, demonstrate the benefits by taking the lead in its implementation in public buildings.

New technological developments for biomass production processes are supported in universities and in association with industry. To meet the demand for new biomass district heating plants, there is already indigenous manufacturing expertise, including boiler and pipework manufacture, and installation services.

Farmers are supportive of new biomass projects as they gain additional income, and wood users such as sawmills also benefit from the additional market for their wood wastes. Together with local energy agencies, these actors have been key in promoting the economic and environmental benefits of using biomass as a fuel.

Source: EEA, 2001

---

the Energy Charter Treaty and Protocol on Energy Efficiency and Related Environmental Aspects (ECS, 2002). In addition, the EU has developed an action plan which aims to deliver a 1 % per year reduction in energy intensity, over and above 'that which would have otherwise been attained' (Council of the European Union, 1998). In this case the energy intensity of a country is defined as its final energy consumption divided by its gross domestic product (GDP). The measures

contained in this plan should encourage developments in countries that have applied for EU membership, as well as in current Member States.

2.1.3.1. Efficiency of fossil-fuelled electricity production

The electricity production sector is of particular importance. Experience shows that the proportion of electricity in final energy consumption increases as economies

| Figure 2.1.3. | Efficiency of electricity production from fossil-fuelled power plant, Europe 1992–1999 |

Source: IEA, 2001

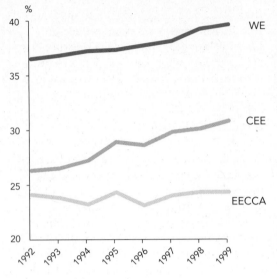

The efficiency of electricity production from fossil fuels improved slightly, but only in western Europe and central and eastern Europe

develop. This is because greater automation in industrial production usually requires a greater use of electricity, while increased wealth results in more electricity use by households and services. Between 1992 and 1999 Europe's share of electricity in final energy demand increased by more than 11 %, reaching 19 % in WE, 15.5 % in CEE and 12.6 % in EECCA. Since this trend is likely to continue, it is vital for the environment that electricity is produced with maximum efficiency, especially when produced from fossil fuels that release substantial quantities of greenhouse gases and other pollutants.

On average, the efficiency of fossil-fuelled electricity production in Europe increased from 29 % to 32 % between 1992 and 1999 (see Figure 2.1.3). This was due mostly to plant replacement in WE (especially switching to inherently more efficient systems such as gas turbines), and technical improvements and refurbishment in CEE. However, production efficiency in both CEE and EECCA remains substantially below WE levels. In CEE countries this is due to high reliance on coal (the source of 74 % of fossil-fuelled electricity production in 1999, compared with 48 % in WE), which is intrinsically less efficient for electricity production than gas, and to the age and low technical standard of many of the plants. In EECCA, 59 % of fossil-fuelled electricity production comes from natural gas, which is capable of higher production efficiencies, but the low efficiency observed in the region indicates the age and poor technical performance of such plant. Significant efficiency improvements in CEE and EECCA will only come from investment in new plant, but few national utilities can afford this. Consequently, many countries are implementing or are planning market liberalisation measures in order to attract private investment.

| Figure 2.1.4. | Final energy intensity, Europe 1992–1999 |

Note: Final energy consumption is the energy consumption of the transport, industry and other (household, services and agriculture) sectors. It includes the consumption of converted energy (i.e. electricity, publicly supplied heat, refined oil products, coke, etc.) and the direct use of primary fuels such as natural gas or renewables (e.g. solar heat, biomass). It excludes petrochemical feedstocks. The final energy consumption of Turkey remained almost constant during the period 1992-99. Excluding Turkey, the largest CEE country, from the aggregated CEE total indicates that in the rest of the region final energy consumption intensity fell by an average of 25 % over this period. Due to incomplete data, western Europe excludes Andorra, Liechtenstein, Monaco and San Marino, and central and eastern Europe excludes Bosnia and Herzegovina and Serbia and Montenegro.

Source: IEA, 2001; World Bank, 2002

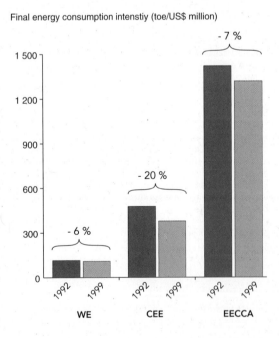

Final energy consumption intenstiy (toe/US$ million)

Energy is being used more efficiently throughout Europe, mainly as a result of changes in central and eastern Europe, the Caucasus and central Asia, but this may not be sustained in the long run without more active support for energy efficiency.

2.1.3.2. Efficiency of energy use

Improvements in the way end-use sectors use energy can be tracked by measuring final energy intensity (i.e. final energy consumption per unit of GDP). The lower the intensity the less energy is used per unit of wealth created.

Energy intensities in CEE and EECCA are substantially higher than in WE (see Figure 2.1.4). This reflects lower efficiency in all end-use sectors due to a combination of factors including older, less efficient industrial plant, inadequate maintenance, older, less efficient vehicle fleets, and the combined effect of poorly insulated building stock, a lack of heating controls in buildings and the comparatively longer and colder winters experienced in some parts of CEE and EECCA. Historically, this situation developed as a result of countries' access to relatively abundant, low-cost energy resources, which made them less exposed to the energy price shocks of the 1970s, and provided less incentive to invest in energy efficiency. The situation persisted due to a shortage of investment, especially in EECCA.

Most EECCA and CEE countries developed policies to encourage and support rational energy saving. This, together with one-off economic restructuring, contributed to reduced energy intensities, particularly in CEE. However, in many countries, the implementation of energy efficiency measures has been weak because priority has been given to economic recovery and social issues, and the institutions needed to drive energy

efficiency policies were poorly supported. Consequently in a number of countries, particularly in EECCA, the improvements have been due mainly to deprivation rather than rational energy saving, and may therefore be reversed as economies develop, unless stronger measures to support energy efficiency are implemented. The slow pace with which energy intensity decreased in WE is the result of low prioritisation of energy efficiency policies due to abundant energy supplies and low fossil fuel prices.

Table 2.1.1 shows that there is considerable potential for energy savings in all sectors throughout Europe and especially in CEE and EECCA. In CEE, improvements in industrial energy intensity resulted from a combination of the closure of some less-efficient plant and investment in new production facilities by international companies. Energy efficiency improvements in households and services resulted from a combination of measures including increased prices, reduced subsidies, metering and billing by consumption, all of which provided a financial incentive to reduce energy consumption. In EECCA, industrial energy intensity actually increased between 1992 and 1999, indicating that, on average, the economic decline and restructuring in these countries has not yielded any improvement in efficiency. The improvements in energy intensity in households and services were due mainly to supply limitations and self-deprivation as price and market reforms have proved difficult to introduce at a time of economic recession and high unemployment.

| (tonnes of oil equivalent /US$ million) | Energy intensities of individual economic sectors | | | | | Table 2.1.1. |
| | Industry | | Transport | | Households and services | |
	1992	1999	1992	1999	1992	1999
Western Europe	126	124	33	33	43	40
Central and eastern Europe	622	418	73	73	202	164
Eastern Europe, the Caucasus and central Asia	924	1 281	242	223	751	615

Notes: The table presents energy intensity data for regional comparison only. Comparisons between different economic sectors should not be made since industrial energy intensity is calculated as the ratio of energy consumption to value added, while the energy intensity of the transport and household and services sectors is calculated as the ratio of energy consumption to GDP. These energy intensities are also not comparable with the final energy intensity of Figure 2.1.4, which is defined as the ratio of final energy consumption to GDP.

Western Europe excludes Andorra, Liechtenstein, Monaco and San Marino, and additionally excludes Iceland, Ireland, Luxembourg and Switzerland from the calculation of industrial energy intensity due to incomplete data. Central and eastern Europe excludes Bosnia and Herzegovina and Serbia and Montenegro, and additionally excludes Cyprus and Malta from the calculation of industrial energy intensity due to incomplete data. Eastern Europe, the Caucasus and central Asia exclude Azerbaijan and Georgia from the calculation of industrial energy intensity due to incomplete data.

Source: IEA, 2001; World Bank, 2002

Box 2.1.2. Energy efficiency: success stories

Case Study — hospital heating system refurbishment in the Czech Republic

The Bulovka teaching hospital in Prague needed a significant upgrade of the central heating system, but the hospital had no available funds. The necessary upgrades were obtained through a performance contract with an energy services company (ESCO). The ESCO provided the finance, which was paid off using the energy savings achieved at the hospital over an eight-year contract period.

The ESCO made four energy saving changes:

- Switching the existing central heating system to district heating that provided space heating and hot water in a more efficient way.
- Installing a small high-efficiency gas boiler for specific uses (other than heating and hot water) including sterilisation and laundry services. Heat had previously been taken from the hospital's main boiler plant.
- Putting in place a new computerised energy management system that gave more precise control of indoor temperatures, hot water and space heating. It also facilitates on-line performance monitoring, which together with preventative maintenance, ensures the long-term efficiency of the system.
- Installing a new air handler recovery system that was more efficient because it used heat exchangers to preheat intake air by absorbing the heat from vented air.

This project cost US$ 2.7 million and will produce savings of US$ 0.7 million/year, illustrating the high potential for energy savings through innovative financial arrangements. The project was awarded best practice status by the World Energy Efficiency Association.

Source: Energy Charter Secretariat, Brussels

2.1.4. Environmental impacts

Greenhouse gas emissions

The reduction of global greenhouse gas emissions is a priority action area for industrialised countries, as agreed under the UN Kyoto protocol (see Chapter 3). There is a clear need for action to reduce emissions arising from energy use since they account for more than 80 % of total emissions. Moreover they only represent a first step, since it is estimated that global emissions need to be reduced by about 70 % in the long term to stabilise greenhouse gas concentrations at an acceptable level (IPCC, 2001). It is therefore important for emissions reductions to be based on lasting measures and actions.

☺ Total energy-related greenhouse gas emissions fell substantially in Europe between 1990 and 1999, due mainly to economic difficulties and restructuring in EECCA and CEE. This improvement may be lost as these economies develop unless economic growth is accompanied by strong energy efficiency measures and the implementaion of low-carbon energy supply options.

Overall, energy-related greenhouse gas emissions in Europe fell considerably between 1990 and 1999 (Figure 2.1.5). This was due mainly to the Russian Federation and Ukraine, two of the biggest energy consumers in Europe, which reduced their total emissions by 36 % and 50 % respectively over the period. These reductions were mostly the result of economic difficulties and restructuring, which resulted in a substantial reduction in the energy use of these two countries over this period. CEE countries achieved a reduction of 4 % due to large cuts in most countries, mainly as a result of economic restructuring, which were partly offset by increased emissions from Turkey (54 %) and Croatia (11.7 %). Energy-related emissions in WE fell by only 1.6 %. Nevertheless, this was achieved against a background of an 18 % increase in economic growth over the same period.

Figure 2.1.5 shows that transport contributes a substantial proportion of greenhouse gas emissions in WE countries but much less in CEE countries. The low energy consumption of the transport sector in EECCA indicates that the contribution of transport emissions in this region is also much less. Transport growth is strongly driven by economic growth and transport emissions are expected to grow substantially in CEE and EECCA as economies recover and the demand for transport increases.

Fugitive methane emissions from energy production amounted to almost 15 % of total greenhouse gas emissions in the Russian Federation and Ukraine in 1999 (reflecting the substantial oil and gas production in these countries) compared to an average of almost 2 % and 4 % in WE and CEE respectively. Other significant oil and gas producers such as the United Kingdom have much lower fugitive emissions (i.e. about 3 % of total emissions in 1999) which indicates the potential for improvement in the Russian Federation and Ukraine.

One option for achieving a lasting reduction in energy-related greenhouse gas emissions is to reduce the greenhouse gas intensity of energy use by switching to energy sources that contain less carbon (e.g. from coal to natural gas or renewable energy sources), and/or by reducing the emissions associated with the production and use of these sources. Figure 2.1.6 shows that all three regions achieved reductions in greenhouse gas intensity between 1992 and 1999. In fact, with total energy consumption growing in

WE, the reduction in its energy-related greenhouse gas emissions was largely due to switching from coal to oil and gas which lead to this cut in greenhouse gas intensity. However, greenhouse gas intensities in CEE and EECCA remain substantially higher than in WE, mainly as a result of a large use of coal in CEE and of substantial fugitive methane emissions in EECCA.

2.1.4.2. Other environmental pressures

In addition to being the most important source of greenhouse gases, energy production and consumption place other pressures on the environment. Fossil fuel combustion is a major source of air pollution (see Chapter 5). Energy production also damages land and water resources through excessive dumping and unplanned discharges of a range of substances such as crude oil, mine tailings, polluted mine waters and coal ash. Nuclear power poses a potential threat to the environment, as there is a risk of radioactive releases (see Chapter 10).

Energy use is the major source of sulphur dioxide (SO_2) and nitrogen oxide (NO_x) emissions, accounting for over 90 % of both emissions in Europe in 1999. Considerable progress has been made in reducing these energy-related acid gas emissions and this has greatly helped all three regions to be on track to achieve their aggregate targets under the UNECE Convention on Long-Range Transboundary Air Pollution (see Chapter 5).

The reductions in acid gas emissions in WE, shown in Figure 2.1.7, were achieved mainly by direct actions including switching to lower sulphur fuels, installing flue gas clean-up systems, introducing catalytic converters in cars and modifying combustion processes. The reductions in CEE were also greatly helped by direct actions. However, the reduction in energy use in CEE, in particular of coal use, also played an important role. Data problems for some EECCA countries prevent precise conclusions being drawn, but judging from the energy consumption data, it is likely that the reduction in acid gas emissions was mostly the result of reduced energy use, with direct actions also contributing.

Energy-related acid gas emissions have been reduced substantially, placing all three regions on track to meet the total emissions targets for 2010.

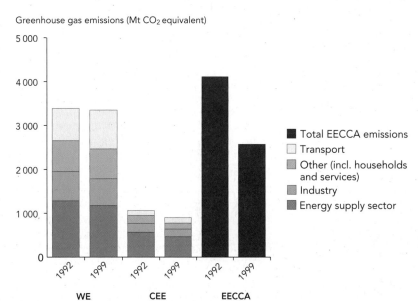

Energy-related greenhouse gas emissions, Europe 1990–1999 — Figure 2.1.5.

Notes: Due to an incomplete sectoral breakdown, data for EECCA cover all sources of carbon dioxide, methane and nitrous oxide, but estimates indicate that energy use accounts for over 80 % of these emissions. CEE excludes Albania, Bosnia and Herzegovina, the former Yugoslav Republic of Macedonia, Romania and Serbia and Montenegro due to missing or incomplete data. EECCA excludes Kyrgyzstan, Tajikistan and Turkmenistan due to missing or incomplete data. Due to an incomplete sectoral breakdown, data are for all greenhouse gas emission sources, not just those from energy-related activities. The Russian Federation and Ukraine accounted for over 82 % of the greenhouse gas emissions from EECCA countries. Energy supply sector emissions include those from coal mining, oil and gas exploration and extraction, public electricity and heat production, oil refining and other industries engaged in converting primary energy into energy products. It also includes fugitive emissions from the exploration, production, storage and transport of fuels. The data are for emissions of carbon dioxide, methane and nitrous oxide, and exclude the fluorinated gases.

Source: EEA/ETC on Air and Climate Change

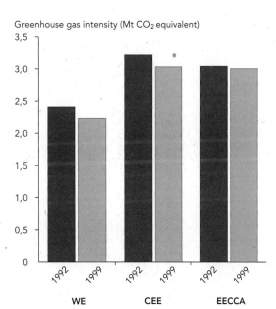

Greenhouse gas intensity of total energy consumption, Europe 1992–1999 — Figure 2.1.6.

Note: Greenhouse gas intensity is defined as the amount of greenhouse gas emissions, expressed in units of carbon dioxide equivalent, released per unit of total energy consumption. EECCA: based on total emissions because energy-related emissions data are not available for most countries in the region.

Sources: IEA, 2001; EEA/ETC on Air and Climate Change

The fact that direct actions contributed significantly to the reductions in Europe, particularly in WE and CEE, is encouraging. Nevertheless, a number of regions in Europe, mostly in CEE and EECCA countries, face serious air pollution problems that need to be addressed urgently and the potential for improvement through direct actions in CEE and EECCA remains large. In addition, the potential for further improvement through energy efficiency measures remains to be explored by all three regions.

Nuclear power is responsible for a steady accumulation of highly radioactive waste which could release radioactivity into the environment if not carefully managed. Some radioactive waste will remain radioactive for hundreds of thousands of years and the favoured long-term solution is at present deep geological disposal. Progress towards this objective has been slow, mainly because of societal concerns. No generally acceptable disposal route has been found.

Nuclear power can have a large impact on human health and the environment, but the risk of operational accidents, such as that experienced at Chernobyl, is reduced with improved safety systems and management procedures. The success of these measures is indicated by a fall in the number of 'unusual events' reported to the incident reporting system operated jointly by the International Atomic Energy Agency (IAEA) and OECD. This shows the number of incidents reported in Europe varying between 177 and 76 during the period 1992–2001, but with no clear improvement trend. Nevertheless, 2000 and 2001 had the lowest number of incidents (see Chapter 10).

The risks need to be balanced against the potential benefits of nuclear power. At the point of electricity production, nuclear power plants do not emit greenhouse or acid gases, but neither does the production of electricity from renewable sources.

Data on the accumulation of radioactive wastes across all three regions is not consistently available. However, OECD (Organisation for Economic Co-operation and Development) data for WE show on average an annual removal of nearly 3 000 tonnes of highly radioactive used nuclear fuel from reactors to stores during the 1985–2010 period (OECD, 1999) (see also Chapter 7).

2.1.5. Policy responses

For at least the next 20–30 years, European energy policy will primarily be driven by the energy policies that result from the Green Paper of the European Commission 'Towards a European strategy for the security of energy supply' and the energy strategy of the Russian Federation for 2020.

Figure 2.1.7.	Energy-related emissions of sulphur dioxide (a) and nitrogen oxides (b), Europe 1992–1999

Notes: Energy-related emissions include emissions from transport. SO_2 emissions for EECCA exclude emissions from Azerbaijan, Georgia, Kyrgyzstan, Kazakhstan, Tajikistan and Turkmenistan, due to incomplete data coverage. SO_2 emissions for CEE exclude emissions from Albania, Bosnia-Herzegovina, Malta and Romania, due to incomplete data coverage. NO_x emissions for CEE exclude emissions from Albania, Malta and Romania, due to incomplete data coverage.

Source: EEA/ETC on Air and Climate Change

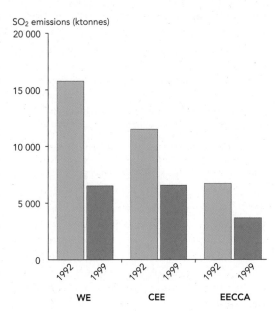

SO₂ emissions (ktonnes)

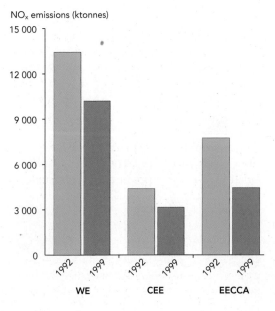

NOₓ emissions (ktonnes)

> 😞 No generally acceptable disposal route has yet been established for the continued build-up of highly radioactive waste from nuclear power production and the risk of radioactivity being released into the environment causes additional concern.

These two main actors launched the EU-Russia Energy Dialogue at the sixth EU-Russian summit on 30 October 2000 in Paris. This cooperation allows the EU and the Russian Federation to pursue areas of 'common interest' by establishing a strategic energy partnership. This will aim to 'share the same concerns for ensuring stable energy markets, reliable and growing imports and exports, a pressing need to modernise the Russian energy sector, to improve energy efficiency and to reduce greenhouse gas emissions from energy production and use in their respective economies'.

A joint declaration adopted at the sixth EU-Russian summit notes that the planned ratification of the Energy Charter Treaty by the Russian Federation will be an important aspect for introducing 'cooperation on energy saving, rationalisation of production and transport infrastructures, European investment possibilities, and relations between producer and consumer countries'. The Energy Charter Treaty has been ratified by most European countries and strives 'towards open, efficient, sustainable and secure energy markets', and 'to promote a constructive climate conducive to energy interdependence on the basis of trust between nations'.

The 'Northern Dimension' aims to address the special regional development challenges of northern Europe (the Baltic Sea region, the Arctic Sea region and the northwest of the Russian Federation). The Northern Dimension action plan includes actions for addressing environmental problems in the region including atmospheric pollution, improving nuclear safety and nuclear waste management, and facilitating cooperation in the energy sector.

Nuclear safety and the management of spent nuclear fuel and radioactive waste remain contentious issues. As yet there are no common rules on nuclear reactor safety or radioactive waste disposal although the European Commission has proposed directives on the safety of nuclear installations and on the management of used nuclear fuel and radioactive waste (European Commission, 2003). Most WE countries that operate commercial nuclear power stations have declared that they will not increase their nuclear power capacity and four countries have declared that their reactors will be phased out. Seven candidate countries use nuclear power. To a large extent, nuclear power replaces the electricity that would otherwise be produced by fossil fuels (and in

particular coal), and so commitments to reducing greenhouse gas emissions make it difficult for some countries to reduce their nuclear power production without a more sustainable alternative energy source. However, the Russian Federation's energy strategy plans to increase coal and nuclear-based electricity production in order to reduce dependence on natural gas.

The three main goals of EU energy policy - security of supply, competitiveness and environmental protection (Council of the European Union, 1995) — are strongly interrelated. Improvements in energy efficiency should benefit security of supply, by reducing the amount of energy consumed, and abate emissions of greenhouse gases and other pollutants, by reducing the consumption of fossil fuels. Market liberalisation and additional price competition will benefit competitiveness through reduced prices, but may act as a disincentive to energy saving and encourage consumption unless external costs are fully internalised and energy demand is better managed.

The environmental integration process was initiated at the European Council Cardiff summit when all relevant formations of the Council were invited to establish their own strategies for giving effect to environmental integration and sustainable development within their respective policy areas. The specific objectives of EU energy policy in the area of environmental integration (European Commission, 1998) are to reduce the environmental impact of the production and use of energy, to promote energy saving and energy efficiency, and to increase the use of cleaner energy and its share of total energy production.

The EU sixth environmental action programme (6EAP) (European Parliament and Council, 2002) encourages renewable and low-carbon fossil fuels for power production as part of the priority actions for reducing greenhouse gas emissions in the energy sector.

The significance of renewable energy sources was recognised at the Johannesburg United Nations World Summit on Sustainable Development (UN, 2002) and in a number of EU policy documents. Notable among these were a renewable energies White Paper (European Commission, 1997) and a directive on the promotion of electricity from renewable energy sources (European Parliament and Council, 2001). The

EU documents set overall targets to derive 12 % of the EU's total energy consumption and 22.1 % of the EU's electricity from renewable sources by 2010. This should also encourage the development of renewable energy sources in countries that have applied for EU membership. Some CEE countries and EECCA have also developed energy and environment policies that include the development of renewable sources, but in most countries this has had a low priority, the necessary investment resources are lacking and the strong institutional structures needed to drive the process have not yet been established.

The Energy Charter Protocol on Energy Efficiency and Related Environmental Aspects has been ratified by most European countries and 'defines policy principles for the promotion of energy efficiency as a considerable source of energy and for consequently reducing adverse environmental impacts of energy systems'.

In addition, the EU 6EAP identifies the promotion of energy efficiency as a priority action to reduce greenhouse gas emissions in the energy sector (European Parliament and Council, 2002) and the Barcelona European Council in 2002 stressed the need to show substantial progress in energy efficiency by 2010. The European Commission's multiannual Intelligent Energy for Europe Programme should support the promotion of renewable energies and energy saving, taking account of the EU strategy for sustainable development approved by the Gothenburg European Council in 2001.

2.1.6. References

Council of the European Union, 1995. 1850th meeting, 1 June 1995. *Council resolution on the Green Paper 'For a European Union energy policy'*.

Council of the European Union, 1998. *Council Resolution 98/C394/01 on energy efficiency in the European Community*.

EEA (European Environment Agency), 2001. *Renewable energies: success stories*. Environmental issue report No 27. EEA, Copenhagen.

EEA (European Environment Agency), 2002. *Energy and environment in the European Union*. Environmental issue report No 31. EEA, Copenhagen.

ECS (Energy Charter Secretariat), 2002. *The Energy Charter Treaty — a reader's guide*. ECS, Brussels.

European Commission, 1997. *Energy for the future: Renewable sources of energy*. White Paper for a Community strategy and action plan. COM(97) 30 final. Commission of the European Communities, Brussels.

European Commission, 1998. *Strengthening environmental integration within Community energy policy*. Communication from the Commission. COM(1998) 571 final. Commission of the European Communities, Brussels.

European Commission, 2002. 2001 *annual energy review*. European Commission, Luxembourg.

European Commission, 2003. *Proposal for a Council (Euratom) directive setting out basic obligations and general principles on the safety of nuclear installations. Proposal for a Council directive (Euratom) on the management of spent nuclear fuel and radioactive waste*. COM (2003) 32 final. Commission of the European Communities, Brussels.

European Parliament and Council, 2001. Directive 2001/77/EC on the promotion of electricity produced from renewable energy sources in the electricity market, September 2001.

European Parliament and Council, 2002. *Decision 1600/2002/EC laying down the sixth Community environment action programme*.

IEA (International Energy Agency), 2001. *Energy balances of OECD countries and energy balances of non-OECD countries*. IEA, Paris.

IPCC (Intergovernmental Panel on Climate Change), 2001 IPCC Working Group I. *Third assessment report, summary for policy makers*.

OECD (Organisation for Economic Co-operation and Development), 1999. *Environmental data compendium 1999*. OECD, Paris.

UN (United Nations), 2002. *World Summit on Sustainable Development — Plan of implementation*. UN, Johannesburg.

World Bank, 2002. *World development indicators 2002*. The World Bank.

2.2. Industry

Industry remains an important sector of the economy in Europe and especially in the 12 countries of eastern Europe, the Caucasus and central Asia (EECCA). Industrial output is growing throughout Europe but eco-efficiency is generally improving. Although industrial energy use in western European countries is growing slowly, value added is growing more rapidly, so energy efficiency is improving. In central and eastern Europe, energy efficiency is improving at a faster rate, but remains well below that in western Europe, while industry in EECCA is still seven times more energy intensive than that in the west.

The main challenge in western Europe is to ensure better protection of the environment while maintaining a competitive industrial base. In central and eastern Europe, major investments are needed to raise the environmental performance of industry to the standards required by the accession process. In EECCA, the main challenge is to build an appropriate regulatory framework and improve enforcement.

2.2.1. Introduction

Industry is an important provider of income and employment in many countries in Europe, but is often associated with pollution. However, industrial pollution has decreased substantially over the past 30 years in most western European (WE) countries and over the past 15 years in the central and eastern European (CEE) countries. As industry consists of large and easy identifiable point sources of pollution, it has always been a prime target of environmental policy.

Data on value added and various pollutants specifically for manufacturing industry are generally sparse. In many countries of CEE and eastern Europe, the Caucasus and central Asia (EECCA), data on manufacturing industry still includes electricity production and mining despite guidelines in the national accounting systems that require them to be separated. This is important because industry in these countries is a large auto-producer of electricity and heat, making it difficult to disentangle a company's energy production from its manufacturing activities. The main developments discussed below are therefore for total industry, which includes mining, manufacturing industries and electricity

production. Developments in manufacturing industry are then discussed in more detail for those countries for which data are available.

2.2.2. Main socio-economic developments

Throughout the region, total industrial output has been growing again since at least the mid-1990s. Since 1993, total industrial value added has grown by 10 % in WE and 30 % in CEE. The industrial sector in EECCA has only recently started to recover from the decline in the early 1990s, with substantial growth in 1999 and 2000.

Despite growing output, employment in total industry is generally falling — in Poland and the Russian Federation by 32 % and 35 % respectively between 1990 and 1999. Even in the EU, industrial employment fell by 13 % during the same period. However, labour productivity has increased substantially, often by more than the increase in nominal wages. Industry therefore remains a dominant sector in Europe, generating 30-40 % of GDP. In CEE and EECCA, this share remained rather stable during the 1990s, while in WE it slowly diminished (Figure 2.2.1). Remarkable is the growth in CEE economies from 1993 to 1997. This supports the view that the first stage of the transition process was characterised by increased utilisation capacities of industries rather than structural shifts in the economy. Devaluation in CEE countries helped by providing cost advantages for companies in international markets. Only after 1997 did growth in the services sector become more dominant. Such

Share of industry in total GDP, Europe 1990–2000	Figure 2.2.1.

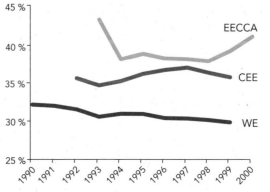

Notes: Data refer to total industry, including mining and electricity production. WE does not include Ireland, Luxembourg, Iceland and Switzerland. CEE does not include Cyprus, Malta, Bosnia-Herzegovina, and Serbia and Montenegro. EECCA does not include Georgia and Tajikistan.

Source: EEA, based on World Bank

developments are still underway in EECCA, where recovery of utilisation capacities only really started in 1999, after the 'rouble crisis' (the 1997 default crisis in the Russian Federation).

The structure of industrial output has changed little in WE but substantially in CEE and EECCA. Figure 2.2.2 shows changes in

Figure 2.2.2.	Changes in value added of industrial sectors in selected countries, 1990–1999 (%)

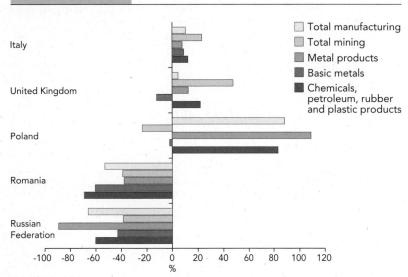

Note: For the Russian Federation, time period is 1990–98.

Source: UN Statistics Division (industrial production index by industry groups)

Figure 2.2.3.	Industrial consumption of energy in Europe, 1993–1999

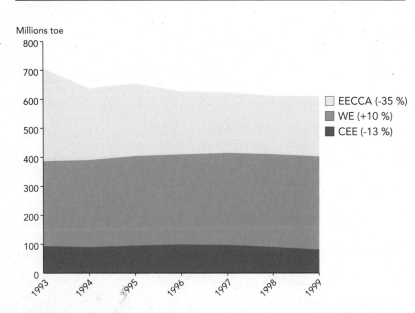

Notes: The percentage change between 1993 and 1999 for the three country groupings is given in brackets. Data refer to total industry, including mining and electricity production and do not include transformation losses in refineries and power and heat generation unless taking place within industries or mines.

Source: IEA

some energy and pollution-intensive sectors for several large countries in Europe. In Italy and the United Kingdom, growth in relatively polluting activities, such as mining and chemical production, was slightly higher than the overall growth in manufacturing industry. Apparently, such activities have been able to cope quite successfully with the growing competition from CEE and EECCA. In Poland, industry has successfully recovered from the economic crisis, with manufacturing industry producing 80 % more value added than in 1990, and an even higher increase in the metal products industries. This is typical for most of the advanced accession countries. In Hungary, industrial output in the metal product sector in 1999 was nine times that in 1990. However, in Romania and the Russian Federation the situation was markedly different. In the Russian Federation, total manufacturing declined by 70 %, but the food industry and the base-metal sector — especially steel production — have shown signs of recovery in more recent years. Raw steel production in 2000 was nearly at the 1992 level.

2.2.3. Environmental developments

Manufacturing industry is responsible for a wide range of environmental pollution: emissions to air (acidifying substances, greenhouse gases, persistent organic pollutants, heavy metals and other types of pollutants), emissions to water, contamination of soil and the generation of wastes. Moreover, industrial activities are connected to disturbances to landscapes, and the generation of noise and hazards.

Many of the environmental problems of industry are sector specific. Concise and comprehensive data on industrial pollution covering the whole region for the various sectors of industry are virtually non-existent. A few indicators can serve as proxies to indicate overall developments. Industrial energy use is the most often used: it can be seen as a proxy for several important air pollutants (in particular carbon dioxide (CO_2) and to a lesser extent sulphur dioxide (SO_2), nitrogen oxides (NO_x), dioxins and airborne heavy metals).

Industrial energy use declined in the whole region during the 1990s (Figure 2.2.3.). In EECCA, industrial energy use declined by 35 %, mainly because of the fall in industrial output. In CEE countries, there was a small increase in energy use between 1993 and 1996, thereafter energy use declined rapidly. In WE, industrial energy use increased by more than 1 % per year. However, industrial value added in WE countries grew more rapidly than industrial energy use, so energy efficiency continued to improve. Efficiency improvements are most pronounced in the CEE countries — by more than 30 % since 1992. Nevertheless, industry in CEE is still three times more energy intensive than that in WE, and the figure is seven times more in EECCA (Figure 2.2.4.). This is explained partly by the relatively low energy prices prevailing in the former socialist republics.

> 😐 Industrial energy use during the 1990s fell in central and eastern European, the Caucasus and central Asian countries and grew slowly in western Europe, where energy efficiency continued to improve. Industry in central and eastern Europe is still three times more energy intensive than that in western Europe, and the figure is seven times more in eastern Europe, the Caucasus and central Asia.

The limited data on industrial pollution, water and energy use, only fully available for some countries, show similar, albeit sharper, improvements in eco-efficiency (Figure 2.2.5). On the basis of these limited data, it can be concluded that an absolute decoupling of industrial growth and environmental pressure was achieved for all the chosen indicators in the EU and in Hungary only. Industrial waste generation increased considerably in Poland and in Norway. Water abstraction by industries and emissions of acidifying substances declined in all countries for which data were available. In Slovakia and the Russian Federation, the decline in these pollutants was higher than the reduction in industrial output; in Latvia, the decline was smaller than the decrease in industrial value added.

> 🙂 Around 75 % of industrial pollution indicators (air emission, water and energy use) show improvement between 1992 and 1999.

The observed decline in some forms of industrial pollution may have different causes for different countries. Some commentators have suggested that economic growth might be the driving force since

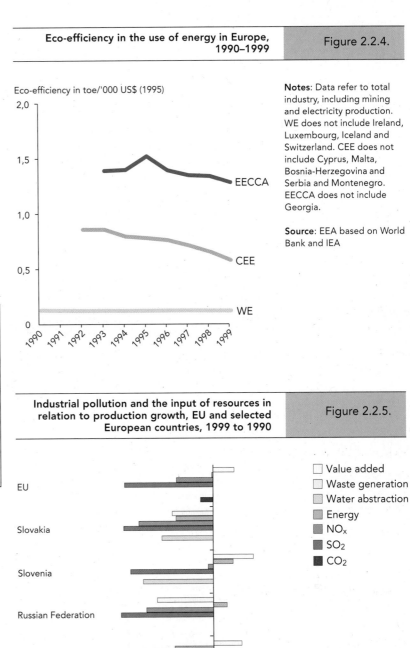

Figure 2.2.4.

Eco-efficiency in the use of energy in Europe, 1990–1999

Eco-efficiency in toe/'000 US$ (1995)

Notes: Data refer to total industry, including mining and electricity production. WE does not include Ireland, Luxembourg, Iceland and Switzerland. CEE does not include Cyprus, Malta, Bosnia-Herzegovina and Serbia and Montenegro. EECCA does not include Georgia.

Source: EEA based on World Bank and IEA

Figure 2.2.5.

Industrial pollution and the input of resources in relation to production growth, EU and selected European countries, 1999 to 1990

☐ Value added
☐ Waste generation
☐ Water abstraction
▨ Energy
▦ NO_x
■ SO_2
■ CO_2

Notes: Energy and value added refer to total industry; emissions, water abstraction and waste to manufacturing industry only. Waste is defined as the total amount of primary waste generated by industrial processes. Data of SO_2 and NO_x refer to categories (3) and (4) of SNAP97: combustion processes in manufacturing industries and production processes (which partially includes building activities). For Slovenia and Slovakia, data on SO_2 and NO_x include only combustion processes in manufacturing industries. CO_2 emissions of the EU refer to net emissions (without sinks). All data for Latvia, Slovenia and the Russian Federation refer to 1992-99. All data for Slovakia refer to 1991-99. Water abstraction for Hungary refers to 1992-98 and for Slovenia to 1992-97.

Source: EEA, based on World Bank (value added), IEA (energy), Corinair (SO_2 and NO_x), Eurostat (New Cronos for waste and water abstraction) and EU data on emissions from EEA (Eurostat)

higher growth rates allow companies to invest in clean technologies and tend to be associated with a more benign attitude towards environmental policies (Grossman and Krueger, 1995).

Figure 2.2.6 shows that for the industry sector throughout Europe virtually no relationship can be found between the change in SO$_2$ emissions and the growth in industrial output (measured as value added). However, it appears that for WE countries high industrial growth rates are associated with less reduction in industrial SO$_2$ emissions in the 1990s.

It is often thought that the transformation in CEE and EECCA countries from heavy industries towards consumer products is responsible for the different relationships as shown in Figure 2.2.6 — industrial structures typically change more rapidly in countries that are experiencing faster growth rates. However, a decomposition analysis into the components of change of SO$_2$ emission intensities (see Box 2.2.1) reveals that this

may not be the case in several countries. It is more likely that higher growth rates allow for more rapid scrapping of out-dated plant, new plant generally having more favourable emission profiles.

2.2.4. Policy outlook

Since the 1970s, much effort at different levels of government has been devoted to controlling industrial pollution. This has resulted in the decoupling of several important pollutants from industrial output. The question is whether such decoupling can be maintained.

A major challenge for industrial pollution control is to improve the cost-effectiveness of environmental regulations in ways that safeguard the environment while maintaining Europe's competitive industrial base. The total cost of environmental protection to manufacturing industry is still only 2 % of industrial value added; however, this figure can be expected to rise. With most relatively inexpensive measures having already been taken in WE, many companies face a steep increase in the marginal costs of further abatement measures. For example, manufacturing industry has, next to households, the highest marginal costs of meeting the Kyoto targets, according to several models (Capros, 1998). Such costs may, however, constitute an opportunity for eco-companies (see Box 2.2.2).

The design of environmental policies has implications for the costs of pollution control. The total costs are determined by the costs of implementing the measures themselves and those of administration, monitoring and enforcement. Virtually nothing is known at present of the magnitude of these costs under different environmental policy arrangements. While simulation studies have reported substantial cost savings from market-based instruments compared to the setting of rigid standards (Tietenberg, 1985), this ignores the fact that industrial regulatory pollution control often mimics cost-equalisation across sectors, for example through the application of the BAT (best available technology) principle. However, application of the BAT principle is not always possible as industry increasingly seeks to abate pollution by complex changes in production processes (i.e. pollution prevention) rather than emission control and waste treatment. This may give rise to an information asymmetry between industries

Figure 2.2.6.	The change in industrial emissions of sulphur dioxide versus changes in industrial value added, selected European countries, 1999 to 1992

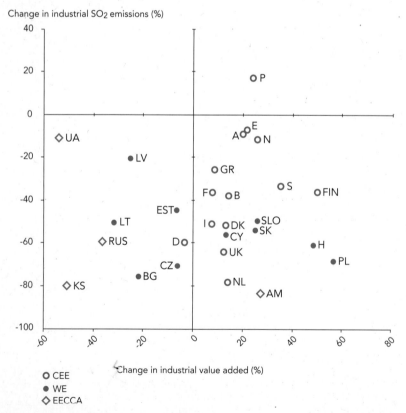

Change in industrial SO$_2$ emissions (%)

Change in industrial value added (%)

○ CEE
● WE
◇ EECCA

Notes: For data and definitions see Figure 2.2.5. For Portugal, Ireland and Greece data cover 1992–98, for Ukra͟ 1992–2000.

Source: EEA, based on World Bank (value added), IEA and Corinair (SO$_2$)

Box 2.2.1. Components of eco-efficiency improvements in Poland, the Netherlands and Sweden

Improvements in the eco-efficiency of manufacturing industry can result from structural changes (the shift towards less pollution-intensive activities) and from technological changes (cleaner technology, end-of-pipe measures or changes in the input mix of raw materials).

Figure 2.2.7 shows the effects of such changes on SO_2 emission intensities for Poland, the Netherlands and Sweden. In all countries, manufacturing emissions of SO_2 declined considerably between 1993 and 2000 (1998 for Sweden), resulting in improvements in emission intensities of 38 % in Sweden, 72 % in the Netherlands and 75 % in Poland. Structural changes contributed to a decline in emissions in the Netherlands and Sweden but hardly at all in Poland. Although there were many structural shifts in the Polish economy, the net effect on the environment was small, as the decline in base metal and refinery industries was offset by substantial increases in the production of chemicals and metal

products. The structural changes in the Netherlands are explained by the relatively low growth in value added from refineries during the period. Other polluting sectors, such as the chemical industries, were growing faster than average. In Sweden, the relative importance of structural changes for the total reduction of emissions is explained mainly by the substantial growth in the relatively clean production of communication equipment.

Technological change seemed to be most dominant in Poland, where emissions declined by 72 % as a result of technological changes. This suggests that environmental policy, which stimulates the application of clean technology, and a higher rate of capital scrapping have been mainly responsible for the reduction of SO_2 emissions in Poland. In the Netherlands, technological changes contributed 43 % of the decline in emission intensities. Technological improvements in Swedish heavy industries were relatively poor between 1993 and 1998.

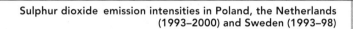

| Sulphur dioxide emission intensities in Poland, the Netherlands (1993–2000) and Sweden (1993–98) | Figure 2.2.7. |

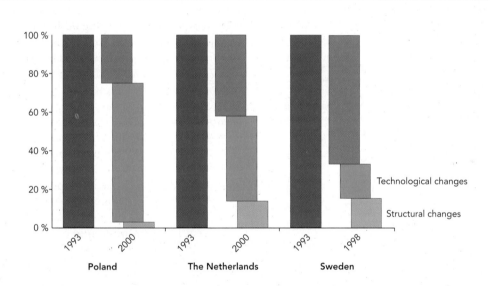

Poland   The Netherlands   Sweden

Notes and **sources**: The components of the decline in emission intensities have been identified with decomposition analysis (Ang, 1994). SO_2 emissions for manufacturing industry only (NACE 15–37). Data for Poland from national statistical office (GUS). Data on SO_2 refer to the main polluters that are obliged to register their pollution. Together they constitute approximately 80 % of total pollution. Data for the Netherlands derived from national statistical office (CBS) using NAMEA statistics. Data for Sweden obtained from national statistical office (SCB). The emission intensities of all sectors have been calculated using sector-specific deflated value-added data. Calculations conducted by CE consulting using the proportional decomposition method, as described in De Bruyn (2000).

and the regulator, which normally involves substantial administration costs to be balanced. Compared with 1994, the share of capital investments in total environmental expenditures has fallen, indicating that more efforts are now devoted to operating costs and to research and development (Ecotec, 2002). This could be a sign of the growing complexity of industrial pollution regulations in WE.

A primary obstacle to the implementation of tighter environmental policy measures is the fear of reduced international competitiveness in pollution-intensive sectors. Although a number of empirical studies (Mulatu *et al.*, 2002) have indicated that the adverse effects of environmental expenditures on competitiveness are small or even absent, many environmental policy plans have special arrangements for

Box 2.2.2. Environmental expenditures and eco-companies — an opportunity

Industry not only contributes to environmental pollution, it also helps to solve environmental problems. 'Eco-industry' is the bundle of activities that produce goods and services (such as consultancy activities) that measure, prevent, limit, minimise or correct environmental damage.

The added value of eco-companies in the EU has risen almost threefold during the past five years (from EUR 35 billion in 1994 to EUR 98 billion in 1999). Around 2.3 % of GDP was generated by eco-companies, suggesting that the importance of eco-companies for income generation is similar to, for example, the base-metal sector in WE economies. Direct employment in the EU in eco-companies amounts to more than 2 million (full-time equivalent) jobs.

Total expenditure on environmental management and protection has increased by 5 % annually since 1994 and reached EUR 183 billion in 1999. Most of the expenditure relates to wastewater treatment and the management of solid waste. In the near future the market for clean technologies is expected to increase further, especially because of the production of equipment for renewable energy plants to meet the EU's Kyoto protocol targets.

In the accession countries, the environmental body of EU law is the main reason for pollution investments. The emphasis is on wastewater measures and end-of-pipe measures for air pollution.

Source: European Commission

Box 2.2.3. Environmental management systems are becoming increasingly popular

The number of environmental management systems (EMS) in Europe grew by 160 % between 1999 and 2002. There are two main systems: the ISO 14001 standards adopted worldwide, and the eco-management and audit scheme (EMAS) which has been set up by the EU. Nearly 40 000 certificates have been issued worldwide: around 36 000 ISO 14001 and nearly 4 000 EMAS. The EU accounts for almost 50 % of these certificates worldwide. Most remarkable is the spectacular growth in ISO 14001 certificates in the accession countries — a sixfold increase since 1999.

The main reason for installing ISO 14001 or EMAS in companies is to achieve better relationships with regulators and clients. They are therefore important marketing tools and help in negotiations with governments on environmental regulations. The total administrative effort (for companies and society) in applying and running a typical company EMAS is between 0.7 and 1.2 person-months of work per year (Lulofs, 2000). Around 20 % of the costs are borne by the companies. Many small companies apply ISO 14001 or EMAS rules without actual certification because of the costs involved. Their numbers are not included in Figure 2.2.8.

Figure 2.2.8.	Development in the application of EMS in Europe

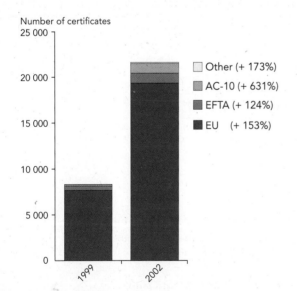

Number of certificates

Other (+ 173%)
AC-10 (+ 631%)
EFTA (+ 124%)
EU   (+ 153%)

Notes: Application of EMS involves both ISO 14001 and EMAS. 1999 refers to the number of certificates in June 1999. 2002 refers to the certificates in January 2002. The figures in brackets next to the keys give the growth in the number of certificates between 1999 and 2002.

Sources: Gergely Tóth, Hungarian Association of Environmentally Aware Businesses (KÖVET-INEM Hungária) and the EMAS Helpdesk, Brussels

pollution-intensive industries. For example, the OECD/EU database on environmental taxes shows that environmentally related taxes are levied almost exclusively on households and the transport sector. Exemptions and rebates for the industrial sector undermine the application of the polluter pays principle and result in less than optimal pollution control because abatement measures are not directed at the areas where they are likely to have the greatest overall effect.

Industry itself tends to have a preference for voluntary approaches, as indicated by a recent survey in the Netherlands (Blok *et al.*, 2001). Environmental management systems (see Box 2.2.3) and environmental and social reporting are important instruments here. However, the total effect on the environment of voluntary approaches is often unknown and difficult to estimate (Starzer, 2001).

> ☺ The number of environmental management systems in Europe grew significantly between 1999 and 2002.

For CEE countries, accession may continue to be the main driving force for environmental policy initiatives in the coming years. Manufacturing industry in CEE countries faces difficult tasks in the accession procedure. The expected effects of accession include increased competition from lowered tariffs, fewer subsidies, cost pressures from rising real wages and, most likely, an appreciating real exchange rate. In addition, substantial costs can be expected from the implementation of the full Community body of EU law (regulation and policies), of which the environmental legislation will be the most costly for the manufacturing and energy production industries (see Box 2.2.4).

The adaptation of current environmental legislation to the body of EU law poses some additional challenges for accession countries. Environmental policy in most countries currently relies more on economic instruments than in EU countries. Figure 2.2.9 gives an overview of the revenues from economic instruments for environmental protection related to industrial value added in some accession countries and compares them with the EU. While initially fees and fines were too low to act as incentives, substantial increases during the 1990s had some effects. Especially in the Czech Republic and Poland, abatement is now often more attractive for companies than paying fines. The revenues from such taxes are earmarked for environmental protection and nature conservation.

The legal approach to transposing and implementing EU legislation carries the risk that the current system of environmental taxes will be replaced by the regulatory framework of the EU without any discussion of the effectiveness of such a tax and fund-raising system in accession countries. Mutually agreed reduction targets may bring the environmental performance of industry more in line with the EU, without necessarily affecting present legislation. Since energy taxes are still fairly low compared with those in WE, an alternative is a gradual switch from pollution taxation towards energy taxation.

In EECCA, the main challenge is to build up legal capacities. Building an appropriate regulatory framework and improved enforcement is crucial here and timing is essential. Current industrial environmental policies in EECCA have evolved mainly around emission limit values laid down in permits. Non-compliance triggers a fine, which is, however, relatively low. Procedures are cumbersome and administrative costs may be greater than the fines. Many companies are therefore permanently in non-compliance. The economy has improved during the past two years, and it is essential that environmental policy now catches up. Increases in fines and taxes for pollution and improved enforcement capacities may be the most straightforward way to guarantee that environmental pollution will develop in similar ways to those observed in CEE countries.

Box 2.2.4. Costs and benefits from EU accession

The total investment needed to meet the EU environmental directives is estimated to be roughly EUR 120 billion, or 32 % of current GDP of the 10 central and eastern European accession countries (Orlowski and Mayhew, 2001). When spread over 20 years such costs will require an annual investment of around 1.5 % of current GDP. Additionally, operating costs may require another 2.5 % of GDP annually. The expenditure on implementation of the air pollution directives will take around 40 % of these costs and mostly be borne by industry and the energy production sector.

The environmental body of EU law will also contribute to benefits: improved health and better environmental services. The benefits of compliance with the environmental body of EU law are estimated to range from EUR 134 to EUR 681 billion (Ecotec et al., 2001), the range being typical of the uncertainties associated with benefit analysis. The major source of these benefits will be industrial pollution control. However, the benefits will arise in the long term and be partly intangible, while the costs are to be borne now. Moreover, benefits do not accrue directly to industry but to society as a whole.

| Revenues from economic instruments for environmental protection in % of industrial value added, EU and selected European countries, 1997 | Figure 2.2.9. |

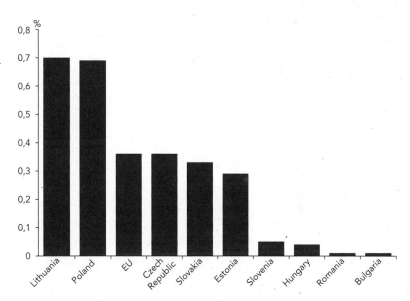

Note: Data refer to pollution charges, fines and taxes only and not to input-related taxes such as energy or motor fuel taxes. Data for Romania refer to 1996.

Sources: REC, 1999; Eurostat, 2000

2.2.5. References

Ang, B. W., 1994. Decomposition of industrial energy consumption: The energy intensity approach. *Energy Economics* 16: 163–174.

Blok, K. *et al.*, 2001. *The effectiveness of policy instruments for energy efficiency improvements in firms.* University of Utrecht, Netherlands.

Capros, P., 1998. *Note on the costs for the EU of meeting the Kyoto target (-8 %).* National Technical University of Athens.

De Bruyn, S. M., 2000. *Economic growth and the environment: An empirical analysis.* Kluwer Academic Publishers, Netherlands.

Ecotec, 2002. *Analysis of the EU eco-industries, their employment and export potential.* Study for the European Commission, DG Environment, Brussels.

Ecotec *et al.*, 2001. *The benefits of compliance with the environmental acquis for the candidate countries.* Study for European Commission, DG Environment, Brussels.

Eurostat, 2000. *Structures of the taxation systems in the European Union 1970–1997.* European Commission, Brussels.

Grossman, G. M. and Krueger, A. B., 1995. *Economic growth and the environment.* Quarterly Journal of Economics 112: 353–378.

Lulofs, K., 2000. *Implementation of EMAS in the Netherlands: A case study on national implementation, environmental effectiveness, productive efficiency and administrative costs.* Research Paper 2000-B-5. European Project IMPOL, Cerna.

Mulatu, A., *et al.*, 2002. Environmental regulation and competitiveness: An exploratory meta-analysis, in Läschel, A. (ed.), *Empirical modeling of the economy and the environment.* Springer-Verlag, Berlin.

Orlowski, W. and Mayhew, A., 2001. *The impact of EU accession on enterprise adaptation and institutional development in the countries of central and eastern Europe.* Sussex European Institute working paper.

REC, 1999. *Sourcebook on economic instruments for environmental policy in central and eastern Europe.* Klarer, McNicholas, Knaus. Szentendre, Hungary.

Starzer, O., 2001. *Towards Kyoto — implementation of long term agreements (LTA) in industry: Which elements make LTA successful and how to integrate them into the policy mix?* ECEEE summer study 2001, 10–15 June,. Mandelieu.

Tietenberg, T. H., 1985. *Emissions trading: An exercise in reforming pollution policy.* Resources for the Future, Washington, DC.

2.3. Agriculture

European agriculture is extremely diverse, ranging from large, highly intensive and specialised commercial holdings to subsistence farming using mainly traditional practices. Consequently impacts on the environment vary in scale and intensity and may be positive or negative. There is a legacy of significant environmental damage associated with agriculture in central and eastern Europe, the Caucasus and central Asia (EECCA), often associated with unique ecosystems, where exploitation of resources (such as freshwater for irrigation) was excessive. The dramatic decline in resource use in these countries, largely due to economic restructuring rather than policy, consumer or technological developments, has scaled back many environmental pressures. However, land abandonment, undergrazing and lack of capital to maintain or improve farm infrastructure are creating new environmental pressures.

The common agricultural policy has been one of the important drivers of farm intensification and specialisation in the EU. Market pressures and technological development have also contributed to these trends which are very strong in some sectors that benefit from little public support (e.g. pigs, poultry, potatoes). Intensive farming has had significant impacts on the environment. Public concerns related to production methods and some reorientation of the common agricultural policy have created new opportunities, for example through labelling and agri-environment schemes, for farmers to reduce pressures on the environment.

For the countries of EECCA, the current window of opportunity for ensuring reduced environmental pressures from agriculture may not remain open for long. Agriculture in the central and eastern Europe countries is likely to intensify when they have full access to the common agricultural policy although there is an evolving agri-environmental policy framework and some opportunities under the special accession programme for agriculture and rural development to address this risk. The common agricultural policy will apply to new Member States in a modified form, which may reduce incentives for increasing production. There is little or no agri-environmental policy framework in the EECCA countries and few possibilities for farmers to address agricultural pressures on the environment.

2.3.1. Introduction

A common policy objective throughout Europe for several decades was to increase food production. Farmers increased agricultural output significantly between the 1940s and the 1990s in response to such policies. Supported by public investment, this resulted in mechanisation combined with the abandonment of traditional practices, reliance on non-renewable inputs such as inorganic fertilisers and pesticides, the cultivation of marginal land and improvements in production efficiency.

In western Europe (WE), the common agricultural policy (CAP) and several national policies encouraged intensification. This took various forms, including the sustained use of chemical inputs, increasing field size and higher stocking densities. Intensified farm management led to discontinuation of traditional fallowing practices and crop rotations resulting in a displacement of leguminous fodder crops with increased use of silage and maize. Specialisation and intensification have resulted in a decrease in the number of farm holdings and numbers employed, as well as a regionalisation of production leading to less diversity of local agricultural habitats.

During the socialist era in central and eastern Europe (CEE) and the 12 countries of eastern Europe, the Caucasus and central Asia (EECCA), government planning determined agriculture and food production with little regard to efficiency or the suitability of production for the environment. The area of land farmed and number of livestock in the former USSR increased as a result of land reforms which were started in the 1930s. The expansion of arable land at the expense of forest and grassland increased the pressure on remaining pastures. The development of huge irrigation and drainage schemes, farm specialisation and investment in animal production were all associated with the push to increase output, and resulted in a greater reliance on non-farm resources. For example the application of fertilisers nearly trebled and pesticide use doubled between 1970 and 1987 (Libert, 1995).

Further specialisation of EU agriculture is expected, but reforms of the CAP are likely to seek further integration of environmental measures into agricultural policy. Implementation of EU environmental legislation, such as the nitrates directive, is also expected to improve. Nevertheless, diverging input/output prices and high labour costs may prevent EU farming from reaching an environmentally sustainable level of intensity due to financial pressures. These trends are also likely to make it difficult for farming to continue the environmental management functions that it currently provides, for example for semi-natural grasslands or landscape elements. Thus, the environmental effects of EU agriculture will require continuing attention, beyond current policy initiatives.

The currently widespread low input and extensive agriculture in CEE provides a window of opportunity for the development of environmentally sustainable agriculture. Future EU membership could result in a return to more intensive agricultural practices unless policies are adapted to promote a more harmonious coexistence of farming with biodiversity, for example through agri-environment measures. There is a large untapped agricultural potential in EECCA that may give rise to intensification as their economies strengthen. For both CEE and EECCA, continued support is needed to integrate the environment into the agricultural sector. This would help to develop an agri-environmental policy framework, strengthen the agricultural advisory services, particularly in the provision of agri-environmental advice and training materials, and provide grants to improve or construct animal waste storage units. Improved monitoring and data are needed to enable a more detailed assessment of the impact of agriculture on the environment in Europe as a whole. For EU Member States and the accession countries, elements of such a monitoring system are under development, but measures should be extended, through cooperation, in order to ensure similar progress in EECCA.

2.3.2. Pressures on the environment

The extent and causes of the environmental impacts of agricultural practices vary significantly across Europe, notably by farm and crop type. Nevertheless, the continuing search for efficiency, lower costs and increased scale of production is resulting in

substantial pressures on the environment, landscapes and biodiversity, particularly in the most intensively farmed areas. At the same time, agriculture remains essential to the maintenance of many cultural landscapes. This dual role is relevant throughout Europe, with farming systems of high nature value found mostly in areas with low input and more traditional agriculture.

Agricultural production throughout the continent continues to rely on non-farm resources such as inorganic fertilisers and pesticides. However, there has been a decline in the use of these resources and, particularly in EECCA and CEE, a reduction in the pressure on the environment.

While agriculture can exert significant pressure on the environment, it is also itself subject to negative environmental impacts linked to air pollution and urban develop-ment. Soil sealing by transport or housing infrastructure eliminates many thousands of hectares of agricultural land every year, in particular in WE (see Chapter 9).

Government programmes have a significant influence on the development of agricultural production capacity and intensity. A particular example of often large-scale public programmes to aid the farming sector is the management of water regimes through river regulation, wetland drainage and irrigation schemes. The development of irrigated area is described hereafter in Section 2.3.2.2. Drainage for agricultural purposes still affects several hundred thousand hectares of land throughout western and eastern Europe, leading to loss of biodiversity, water purification and retention capacity (IUCN, 1993). Though the amount of new drainage declined drastically throughout the region during the 1990s, existing drainage programmes continue to exert a negative impact on 15 % of all important bird areas in Europe (Heath and Evans, 2000).

2.3.2.1. Fertiliser and pesticide consumption
Enrichment of waters by nitrogen and phosphorous is widespread despite reductions in fertiliser use (Figure 2.3.1.). Diffuse losses from agriculture continue to be the main source of nitrate pollution in European waters as the treatment of sewage and industrial effluent has become very effective (see Chapter 8). For instance, more than half of all nutrient inputs to the Danube River were from agriculture (Haskoning, 1994) and fertiliser inputs to

the Danube basin will have to be maintained at about half of their 1991 levels in Bulgaria, Romania and Hungary to prevent further eutrophication of the Black Sea (WWF, 2000). Substantial amounts also enter the Baltic Sea from the nine bordering countries (Baltic 21, 2000). Chapter 8 describes the negative impact of phosphorus enrichment from diffuse agricultural sources on the water of eutrophic lakes in western and central Europe.

EU legislation, such as the nitrates directive (Directive EC 91/676), seeks to limit nutrient losses from farming to freshwater bodies by restricting nutrient use in designated nitrate vulnerable zones. However, more progress by Member States is required before this policy response can be considered fully satisfactory (EEA, 2002a). The decline in fertiliser use in CEE countries and EECCA is more attributable to reduced market opportunities for agricultural products, the declining profitability of agriculture, reduced state support and the widespread reorganisation of farming in the region. However, inorganic fertiliser consumption in CEE is expected to increase as a response to expected new market opportunities and integration with the CAP (EFMA, 2000).

> 😐 Overall consumption of fertilisers has stabilised in recent years, following a significant decline during the first half of the 1990s in CEE and EECCA. Without appropriate management, current fertiliser input in western and eastern Europe may still be too high to be environmentally sustainable in the longer term.

Pesticides may pollute drinking water, surface water and groundwaters. Many groundwater supplies in EU countries exceed the drinking water directive (Directive 98/83/EC) maximum of 0.1 ug/l for a single pesticide (EEA, 2002b). Soils can also be affected: in Ukraine more than 20 % of the investigated agricultural lands are polluted by DDT and its degradation products, about 4 % are polluted by hexachlorine-cyclohexane (Ukrainian NCP, 2002).

New management practices, such as integrated crop management (ICM), have evolved as a response to the need to reduce dependence on pesticides (Figure 2.3.2.). ICM aims at environmentally sensitive crop management, including a reduced use of inputs, while maintaining agricultural

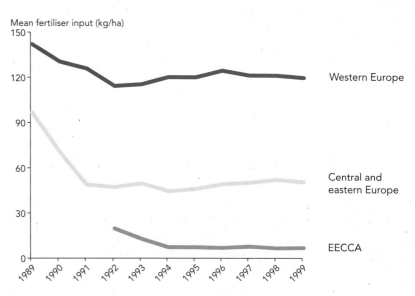

| Fertiliser input per hectare of agricultural land in Europe, 1989–1999 | Figure 2.3.1. |

Notes: Both fertiliser and agricultural area data are available for Estonia, Latvia, Lithuania and Slovenia from 1992; for Slovakia and the Czech Republic from 1993; and for members of the EECCA country group from 1992. The graph expresses total inorganic fertiliser consumption (N, P and K) per hectare of agricultural land (a complete time series of utilised agricultural area (UAA) was not available) for all countries with data.

Source: FAO

productivity and profitability. Although covering only about 3 % of utilised agricultural area (UAA) in the EU, ICM encourages more targeted use and reductions in application rates of pesticides (see Box 2.3.1.) In EECCA and CEE, there are initial training programmes to support the uptake of ICM practices although the main reason for reduced pesticide use is economic restructuring. However, there is a significant environmental legacy in many of the CEE countries and

---

Box 2.3.1. Changes in pesticide use in Kazakhstan and the EU

Kazakhstan
The use of pesticides has been an important feature of agricultural production in Kazakhstan. The government financed pest control campaigns against exotic insects such as locusts and Colorado beetle. However, since 1992 farmers have had to buy the pesticides themselves and, due to economic circumstances, this resulted in a dramatic reduction in pesticide consumption. Between 1985 and 1997, pesticide input decreased from 0.57 to 0.13 kg of active ingredient per hectare. Despite the reduced pressure from pesticides their legacy persists, with many water courses, including the Syr-Darya, heavily polluted with DDT, DDD and DDE. The same is also true for large expanses of soil contaminated with organo-chlorine pesticides.

...and the EU
The integrated crop management concept is slowly gaining acceptance in the EU countries and integrated crop management methods are now applied on about 3 % of the utilised agricultural area. Evidence suggests that practising integrated crop management can lead to a reduction in pesticide leaching and, through general reductions in the application of pesticides, to a reduction in the risk of pesticide residues building up in the soil. Since integrated crop management systems promote a reduction in the use of pesticides and fertilisers, they are also likely to have positive side effects for biodiversity.

Sources: Pak, 1998 (Kazakhstan); European Commission, 2002 (EU)

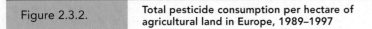

Mean consumption (kg/ha$_2$)

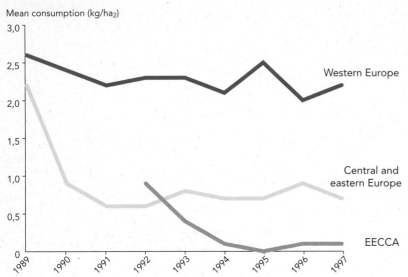

Figure 2.3.2. Total pesticide consumption per hectare of agricultural land in Europe, 1989–1997

Notes: The graph expresses mean consumption of pesticides (active ingredients classed as insecticides, herbicides, fungicides and others) as a percentage of total agricultural land (a complete time series of UAA was not available). The pesticide and agricultural land area dataset has an incomplete time series for all EECCA and CEE countries and for all WE countries except Finland and Denmark. Data for 1998 and 1999 are too sparse to be plotted on a country group basis.

Source: FAO

Figure 2.3.3. Average irrigated land area as percentage of agricultural land area in Europe, 1989–1999

% agricultural land irrigated

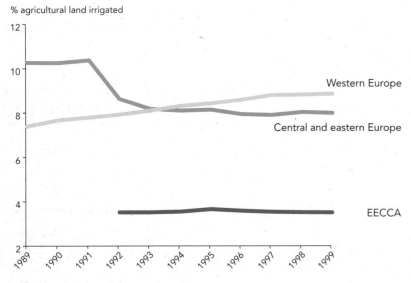

Notes: The graph expresses total irrigated area as a percentage of total agricultural land (a complete time series of UAA was not available). No distinction was made between total areas equipped for irrigation and actually irrigated surface. Irrigated area data were not available until 1992 for Estonia, Latvia, Lithuania, Slovenia, Bosnia-Herzegovina, Serbia and Montenegro, FYR of Macedonia, Croatia and EECCA and until 1993 for Czech Republic and Slovakia.

Source: FAO

EECCA where localised hot spots of contamination are commonly associated with the storage and disposal of pesticides. For example, there are estimated to be up to 60 000 tonnes of obsolete stocks of pesticides in Poland, 20 000 tonnes in the Russian Federation and 15 000 tonnes in Ukraine (IHPA, 2001; see also: Danish Environmental Protection Agency, 2001; SYKE, 2002). Improved monitoring and disposal programmes for obsolete pesticide stockpiles are clearly required to avoid significant environmental problems in the future (see also Chapter 6).

The intensity of pesticide use has declined in many countries as a result of public environmental concern, legislation, economic pressures and the introduction of active ingredients with lower dosage requirements. However, much agricultural production still relies heavily on pesticide application to achieve higher economic returns.

2.3.2.2. Irrigated area

In southern Europe and central Asia, irrigation is essential for achieving economic yields and results in high water demand. In central and western Europe, irrigation is often used to ensure yields in dry summers. The largest irrigated areas are in the Russian Federation, Kazakhstan, Ukraine, Uzbekistan, Romania and Turkey. The scale and importance of irrigation in the EU is substantially greater in the southern countries but it is also significant in several northern regions. The irrigated area has increased most notably in France, Greece and Italy. There has been an overall decrease in the accession countries (see Figure 2.3.3).

Many heavily irrigated regions of southern and eastern Europe are characterised by a lowering of water tables, land degradation and desertification, salinisation and the destruction or degradation of wetlands and aquifers (see Box 2.3.2).

Irrigated land has a significant share of the agricultural area in western, central and eastern Europe. Substantial increases in irrigated area are still occurring in some western and Mediterranean countries. Eastern Europe, the Caucasus and central Asia has the largest area of irrigated land with serious implications for demand on limited water resources.

2.3.2.3. Livestock numbers

The total numbers of cattle, pigs, sheep and goats in CEE and EECCA have decreased; numbers in the EU have been nearly stable since 1990 (see Figure 2.3.4). High livestock population densities are associated with excessive concentrations of manure, leading to an increased risk of water pollution. In the EU, legislation and national programmes seek to minimise this problem with some success. Underdeveloped programmes and/ or lack of legislative enforcement coupled with poor or non-existent containment of manure in CEE countries such as Poland (JRC, 2001) and Romania are still giving rise to localised hot spots of nutrient loading. This is also the case in EECCA, particularly in Belarus and regions of Ukraine and the Russian Federation specialising in animal production.

The loss or intensification of traditional extensive livestock grazing systems has had particularly negative effects on biodiversity. Overgrazing in certain vulnerable environments (such as parts of the UK uplands and heather moorlands) has damaged these habitats. The contribution of livestock to gaseous emissions is also significant: 94 % of total EU ammonia emissions (from housed animals) and 49 % of total methane emissions arise from animal husbandry (EEA, 2002c).

Livestock production in the EU has become more specialised and intensive. Overstocking can be attributed partly to the provision of production incentives, including payments per head of livestock under the CAP, although socio-economic drivers have also encouraged some regionalisation of livestock production and localised overgrazing.

Livestock numbers fell markedly between 1989 and 2001 in central and eastern Europe, the Caucasus and central Asia. However, high pressures on the environment from intensification and the concentration of livestock production in large units with poor animal waste management persist, especially in eastern Europe, the Caucasus and central Asia and the accession countries.

2.3.2.4. Biodiversity and semi-natural grasslands

Much of the biodiversity in Europe is found on or adjacent to farmland and is therefore considerably affected by agricultural practices (see also Chapter 11). Agricultural

Box 2.3.2. Irrigation issues

Southern Europe
Arable production in Spain has become more intensive through the expansion of irrigated crops, resulting in a loss of dry-steppic habitats, traditional dryland crops, and breeding areas for birds such as the great bustard (Otis tarda). In spite of recent reductions in water use (see Chapter 8, Figure 8.3.), the wetland area of Las Tablas de Daimiel, which is a Natura 2000 and Ramsar site, has been reduced by 60 % as a result of agricultural overexploitation of the aquifer that feeds the La Mancha wetlands. Salinisation of the subterranean water and contamination and eutrophication of the surface water has also occurred, in addition to a reduction in nesting areas due to changes in vegetation, including peat fires, and land subsidence.

Central Asia
Central Asia, under the former USSR, was allocated the role of raw material supplier, principally cotton. An extensive irrigation scheme encompassing the Amu-Dar and Syr-Dar river catchments was undertaken to ensure competitive yields. The irrigated area increased from 4.5 million ha to 8 million ha between 1960 and 1995. Among irrigated crops, cotton has the highest requirement of freshwater per kilogram of product. In Uzbekistan, freshwater consumption by agriculture amounted to 84 % of total water use in 1989, largely attributable to cotton production.

Drainage systems are used to avoid water-logging and salinity of soils, and the fields are irrigated with additional freshwater to remove salts from the soil. The returned salt-contaminated drainage water contains pesticide residues and fertiliser and has a severe impact on rivers and wetlands. The traditional ecosystems of the two deltas of the Amu-Dar and Syr-Dar have perished and the Aral Sea is drying up as a result of excessive water demands. Since the 1990s, some initiatives have been under way to improve the environmental and water management in the Aral Sea catchment area. For various reasons the area planted with cotton has also decreased during the same period, although Uzbekistan is still one of the largest cotton producers in the world. However, the environmental situation in and around the Aral Sea remains very serious (See Chapter 8, Box 8.1. and Chapter 9, Box 9.2.).

Sources: Baldock et al., 2000 and WWF, 2000 (southern Europe); http://www.fao.org/ag/AGL/aglw/aquastat/regions/fussr/index.htm and WWF, 1999 (central Asia)

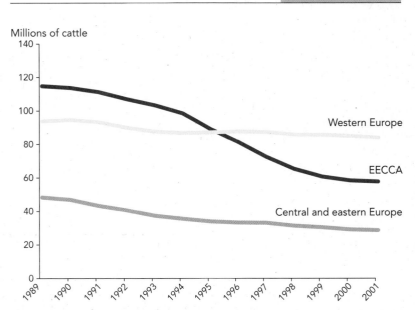

Number of cattle in Europe, 1989–2001 — Figure 2.3.4.

Note: Similar declining trends are reported for pigs, sheep and goats in CEE and EECCA, while in the EU there was little net change in pig, sheep or goat numbers.

habitats support the largest number of bird species of any broad habitat category in Europe, including the greatest number of threatened species (Heath and Tucker, 1994) (see Chapter 11). Species dependent on farmland are, however, threatened by changes in management practices, such as the time of sowing and harvesting of crops, intensification, abandonment, loss of field boundaries, conversion of grassland into arable land (see Box 2.3.3), and a decline in habitat diversity due to increased mechanisation (Nagy, 2002).

The surviving natural steppe grasslands in EECCA remain threatened by conversion to arable land and by local overgrazing, but the collapse of many collective farms has led to the re-establishment of communal, semi-subsistence pastoral systems. This extensive land use favours the maintenance of biodiversity-rich semi-natural grassland systems that depend on traditional grazing and/or haymaking. Case studies from Ukraine and elsewhere show the high plant and butterfly diversity of such systems, most of which has already been lost in WE (Elligsen *et al.*, 1998).

Box 2.3.3. Agriculture in semi-natural grasslands

Due to the relatively small area of undisturbed natural habitat that remains in Europe, semi-natural habitats are particularly important for nature conservation. Semi-natural grassland depends for its maintenance on appropriate management by farmers through mowing and/or grazing, and is therefore particularly sensitive to intensification or abandonment. The area of semi-natural grassland has fallen in recent decades across Europe. In the United Kingdom, for instance, semi-natural acid grassland declined by 17 % between 1990 and 1998 in England and Wales (DEFRA, 2002). In spite of the generally extensive nature of agriculture in Finland, many areas of semi-natural grassland have been converted into arable land. Thus, the area of hay fields fell from 13 000 ha in 1970 to just 6 000 ha in 1997 (Pitkänen and Tiainen, 2001).

The proportion of semi-natural grassland in CEE and EECCA is high relative to most EU countries, and the total area far exceeds that in the EU. However, agriculture has become significantly more intensive and, in Turkey for instance, the area of steppe grassland fell from 60 % to 31 % of total agricultural land between 1950 and 1984. Some central and eastern European countries have a relatively high proportion of semi-natural grassland, for instance in Slovenia it amounts to more than half of the UAA (Veen, 2001).

Such habitats will, however, come under considerable pressure if agriculture becomes more intensive, giving rise to significant biodiversity loss (Donald *et al.*, 2001). On the other hand, land abandonment is currently a bigger problem in the region, and is likely to remain so during the transitional years after EU membership. In Estonia, for example, about 30 % of the 1.5 million ha of farmland is currently abandoned (Estonian Ministry of Agriculture, 2001). This proportion is even higher for permanent grasslands (56 %). Among semi-natural grasslands of medium or high nature value (37 000 ha), only 40 % is still under management (Mägi and Lutsar, 2001).

Table 2.3.1.	Estimated distribution of agricultural areas, permanent grassland, semi-natural and natural grasslands in CEE countries in 1999

Country	Total utilised agricultural area (UAA)	Total area of permanent pasture	Total semi-natural grassland area	Total mountain grassland area	Semi-natural grassland in total UAA
	(ha)	(ha)	(ha)	(ha)	%
Bulgaria	6 203 000	1 705 000	444 436	332 071	7.2
Czech Republic	4 282 000	950 000	550 000	1 750	12.8
Estonia	1 434 000	299 000	73 200	0	5.1
Hungary[1]	6 186 000	1 147 000	960 000	0	15.5
Latvia	2 486 000	606 000	117 850	0	4.7
Lithuania	3 496 000	500 000	167 933	0	4.8
Poland	18 435 000	4 034 000	1 955 000	413 600	10.6
Romania	14 781 000	4 936 000	2 332 730	285 000	15.8
Slovakia	2 443 000	856 000	294 900	13 100	12.1
Slovenia	500 000	298 000	268 402	29 822	53.7

Source: Adapted from Brouwer *et al.*, 2001, on the basis of FAO data; data for Hungary: Demeter and Veen, 2001

In CEE and EECCA the status of farmland biodiversity is better than in the EU although a problem is emerging with land abandonment and undergrazing. This is resulting in forest and shrub encroachment on flower-rich grassland areas and a consequent loss in biodiversity. In general, it may be assumed that land abandonment affects semi-natural grasslands and other extensive farmland important for biodiversity more often than the available land abandonment data suggest.

Semi-natural grassland can also be threatened by conversion to arable land. In Hungary, a return to private ownership and market pressures have provided an incentive to convert extensive semi-natural grassland ('puszta') areas to the production of cash crops such as maize and sunflowers. A comparison of maps and satellite images for the area between the Danube and Tisza rivers (about one sixth of the country) showed that 44 000 ha of such grasslands were lost between the mid-1980s and 1998 (Molnár and Vajda, 2000). Conversion to arable land is a continuing threat to the high ecological value of semi-natural grasslands in a country which still harbours the great bustard (*Otis tarda*) and imperial eagle (*Aquila heliaca*), among many other species.

2.3.3. Policy response

Recent shifts to environmentally friendly production systems, such as organic production, are apparent and contribute to reducing agriculture's dependence on external chemical inputs. Organic farming covered about 3 % of the total agricultural area of the EU in 2000. The development of certified organic farming in the accession countries and EECCA still lags significantly behind this figure (EEA, 2002a) in spite of a high share of low-input systems that could facilitate such a shift.

Reforms of the CAP (e.g. in 1992 and Agenda 2000 of the European Union) aim to shift the emphasis of the policy from market-based support (e.g. intervention to maintain producer prices) towards direct income support (e.g. payment per hectare or unit of livestock). These changes, together with public concerns related to production methods, have encouraged the EU to provide new opportunities to finance agri-environment schemes as part of rural development programmes. These are

obligatory under the EU rural development regulation (Regulation 1257/1999) and take up about 50 % of planned rural development expenditure in the EU Member States in 2000–06. By 1998, such schemes already covered more than 20 % of the agricultural area of the EU although farmer participation varied greatly between countries and did not necessarily coincide with the areas of highest environmental value or need (Petersen, 1998).

Throughout CEE and EECCA, increased environmental awareness and recognition of the complexity of rural socio-economic problems is apparent, but agri-environmental policy development is still at an early stage. There are also significant regional disparities, with accession to the EU being a major influence on agricultural policy and activities in all accession countries. Pre-accession instruments, notably the special accession programme for agriculture and rural development (SAPARD) are assisting this process in CEE countries although most countries have chosen to give higher priority to improving the competitiveness of the agri-food sector than to agri-environment measures. Nearly all CEE countries included agri-environment measures in their proposed SAPARD programmes, but there have been considerable delays with implementation, and some countries have abandoned the measure altogether. The obligation to implement EU legislation such as the water framework, nitrates, birds and habitats directives after accession will, however, make it necessary to integrate environmental considerations into agriculture policy.

For EECCA, it has been market reforms, rather than agri-environmental policy or the integration of environmental actions into the agricultural sector that have been the principal drivers of change. Many of the international financing institutions cooperate with EECCA in providing grants and loans to develop strategies and actions to mitigate the impacts of agriculture on the environment.

The situation in the Mediterranean accession countries is different, with wide variations in the economic significance of agriculture, production patterns and environmental problems. Unlike CEE and EECCA, which have gone through major reductions in the use of inputs, one of the main issues for Cyprus, Malta and Turkey is prevention or control of the detrimental effects of likely future agricultural development on water resources and other aspects of the environment. Few agri-environment initiatives have been established in these countries, partly because so far they have not been eligible for EU funds for developing agricultural methods that protect the environment.

2.3.4. References

Baldock *et al.*, 2000. *The environmental impacts of irrigation in the European Union.* Report for DG Environment by the Institute for European Environmental Policy (IEEP), London.

Baltic 21, 2000. *Development in the Baltic Sea region towards the Baltic 21 goals — an indicator based assessment.* Baltic Series No 2/2000. ISSN: 1029–7790.

Brouwer *et al,.* 2001. *The relation between agriculture and nature management.* High level conference on EU enlargement. Wassenaar, 22–24 January 2001.

Danish Environmental Protection Agency, 2001. *Review on obsolete pesticides in eastern and central Europe.* www.mst.dk/chemi/Chemicals/Appendix_Report_2304.DOC

DEFRA (Department for Environment, Food and Rural Affairs), 2002. *Countryside Survey 2000.* DEFRA, United Kingdom. www.defra.gov.GB/wildlife-countryside/cs2000/02/05.htm

Demeter, A. and Veen, P. (eds), 2001. *Final report on natural and semi-natural grasslands in Hungary. A national grassland inventory project 1997–2001.* Report for the Authority for Nature Conservation, Ministry of Environment, Hungary and the Royal Dutch Society for Nature Conservation.

Donald, P. *et al.,* 2001. Agricultural intensification and the collapse of Europe's farmland bird populations. *Proceedings of the Royal Society London*, 268: 25-29.

EEA, 2002a. *Environmental signals 2002.* Chapter 6 on agriculture. European Environment Agency. Copenhagen.

EEA, 2002b. *Water indicator report: Pesticides in groundwater (fact sheet 17).* European Environment Agency. Copenhagen.

EEA, 2002c. *Environmental signals 2002 (fact sheets AP3a — total NH3 emissions; AP3b — total emissions of acidifying substances; CC2 — total EU CH4 emissions.* European Environment Agency. Copenhagen.

EFMA (European Fertilizer Manufacturers Association), 2000. *Forecast of food, farming and fertilizer use in the European Union — 2000 to 2010.* EFMA, Brussels.

Elligsen,H, Beinlich, B and Plachter, H (1998). *Large-scale grazing systems and species protection in the Eastern Carpathians of Ukraine.* La Cañada, Number 9; EFNCP, Gruinart, Islay, UK.

Estonian Ministry of Agriculture, 2001. *Agriculture and rural development in Estonia.* Ministry of Agriculture, Tallinn.

European Commission, 2002. *Integrated crop management systems in the EU.* Brussels.

SYKE (Finnish Environment Institute), 2002. *Report on obsolete pesticides in Russia.* http://www.vyh.fi/eng/current/press/syke/2002/r020731.htm

Haskoning, N., 1994. *Danube integrated environmental study. Final report of the EU-Phare environmental programme for the Danube Basin.* Haskoning Royal Dutch Consulting Engineers and Architects, Nijmegen.

Heath, M. and Tucker, G., 1994. *Birds in Europe: Their conservation status.* BirdLife International, Cambridge.

Heath, M. F. and Evans, M. I. (eds), 2000. *Important bird areas in Europe: Priority sites for conservation.* BirdLife Conservation Series No. 8. Cambridge.

IHPA (International HCH and Pesticides Association), 2001. Technical summary of sessions. *Proceedings of 6th International HCH and Pesticides Forum, 20–22 March 2001, Pozna, Poland.*

IUCN (IUCN-The World Conservation Union), 1993. *The wetlands of central and eastern Europe.* IUCN, Gland and Cambridge.

JRC (2001). 'Agriculture in the CEEC: options for agriculture in the new member states — the case of Poland'. Unpublished report prepared by ADAS for the JRC (IPTS) Contract No. 15585/1999/12. FIED SEV GB.

Libert, B., 1995. *The environmental heritage of Soviet agriculture.* CAB International, Oxford.

Molnár, Zs. and Vajda, Z., 2000. *Actual habitat mapping of the Duna-Tisza köze.* Kecskemét-Vácrátót. Report for the Ministry for the Environment, Budapest.

Mägi, M. and Lutsar, L., 2001. *Inventory of semi-natural grasslands in Estonia 1999–2001.* Estonian Fund for Nature and Royal Dutch Society for Nature Conservation.

Nagy, S., 2002. *The status of biodiversity on farmland in Europe (birds).* For the high level pan-European conference on agriculture and biodiversity, Paris, 5–7 June 2002.

Pak, L., 1998. United Nations Environment Programme, Division of Technology, Industry and Economics, Chemicals Unit. *Proceedings of the regional awareness raising workshop on persistent organic pollutants (POPs). Abu Dhabi, United Arab Emirates, 7–9 June 1998.*

Petersen, J-E., 1998. *Agro-environment schemes in Europe - lessons for future rural policy.* Institute for European Environmental Policy (IEEP), London.

Pitkänen, M. and Tiainen, J., 2001. *Biodiversity of agricultural landscapes in Finland.* Birdlife, Helsinki.

Ukrainian NCP (national contact point), 2002. Communication by the Ukrainian national contact point on the basis of information provided by the Ukrainian National Academy of Agricultural Sciences.

Veen, P., 2001. *Semi-natural grasslands in candidate countries — a contribution to the background papers for the conference 'Agriculture and nature conservation in the Candidate Countries: perspectives in interaction',* Wassenaar, January 2001. LEI, Wageningen.

WWF, 1999. *The impact of cotton on freshwater resources and ecosystems — background paper, a preliminary synthesis.* WWF-Switzerland, Zurich.

WWF, 2000. 'Implementing the water framework directive — a seminar series on water'. A synthesis note by Tim Jones. www.panda.org/europe/freshwater/seminars/sem1/seminar1syn.html

2.4. Forestry

The total area of forest in Europe is increasing and the annual increment of growing stock has been larger than annual felling in nearly all countries. The timber resource is therefore increasing. The expansion of forest area has been mainly in the Mediterranean region and the southeastern countries of eastern Europe, the Caucasus and central Asia. In the Russian Federation, there has been an annual decline of forest area, but the combined area of forest and 'other wooded land' has been increasing.

About three quarters of the total forest area is considered 'undisturbed'; most of this is located in the Russian Federation. Recent studies suggest, however, that only about 26 % of the forest zone in the Russian Federation remain as large, intact forest landscape. About 7 % of the European forest area is under some form of protection and about 3 % under strict protection. A general strategy has been to expand existing protection networks, such as Natura 2000 in the European Union, in order to improve to improve protection in all regions.

Crown condition in European forests deteriorated considerably during the 10 years that followed the setting up of monitoring in 1985 as response to the UNECE Convention on Long-range Transboundary Air Pollution. After some recovery in the mid-1990s, deterioration has resumed in recent years with more than 20 % of trees now classified as damaged.

The relatively low utilisation of Europe's valuable timber resources provides opportunities for policy-makers and forest managers to diversify the functions of Europe's forests and achieve a better balance between environmental, social and economic interests in forest areas. In extensive forests, generally far from human settlements, current sustainable management practices should continue while allowing the protection of biodiversity, soil and water catchments. The smaller forests areas, in countries not highly dependent on forestry or where opportunities for commercial use are more limited, could increasingly satisfy functions other than production, including recreation, education, nature protection and buffer zones between built-up areas.

2.4.1. Introduction

Forests and 'other wooded land' (see definition in Section 2.4.5) constitute an important natural resource. They cover about 38 % of the land area of Europe and provide a wide range of goods and services for society. These include renewable fibre and timber resources and non-wood goods and services. Forests are a major reserve for Europe's biodiversity, provide important general ecological functions, since they serve as carbon sinks, protect water quality and soils. They are also of great value for tourism, recreation and education.

An important characteristic of European forests is that each country has its own management culture and specific goals, different ownership structures and particular societal demands and pressures on forests (e.g. climate change, biodiversity loss, illegal logging). This is one of the reasons why European forests are subject to many political initiatives and processes at different levels. These include a number of international conventions and two ministerial processes at the European level — 'Environment for Europe' and the Ministerial Conference on the Protection of Forests in Europe (MCPFE) — which aim at identifying common denominators and necessary actions.

In particular, an integrated approach is needed for maintaining biodiversity; this is reflected in the MCPFE process, in which biodiversity is regarded as part of sustainable forest management. MCPFE uses one biodiversity criterion for protected forests and eight (biodiversity) criteria for other forests.

In the EU, these initiatives are implemented through a set of strategies, action plans, directives and regulations. This policy framework reflects the long silvicultural tradition of the Member States and ensures that the forest resource is relatively well controlled and protected, although environmental challenges remain (halting the gradual loss of biodiversity, improving carbon sink capacities, etc.).

On a European scale, the situation is more complex. For example, forests in countries

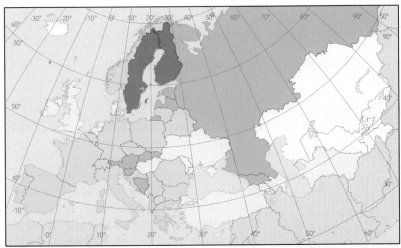

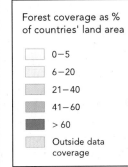

Forest coverage as %
of countries' land area

☐ 0–5
☐ 6–20
☐ 21–40
☐ 41–60
■ > 60
▨ Outside data
   coverage

Notes: Based on remote
sensing technologies and
forest inventory statistics.
Most of EECCA (including
parts of the Russian
Federation), Turkey and
Cyprus are visualised by one
%-class for the whole
country as the current forest
map does not cover the
entire region.

Sources: Schuck *et al.*, 2002;
Päivinen *et al.*, 2001;
UNECE/FAO, 2000

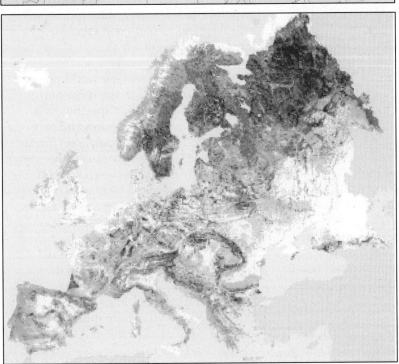

with economies in transition are
experiencing many changes resulting from
the opening-up of new export markets,
institutional restructuring and changes in
ownership structures. The amount of virgin
forest in the Russian Federation, in
particular, is declining, most visibly in the
western areas, western Siberia, the southern
parts of eastern Siberia and the Russian far
east. This is due mainly to fundamental
transformation of the forest vegetation by
human activity having considerable impact
on the existing areas of intact natural forest
ecosystems and the biodiversity within them
(Aksenov *et al.*, 2002).

Evaluating the development of forests and
forestry requires indicators that reflect the

various functions of the forest resource:
forest area and composition, the volume and
increment of the timber resource, markets
and use of forest products, socio-economic
factors and environmental conditions. The
information base should improve
significantly as a result of the set of
indicators for sustainable forest management
that has been prepared for adoption at the
2003 Ministerial Conference on the
Protection of Forests in Europe.

2.4.2. Forest area

2.4.2.1. Total forest area
The total forest area of Europe (excluding
'other wooded land') amounts to 10.3

million km². Even without taking into account the vast resources of the Russian Federation, the forest area is 2.1 million km².

Figure 2.4.1 shows the recent average annual change in forest area based on two reference periods for different country groupings and separately for the Russian Federation.

> 😐 The total forest area of Europe, excluding the Russian Federation, is increasing by about 11 000 km²/year. Expansion has been mainly in the Mediterranean region and the southeastern countries of eastern Europe, the Caucasus and central Asia. The Russian Federation reported a decrease in forest area at a very similar rate. This, however, was more than offset by an increase of about 16 000 km²/year in the area of 'other wooded land'. The increase in forest area (excluding the Russian Federation) has taken place mainly in forest not available for wood supply (around 7 700 km²/year).

The largest increases are reported in EECCA (in particular Belarus and Kazakhstan) and countries in the Mediterranean region (Spain, France, Portugal, Greece and Italy). The only countries indicating a slight decline in forest area are Serbia and Montenegro, Albania and Belgium. Countries with an expanding forest area in the EU are mainly those that have

implemented afforestation programmes through planting or by allowing 'other wooded land' to be converted to forest.

A problem related to monitoring developments in forest areas is the lack of comparability between inventories in different countries, especially for changes over time because of changes in definitions between assessment periods. Land-use change is an important indicator related, for example, to biodiversity and carbon sequestration; frequent reporting is therefore likely to be demanded in future. In the near future, more emphasis will need to be put on using remote sensing technologies and combined approaches (remote sensing and inventory statistics) in order to guarantee continuous and harmonised monitoring of changes in forest area.

2.4.2.2. Composition trends

In Europe, broadleaved forests dominate in several countries of EECCA (Republic of Moldova, Ukraine, Azerbaijan, Turkmenistan, Uzbekistan) and in the Balkans (Serbia and Montenegro, Croatia). Coniferous forests dominate in the densely forested countries, particularly the Nordic countries (Sweden and Finland: more than 75 %) but also western and central Europe (e.g. Austria: around 70 %). Some countries have a roughly equal share of broadleaved and coniferous forest (e.g. Belgium, Greece, the Netherlands and Ukraine).

Forest management in many parts of Europe during the past two centuries has often favoured single-species stands. Currently, there is a general trend, especially in western and central Europe, to increase the share of mixed forests by converting monocultural stands (Bengtsson et al., 2000). Natural regeneration is becoming a more common forest management practice and often increases the amount of mixed forests (Bartelink and Olsthoorn, 1999). According to UNECE/FAO (2000), however, only about 17 % of the forests are considered mixed for all Europe (excluding the Russian Federation, in which 41 % are reported as mixed). In the EU, 13 % of the forest is mixed.

Even active tree species policies result in only slow changes in forest composition. They depend, for example, on the rotation period of forest stands and the area available for regeneration. The multiple functions of forests imply that there are many different targets that relate to the composition of

| Figure 2.4.1. | **Average annual change of forest area in Europe between two reference periods** |

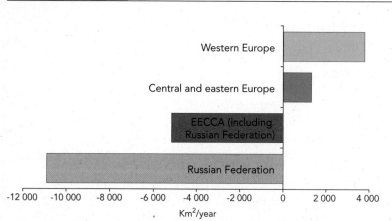

Western Europe

Central and eastern Europe

EECCA (including Russian Federation)

Russian Federation

-12 000   -10 000   -8 000   -6 000   -4 000   -2 000   0   2 000   4 000

Km²/year

Notes: Calculation of annual change is based on two reference periods; most countries compared data for a period of 1-5 years in the mid-late 1990s with a reference period that was generally 5-10 years earlier.

Source: UNECE/FAO, 2000.

forests which will also influence the rate of change. For example demands for more stability of forests against natural disturbances, biodiversity issues, forest protection and the use of forests as carbon sinks may target different tree species or mixes of species.

2.4.2.3. Naturalness

About three quarters of the forest area of Europe is considered to be undisturbed. However, nearly all of this lies within the Russian Federation, mainly in its northern regions. According to UNECE/FAO (2000) 92 % of Russian forests are considered undisturbed.

In contrast, a study by Aksenov *et al.* (2002) shows that about 290 million hectares, or 26 % of the forest area in the Russian Federation remain as large, intact forest landscape. The eastern Siberian region is least affected by modern land use. The western part of the Russian Federation has only small amounts of intact forest landscape (9 %). More than 80 % of the intact forest landscapes are located in the boreal forests/taiga of the Russian Federation. The forests in these areas mostly have a very low production potential (often less than 1 m³/ha/year) and are therefore not suitable for sustainable wood production (Yaroshenko *et al.*, 2001).

The main causes of fragmentation, according to Aksenov *et al.* (2002), are industrial forest harvesting and the fires that follow logging, agricultural use and road construction. This applies in particular to the western part of the Russian Federation. Extraction of mineral resources can be a further cause of forest fragmentation. The financial crisis of 1998 led to the highest rates of forest utilisation for a decade, as it became more profitable to harvest and export raw material; this caused a real threat to the remaining intact forests (Yaroshenko *et al.*, 2001).

With the exception of the Russian Federation and the Nordic countries (northern Sweden, Finland and Norway), the proportion of forest 'undisturbed' by human activities in most European countries is less than 1 %. The undisturbed boreal forest area of northwestern Europe, with its continuation into the Russian Federation, is therefore quite outstanding. The smallness of the area of totally undisturbed forests that remains in Europe reflects the long tradition of forest use and management. However,

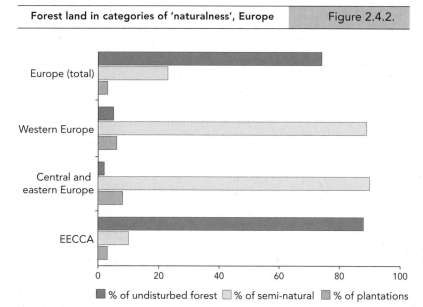

Forest land in categories of 'naturalness', Europe   Figure 2.4.2.

Note: No data available for Greece and Luxembourg.

Source: UNECE/FAO, 2000

such small remnants may be of high importance for nature protection and the conservation of biological diversity. A number of prominent examples are the Bialowieza forest in Poland and Belarus, strict forest reserves in the Carpathian mountains of Romania and the protected laurel forests in Atlantic islands such as Madeira (Portugal) and La Gomera (Spain).

Forest classified as 'semi-natural' dominates in Europe (excluding the Russian Federation). Some countries in WE (Germany, Austria, Switzerland, Italy), CEE (Czech Republic, Slovakia, Poland, and Serbia and Montenegro) and EECCA have reported their forests to be between 98 % and 100 % semi-natural. Overall, semi-natural forests comprise only about 23 % of the total forest area when including the Russian Federation (Figure 2.4.2.).

'Plantations' are defined as forest areas established by planting or/and seeding in the process of afforestation or reforestation. They can consist of non-native tree species or intensively managed stands of indigenous species which meet three criteria: one or two species, even age class, and regular spacing (UNECE/FAO, 2000). They comprise only 3 % of the total forest area. Countries with large proportions of plantations are Ireland, Denmark and the United Kingdom. Other countries with notable amounts of plantation area are Bulgaria, France, Portugal, Spain and Turkey. In the Nordic countries, the plantation criteria may apply to large areas of forest, but since these are also characteristic of semi-natural and natural boreal forests they have not been reported as plantations but under one of the other categories.

2.4.2.4. Forest condition

Forest condition is assessed annually in 37 European countries participating in the international cooperative programme on forests set up in 1985 under the United Nations Economic Commission for Europe (UNECE) Convention on Long-range Transboundary Air Pollution (CLRTAP).

Crown condition in European forests deteriorated considerably during the first decade of monitoring. After some recovery in the mid-1990s, deterioration resumed in recent years with more than 20 % of trees now classified as damaged. Significant deterioration in crown condition is to be found in southern Finland, Estonia and Latvia. Increasing defoliation was registered in central Romania, Bulgaria and the west of the Iberian Peninsula. Improving crown condition was observed mainly in southern Poland, western Romania and in Slovakia, after considerable damage in the past.

Results from intensively monitored plots indicate a continuing threat to forests from deposition of nitrogen and acidity, particularly in central Europe. Nitrogen deposition constitutes a particular risk in WE. Sulphur depositions were reduced on many plots — a clear result of the drastic reduction in sulphur emissions in Europe resulting from CLRTAP and other pollution-abatement strategies (UNECE, 2002).

2.4.2.5. Protected areas

Concerns about a decline in natural forests, accompanied by a loss of biological diversity, created a political momentum, particularly during the 1980s, to increase the area of protected forest. The initiatives have aimed mainly at protecting biodiversity but also take related social and cultural values into consideration. A general strategy has been to expand existing protection networks, such as Natura 2000 in the EU, in order to improve protection in all regions.

Including all IUCN-The World Conservation Union categories of protection, 7.3 % of forest land in Europe was reported to the Temperate and Boreal Forest Resources Assessment 2000 as being protected (UNECE/FAO, 2000). About 3 % was classified as being under stricter protection (IUCN categories I and II).

A European project, the 'Forest reserves research network', reported that 1.6 % of the overall forest area in 27 participating European countries was strictly protected (European Commission, 2000). Work is in hand to harmonise definitions and data collection on protected areas in the EU and at the pan-European level.

2.4.3. Annual fellings and total annual increment of growing stock

The Russian Federation has a growing stock of about 85 billion m^3, or three quarters of the total resource of Europe. Together with the growing stock in Finland, Sweden, Germany, France, Poland, Italy and Ukraine this represents 88 % of all forest resources in Europe.

The net annual increment (NAI) of forest available for wood supply in the Russian Federation is about 740 million m^3. By comparison, the remaining European countries (excluding those for which no data were available) have an NAI of 708 million m^3. NAI does not include natural losses, for example from windblow that can be harvested and counted as felling. This can be substantial and lead to 'felling' exceeding NAI without any depletion of the growing stock.

> ☺ In general, both net annual increment and annual felling have increased during recent decades, with annual felling rising much more slowly. The balance between NAI and annual felling is a major indicator of the long-term sustainability of forestry with respect to the overall timber resource.

NAI is generally well above annual felling in most of Europe (Figure 2.4.3). The Russian Federation uses about 16 % of its NAI. This is mainly explained by the collapse of felling after the break-up of the USSR in the early 1990s. This becomes clearer when looking at the figures of the previous (1990) forest resources assessment, for which the former USSR reported felling reaching about 74 % of the NAI in forests available for wood supply (UNECE/FAO, 1992).

The net annual increment of Europe's forests available for wood supply started to exceed annual fellings significantly in the 1960s (Kuusela, 1994; Silva Network, 1999). Possible causes for the increase (Spiecker *et al.*, 1996; Päivinen *et al.*, 1999) include:

- increased growing stock and expansion of the forest area;
- improved forest management practices and changes in forest structure aimed at higher wood production;
- environmental changes;
- changes in forest definitions and more accurate inventory methods.

The gap between the NAI and annual felling may also be increasing for reasons related to the economic profitability of harvesting and large-scale use of the entire NAI.

If current supply/demand structures stay in place, the growing stock will continue to increase. However, wood supply/demand patterns are dynamic: both market and policy forces can have measurable impacts on felling levels. One example of increasing demand for timber can be related to the aim of the European Commission to increase the share of renewable energy in the EU by 50 % (based partly on wood), to 12 % of total energy use by the year 2010 (European Commission, 1997) (Figure 2.4.4.).

Further increases in private ownership of forests in countries with economies in transition may lead to an increase in felling as the owners continue to see the forest as a potential source of income (Csoka, 1998). However, concerns are also expressed that in these countries where privatisation and restitution are expected to yield some 2.3 to 3.5 million forest owners, many will receive very small holdings for which they may show only limited interest with regard to management.

A recovery of the Russian forestry sector and active consumer behaviour (e.g. increased demand for products from sustainably produced timber) should contribute to an increase in supply and demand for wood and wood products. Other issues related to conservation and biodiversity, social functions of forests, environmental changes and carbon sequestration might result in an adaptation of forest management procedures in ways that enable the demands of various stakeholders to be met simultaneously.

It is the currently low use of the available resources that is providing scope for European policy-makers to design more socially, economically and environmentally balanced options for forest management and utilisation (Nabuurs *et al.*, 2003).

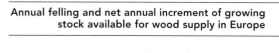

| Annual felling and net annual increment of growing stock available for wood supply in Europe | Figure 2.4.3. |

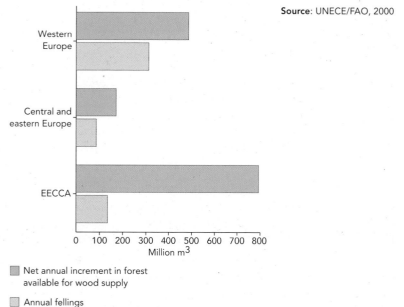

Source: UNECE/FAO, 2000

Net annual increment in forest available for wood supply

Annual fellings

| Net annual increment (NAI) and annual felling (AF) of the growing stock of forest for the EU | Figure 2.4.4. |

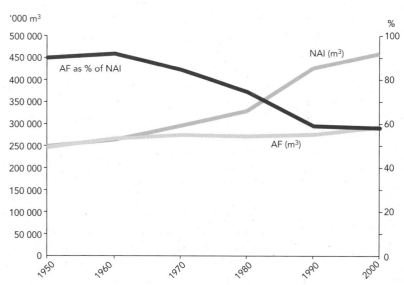

Sources: Kuusela, 1994; UNECE/FAO, 2000

2.4.4. The forestry sector as part of the national economy

The possibilities for changing production forests into forested areas that are able to satisfy a number of functions, including recreation, education, nature protection and buffer zones between built-up areas, are dependent on the importance of forestry for the national economies. The most-used indicator for assessing the role of the forestry sector in the national economy is the ratio of the value added by the sector to the country's GDP (Figure 2.4.5.).

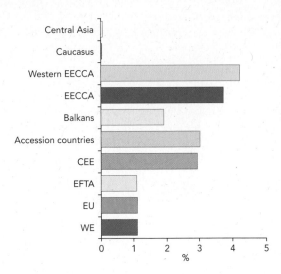

Figure 2.4.5.   Forestry sector share of gross domestic product in Europe, 2000

Sources: FAOSTAT, 2002; World Bank, 2000

The contribution of the forestry sector to GDP is generally relatively low, below 2 %, but substantially higher, typically more than 10 %, in some western Europe countries like Finland and Sweden and some central and eastern Europe countries like Latvia, Estonia and Lithuania. Even in these countries, however, the ratio has decreased substantially — in Finland, for example, from about one third in the late 1980s to 12 % in 2000.

This decrease in relative importance is often the result of faster growth in other sectors, with the value added by the forest sector remaining stable. Forest industries in the EU typically invest less than industries such as telecommunications or other sectors that

aim for fast growth. This may reflect the economic maturity of the sector and changes in the geographical distribution of investment following the estimated future consumption of forest products, but may also reflect the availability of raw materials or energy for the processing industries of Europe.

Most trade in forest products in Europe is internal, but many European countries are important exporters, the five largest being Finland, Sweden, Germany, France and Austria (Peck, 2001; EFI/WFSE, 2002). The revealed 'comparative advantage index' (Figure 2.4.6) shows the ratio of net exports of forest products to national GDP. The index follows the logic that if a country devotes more of its total resources to the production of a good than its domestic demand, it will have a comparative advantage with respect to this product in international trade. Thus, the comparative advantage index illustrates the country's position in international markets (Palo and Lehto, 1999). Among the WE and CEE countries, the index was highest (in 2000) in Latvia, Finland, Estonia and Sweden, where the relative share of forest products exports was also highest.

Based on trade indicators, there are countries where the forest sector has a high comparative advantage, a high share of exports and a clearly positive net trade value, e.g. Finland, Sweden, Austria and Norway (WE); Latvia, Estonia, Lithuania Slovenia, Slovakia and the Czech Republic (CEE); and the Russian Federation (EECCA). Other countries have a low comparative advantage and a relatively high share of import of forest products, e.g. Germany, France, Spain, the Netherlands and Italy (WE); Poland, Turkey, and Serbia and Montenegro (CEE). Finally, some countries have little forest product production and nearly total dependency on imports, e.g. Uzbekistan, Turkmenistan, Armenia and Azerbaijan (EECCA).

The rather low exploitation of Europe's timber resources and the limited contribution to GDP and export earnings in many European countries provide opportunities for diversifying the functions of Europe's forests. In countries with large forests, generally far from human settlements, current management activities could coexist alongside ensuring the protection of biodiversity, soil and water catchments. This can only be guaranteed if unsustainable use of forest resources by over-cutting or illegal logging is prevented. These practices have been

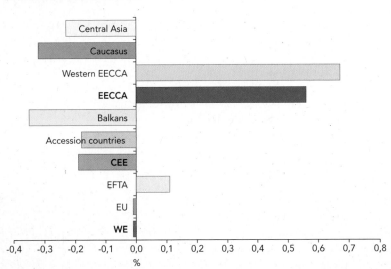

Figure 2.4.6.   Revealed forestry comparative advantage index in Europe, 2000

Sources: FAOSTAT, 2002; World Bank, 2000

receiving increased attention and have been mentioned in particular with regard to EECCA. Smaller-scale forests in countries not strongly dependent on forestry, or where opportunities for commercial forest management are more limited, could increasingly satisfy functions other than production, including recreation, education, nature protection and buffer zones between built-up areas.

2.4.5. Definitions

Terms used in this chapter are based on the following definitions:

Other wooded land
Land either with a tree crown cover (or equivalent stocking level) of 5–10 % of trees able to reach a height of 5 m at maturity in situ; or a crown cover (or equivalent stocking level) of more than 10 % of trees not able to reach a height of 5 m at maturity in situ (e.g. dwarf or stunted trees) and shrub or bush cover.

Forest available for wood supply
Forest where any legal, economic, or specific environmental restrictions do not have a significant impact on the supply of wood.

Forest not available for wood supply
Forest where legal, economic or specific environmental restrictions prevent any significant supply of wood.

Forest/other wooded land undisturbed by humans
Forest/other wooded land which shows natural forest dynamics, such as natural tree composition, occurrence of dead wood, natural age structure and natural regeneration processes, the area of which is large enough to maintain its natural characteristics and where there has been no known significant human intervention or where the last significant human intervention was long enough ago to have allowed the natural species composition and processes to have become re-established.

Semi-natural forest/other wooded land
Forest/other wooded land which is neither 'forest/other wooded land undisturbed by humans' nor 'plantation' as defined separately.

Plantation(s)
Forest stands established by planting or/and seeding in the process of afforestation or reforestation. They are either:

- of introduced species (all planted stands), or
- intensively managed stands of indigenous species which meet all the following criteria: one or two species at plantation, even age class, regular spacing.

Excludes: stands which were established as plantations but which have been without intensive management for a significant period of time. These should be considered semi-natural.

2.4.6. References

Aksenov, D., *et al.*, 2002. *Atlas of Russia's intact forest landscapes.* Global Forest Watch. Moscow. p. 185.

Bartelink, H. H. and Olsthoorn, A. F. M., 1999. Introduction: mixed forests in western Europe. In: Olsthoorn, A. F. M., Bartelink, H. H., Gardiner, J. J., *et al.*, *Management of mixed-species forest: Silviculture and economics.* IBN Scientific Contributions 15. Wageningen.

Bengtsson, J. *et al.*, 2000. Biodiversity, disturbances, ecosystem function and management of European forests. *Forest Ecology and Management* 132(1): 39–50.

Csoka, P., 1998. Forest policy activities in the countries in transition in their preparation for the EU. In: Glück, P., Kupka, I. and Tikkanen, I. (eds). *Forest policy in countries with economies in transition — ready for the European Union?* EFI Proceedings No 21. Joensuu, Finland. pp. 9–20.

EFI/WFSE, 2002. Forest products trade flow database (based on United Nations COMTRADE data). http://www.efi.fi/efidas/

European Commission, 1997. *Energy for the future: Renewable sources of energy.* COM (97) 599. Brussels.

European Commission, 2000. *COST Action E4 — Forest reserves research network.* EUR 19550. Directorate General for Research, Luxembourg. p. 377.

FAOSTAT (forestry data), 2002. http://www.fao.org/forestry/include/frames/english.asp?section=http://apps.fao.org/page/collections?subset=forestry

Kuusela, K., 1994. *Forest resources in Europe 1950–90.* EFI Research Report 1. Cambridge University Press. p. 154.

Nabuurs, G. J., *et al.*, 2003. *Development of European forests until 2050 — a projection of forest resources and forest management in thirty countries.* EFI and ALTERRA. European Forest Institute. Research Report 15. Brill Leiden, Boston.

Palo, M. and Lehto, E, 1999. Revealed comparative advantage trends of forest products in 12 countries, 1980–1996. In: Palo, M. and Uusivuori, J. (eds). *World forests, society and environment. Volume I.* Kluwer Academic Publishers. pp. 302–303.

Päivinen, R., *et al.*, 1999. Growth trends of European forests — what can be found in international forestry statistics? In: Karjalainen, T., Spiecker, H. and Laroussinie, O. (eds). *Causes and consequences of accelerating tree growth in Europe.* EFI Proceedings No 27. pp. 125–137.

Peck, T., 2001. *The international timber trade.* Woodheal Publishing Limited, Cambridge. p. 325.

Päivinen, R., *et al.*, 2001. *Combining Earth observation data and forest statistics.* EFI Research Report 14. European Forest Institute, Joensuu, Finland. Joint Research Centre, European Commission.

Schuck, A., *et al.*, 2002. Internal Report 13. European Forest Institute, Joensuu, Finland. EUR 20546 EN. 44 pages plus annexes.

Silva Network, 1999. *Forestry in changing societies in Europe. Part I: Information for teaching module.* Pelkonen, P., Pitkänen, A., Schmidt, P., *et al.* (eds.). University Press, University of Joensuu. p. 82.

Spiecker, H., *et al.* (eds), 1996. *Growth trends in European forests — studies from 12 countries.* Springer-Verlag, Heidelberg. ISBN 3-540-61460–5. 354 pages.

UNECE/FAO, 1992. *The forest resources assessment of the temperate zones, 1990.* Volume 1. ECE/TIM/62. UNECE/FAO, New York. 348 pages.

UNECE/FAO, 2000. Forest resources of Europe, CIS, North America, Australia, Japan and New Zealand. (Industrialised temperate/boreal countries.) UNECE/FAO contribution to the *Global forest resources assessment 2000. Main report.* ECE/TIM/SP/17. New York and Geneva.

UNECE, 2002. 'The condition of forests in Europe'. Executive report. Geneva and Brussels, p. 35

World Bank, 2000. *Gross domestic product at market prices.* EEA data service. Access to datasets used in EEA periodical reports.

Yaroshenko, A., *et al.*, 2001. *The last intact forest landscapes of northern European Russia.* Greenpeace Russia and Global Forest Watch, Moscow. p. 75.

2.5. Fisheries and aquaculture

A complex set of driving forces has resulted in overexploitation of most of the capture fisheries of Europe, leading in turn to increased catches of compensating species. Many stocks are now considered to be outside safe biological limits, and some are in a critical state. A range of alternative management regimes has been introduced, but most of these have failed to achieve policy objectives, primarily because the forces driving overexploitation have not been addressed. Indeed, government subsidies to the sector may have exacerbated the problem.

It is this aspect of persistent chronic overexploitation that is the greatest current environmental concern. Care is also needed to ensure that the current overcapacity in Europe is not exported to other countries, either through the sale of fishing vessels or through fishing agreements with third-party countries. The new common fisheries policy of the EU, which entered into force on 1 January 2003, aims to tackle this as well (European Commission, 2002a).

While fisheries economic production is generally in decline, aquaculture has grown dramatically, especially marine aquaculture in western Europe. The main aquaculture-related environmental concerns are associated with intensive cultivation of salmon and other marine finfish species and with trout or carp in freshwater. Also, intensification of aquaculture increases the demand for fish feed, which then increases fishing pressure on wild stocks. The local effects of aquaculture practices on the aquatic environment are well understood and highly regulated and monitored in the main producing countries. The wider impacts on the nutrient status of receiving waters, and effects on wild populations via escapees and parasites are, however, less well understood and more difficult to monitor and manage. In the European Union, these concerns should be more effectively addressed under the water framework directive and under the European Union recommendations on integrated coastal zone management and strategic environmental assessment.

2.5.1. Introduction

The Food and Agriculture Organization of the United Nations (FAO) code of conduct for responsible fisheries, agreed by all major countries of the world, defines a responsible fisheries policy as follows. It is one which ensures 'effective conservation, management and development of living aquatic resources with due respect for the ecosystem and bio-diversity in order to provide, both for present and future generations, a vital source of food, employment, recreation, trade, and economic well-being for people'.

Greater integration of environmental concerns, and the application of the 'precautionary principle' to fisheries and aquaculture management are key elements of EU fisheries policy and are specifically mentioned in the EU's plans for the reform of the common fisheries policy (CFP) (European Commission, 2002b). Most of these elements are reiterated in other national, bilateral and regional agreements and conventions. Commitments are increasingly being made, at national, international and EU levels to a more ecosystem-based approach to fisheries and aquaculture management.

Management regimes are normally designed to control pressures (e.g. fishing capacity) and impacts through a combination of quotas, gear controls, closed areas, and vessel restrictions. Controls on the economic driving forces (e.g. capping prices, sales or salaries) are rarely considered - indeed, subsidies are often available which may undermine other management initiatives.

Membership of international fisheries organisations (IFOs) (see Figure 2.5.1) gives a rough indication of a country's commitment to fisheries management.

Membership of IFOs is high in western European (WE) and central and eastern European (CEE) countries but low among the countries of eastern Europe, the Caucasus and central Asia (EECCA). Many of the fisheries in EECCA are in large transboundary inland lakes or seas (e.g. Caspian Sea, Aral Sea, Lake Peipus). It is not necessary to form an IFO in these situations, but coordinated management is required. This is becoming more common, which is encouraging. The role of IFOs in the management of international fisheries is expected to expand with increasing monitoring and the application of sanctions in cases of non-compliance.

| Figure 2.5.1. | European membership of international fisheries organisations with a European area of operation 2002 |

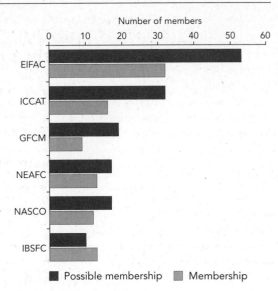

Notes: EIFAC: European Inland Fisheries Advisory Commission. ICCAT: International Convention for the Conservation of Atlantic Tuna. GFCM: General Fisheries Commission for the Mediterranean (responsible for the Mediterranean Sea, Black Sea and connecting waters). Georgia, the Russian Federation and Ukraine are not members of GFCM, but experts participate at GFCM meetings concerning the Black Sea. NEAFC: North East Atlantic Fisheries Commission. NASCO: North Atlantic Salmon Conservation Organization. IBSFC: International Baltic Sea Fishery Commission. Possible membership: the number of countries with fisheries relevant to the international fisheries organisations' area of operation. Membership: the number of countries that are members of the international organisation. Some EU countries are not represented on international organisations individually but by the European Union. Countries represented by the EU are included in the number of countries counted as being 'members'. Some countries are also members of other international fisheries organisations, which have a remit for fisheries in other areas of the world, e.g. the North West Atlantic, the Antarctic.
Sources: EIFAC, GFCM, IBSFC, NEAFC, NASCO, ICCAT

| Figure 2.5.2. | Western European fisheries economic production index |

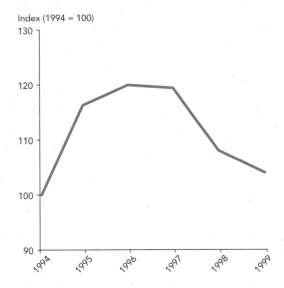

Notes: The economic fisheries production index provides a signal of income levels derived from fishing. Under the circumstances of a falling index fishermen and vessel owners are more likely to seek to increase income from further fishing activity, while others may choose to leave the industry. The reverse is likely in a rising index. The index has been calculated using the first-hand value of fish catch expressed in terms of value per full-time fisherman, modified by the strength of the local economy, and the technological scale (power) of the local fleet, indexed against a base year of 1994. Includes only Belgium, France, Greece, Netherlands and United Kingdom as all required data were only available for these. 1999 data point should be approached with caution as not all data are available for all countries.
Sources: Anon, 2000 and 2001b; FAO, 2002; OECD, 2001; Eurostat New Cronos database, 2002; Pacific Exchange Rate Service, no date; Anon, 2001b; World Bank, 2001

2.5.2. Fisheries

2.5.2.1. Economic drivers and pressures

Most of the fisheries in Europe are overexploited and declining catches have not reduced fishing pressures. In some cases, the profitability of fisheries has decreased and those with significant committed investment have had little choice but to fish harder to pay off their investment. This type of influence is represented in the fisheries economic production index shown in Figure 2.5.2, which suggests that income has declined in recent years following a peak in the mid-1990s. This may elicit a variety of responses from fishermen: to fish harder in order to maintain income; to circumvent legal constraints on fishing activity; to leave the industry if suitable alternatives exist; or to shift to other fisheries, such as shellfisheries. Subsidies, and especially capital subsidies, have exacerbated the problem.

On a more positive note, technical advances and improved labour productivity have, to some extent, compensated for declining catches. Further, rising prices associated with declining catches have tended to stabilise earnings, but these same factors can also facilitate and encourage substantial increases in effort and levels of exploitation. Profitability, tradition and, in some places, lack of alternatives remain the main incentives to invest in fishing enterprises and continue fishing.

> The decline in the fisheries economic production index for the third year running indicates the worsening economics of marine fishing in western European countries at a general level, and signals rising incentives to increase fishing effort and work round control regulations in order to maintain economic benefits at previous levels, or to leave the industry.

One of the most commonly used indicators of fishing pressure — fishing capacity measured in terms of the combined main engine power of the fleet — has decreased since 1990 (Figure 2.5.3.). The largest reductions have been in the EU fleet, driven by EU fisheries policy and financial assistance for decommissioning. The EECCA fleet size has also decreased following the collapse of many previously state-operated fishing enterprises.

Although some fleet capacity reductions in terms of engine power have been achieved in the EU, this positive influence may be neutralised by increases in fishing efficiency or effort (for example days at sea). Much larger reductions are needed as a matter of urgency to reduce overfishing. The current process of reform of the CFP indicates that a further reduction of around 40 % is still required (European Commission, 2001; 2002b). This will require strong political will and some measures to reduce the adverse short-term socio-economic impacts.

The increases in the capacity of the Norwegian and Icelandic fleets suggest a worsening of the situation, but it should be noted that these changes are taking place in the context of national management regimes and practices that are the most advanced in Europe in supporting and encouraging responsible and sustainable fisheries.

☺ Compared with the indicative policy objectives, only modest reductions in the capacity of the European fleet as a whole have been achieved over the past decade.

In the past, some of the overcapacity of the European fleet, and in particular the EU fleet, has been 'exported' to third-party countries, either through fishing agreements (the EU has concluded around 20 such agreements) or through the sale of fishing vessels. This has undoubtedly increased fishing pressure in some other parts of the world, and may have had knock-on socio-economic effects.

2.5.2.2. Impacts of fishing

The most direct impact of fishing is the removal of a significant proportion of target fish populations — the catch (see Box 2.5.1.). Since 1990, total landings of marine catch have increased by 25 % (Figure 2.5.4), although longer time-series data show catches may be returning to pre-1990 levels. This increase has occurred throughout Europe and for most major types of fish and shellfish. Landings of many key stocks, e.g. Atlantic cod, Atlantic mackerel and blue-fin tuna, have declined significantly in recent years and alternative species have been caught e.g. Alaskan pollock as a substitute for cod. The overall increase in landings is due to fishing fleets catching species that were not caught previously, such as industrial and deep-water species, some of which are used to underpin the growth of aquaculture (see Section 2.5.3).

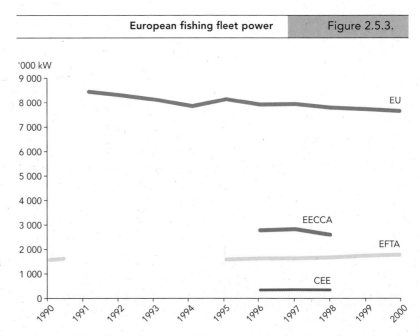

European fishing fleet power | **Figure 2.5.3.**

Notes: EU includes all coastal countries. EFTA is represented in these figures by Norway and Iceland only. Of the CEE countries, figures were only available for Croatia, Cyprus, Estonia, Latvia, Romania and Slovenia. EECCA includes Azerbaijan and the Russian Federation. Other countries not included due to lack of data or absence of fishing fleet. FAO data on CEE and EECCA countries' fleets only include information on decked vessels.

Sources: Eurostat; Anon, 2001b; Norwegian Directorate of Fisheries; FAO, 2002

Box 2.5.1. Discards and by-catch

The catch is composed not only of fish that are landed and sold, but fish that are discarded and subsequently die, as most do, and non-targeted species such as starfish, marine mammals and seabirds. These discards form a source of food for many scavenging sea creatures and seabirds. In fact, discards of fish form a large proportion of the diet of many seabirds in the North Sea.

The level of discarding is very variable and depends on the interaction of a range of factors. High levels of discarding may occur if there are lots of juvenile fish in the sea. This may be due to natural fluctuations in breeding.

Discarding is affected by the net mesh size and minimum landing size (MLS) allowed. If mesh sizes are such that large numbers of fish just below the legal minimum landing size are caught, then discarding will be high. Ensuring that regulations are complementary and do not undermine or contradict each other can alleviate this problem.

Quotas can also affect discard rates. Low quotas mean that fishermen have to discard all fish of a particular species once their quota for that species has been fulfilled. Low quotas can also lead to 'high grading', whereby low-value (e.g. small or damaged) fish are discarded in the hope that higher-value examples can be caught in the future, in order to gain the most income from a given quota. Other management regimes, such as that in Norway, prohibit any discarding.

Economics and market conditions can also affect the level of discards. If a previously discarded species becomes marketable, then discards will decrease, but overall the amount of fish caught will remain the same since that species is now being caught and sold instead of caught and discarded.

Illegal landings of sturgeon in the Caspian Sea are many times greater than legal landings and illegal trade in sturgeon products, especially caviar, continues to fuel illegal fishing. Official landings of sturgeon have fallen dramatically since 1992 (see Box 2.5.2).

The indirect and less easily observable impacts of fishing are those on the wider

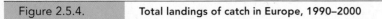

Figure 2.5.4.	Total landings of catch in Europe, 1990–2000

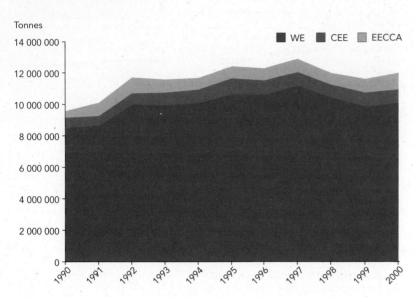

Notes: All catches of all species in North East Atlantic Ocean (includes Baltic Sea), Mediterranean Sea and Black Sea (including the Azov Sea) and Arctic Ocean . Caspian Sea and Aral Sea not included, as these are considered to be 'inland waters' by FAO. WE: Belgium, Denmark, Finland, France, Germany, Greece, Iceland, Ireland, Italy, Monaco, Netherlands, Norway, Portugal, Spain, Sweden, United Kingdom. CEE: Albania, Bosnia-Herzegovina, Bulgaria, Croatia, Cyprus, Estonia, Latvia, Lithuania, Malta, Poland, Romania, Slovenia, Turkey, Serbia and Montenegro. EECCA: Georgia, Russian Federation, Ukraine. Other European countries not included due to either a lack of fishing activity or a lack of data.

Source: FAO Fishstat Plus, no date

Box 2.5.3. The spawning stock biomass indicator

The total biomass of spawning stock (SSB) is one of the indicators used by ICES, the International Convention for the Conservation of Atlantic Tuna (ICCAT) and other fisheries organisations to assess the status of fish stocks. The level of fishing mortality (F) is used in conjunction with SSB. Reference points for SSB and F have been established, which indicate whether a stock is healthy or at risk of collapse.

Stocks are assessed in terms of the level that is considered to be sustainable. If SSB is too low, the stock is more likely to collapse. If fishing mortality is too high (i.e. too much of the stock is being removed by fishing activity), then the stock may also be more likely to collapse. The precautionary level of SSB (SSBpa) is the size of spawning stock below which management measures should be taken. Every effort should be made to ensure that SSB does not fall below this limit level (SSBlim). When SSB is below SSBlim, recruitment is likely to be affected and the risk of stock collapse is increased.

SSBpa and SSBlim do not take fisheries economics into account. They are purely biological reference points for sustainability against which the current state of the stock can be compared.

Overall, total European marine landings have increased by 25 % (2.4 million tonnes) since 1990. Landings of Atlantic cod, Atlantic mackerel and blue-fin tuna have declined in recent years, which has been compensated for by increased catches of Alaskan pollock, industrial and deep-water species.

A recent International Council for the Exploration of the Sea (ICES) working group on the ecosystem effects of fishing activity (WGECO) states that the level of beam trawling activity in some areas of the North Sea (10 or more trawls per year) may be comparable to the effect of dredging for marine aggregate (ICES, 2002). Deep sea trawling operations off the west coasts of Scotland and Ireland are causing concern due to their potential to damage the fragile deep-sea coral beds in these areas. Other environmental problems that may affect the sector, such as the effects of climate change, pollution and habitat destruction on fish stocks, are poorly understood. Nonetheless, it is now well established that certain organic pollutants contaminate fish to a level where it is no longer suitable for human consumption.

2.5.2.3. Status of fish stocks

ICES considers all European stocks of Atlantic cod and Atlantic mackerel to be at risk, either because the spawning stock biomass is too low (see Box 2.5.3 and Figure 2.5.6), or because fishing mortality is too high. Stocks of eastern North Atlantic blue-fin tuna are also a cause for concern. Until now, more fishing has been allowed than is recommended by scientific advice due to the lobbying influence of the fishing industry on governments. Only some commercially important fish stocks are monitored. ICES only monitors stocks in the North East Atlantic Ocean and adjacent seas such as the Arctic Ocean, Baltic Sea and North Sea. Stocks in other areas such as the Mediterranean Sea and Black Sea are not closely monitored, although this is improving. The General Fisheries Council for the Mediterranean (GFCM) does, however, report annually on the state of key stocks although the spatial coverage of these assessments is limited — hake and red mullet are considered overfished whilst sardine and anchovy are within safe limits. Biological reference points have only been set for a few commercially exploited species.

marine ecosystem, such as the effects of removing large quantities of fish that form the food for other species (e.g. sand eels), removing predators (e.g. cod) or causing disturbance to the seabed and its animal communities. These ecosystem impacts are poorly understood, but may have knock-on effects on other commercial fish species, marine mammals and seabirds. These issues are now being intensively researched.

Box 2.5.2. Caspian Sea sturgeon

Sturgeon is the most valuable fish in the world and forms an important economic component of the catch in the eastern Europe, the Caucasus and central Asia. The Convention on International Trade in Endangered Species of Wild Fauna and Flora (CITES) lists 25 of the 27 species of sturgeon and paddlefish ('cousins' of sturgeon) in Appendix II of the convention, meaning that international trade requires special documentation. The remaining two species - including the Baltic or common sturgeon (*Acipenser sturio*) — are listed in Appendix I of the convention, which bans all international trade in these species or products derived from them (CITES, 2000).

Somewhere between 60 % and 90 % of the world's caviar production comes from the Caspian Sea. The Caspian sturgeon fishery is split between five coastal countries — the Russian Federation, Azerbaijan, Kazakhstan, Turkmenistan and the Islamic Republic of Iran. The northern part of the Caspian Sea supports the major commercial stocks and it is the northernmost countries that catch most of the sturgeon.

Despite the general trend of increased landings in most European fisheries, official sturgeon landings from the Caspian Sea have fallen dramatically since 1992. This decline is not due to reduced fishing, but to a lack of available fish and to illegal landings not being included in the data. Illegal and unrecorded landings are estimated to be approximately 10 times the legal landings. The former USSR closely controlled sturgeon fishing, banning fishing at sea and attempting to rebuild stocks with extensive hatchery and restocking programmes, but its dissolution led to fishing restrictions being lifted

or not properly enforced and hatcheries being abandoned due to lack of funding. Caspian Sea sturgeon have not only been affected by fishing but have suffered greatly from pollution and access to spawning grounds being reduced or blocked by the construction of hydroelectric dams across the rivers that form their main migratory pathways.

To tackle these problems, Azerbaijan, Kazakhstan, Turkmenistan and the Russian Federation set up the Commission on Caspian Aquatic Bioresources in 1992 to control the sturgeon fishery. The commission assesses stocks and sets fishing quotas, and the Islamic Republic of Iran, where illegal fishing and trade in sturgeon is tightly monitored, undertakes a similar process. In June 2001, the five countries bordering the Caspian Sea agreed to build a management system for sturgeon stocks and to implement a commercial ban on fishing until the end of 2001. The authorities have also undertaken intensive enforcement operations against poachers, seizing illegally caught sturgeon and caviar.

Similar problems of overfishing, illegal fishing, and loss of habitat are found in the other major sturgeon fishing areas of the Black Sea (fished by Romanian, Bulgarian and Ukrainian fishermen) and the Azov Sea (fished by Ukrainian and Russian fishermen). However, increased enforcement, cooperation with CITES, intensive scientific research, restocking programmes and habitat improvement programmes are all under way in these areas, and international cooperation among the sturgeon fishing nations and the international community is continually improving.

| Catch of Caspian Sea sturgeon | Figure 2.5.5. |

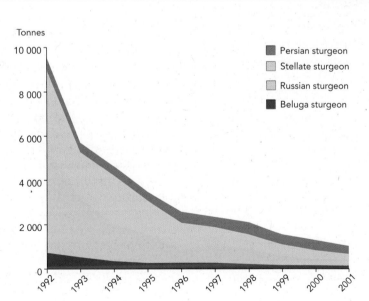

Notes: Data from the Russian Federation and the Islamic Republic of Iran have been combined to give sturgeon landings for the Caspian Sea. Landings from other countries are not included due to lack of reliable and comprehensive data. Landings of sterlet sturgeon (*Acipenser ruthenus*) and ship sturgeon (*Acipenser nudiventris*) have not been included as they are caught in only small amounts (<2 tonnes and < 25 tonnes in any one year respectively). All landings of Persian sturgeon (*Acipenser persicus*) are made by the Islamic Republic of Iran. Landings do not take into account illegal/unrecorded landings.

Source: The Management Authority for Sturgeon of the Russian Federation, 2000

Figure 2.5.6.   Spawning stock biomass of European Atlantic cod stocks

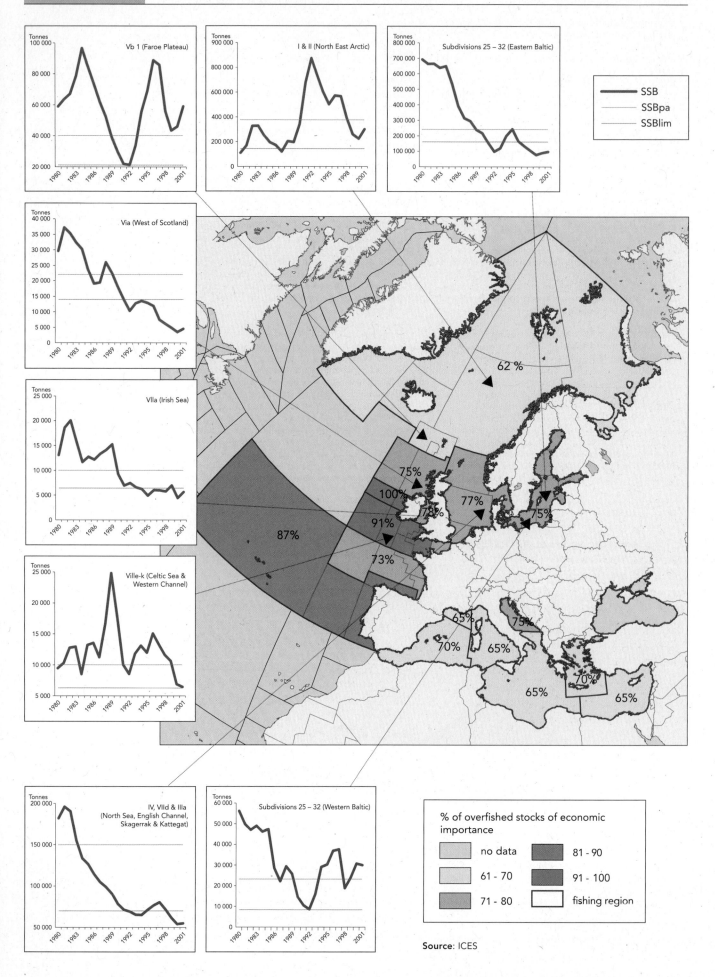

Source: ICES

Most European cod stocks have declined significantly since 1980 and most are considered to be at risk of collapse.

2.5.2.4. Inland fisheries

Inland fisheries provide an important source of fish for consumption and trade, and recreational fisheries are becoming increasingly important economically. Inland waters are subject to many pressures — fishing, abstraction, pollution, aquaculture, damming, irrigation, climate change and land-use change (see Chapter 8). Although overfishing may be a problem in some areas, FAO considers environmental degradation, not overexploitation of fish stocks, to be the greatest threat to inland fisheries (FAO, 1999), as in the case of the Caspian Sea sturgeon (see Box 2.5.2). This reinforces the view that more integrated environmental management of watersheds is required especially as demand for the utilisation of inland waters is expected to increase.

Commercial inland fisheries catches have fallen by 32 % (258 000 tonnes) since 1990 while recreational fishing is increasing. Data relating to the scale of these fisheries are very limited.

2.5.3 Aquaculture

2.5.3.1. Economic drivers and pressures

The rapid increase in the production of farmed fish is driven by strong market demand, and made possible through technical advances. Strong market demand is due mainly to:

- population growth and increased income;
- the worldwide popularity of seafood as a healthy food and as a luxury food;
- declining wild catches of high-value fish species;
- cheaper and easier international trade, transport and communications.

Total production in 2000 was just over 2 million tonnes (Figure 2.5.7.). Most of the increase during the 1990s was from marine salmon culture in northwest Europe, and to a lesser extent trout culture (throughout WE and Turkey), sea bass and sea bream cage culture (mainly Greece and Turkey), and mussel and clam cultivation (throughout WE). Inland aquaculture of carp (mainly common and silver carp) declined

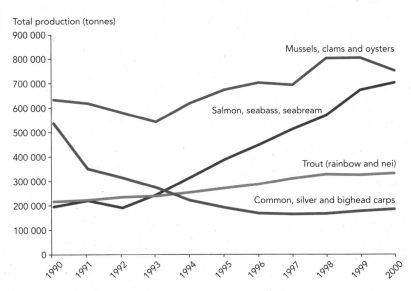

European production of major commercial aquaculture species, 1990–2000   Figure 2.5.7.

Total production (tonnes)

Mussels, clams and oysters

Salmon, seabass, seabream

Trout (rainbow and nei)

Common, silver and bighead carps

Note: Includes all countries and production environments for which data are available
Source: FAO Fishstat Plus, no date

significantly throughout CEE, resulting partly from political and economic changes.

Aquaculture has also been promoted in many parts of Europe as an alternative to fisheries where these are in decline or where other development options are limited in remote regions.

Intensive aquaculture currently depends on high quality pelleted feeds containing a significant proportion of fish meal. This is boosting demand for fish meal and generating strong incentives to increase fishing pressure on wild stocks throughout the world. This pressure should be understood in the context of global demand and trends for fish meal and oil for animal feeds generally.

The price of farmed marine finfish has declined significantly over the past decade as production has increased rapidly. This has stimulated substantial rationalisation of the industry. The bulk of production is now produced by a few major multinational enterprises. Small-scale producers find it increasingly difficult to survive.

Intensification of aquaculture and the related increase in demand for fish feed affect the fishing pressure on wild stocks. Fishing for food becomes fishing for feed.

Recent negative publicity relating to intensive farming of marine species may lead to some fall in demand and prices unless the industry demonstrates better environmental and product-quality management.

2.5.3.2. Environmental impacts

Different types of aquaculture generate different pressures on the environment. Intensive finfish production in marine waters and freshwater where production has increased most rapidly in recent years generates the greatest environmental pressure.

For intensive finfish aquaculture in marine and brackish waters and freshwater, pressures include discharge of organic matter, nutrients, chemicals and the escape of cultured organisms, and possibly increased density of pathogens. Inland pond aquaculture of carp usually requires less intensive feeding, and in most cases a greater proportion of the nutrients discharged are assimilated locally. In the case of bivalve molluscs, pressures include removal of plankton, and local concentration and accumulation of organic matter and metabolites.

Nutrients, organic matter, and chemicals discharged from intensive cultivation of finfish have well-understood effects in the immediate vicinity of cages or pond discharges, but also contribute to the overall load on the inland and coastal environment from agriculture, forestry, industry and domestic waste. Wider impacts on water quality and ecology can only be considered in the context of this wider pressure (see Box 2.5.4.). Figure 2.5.8 shows the relative significance of nutrient discharges from marine cage culture in some important producing countries. Although the figures should be treated as indicative only, it is clear that where aquaculture is a major industry in otherwise relatively undeveloped coastal areas, it can become the major anthropogenic source of nutrients. This is particularly the case within those aquatic systems (such as fjords, sea lochs, archipelagos) most suited to aquaculture. However, this does not necessarily imply a problem if well managed; for instance HELCOM (Helsinki Commission) has recently removed the major Finnish fish farming areas (archipelago and Åland Sea) from its list of 'hot spots'.

The point at which the pressure from organic matter, nutrients or chemicals triggers undesirable changes in the wider coastal environment, such as harmful algal blooms or other changes in ecology, is not well understood. In this process, there is no clear evidence that aquaculture has contributed to such problems (Scottish Association for Marine Science and Napier University, 2002). Indeed, aquaculture (especially of salmonids) generally takes place in relatively pristine waters, in which water quality historically has remained well within environmental quality standards. In most cases, however, monitoring programmes do not sample coastal waters systematically in relation to existing pressures.

Figure 2.5.8.	Contribution of marine and brackish water finfish culture to total anthropogenic coastal discharges in selected countries

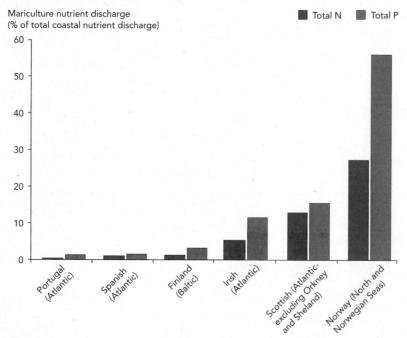

Mariculture nutrient discharge
(% of total coastal nutrient discharge)

■ Total N   ■ Total P

Notes: The data on 'other coastal nutrient discharges' comprise riverine inputs and direct discharges as reported for 1999 in the OSPAR Study on Riverine Inputs and Direct Discharges (RID). Nutrient discharge from mariculture is estimated from production using the mid-range of values stated in the OSPAR report (Ospar Commission, 2000) (55g N/kg production and 7.5g P/kg production). The figures for Finland are based upon the HELCOM 1998 data. Nitrogen limited to riverine discharge only (no data on direct inputs). Phosphorus discharge: average of lower and upper estimates. Total N for riverine discharge estimated as NH$_3$-N+NO$_3$-N. This will overestimate the relative N discharge from aquaculture. Nutrient discharge applicable to sea areas in which the bulk of marine and/or brackish water finfish aquaculture takes place have been used. These figures do not include N and P discharges from inland aquaculture production. Production figures relate to marine species only, except Finland, which refer to brackish water production.

Sources: FAO Fishstat Plus, no date; Jonsson and Alanara, 1998; Ospar Commission, 2000; Haugen and Englestad, 2001; Beveridge, pers. comm.; HELCOM, 1998

Marine finfish culture (mainly Atlantic salmon) now makes a significant contribution to nutrient discharge in some coastal waters, but there is no clear evidence that this has resulted in significant undesirable changes in the wider coastal environment.

2.5.3.3. Environmental management

Aquaculture is relatively highly regulated in WE and less well regulated elsewhere (Figure 2.5.9.). Regulation is strongest in those countries where the growth of aquaculture has been most rapid, suggesting that governments have taken a precautionary approach.

However, assessment, regulation and monitoring have been concerned mainly with the micro-impacts of organic matter in the immediate vicinity of farms and have not addressed the potentially more serious impacts on wild fish populations and the wider environment (see Box 2.5.4.). These can only be addressed through comprehensive monitoring and integrated management of aquatic systems, taking account of the pressures from aquaculture and other economic activities.

> 🙁 Aquaculture is highly regulated in many major producing countries, but generally at the individual farm level with little attention to diffuse and cumulative impacts and few links between monitoring and regulatory response.

The industry itself has responded with technical and management measures to reduce waste and other environmental pressures. The efficiency of nutrient utilisation in intensive salmonid aquaculture has increased steadily. Industry sources suggest that the quantity of nitrogen discharged per tonne of production has decreased from almost 180 kg/tonne of production in the late 1970s to less than 40 kg/tonne in the mid-1990s. While these improvements have come mainly from improved feed quality, future progress is more likely to come from improved feed management systems.

Intensive work is continuing to reduce nutrient loads from aquaculture as in agriculture. In several European countries, closed system fish farms are in operation. While these do not directly pollute aquatic systems, they still generate waste that requires careful management. Some sectors of the industry have also responded to consumer concern by initiating codes of practice and joining quality management and organic certification schemes.

Box 2.5.4. Escaped fish from fish farms

Significant numbers of farmed fish escape from fish cages and may affect wild populations through competition, genetic change and disease transmission. The largest producer of salmon, Norway, recorded 276 000 escapes in 2000 (NDF, 2000), corresponding to just under one escape per tonne produced — a ratio significantly lower than that achieved in the early 1990s. This should be seen in relation to the wild stocks numbering about 1 million wild salmon. In Scotland, total recorded escapes from cages varied between 67 000 in 1998 and 420 000 in 2000 (SERAD, 2002); these have been released into an area that probably supports about 60 000 wild salmon. Salmon farming could be contributing, along with other important pressures, to the current poor state of wild salmon and sea trout stocks. Direct indicators of competition, genetic change or disease incidence in wild stocks are currently not available or reliable enough to illuminate these issues.

| Levels of aquaculture regulation, monitoring and policy in selected European countries | Figure 2.5.9. |

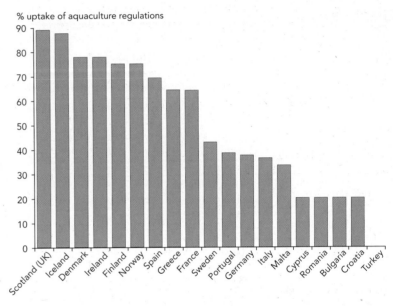

Notes: The regulations, policy and monitoring requirements for which data are available are capacity limits, environmental quality standards, food standards, medicinal and pesticide regulation, self-testing of food and environmental quality, authority testing of food and environmental quality, specific aquaculture policy, national aquaculture plans, centralised administrative framework, established aquaculture zones, environmental impact assessment and genetically modified organism (GMO) legislation. The percentage score refers to the percentage of these 15 key regulatory tools that have been reported as implemented by each country. The percentage is based only on those tools for which information is available for each country. The relative figure provides an indicative value only and should therefore be treated with caution.

Source: Adapted from Fernandes *et al.*, 2000; Christofilogiannis, 2000

2.5.4. References

Anon, 2000. *Economic performance of selected European fishing fleets annual report 2000*. EU Concerted Action (FAIR PL97-3541) Promotion of Common Methods for Economic Assessment of EU Fisheries.

Anon, 2001a. Economic and biological key figures from the Norwegian fisheries. Directorate of Fisheries, Norway. http://www.ssb.no/english/subjects/10/05/fiskeoppdrett_en/tab-2001-08-22-02-en.html

Anon, 2001b. *Icelandic fisheries in figures*. Ministry of Fisheries, Iceland.

Beveridge, M., pers. comm. University of Stirling, Institute of Aquaculture.

CITES, 2000. Implementation of Resolution Conf. 8.9 (Rev.) — Acipenseriformes. Sixteenth meeting of the CITES Animals Committee, USA, 11–15 December 2000.

European Commission, 2001. *Green Paper on the future of the common fisheries policy*. COM (2001) 135 final.

European Commission, 2002a. Outcome of the Fisheries Council of 16-20 December 2002. http://europa.eu.int/comm/fisheries/news_corner/press/inf02_61_en.htm

European Commission, 2002b. Communication from the Commission on the reform of the common fisheries policy ('roadmap'). COM(2002) 181 final. Brussels.

Eurostat New Cronos database, 2002. Agriculture and fisheries, theme 5, employment in the fishery sector. Last update available: 29/01/2002.

FAO FISHSTAT Plus, no date. As available in EEA data service.

FAO, 2002. FAO Fishery Country Profiles. http://www.fao.org/fi/fcp/fcp.asp

FAO, 1999. *Review of the state of world fishery resources: Inland fisheries*. FAO Fisheries Circular No 942, FIRI / C942. FAO, Rome.

Fernandes, T. F., *et al.*, 2000. Monitoring and regulation of marine aquaculture in Europe. *J. Appl. Ichthyol.* 16: 138–143.

Christofilogiannis, P., 2000. *Codes of practice in southern Europe*. http://www.lifesciences.napier.ac.uk/maraqua/christo.htm

Haugen, A. S. and Englestad, M., 2001. *Fish farming in tune with the environment*. Ewos Perspective n° 3, Norway

HELCOM (Helsinki Commission), 1998. *The third Baltic Sea pollution compilation*. Baltic Sea Environment Proceedings. Baltic Marine Environmental Protection Commission

ICES, 2002. *Report of the working group on ecosystem effects of fishing activities*. Advisory Committee on Ecosystems. ICES CM 2002/

ACE:03 Ref D,E,G. ICES Headquarters.

Jonsson, B. and Alanara, A., 1998. *Svensk fiskodlings närsaltsbelastning*. Vattenbruksinstitutionen. SLU Report 18. 26 pages.

NDF, 2002. *Key Figures from the Norwegian Aquaculture Industry 2000*. Norwegian Directorate of Fisheries. Norway. http://www.fiskedir.no/english/pages/statistics/key_aqua/keyfigures_aqua_00.pdf

OECD, 2001. Review of fisheries in OECD countries: Policies and summary statistics. OECD, Paris.

Ospar Commission, 2000. Nutrient discharges from fish farming in the OSPAR Convention area.

Pacific Exchange Rate Service, no date. http://pacific.commerce.ubc.ca/xr/

Scottish Association for Marine Science and Napier University, 2002. *Review and synthesis of the environmental impacts of aquaculture*. Prepared for the Scottish Executive Central Research Unit.

SERAD, 2001. *Scottish Fish Farm Annual Production Survey*, Scottish Executive Environment and Rural Development Department. Official Aquaculture Statistics. Scotland. http://www.marlab.uk/PDFs/ProdSurvey/survey2001.pdf

The Management Authority for Sturgeon of the Russian Federation, 2000. *Total allowable catch (TAC) estimation for sturgeon species in the Caspian Sea*. Sixteenth Meeting of the CITES Animals Committee, Shepherdstown (United States of America) 11–15 December 2000. http://www.cites.org/eng/cttee/animals/16/16-07-2.pdf

World Bank, Economy and Finance, 2001. Theme 2: National accounts - aggregates; GDP and main aggregates; GDP and main components. Last update available: 09/11/2001.

2.6. Transport

The dramatic increase in transport demand, and in particular for road transport and aviation, has made the sector a major contributor to several health and environmental problems in Europe. Western European transport systems comply with stricter environmental and safety standards than those in central and eastern Europe and certainly than those in the 12 countries in eastern Europe, the Caucasus and central Asia (EECCA). However, western European citizens use about three times as much transport fuel and face approximately the same probability of death in a transport accident as those in the east.

EU experience shows that vehicle technology and fuel improvements can, through environmental regulation, help to reduce certain impacts per unit of transport significantly, particularly air pollution. But such gains in eco-efficiency seem not to have been sufficient to mitigate the impacts of the rapid growth of transport and infrastructure volumes on greenhouse gas emissions, noise and habitat fragmentation. In addition to technological solutions, better integrated transport and environmental strategies are needed to restrain traffic growth and promote the use of more environmentally friendly modes - two of the key objectives of the EU sustainable development strategy.

The most important short-term challenges for the Balkan countries and the countries of EECCA are to phase out leaded petrol (most countries), abolish fuel subsidies (three countries only), introduce self-financing of the transport system via fuel taxes, and move towards cleaner vehicles and better inspection and maintenance regimes. For the accession countries, the main short-term challenge is complying with the complex and extensive EU environment and transport legislation. The upgrading of their infrastructure networks — while at the same time maintaining their high share of rail transport — is another major challenge.

Despite regular increases in tax, fuel for road transport remains cheaper in real terms than it was 20 years ago. The EU recognises the need to internalise the external costs of transport on society in its common transport policy. Some Member States have begun to introduce instruments to achieve this, but a number of barriers to implementation remain. There is little evidence of similar measures being developed or introduced in other parts of Europe.

Investment in infrastructure remains a priority of transport policy. Investment in western Europe has focused on extending the infrastructure, particularly roads, and investment in the accession countries is moving in the same direction. The multi-modal trans-European transport network and its extension to the east constitute a major pillar of the common transport policy. Although trans-European transport network investments were originally targeted to have a dominant rail share, road network development is currently ahead of the railway network.

Strategic environmental assessment is a useful tool to help integrate environmental concerns at various policy and planning levels. A recent EU directive requires that transport plans and programmes be subject to environmental assessment prior to their adoption as from mid-2004. Large variations exist across the EU; some countries have an established history of strategic environmental assessment of transport plans or policies and others are moving towards systematic strategic environmental assessment of transport. Some accession countries are considering strategic environmental assessment of national transport plans, but these are either non-existent or still optional in others.

2.6.1. Introduction

Transport is essential for the functioning of modern societies. A well-developed transport system should enable the free movement of goods, services and people, and promote inter- and intra-regional communication. It should also allow businesses and people a greater choice of location for work, trade, living, shopping, learning and leisure.

The sector's contribution to air pollution was reduced substantially across Europe but transport also contributes significantly to several environmental (and health) problems, particularly climate change, acidification, local air pollution, noise, land take and the fragmentation and disruption of natural habitats. It is a major consumer of fossil fuels and other non-renewable resources. Transport accidents kill more than 100 000 people every year in Europe.

The challenge for transport policy is to strike a balance between the economic and social benefits of transport and its negative impacts on society and the environment.

2.6.2. Transport growth

Growth in transport is often linked to economic growth and political openness, and to the price and quality of transport. Growth in incomes, opening of borders and better technology (resulting in lower prices and higher speeds) have all contributed to growth in transport. Increases in transport infrastructure and car ownership form a circle of demand: more road infrastructure leads to greater car ownership and use, in turn fuelling demand for more infrastructure.

The patterns of growth have differed markedly between Europe's regions (Figures 2.6.1. and 2.6.2.), reflecting differences in economic and political development. A key factor is the quantity and rate of increase in the number of private cars.

In western Europe (WE) both freight and passenger volumes have more than doubled

since 1970. The increases in WE in the 1990s were primarily in road and air transport. Total European Union (EU) freight transport increased by 33 % over the 1991-99 period (including road, rail, inland waterways and air transport — the latter excluding Luxembourg) explained mainly by a 44 % increase in road transport. Total EU passenger transport, including passenger car, bus/coach, rail, and domestic, intra- and extra-European aviation, increased by 19 %, due mainly to the 15 % growth in passenger car transport and 97 % growth in aviation (including domestic, intra- and extra-European aviation). Further increases of 38 % in freight and 24 % for passenger transport in WE are expected between 1998 and 2010 (European Commission, 2001a).

Important factors behind the increase in passenger transport by road over the past 20 years in the EU are growing car ownership (increasing affordability), transport prices (in a number of countries private car use has become relatively cheaper than rail and bus use), infrastructure investments that prioritise roads (better flexibility), and the worsening quality of public transport and rail (EEA, 2001; 2002a). Urban sprawl has enhanced this trend. A Dutch case study (SEO, 1991) helps to explain the success of the passenger car. It shows that the price/quality ratio of the Opel Kadett improved by almost 1 % per year over the entire 30-year life span of the model, demonstrating the impressive improvement in the competitive position of the car.

In central and eastern Europe (CEE) and the 12 countries of eastern Europe, the Caucasus and central Asia (EECCA) there was a sharp decline in transport volumes after 1989 following economic recession. Freight transport in both regions is back at the level of the mid-1970s and still well below that in the 1980s. In CEE freight volumes have been on the rise again since the mid-1990s, following economic recovery. The limited passenger transport data show a more mixed picture: volumes in EECCA are currently at about 1970 levels, whereas in CEE they are back at 1990 levels and rising rapidly. The figures given for CEE and EECCA may be unreliable because of data limitations — data on car use are lacking for most of the countries. However, judging from the steady growth in passenger car ownership in these regions, demand for passenger car use is likely also to have risen rapidly, especially in CEE.

Figure 2.6.1.	**Annual changes in demand for passenger transport by mode in Europe, over the 1990s**

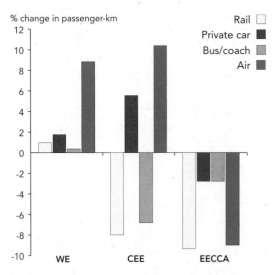

Notes: Waterborne passenger transport excluded as it has such a small share. WE figures apply to EU over 1991–99 period (including passenger car, bus/coach, rail, and domestic, intra- and extra-European aviation). CEE figures exclude Cyprus, Albania, Bosnia-Herzegovina, Serbia and Montenegro, and Malta and apply to 1990-99, except the air figure which applies to 1993–98 period. CEE data on car passenger transport apply to Hungary and Poland only. EECCA figures apply to 1994–98 period, and include all countries for rail passenger transport and all except Armenia for air passenger transport. Bus and coach passenger transport figures apply to Armenia, Azerbaijan, Republic of Moldova, Russian Federation, Kazakhstan and Kyrgyzstan. Private car passenger transport only applies to Azerbaijan, Republic of Moldova, Kazakhstan and Kyrgyzstan.

Sources: Eurostat, 2002 (EU); ECMT, 2002 (CEE); UNECE, 2002a (EECCA)

As well as transport volumes, shares of road, rail, waterways and air transport differ markedly across the regions (Figure 2.6.3). Road has been increasingly dominant in WE for many decades. The stabilisation of its share in passenger transport in the EU in the 1990s at around 80 % is mainly due to strong growth in air transport. For freight transport, road is also dominant with a 74 % share. The share of road in inland freight transport is still growing (from 68 % in 1991), while that of the alternative modes (rail, inland waterways) continues to decline. Short sea shipping in western Europe is also quite successful, carrying almost the same amount of tonne-km as road. While rail and public transport dominated the transport system in the CEE countries in the early 1990s, road is gaining rapidly at the expense of rail. The market share of rail in CEE is however still much higher than in WE. In EECCA, the position of rail remains strong, with no signs of decline. Aviation is the fastest growing mode. Its EU passenger market share (5 %) is about to overtake that of rail, but its share in other regions is still much smaller.

In order to combat the environmental, safety and congestion problems resulting from the continuing growth in transport, the EU's sustainable development strategy, adopted at the Gothenburg Council in 2001, contains policy objectives to break the link between economic growth and the growth of transport, to stabilise modal shares at the 1998 level by 2010, and to shift transport from road to rail, inland waterways and shipping from 2010 onwards.

> 🙁 Transport volumes grew at a fast rate in western Europe in the 1990s. They fell in central and eastern Europe and EECCA in the first part of the decade but are again beginning to rise.
>
> 🙁 At the same time transport volumes shifted away from the more environmentally friendly modes, towards road and aviation. Rail and public transport still have a higher share in central and eastern Europe and EECCA countries than in western Europe.

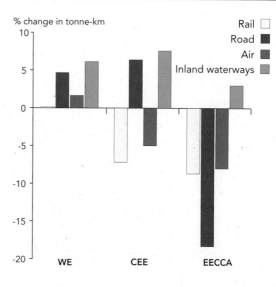

Typical annual changes in demand for freight transport by mode in Europe, over the 1990s

Figure 2.6.2.

Notes: WE data apply to EU over 1991–99 period (including road, rail, inland waterways and air transport — the latter excluding Luxembourg). CEE figures exclude Cyprus, Albania, Bosnia-Herzegovina, Serbia and Montenegro, and Malta and apply to 1990–99 period, except air transport figure which applies to 1994–2000 period. EECCA figures only include Republic of Moldova, Russian Federation, Ukraine and Kyrgyzstan and apply to 1993–98 period except air transport figure which applies to 1993–2000 period.

Sources: Eurostat, 2002 (EU), ECMT, 2002 (CEE); UNECE, 2002a (EECCA); World Bank (ICAO), 2002

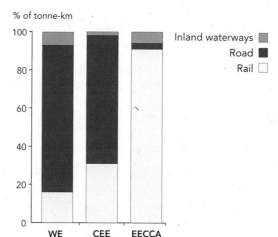

Modal shares in tonne-kilometres in Europe, 1998 (EECCA) and 1999 (WE and CEE)

Figure 2.6.3.

Notes: WE figures refer to EU and apply to 1999. CEE figures exclude Cyprus, Albania, Bosnia-Herzegovina, Serbia and Montenegro, and Malta and apply to 1999. EECCA figures only include Republic of Moldova, Russian Federation, Ukraine and Kyrgyzstan and apply to 1998.

Sources: Eurostat, 2002 (EU), ECMT, 2002 (CEE and EECCA)

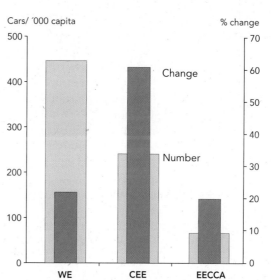

Car ownership in Europe and changes 1999 to 1990

Figure 2.6.4.

Notes: All countries included except Bosnia-Herzegovina. WE: data only for EU.

Source: UNECE, 2002a

Figure 2.6.5.	Total energy consumption by transport in Europe (a) and split of EU transport energy consumption between modes (b), 1990–1999

Note: Transport by oil pipelines is responsible for between 1 and 1.5 % of total energy consumption by transport and is therefore omitted. Marine bunkers: fuel oil sold for international seaborne shipping.

Source: IEA energy balances, 2002 ; Eurostat, 2002

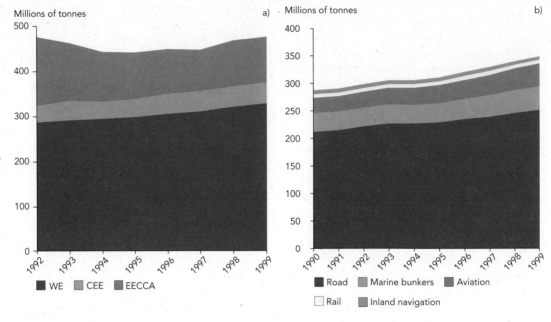

2.6.3. Environmental impacts

The most important environmental impacts of transport are climate change (greenhouse gas), loss of biodiversity due to habitat disruption, and effects on human health (e.g. local air pollution) and well-being due to accidents, air quality and noise.

2.6.3.1. Greenhouse gas emissions
Greenhouse gas emissions from the transport sector are almost entirely dependent on the amount of energy used.

For Europe as a whole, energy consumption by transport in 1999 was the same as in 1992 (Figure 2.6.5.), mainly because of the economic downturn in EECCA, which drastically reduced consumption between 1992 and 1997. In WE transport is the second largest energy consumer (with 30 % in 1999), and — given its almost entire reliance on fossil fuels — also a major contributor to carbon dioxide (CO_2) emissions (see Chapter 2.1). The sector's share in energy consumption is much lower in CEE countries (22 % in 1999) and EECCA (17 % in 1999). There are also large differences between the regions in transport energy use per person (about 840 kg of transport fuel in WE, 240 kg in CEE and 360 kg in EECCA). Following the dramatic growth in road transport and aviation, transport energy consumption rose by almost

2 %/year in WE (1990-99) and almost 3 %/year in CEE. As a result, the sector's greenhouse gas emissions are growing dramatically, thus jeopardising achievement of the reduction targets set by the Kyoto protocol (see Chapter 3). Energy consumption and CO_2 emissions are expected to grow in EECCA as economies recover and the demand for transport increases. Achieving economic growth while reducing greenhouse gas emissions from transport therefore poses a major policy challenge; furthermore, there are no sectoral transport greenhouse gas emissions targets.

Aviation requires special attention. It is the fastest growing energy user in the sector, and the impact on the climate of all aviation

---

☹ Transport energy consumption and greenhouse gas emissions in Europe are now growing strongly along with traffic volumes after a drop in the early 1990s in central and eastern Europe and EECCA.

☺ The sector's contribution to air pollution was reduced substantially across Europe due to a mixture of policy-driven technological improvements, fleet renewal and reduced transport volumes.

emissions is estimated at two to four times that of the CO_2 alone, mainly because of nitrogen oxide (NO_x) emissions and condensation trails at higher altitudes (IPCC, 1999).

2.6.3.2. Air and noise pollution

Transport is a significant source of emissions of acidifying pollutants, eutrophying compounds, ozone precursors and particulate matter (see Chapter 5). In WE, regulations on vehicle technology (e.g. introduction of catalysts) and fuel quality have helped to reduce emissions substantially. Substantial reductions are also expected in CEE, with gradual fleet renewal and uptake of EU regulation. However, the environmental benefits of technological improvements are being partly offset by growth in road transport, and air quality in most European cities remains poor.

Road, rail and air transport are also major causes of noise nuisance. Data are however scarce and not harmonised. In the EU, it is estimated that more than 30 % of citizens are exposed to road noise levels, and around 10 % to rail noise levels, above 55 Ldn dB(A) (EEA, 2001). Data on noise nuisance by aircraft are the most uncertain, but 10 % of the total EU population may be highly disturbed by air transport noise. Noise levels around several large airports in the EU have dropped in recent years as a result of the phasing out of noisier 'Chapter 2' (International Civil Aviation Organization noise category) aircraft. However, this trend is expected to reverse as the growth in aircraft movements is no longer compensated for by the use of quieter aircraft.

2.6.3.3. Accidents

Road transport accidents are now the largest cause of death for people under 45 in Europe (the impacts of transport emissions on human health are discussed in Chapter 12, Box 12.2).

More than 100 000 people died on European roads in 2000 (ECMT, 2002) and almost 2 million people were reported injured in the EU alone (European Commission, 2001a), but there are signs that the latter figure is largely underestimated. All regions show a gradual reduction in the annual number of fatalities — although levels have remained more or less stable in WE and EECCA during the last two to three years. The numbers of injuries and accidents in WE, however, are still rising. Annual fatality rates per million road vehicles range from 100 to 150 for the 'best' WE countries (United Kingdom, Sweden, Switzerland, Norway, Netherlands) to more than 1 000 for some EECCA and Balkan countries. Fatality rates per million inhabitants give a different and more mixed picture of 'worst performers' — Latvia, the Russian Federation, Greece and Portugal (180 to 270) have three to four times the rate of the best countries (ECMT, 2002).

In WE, one accident in two occurs in the urban environment (European Commission, 2001a). Pedestrians, cyclists and motorcyclists are the most vulnerable so their protection, for example via separate infrastructure, is of vital interest for road safety.

Lack of harmonisation and enforcement of speeding and 'drink-driving' rules hinder efforts to reduce driver-related accidents and their consequences. The European Commission has adopted a target of halving the annual number of road fatalities by 2010 (European Commission, 2001a).

2.6.3.4. Infrastructure and biodiversity

Trends in infrastructure lengths indicate that infrastructure investments are gearing the accession countries' road density in the direction of EU road density. While the motorway length in accession countries is less than 10 % of the EU's, it almost doubled between 1990 and 1999. In both regions the length of railways is decreasing (Figure 2.6.6).

The road and rail density in the accession countries remains lower than in the EU, and their territory therefore less fragmented. The expansion of transport infrastructure networks — in WE as well as CEE — leads however to increasing land take and fragmentation, and increases the pressure on designated nature conservation sites (Figure 2.6.7.). Fragmentation by transport infrastructure in the Czech Republic, Hungary and Slovakia is already more severe than the EU average. The needed development of the trans-European transport network, and its extension to the east, risks aggravating further the conflicts between infrastructure development and nature conservation.

> The development of infrastructure throughout Europe continues to increase pressure on habitats and ecosystems due mainly to fragmentation, and to disturb a large proportion of the population by traffic noise.

| Figure 2.6.6. | Changes in transport infrastructure length, 1990-99, accession countries (a) and EU Member States (b) |

Notes: Road, excluding motorways, excluding Czech Republic, Estonia and Turkey. Due to incomplete time series oil pipelines and inland waterways remained more or less stable and are therefore left out of the chart.

Sources: UNECE, 2001; Eurostat, 2002

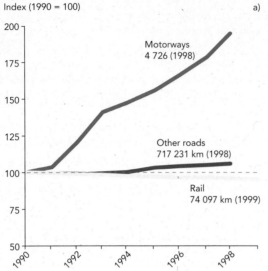
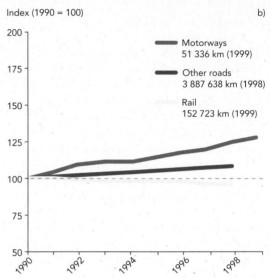

| Figure 2.6.7. | Average size of non-fragmented land, 1998, EU accession countries (a) and EU Member States (b) |

Source: EEA, 2002b

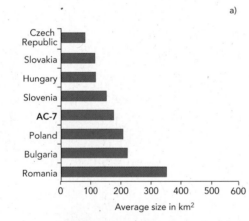
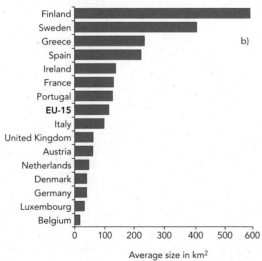

2.6.4. Policy prospects

2.6.4.1. Cleaner vehicles and fuels

Introduction of cleaner vehicles and fuels has proved to be extremely effective in reducing air pollution from transport. In the 1970s, WE gradually started introducing environmental standards in transport, following the US example. Harmonised and binding EU legislation for road vehicles (passenger cars, vans, trucks) has been coming into force since 1993, accompanied by the gradual phase-out of leaded petrol, which was completed in the EU in 2002.

During the past five years, the EU has taken several steps to reduce the sulphur content of road fuels to almost zero (by 2009). This increases the possibility of using the highly effective $DeNO_X$ catalysts and particle filters, which further reduce air pollution and enable the fuel efficiency of vehicle engines to be optimised. As a result, emissions of NO_X, HC and PM_{10} (particulate matter with a diameter less than 10 µm) from the newest generation of vehicles will be only a few per cent of those from the vehicles of the 1980s. Improvements are also needed for other transport modes, but pollutant emissions standards for rail, aviation and shipping are generally less regulated or lacking.

For CEE and EECCA, the most important measures needed in the short term are the phase-out of leaded petrol (for direct health benefits and to avoid catalyst poisoning), the adoption of stricter standards for new vehicles (sometimes difficult because of the

outdated technological level of domestic
vehicle production) and an effective
inspection and maintenance regime for the
existing fleet (particularly important as old
vehicles often have very high emissions).

The average age of the passenger car fleet is
currently 7.3 years in the EU and 11.5 in the
accession countries. Most accession countries
have already introduced higher taxes on
leaded petrol or banned it completely. They
are in the process of adopting the strict EU
environmental standards and inspection
regimes. Non-accession countries do not feel
the pressure of the EU body of legislation
and therefore generally lag behind.

Most of the EECCA countries have not yet
banned leaded petrol but are planning to do
so; Belarus and Turkmenistan banned leaded
petrol in 1998 and 2000, respectively. A
number of EECCA countries have signed a
resolution which states that they support the
total phase-out of leaded petrol by 2005
(2008 in Uzbekistan). Support was also
expressed for better vehicle and fuel
inspection and maintenance and air quality
monitoring. They also requested that these
recommendations be included in the agenda
of the Kiev environment ministers
conference (World Bank, 2001).

Despite efforts at the EU level to promote
alternative and renewable transport energy
sources, such as natural gas, biofuels or
electricity, their use and penetration remains
low. The Commission proposes that 5.75 % of
fossil-based fuels should be replaced with
biofuel substitutes by 2010 (COM(2001)547).
The environmental impact of this is highly
dependent on how and where such fuels are
produced and any resulting emissions from
the production plant and vehicles.

Emission and fuel quality standards
have greatly contributed to the
reduction of air pollution from road
vehicles in western Europe. The
implementation of such standards in
central and eastern Europe and EECCA
countries is in progress but needs an
effective enforcement and inspection
regime to fully benefit from these
developments.

2.6.4.2. Infrastructure investments
Infrastructure investment is another long-
standing priority of transport policy. A good
quality transport infrastructure network is an
essential backbone for society and the

Box 2.6.1. Transport infrastructure funding by the European Investment Bank and European Bank for Reconstruction and Development

Looking at loans by the European Investment Bank (EIB) and investments by the European Bank for Reconstruction and Development (EBRD) can tentatively indicate more recent investment trends. Even though these account for only a part of the total financing for transport infrastructure, funding by international banks is often a catalyst to attract funding from the private sector and other international financial institutions. Both the loans signed and the investments made by the EIB and EBRD incline towards road, in the accession countries as well as in the EU. Despite the EIB being an important contributor to almost all major railway investment projects in the accession countries (EIB, 2001b), rail investments cover 24 % of all loans signed by the bank, versus 59 % for road. EBRD loans to EECCA countries between 1992 and 2002 amounted to EUR 656 million in total; 50 % for road, 14 % for rail, 20 % for air, and 17 % for ports.

The imbalance between road and rail investments has worsened in the accession countries since 1995, when road transport volumes rapidly recovered and rail traffic continued to decline. Under these circumstances, funding for road improvements was probably easier to obtain than for rail.

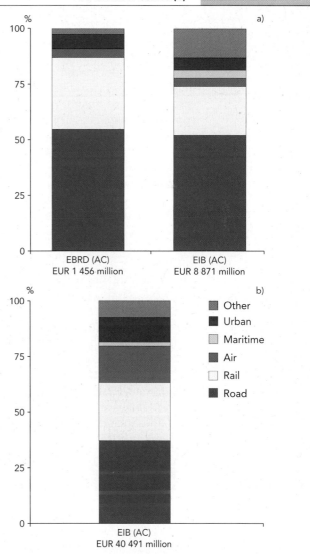

Modal distribution of transport infrastructure funding by European Investment Bank and European Bank for Reconstructions and Development, EU accession countries (a) and EU Member States (b) Figure 2.6.8.

Notes: EIB data for the accession countries refers to 1990 to June 2002, for the EU to 1995-2001. 'Other' for accession countries refers to repairs of different infrastructure after floods (Czech Republic, Hungary and Poland), oil pipelines (Czech Republic and Slovakia), multi-modal (road-rail) transport (Czech Republic) and improvement of navigation on the Sulina Canal in the Danube Delta (Romania).
Sources: EBRD, 2002; EIB, 2001a; EIB, 2002

economy. Transport investment policies in the EU have traditionally focused on extending infrastructure, particularly roads, as a response to increasing traffic demand. Better road networks, in turn, have further boosted road transport.

The few statistics available on transport infrastructure investments show that between 1993 and 1995 47 % of infrastructure spending in the accession countries went to roads and 42 % to railways. In the EU, road received 62 % of total investment, and rail 29 %, i.e. a larger share than its share of transport volume. This has, however, not been sufficient to make rail flexible enough to meet new transport demands. Maintenance budgets are allocated mainly to railways in the accession countries (54 %) and to roads in the EU (72 %). More up-to-date figures on investments by international banks indicate more bias towards road funding in the accession countries as well as in the EU (see Box 2.6.1).

The multi-modal trans-European transport network (TEN-T), and its extension to the east, constitutes a major pillar of the common transport policy (European Commission, 2001a). Total TEN-T investments were estimated to exceed EUR 400 billion by 2010. Although these investments were originally targeted to have a dominant rail share, to support, in particular, the development of the high-speed rail network, the building of the TEN-T road network is currently running ahead of the railway network development. In 2001, only 2 800 km of high-speed railway lines were in service, and it is expected that the completion of this 12 600 km network will take 10 years longer than planned (i.e. until 2020) (European Commission, 2001a). At the same time, the average speed of international rail freight transport is only 18 km/hour (European Commission, 2001a). The recently revised TEN-T guidelines include measures to tackle this problem, in particular by giving investment priority to the creation of a dedicated rail freight network, including port connections (European Commission, 2001b).

The network's extension to the east relies heavily on the transport infrastructure needs assessment (TINA) process. This has resulted in the definition of a network centred on 10 trans-European corridors but also including some additional links and all international air and seaports. By 2015, the TINA rail network is planned to extend to 21 000 km and the motorway network to 19 000 km. The network's costs are estimated at EUR 91.5 billion, with 48 % for the motorway network and 40.5 % for the rail network (European Commission, 2001c).

An overall assessment of the transport, economic, social and environmental impacts and benefits of the TEN-T or the TINA has not yet been made.

2.6.4.3. Fuel taxes

Fuel taxation is an important policy tool that provides a direct incentive to improve the energy efficiency of transport and thereby reduce greenhouse gas emissions. Fuel tax can also serve as a tool for payment of the costs of infrastructure and the external costs of infrastructure, congestion, accident risks, air pollution and noise, but a differentiated kilometre charge is generally considered a more effective tool for internalising and reducing these costs (see Section 2.6.4.4). Finally, increasing fuel taxes provides an opportunity to lower other taxes, such as those on labour, which reduces unemployment.

Figure 2.6.9 shows European petrol and diesel fuel prices in November 2000 (GTZ, 2001). The figures also show the pre-tax retail price of petrol and diesel (i.e. world market price plus distribution costs). Some countries actually subsidise their transport fuels, in the sense that the fuel is sold below the world market price plus distribution costs. In November 2000, Turkmenistan and Uzbekistan subsidised both petrol and diesel and Cyprus and Azerbaijan subsidised diesel. Cyprus intended to abolish the diesel subsidy by January 2003. A number of countries, particularly in EECCA, levy hardly any tax on petrol or diesel. Despite regular rises in fuel tax, the weighted average EU road fuel price is still 10–15 % lower than it was 20 years ago and has remained fairly stable over the past 15 years, with the exception of a price hike in autumn 2000 (EEA, 2002a).

> ☺ Rail infrastructure is generally better developed in central and eastern Europe, but the apparent prioritisation of road investments may jeopardize a balanced development of transport modal split.

> ☹ Trends in transport fuel prices are not encouraging the use of more fuel-efficient transport modes.

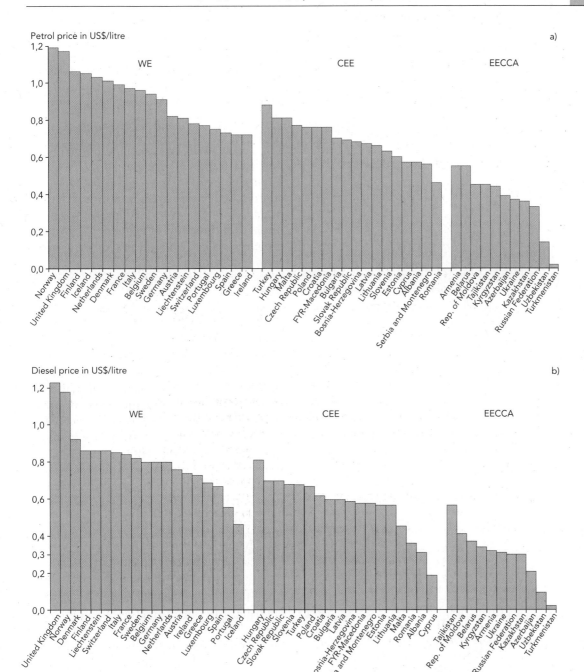

Petrol (a) and diesel (b) prices in Europe as of November 2000, in US$/litre   Figure 2.6.9.

Shipping and aviation fuels are not taxed at all. Railway diesel and electricity are either not taxed or relatively mildly taxed. This distorts competition between transport modes and the untaxed sectors face no extra incentives to reduce their greenhouse gas emissions.

2.6.4.4. Internalisation of external costs

Every transport user poses a burden of unpaid costs on other people, including the costs of accidents, pollution, noise and congestion. In the EU, these costs are estimated at 8 % of GDP (INFRAS/IWW, 2000). At the same time, many transport taxes are poorly targeted and unequal. They do not differentiate between

users and their different impacts on infrastructure, contributions to pollution, accidents and bottlenecks.

A restructuring (and in many cases increase) of transport taxes and charges could contribute to making individual users pay the true costs imposed on society. With such internalisation of external costs, users would have incentives to drive cleaner and safer vehicles and avoid peak hours, and accidents and congestion should decrease.

Switzerland is the only country to have introduced a kilometre-dependent transport

Figure 2.6.10.	Specific test-cycle fuel consumption of passenger cars in the EU, 1990–2000

Notes: Source for test values: national agencies, except Ireland, Luxembourg and Portugal. For these countries the data are elaborated for ODYSSEE from data provided by Association of Car Manufactures from Europe (ACEA), Japan (JAMA) and Republic of Korea (KAMA). Data based on the new test cycle according to Directive 93/116/EC. For 1995, data were initially based on the old cycle; they have been adjusted by the ACEA applying a 9 % adjustment 'across the board'. For previous years, data have been adjusted to be consistent within the new cycle. Please note that fuel consumption in practice, i.e. outside the test cycle, is different from the test values, because the test cycle does not account for factors like harsh driving and air conditioning.

Source: ODYSSEE, 2002

Litres/100 kilometres

All passenger cars

New passenger cars

charge in its whole territory. A heavy goods vehicle (HGV) charge is dependent on distance driven in Switzerland, size of truck and the environmental class of the engine. Germany has planned for the introduction of such charges in August 2003. London has introduced a congestion charge for its centre, starting 17 February 2003, of around 8 EUR (www.cclondon.com).

The European Commission intends to publish a framework directive on infrastructure charging which aims to coordinate the principles on which transport pricing should be based. Following this framework directive, subsequent daughter directives are to be published for each mode, starting with road freight.

Some western European countries pave the way for internalisation by restructuring transport taxes and charges.

2.6.4.5. Voluntary agreements

The EU focuses its policy efforts mainly on the Community strategy to reduce CO_2 from passenger cars, which includes three pillars: the voluntary agreement with the European car manufacturers, car labelling and fiscal measures for new passenger cars. Other transport modes are as yet much less addressed by EU policies.

The voluntary agreement between car manufacturers and the European Commission aims to reduce average CO_2 emissions from new vehicles sold on the EU market (European Commission, 2001d). The target for European manufacturers is 140 g CO_2/km by 2008 (compared with 186 in 1995) and by 2009 for manufacturers in Japan and the Republic of Korea. The car manufacturers are on track to meet their intermediate targets — CO_2 emissions from new cars were reduced by 10 % between 1995 and 2001 — but extra efforts are needed to reach the 120 g CO_2/km target for 2010. By 2001 the intermediate target range (165–170 g CO_2/km) envisaged for 2003 was achieved (European Commission, 2001b). The improvement of fuel efficiency of new cars (Figure 2.6.10) has contributed to a 2 % improvement of energy efficiency of the entire EU car fleet (Figure 2.6.11). However, the increased share of diesel cars in sales, which partly explains the energy consumption reduction, raises concerns regarding higher emissions of particulates

Figure 2.6.11.	Energy efficiency of car, rail and air passenger transport, EU, 1990–1999

Notes: EU-3 refers to Denmark, Germany and Finland

Source: ODYSSEE, 2002

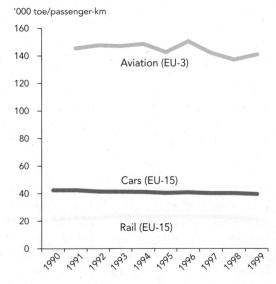

'000 toe/passenger-km

Aviation (EU-3)

Cars (EU-15)

Rail (EU-15)

and NO_x. General technical improvements have also led to improvements in the energy efficiency of road freight transport in a number of Member States. Trucks and vans are not yet included in the voluntary agreement. The Commission has however submitted a proposal to measure CO_2 emission and fuel consumption from light commercial vehicles (European Commission, 2001e) and is currently studying measures to reduce their CO_2 emissions.

There are no voluntary requirements (or, indeed, legal requirements) for air and rail transport to reduce their CO_2 emissions. There have been no improvements in the energy efficiency of rail, but this remains the most energy-efficient mode. Despite improvements during the 1990s, aviation is generally the least energy-efficient mode. Meanwhile, transport energy consumption continues to grow dramatically (see Section 2.6.3.1), indicating that technology improvements are being offset by growth in transport.

> The voluntary agreement between car manufacturers and the European Commission has contributed to a 10 % improvement of energy efficiency of new cars in the EU. However, there are no voluntary requirements for air and rail transport to reduce their CO_2 emissions.

2.6.4.6. *Strategic environmental assessment and monitoring*

Strategic environmental assessment (SEA) can be a useful tool to help integrate environmental concerns at various policy and planning levels. According to the recently adopted SEA directive (Directive 2001/42/EC) — to be implemented by EU Member States by 2003 — transport plans and programmes should be subject to environmental assessment prior to their adoption. UNECE is developing a protocol on SEA. This would also require countries to establish mechanisms for SEA at international, national, regional and local levels as well as in transboundary and non-transboundary contexts (UNECE, 2002b).

Large variations exist across the EU, with Denmark, Finland, Sweden and the Netherlands having an established history of SEA of transport plans or policies, supported by legal instruments. Seven other countries

are moving towards systematic SEA of transport (EEA, 2002a). Bulgaria, the Czech Republic, Poland and the Slovak Republic are considering SEA of national transport plans, but these are either non-existent or still optional for most accession countries (EEA, 2002a).

In addition to the necessary legal requirements, practical implementation also requires sufficient administrative capacity to perform the SEA, which is often not present. Moreover, to be effective, the findings of SEAs should also be taken into account in decision-making, which is as yet rarely the case — in the EU as well as in the accession countries (IEEP, 2001).

One of the strengths of SEA is that it would also provide for a trans-boundary assessment of international transport planning. It is therefore indicative that major infrastructure programmes such as the TEN-T and TINA have not yet been assessed at a strategic level.

Finally, regular monitoring is crucial to asses whether transport and environment policies are successful or not, and whether adjustments are needed. In order to do so the EU has established the transport and environment reporting mechanism (TERM), in which indicators are used to track progress in various policy areas. TERM's aim is to build up a policy-oriented system of data generation, integration and interpretation.

2.6.5. References

EBRD (European Bank for Reconstruction and Development), 2002. *EBRD Investments 1991–2001 — moving towards a better future.* EBRD, London. http://www.ebrd.org/pubs/general/invest.pdf

EIB (European Investment Bank), 2001a. *Development of trans-European transport networks: The way forward.* EIB, Luxembourg.

EIB (European Investment Bank), 2001b. *The Bank's operations in the accession countries of central and eastern Europe: Review of current and future lending policy.* EIB, Luxembourg.

EIB (European Investment Bank), 2002. Web site of the EIB. http://www.eib.org/

European Commission, 2001a. *European transport policy for 2001: Time to decide.* COM(2001)370. European Commission, Brussels.

European Commission, 2001b. *Proposal for a decision of the European Parliament and of the Council amending Decision No 1692/96/EC on Community guidelines for the development of the trans-European transport network*. Commission of the European Communities, Brussels. http://europa.eu.int/comm/transport/themes/network/english/ten-t-en.html

European Commission, 2001c. *Report from the Commission. Annual report of the instrument for structural policy for pre-accession (ISPA)* 2000. COM(2001) 616 final.

European Commission, 2001d. *Implementing the Community strategy to reduce CO_2 emissions from cars: Second annual report on the effectiveness of the strategy, reporting year 2000*. COM(2001)643, final. European Commission, Brussels.

European Commission, 2001e. *Proposal for a directive of the European Parliament and of the Council amending Council Directives 70/156/EEC and 80/1268/EEC as regards the measurement of carbon dioxide emissions and fuel consumption of N1 vehicles.* COM(2001) 543 final. Brussels.

Eurostat, 2002. 'Transport and environment: Statistics for the transport and environment reporting mechanism (TERM) for the European Union, data 1980–2000'. Unpublished electronic update, January 2002.

ECMT (European Conference of Ministers of Transport), 2002. Statistical trends in transport 1970–2002. Paris.

EEA (European Environment Agency), 2001. *TERM 2001, transport and environment reporting mechanism*. Environmental issue series No 23. EEA, Copenhagen.

EEA (European Environment Agency), 2002a. *Paving the way for enlargement. Indicators on transport and environment integration. TERM 2002.* Environmental issue series No 32. EEA, Copenhagen.

EEA (European Environment Agency), 2002b. European Topic Centre on Terrestrial Environment of the European Environment Agency. http://terrestrial.eionet.eu.int

GTZ (Deutsche Gesellschaft für Technische Zusammenarbeit GmbH), 2001. *Fuel prices and vehicle taxation, with comparative tables for 160 countries*. Second edition. GTZ, Eschborn.

IEEP, 2001. *Background for the Integration of Environmental Concerns into Transport Policy in the Accession Candidate Countries.* Final report to DG Environment. Institute for European Environmental Policy (IEEP). http://europa.eu.int/comm/environment/trans/ceec/index.htm

INFRAS/IWW, 2000. *External costs of transport (accidents, environmental and congestion costs) in western Europe*. Study on behalf of the International Railway Union. Paris. INFRAS, Zurich, IWW, University of Karlsruhe.

IPCC (Intergovernmental Panel on Climate Change), 1999. *Aviation and the Global Atmosphere*. IPCC, Geneva.

ODYSSEE, 2002. ODYSSEE database. ADEME/SAVE project on energy efficiency indicators. http://www.odyssee-indicators.org

SEO (Stichting Economisch Onderzoek), 1991. *De kosten van de auto en het openbaar vervoer vergeleken 1962–1990* (Comparing costs of the car and public transport 1962-1990). Bennis, et al. SEO, University of Amsterdam.

UNECE (United Nations Economic Commission for Europe), 2001. *Annual bulletin of transport statistics for Europe and North America*. UNECE, Geneva. Data received electronically, July 2001.

UNECE (United Nations Economic Commission for Europe), 2002a. Transport statistics from UNECE, provided through EEA's data service.

UNECE (United Nations Economic Commission for Europe), 2002b. Further updated version of the substantive provisions of a protocol on strategic environmental assessment. Ad hoc working group on the protocol on strategic environmental assessment. MP.EIA/AC.1/2002/8. http://www.unece.org/env/eia/ad-hocwg.htm

World Bank, 2001. *Cleaner transport fuels for cleaner air in central Asia and the Caucasus.* Kojima, M. Report No 242/01.

World Bank (ICAO), 2002. *World development indicators 2002, using ICAO.* Provided through EEA's data service.

2.7. Tourism

Tourism is one of Europe's fast-growing sectors and is an increasing source of pressure on natural resources and the environment. Continuing growth may jeopardise the achievement of sustainable development and, unless properly managed, may affect the social conditions, cultures and local environment of tourist areas; it may also reduce the benefits of tourism to the local and wider economy. The main pressures come from transport, the use of water and land, energy use by buildings and facilities, and the generation of wastes. Erosion of soils and impacts on biodiversity are also tourism-related issues. In some popular destinations, these pressures have resulted in irreversible degradation of the local environment.

Tourism is the main driver behind the increase in the demand for passenger transport, with its associated environmental impacts. This demand is expected to continue to grow, including a significant contribution to doubling of air traffic over the next 20 years. Cars and planes, the most environmentally damaging modes, remain the most used forms of transport.

The high concentration and seasonal nature of tourism create some direct environmental impacts at destinations. The seaside and mountains remain the favourite destinations. Tourism is taking a growing share of household expenditure as relative prices continue to fall.

There has been limited progress in the implementation of policies for more sustainable tourism, with minimal penetration of schemes such as eco-labelling within the tourism industry.

Unfortunately, the lack of relevant data makes it difficult to evaluate the overall contribution of the tourism sector to environmental problems; the assessment presented in this chapter is therefore based on rather fragmented information.

2.7.1. Introduction

Tourism in Europe is increasingly seen as a sector that interacts strongly with other policies such as transport, environment, regional planning, energy, trade and business, and information technology. The sector is highly fragmented and has long been regarded as a local management issue. Until recently, there has been little policy attention at the national and European levels and little realisation of the need for more sustainable management.

Different European countries have different institutional frameworks for tourism, from regional boards to state ministries, and some programmes that are designed to encourage sustainable tourism are being developed. However, most of the environmental measures that have so far been implemented have been initiated by major tour operators and local stakeholders and are based on voluntary approaches. There are examples of good practices in many countries (e.g. Austria, France, Germany, Spain, Switzerland and the United Kingdom) but most remain marginal (e.g. eco-label schemes or eco-taxes). There is a general lack of broad environmentally integrated strategies for the sector.

The tourism industry recognises the need to maintain its main assets, for example the attractiveness of destinations. While it is now generally recognised that tourism will be a successful industry only if it is managed in an ecological and sustainable manner, some efforts are still needed to move towards a broader and more integrated approach. At the international level, the United Nations Commission on Sustainable Development (UNCSD, 1999) and the Convention on Biological Diversity (CBD, no date) have targeted tourism as a priority policy area. At the regional level, the Mediterranean countries, the Alpine countries and the Baltic countries have initiated actions to promote sustainable tourism. The European Union (EU) Council adopted a resolution in May 2002 on the need to improve the coordination of policies that affect tourism. An Agenda 21 programme includes an integrated evaluation of tourism activity throughout the EU, the development of an integration strategy for the sector and the elaboration of harmonised indicators of sustainable development for tourism.

2.7.2. Major tourism patterns

2.7.2.1. Growth in demand

Tourism is an important industry in Europe; the region has long been the world's favourite tourist destination, with almost 60 % of the world market share. International arrivals are

| Figure 2.7.1. | Trends in international tourism arrivals, SW and NW Europe, EU accession countries and Russian federation and western EECCA (1985–2000) (a), Balkans, Caucasus and central Asia (1991–2000) (b) |

Notes: Here and throughout this chapter, northwestern Europe (NW Europe): Austria, Belgium, Denmark, Finland, Germany, Iceland, Ireland, Liechtenstein, Luxembourg, the Netherlands, Norway, Sweden, Switzerland and United Kingdom; southwestern Europe (SW Europe): France, Greece, Italy, Portugal and Spain. Central Asia: no data available for Tajikistan and Kazakhstan.

Source: World Tourism Organisation, 2001a

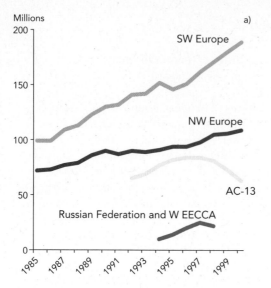

expected to grow by 50 % to around 720 million per year by 2020, with a doubling of air traffic in Europe. In the EU, the sector represents 30 % of total external trade in services, 6 % of employment and contributes 7 % of GDP (12 % if indirect effects are included) (EEA, 2001).

> 390 million foreign tourists visited Europe in 2000, 56 % of the world's tourism market. Of these, 360 million were to western Europe, and 190 million to southwestern Europe alone, where tourist arrivals increased by 91 % between 1985 and 2000.

During the past two decades, international tourism in Europe increased by an average of 3.8 % per year (Figure 2.7.1). The World Tourism Organisation (WTO, 2001b) forecasts an annual increase of 3.1 % over the period 1995–2020, which is one percentage point more than the anticipated economic growth. The three most visited countries in the world, France, Spain and Italy, already accounted for 24 % of the world's total arrivals in 1999 and will remain in this position even if their total share is expected to fall. At the same time, some other regions are becoming more attractive as a result of economic transition and the opening of borders, with a huge potential for tourism development. The countries of eastern Europe, the Caucasus and central Asia (EECCA), recorded the biggest growth over the period 1995–99, with tourist arrivals approximately doubling. The biggest growth (4.8 % per year up to 2020) is expected in

central and eastern Europe (CEE). Poland, the Czech Republic, Hungary and Turkey accounted for 81 % of CEE arrivals in 1999.

However, most tourist trips are not international, but within the country of origin. In 1995, WTO estimated that total domestic tourist arrivals numbered about 5.6 billion worldwide, with 567 million tourists travelling outside their own country (699 million in 2000). In Europe, domestic tourism accounts for 20–90 % of all tourist trips, from less than 20 % in Luxemburg, Croatia and the Czech Republic to around 90 % in Germany, Finland and Romania. More development of this form of tourism is expected as a result of increasing welfare levels in all countries.

2.7.2.2. Tourism expenditure
Many factors affect the demand for tourism, including increases in time for leisure activities and their social importance, economic growth, and changes in demographic factors, behaviour and expectations (EEA, 2001). The choice of destination remains determined mainly by scenery and climate. Europe offers the greatest diversity and density of attractions — coastal zones, islands, mountains, historical sites and countryside. European tourists chose the sea (63 %), mountains (25 %), cities (25 %) and the countryside (23 %) as holiday destinations in 1997 (European Commission, 1998). However, tourists are becoming more interested in higher quality tourism experiences, particularly in natural and cultural sites; nature, beauty and calm are the first criteria for choosing a destination, before price.

During recent years, the length of vacations has increased, which gives more time for tourism and leisure. Europeans now take multiple holidays rather than extending the length of their main holiday. In the Netherlands for instance, the average number of vacations per person increased from 1.21 to 1.71 between 1966 and 1997, and the number of short breaks doubled in comparison to long vacations. UK residents who travelled within their own country spent 4.1 nights away from home on average in 1989 and 3.6 nights in 1997; most tourists (70 %) now take short holidays (less than 4 nights). In France, the decrease in working hours, from 39 to 35 hours, has resulted in more days for holidays. There have been similar developments in several other European countries.

> 🙂 Tourism expenditure on international travel increased by 7 % between 1995 and 1999 in Europe, and by a factor of four between 1985 and 1999 in the western European countries only (they accounted for 87 % of total European tourism expenditure).

Tourism, and particularly mass tourism to some destinations, has become more attractive and easily accessible as a result of more packaged holidays being on offer, strong marketing strategies, low prices (particularly transport costs), the developing use of the internet for reservations, and the introduction of the euro currency in 12 EU countries. All this has led to more journeys per person and per year. As people become more affluent and the relative costs of travel and holidays fall, tourism is taking a larger and larger share of household expenditure on leisure. In the EU, expenditure for recreation and culture increased by 60 % between 1990 and 2000, with EUR 435 billion spent in 2000, while the share of total expenditure increased from 9.2 % to 10.3 % over the same period. According to the Swiss Federal Statistical Office (2002), half of expenditure by Swiss citizens on transport, meals and beverages in 1998 was for leisure. The growth in tourism expenditure by households results mainly from the increase in transport, which accounts for the largest share of tourism expenditure (for tour packages, about 45 % of the overall cost is for travel and 37 % for accommodation) (Eurostat, 2000) (Figure 2.7.2).

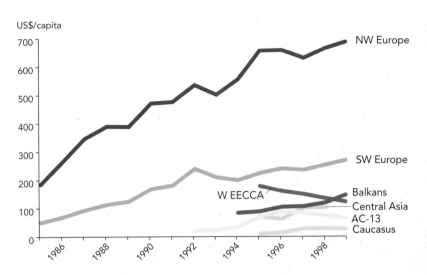

| Tourism expenditure on travel abroad (excluding international transport) | Figure 2.7.2. |

US$/capita

NW Europe
SW Europe
W EECCA
Balkans
Central Asia
AC-13
Caucasus

Note: No data available for Bosnia-Herzegovina, Serbia and Montenegro, Russian Federation and Turkmenistan.

Source: World Tourism Organisation, 2001a

2.7.3. Tourism and the environment

2.7.3.1. Transport

The most important regional environmental impact of tourism is from the associated transport (see Chapter 2.6). Travel to and from destinations is responsible for 90 % of the energy used in the tourism sector. In the EU, tourist travel represents 9 % of total passenger travel (including business travel, which constitutes 25–30 % of total passenger-km), and about 70 % of air transport is for holiday travel. For the whole EU, holiday transport is responsible for half of all passenger transport energy use, and 11 % of the overall energy consumption of the transport system (including freight). In France, transport for domestic tourism contributes from 5 % to 7 % of all greenhouse gas emissions (IFEN, 2000). As tourism is growing more rapidly than overall traffic, the associated problems are likely to increase.

The car offers a high degree of freedom for holidays and has also become cheaper relative to public transport than it was 20 years ago, giving it a special attractiveness for holiday travel (OECD, 2000). Some 340 million tourists arrived by road in southwestern Europe (Figure 2.7.3) and EU accession countries in 1999. The modal shares of international tourist travel to southwestern European countries in 1997 were 61 % road, 30 % air, and only 4 % rail, putting especially high pressure on some

| Figure 2.7.3. | Modes of transport used by international tourists, southwestern Europe and EU accession countries |

Note: The EU accession countries exclude Estonia, Latvia, Lithuania, Slovakia, and Slovenia.

Source: World Tourism Organisation, 2000a

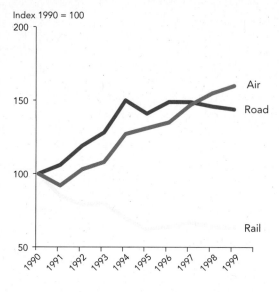

| Figure 2.7.4. | Changes in modes of transport used for tourism by residents for France, United Kingdom and Flanders (Belgium) |

Notes: France: all tourism trips (holidays and business) by residents; United Kingdom: all holiday trips by UK residents in England; Flanders: long holiday trips (more than three nights) by residents.

Sources: France: Direction du Tourisme/Sofres — cited in IFEN, 2000; United Kingdom: United Kingdom Tourism Survey 1999 — cited in English Tourism Council, 2001; Flanders: WES — cited by VMM in MIRA, 2001

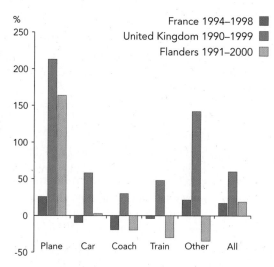

1999 (20 % of all arrivals), an increase of 60 % from 1990.

> :(Tourist travel continues to grow and is increasingly dominated by road and air transport, the most environmentally damaging modes.
>
> :| Vacation patterns are changing, with more vacations, particularly short breaks; people are travelling more often, for shorter stays and further from home.

Of the 2 200 million day-trip journeys by UK tourists in 1998, the share of the train was less than 5 % (10 % for overnight trips) while that of the car remained above 80 %. Tourist trips in England made by UK residents increased by 60 % between 1990 and 1999, with air transport increasing by 213 % (Figure 2.7.4). Some subregions of the British rail network are already running at 90 % of capacity and most routes out of London will reach the same level by 2011 (English Tourism Council, 2001). There are similar developments in many countries and for all transport systems. Routes of strategic importance for tourism will need to be further considered if the transport system is to cope with the continuous growth of tourist flows expected during the next 10–20 years.

Travel patterns are changing: tourists are travelling more often, for shorter stays, and further from home, and the average round-trip is getting longer than that for other purposes. In France, for example, the annual average distance travelled for tourism is 917 km per capita compared with 770 km for other purposes. The average person in the EU makes 0.8 tourist trips per year, travelling about 1 800 km; both these figures are likely to increase, with added impacts on the environment and on 'normal' traffic conditions.

2.7.3.2. Destinations
The direct local impacts of tourism on people and the environment at destinations are strongly affected by concentration in space and in time (seasonality). They result from the intensive use of water and land by the tourism and leisure facilities; the delivery and use of energy; changes in the landscape from the construction of infrastructure, buildings and facilities; air pollution and wastes; the compaction and sealing of soils (damage and destruction of vegetation); and the disturbance of fauna and local people

areas. For example, up to 80 % of all tourist journeys to the Alps, where public transport is crucially lacking, are by car. In the accession countries, 92 % of visitors come by road although the region has good access by train. Tourist travel is also highly concentrated in time, and the resulting seasonal saturation of road transport infrastructures often leads to decisions to supply more infrastructures and services.

Although most air travel remains relatively short-distance, long-haul travel is the most rapidly growing form of tourist travel, both in absolute and percentage terms. There were 80 million arrivals by air in the southwestern and accession countries in

(for example by noise). The growing number of tourists visiting sensitive natural areas, heightened by developments such as rural tourism around biosphere reserves, may jeopardize nature conservation. Some conflicts may also arise between tourism development and other sectors such as agriculture and forestry. The uncontrolled development of tourism over recent decades has led to a dramatic degradation of the quality of the environment, especially around the Mediterranean and in the Alps. About 35 % of international tourist trips by Europeans are to the European Mediterranean countries (mostly to coastal areas) and 8 % to the Alps.

Every year in the 1990s, it was estimated that nearly 135 million tourists (international and domestic) visited the Mediterranean coasts, doubling the local population. The impacts of the use of leisure boats and marinas are increasingly raising concerns in terms of pollution, over-use of natural sites and coastal zone management. It is estimated that tourism contributes to 7 % of all pollution in the Mediterranean (industrial and urban wastes including sewage, polluted rivers draining into the sea, crude oil dumped by all activities, detergents, mercury, phosphates, eutrophication). Health problems such as infections of the ear, nose and throat, hepatitis, enteritis and dysentery can all result from swimming in some areas.

Some destinations have become the victims of their own attractiveness. Islands such as Mykonos (Greece), Porquerolles and Ré (France), and Capri (Italy) that are experiencing increasing pressures have already exceeded their carrying capacity. The coastal strip (500 m from the shore) of Majorca, one of the most popular destinations, was already 27 % urbanised in 1995.

The over-use of water by hotels, swimming pools and golf courses is of particular concern in the Mediterranean and other regions where water is scarce. Tourists consume up to 300 litres (up to 880 litres for luxury tourism) and generate around 180 litres of wastewater per day. In the Balearic Islands, water consumption during the peak tourist month in 1999 (July) was equivalent to 20 % of that by the local population in a whole year, having increased by about 80 % since 1994. In the Rimini province (Italy), the production of wastes and wastewater in summer is three times higher than in winter, leading to some management problems.

The Alps are the second most favoured destination in Europe with 60 million arrivals per year, mainly because of the skiing facilities. Tourism is a key industry in many alpine areas, but it is also embedded in a wider socio-economic structure, with strong links with agriculture and other sectors. Tourism intensity can be considered as medium (0.1–0.5 tourist beds per local inhabitant) for 40 % of the Alpine communities and high (more than 0.5 beds per inhabitant) for approximately 20 % (EEA, 1999). Tourism in mountain areas is responsible for changing the appearance of the landscape through buildings and facilities and disturbing fauna (for example by noise). The tracks of the heavy equipment that tend the ski slopes erode the thin topsoil on which the vegetation cover depends, and over-fertilization in summer causes severe losses of biodiversity. Tourism also results in water supply problems (including from the production of artificial snow, with snow blowers consuming 1 m^3 of water for 2 m^3 of produced snow), and in sewage and waste disposal management difficulties. The waste generated in the isolated and high-altitude refuges is a crucial problem that may require special management such as transportation by helicopters. The functioning of the ski lifts needs a great deal of energy (equivalent in the French Alps alone to one-third of the annual production of a nuclear power plant (IFEN, 2000).

Accommodation (80 % of all tourism and leisure buildings) is a major source of impact, particularly on water resources, land use and ecosystems. Hotels are high consumers of water, as a tourist staying in a hotel uses on average one third more water per day than a local inhabitant. Energy consumption per m^2 per year by a one star hotel is 157 kWh (380 kWh in a four star hotel). Some tourism businesses are starting to implement energy-efficiency measures, for example hotels in the United Kingdom 'saved' up to 9 000 tonnes of carbon dioxide per year each between 1997 and 1999. Campsites are supposed to be a reversible form of land use, but water supply, sewage and waste disposal problems can arise if the infrastructure is not designed to cope with peak periods.

The growth in the number of second homes during the 1990s constitutes another major problem. The land area required by such a home, estimated at around 100 m^2 per person, represents 40 times that for a flat

Figure 2.7.5.	Stays in European tourism establishments - residents and non-residents, 2000 (a) and total residents, 1994–2000 (b)

Notes: (a) Balkans: 3.8 million residents. No data available for Cyprus, Turkey, Malta, and Serbia and Montenegro. (b) Data include residents and non-residents. No data available for Malta, and Serbia and Montenegro.

Source: Eurostat, 2000

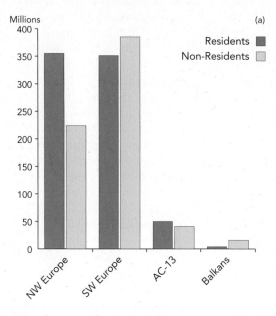

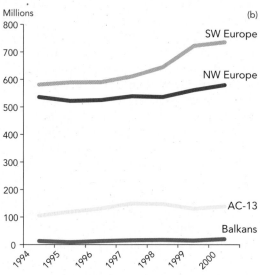

rental and 160 times that for an 80-bed hotel in a year (20 times that for an 80-bed hotel when garden areas are excluded). Most construction is in coastal zones and skiing areas. In Sweden, about one third of second homes are 100 m from the shore. In France, the world's top tourist destination, almost 335 000 new second homes have been built during the past two decades, covering more than 22 million m² of land; second homes now represent 73 % of total tourist lodging capacity, and 18 % of all nights spent by residents in 1999 were in their second home. Moreover, most second homes are seldom used: often only two weeks a year compared to more than 20 weeks for hotels. In Portugal, some families travel every summer weekend to a second home, at a considerable distance (more than 200 km).

> 🙁 Construction of second homes is increasing rapidly (by 10 % in France between 1990 and 1999), creating more intensive pressures on land and the environment, especially in coastal and mountain zones.

The continuing demand for high quality, luxurious and comfortable accommodation is expected to result in a steady growth in the number of holidays spent in hotels and second homes (Figure 2.7.5).

2.7.4. Management policies

Progress in addressing the sustainable development of tourism is mainly at the destination level, generally with a regulatory approach in the southwestern European countries and a more market-based approach in the northwestern countries, through voluntary agreements and eco-labelling schemes. At the regional level, tourism is covered in the Mediterranean area by the Barcelona convention and the Mediterranean action plan, in the Alps by the additional protocol on tourism to the Alpine convention, and in the Baltic by Agenda 21 for the Baltic Sea region.

Most policy developments at the local level are through Local Agenda 21, with up to 35 % of European municipalities committed to plans that stress tourism as a priority (ICLEI, 1997).

Vital public/private sector collaborative links are being developed at a number of leading destinations. For instance, and as a trans-national experiment, 13 natural parks in six western European countries have committed to the criteria of the 'Charter on sustainable tourism in natural protected areas' that is supported by the Europarc Federation. Hoteliers and other tourism businesses could play a significant role in the development of sustainable tourism and benefit directly from environmental initiatives, but very few have adopted environmental management systems.

Eco-labelling has shown some potential but its use, while growing, remains small (e.g. 0.1 % penetration in Austria) (Figure 2.7.6). Recent surveys suggest that many people would pay extra for accommodation that was part of a green accreditation scheme.

The external costs that tourism imposes on the local and regional environment and population are complex and depend on the characteristics of tourism in each type of destination. The impacts on society as a whole are associated with transport systems (see Section 2.6.3). Economic instruments such as environmental taxes are used in some countries, with visitors paying direct and indirect taxes on tourism products and services, but the revenues are not generally directed to environmental protection or improvement. At the same time, some popular destinations receive special subventions from the state for tourism infrastructures. In 1995, the European Council in its Recommendation R(95)10, relating to a policy for the development of sustainable tourism in natural protected areas, recommended allocating part of the tax on overnight stays to financing environmental infrastructures and the preservation of the environment. In Austria, the Land of Salzburg instituted in 1992 a tax on second homes ('Besondere Kurtaxe') that is allocated to local actions for preserving the landscape. The Balearic Islands levy an eco-tax on hotel stays (see Box 2.7.1) and a tax on passenger transport to small islands is levied in France. A diving tax (EUR 2.30 per dive) in the natural reserve in Medes Islands (Catalonia, Spain) generated EUR 130 000 in 1996, i.e. 68 % of the budget of the reserve (Afit, 2000).

Some more general responses could be developed to cope with the environmental impacts of tourism. Examples include spreading the vacation calendar at the European level to reduce the high seasonality of tourism, strengthening

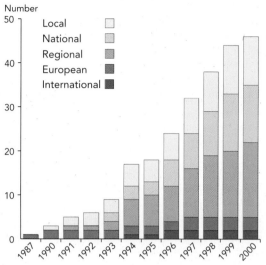

Eco-labels for accommodation in Europe, 1987–2000 Figure 2.7.6.

Source: ECO-TIP database

regional management plans, setting up some strategic environmental assessments for tourism projects, and generalising integrated quality management systems to tourist destinations. These include IQM (Integrated Quality Management) methodologies which have been developed for coastal, rural, and urban tourist destinations by the European Commission (2000).

2.7.5. References

Afit (Agence française de l'ingénierie touristique), 2000. *Sites naturels, contribution du tourisme à leur gestion et à leur entretien.* Les Cahiers de l'Afit, Guide de savoir-faire, Paris.

CBD, no date. Decision V25. 'Tourism in protected areas'. UN Convention on Biodiversity. http://www.biodiv.org/decisions/

> ☹ There has been a significant increase since 1990 in the use of eco-labels for tourism at the national and subregional level but their implementation remains marginal.

Box 2.7.1. Tourism eco-tax in the Balearic Islands

Almost 12 million people arrive at the Balearic Islands in Spain each year, compared with a permanent population of only 760 000. The tourists contribute significantly to the local economy, but there are social and environmental costs. The regional government wants to move to a more sustainable form of tourism and plans to finance its programme through a tax on hotel stays. From May 2002, tourists are charged EUR 1 per night eco-tax on all hotel bills. The EUR 24 million that this is expected to raise in the first year will be spent on environmentally friendly projects. The hotel industry was required to cooperate with the introduction of the new measure when it became apparent that the tax enjoyed strong support among residents. Tourists appear to agree with the aim of the tax once it is explained to them.

Source: http://www.caib.es

ECO-TIP database, no date. http://www.eco-tip.org

EEA, 1999. 'Tourism and the environment at European level — a practical framework for assessing the issues with particular reference to coastal Mediterranean and alpine regions'. Consultant report, March 1999.

EEA, 2001. *Environmental signals 2001.* Environmental assessment report No 8. European Environment Agency, Copenhagen.

English Tourism Council, 2001. http://www.wisegrowth.org.uk

European Commission, 1998. *Facts and figures on the Europeans on holiday 1997–1998.* A Euro barometer survey.

European Commission, 2000. *Towards quality coastal tourism: Integrated quality management (IQM) of coastal tourist destinations.* Brussels.

Eurostat, 2000. *Tourism in Europe — trends 1995–1998.* Luxembourg.

IFEN, 2000. *Tourisme, environnement, territoires: Les indicateurs.* Institut français de l'environnement, Orléans. An outline of the main findings is available in English. http://www.ifen.fr

ICLEI (International Council for Local Environmental Initiatives), 1997. http://www.iclei.org

MIRA (Milieu- en natuurrapport Vlaanderen), 2001. Flamish Environment Ministry, Belgium. http://www.milieurapport.be

OECD, 2000. *Tourism and travel patterns: Part I: Tourism travel trends and environmental impacts.* Organisation for Economic Co-operation and Development, Paris.

Swiss Federal Statistical Office, 2002. *Environment Switzerland 2002: Statistics and analysis,* Neuchâtel. 322 pages.

UNCSD, 1999. *Report on the seventh session, New York: Sustainable tourism.* United Nations Commission on Sustainable Development., New York. http://www.un.org/esa/sustdev/report99/csd7report_en.htm

WTO, 2001a. *Tourism Highlights 2001.* World Tourism Organisation, Madrid. http://www.world-tourism.org/market_research/data/pdf/highlightsupdatedengl.pdf

WTO, 2001b. *Tourism 2020 vision: Global forecasts and profiles of market segments.* Volume 7. World Tourism Organisation, Madrid.

3. Climate change

Global mean temperature has increased by 0.6 °C (in Europe by about 1.2 °C) over the past 100 years, and the 1990s was the warmest decade for 150 years. Global and European mean temperatures are projected to increase by 1.4–5.8 °C between 1990 and 2100 with larger increases in eastern and southern Europe in most projections. The proposed European Union target to limit temperature increase to a maximum of 2 °C above pre-industrial levels will therefore be exceeded during this century.

Sea level rose by 0.1–0.2 meters, globally and in Europe, during the last century. It is projected to rise by an additional 0.1–0.9 meters by 2100. Global precipitation increased by about 2 % during the last century, with northern Europe and the western part of the Russian Federation getting 10–40 % wetter with a further projected increase of 1–2 % per decade. In southern Europe and most of the countries of eastern Europe, the Caucasus and central Asia, precipitation in summer is projected to decrease by up to 5 % per decade, while the winters may become wetter. In summer 2002, heavy rainfall caused floods in central Europe, which cannot be attributed to climatic change alone, but can be considered an example of what may happen if climate change continues. The risk of floods is projected to increase, but river management and urban planning are also contributory factors. Droughts are likely to become more frequent in other areas of Europe such as southern Europe.

Greenhouse gas emissions in the EU fell by 3.5 % between 1990 and 2000, about halfway to the Kyoto target for 2008–12, assuming the use of domestic measures alone. Decreases from energy industries, the industry sector, agriculture and waste were partly offset by increases from transport. Substantial further reductions are needed to reach the national (burden-sharing) targets. Emissions in central and eastern European countries fell by 35 % between the base year 1990 (or earlier years for five countries) and 2000; most of these countries are on track to reach their Kyoto targets. Emissions in some countries, however, have started to increase again as their economies recover. Emissions in eastern Europe, the Caucasus and central Asia fell by about 38 %, mainly due to economic and structural change.

Many European countries have adopted national programmes that address climate change. Key policies and measures include carbon dioxide taxes, renewable energy for electricity production (wind, solar, biomass) combined heat and power, domestic emissions trading schemes, abatement measures in industry and measures for reducing emissions from landfills. A key policy is the directive on an EU-wide emissions trading scheme, which is expected to lower the compliance costs of the Kyoto protocol.

The costs of climate mitigation in western Europe can be reduced significantly through the use of the Kyoto mechanisms (joint implementation, clean development mechanism and emissions trading). In many economies in transition in eastern Europe, the Caucasus and central Asia investments in the energy sector are needed, and greenhouse gas mitigation costs in eastern Europe are expected to be lower than in western Europe. The Russian Federation, which is likely to have a significant surplus of emission allowances by 2010, could have a central role in the future market for greenhouse gas allowances. The costs of domestic measures in western Europe have been estimated in a recent study to be about EUR 12 billion per year. Assuming optimal banking of allowances by the Russian Federation would decrease the costs to a total of about EUR 4 billion per year, but lead to higher global greenhouse gas emissions by 2008–12 due to the use of surplus allowances. Climate change policies can have significant positive effects ('co-benefits') by also reducing emissions of air pollutants and thus the costs of abating air pollution.

Sequestration through land-use change and forestry ('carbon sinks') can be used to meet Kyoto targets, under some circumstances, with additional allowances amounting to about 1–4 % of 1990 emissions for some EU countries.

3.1. Introduction

Global and European average temperatures are increasing, sea levels are rising, glaciers are melting, and the frequencies of extreme weather events and precipitation are changing. Most of the warming can be attributed to emissions of greenhouse gases from human activities. Climate change is expected to have widespread consequences including an increased risk of floods, and impacts on natural ecosystems, biodiversity, human health and water resources as well as on economic sectors such as forestry, agriculture (food productivity), tourism and the insurance industry.

Climate change is addressed by the United Nations Framework Convention on Climate Change (UNFCCC), and the Kyoto protocol set binding targets for industrialised countries to reduce their greenhouse gas emissions. The protocol is a first step towards the more substantial global reductions (about 50 % by the middle of the 21st century) that will be needed to reach the long-term objective of achieving 'sustainable' atmospheric greenhouse gas concentrations.

Many countries have adopted national programmes that focus on reducing greenhouse gas emissions. However, even immediate large reductions in emissions will not prevent some climate change, and environmental and economic impacts, because there is a considerable time delay between the reduction of emissions and the stabilisation of greenhouse gas concentrations. Measures in various socio-economic sectors will therefore be necessary to adapt to the consequences of climate change in addition to emission reduction measures.

Although there have been some successes in reducing emissions, with some countries on track to achieving their Kyoto protocol targets, many of the improvements have resulted from one-off changes. Further action at all levels, affecting all economic sectors, will be needed if national Kyoto targets are to be met. Beyond Kyoto, the challenges of achieving 'sustainable' greenhouse gas concentrations are large, particularly if the economies and lifestyles of the countries of central and eastern Europe, the Caucasus and central Asia (EECCA) move towards the levels currently enjoyed by most western European (WE) countries.

3.2. Climate change and sustainability

Signs of a changing climate have been observed at global and European levels. The clearest indicator is the considerable increase in temperature over the past 150 years (ECA, 2002). A rise in sea level and changes in precipitation and extreme weather and climate events have also been observed in Europe during the past 50 years. Other signs include a retreat of mountain glaciers and a decrease of snow cover (IPCC, 2001a) (see also Box 3.1).

3.2.1. Sustainable targets for climate change
The ultimate objective of the UNFCCC is to reach atmospheric concentrations of greenhouse gases that prevent dangerous anthropogenic interference with the climate system, but allow sustainable economic development. Achieving such 'sustainable' levels would require substantial (about 50 % by the mid-21st century) reductions of global greenhouse gas emissions (IPCC, 2001a). The European Union (EU), in its sixth environment action programme (6EAP), has proposed that global temperatures should not exceed 2 °C above pre-industrial levels, which means 1.4 °C above current global mean temperature (European Parliament and Council, 2002). A study (Leemans and Hootsmans, 1998) proposed additional 'sustainable' targets: to limit anthropogenic warming to 0.1 °C per decade and sea level rise globally to 20 mm per decade.

Comparing these proposed indicative targets with projections of temperature increase and sea level rise shows that it is likely that these targets will be exceeded during the next 50-100 years if no further steps to mitigate climate change are taken. Achieving 'sustainable' levels of greenhouse gas concentrations and related climate change is likely to be one of the most difficult environmental challenges of the century.

3.2.2. Temperature increase
Globally, surface air temperatures have been recorded systematically since the middle of the 19th century. There is new and stronger evidence that most of the warming observed over the past 50 years is attributable to human activities. Confidence in climate models has increased: when fed with data on past anthropogenic emissions they calculate changes similar to those that have actually been observed (IPCC, 2001a).

Over the past 100 years, global mean temperature has increased by 0.6 °C with land areas warming more than oceans (Figure 3.1). Of the past 150 years, 1998 was the warmest, and 2002 the second warmest (WMO, 2002). The 1990s was the warmest decade since the middle of the 19th century, and probably also the warmest decade of the millennium. It is likely that the increase in northern hemisphere surface temperatures in the 20th century was greater than during any other century in the last 1 000 years (IPCC, 2001a).

The data for Europe (including Siberia) show that the temperature increase up to

2002 is consistent with the global trend and amounts to about 1.3 °C over the past 100 years. The increase in the countries of EECCA was up to 1.3 °C with the increase in Siberia amongst the highest in Europe (IPCC, 2001c; UNFCCC, 2002a). Observations show that 2002 was also the second warmest year in Europe (including Siberia). The temperature was 1.25 °C higher than the average (from 1961 to 1990) and only 1995 was warmer (1.46 °C above the average). Especially the beginning of 2002 was warm (3.9 °C above the average), while 2002 had the coldest December month in the last 100 years (3.1 °C below the average).

The warming in Europe has been largest over the Russian Federation and the Iberian Peninsula and least along the Atlantic coastline. The temperature changes are larger in the winter season in line with the global trend. In the summer season, southern Europe warms at twice the rate of northern Europe. Cold winters are expected to nearly disappear during the next century, and hot summers are expected to become much more frequent (Parry, 2000).

According to the Intergovernmental Panel on Climate Change (IPCC), global mean temperature is projected to increase by 1.4–5.8 °C from 1990 until 2100 (IPCC, 2001a). The range reflects not only the uncertainty of climate change models, but also the differences in scenarios for greenhouse gas and sulphur dioxide emissions over the next 100 years based on different assumptions on population growth and socio-economic development. These scenarios imply an increase in average temperature in Europe of 0.1–0.4 °C per decade over the next 100 years. The largest increase is projected for southern Europe (Spain, Italy, Greece), northeast Europe (Finland and the western Russian Federation) and some of EECCA, and the smallest increase along the Atlantic coastline. The projected increase in the annual average temperature in EECCA varies, with an average of about 4.5 °C by 2080 (IPCC, 2001c). In the winter season, the continental interior of eastern Europe, the western Russian Federation and some other areas in EECCA warms more rapidly than elsewhere (Parry, 2000; IPCC, 2001a; UNFCCC, 2002a).

Comparing these projections with the proposed 'sustainable' targets suggests that the EU target for absolute global temperature increase might be exceeded by

Observed annual average temperature deviations (global and European)	Figure 3.1.

Temperature deviation, compared to 1961–1990 average (°C)

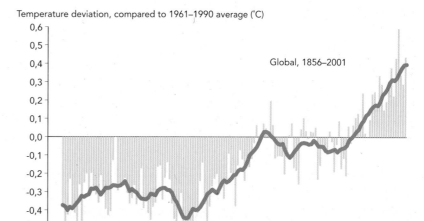

Temperature deviation, compared to 1961–1990 average (°C)

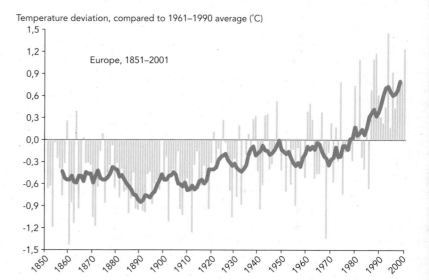

Notes: The bars show the annual average and the line the 10-year smoothed trend. Europe includes Siberia.

Source: Climatic Research Centre (CRU)

about 2050, and the proposed target of not more than 0.1 °C increase per decade might be exceeded even earlier.

> Over the past 100 years, global mean temperature has increased by 0.6 °C (in Europe about 1.2 °C). Global and European mean temperatures are projected to increase by 1.4–5.8 °C between 1990 and 2100.

3.2.3. Sea level rise
The sea level, globally and for Europe, rose between 0.1 m and 0.2 m during the 20th century (IPCC, 2001a; Parry, 2000). Global sea level is projected to rise by 0.09–0.88 m between 1990 and 2100, taking into account the full range of emission scenarios (IPCC,

2001a). Future sea level rise in Europe is expected to be similar (Parry, 2000). Due to long-term movements in the Earth's crust, there are regional differences, because most of southern and central Europe is slowly sinking (typically by 5 cm by the 2080s) and much of northern Europe is rising out of the ocean (Parry, 2000).

Comparing this projection with the proposed 'sustainable' target suggests that the target will be exceeded during the next 100 years.

3.2.4. Precipitation change

Global precipitation increased by about 2 % during the last century (IPCC, 2001a) with large variations between continents and also within Europe. Northern Europe and the western Russian Federation are getting wetter with an increase of 10–40 % over the last century; southern Europe and many EECCA countries are changing little or getting dryer by up to 20 % in some parts (IPCC, 2001a; IPCC, 2001c; ECA, 2002).

The intensity of precipitation has also changed. Several indicators show that more intense precipitation events are occurring over many areas in Europe whereas other areas are experiencing more droughts (ECA, 2002). In Kazakhstan, for example, rainfall intensities increased although annual precipitation decreased (IPCC, 2001c). In addition, increasing intensities may result in extreme events like floods (see Chapter 10). In the United Kingdom, for example, the contribution of short-duration precipitation events has increased significantly during the past 40 years (Hulme et al., 2002).

A third factor related to precipitation is its seasonal variation. Precipitation in winter has changed most (IPCC, 2001a). As a result, water losses in summer, due to increasing temperatures, are compensated for by precipitation increases in winter, but may lead to more severe summer droughts.

Climate models project a further increase in precipitation of 1–2 % per decade in northern Europe during this century. In southern Europe, especially in parts of Spain, Greece and Turkey, precipitation in the summer is projected to decrease by up to 5 % per decade (depending on the region

and the climate model used), while the winters may become wetter (Parry, 2000, IPCC, 2001c). In most EECCA countries, precipitation is also projected to decrease in summer, for example with a 5–10 % decrease in Kazakhstan by 2080 whereas the winters are projected to become wetter. The annual decrease is projected to be 1–4 % by 2050 (IPCC, 2001c).

3.2.5. Extreme weather and climate events

Changes in the frequency and characteristics of extreme weather and climate events were observed in the second half of the 20th century. These extreme events cannot be attributed to long-term climate change, but may provide a picture of the future since climate models predict that the frequency and intensity of extreme events are very likely to increase as a result of climate change. Climate change models project that further changes are likely in this century (IPCC, 2001a). In Europe, extremely cold winters have become less frequent in recent decades and may become rare by the 2020s, whereas hot summers are likely to become more frequent (Parry, 2000). An increase in maximum temperatures and the number of hot days was observed during the second half of the 20th century in various locations in Europe (e.g. the United Kingdom, Scandinavia and the Russian Federation). In the northern hemisphere, the proportion of total annual precipitation derived from heavy and extreme precipitation events has increased (IPCC, 2001a). In 1995, for example, large parts of northwest Europe became flooded. Likewise, in summer 2002 heavy rainfall in the Erz Mountains in central Europe caused a 'flood of the century' in Germany, the Czech Republic and Austria.

3.2.6. Uncertainties

There has been significant progress in the scientific understanding of climate change, its impacts and the human response to it (IPCC, 2001d). Many of the available robust findings relate to the existence of climate change, while uncertainties are concerned with quantifying the magnitude and the timing of these changes. Important areas for further scientific work, aimed at reducing uncertainties and increasing knowledge, are (IPCC, 2001d):

- detection and attribution of climate change;
- understanding and prediction of regional changes in climate and climate extremes;
- quantification of climate change impacts at the global, regional and local levels;

> Global and European sea level rose by 0.1–0.2 m during the last century and is projected to rise by an additional 0.1–0.9 m by 2100.

- analysis of adaptation and mitigation activities;
- integration of all aspects of the climate change issue into strategies for sustainable development;
- investigations to support the judgement of what constitutes 'dangerous anthropogenic interference with the climate system'.

3.3. Impacts and adaptation

Climate change is expected to have significant impacts in Europe. Generally, the south and the European Arctic are the most vulnerable areas (IPCC, 2001c; Parry, 2000; IPCC, 1997). Impacts can be expected in particular with respect to:

- hydrology and water resources (see also Chapter 8);
- mountain regions and coastal zones;
- land and soil resources (see also Chapter 9);
- forestry and agriculture (see also Chapter 2.4 and Chapter 2.3);
- natural ecosystems and biodiversity (see also Chapter 11);
- economic sectors (see also Chapter 10);
- human health (see also Chapter 12).

3.3.1. Hydrology and water resources
Total annual flow and its variations through the year are likely to be affected by climate change. Changes in precipitation are projected to increase annual flow in northern Europe and decrease it in the countries around the Mediterranean Sea. Decreasing flows are also projected for the EECCA countries (see Box 3.1). In mountainous and continental regions more precipitation will fall as rain instead of snow. These effects will also increase the risk of floods and summer droughts in the downstream areas of rivers. More intense precipitation events may affect large areas as in the 'flood of the century' mentioned above. Many large towns and industrial areas are in the catchments of large rivers. For example in Germany about 17 000 people were evacuated and many cities along the rivers were severely damaged, with estimated costs of about EUR 15 billion (Die Zeit, 2002). The demand for water for irrigation will increase, but availability will be reduced during the summer.

Adaptation will involve measures on both the demand and the supply side, and will require the development of management systems that allow short-term actions as well as

measures affecting urban planning and building standards.

3.3.2. Mountain regions and coastal zones
Mountain regions and coastal zones are particularly vulnerable to climate change. Changes in rain and snow precipitation in mountain areas will also have significant impacts on more lowland populations (see Section 3.3.1). Landslides, rockslides and avalanches are likely to increase due to sudden and strong precipitation and endanger human settlements (as occurred in Italy in 2000). Furthermore, the area covered by European glaciers has decreased in recent decades (e.g. already by 50 % in the Alps). Projections show that as much as 50–90 % of alpine glaciers could disappear by the end of the 21st century, and the snowline is expected to rise by 100–150 m for every degree of warming (Parry, 2000). Coastal zones already face several pressures such as flood risk and coastal erosion. Climate change will increase the risk of floods and the erosion of coasts due to the rising sea level, a higher frequency of storms (especially in northwest Europe) and increased precipitation intensity. In both mountain regions and coastal zones, human settlements, important sectors of the economy (e.g. tourism) and natural areas (e.g. wetlands, especially in the Baltic and Mediterranean regions) will be affected.

There are various policy options for limiting the potential impacts and adapting to the adverse effects of climate change in coastal areas. The policies implemented depend on local and national circumstances, recognising the economic and ecological importance of coastal zones and taking account of technical capabilities (Parry, 2000). Fewer policies have as yet been implemented in mountain regions. One option often mentioned is to change the approach to forest management to 'support' mountain forests and enable them to adapt to climate change resulting in conservation of the soil and improved water storage and land protection (Parry, 2000).

3.3.3. Land and soil
Climate change will affect land and soil directly as well as indirectly through impacts on land use. Changes in the use and management of land are likely to have bigger effects on soils than climate change itself. Nevertheless, climate change is likely to result in the deterioration of soil quality. Likely effects include salinisation, peat loss and erosion by wind or water (see Chapter

---

Box 3.1. Climate change impacts in some eastern European, Caucasus and central Asian countries

Many of the countries in eastern Europe, the Caucasus and central Asia (EECCA) are vulnerable to climate change especially in relation to water resources and agriculture. The agriculture sector is important in most of EECCA because of the significant contribution to gross domestic product (GDP) (e.g. about one third in Tajikistan). Agriculture and livestock production depend significantly on the availability of water for irrigation. Water is already a scarce resource in many EECCA countries, and small decreases in water availability can have severe effects.

Periods with significant changes in annual river flow and flood events are occurring, for example in Tajikistan. These are caused by a combination of effects including decreased precipitation in summer and increased precipitation in winter. Further, reduced snowfall in winter, due to increased temperature, results in increased runoff in winter and reduced runoff in summer. Rapid snowmelt was one of the main causes of the disastrous floods in Tajikistan in the 1990s. Finally, significant retreat of glaciers affects annual river flows and flood events.

In some EECCA countries, glaciers play a crucial role in the hydrological cycle. In Tajikistan, for example, glaciers occupy about 6 % of the total land, providing about a quarter of Tajikistan's annual water flow. Increasing temperatures have already caused significant retreat of glaciers in several EECCA countries with various impacts on water availability, flood risk, agriculture and livestock production. Some glaciers are projected to retreat further, which is thought initially to increase water availability and to contribute to increasing flood risks. The increase in runoff will, however, be followed by a strong decrease after the disappearance of the glacier, which can take decades or centuries for large glaciers. This is projected to reduce the water availability in downstream areas with considerable consequences. Grassland production in many EECCA countries, for example, might decrease 40-90 % by 2080, mainly due to high water stress in summer. Considerable impacts are also projected for the power supply in Tajikistan, which relies largely on hydropower.

Observed and projected changes in temperature also have direct negative effects on particular sectors in some of the EECCA countries. Kazakhstan, for example, reported decreasing trends in grassland production, mainly due to unfavourable temperature conditions in summer. The projected temperature increases might lead to an additional 30–90 % loss by 2050.

An example of a combined effect of temperature and precipitation change is the recent rise in the Caspian Sea level by 2.5 m, which resulted in severe floods. By 2020–40 an additional 1.2–1.5 m increase is projected, which could result in about US$ 4 billion damage.

Source: UNFCCC, 2002a; IPCC, 1997 and 2001c; national communications

---

9). Mediterranean forest soils are already facing a loss of carbon through wildfires, which are likely to increase.

Adaptation will require the development of policies to preserve the quality of land and soil and promote a sustainable use of land, for example through afforestation.

3.3.4. Forestry and agriculture

A higher carbon dioxide (CO_2) concentration in the atmosphere may lead to an increase in net productivity in most European forests and agricultural systems, though there will be regional differences depending mainly on water availability. For example, productivity in the forestry sector in Germany may fall (by up to 9 %) at forest sites where drought stress increases. However, where precipitation is not the limiting growth factor, forest productivity may increase by 5 % (Lindner et al., 2002). The risks of climate change will be considerably higher and less manageable in countries that already suffer significantly from drought stress such as the Mediterranean countries. In agriculture, increasing temperatures are likely to result in a reduction in the growing period of crops like cereals. In contrast, warming could lead to a lengthening of the growing season for root crops like sugar beet. An unclear, but important issue is how pests and diseases will be affected by climate change. Both are expected to increase, but it is not yet known to what extent. Agricultural systems and forests are vulnerable to extreme weather events such as droughts, storms or fires which are likely to increase with climate change.

Adaptation measures will require more flexibility of land use, crop production and farming systems.

3.3.5. Natural ecosystems and biodiversity

Climate change is expected to affect ecosystems and biodiversity, though it is difficult to attribute changes that have already occurred to climate change alone. The impacts may threaten the habitats of some plant and animal species, which may lead to their extinction if they are not able to adapt or migrate. For example, wintering shorebird and marine fish diversity are seriously endangered by a loss of coastal wetlands. Ecosystems that thrive in the warm humid conditions of northern Iberia may appear in northern France and the southern British Isles. The tree line has already moved upwards and this is projected to continue in many mountainous regions.

Adaptation measures will have to protect endangered species, and include monitoring the productivity of other species, as changes in these may disrupt ecological balances.

3.3.6. *Economic and health-related impacts*

Economic activities in coastal areas

The increased risk of flooding, erosion and wetland loss in coastal areas will have impacts on human settlements, industry, tourism and agriculture. Southern Europe appears most vulnerable (Parry, 2000). Management systems which safeguard human activities and preserve coastal ecosystems will need to be developed; these should include measures to lessen flood peaks and keep floods away from properties.

Insurance

The insurance industry is already facing claims for growing property damage due to more extreme weather events such as windstorms and flooding. Worldwide, economic losses from catastrophic events have increased more than 10-fold during the past 50 years although only a part of this increase can be linked to climatic factors (IPCC, 2001c). Properties at risk in some regions of Europe may become uninsurable. Adaptation measures include risk transfer into wider financial markets and generally better cooperation between stakeholders.

Tourism

Climate change is likely to have significant consequences, both positive and negative, for tourism. Higher temperatures are likely to change summer destination preferences since outdoor activities in northern Europe may be stimulated, while summer heat waves in the Mediterranean region may lead to a shift of tourism to spring and autumn. Higher temperatures will also result in less reliable snow conditions and affect winter tourism. Regional policies will have to respond to changes in tourism patterns, for example new destinations may need specific infrastructure (Parry, 2000).

Human health

Climate change is likely to have considerable effects on the spread of vector-, food- and water-borne infections. Some vector-borne diseases may expand their range northwards. For example, there is some evidence that the northward migration of tick vectors in Sweden is due to the observed warming. An increase in heat waves, accompanied by a rise in urban air pollution, can cause an increase in heat-related deaths and periods of illness, but winter mortality is likely to be reduced.

Adaptation measures should include specific public health programmes and the development of pan-European surveillance systems which allow the early detection of infectious diseases (Parry, 2000).

3.4. Greenhouse gas emissions

3.4.1. *Overview*

For international comparisons purposes, 1996 is the latest year which provides complete data. On this basis, total greenhouse gas emissions in the EU (excluding land use change and forestry) are about 4 160 million tonnes of CO_2 equivalent per year (24 % of the total for industrialised countries). In EFTA countries they are about 110 million tonnes (less than 1 % of the total of industrialised countries) and in the EU accession countries about 1 070 million tonnes (6 % of the total of industrialised countries). In the EECCA countries they are about 2 900 million tonnes (17 % of the total of industrialised countries, out of which 12 % for the Russian Federation). Other industrialised countries in the world contribute as follows to the total greenhouse gas emissions of industrialised countries (excluding land use change and forestry): US (39 %), Japan (8 %) and Canada (4 %).

Significant reductions in total greenhouse gas emissions occured during the 1990s, ranging from 3.5 % in the EU, to 34 % in CEE and 38 % in EECCA (Figure 3.2).

CO_2, the most important greenhouse gas, contributes about 82 % of total greenhouse gas emissions in WE, about 84 % in the accession countries and about 75 % in EECCA.

Figure 3.3 shows that:

- Combustion in the energy industries, industry, transport and 'other' sectors (mainly heating in commercial and residential areas) is the dominant source of greenhouse gas emissions in all of Europe.
- Emissions from energy industries (electricity and heat production) are more important in the accession countries (including Cyprus, Malta and Turkey) and the EECCA countries than in WE, partly because of the lower share of other sources such as road transport. In the European Free Trade Association (EFTA) countries, emissions from energy industries are relatively low due to a high

| Figure 3.2. | Greenhouse gas emissions by gas in Europe, 2000 |

Source: UNFCCC, 2002a

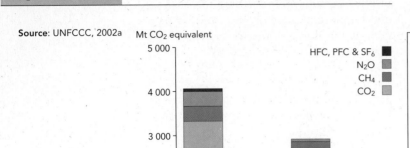

caused mainly by methane leakages in natural gas transport systems.

> 😐 In the EU, decreases in emissions from energy industries, the industry sector, agriculture and waste management have been partly offset by increases from transport.
>
> 😐 In the accession countries, emissions from energy industries, the industry sector, agriculture and waste management also decreased; emissions from transport fell between 1990 and 1995, but increased significantly thereafter.

3.4.2. Energy industries

Energy industries (electricity and heat production, refineries, mining and distribution of energy carriers) are the most important sources of greenhouse gases in Europe, contributing 29 % of total emissions in WE; 42 % in the accession countries and about 20 % in the EECCA countries.

In the EU, CO_2 emissions from electricity supply fell by 5 % between 1990 and 2000, corresponding to 55 million tonnes, mainly due to switching from coal to gas in the United Kingdom and efficiency improvements in Germany, while consumption of electricity increased by 19 % (EEA, 2002a). The increase in combined heat and power generation in several Member States, as well as increasing wind power generation in Denmark and Germany, also contributed to the reductions. Significant reductions of fugitive emissions from methane (by 34 %) were a result of reduced coal production, better control of coalmines and reduction of leaks in the natural gas distribution system.

In the EU accession countries, emissions from energy industries fell by about 8 %, corresponding to 50 million tonnes of CO_2 equivalent, between 1990 and 2000. This was due to economic restructuring, an associated decrease or stabilisation of electricity consumption, changes in fuel use (less coal, more nuclear) and considerable efficiency improvements in power plants. Fugitive methane emissions also decreased significantly by 23 %, corresponding to 64 million tonnes of CO_2 equivalent.

Greenhouse gas emissions from energy industries also fell significantly in the EECCA countries between 1990 and 2000 resulting

| Figure 3.3. | Greenhouse gas emissions by sector in Europe, 2000 |

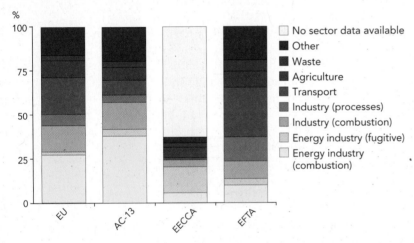

Note: Data for EECCA countries are incomplete: for 63 % of the reported emissions the sectors are not known.

Source: UNFCCC, 2002a

share of electricity from hydropower plants.

- In the EU, transport contributes to about 20 % of total greenhouse gas emissions, whereas in the EU accession countries, the contribution is considerably less since there is less road transport.
- Emissions from industry contribute to about 20 % of total greenhouse gas emissions in most of Europe. Fuel combustion for power and heat generation is the main source. Process emissions are more important in the EFTA countries.
- Although data for the EECCA countries are limited, fugitive emissions from energy industries appear to contribute significantly to total emissions. This is

mainly from reduced electricity generation due to economic restructuring.

3.4.3. Industry

The industry sector is the second largest source of greenhouse gas emissions in western and central Europe. Combustion of fossil fuels is the most important industrial source: about 70 % of emissions from industry in the EU and about 75 % in the accession countries. Information for the EECCA countries is not available. CO_2 emissions from the production or use of mineral products (e.g. cement production) is the other main source, followed by nitrous oxide (N_2O) emissions from the chemical industry, mostly from adipic and nitric acid production and the use of fluorinated gases used for various purposes in industry as substitutes for ozone-depleting substances banned by the Montreal protocol.

In the EU, annual CO_2 emissions from industry fell by 8 % between 1990 and 2000, corresponding to 55 million tonnes, mainly as a result of improvements in industrial processes, economic restructuring and efficiency improvements in German manufacturing industry after reunification. Large reductions of 56 % between 1990 and 2000, corresponding to 59 million tonnes, were achieved in nitrous oxide emissions from the chemical industry, because of specific measures at adipic acid production plants in Germany, the United Kingdom and France (EEA, 2002a). Emissions of fluorinated gases increased by 36 % between 1990 and 2000. Emissions of hydrofluorocarbons (HFCs) increased by 94 % over the same period, although during recent years large reductions of HFC emissions were achieved in the United Kingdom. It is expected that emissions of fluorinated gases will increase further by a significant amount (EEA, 2002b).

CO_2 emissions from industry in the EU accession countries fell by 25 %, corresponding to 60 million tonnes, between 1990 and 2000. Some countries reduced industrial nitrous oxide emissions from chemical plants. However, there was no overall reduction in emissions from industry in the accession countries. No information is available on emissions of fluorinated gases. No data are available on trends in emissions from industry in the whole of the EECCA region.

3.4.4. Transport

The transport sector contributed more than 20 % of overall greenhouse gas emissions in the EU in 2000. In the accession countries, emissions from transport are the third largest contributor (about 8 %), with a far smaller share in the EECCA countries. Road transport is the largest source. CO_2 from fuel combustion is by far the most important greenhouse gas, followed by nitrous oxide, mostly generated as a by-product in catalytic converters.

Of particular concern in the EU is the 18 % increase in CO_2 emissions from transport between 1990 and 2000, corresponding to 128 million tonnes. This was due to a growing volume of traffic, both passenger car and freight transport, and no substantial improvement in energy use per vehicle-km for the whole vehicle fleet. However, recent years show a decreasing trend in CO_2 emissions per vehicle-km for new passenger cars, due to an agreement to reduce such emissions with European and other car manufacturers (see Chapter 2.6, Section 2.6.4.5). Only Finland achieved slight emission reductions and the United Kingdom and Sweden managed to limit growth to less than 10 % from 1990 to 2000. Although only responsible for 0.6 % of greenhouse gas emissions, nitrous oxide emissions from transport increased after the introduction of the catalytic converters in most WE countries. CO_2 emissions are expected to increase by about 25-30 % between 2000 and 2010 (EEA, 2002b).

Emissions in the 10 accession countries fell by 19 % between 1990 and 1995, but increased significantly thereafter. Emissions in 2000 were only about 5 % below the 1990 level. Economic growth and the continued shift towards road transport will further significantly increase emissions. Although CO_2 is currently the main greenhouse gas emission from the sector (98 %), nitrous oxide emissions are expected to increase rapidly due to the growing penetration of cars with catalytic converters.

Transport is a smaller contributor to greenhouse gas emissions in the EECCA countries. However, large increases are expected as the number of cars and transport demand rise (see Chapter 2.6).

3.4.5. Agriculture

Agriculture contributed about 10 % of overall greenhouse gas emissions in all three groups of countries in 2000. Nitrous oxide emissions from agricultural soils (mainly due to the application of mineral nitrogen fertilisers) and methane emissions from enteric fermentation (mainly from cattle) are the largest sources.

In the EU, nitrous oxide emissions fell by 4 % from 1990 to 2000 mainly as a result of a decrease in the use of nitrogen fertilisers. Methane emissions from ruminant animals fell by 9 % between 1990 and 2000 due to falling cattle numbers and changes in manure management (EEA, 2002a). Methane emissions may fall by 18–40 % by 2010 compared with 1990 due to a further reduction in livestock numbers and changes in manure management (EEA, 2002b).

In the 10 accession countries, relatively large reductions in methane emissions from enteric fermentation were achieved (46 %) due to falling cattle numbers. Nitrous oxide emissions do not show a clear trend, and in 2000 were at about the same level as in 1990. No data are available on trends in emissions from agriculture in EECCA.

3.4.6. Waste
The waste sector contributes only about 3–5 % of total greenhouse gas emissions in the different country groups within Europe. The main source is methane resulting from solid waste disposal on land.

In the EU, substantial reductions (26 %) in methane emissions were achieved (from 1990 to 2000) as a result of landfill emission control measures (EEA, 2002a) through early implementation of the landfill directive. Similar trends can be observed in the 10 accession countries, where methane emissions fell substantially (by 27 %) between 1990 and 2000. Methane emissions from the waste sector may decline much further by increasing use of methane and energy recovery and the diversion of biodegradable waste from incineration to composting or anaerobic treatment.

3.5. Kyoto protocol targets

3.5.1. Kyoto protocol targets
Negotiations on an international convention addressing climate change resulted in the adoption of the UNFCCC in 1992. The Kyoto protocol, adopted in 1997, sets binding targets for industrialised countries (Annex I Parties) to reduce their collective greenhouse gas emissions by about 5 % by 2008–12 compared with 1990. This is generally seen as a first step towards the ultimate objective of the UNFCCC. The Kyoto protocol covers the greenhouse gases carbon dioxide (CO_2), methane (CH_4), nitrous oxide (N_2O), hydrofluorocarbons (HFCs), perfluorocarbons (PFCs) and sulphur hexafluoride (SF_6).

Most of the detailed provisions of the Kyoto protocol were finally agreed in 2001 with the Marrakech accords. These contain concrete rules for the use of the flexible mechanisms — joint implementation, clean development mechanism and emissions trading — and on the extent to which carbon sequestered by land-use change and forestry activities ('carbon sinks') can be accounted for the fulfilment of reduction commitments.

Under the Kyoto protocol, the EU has an emission reduction target of 8 % from 1990 levels for 2008–12. According to Council Decision 2002/358/EC, the EU and its Member States agreed on different emission limitation and/or reduction targets for each Member State according to economic circumstances — the 'burden-sharing' agreement. According to this, some Member States have to cut their emissions, while others may increase them (Table 3.1).

The Russian Federation and Ukraine are committed to keeping their emissions at the 1990 level by 2008-12, Norway may increase

Table 3.1.	EU Member States' burden-sharing targets (EU Council Decision 2002/358/EC)

Member State	Commitment (% change in emissions for 2008-12 relative to base-year levels)
Austria	-13
Belgium	-7.5
Denmark	-21
Finland	0
France	0
Germany	-21
Greece	+25
Ireland	+13
Italy	-6.5
Luxembourg	-28
Netherlands	-6
Portugal	+27
Spain	+15
Sweden	+4
United Kingdom	-12.5

its emissions by 1 %, Iceland by 10 %. Switzerland and eight accession countries (Bulgaria, Czech Republic, Estonia, Latvia, Lithuania, Romania, Slovakia and Slovenia) have to reduce their emissions by 8 %; Hungary and Poland by 6 %, and Croatia by 5 %. Other European countries do not have binding targets. Non-European countries with a commitment under the Kyoto protocol are Australia (+8 %), Canada (-6 %), Japan (-6 %) and New Zealand (0 %). The US has a target of -7 %, but announced in 2001 that it does not intend to ratify.

By January 2003, more than 100 countries (28 from Annex I industrialised countries), responsible for 44 % of the emissions of industrialised countries in 1990, had ratified the protocol (UNFCCC, 2002a). The Kyoto protocol will enter into force when it has been ratified by at least 55 countries including industrialised developed countries that together accounted for at least 55 % of CO_2 emissions from this group in 1990. In practice, this means that the United States or the Russian Federation would need to ratify for the protocol to enter into force.

3.5.2. Progress towards targets
European Union
Greenhouse gas emissions in the EU fell by 3.5 % between 1990 and 2000. The EU is about halfway towards reaching its Kyoto target (see EEA, 2002a) assuming that this will be reached through domestic policies and measures in the EU alone (Figure 3.4). The possible use of the Kyoto mechanisms and carbon sinks to meet the EU Member States' burden-sharing targets is discussed in Section 3.6.4.

EU greenhouse gas emissions fell by 3.5 % between 1990 and 2000, about halfway to the Kyoto target for 2008–12. Emissions were reduced partly due to favourable circumstances in Germany and the United Kingdom. Projections show that substantial further action is needed to reach many national (burden-sharing) targets.

During the past 10 years, considerable cuts in emissions were achieved, mainly in Germany (by 19.1 %) and the United Kingdom (by 12.9 %), while emissions increased in eight Member States. About half of the emission reductions in Germany and the United Kingdom were due to one-off factors (Eichhammer *et al.*, 2001; Schleich *et al.*, 2001). In Germany, economic

restructuring of the five new Länder after reunification resulted in significant emission reductions, particularly in the electricity production sector due to energy efficiency improvements. In the United Kingdom, energy markets were liberalised and electricity utilities switched from oil and coal to gas.

Figure 3.5 compares greenhouse gas emissions of EU Member States in 2000 with their linear target path for 2008–12. Nine Member States are well above their Kyoto target path and six are below.

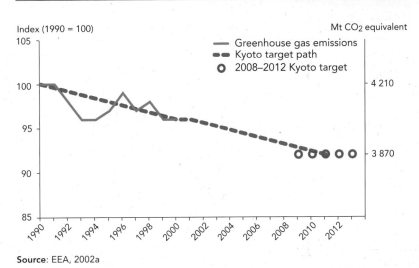

European Union greenhouse gas emissions compared with target for 2008-12 (excluding land-use change and forestry) — Figure 3.4.

Source: EEA, 2002a

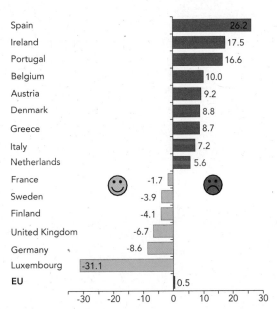

Distance to target indicators (in index points) in 2000 for the Kyoto protocol and burden-sharing targets of EU Member States — Figure 3.5.

Notes: The distance-to-target indicator (DTI) measures the deviation of actual emissions in 2000 from the (hypothetical) linear target path between 1990 and 2010. The DTI gives an indication of progress towards the Kyoto and Member States' burden-sharing targets. It assumes that the Member States meet their target entirely on the basis of domestic measures. However, Member States may also use the flexible mechanisms and sinks to fulfil their commitments (see Sections 3.6.3 and 3.6.4).

Source: EEA , 2002a

02

Europe's environment: the third assessment

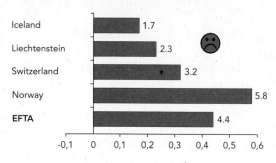

Figure 3.6. Distance-to-target indicators (in index points) in 2000 for the Kyoto protocol of EFTA countries

Notes: The distance-to-target indicator (DTI) measures the deviation of actual emissions in 2000 from the (hypothetical) linear target path between 1990 and 2010. The DTI gives an indication of progress towards the Kyoto targets. It assumes that countries meet their target entirely on the basis of domestic measures. However, countries may also use the flexible mechanisms and sinks to fulfil their commitments (see Sections 3.6.3 and 3.6.4).
Source: UNFCCC, 2002a

Figure 3.7. Greenhouse gas emissions in 10 EU accession countries compared with Kyoto target for 2008–12 (excluding fluorinated gases and land-use change and forestry)

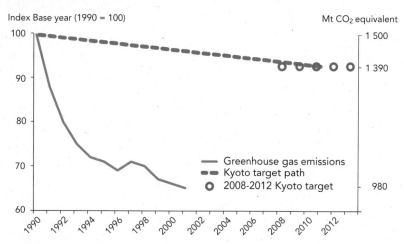

Note: Article 4.6 of the UNFCCC allows countries undergoing the process of transition to a market economy some flexibility in choosing the base year. For Bulgaria the base year is 1988, for Hungary the average of 1985-87, for Poland 1988, for Romania 1989 and for Slovenia 1986.
Source: UNFCCC, 2002a

Figure 3.8. Distance-to-target indicators (in index points) in 2000 for the Kyoto protocol of 10 EU accession countries

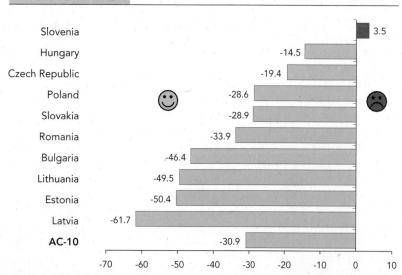

Note: See note to Figure 3.6. For countries with other base years than 1990 (Bulgaria, Hungary, Poland, Romania and Slovenia), base-year emissions have been taken into account.
Source: UNFCCC, 2002a

According to the latest EU projections, total greenhouse gas emissions in the EU are expected to fall by 4.7 % from the 1990 level by 2010 assuming adoption and implementation of current, but no additional, policies and measures (EEA, 2002a). This leaves a shortfall of 3.3 % to the target of an 8 % reduction. Only the United Kingdom, Germany and Sweden are projected to achieve their Kyoto burden-sharing targets without additional policies or measures or the use of the flexible mechanisms. The transport sector is of particular concern with emissions projected to increase by more than 25–30 % between 1990 and 2010 (EEA, 2002a). Substantial further action is therefore needed if the EU is to reach its Kyoto target.

EFTA countries
Greenhouse gas emissions in Iceland, Liechtenstein, Norway and Switzerland fell slightly during the first half of the 1990s. During the second half, emissions increased significantly in Iceland and Norway, but hardly changed in Switzerland and Liechtenstein. In total, between 1990 and 2000, greenhouse gas emissions increased in Iceland (by 6.7 %) and Norway (by 6.3 %) and decreased in Switzerland (by 0.9 %) and Liechtenstein (by 1.7 %). All these countries are some percentage points above their linear Kyoto target (Figure 3.6).

EU accession countries
In the accession countries, greenhouse gas emissions fell altogether by 34.7 % between the base year and 2000 (Figure 3.7). The reductions were mainly due to the transition to a market economy and economic restructuring during the first half of the 1990s. During the second half, emissions in Slovenia, the Czech Republic, Poland and Hungary increased, while those in the other countries stabilised or continued to fall.

Total accession country greenhouse gas emissions in 2000 were far (30.9 %) below their linear Kyoto targets, except for Slovenia which is above (Figure 3.8.).

> Greenhouse gas emissions in the accession countries fell by 35 % between the base year (1990, or earlier years for five countries) and 2000, and most countries are well on track to reach their Kyoto targets. However, in some countries emissions have started to increase again.

Eastern Europe, the Caucasus and central Asia
Greenhouse gas emissions in the EECCA
countries fell by about 38 % between 1990
and 2000 (Figure 3.9). As in the accession
countries, this was mainly due to economic
and structural changes following the collapse
of the former USSR.

Within EECCA, only the Russian Federation
and Ukraine currently have Kyoto targets.
Both countries are far below their linear
Kyoto target path, and emissions are
expected to be substantially below their
Kyoto target by 2010. This will generate
significant surpluses of emission allowances
(see also Section 3.6.3).

3.6. Policy responses

Most WE countries will need additional
efforts to fulfil their commitments under the
Kyoto protocol, while most accession
countries and the EECCA countries expect
to be below their Kyoto targets. Most
European countries will need to prepare for
climate change by selecting and
implementing appropriate adaptation
strategies. WE countries are expected to
reduce greenhouse gas emissions primarily
by domestic action, policies and measures,
although the Kyoto protocol gives Parties
additional flexibility in fulfilling their
commitments by the use of flexible
mechanisms and 'carbon sinks'.

Programmes, policies and measures
addressing climate change, mainly for the
period up to 2008–12, are described in the
next section while the possible use of the
flexible mechanisms and sinks is analysed
separately. In addition, the costs and benefits
of climate change policies are analysed.

A long-term climate change strategy for the
period after 2012 will also be needed.

Many European countries have
adopted national programmes
addressing climate change. Key policies
and measures include carbon dioxide or
energy taxes, promotion of renewable
energy (wind, solar, biomass) and
combined heat and power, abatement
measures in industry and measures to
reduce emissions from landfills. A new
policy instrument is emissions trading
which has been put in place in a few
countries.

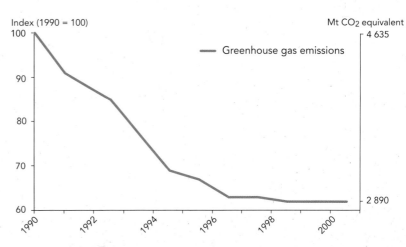

Greenhouse gas emissions in eastern Europe, Caucasus and central Asia (excluding fluorinated gases and land-use change and forestry)

Figure 3.9.

Index (1990 = 100)

Mt CO$_2$ equivalent

— Greenhouse gas emissions

Source: UNFCCC, 2002a

Projections show that emissions are expected
to increase, particularly in the transport
sector, if no additional efforts are undertaken.
Also the massive nuclear decommissioning
which is anticipated to take place after 2010
will challenge climate policy responses.
Future climate change policy will require
structural changes of the economy to bring
down emissions in the long term. Expansion
of the use of renewable energy and increase
in energy efficiency will need to be a focus of
such a future climate change policy, along
with adaptation measures in a wide range of
socio-economic sectors.

3.6.1. National programmes
Many European countries have adopted and
partly implemented programmes that
address climate change. The energy sector,
the largest contributor to greenhouse gas
emissions, is a focus of policies and measures
in many countries.

- *Energy and CO$_2$ taxes.* Several countries
  (Denmark, Finland, Germany, Italy, the
  Netherlands, Norway, Slovenia, Sweden
  and the United Kingdom) have
  introduced or increased taxes on energy
  use and/or CO$_2$ emissions.
- *Promotion of renewable energy.* In WE,
  many countries have adopted legislation
  to further increase the share of
  renewables. The rapid expansion of wind
  power (38 % per year in the EU between
  1990 and 1999), driven by Denmark,
  Germany and Spain, was the result of
  support measures including 'feed-in'
  arrangements that guarantee a fixed

favourable price for renewable electricity producers. Germany and Spain are leading countries in the growth of solar (photovoltaic) electricity, mainly as a result of a combination of 'feed-in' arrangements and high subsidies (EEA, 2002c). Biomass for electricity and heat production has also expanded significantly in some countries, especially in Finland, Sweden, Austria and the Baltic countries (EEA, 2002c).

- *Promotion of combined heat and power (CHP).* Several countries have promoted the use of CHP plants by regulatory, economic and fiscal policies. A particularly high penetration of CHP was achieved by 1998 in Denmark (62.3 %), the Netherlands (52.6 %) and Finland (35.8 %) (European Commission, 2002).
- *Carbon dioxide emissions trading schemes in the United Kingdom and Denmark.* The United Kingdom is the first country in the world to set up a domestic emissions trading scheme for the basket of six Kyoto gases. Companies may voluntarily take on legally binding obligations to reduce their emissions from 1998–2000 levels. The government is making up to USD 340 million available over five years to participating companies. Denmark is experimenting with emissions trading on a pilot basis in the electricity generation sector. This system is expected to cover approximately 30 % of the country's CO_2 emissions.

Regarding transport, with emissions projected to rise significantly, some policies and measures are in place in several countries. For example, in Denmark, the Netherlands and the United Kingdom, the use of less fuel-consuming cars is promoted through tax-differentiation schemes (in Sweden such a system is under consideration). The promotion and development of inter-modal transport, rail transport and public transport are an important part of Finnish transport policy.

Few policies and measures are in place to reduce greenhouse gas emissions in the agricultural sector. Some policies and measures may help to reduce emissions as a side effect rather than directly. For example, in Finland, an agri-environmental support programme aimed at decreasing nutrient inputs to surface waters and groundwaters is being implemented by about 90 % of farmers, which is also expected to reduce nitrous oxide emissions as a side effect.

In industry, large reductions of nitrous oxide emissions can be achieved by measures in the manufacture of adipic and nitric acid. Emission reductions ranging from 45 % to 75 % are projected in the United Kingdom, Germany and France from such measures.

Large reductions may be achieved in the waste sector by implementing the landfill directive, leading to reductions of methane emissions of up to 80 %.

3.6.2. European Union

 In the EU, several common and coordinated policies and measures have been developed including an agreement with car manufacturers to limit emissions of CO_2 from new passenger cars and a directive on an EU-wide emissions trading scheme.

In the EU, common and coordinated policies and measures have been developed in several sectors, for example the Green Paper on the security of energy supply (see Chapter 2.1) and the White Paper on a common transport policy (see Chapter 2.6) (see also European Commission, 2001a; European Commission, 2001b; European Parliament and Council, 2002).

In June 2000, the EU established the European climate change programme (ECCP) to help identify the most cost-effective additional measures to meet the Kyoto target and national burden-sharing targets. Several measures are at an advanced stage of preparation, including directives on:

- an EU emissions trading scheme;
- promotion of renewable energy;
- combined heat and power;
- biofuels;
- energy performance of buildings;
- energy efficient public procurement;
- fluorinated gases.

In the transport sector, the 1999 agreement with the European car manufacturers association (ACEA agreement) is expected to significantly limit the increase of CO_2 emissions from road passenger transport.

An important new EU policy instrument for the mitigation of climate change is a greenhouse gas emissions trading scheme, which was agreed in December 2002 (European Commission, 2001c). The scheme is limited to CO_2 and to energy-intensive sectors. The proposal covers about 46 % of the EU CO_2 emissions. A first phase will be established for the period 2005–07. The scheme is expected to lower the compliance costs of the Kyoto protocol for the EU significantly (by 35 %) compared with Member States meeting their commitments without trading across borders. The price for allowances for 1 tonne of CO_2 is estimated to fall in the range of EUR 20–33 (European Commission, 2001c).

3.6.3. Emissions trading and joint implementation

The Kyoto protocol and the Marrakech accords provide for three flexible mechanisms, which Parties may use to supplement domestic measures to facilitate compliance with their commitments:

- By *joint implementation*, industrialised countries (Annex I countries) may conduct joint projects to reduce greenhouse gas emissions or to increase take-up by sinks (including soils and forests). The mechanism invites western economies especially to invest in projects to reduce greenhouse gas emissions in countries in transition in eastern Europe and the Russian Federation. The achieved emission reduction units, or parts of them, are transferred to the investing Party, which can use them to fulfil its reduction commitments.
- The *clean development mechanism* invites industrialised countries (Annex I countries) to invest in projects to reduce greenhouse gas emissions in developing countries (non-Annex I countries). According to the reduction achieved, certified emission reduction units are issued which industrialised countries can use to fulfil their commitments. Projects that enhance the uptake of carbon are limited to afforestation and reforestation activities and may not exceed 1 % (annually) of a Party's base-year emissions.
- *Emissions trading* allows industrialised countries to trade emission allowances among each other.

The three flexible mechanisms are expected to become important instruments for reducing compliance costs by channelling investments into cost-effective greenhouse gas mitigation options. Joint implementation is particularly interesting for cooperation between western and eastern European countries. In many countries in transition in eastern Europe, investments in the energy sector are needed. At the same time, greenhouse gas mitigation costs in eastern

Europe are mostly expected to be lower than in western Europe. Such projects could also help accession countries to integrate into the EU (Fernandez and Michaelowa, 2002). During a pilot phase for project-based activities to reduce greenhouse gas emissions under the UNFCCC, more than 80 projects under 'activities implemented jointly' have been reported in eastern Europe, including many cooperative projects between Sweden and Latvia, Estonia and Lithuania. The Netherlands has also implemented many projects in eastern Europe and EECCA (UNFCCC, 2002b).

The Russian Federation and Ukraine could have a central role in the future market for greenhouse gas allowances. Both had relatively large emissions (the Russian Federation about 3 040 million tonnes of CO_2 equivalent in 1990), which fell until 1996 due to economic restructuring and a decrease in economic activity (Russian emissions fell by approximately 35 % (DIW, 2002)). By 2010, Russian emissions are projected to be far below the Kyoto target, which is to keep emissions at the 1990 level. Consequently, the Russian Federation and also some other eastern EECCA countries are likely to have a surplus of emission allowances in 2008-12, which is estimated to range from 750 to 1 340 million tonnes of CO_2 equivalent annually by 2010 (Grüttner, 2001a). In addition, if Kazakhstan agrees a Kyoto protocol commitment, this could lead to substantial additional surplus emission allowances. Following negotiation in Marrakech, the Russian Federation is allowed to account up to an additional 121 million tonnes of CO_2 annually during the first commitment period (or a total of 605 million tonnes of CO_2 during the five years from 2008 to 2012) for forest management activities. This may lead to an increase in the amount of surplus emission allowances available from the Russian Federation.

Trading of surplus allowances would increase physical greenhouse gas emissions during the first commitment period. However, there is a substantial potential in many EECCA countries for further emission reduction through improvements in energy efficiency, which may be facilitated through joint implementation projects. The 'green investment scheme' which is currently being developed aims to use funds from the flexible mechanisms to invest in reforming the Russian energy sector. It could create a framework to make Russian surplus emission allowances both economically effective and environmentally legitimate by ensuring investment in real emission-reduction projects (Moe *et al.*, 2001).

Following the United States withdrawal from the Kyoto protocol and with the additional flexibility of accounting for carbon sinks, projected prices in the future greenhouse gas market have dropped from a range of USD 3-27 to a range of USD 0–8 per tonne of CO_2 (Grüttner, 2001b; den Elzen and de Moor, 2001; Vrolijk, 2002). The Russian Federation, as a potential main supplier of greenhouse gas allowances, has an economic interest in reducing the supply of its allowances by banking them to the next commitment period after 2012, which would lead to a reasonable price in the first commitment period (see also Chapter 5). However, prices would be difficult to control, because they will depend on economic growth, on the amount of allowances banked and on the extent to which countries use domestic policies and measures, flexible mechanisms and carbon sinks to meet their targets.

Altogether, the effect of the Kyoto protocol after Marrakech is estimated to bring emissions of Annex I countries (without the United States) to 0–3 % under the base-year levels (den Elzen and de Moor, 2001).

3.6.4. Carbon sinks

> 😐 Sequestration in land-use change and forestry ('carbon sinks') can be used to meet Kyoto targets, under some circumstances, with additional allowances amounting to about 1–4 % of 1990 emissions for EU countries (with an EU average of 2 %).

Terrestrial ecosystems contain large carbon stocks, amounting to about 2 500 000 million tonnes of carbon globally (IPCC, 2001b). In the past, land management has often resulted in the depletion of carbon pools, but in many regions, like WE, carbon pools are now recovering (IPCC, 2001b). Recent calculations indicate that terrestrial carbon sinks may turn into a source of CO_2 in the second half of the 21st century (Cox *et al.*, 2000).

Management of land may also lead to considerable carbon uptake and consequently mitigate climate change by lowering CO_2 concentrations in the atmosphere. However, the effectiveness and security of such sequestration may be only temporary.

Under the Kyoto protocol, carbon sequestration from human-induced afforestation, reforestation and deforestation (ARD) as well as from other land use, land-use change and forestry activities (revegetation, forest management, cropland management and grazing land management) since 1990 can be used to meet the targets. The extent to which Parties can account for carbon sequestration by specific land use, land-use change and forestry activities is limited to the first commitment period (2008–12). Accounting of forest management activities is subject to an individual cap for each Party.

There are large differences between countries' emission/removal estimates from land-use change and forestry for the year 2000 (Figure 3.10). The United States shows the largest uptake of about 900 million tonnes of CO_2. Within the EU, the largest CO_2 uptake occurs in France (about 36 million tonnes), followed by Spain (29 million tonnes). The United Kingdom and Greece have net emissions from land-use change and forestry. The amount of

| Figure 3.10 | Reported emissions/removals of greenhouse gases from land use, land-use change and forestry for the year 2000, Annex 1 Parties to UNFCCC |

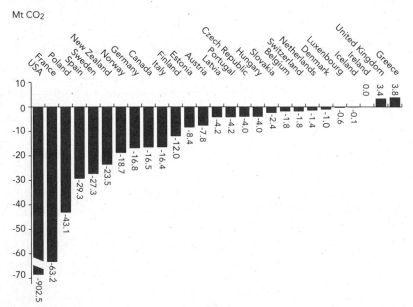

Mt CO2

Notes: Positive values indicate a net emission, negative values a net uptake of CO_2. Several Annex I Parties have not reported inventories on land-use change and forestry or not complete inventory data.

Source: UNFCCC, submitted greenhouse gas inventories by Annex I Parties for the year 2000

removals which can be accounted for under the protocol will be lower than the removals currently reported, because of the limits agreed for several activities and because only activities initiated after 1990 can be accounted for.

Comprehensive methods for estimating changes of carbon pools under the protocol are currently being developed by IPCC. Projections for the relevant carbon pool changes during the first commitment period are therefore difficult to perform with the existing inventory data.

The maximum potential of the contribution of sinks may be estimated. However, this does not imply that Parties will actually use the maximum potential, some countries have even indicated that they expect not to use their maximum (Petroula, 2002).

Figure 3.11 compares the maximum contributions from the potential carbon removal activities with the EU Member States targets under the burden-sharing agreement. With the use of carbon sinks, Spain can increase its emissions target of an allowed increase of 15 % by approximately 4.2 %. Similarly, Sweden can increase its emissions target of an allowed increase of 4 % to 8 % by using all of its potential for sinks. In Austria and Ireland, sinks could contribute about 4 % (of base-year emissions) to the achievement of their burden-sharing target. For the rest of the EU, the sink potential is less than 2 % of base-year emissions. The EU average is about 2 % of base-year emissions (Petroula, 2002). Most EU countries have not yet provided final estimates for the carbon sink potential of their agriculture activities, which are therefore not included in Figure 3.11. This could further increase the contribution of sinks to the achievement of the Kyoto targets.

For some non-EU Parties, sinks could contribute to a much larger extent to the achievement of the Kyoto targets (Figure 3.12). In New Zealand, sinks would allow for an emission growth by 40 % above the stabilising target if maximum potentials were used. For Canada, potential effects from removals are considerably larger (11 %) than the reduction target (-6 %). For Iceland and Norway, potential credits from sinks can also considerably increase the allowed emission growth, but Norway has indicated that it will not use sink credits from agricultural activities and forest management (Petroula, 2002). Japan, Switzerland and the Russian

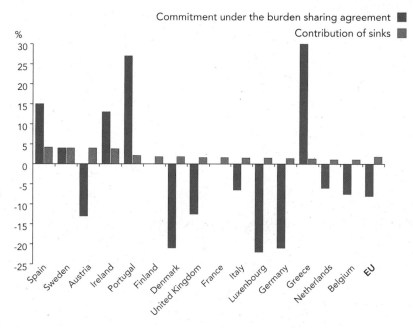

Comparison of potential contributions from land use, land-use change and forestry with burden-sharing targets for EU (percentage change from the base year)   Figure 3.11.

Notes: Agreed caps were considered. Estimates include the maximum contribution of sink clean development mechanism projects. This contribution was calculated on the basis of base-year data from 2002 inventory submission.

Sources: Data for ARD activities, forest management and additional activities were taken from Parties' submissions to UNFCCC; FAO data and country specific data were used for calculation of the debit compensation

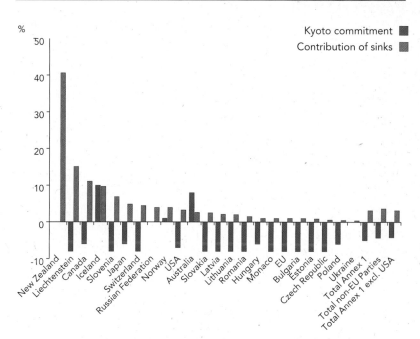

Comparison of potential contributions from land use, land-use change and forestry with targets for non-EU industrialised countries (percentage change from the base year)   Figure 3.12.

Notes: See note in Figure 3.11. For clean development mechanism potential it was assumed that CEE and EECCA countries will not use the mechanism.

Sources: id. Figure 3.11.

Federation can potentially increase their emissions by 4–5 percentage points. For most accession countries (with the exception of Slovenia) sinks will not contribute significantly to achieving emission targets.

3.6.5. Costs and benefits of climate change policies

Costs

In general, there is still a considerable range in the estimated cost of implementing the Kyoto protocol. The estimates for the EU range from about EUR 4 to EUR 30 billion per year. Important factors that influence the estimates include differences in cost definitions and baseline scenarios, the assumed effectiveness of policies and measures for reduction of emissions, and the greenhouse gases that have been taken into account (only carbon dioxide or all gases). A further important factor is different assumptions about using the Kyoto mechanisms: joint implementation, clean development mechanism, emissions trading and the EU internal emissions trading scheme. Using these mechanisms can significantly reduce the costs of climate change mitigation.

In a detailed study (Blok et al., 2001), the costs of domestic implementation of the Kyoto protocol in the EU were estimated to vary between EUR 4 and EUR 8 billion per year with the lower estimate assuming EU-wide emissions trading. The study covered all greenhouse gases, which generally leads to a somewhat lower cost estimate than studies that only take CO_2 into account.

Another relevant study, which analysed European environmental priorities (RIVM et al., 2001) and used the EU-wide PRIMES energy model, estimated costs for the EU for domestic implementation of the Kyoto protocol at EUR 13.5 billion per year. The study also included a cost estimate, taking into account the use of Kyoto mechanisms, of EUR 6.3 billion per year. This study also included macro-economic cost estimates (welfare loss), which are higher due to impacts on foreign trade and the competitive position of EU industries, and which could lead to displacement of industries to countries outside the EU. These macro-economic costs of domestic implementation of the Kyoto protocol in the EU were estimated to be about EUR 30 billion per year.

Another more recent study (EEA, 2003) has estimated the costs of achieving the Kyoto targets for WE, taking into account only CO_2,

and analysed the ancillary benefits of climate change policies on air pollution (see also Chapter 5). This study uses a similar cost estimation method to RIVM et al. (2001) and leads to similar cost estimates (Table 3.2). In one scenario within the study, it is assumed that the Kyoto targets would be achieved by using only domestic action in WE. This baseline scenario results in an 8 % increase in CO_2 emissions compared to the 1990 level, which implies, assuming domestic action only, a 13 % decrease in energy-related CO_2 emissions by 2010 from 1990 levels (including 2 % for sinks). Measures would include a number of the policies and measures mentioned above, including the improvement of energy efficiency, the substitution of coal by gas in electricity production and measures in some end-use sectors. Measures in the transport sector would be limited. The costs of these measures in WE would be about EUR 12 billion (1995) per year. The study also analysed two additional scenarios of use of the Kyoto mechanisms; more details on the assumptions are given in Chapter 5.

One of these additional scenarios ('optimal banking') assumes that it is beneficial for the Russian Federation and Ukraine to 'bank' a large share of their available surplus emission allowances and supply only 25 % of their potential to the market. In such a scenario, the use of all flexible instruments (emissions trading, joint implementation and clean development mechanism) would result in a 3 % emission reduction (instead of 13 %) compared with the baseline in WE, a 5 % reduction in central Europe and a 5 % reduction in the EECCA countries. This implies that about 80 % of the reductions in WE would be met by the use of flexible mechanisms, resulting in significantly reduced implementation costs. Costs for domestic policies and measures in WE would decrease to EUR 1 billion per year. However, at the same time about EUR 3 billion per year would be spent on permits (both emissions trading and joint implementation), giving a total of EUR 4 billion per year.

In a second scenario, the maximum potential for ancillary benefits, in terms of reduced emissions of air pollutants, was explored by excluding trading of surplus emission allowances. In this scenario, 55 % of the total emission reduction of CO_2 does not take place in WE but in central Europe and EECCA. The total expenditure for WE then is about EUR 7 billion per year.

😊 Climate mitigation costs in western Europe can be reduced significantly through the use of cost-effective policies and measures and the use of the Kyoto mechanisms (joint implementation, clean development mechanism and emissions trading).

Total annual costs for implementation of the Kyoto protocol in western Europe (EUR billion/year)			Table 3.2.
Scenario	Domestic policies and measures	Kyoto mechanisms	Total
Domestic action only	12	0	12
Kyoto mechanisms with optimal banking	1	3	4
Kyoto mechanisms without trading of surplus emission allowances	2	5	7

Note: Costs in central and eastern Europe and EECCA are zero in all scenarios.
Source: EEA, 2003

Benefits
Policies and measures to abate greenhouse gas emissions result in lower emissions and lower concentrations in the atmosphere, which is expected to slow down climate change. However, there is a considerable time delay between the reduction in emissions and stabilisation of the concentrations. Many impacts of the greenhouse gases emitted during the past 150 years will only become apparent during the second part of this century or even beyond. Assessment of the benefits (or the avoided costs of damages) of abatement policies is therefore difficult. Furthermore, today's costs of reducing greenhouse gases are difficult to compare with the future costs of adaptation to climate change. Because of uncertainties in the quantification of climate change impacts and difficulties in expressing these in monetary terms it is not possible to compare benefits (now and in future) directly with mitigation costs with sufficient degree of accuracy.

Climate change policies can have significant positive effects on other environmental issues, in particular acidification, tropospheric ozone and urban air quality (primary particulate matter) in terms of reduced emissions of air pollutants (nitrogen oxides, sulphur dioxide, particulate matter) and reduced costs (see also Chapter 5). Climate change policies in the EU may lower the cost of reaching acidification and ozone targets by EUR 2–7 billion per year.

😊 Climate change policies can have significant positive effects (ancillary benefits) by also reducing emissions of air pollutants and thus the costs of abating air pollution.

3.7. References

Blok, K., *et al.*, 2001. *Economic evaluation of sectoral emission reduction objectives for climate change — summary report for policy makers.* Ecofys Energy and Environment, Utrecht.

Cox, P. M., *et al.*, 2000. Acceleration of global warming due to carbon-cycle feedbacks in a coupled climate model. *Nature 408*: 184–187.

den Elzen, M. G. J. and de Moor, A .P. G., 2001. *The Bonn agreement and Marrakech accords: An updated analysis.* RIVM Report 728001017/2001. Bilthoven.

Die Zeit, 2002. *Deutschlands Dämme brechen.* No. 34/2002, pp. 1 ff. Hamburg.

DIW (Deutsches Institut für Wirtschaftsforschung), 2002. Internationale Klimaschutzpolitik vor großen Herausforderungen. *DIW-Wochenbericht* 69(34): 555–568.

ECA (European Climate Assessment), 2002. *The European climate assessment and dataset.* KNMI, Netherlands. www.knmi.nl/samenw/eca

EEA (European Environment Agency), 2002a. *Greenhouse gas emission trends and projections in Europe.* Environmental issue report No 33/2002. EEA, Copenhagen.

EEA (European Environment Agency), 2002b. *Greenhouse gas emission projections for Europe.* Technical report No 10/2002. EEA, Copenhagen.

EEA (European Environment Agency), 2002c. *Energy and environment in the European Union.* Environmental issue report No 31. EEA, Copenhagen.

EEA (European Environment Agency), 2003. *Co-benefits of climate change policies in Europe: The impacts of using flexible instruments under the Kyoto protocol.* Van Vuuren, D. P., Cofala, J., Eerens, H., et al., for European Environment Agency, Technical report (forthcoming). Copenhagen.

European Commission, 2001a. *Third communication from the European Community under the UN Framework Convention on Climate Change.* SEC(2001) 2053. 20.12.2001. Commission of the European Communities, Brussels.

European Commission, 2001b. *Communication from the Commission on the implementation of the first phase of the European climate change programme.* COM(2001) 580 final. 23.10.2001. Commission of the European Communities, Brussels.

European Commission, 2001c. *Proposal for a directive of the European Parliament and of the Council establishing a framework for GHG emissions trading within the European Community and amending Council Directive 96/61/EC.* COM(2001) 581 final. 23.10.2001. Commission of the European Communities, Brussels.

European Commission, 2002. *Directive of the European Parliament and the Council on the promotion of cogeneration based on a useful heat demand in the internal energy market.* COM (2002) 415 final. 22.07.2002. Commission of the European Communities, Brussels.

European Parliament and Council, 2002. *Decision on the sixth Community environment action programme.* Decision 1600/2002/EC, July.

Eichhammer, W. *et al.*, 2001. *Greenhouse gas reductions in Germany and the UK: Coincidence or policy induced? An analysis for international climate policy.* Study for the German Federal Ministry of the Environment (BMU) and the German Federal Environmental Agency (UBA) by the Fraunhofer-Institute Systems and Innovation Research (ISI, Germany), Deutsches Institut für Wirtschaftsforschung (DIW, Germany) and Science Policy and Technology Policy Research (SPRU, UK).

Fernandez, M. and Michaelowa, A., 2002. *Joint implementation and EU accession countries.* HWWA discussion paper No 173. Hamburg.

Grüttner, J., 2001a. *The GHG market after Bonn.* Andwil, Switzerland.

Grüttner, J., 2001b. *World market for GHG emission reductions.* Prepared for the World Bank's National AIJ/JI/CDM Strategy Studies Program. World Bank, New York.

Hulme, M., *et al.*, 2002. *Climate change scenarios for the United Kingdom.* Tyndall Centre for Climate Change Research, University of East Anglia, Norwich.

IPCC (Intergovernmental Panel on Climate Change), 1997. *The regional effects of climate change: An assessment of vulnerability.* Special Report of IPCC Working Group II. Watson, R. T., Zinyowera, M. C., Moss, R. H. (eds). Cambridge University Press. 517 pages.

IPCC (Intergovernmental Panel on Climate Change), 2001a. *Climate change 2001: The scientific basis.* Contribution of Working Group I to the Third Assessment Report of the Intergovernmental Panel on Climate Change. Cambridge University Press, Cambridge, UK and New York. 881 pages.

IPCC (Intergovernmental Panel on Climate Change), 2001b. *Climate change 2001: Mitigation.* Contribution of Working Group III to the Third Assessment Report of the Intergovernmental Panel on Climate Change. Cambridge University Press, Cambridge, UK and New York. 752 pages.

IPCC (Intergovernmental Panel on Climate Change), 2001c. *Climate change 2001: Impacts, adaptation, and vulnerability.* Contribution of Working Group II to the Third Assessment Report of the Intergovernmental Panel on Climate Change. Cambridge University Press, Cambridge, UK and New York. 1 032 pages.

IPCC (Intergovernmental Panel on Climate Change), 2001d. *Climate change 2001: Synthesis report.* WMO/UNEP.

Leemans, R. and Hootsmans, R., 1998. *Ecosystem vulnerability and climate protection goals.* RIVM, Bilthoven.

Lindner, M. *et al.*, 2002. *Integrating forest growth dynamics, forests economics and decision making to assess the sensitivity of the German forest sector to climate change.* Forstwissen-schaftliches Centralblatt 121(1): 191–208.

Moe, A. *et al.*, 2001. *A green investment scheme. Achieving environmental benefits from trading with surplus quotas.* Briefing paper presented at a special event in COP 7, November.

Parry, M. L. (ed.), 2000. *Assessment of potential effects and adaptations for climate change in Europe: The Europe ACACIA project.* Jackson Environment Institute, University of East Anglia, Norwich.

Petroula, T., 2002. *Sinks as an option to meet CO_2 emission reductions targets in Europe.* RIVM Report 500005001. Bilthoven.

RIVM, EFTEC, NTUA and IIASA, 2001. *European environmental priorities: An integrated economic and environmental assessment.* RIVM Report 481505010. Bilthoven.

Schleich, J., *et al.*, 2001. *Greenhouse gas reductions in Germany — lucky strike or hard work?* Climate Policy 1(3): 363–380.

UNFCCC, 2002a. N*ational communications by Parties* (including Azerbaijan, 1998; Kazakhstan, 1998; Tajikistan, 2002). http://unfccc.int/resource/natcom/nctable.html

UNFCCC, 2002b. *AIJ under the pilot phase. List of reported projects.* http://www.unfccc.int/program/coop/aij/aijproj.html

Vrolijk, Ch., 2002. *A new interpretation of the Kyoto protocol. Outcomes from The Hague, Bonn and Marrakech.* Royal Institute of International Affairs (RIIA) Briefing Paper No 1.

WMO (World Meteorological Organisation), 2002. *WMO statement on the status of the global climate in 2002: Global surface temperatures second warmest on record.* WMO, Geneva.

4. Stratospheric ozone depletion

The thickness of the ozone layer above Europe has decreased significantly since the beginning of the 1980s, and is declining at a rate of 4–5 % per decade.

The gradual fall in the concentration of chlorine-containing ozone-depleting substances in the troposphere (on their way to the stratosphere) shows that international policies to control emissions of ozone-depleting substances are succeeding.

Production, sales and consumption of ozone-depleting substances in European countries have fallen significantly since 1989. However, the long life of these substances in the atmosphere means that the ozone layer may not recover fully until after 2050.

The remaining policy challenges for European countries are to tighten control measures, reduce the production and use of hydrochlorofluorocarbons and methyl bromide, to manage the remaining stocks of ozone-depleting substances, and to support developing countries in their efforts to reduce their production, use and emissions of ozone-depleting substances.

4.1. Introduction

4.1.1. The issue
The ozone layer in the stratosphere, albeit very dilute, is an essential component of the Earth's atmosphere. It protects humans, animals and plants from damaging short-wave ultraviolet (UV) radiation. Ozone is also a greenhouse gas, but most of the warming effect comes from the ozone in the troposphere.

Ozone is produced in the upper stratosphere by the interaction of short-wave solar UV radiation with oxygen. It is destroyed (dissociated) by reactions with certain compounds (ozone-depleting substances) in the presence of somewhat longer wavelength UV radiation. The dynamic balance between production and destruction determines the concentration and total amount of ozone in the stratosphere, or the 'thickness' of the ozone layer. Anthropogenic emissions of ozone-depleting substances that contain chlorine and bromine disturb this balance. A single chlorine or bromine atom can destroy

thousands of ozone molecules before being removed from the atmosphere.

The dramatic depletion of stratospheric ozone which is observed in polar regions is caused by a combination of anthropogenic emissions of ozone-depleting substances, stable circulation patterns, extremely low temperatures and solar radiation.

Compounds that cause significant ozone depletion include chlorofluorocarbons (CFCs), carbon tetrachloride, methyl chloroform, halons, hydrochlorofluoro-carbons (HCFCs), hydrobromofluoro-carbons (HBFCs) and methyl bromide. They are used as solvents, refrigerants, foam-blowing agents, degreasing agents, aerosol propellants, fire extinguishers (halons) and agricultural pesticides (methyl bromide). The extent to which an ozone-depleting substance affects the ozone layer (its 'ozone-depleting potential' or ODP) depends on its chemical characteristics. Other factors which affect the ozone layer include natural emissions, large volcanic eruptions, climate change, and the greenhouse gases methane and nitrous oxide.

The ozone column (a measure of the thickness of the ozone layer) above Europe has decreased significantly since the beginning of the 1980s. The average ozone column over Europe in March for 1997–2001 was about 7 % lower than that for 1979–81 (Figure 4.1). This decrease is larger that the global average decrease (about 4 %) at northern mid-latitudes for winter-spring (WMO, 2003).

International measures to protect the ozone layer were triggered by the dramatic discovery of a hole in the layer above the Antarctic. The effect of these measures, introduced in the Montreal protocol (1987) and subsequent actions to reduce emissions of ozone-depleting substances, is observed first in the lower part of the Earth's atmosphere. The total potential chlorine concentration in the troposphere has fallen since 1994 mainly because of a large decrease in the concentration of methyl chloroform. The concentration of some CFCs is decreasing, while the increase in the concentration of other CFCs is levelling off.

However, concentrations of HCFCs (used as an alternative to CFCs) are increasing. The changes in concentrations of ozone-depleting substances in the stratosphere follow the changes of concentrations in the troposphere with a delay of three to five years.

As for the concentration of hydrogen chloride in the stratosphere, which is a measure of the total amount of chlorine in the stratosphere, the annual increase has been substantially less since 1997 than before that year (WMO, 2003). Contrary to earlier expectations, the total potential bromine concentration in the troposphere is still rising as a result of increased concentrations of halons.

> The thickness of the ozone layer over Europe in March has decreased significantly since the beginning of the 1980s by 4–5 % per decade.

Because ozone-depleting substances have a very long lifetime in the stratosphere, detectable recovery of the ozone layer is not expected before 2020 as a result of the Montreal protocol. Complete recovery is not expected until after 2050 (WMO, 1999). Over the polar regions, extensive ozone depletion will continue to be observed in spring for many decades.

Ground-based measuring stations have recorded increases in the amount of UV radiation in recent years. Satellite-derived UV data and ground measurements generally agree. Increased UV radiation will continue until ozone recovery is complete, but the damaging effects of UV on human health and ecosystems are likely to persist even longer. Ecosystems in mountain regions, which have high natural background levels of UV radiation, are particularly vulnerable to increases. Skin cancers only appear many years after exposure to UV (see Chapter 12). However, if the current control measures are implemented, the increase in future skin cancer incidence caused by ozone depletion will be very limited (with the maximum impact expected around 2050 (see also EEA, 1999)). Changes in lifestyle, involving more exposure to the sun, may have a much larger effect.

4.1.2 Policies

The Montreal protocol of 1987 (and subsequent amendments and adjustments)

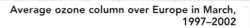

| Average ozone column over Europe in March, 1997–2002 | Figure 4.1. |

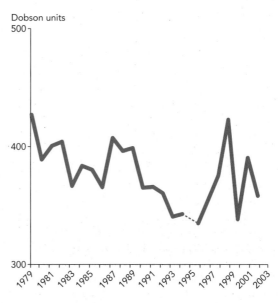

Notes: 1 Dobson unit = 0.01 mm ozone column thickness at standard temperature and pressure. Monthly average ozone data derived from satellite instruments, averaged from 35 °N to 70 °N and from 11.2 °W to 21.2 °E.

Source: EEA (calculations from published data)

aims to eliminate the production and use of ozone-depleting substances (ODS) worldwide. Council Regulation 2037/2000 is the European Union's (EU) current legislative instrument for phasing out ODS in line with the requirements of the Montreal protocol. The regulation includes controls on the production, import, export, supply, use, leakage and recovery of controlled substances. It also establishes a licensing procedure for all imports of ODS.

Current policy challenges include:

*   ensuring full compliance by all countries, notably developing countries and economies in transition;
*   reducing the remaining production of ODS for essential uses and for supply to countries which have an authorization in accordance with the protocol;
*   stopping 'dumping' in developing countries and countries with economies in transition of second-hand equipment which uses CFCs;
*   taking action against smuggling of CFCs and halons;
*   reducing emissions of halons and CFCs from existing equipment, especially in developed countries;
*   discouraging the use of HCFCs as replacements for CFCs;
*   preventing the increased use of methyl bromide in developing countries;

- preventing the production and marketing of new ozone-depleting substances.

Europe's successes and the recovery of the ozone layer will be jeopardised unless developing countries also meet their commitments under the Montreal protocol. These came into effect in 1999.

In 1990, the Parties to the Montreal protocol established a multilateral fund to help developing countries implement the protocol. Developed countries contribute to this fund, while developing countries can apply for financial assistance for particular projects.

Western European countries contributed about USD 560 million to the multilateral fund between 1991 and 2000. This amount is about 48 % of total global payments to the fund. The total amount spent so far by the fund (USD 936 million) is expected to result in the phasing out of the use of 122 million ODP kg (more than twice the 1997 production in western Europe) and the phasing out of the production of about 42 million ODP kg of ozone-depleting substances. European countries operating under Article 5 of the Montreal protocol are Albania, Bosnia-Herzegovina, Croatia, Cyprus, the Former Yugoslav Republic of Macedonia, Georgia, Malta, Republic of Moldova, Romania, Turkey and Serbia and Montenegro.

4.1.3. The interaction between climate change and ozone depletion

Ozone is itself a greenhouse gas, but most of its warming effect comes from tropospheric ozone. Some ozone-depleting substances e.g. CFCs and HCFCs are also potent greenhouse gases. Stratospheric ozone depletion and climate change therefore have some common sources. CFCs, HCFCs and related compounds contribute about 13 % to total radiative forcing (the net extra radiation giving rise to global warming) from all greenhouse gases (Figure 4.2). However, their emissions are not regulated under the Kyoto protocol (see Chapter 3, Section 3.6) but under the Montreal protocol. Hydrofluorocarbons (HFCs), which are increasingly used as substitutes for ozone-depleting substances, are also potent greenhouse gases. HFCs are covered by the Kyoto protocol. One of the current policy challenges is to find ways to use HFCs, which can be applied to substitute Montreal protocol gases, in a way that would minimise their contribution to global warming.

The radiative forcing of ozone-depleting substances is still increasing but less than in the 1980s. There are a number of reasons for this. The phasing out of methyl chloroform under the Montreal protocol is largely responsible for the decrease in total potential chlorine. However, methyl chloroform contributes less to radiative forcing than CFCs and HCFCs. In addition, the contribution from CFCs is levelling off as a direct result of the Montreal protocol, and the radiative forcing of HCFCs is increasing as their concentrations in the troposphere increase.

In addition to the radiative effects of ozone-depleting substances, there are further interactions between climate change and ozone depletion through atmospheric chemistry, possible changes in troposphere-stratosphere exchange, emissions of the greenhouse gases nitrous oxide and methane, etc.

The interaction between climate change and ozone depletion could be especially important for the polar regions. The depth,

| Figure 4.2. | Radiative forcing of ozone-depleting substances at the global level |

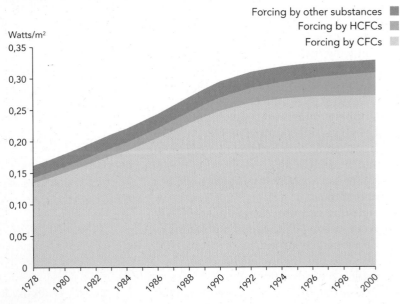

Forcing by other substances
Forcing by HCFCs
Forcing by CFCs

Watts/m²

Source: RIVM

> ☺ The radiative forcing of ozone-depleting substances is still increasing. This is because the radiative forcing of HCFCs is increasing, while that of CFCs is levelling off.

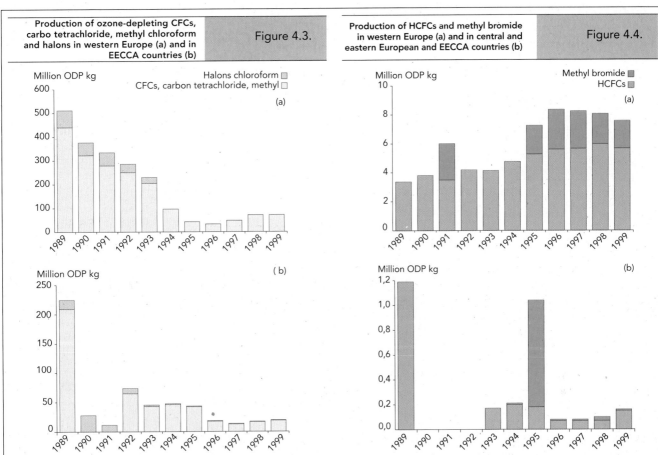

Notes: Production is defined as actual manufacture in the EU for dispersive uses, but excluding: imports, production for use as a raw material for the production of other chemicals, and used material recovered, recycled or reclaimed. Production data are weighted according to ozone-depleting potential (ODP). Production data are weighted according to ozone-depleting potential (ODP). Some data gaps as countries were only required to report data on HCFCs and methyl bromide in certain years.
Source: European Commission, 1999; UNEP, 1998

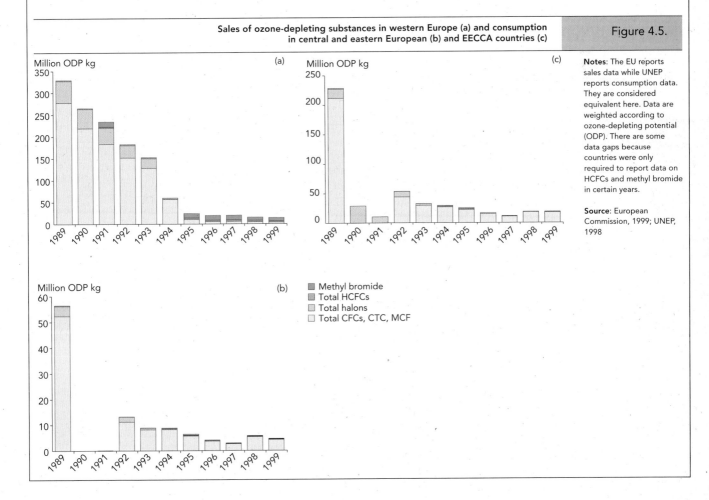

duration and extent of the ozone holes at the north and south poles could increase as a result of lower stratospheric temperatures associated with climate change.

UNFCCC has requested the Intergovernmental Panel on Climate Change (IPCC) and the Technological and Economic Assessment Panel of the Montreal protocol to develop a special report on options to limit the contribution of HFCs to climate change.

4.2. European production, sale and consumption of ozone-depleting substances

The production of CFCs, carbon tetrachloride, methyl chloroform and halons in Europe fell substantially between 1989 and 1999, while production of HCFCs increased (Figures 4.2 and 4.3). The sale and consumption of all ODS shows a similar pattern (Figure 4.4). This overall decline in the production and sale of ODS is a direct result of the Montreal protocol and EU and national regulations. Halon production has been banned in the EU since 1994 and production of CFCs, carbon tetrachloride and methyl chloroform since 1995. Limited production and use of certain compounds (mainly CFCs) is still allowed for designated essential uses (e.g. metered dose inhalers for medical purposes) and to meet the basic needs of developing countries. Production for sale to developing countries accounts for the increase in 1997. HCFCs and methyl bromide may still be produced and sold in the EU subject to mandatory limits.

The production of ODS in western Europe (WE) varied between 20 % and 30 % of global production in the years 1996–99. In all countries in WE, the use of ODS has fallen faster than required under the Montreal protocol.

Global production and emissions of ODS have also decreased significantly. However, existing equipment and products still contain large amounts of CFCs and halons, generating emissions when these are released. Emissions of ODS can occur within a few months of production, e.g. during the manufacture of open-cell foams or after several years. e.g. from refrigerators, closed-cell foams and fire extinguishers.

Illegal production and smuggling of ODS is estimated at 10 % of 1995 global production.

These illegal activities will delay the recovery of the ozone layer by several years.

> Production of ozone-depleting substances in western Europe has decreased by almost 90 %. However, production of hydrofluorocarbons — with low ozone-depleting potential but high global warming potential — is increasing.

4.3. References

EEA (European Environment Agency), 1999. *Environment in the European Union at the turn of the century*. EEA, Copenhagen.

European Commission, 1999. *Statistical factsheet — ozone-depleting substances*. European Commission, Brussels.

UNEP, 1998. *Production and consumption of ozone-depleting substances 1986–1996*. UNEP United Nations Environment Programme, Nairobi, Kenya.

WMO, 1999. *Scientific assessment of ozone depletion: 1998*. Global Ozone Research and Monitoring Project — Report 44. World Meteorological Organization, Geneva.

WMO, 2003. *Scientific assessment of ozone depletion: 2002*. Global Ozone Research and Monitoring Project. World Meteorological Organization, Geneva. (In press.).

5. Air pollution

Emissions of acidifying and eutrophying substances and ground-level ozone precursors have fallen substantially since 1990 — in particular in central and eastern Europe and the 12 countries of eastern Europe, the Caucasus and central Asia (EECCA) as a result of economic restructuring. Reductions in western Europe have resulted mainly from fuel switching, flue-gas treatment and the introduction of three way catalysts for cars.

In consequence, most of Europe's ecosystems are now protected against further acidification but a number of hot-spot areas remain at risk especially in central Europe. Eutrophication remains a substantial problem with large areas unprotected throughout Europe especially in western Europe and central and eastern Europe. Furthermore, most of the monitored vegetation and agricultural crops in western Europe and central and eastern Europe are exposed to ozone concentrations above the long-term European Union target.

Air pollution remains a problem in most cities. Long-term average ground-level ozone concentrations continue to increase although short-term peak concentrations are falling. Exposure to particulate matter may be the largest potential health problem from air pollution in most cities. Although concentrations have been falling since monitoring began, a significant proportion of the urban population experiences concentrations above limit values. Exposures to concentrations of nitrogen dioxide and sulphur dioxide above limit values have fallen since 1990 and further notable reductions are expected. These reductions will focus attention to a greater extent on cities in the EECCA countries where air pollution remains a serious problem, and where implementation of better policies, monitoring and assessment are needed.

Baseline projections to 2010 suggest that while exposure to ground-level ozone at concentrations in excess of the EU threshold will fall in almost all western European and central and eastern European cities, the target levels are nevertheless unlikely to be attained. Similarly, concentrations of particulates will remain above the limit values. The fraction of the urban population exposed to air concentrations in excess of the most stringent of the nitrogen dioxide limit values will fall to about half compared to 1995, and exceedance of sulphur dioxide threshold will be observed only in EECCA.

Baseline projections for 2010 also suggest that economic restructuring and switching to cleaner fuels should enable the Russian Federation and the western countries of EECCA to fulfil their emission ceilings targets. Implementation of EU legislation in central and eastern Europe should result in countries attaining their national emission ceilings for all air pollutants except ammonia. In western Europe, additional measures beyond current legislation will be needed to reach the national emission ceilings of nitrogen oxides, volatile organic compounds and ammonia.

The same projections suggest that the total area of ecosystems protected from further acidification will increase to cover nearly all the ecosystem area. Recovery from past impacts, however, cannot be expected so rapidly. Protection from further eutrophication will also improve but still leave about half of the area in western, and central and eastern Europe unprotected. Regional ground-level ozone concentrations will fall below the threshold for vegetation.

Assuming a reduction of carbon dioxide emissions to comply with the Kyoto protocol, there will be significant ancillary benefits in terms of additional reduced emissions of air pollutants and reduced costs of air pollution abatement. The use of flexible mechanisms to implement the Kyoto protocol, compared to implementation primarily by means of domestic measures, will shift the additional reductions of air pollutant emissions from western to central and eastern Europe, the Russian Federation and the western countries of EECCA. It will also reduce the ancillary benefits in terms of control costs for air pollution in Europe and result in higher ecosystem protection in the whole of Europe. Using surplus emission allowances will reduce ancillary benefits in particular for central and eastern Europe, the Russian Federation and the western countries of EECCA.

5.1. Introduction

5.1.1. The issue
Air pollution is a transboundary, multi-pollutant/multi-effect environmental problem. Although significant and well-directed efforts over more than two decades have led to a reduction in emissions, air pollution in Europe continues to pose risks and have adverse effects on human health and on natural and man-made environments.

Box 5.1 summarises various important air pollution issues. These arise either from atmospheric deposition of pollutants or from direct exposure to ambient concentrations of pollutants i.e. from air quality.

The main deposition issues for this chapter are:

- acidification of soils and freshwater through the deposition of sulphur and nitrogen compounds;
- eutrophication of terrestrial, freshwater and marine ecosystems through the deposition of nitrogenous nutrients.

The main air quality issues addressed are:

- human health effects resulting from ground-level (tropospheric) ozone, particulate matter and other pollutants, including nitrogen oxides, benzene and sulphur dioxide;
- adverse effects on vegetation and crops resulting from ground-level ozone, nitrogen oxides and sulphur dioxide.

Ground-level ozone, acidification and eutrophication are issues of European scale because of atmospheric transboundary transport of pollutants. Air quality issues such as nitrogen dioxide and benzene are more subregional or local. Particulate matter and ozone have both local and transboundary

aspects. Policy measures must be targeted accordingly at European, national and local levels.

The issues of stratospheric ozone depletion and dispersion of chemicals such as organic compounds or heavy metals are addressed in Chapters 4 and 6 respectively.

 Emissions of acidifying and eutrophying substances and ground-level ozone precursors have fallen substantially since 1990, but these pollutants continue to pose risks to health and the environment.

5.1.2. The policy framework
Air pollution issues are addressed by:

- European Community legislation and strategies;
- the United Nations Economic Commission for Europe (UNECE) Convention on Long-Range Transboundary Air Pollution (CLRTAP).

A key element of EU legislation on emissions is the national emission ceilings directive (NECD) (European Community, 2001a), which sets emission ceilings for sulphur dioxide (SO_2), nitrogen oxides (NO_x), and ammonia (NH_3) and volatile organic compounds (VOCs). These have to be achieved through EU-wide and national policies and measures aimed at specific sectors. Member States are obliged to prepare a national programme presenting their approaches to achieving the emission ceilings. EU sectoral emission legislation sets emission standards for specific source categories. There are a number of EU directives controlling emissions from vehicles (European Community, 1998), large combustion plants (European Community, 2001b) and industry (VOC directive — European Community, 1999 and integrated pollution prevention and control directive — European Community, 1996).

National emission ceilings for non-EU countries have been agreed under the CLRTAP Gothenburg protocol (UNECE, 1999). These ceilings represent cost-effective and simultaneous reductions of acidification, eutrophication and ground-level ozone. The EU NECD ceilings were developed using a similar approach.

The EU air quality framework directive (Directive 96/62/EC) and daughter directives (SO_2, NO_X/NO_2, PM_{10}, Pb, CO, C_6H_6 and O_3) set concentration limit values to protect human health and the environment. If these limit values are exceeded, Member States are obliged to set up, implement and report abatement plans.

EU air policy is evaluated and new policies are being developed under CAFE, the European Commission's clean air for Europe programme, which is part of the sixth environment action programme (6EAP). This should lead to a thematic strategy for air pollution in 2005.

Almost all European countries that are parties to CLRTAP have signed protocols under this convention. However, in many countries the protocols await ratification. By January 2003, only four parties had ratified the 1999 Gothenburg protocol (31 signatures), and 14 parties the 1998 heavy metal protocol (36 signatures) and the 1998 protocol on persistent organic pollutants (36 signatures).

Long-term environmental targets within the EU and the CLRTAP policy frameworks are derived from an effect-oriented approach based on critical thresholds that define the extent to which deposition and ambient concentrations should be reduced to maintain the structure and function of ecosystems. The level of protection afforded to ecosystems may therefore be expressed in terms of the fraction of total ecosystem areas where critical thresholds are not exceeded and hence protected from further impact (this does not reflect recovery from past damage, which typically only occurs over an extended time period) (see CCE, 2001; 1999).

The emission targets set in the EU NECD and Gothenburg protocol correspond to interim environmental targets where ecosystem protection will be improved but critical thresholds will still be exceeded in some areas (Table 5.1).

5.2. Current status and trends of regional air pollution

5.2.1. Acidification — emission reductions and ecosystem protection

Agriculture, energy production and transport are the main sectors that contribute to acidification (Table 5.2).

Emissions of acidifying compounds in Europe have decreased significantly since 1990 (Figure 5.1). In particular, emissions in

Emission reduction targets for 1990–2010 (%)			Table 5.1.
	Western Europe	Central and eastern Europe	Eastern Europe, Caucasus and central Asia
Acidification	-56	-40	-40
Eutrophication	-36	-10	-25
Ozone precursors	-53	-21	-36

Notes: Percentage change between the emissions in the base year 1990 and the emission ceilings of the EU NECD or the CLRTAP protocols. The following weighting factors to convert to acid equivalents: sulphur dioxide $* 1_{/32}$, nitrogen oxide $* 1_{/46}$ and ammonia $* 1_{/17}$. These factors represent a simplified approach to complex atmospheric processes. Western Europe: excluding Iceland. Central and eastern Europe: excluding Cyprus, Malta, and Turkey. Eastern Europe, Caucasus and central Asia: the targets refer to Belarus, Republic of Moldova, the Russian Federation and Ukraine.

Sources: EMEP/MSC-W, 2002; EEA-ETC/ACC

Contribution to emissions of acidifying pollutants in 2000 (% of total emissions from all sectors)			Table 5.2.
	Western Europe	Central and eastern Europe	Eastern Europe, Caucasus and central Asia
Agriculture	31	13	17
Energy industries	25	48	41
Transport	24	12	21

Sources: EMEP/MSC-W, 2002; EEA-ETC/ACC

Change in emissions of acidifying substances for 1990–2000 compared to EU NECD and CLRTAP targets for 2010	Figure 5.1.

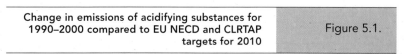

■ 1990 - 2000   □ 2010 targets NECD, CLRTAP   Source: EMEP/CLRTAP and EEA-ETC/ACC

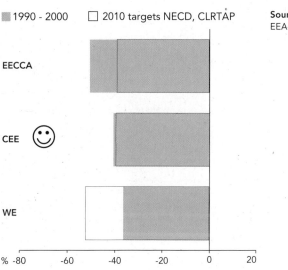

Figure 5.2.

Sources: CCE, 2001; EMEP/
MSC-W, 2002

**Calculated estimates of ecosystem protection
against further acidification in 2000**

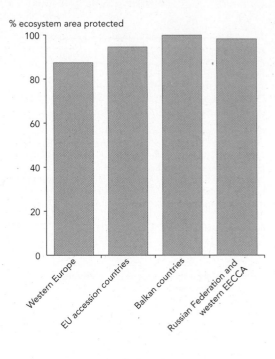

% ecosystem area protected

central and eastern Europe (CEE) and the
countries of eastern Europe, the Caucasus
and central Europe (EECCA) fell, by 39 %
and 52 % respectively, mainly as a result of
economic restructuring, switching from coal
to gas and more desulphurisation of
emissions from power plants. At present,
EECCA and CEE emissions are below targets
whereas western Europe (WE) will need to
reduce emissions further to reach the 2010
targets.

In 2000, more than 90 % of the ecosystems
in CEE and EECCA were estimated to be
protected against further acidification
(Figure 5.2). In WE, more than 10 % of the
ecosystem area remains unprotected — i.e.
acidifying deposition exceeds the thresholds
for these ecosystems.

The geographical distribution of ecosystem
protection suggests significant differences
between areas (Map 5.1). Areas in southern
Scandinavia, central Europe and the United
Kingdom are believed to have relatively low
ecosystem protection whereas ecosystem
protection in southern WE and the EECCA
countries is relatively high. Central Asian
soils are less sensitive than those in Siberia,
but acidification in these areas is still
believed to be worsening as a result of rising
emissions.

Map 5.1.   **Calculated estimate of the distribution of ecosystem protection against further acidification in 2000**

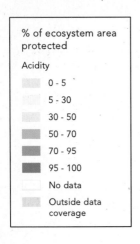

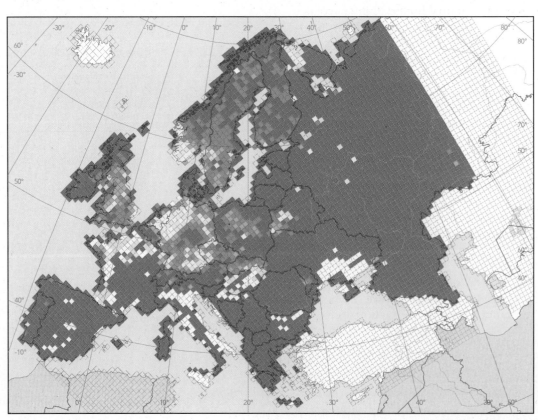

Sources: CCE, 2001; EMEP/
MSC-W, 2002

More than 90 % of the ecosystem areas of Europe overall are calculated to have been protected against further acidification as a result of general emission control. However, many hot-spot areas remain at risk especially in central Europe.

Contribution to emission of eutrophying compounds in 2000 (%)			Table 5.3.
	Western Europe	Central and eastern Europe	Eastern Europe, Caucasus and central Asia
Agriculture	24	20	21
Energy industries	13	22	41
Transport	47	33	16

Sources: EMEP/MSC-W, 2002; EEA-ETC/ACC

5.2.2. Eutrophication — emission reductions and ecosystem protection

Emissions of eutrophying substances originate mainly from the energy, transport and agriculture sectors (Table 5.3).

Emissions of nitrogen compounds that cause eutrophication have fallen since 1990 (Figure 5.3). Reductions in nitrogen oxide emissions resulted from the introduction of three-way catalysts in passenger cars, fuel switching from coal to gas, and measures to improve energy efficiency in industry and power plants. In CEE and EECCA, the main underlying factor was economic restructuring. Reductions in emissions of ammonia from the agriculture sector in WE and CEE are the result of falling animal numbers rather than abatement measures. Although now stabilising, these emissions have generally proved difficult to control. The reduction of nitrogen oxide emissions from the transport sector has to some extent been offset by increased road traffic.

In WE, substantial further reductions of nitrogen emissions are believed necessary to reach the 2010 Gothenburg protocol and NECD targets. In 2000, ecosystem protection against eutrophication was below 50 % in WE and below 30 % in CEE. In EECCA, however, ecosystem protection was high above 80 % (Figure 5.4). Thus the area calculated to be unprotected against eutrophication is larger than that unprotected against acidification. Ecosystems are therefore exposed to a higher long-term risk of eutrophication than of acidification. Areas of low protection levels against eutrophication are more widespread and extend over most of WE and CEE (Map 5.2).

Eutrophication of ecosystems remains a significant problem with large areas throughout Europe unprotected especially in western Europe and central and eastern Europe.

Change in emission of eutrophying substances for 1990–2000 compared to EU NECD and CLRTAP targets for 2010	Figure 5.3.

■ 1990 - 2000 □ 2010 targets NECD, CLRTAP

Source: EMEP/MSC-W, 2002; EEA-ETC/ACC

EECCA
CEE
WE

% -40 -30 -20 -10 0 10

Calculated estimates of ecosystem protection against eutrophication in 2000	Figure 5.4.

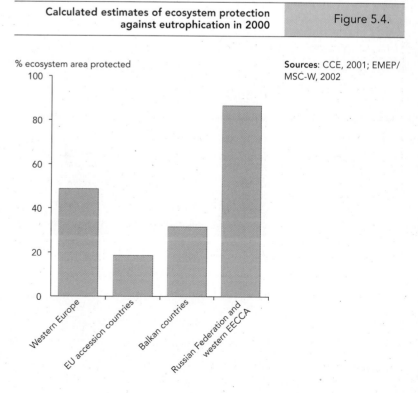

% ecosystem area protected

Sources: CCE, 2001; EMEP/MSC-W, 2002

Western Europe
EU accession countries
Balkan countries
Russian Federation and western EECCA

Map 5.2.   **Calculated estimate of the distribution of ecosystem protection against eutrophication in 2000**

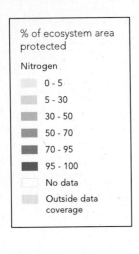

% of ecosystem area protected

Nitrogen

- 0 - 5
- 5 - 30
- 30 - 50
- 50 - 70
- 70 - 95
- 95 - 100
- No data
- Outside data coverage

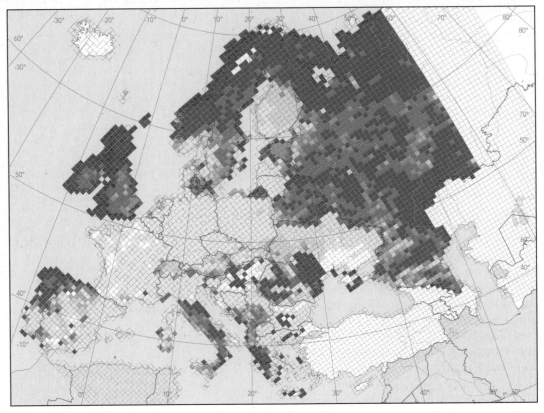

Sources: CCE, 2001; EMEP/MSC-W, 2002

5.2.3. Ground-level ozone — emissions and exposure

Emissions of ozone precursors come mainly from the transport sector and constitute for EECCA 38 %, for CEE 37 % and for WE 52 % of the total emissions in these regions.

In CEE, and particularly EECCA, emissions of ozone precursors have fallen mainly as a result of economic restructuring (Figure 5.5). In WE, the reductions resulted mainly from the introduction of catalysts on new cars, and implementation of the solvents directive in industrial processes and other uses of solvents.

In WE, substantial further reductions of emissions of ozone precursors, particularly NO_x and non-methane volatile organic compounds (NMVOC), are expected to be needed to reach the 2010 Gothenburg protocol and NECD targets.

In 1999, almost 90 % of agricultural crops covered by monitoring in WE and CEE were subject to ground-level ozone concentrations above the EU long-term critical level (Figure 5.6). In 1999, the monitored area covered

Figure 5.5.   **Change in emission of ozone precursors for 1990–2000 compared to EU and CLRTAP targets for 2010**

Source: EMEP/MSC-W, 2002; EEA-ETC/ACC

■ 1990 - 2000   □ 2010 targets NECD, CLRTAP

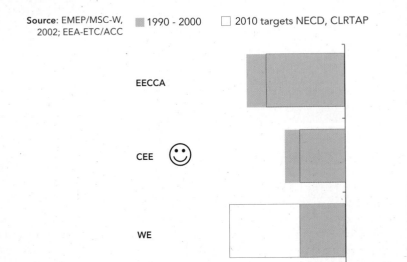

EECCA

CEE ☺

WE

%   -80   -60   -40   -20   0   20

> ☹ Almost 90 % of the monitored vegetation and agricultural crops in western Europe and central and eastern Europe are exposed to ozone concentrations above the long-term EU target.

more than 50 % of the total arable area, compared with about 30–35 % in previous years. In addition, a significant fraction of crops were exposed to concentrations in excess of the less strict EU interim target for 2010 — especially in WE. No data are available for EECCA.

5.3. Urban air pollution

The information in this section is derived from the Auto-Oil II air quality study (European Commission, 2000; EEA, 2001). Urban air quality across Europe is managed at different levels — European, national and local. EU Member States and accession countries have to comply with air quality limit values for the protection of human health and the environment as set in daughter directives to the air quality framework directive. These are based on the World Health Organization air quality guidelines for Europe. Where limit values are exceeded, countries must prepare abatement programmes. These generally include local, essentially urban and sometimes industrial, measures, since national emission ceilings, policies and measures should be included in the national programmes required under the EU NECD and CLRTAP Gothenburg protocol. No national emission ceilings have been set for particulate matter.

Figure 5.7 shows the fraction of urban population in WE and CEE exposed to peak air pollution in excess of short-term EU limit values. The fraction is estimated from calculating the total population of those cities experiencing days of exceedance of the limits divided by the total population of all cities with monitoring stations. Problems from sulphur dioxide (SO_2) and nitrogen dioxide (NO_2) affect 10 % or less of the urban population. During occasional years exceedance of short-term limits is not observed (as for NO_2 in 1996). About half of the urban population is exposed to elevated particulate concentrations, and more than 95 % to excess ozone concentrations (all in terms of the threshold in the old ozone directive (Directive 92/72/EEC)).

Coverage of monitoring stations from which data are reported at European level increased considerably between 1990 and 1995 partly because of the establishment of the EuroAirNet network (EEA, 2002a). Monitoring coverage in EECCA is probably less.

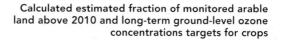

| Calculated estimated fraction of monitored arable land above 2010 and long-term ground-level ozone concentrations targets for crops | Figure 5.6. |

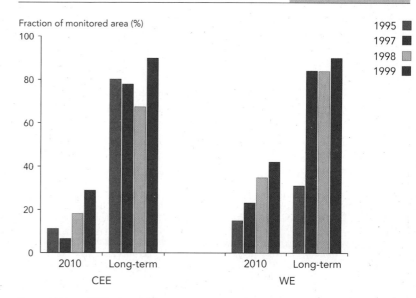

Fraction of monitored area (%)

1995 ■
1997 ■
1998 ■
1999 ■

Notes: 2010 = AOT40 18mg/m³.h. Long term = AOT40 6mg/m³.h. AOT40 stands for accumulated exposure to ozone above 40 ppb.

Source: EEA

| Urban population fraction in western Europe and central and eastern Europe exposed to short-period air quality above limit values | Figure 5.7. |

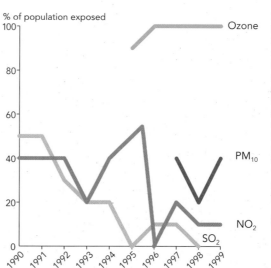

% of population exposed

Notes: Based on an estimate from data in 21 western European and central and eastern European countries. Limit values referred to are: ozone 110 µg/m³ 8-hour average not to be exceeded; PM_{10} 50 µg/m³ 24-hour average not to be exceeded on more than 35 days; NO_2 200 µg/m³ 1-hour average not to be exceeded more than 18 times a year; SO_2 125 µg/m³ 24-hour average not to be exceeded more than 3 times a year.

Source: EEA

5.3.1. Ground-level ozone

The new EU target of 120 µg/m³ (8-hour average to be exceeded on no more than 25 days per year) (Directive 2002/3/EC) has seldom been met in recent years. In 1999, a third of the urban population was exposed to over 30 exceedances a year, and about 30 % of cities exceeded the target (rural concentrations are generally higher than urban - see Section 5.2.3). Most exceedances are in central and southern European countries. There appear to be decreasing short-term peak concentrations across WE but increasing long-term averages. This would reduce the effects of acute ozone exposure, which the limit values address, but increase low-level chronic exposure.

In the Auto-Oil II air quality project, projections of ozone concentrations have been estimated for major conurbations across the EU, accession and EFTA countries under a scenario developed for 2010. These estimates indicate that reductions in the emissions of ozone precursors between 1990 and 2010 could be expected to result in significant improvement in health protection. Exceedances of the 8-hour 120 µg/m³ threshold should decrease by 20–85 % between 1990 and 2010 in almost all cities as a result of reductions in emissions of ozone precursors. However, these reductions are unlikely to be enough to reach target concentrations over the whole of Europe. The limit value is expected to be exceeded on about 25 days per year in 2010 in northwest Europe (see Section 5.4).

5.3.2. Particulate matter

Exposure to particulate matter may be the largest potential health problem from air pollution in all areas (see Chapter 12). The EU has set the following limit values for PM_{10} (particle diameter less than 10 µm): an annual mean of 40 µg/m³ by 2005, to fall to 20 µg/m³ by 2010, and exceedances of a 24-hour peak value of 50 µg/m³ on no more than 35 days per year, to fall to 7 days per year by 2010.

A significant fraction of the urban population in WE is currently exposed to PM_{10} concentrations in excess of the limit value of 50 µg/m³ 24-hour average not to be exceeded on more than 35 days (Figure 5.7).

Analysis of the PM_{10} data in AIRBASE, the European air quality information system (van Aalst, 2002), suggests that concentrations at almost all stations have been falling in recent years (Figure 5.9).

Nevertheless, projections carried out under the Auto-Oil II programme suggest that concentrations of PM_{10} in most urban areas in the EU will remain well above limit values up to 2010.

5.3.3. Nitrogen dioxide

The most stringent of the EU limit values for NO_2 proves to be the annual average concentration of 40 µg/m³ as its attainment will generally also mean achievement of short-term limits. Concentrations at urban street hot spots have declined since the end of the 1980s as a result of the growing penetration of catalysts in the car fleet. Exposure to NO_2 has decreased and may now be stable. Nevertheless, at present the annual limit is exceeded in about 30 European cities which report data, and substantial numbers of people are exposed to NO_2 concentrations above health protection-based limit values. According to

---

Box 5.2. Air emissions in cities of eastern Europe, the Caucasus and central Asia

Rapidly increasing private transport is a major problem for the urban environment in EECCA. In capital cities such as Ashgabat, Dushanbe, Moscow, Tbilisi and Tashkent transport is the dominant source of air pollutants — more than 80 % of the total (Figure 5.8). Mobile sources are also a major source of emissions in other large cities in eastern Europe, the Caucasus and central Asia including Baku, Bishkek, Chisinau, Kiev, Minsk and Yerevan. The main causative factors include the age of the vehicle fleet, low quality and high sulphur content fuel, and declining public transport. Industrial sources have declined in importance, but remain relevant and difficult to address.

Figure 5.8.	Development of total emissions of air pollutants in Moscow, 1990-96

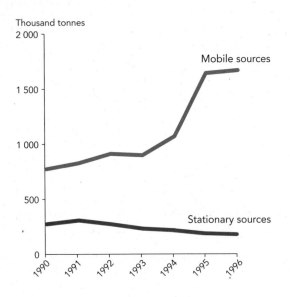

Thousand tonnes

Source: WHO, 2002

Abatement measures
The level of implementation of abatement measures in eastern Europe, the Caucasus and central Asia varies greatly. Mobile source abatement began in Moscow in 1996 with control of the technical condition of cars more than 15 years old. In Dushanbe, emission permits are given to vehicles that meet required standards. Turkmenistan has set a reduction by 2005 for emissions from mobile sources. In Kiev, however, it is expected that air pollution from road transport will continue to be a problem for at least 10–15 years due to the slow change in the car fleet. For stationary sources, the aim is reconstruction and modernisation, often with international assistance, but environmental control under conditions of intermittent operation is complicated. Lack of finance and a focus on energy issues has meant that no environmental programme exists in Tbilisi.

Economic growth, which is now expected, will not immediately bring in new technology for industrial sources. Growth in transport and a greater proportion of new vehicles can be expected, but improvements in air quality will take many years. In some countries, serious economic problems will preclude strong abatement measures. Emissions can therefore be expected to rise, with consequent effects on air quality.

the Auto-Oil II study, NO_2 concentrations are expected to fall considerably by 2010. The fraction of the urban population affected is estimated to be 45-60 % below its 1995 value by 2010 (EEA, 2001).

5.3.4. Sulphur dioxide

Increased use of low-sulphur fuel and successful implementation of abatement measures have reduced concentrations in WE considerably since the 1980s. Limit values in the EU have more than halved to 125 µg/m³ (98th percentile of daily values). Since 1995, less than 20 % of the population has been exposed to SO_2 concentrations above the limit value, and the number of exceedance days continues to fall. Similar reductions have occurred more recently in CEE and EECCA as a result of economic restructuring and abatement measures; though information is scarce, World Health Organization (WHO) guideline values appear to be widely exceeded.

Further reductions in urban SO_2 exposure in WE by 2010 will shift attention to CEE and EECCA. In some cities, air quality may deteriorate between 2010 and 2020 if emissions from traffic and heating increase as expected.

National reduction plans may not have a large impact on local air quality, since the major industrial emissions from high stacks have little influence on urban concentrations.

5.4. Air pollution in Europe in 2010

5.4.1. Regional air pollution in 2010 — a baseline scenario

This section presents a baseline scenario for 2010, which has been derived to assess the effects of the implementation of current legislation. It includes policies as decided by December 2001, national emission ceilings on future emissions of air pollutants and ecosystem protection. The section is based on a study performed by the European Environment Agency (EEA, 2003). The baseline scenario covers WE, CEE, the Russian Federation and the western countries of EECCA.

The scenario includes emission control policies and measures, including fuel standards, according to current legislation, and emission ceilings from the EU NECD and the Gothenburg protocol. For each country the more stringent value of current

The EU target value for ground-level ozone is exceeded in many European cities. Average ozone concentrations have continued to increase since 1995, but short-term peak values have fallen.

A significant proportion of Europe's urban population is exposed to concentrations of fine particulates, PM_{10}, above limit values. However, concentrations have fallen since monitoring began.

Exposures of urban citizens in western Europe and central and eastern Europe to concentrations of nitrogen dioxide and sulphur dioxide above the EU limit values have fallen since 1990.

| Distribution of change coefficients for 210 stations monitoring PM_{10} in 12 western European and central and eastern European countries | Figure 5.9. |

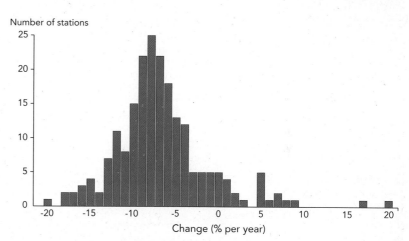

Number of stations

Change (% per year)

Note: Time series of daily data from 1999 or before to 2000.
Source: EEA

legislation or national ceiling was used. The baseline scenario does not assume implementation of any recent adopted or foreseen climate change policies after 1999 (this is addressed in Section 5.4.2).

Main assumptions

The baseline scenario is characterized by a continuation of the dominant 1990s trends: increasing globalisation, further liberalisation and average assumptions regarding population growth, economic growth and technology development (EEA, 2002b). The baseline was developed to ensure consistent CO_2 projections at the EU level with previous energy projections developed for the European Commission

Box 5.3. Urban air quality in eastern Europe, the Caucasus and central Asia

Air pollution is among the most serious of the environmental problems faced by cities in eastern Europe, the Caucasus and central Asia.

Lack of monitoring data precludes in-depth assessment of the state of air quality in this region though air quality has been monitored in all the countries for many years. After decentralization, the countries redesigned their monitoring systems, but lack of funds has inhibited any major progress. Obsolete measuring methods are therefore still widely in use. Monitoring is under the control of different authorities with often poorly defined responsibilities (WHO, 2002) and/or quite different functional competences.

During the 1990s, pollutant concentrations fell in many states before rising again with economic growth and related increased road transport. By 1998 in the Russian Federation, 72 of the observed cities exceeded annual average concentration limits for at least one pollutant and more than 24 exceeded annual limits for three or more pollutants. Acute exposure was extensive. Up to 95 cities exceeded short-term limits for at least one substance. Elsewhere the picture is similar. Concentrations several times above limit values have been observed in a number of cities, examples being Tbilisi and Dushanbe (SO_2 and PM_{10}), Bishkek (NO_x and PM), Kiev and Chisinau (NO_x), Almaty (formaldehyde) and Ashgabat (formaldehyde and PM) (Figure 5.10). Large industrial centres regularly exceed limits, e.g. Ust-Kamenogorsk, Ridder and Temirtau in Kazakhstan, and Donetsk, Lutsk, Odessa in Ukraine. Ozone smog events are reported from Georgia, but a lack of monitoring data means that the scale of the problem is unknown.

Effects on health cannot currently be quantified partly because of the lack of monitoring data, e.g. for PM_{10} and $PM_{2.5}$. There are some indications that respiratory disease occurs in cities such as Kiev at twice the rate found in other monitored cities. The link with air pollution, however, can only be assumed, not demonstrated. Tbilisi reports increased illness as the major impact of air pollution.

Approximately 30 % of Russian cities exceeded limits for particulate matter in 1998. In Ukraine in 2000 over 40 % of monitored cities exceeded PM limits. Limits were exceeded in the central Asian Republics, where elevated natural concentrations from desertification, desert dust and the dried Aral Sea bed enhance the impact of particulates from cheap low-quality coal used for power generation and from road transport . Emissions of PM in central Asia are expected to increase with growing energy use as control measures for low-quality coal burning or road transport are not expected to reduce emissions sufficiently.

Sources: State of environment reports, various dates

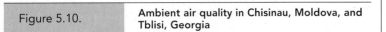

| Figure 5.10. | Ambient air quality in Chisinau, Moldova, and Tblisi, Georgia |

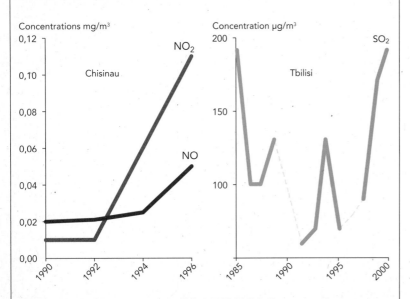

Sources: 'State of the environment in Tbilisi', 2000 (Tbilisi); 'Summary environment state in the Republic of Moldova', 1998 (Chisinau)

and used in several other scenarios for European assessments (EEA, 2002c; Capros, 1999; Criqui and Kouvaritakis, 2000; IMAGE-team, 2001). The baseline projection shows somewhat higher CO_2 emissions than the most recent projections that include the latest measures adopted by Member States.

The most important changes in primary energy consumption and emission control legislation in individual regions included in this baseline are:

Western Europe: Between 2000 and 2010, energy use will continue to increase in absolute and per capita terms. Natural gas shows the fastest growth rates but oil remains the most important fuel. The share of coal declines further. Implementing current legislation (including the large combustion plant directive adopted in 2001) allows the national emission ceilings for SO_2 to be reached. In the case of other pollutants (NO_x, VOC and NH_3), additional measures are needed and assumed to be implemented.

Central and eastern Europe: Total energy use is expected to grow considerably after 2000 but not to reach the levels of the late 1980s. Coal is replaced by natural gas in the residential sector and power plants. Oil consumption increases due to rapid growth of road transport. The region will adopt EU emission and fuel standards for mobile and stationary sources in 2006-08.

The Russian Federation and western countries of EECCA: Natural gas has become by far the most important energy carrier since the early 1990s. From 2000 to 2010, coal use decreases further and natural gas and oil grow modestly. Total energy use in 2010 remains more than one third below the 1990 level. Regarding SO_2 emission, standards for new sources and low sulphur gas oil are assumed to be implemented (second sulphur protocol — CLTRAP). The Gothenburg protocol does not specify any national emission ceilings for the Russian Federation but only the control of emissions in the pollution emissions management areas (PEMA). Emissions ceilings will be reached mainly through economic restructuring and switching to cleaner fuels. Emission volumes from transport remain uncontrolled.

Emissions and ecosystem exposure in 2010
The baseline scenario indicates that emissions of air pollutants will fall significantly throughout Europe (Table 5.4), a continuation of the recent trend. In

particular, SO_2 emissions will fall to 25 % of the 1990 level, mostly as a result of emission control policies. Emissions of NO_x and VOC will fall by more than 40 % and fine particulates by more than 35 %. Reduction of ammonia emissions is much more limited (around 15 %) and will result mainly from the decrease in livestock farming. In contrast to regional air pollution, CO_2 emissions will increase in all regions compared to 2000, but in CEE, the Russian Federation and western countries of EECCA their levels will not (yet) return to their 1990 levels. CO_2 emissions from WE will increase by 8 % compared to 1990.

For Europe as a whole, implementation of national emission ceilings (in addition to the current legislation controls) decreases the emissions of NO_x and SO_2 by 2 % and emissions of VOC by 7 %.

The emission controls implemented up to 2010 will significantly increase the area of ecosystem protected against acidification and eutrophication. Protection against acidification will be high throughout Europe in 2010 leaving 1.5 % of the ecosystem area unprotected. However, relatively large areas (more than 57 %) will remain unprotected against eutrophication in particular in CEE. Realisation of the baseline scenario will also reduce vegetation and population exposure to elevated regional ozone levels by 50 % and 74 % respectively.

Emission control costs

The emission control costs for each region (Table 5.5) include the costs of measures necessary to reach the emission reductions displayed in Table 5.4. The costs of controlling all air pollutants in the baseline scenario will increase to about EUR 89 billion/year in 2010. The high costs of NO_x and VOC controls are due to relatively expensive measures for mobile sources (57 % of the total costs). Fine particulates control costs for stationary sources contribute about 11 % and for SO_2 21 %. The policies and emission ceilings for ammonia are still relatively liberal and the costs of controlling ammonia are only 2 % of the total cost.

Western Europe bears 81 % of total European costs. This is because of more stringent emission ceilings than in other parts of Europe and high emissions in the base year. The marginal reduction costs in WE are higher than in CEE and the Russian Federation and western countries of EECCA.

Emissions changes in 2010 as compared with 1990 (%)						Table 5.4.
	CO_2	NO_x	SO_2	NH_3	VOC	PM_{10}
Western Europe	+8	-52	-81	-15	-54	-56
Central and eastern Europe	-10	-42	-68	-15	-22	-67
The Russian Federation and EECCA	-32	-32	-71	-36	-26	-68
Total	-7	-45	-74	-18	-44	-64

Notes: Western Europe includes EU, Norway and Switzerland and excludes Iceland, Liechtenstein, Andorra, Monaco and San Marino. Central and eastern Europe does not include Cyprus, Malta and Turkey. The Russian Federation includes the European part within the EMEP region. The energy projections were generated with the PRIMES energy model. PRIMES results as well as TIMER/RAINS results (used in this study) compared fairly well with country estimates. For details see EEA, 2003.

Sources: IIASA, RIVM

Annual emission control costs for the baseline scenario (1995 prices)						Table 5.5.
	Cost EUR billion (1995)/year	NO_x + VOC (stationary sources only)	SO_2	NH_3	PM_{10}	Mobile sources
Western Europe	72	11	22	1	8	59
Central and eastern Europe	14	2	14	7	15	61
The Russian Federation and EECCA	3	2	35	1	63	0
Total	89	9	21	2	11	57

Notes: Control costs (as calculated by the RAINS model) may be compared with the costs of complying with the Kyoto protocol in Chapter 3, but with care. The latter were calculated by the TIMER model and include the costs of energy system measures such as energy efficiency improvement and fuel switching. The RAINS model includes only the costs of add-on technologies. Since TIMER and RAINS use different technology databases, the assumptions and methodologies may not be fully comparable.

Source: IIASA (RAINS model)

Implementing EU legislation, mainly for NO_x and VOC emissions from mobile sources, will drive the control costs in CEE. The control costs more than double compared with the legislation from the mid-1990s (i.e. with emission and fuel standards adopted before the accession negotiations began). Costs for the Russian Federation and western countries of EECCA are driven by the need to comply with the emission and fuel standards specified in the second sulphur protocol.

5.4.2. Exploring ancillary benefits of implementing the Kyoto protocol

This section presents the way that different use of Kyoto mechanisms could affect emissions of air pollutants, their associated control costs and ecosystem protection in 2010. It focuses solely on CO_2 emissions, and does not consider the other greenhouse gasses. As a result, the actual ancillary benefits can change when the other greenhouse gasses (especially methane — CH_4 and nitrous oxide — N_2O) are considered.

It should be noted that the results are of a descriptive 'what-if' character and are not intended to be prescriptive for any future implementation of the Kyoto protocol and air pollution policies. The purpose is to explore the possible ancillary benefits in larger European regions. This section is based on a study performed by the European Environment Agency (EEA, 2003).

There are potential ancillary benefits of climate policies for regional air pollution in Europe in 2010. In particular, reducing CO_2 emissions through structural changes in the energy sector or energy efficiency measures are likely to have beneficial spill-over effects on emissions of air pollutants. Different ways of meeting the Kyoto targets (in terms of the use of flexible instruments) will affect the potential for these ancillary benefits. In principle, reaching some of the required greenhouse gas emission reductions in WE by using emissions trading and/or joint implementation with CEE or the Russian Federation and western countries of EECCA would shift the ancillary benefits (additional reduction of air pollutants or reduced control costs) to these regions.

There are important differences between abatement strategies for climate change and regional air pollution that affect the actual ancillary benefits. In principle, the effects of climate change policies on global temperature and other climate change indicators do not depend on where emissions are reduced. Climate change policies therefore aim for the most cost-effective reductions worldwide. Policies to combat regional/local air pollution have to address the location of the emission sources. In a European context, it is mainly WE which needs to implement policies to meet its Kyoto target, the other two regions already meet their target under the baseline scenario. There are several options available for meeting the WE target (see Chapter 3).

These include reduction of CO_2 emissions from the energy sectors, reducing other greenhouse gases (methane, nitrous oxide and gases with a high global warming potential), sinks enhancement and the use of Kyoto mechanisms such as emissions trading, joint implementation and the clean development mechanism. The use of the Kyoto mechanisms can lead to emission reductions in the selling regions, but can also involve trade of so-called surplus emission allowances.

Below, three different climate change policy regimes are compared with the baseline scenario (see Section 5.4.1). The scenarios involve the same assumptions regarding air pollution control as the baseline scenario. Implementation of the Kyoto target is limited to addressing CO_2 emissions and does not consider the other greenhouse gases.

The following trading scenarios are explored and compared with the baseline:

1. Scenario: *Domestic action only (DAO)*. All Annex 1 Parties (countries from western and central Europe as well as EECCA, Canada, Australia, New Zealand and Japan) implement their Kyoto targets domestically, i.e. without use of the Kyoto mechanisms. The exception is trade within the regions considered, for example among the current EU Member States.
2. Scenario: *Trade — no use of surplus emission allowances (TNS)*. This scenario assumes full use of Kyoto mechanisms among Annex 1 Parties, but without any use of the 'surplus emission allowances'. This scenario explores the maximum ancillary benefits that can be obtained under a trade case.
3. Scenario: *Trade with surplus emission allowances (TWS)*. This scenario assumes full use of Kyoto mechanisms among Annex 1 Parties and includes the use of 'surplus emission allowances'. However, the supply of these allowances is limited to the level that maximizes the profits of the Russian Federation and Ukraine from selling the emission permits. According to calculations performed by the FAIR model, the supply of tradable permits on the basis of the 'surplus emission allowances' of some of the CEE countries and EECCA is 25 % of the total available potential.

In summary, the DAO scenario requires physical policies and measures at the domestic level whereas the TNS also involves physical policies and measures abroad, mainly through joint implementation (in CEE, the Russian Federation and western countries of EECCA) and the clean development mechanism (in developing countries). The TWS scenario reduces the need to use joint implementation/clean development mechanisms compared to the TNS scenario, and increases the use of emission trading.

Table 5.6 shows that climate policies, irrespectively of the scenario, can have important ancillary benefits by reducing emissions of air pollutants in Europe. In the DAO scenario, climate policies are implemented only in WE, so all ancillary benefits in terms of emissions are restricted to this region.

For the trading scenarios (TNS and TWS), the ancillary benefits of climate policies are partly shifted to CEE and the Russian Federation and western countries of EECCA. The main reason for this is that WE as well as other industrialised countries will use cost-effective emission reduction options by means of joint implementation in CEE, the Russian Federation and western countries of EECCA. The resulting CO_2 reduction will have consequences for air pollutant emissions and particularly for SO_2. Parts of the ancillary benefits are a result of a fuel switch from coal to gas, which reduces both CO_2 and SO_2 emissions. Fuel savings will also result in a decrease of emissions of NO_x and fine particulates, although smaller than for SO_2. Ancillary benefits for VOC emissions are low.

The emission reductions of atmospheric pollutants are more strongly coupled to the reduction of CO_2 in CEE than in WE (because of less strict environmental policies and more coal use). The net result of the trading scenarios is that the ancillary benefits in terms of emission reductions for Europe

		Emissions					Energy use			
Scenario	Region	CO_2	SO_2	NO_x	VOC	PM_{10}	Coal	Oil	Gas	Total
Domestic action only	WE	-12	-15	-7	-1	-5	-38	-9	-2	-7
	CEE	0	0	0	0	0	0	0	0	0
	Russian Federation and EECCA	0	0	0	0	0	0	0	0	0
	Total	**-7**	**-5**	**-4**	**-1**	**-2**	**-20**	**-7**	**-1**	**-5**
Trade — no use of surplus emission allowances	WE	-4	-7	-3	0	-3	-21	-3	3	-2
	CEE	-8	-16	-7	-2	-9	-23	-2	7	-4
	Russian Federation and EECCA	-11	-19	-12	-6	-7	-32	-9	-7	-9
	Total	**-6**	**-14**	**-6**	**-2**	**-6**	**-23**	**-4**	**0**	**-4**
Trade with surplus emission allowances	WE	-3	-4	-1	0	-2	-14	-2	3	-1
	CEE	-5	-11	-4	-1	-7	-17	0	6	-2
	Russian Federation and EECCA	-5	-15	-8	-4	-6	-26	-6	-3	-5
	Total	**-4**	**-10**	**-4**	**-2**	**-4**	**-17**	**-2**	**1**	**-2**

Change in 2010 emissions and energy mix compared to the baseline scenario (%)   Table 5.6.

Notes: The scenarios assume full use of land use, land-use change and forestry activities and clean development mechanisms for achieving carbon credits for sinks as agreed in Marrakech in 2001. This means that the Annex 1 countries could use a total amount of sink credits of 440 million tonnes CO_2, of which 270 million tonnes CO_2 could be used by the regions included in our study. The remaining total emission reduction obligation in Europe, after taking into account these sink credits, is about 500 million tonnes CO_2 (see also den Elzen and Both, 2002). We have assumed that the United States will implement the targets indicated in the Bush climate change initiative, which does not result in any improvement over our baseline scenario. At the time of the analysis, Australia had not indicated that it was not going to implement the Kyoto protocol. The rejection of the Kyoto protocol by Australia, however, has only a very small impact on the international permit market and thus on the analysis presented here (see Lucas et al., 2002). It should be noted that the total available 'surplus emission allowances' is larger than the required emissions reductions by Annex 1 Parties (from the baseline), a scenario that would assume trade with full use of 'surplus emission allowances' would simply equal the baseline.

Source: RIVM, IIASA

as a whole are higher than in the DAO scenario.

The difference in ancillary benefits between the trading scenarios TNS and TWS is a reduction of the emissions of SO_2 by 10 % instead of 14 % (see Table 5.6). Thus the introduction of a limited amount of surplus emission allowance on the market, based on maximizing profits, reduces the ancillary benefits by around one third. The trading scenarios increase ecosystem protection against acidification and eutrophication throughout Europe. The transboundary character of air pollution is reflected in the DAO scenario, where ecosystem protection increases in CEE and the Russian Federation and western countries of EECCA, and in the trading scenarios where most of the emission reductions take place outside WE but which still yield substantial increased ecosystem protection in WE.

In the scenarios with constraints on CO_2 emissions, the costs of controlling emissions that contribute to regional air pollution are clearly lower than in the baseline scenario (Table 5.7). The reductions in air pollution control costs again illustrate the synergistic effects of global and regional air pollution control policies. In the DAO scenario, which requires the strongest domestic climate policies, the costs of controlling CO_2 emissions are estimated at approximately EUR 12 billion/year. Expenditure on regional air pollution mitigation in WE decreases at the same time by approximately 9 % (EUR 7 billion/year in 2010). As expected, the trading scenarios involve less cost for controlling CO_2 emissions. Costs are

EUR 7 billion/year (of which EUR 2 billion/year is for domestic action) in the TNS scenario and EUR 4 billion/year (of which EUR 1 billion/year is for domestic action) in the TWS trading scenario. This is EUR 5–8 billion/year less than calculated for the DAO scenario. At the same time, the reduction in costs of controlling air pollution emissions reduces: EUR 2.5 billion/year less is saved by going from DAO to TNS scenario, and a further 1.6 billion less by going to TWS scenario.

The main conclusions of the analysis show that:

- Implementation of climate change policies to comply with the Kyoto protocol is likely to yield substantial ancillary benefits for air pollution in Europe. The ancillary benefits are expected to result in a decrease in air pollution emissions and control costs but also an increase in environmental protection. The realization of ancillary benefits depends on how the flexible mechanisms and surplus emission allowances are used to reach the Kyoto targets.
- The use of the flexible mechanism and surplus emission allowance is intended to, and will, reduce the costs of implementing the Kyoto protocol. However, using flexible mechanisms will also reduce the ancillary benefits in terms of control costs for air pollution in Europe.
- Using flexible mechanisms will shift ancillary benefits in terms of emissions reductions of air pollutants from WE to CEE and the Russian Federation and

Table 5.7.	Change in air pollutant emission control costs in 2010 compared to the baseline scenario					
	(EUR billion/year)			(%)		
	Domestic action only	Trade — no use of surplus emission allowances	Trade with surplus emission allowances	Domestic action only	Trade — no use of surplus emission allowances	Trade with surplus emission allowances
WE	-6.6	-2.9	-1.7	-9	-4	-2
CEE	0.0	-0.9	-0.6	0	-7	-5
Russian Federation and EECCA	0.0	-0.2	-0.2	0	-9	-7
Total	-6.6	-4.0	-2.5	-7	-5	-3

Source: IIASA

western countries of EECCA. For Europe, emission trading could lead to further emission reductions of regional air pollutants, which will also increase ecosystem protection in WE. Using surplus emission allowances will reduce these ancillary benefits, in particular for CEE and the Russian Federation and western countries of EECCA.

5.5. References

Capros, P., 1999. *European Union energy outlook to 2020.* DG for Energy, European Commission. Brussels.

CCE (Coordination Center for Effects), 1999. Posch, M., de Smet, P. A. M, Hettelingh, J-P., Downing, R. J. (eds). *Calculation and mapping of critical thresholds in Europe. Status report 1999.* CCE, National Institute of Public Health and the Environment (RIVM), Bilthoven, The Netherlands.

CCE (Coordination Center for Effects), 2001. Posch, M., de Smet, P. A. M, Hettelingh, J-P., Downing, R. J. (eds). *Modelling and mapping of critical thresholds in Europe. Status report 2001.* CEC, National Institute of Public Health and the Environment (RIVM), Bilthoven, The Netherlands.

Criqui, P. and Kouvaritakis, N., 2000. *World energy projections to 2030.* International Journal of Global Energy Issues 14(1, 2, 3, 4): 116–136.

EEA (European Environment Agency), 2001. *Air quality in larger cities in the European Union — A contribution to the Auto-Oil II programme.* Topic report No 3/2001. EEA, Copenhagen.

EEA (European Environment Agency), 2002a. *EuroAirNet status report 2000.* Larssen, S. and Kozakovic, L. European Topic Centre on Air Quality. EEA, Copenhagen

EEA (European Environment Agency), 2002b. *Greenhouse gas emission projections for Europe.* Technical report No 10/2002. EEA, Copenhagen.

EEA (European Environment Agency), 2002c. *The ShAir scenario. Towards air and climate change outlooks, integrated assessment methodologies and tools applied to air pollution and greenhouse gasses.* Albers, R., de Leeuw, F., Van Woerden, J. and Bakkes, J. EEA, Copenhagen.

EEA (European Environment Agency), 2003. van Vuuren, D. P., Cofala, J., Eerens, H. C., *et al. Exploring the ancillary benefits of the Kyoto protocol for air pollution in Europe.* EEA, Copenhagen. (Forthcoming.)

den Elzen, M. G. J. and Both, S., 2002. *Modelling emissions trading and abatement costs in FAIR 1.1.* National Institute for Public Health and the Environment, Bilthoven.

European Commission, 2000. *AOP II air quality report.* Brussels.

European Community, 1996. *EU Council Directive 96/61/EC concerning integrated pollution prevention and control.* OJ L257, 10/10/1996.

European Community, 1998. *EU Directive on the quality of petrol and diesel fuels 98/70/EC.* OJ L350.

European Community, 1999. *EU Directive 1999/13/CE on reduction of emissions of volatile organic compounds from use of organic solvents in certain activities and installations.* OJ L 163 29.06.1999.

European Community, 2001a. *Directive 2001/81/EC of the European Parliament and of the Council of 23 October 2001 on national emissions ceilings for certain atmospheric pollutants.* OJ L309. 27/11/2001.

European Community, 2001b. *Directive 2001/80/EC of the European Parliament and of the Council of 23 October 2001 on the limitation of certain pollutants into the air from large combustion plants.* OJ L309. 27/11/2001.

EMEP/MSC-W, 2002. *Emissions data reported to UNECE/EMEP — Quality assurance and trend analysis and presentation of WebDab.* Note 1/02, July 2002. Status EMEP/Meteorological Synthesising Centre-West, Oslo.

IMAGE-team, 2001. *The IMAGE 2.2 implementation of the IPCC SRES scenarios. A comprehensive analysis of emissions, climate change and impacts in the 21st century.* National Institute for Public Health and the Environment, Bilthoven.

Lucas, P., den Elzen, M. J. E. and van Vuuren, D. P., 2002. *Multi-gas abatement analysis of the Marrakesh accords.* Paper prepared for the CATEP workshop 'Global Trading' at the Kiel Institute for World Economics, Kiel, September 30-October 1, 2002. National Institute of Public Health and the Environment (RIVM), Bilthoven, The Netherlands

State of environment reports, various dates. Russian Federation, 1998. http://ceeri.ecoinfo.ru/state_report_98/eng/introduction/htm; http://ceeri.ecoinfo.ru/state_report_98/eng/town/htm
Ukraine, 2000. Kyiv, 2001.
Uzbekistan. http://www.grida.no/enrin/htmls/uzbek/report/index.htm
Turkmenistan. http://www.grida.no/enrin/htmls/turkmen/soe/indexen.htm
Kazakhstan. http://www.grida.no/enrin/htmls/kazahst/soe
Tajikistan. http://www.grida.no/enrin/htmls/tadjik/soe/air
Armenia. http://www.grida.no/enrin/htmls/armenia/soe2000/eng/index.htm

'State of the environment in Tbilisi,' 2000. http://www.ceroi.net/reports/tbilisi/issues/air_quality/sor.htm

'Summary environment state in the Republic of Moldova', 1998. http://www.grida.no/enrin/htmls/moldova/soe/urban/air.htm

UNECE, 1999. *Protocol to the 1979 Convention on Long-Range Transboundary air pollution (CLRTAP) to abate acidification, eutrophication and ground-level ozone.* 1 December 1999. Gothenburg, Sweden.

Van Aalst, R., 2002. *Analysis of the PM$_{10}$ data in AIRBASE.* European Environment Agency, Copenhagen

WHO (World Health Organization), 2002. *Structure of emissions 1990–1996.* http://www.md.mos.ru (in Russian).

6. Chemicals

During the past decade, growth of the European Union chemical industry has been higher than that of EU gross domestic product and than that of the chemical industry in either the United States or Japan. The chemical sector in central and eastern Europe, the Caucasus and central Asia experienced significant downturns during the early 1990s.

Emissions of many heavy metals and persistent organic pollutants in Europe have fallen during the past decade mainly as a result of the introduction of stricter national and regional regulatory frameworks, the use of improved pollution abatement systems by industry and the development of cleaner technologies.

There is a need for further global initiatives on mercury. High concentrations continue to be found in the Arctic environment despite cuts in European emissions. The neurological development of children in several native Arctic populations may be suffering damage as a result of dietary exposure to this toxic element.

Although there is much 'good news' about the effectiveness of policies leading to decreasing concentrations of several chemicals in the environment, there remain a number of instances where target levels are exceeded and which, for example, necessitate food recommendations for pregnant women. Dioxins and mercury in fish are two examples.

Monitoring and reporting of chemicals in Europe is uncoordinated with an imbalance between different substances. Pharmaceuticals and their metabolites are monitored occasionally. A relatively few selected heavy metals, persistent organic pollutants and pesticides seem to be the only groups of substances that are frequently monitored in most environmental areas, food, consumer products and human tissues. Integrated monitoring and exposure assessment should ideally consider all relevant sources during the life cycle of a product, emphasise the complete sequence of direct and indirect routes of exposure, and especially consider the exposure of sensitive groups. Most of these data are currently lacking.

Despite more than 25 years of regulation of chemicals in Europe, there remains a general lack of information and knowledge about the end uses and hazardous properties of most of the circa 30 000 existing substances currently on the EU market. With regard to existing chemicals, i.e. chemicals that were identified on the European market in 1981, current EU legislation only requires primary chemical producers and importers to provide limited information. Downstream users, e.g. industrial users, formulators and product manufacturers, do not have to provide any data. Information on the uses of specific substances is therefore difficult to obtain, and knowledge about subsequent environmental and human exposures from use of downstream products is scarce.

Current policy approaches to chemicals do not adequately address a number of issues that are of public concern e.g. combined exposures to multi-pollutants, and the impacts of some pollutants, e.g. endocrine disruptors and certain flame retardant chemicals present at low concentrations. Recognising the inadequacy of current procedures for chemical risk management, two recent and contrasting initiatives (the Stockholm convention on persistent organic pollutants and the EU chemicals policy White Paper) both incorporate precautionary-based approaches to risk prevention. The EU White Paper also places the burden of providing hazard information on the producer — a change in the development of European policy on chemicals.

6.1. Introduction

The chemical industry supplies a vast range of chemicals to virtually all sectors of the economy although the exact number of substances marketed within Europe is not known. The European inventory of existing chemical substances (EINECS) compiled by industry in 1981 identified 100 195 chemicals that year (although it is uncertain how many were actually marketed) and approximately 3 000 'new' substances have been brought onto the European market since that time (European Commission, 2001). A large proportion (about 30 %) of manufactured chemical products are consumed or further processed within the chemical industry itself. Basic chemicals undergo further treatment to be converted into chemical additives suitable for a variety of industrial, agricultural and consumer products. These include high value-added products such as medicines, adhesives, paints, dyes, plastics, fertilisers, pharmaceuticals, cosmetics and household products.

However, lack of access to information on chemical production, especially for hazardous chemicals, continues to impede policy-making in this field across Europe. The European coverage of monitoring data for halogenated organics in general and persistent organic pollutants (POP) in particular is rather patchy. Information on degradations, transformations, by-products and exposures to mixtures is also poor.

There is also increasing concern over the rising concentrations of a number of newly identified pollutants in the environment, such as alkoxy phenols, chlorinated paraffins and polybrominated flame retardants. Controls on the use and emissions of these substances may be required to prevent further wildlife and human exposure occurring.

This chapter reviews some of the key issues concerning the release of hazardous chemicals into the European environment. Trends in chemical production within the European region are discussed together with information on the key uses and routes leading to environmental releases. The state and impacts of chemical pollution within the environment are illustrated with selected examples that show the effectiveness of previous policy responses to these impacts. A number of areas are identified where better quality information is required (see Box 6.1.), and an assessment is made of the

current main challenges to the reduction of risks resulting from environmental exposure to hazardous chemicals.

6.2. Production and uses of chemicals

The EU is the largest chemical producing area in the world, accounting for 32 % of an estimated global turnover for chemical production of EUR 1 632 billion in 2001 (CEFIC, 2002). During much of the 1990s, the EU chemical industry grew faster than GDP (Figure 6.1), with total chemical production growing more strongly than other EU industry sectors over the past 10 years (3.2 % per year), and faster than the chemical sectors of the US (2.4 % per year) and Japan (1.4 % per year) (CEFIC, 2002). The drivers behind this growth are the stimulation of consumer demand for products based on new uses of chemicals, and the availability of many feedstocks (ethylene, benzene, propylene etc.) that are produced by the petrochemical industry (EEA, 1998).

In contrast to most western European (WE) countries, many countries in central and eastern Europe (CEE) experienced large falls in chemical production during the early 1990s in line with significant decreases in GDP that occurred during that time. Most CEE countries have since seen a recovery in chemical production although annual growth is generally lower than that in the WE countries. The chemical industry in eastern Europe, the Caucasus and central Asia (EECCA) has stabilised due to growth of exports (Breiter, 1997), but its competitiveness remains comparatively low with exports largely comprising raw materials rather than high value-added products.

The use and disposal of products containing hazardous chemicals has been linked to a range of potential impacts on the environment and human health. Concern is greatest for highly persistent chemicals which may remain in the environment for many years, and particularly those that can bioaccumulate in wildlife and humans. Table 6.1 provides some examples of environmentally persistent chemicals and their main uses.

Despite these concerns and the availability of some key data within the chemical industry, there is still very little robust and detailed information on pan-European production and import/export volumes of 'hazardous'

Figure 6.1.	Production volumes of chemicals relative to GDP for EU Member States 1991–1999

Sources: EU toxic CMR (carcinogenic, teratogenic, mutagenic and reprotoxic chemicals) production data: Eurostat, 2001a; total EU chemical production volumes: CEFIC, 2000; GDP: Eurostat, 2001b

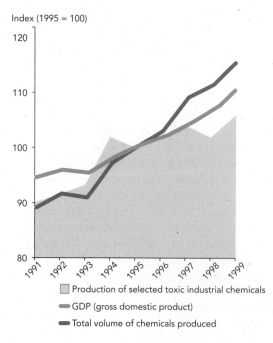

Index (1995 = 100)

- ▢ Production of selected toxic industrial chemicals
- ▬ GDP (gross domestic product)
- ▬ Total volume of chemicals produced

	Main sources and uses of some environmentally persistent chemicals		Table 6.1.

Abbreviation	Type of chemical	Applications/sources	
ACB	Alkylated chlorobiphenyls	PCB substitutes	Source: Based on Swedish EPA, 1993
CP	Chlorinated paraffins	C_{10}-C_{30} alkanes with 30–70 % chlorine, plasticisers for use in polymer manufacture, metal working fluids, flame retardants, paint additives	
Cyclodienes	Aldrin, endrin, dieldrin, endosulfan, chlordane, heptachlor	Pesticides	
DDE	4, 4-dichloro-diphenyl-dichloroethene	Degradation product of DDT	
DDT	4, 4-dichloro-diphenyl-trichloroethane	Insecticide (still used in tropical developing countries)	
HAC	Halogenated aliphatic compounds	Volatile halogenated solvents such as tri- and tetrachloroethylene and ethylene dichloride tar	
HCB	Hexachlorobenzene	Formerly used as a fungicide; also a combustion by-product	
HCH	Hexachlorohexanes	Used as insecticide. Several persistent isomers including lindane (gamma isomer)	
HMs	Heavy metals	Large numbers of potential sources e.g. combustion by-products, industrial processes, water treatment sludges, batteries, paints, anti-fouling coatings, zinc and cadmium from car tyres, mercury in dental amalgam, nickel from diesel, cadmium from phosphate fertilisers, arsenic, copper and chromium from wood preservatives	
NPN	Nonylphenol	Stable degradation intermediate of nonylphenol ethoxylates used as detergents and additives in latex and plastic goods	
Oms	Organo-metallic compounds	Mainly mercury, lead and tin compounds; mercury in paints; seed disinfectants; anti-sliming agents; lead in petrol; tin in marine anti-fouling agents	
PAC	Polycyclic aromatic compounds	Heterocyclic aromatic compounds, derivatives of PAHs (such as nitro-, chloro- and bromo-PAHs)	
PAE paint	Phthalatic acid esters (phthalates)	Plasticisers (e.g. in PVC — polyvinyl chloride); additives, varnishes; cosmetics; lubricants	
PAH	Polycyclic aromatic hydrocarbons	Crude oil; by-products of incomplete combustion by-products of fuel and wood; creosote wood preservative; coal tar	
PBB/PBDE	Polybrominated biphenyls/diphenyl ethers	Intermediates for chemical industry; brominated flame retardants	
PCB	Polychlorinated biphenyls (and their degradation products)	More than 200 substances (but not all congeners are found in technical product or in the environment); insulating fluid in transformers; cables; plasticisers; oil and paint additives; hydraulic fluids; combustion by-products	
PCC	Polychlorinated camphenes	Pesticides e.g. toxaphene, campechlor	
PCDD/F	Polychlorinated dibenzo-p-dioxins/dibenzofurans, collectively referred to here for simplicity as 'dioxins'	More than 200 substances; mainly by-products from combustion and other chemical processes, such as incineration; paper pulp bleaching and metal refining; as contaminants impurities in PCBs, PCP, transformer oils; and chlorinated phenolic herbicides; contaminants; incinerators; paper pulp bleaching	
PCDE	Polychlorinated diphenyl ethers	By-products of PCP manufacture; PCB substitutes; pesticide additives	
PCN	Polychlorinated napthalenes	Insulating fluids in capacitors; flame retardants; oil additives; wood preservatives, pesticides; combustion by-products	
PCP	Pentachlorophenol	Fungicides; bactericides; wood preservatives	
PCS	Polychlorinated styrenes	By-products of chemical processes	
PCT	Polychlorinated terphenyls	PCB substitutes	

chemicals accessible to policy-makers and the public. However, EU production volumes of selected toxic chemicals (i.e. those classified as carcinogenic, teratogenic, mutagenic and reprotoxic, CMR substances, according to EU Directive 67/548/EEC) increased during the 1990s, together with total chemical production as shown in Figure 6.1.

It should be noted that production volume alone is not necessarily an indicator of potential human exposure or environmental risk. In particular, as toxic chemicals will be used in various economic activities, emissions may take place during any stage of the chemical life cycle, from production and use through to waste treatment and disposal. Emissions may therefore vary on a case-by-case basis. Knowledge of both the production processes and subsequent emissions is therefore necessary in order to support activities aimed at reducing exposures. New mechanisms to inform consumers on the exposure to chemicals from product use have been proposed in the EU chemicals policy White Paper (European Commission, 2001).

> 🙁 Chemical production within the EU is increasing faster than GDP, illustrating an increasing 'chemical intensity' of EU GDP. The volume of selected hazardous chemicals produced is also increasing, albeit at a slower rate than the production of all chemicals.

6.3. Chemicals in the environment: emissions and concentrations of selected chemicals

Table 6.1 shows that environmentally persistent chemicals have a range of diverse uses, and hence the potential to be released into the environment (together with their degradation products) during production or product life cycles i.e. from raw material acquisition to final waste treatment and disposal. Actual emissions, concentrations and exposures of ecosystems, wildlife and humans will, however, vary between chemicals.

6.3.1. Emissions — heavy metals
Of the many heavy metals released from various products and processes, cadmium, lead and mercury are of great concern to human health because of their toxicity and their potential to cause harmful effects at low concentrations and to bioaccumulate.

Significant progress has been made in reducing emissions to air of these metals in the European region with 1995 emissions being about 50 % of 1990 levels and decreasing further to 40 % by 1999. Lead emissions in 1999 were down to about 17 000 tonnes/year and mercury and cadmium to 200 and 400 tonnes/year, respectively (EMEP, 2002).

All three groups of countries in the European region achieved absolute decreases of emissions (on a tonnage basis) for the three heavy metals over the period 1990–99. Figure 6.2. presents the data for the country groupings weighted by GDP. On this basis, WE released significantly lower amounts of the pollutants in 1999 than either CEE or EECCA. WE also exhibited the greatest percentage reduction in emissions for the period 1990-99.

Although controlling diffuse emissions of cadmium and mercury remains problematic (e.g. batteries), point source emissions of these metals have declined as a result of improvements in sectors such as wastewater treatment, incinerators and the metals sector. Factors contributing to this include large decreases of lead emissions from the transport sector following the introduction of unleaded petrol in the early 1990s (see Chapter 2.6.); continuing moves away from the use of lignite in the eastern European energy sector; and the introduction of improved pollution abatement technologies across a range of industrial and waste treatment sectors.

> 😊 Emissions of the toxic metals cadmium, lead and mercury decreased during the1990s, with emissions in 1999 being 40 % of those in 1990.

A number of recent policy initiatives has been introduced at the international level to address concerns raised by heavy metal emissions. The United Nations Economic Commission for Europe (UNECE) Convention on Long-Range Transboundary Air Pollution (CLTRAP) 1998 Aarhus protocol on heavy metals targets cadmium, lead and mercury and requires countries to reduce their emissions of these three metals to below their 1990 levels (or an alternative year between 1985 and 1995).

Similarly, the Fourth Ministerial Conference of the North Sea States committed signatory countries to end discharges, emissions and losses of hazardous substances, including cadmium, lead and mercury compounds by the year 2020. This target was incorporated into the Convention for the Protection of the Marine Environment of the North-East Atlantic (OSPAR convention) and the Helsinki Convention on the Protection of the Marine Environment of the Baltic Sea Area (HELCOM convention) in 1998. Although atmospheric emissions of these three metals are decreasing, there is clearly still much to be done under the OSPAR and HELCOM conventions. Through cessation of anthropogenic emissions of hazardous substances by 2020, these conventions aim to achieve concentrations close to background levels for those substances occurring naturally e.g. the heavy metals, or close to zero for man-made substances. Selected heavy metal emissions to inland and marine waters are addressed in Chapter 8.

The need for further global initiatives on mercury has also recently been highlighted (TemaNord, 2002; UNEP, 2002). Some European countries have had success in reducing emissions of this metal (Table 6.2) through a combination of substitution, e.g. of mercury cells used in chlorine production, and improvement in abatement technologies especially flue-gas cleaning.

More worryingly, however, a new report from AMAP (2002) raises concern over increasing levels of mercury in the Arctic, which may be acting as a global sink for the metal transported over long distances through the atmosphere. The most significant global man-made source is combustion, particularly of coal in Asia, which as a region is now responsible for half the world's mercury emissions, and Europe. Although European and North American emissions have decreased significantly since the 1980s, mercury concentrations have clearly continued to rise in some Arctic areas, and neurological development in the children of some native Arctic populations may be suffering damage through dietary exposure to the metal.

The TemaNord (2002) assessment notes that mercury and its compounds share many properties with some of the persistent organic chemicals listed in Table 6.1. The problem of mercury remains under active consideration by the United Nations Environment Programme (UNEP). Its Global Mercury Assessment Working Group meeting in September 2002 concluded that

there was sufficient evidence of significant global adverse impacts to warrant international action to reduce the risks to human health and/or the environment arising from the release of mercury into the environment. It agreed on an outline of possible options to address the adverse impacts of mercury at the global, regional, national and local levels and identified a

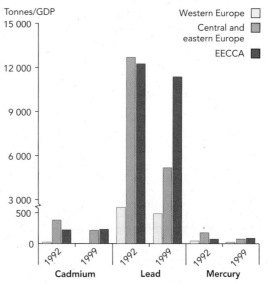

European emissions (tonnes/GDP) of cadmium, lead and mercury in 1990 and 1999 — Figure 6.2.

Notes: GDP as trillion US$. Data were not available for the following countries: Andorra, Kyrgyzstan, Liechtenstein, Malta, Monaco, San Marino, Tajikistan, Turkmenistan and Uzbekistan. Negative GDP growth was observed for eastern Europe, the Caucasus and central Asia during 1990–99.

Source: UNECE/EMEP Convention on Long-Range Transboundary Air Pollution

Trend of mercury emissions in Nordic countries (tonnes)		Table 6.2.	
Denmark		1982–83	1992–93
	Air	4.0-7.4	1.9-2.5
	Water	1.4	0.25
	Soil	1.4-1.6	0.2-0.3
	Total	6.8-10.4	2.4-3.1
Finland		1990	1997
	Air	1.1	0.6
Norway		1995	1999
	Air	1.1	1.1
	Water	0.6	0.4
	Soil	0.5	0.3
	Total	2.2	1.8
Sweden		1990	1995
	Air	1.5	0.9
	Water	0.2	0.6
	Total	1.7	1.5

Source: TemaNord, 2002

Box 6.1. Monitoring chemicals in the environment

There are many established regional or localised monitoring programmes that sample marine or land-based environmental media to monitor temporal trends in persistent organic pollutant (POP) concentrations e.g. the UNECE collaborative monitoring programmes, and EMEP initiatives based around the Convention on Long-Range Transboundary Air Pollution. However, there remains no comprehensive source of comparable pan-European data that would enable a clear picture of the extent of pollution by POPs to be established. Acknowledging the lack of comparability of present monitoring schemes due to the varied methodologies used, UNEP Chemicals has recently established a global network for monitoring of chemicals in the environment which aims to harmonise the methodologies and analyses of chemicals in the environment.

A joint EEA/European Science Foundation study on European monitoring of chemicals (EEA, 2003) concludes that: 'Monitoring is partial, uncoordinated, sometimes out of date, and, on many occasions, irrelevant to current policy needs; centralised knowledge about chemical monitoring activities that are conducted for different purposes is incomplete; there is a lack of integrated exposure assessments that consider all relevant exposure routes; there are huge data gaps in information on chemical exposures and impacts, especially concerning vulnerable groups and ecosystems; filling the data gaps adequately, via conventional approaches, would take several decades and millions of euro.'

New approaches to monitoring and exposure assessments are therefore needed to complement conventional approaches, which have focused mainly on monitoring the environmental media of air, water and soil. These now need to be streamlined and supplemented by macro-monitoring which focuses on material flows of chemicals into and through the environment, and micro-monitoring which focuses on micro-pollutants in biological issues or in sensitive parts of the technosphere such as sewage effluent and the stratosphere. These more integrated exposure assessments would cover a product's life cycle, focus on the intrinsic properties of priority chemicals, for example bioaccumulation and persistence, and make intelligent use of 'proxies' for the mixtures and other complexities that bedevil the control of chemicals in the environment.

range of possible immediate actions in light of findings on the impacts of mercury. The UNEP Governing Council addressed the matter at its session in February 2003.

6.3.2. Emissions — persistent organic pollutants

Persistent organic pollutants (POPs) are a group of specific chemicals regulated under international agreements to reduce or eliminate their use and release to the environment. The CLTRAP POPs protocol (UNECE, 1998) lists 16 substances as POPs, and the Stockholm convention on persistent organic pollutants (2001) identifies a subset of 12 of these substances targeted for release reduction or elimination. The manufacture, use or importation of 11 POPs has already been banned under EU legislation. The 16 POPs identified under the UNECE protocol are: aldrin*, chlordane*, [chlordecone*], DDT*, dieldrin*, endrin*, heptachlor*, hexachlorobenzene (HCB*), [hexachloro-cyclohexane (HCH)], mirex*, toxaphene*, polychlorinated biphenyls (PCBs*), [hexa-brominated biphenyls (HBBs)], poly-chlorinated dibenzodioxins and the related furans — known collectively as dioxins — and [polyaromatic hydrocarbons (PAHs)]. All the substances listed are also defined as POPs under the UNEP POPs convention, except those shown in [square brackets] and * denotes substances whose manufacture, importation or use within the EU has been prohibited.

The international agreements also have mechanisms by which other chemicals that meet defined criteria of toxicity, persistence and ability to bioaccumulate can be added to the defined POPs list. POPs are released into the environment either as a result of their intentional use e.g. as pesticides such as lindane or DDT, as contaminants of other products, or as by-products from industrial

Figure 6.3.	Total HCB emissions in Europe and concentrations in human milk in Sweden

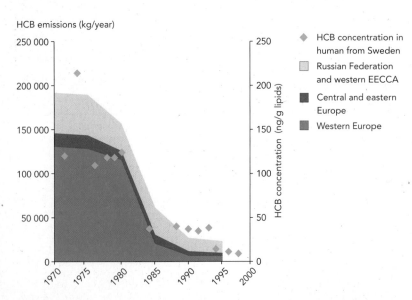

HCB emissions (kg/year)

HCB concentration (ng/g lipids)

- ◆ HCB concentration in human from Sweden
- ☐ Russian Federation and western EECCA
- ■ Central and eastern Europe
- ■ Western Europe

Notes: Data were not available for: Andorra, Armenia, Azerbaijan, Cyprus, Georgia, Kazakhstan, Kyrgyzstan, Liechtenstein, Malta, Monaco, San Marino, Tajikistan, Turkey, Turkmenistan and Uzbekistan. Data available for the former German Democratic Republic (to 1990) were included in the western European country grouping.

Sources: HCB emission data: Münch and Axenfeld, 1999 ; human milk data: Norén and Meironyté, 2000

☺ Although hexachlorobenzene emissions have decreased throughout Europe, the rate of decrease has slowed markedly since 1990. Further reductions in hexachlorobenzene emissions with its eventual elimination from use should be feasible.

☹ Hexachlorobenzene remains widely dispersed throughout the region due to long-range atmospheric transport processes and local 'hot spots' that reflect high levels of local use or contamination.

processes e.g. dioxins, PAHs, HCB. The long-range transportation and transboundary distribution of POPs means that they pose an environmental threat not only within the country in which they are used but also to geographically distant countries (Swedish EPA, 1998a). For example, residues from past global use of POPs are found in many remote regions of the Arctic, Baltic and other areas despite their use or emission never having taken place in these regions. Environmental and health monitoring programmes, especially in remote environments, are crucial in identifying future problems resulting from long-range transport of pollutants.

Concentrations of several of the priority POPs have decreased over recent decades due to a reduction in their production and use, accompanied by bans and other restrictions. Hexachlorobenzene (HCB) provides one example of recent reduction trends, and the link between decreased emissions and reduced concentrations in

breast milk (Figure 6.3). HCB is a potential human carcinogen that was used as a pesticide/fungicide from the 1950s until the early 1980s. Its use as an agricultural chemical was banned in many European countries by the mid-1980s (Münch and Axenfeld, 1999). The presence of hazardous chemicals in breast milk is of concern since babies are particularly sensitive to low doses of chemicals and breast milk is, in most cases, their main source of early nutrition.

Despite the banning of HCB as an agricultural chemical, it continues to be released via a number of other pathways e.g. via chlorinated solvent manufacture, as a contaminant in other pesticide formulations and from combustion processes, and therefore remains widely dispersed in the environment (Figure 6.4).

There are also positive trends in other parts of the European environment as regards chlorinated organic compounds. The pulp and paper industry is very important to the

Modelled HCB background soil concentrations in Europe, 1998   Figure 6.4.

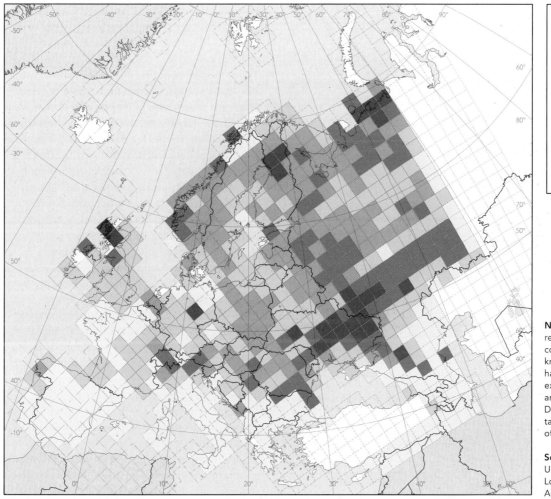

HCB soil concentration

1998 (ng/g)

- 0.01 - 0.05
- 0.05 - 0.08
- 0.08 - 0.10
- 0.10 - 0.20
- 0.20 - 0.35
- No data
- Outside data coverage

Notes: Concentrations represent the average soil concentration in a 150 x 150 km area. Localised areas having high HCB levels will exist within these larger areas. As a reference, the Dutch government has a target value for HCB in soil of 2.5 ng/g.

Sources: EMEP/MSC-East; UNECE Convention on Long-Range Transboundary Air Pollution programme

Finnish economy, but the industry uses a lot of water and different chemicals in the production processes. One of the main sources of the harmful organic compounds discharged to watercourses has been bleaching processes. Before the early 1980s, bleaching processes were conventional, using elemental chlorine with partial substitution with chlorine dioxide. Between 1985 and 1995, the use of elemental chlorine was phased out and effluent treatment was improved. As a result, the amount of chlorinated organic compounds found in receiving waters has decreased markedly (Figure 6.5).

| Figure 6.5. | The concentration of organic chlorine compounds originating from pulp bleaching in incubated mussels |

Source: Herve et al., 2002

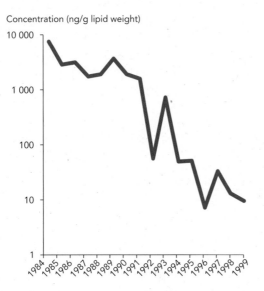

Concentration (ng/g lipid weight)

Box 6.2. Survey of dioxin sources in the Baltic region

Dioxins and furans are very toxic, lipophilic and persistent. In order to establish an overview of the situation concerning dioxin sources in the Baltic region, the Danish Environment Protection Agency initiated and financed a survey of dioxin releases in the year 2000 from some countries for which detailed dioxin surveys did not already exist. The main route for direct releases to the environment is emission into air. The air emissions from the Baltic countries were previously estimated in the EU financed project entitled POPcycling Baltic. Releases from eastern European countries have been relatively low compared to the western European countries, due mainly to the more widespread use of waste incineration in western Europe.

From the middle of the 1980s, releases from the western European countries decreased considerably — a trend that continued during the 1990s. However in 1993–95 per capita emission from the western European countries was still higher than from eastern European countries.

New studies of air emissions in Poland show that the main sources are waste incineration and uncontrolled combustion processes such as landfill fires and burning of household waste.

Air emissions are also the main source in Estonia, Latvia and Lithuania; 'power generation and heating' and 'uncontrolled burning processes' are the most important source categories in all three countries.

Source: Lassen, et al., 2003

Mirroring the reduced emissions and concentrations of many POPs, human exposure to POPs and other substances with similar properties has also decreased over the past few decades (Figure 6.6; see also Box 6.2.).

With the exception of the flame retardant polybrominated diphenyl ethers (PBDEs — see Box 6.3.), all substances declined in absolute concentration values during this time. The spatial distribution of the contaminants also changed over the time period studied.

Although the environmental concentrations of some chemicals currently defined as POPs have fallen, this is not so for all of them. For example, PCB concentrations remain sufficiently high in several Arctic areas to raise concerns about the possible ecological effects of disturbances that they may cause to the immunological, reproductive and neurobehavioural systems of marine mammals and other animals (AMAP, 2002). Elevated levels of PCBs in maternal pregnancy serum have also been observed in the Faroe Islands' population where exposure levels were three to fourfold higher than in other studies performed in the United States, the Netherlands, Germany and in northern Quebec (Longnecker et al., 2003).

There is also concern about the wide dispersion and increasing environmental concentrations of persistent, bioaccumulative and toxic (PBT) chemicals that are not currently classified as POPs such as chlorinated paraffins and certain flame retardants (Figure 6.7). A number of such chemicals are included in the OSPAR and HELCOM conventions which aim for the cessation of emissions, discharges and losses of these substances within a generation i.e. by 2020. For example, the extremely persistent fluorinated compound used as a stain repellent and in other applications, has been measured in some Arctic animals (AMAP, 2002). The principal manufacturer announced a voluntary phase-out of this chemical in 2000, after its persistency and bioaccumulative properties in humans were demonstrated. Several bodies currently advocate the classification of these PBT substances as 'new' POPs under the POPs protocol and the Stockholm convention.

Another potentially significant environmental problem arises from the large quantities of old and out-dated pesticides (some of which

☺ Concentrations of a variety of contaminants in human milk from Sweden have decreased significantly since the 1970s. The contaminant levels reflect the decreasing levels of general environmental contamination and background levels in the population.

☹ There is concern over the dispersion of polybrominated flame retardants in the environment. Concentrations of polybrominated diphenyl ethers have risen steeply in Swedish human milk since the 1970s despite these substances never having been manufactured in that country. Although concentrations are now declining, they remain many times higher than previously.

are POPs) that are known to be stockpiled in many CEE countries and EECCA (see Table 6.3). Storage facilities for these chemicals are frequently inadequate, ranging from simple holes in the ground and open sheds in fields to decomposing concrete bunkers. In many cases the poor storage facilities create high levels of potential risk to both the environment and humans (Klint, 2001). Factors contributing to the build-up of unwanted pesticide stocks include poor stock management, inappropriate marketing, lack of adequate regulatory infrastructures, poor product packaging, purchases (or donations) of unsuitable products in impractical quantities, and prohibition of use (Jensen, 2000).

Progress in destroying stocks of unwanted pesticides is impeded by a lack of information on quantities and location. Although the quantities referred to in Table 6.3 are from the latest official compilation produced by the International HCH and Pesticides Association (IHPA), it is recognised that they are subject to great uncertainty. The estimates will be revised by IHPA in June 2003 taking into account newly available data, although developing an accurate inventory will necessarily be a long-term goal for some countries.

A number of international organisations have programmes for the collection and disposal of obsolete pesticides in developing countries and those with economies in transition. These include the Food and Agriculture Organization of the United Nations (FAO), UNEP, Inter-Organization Programme for the

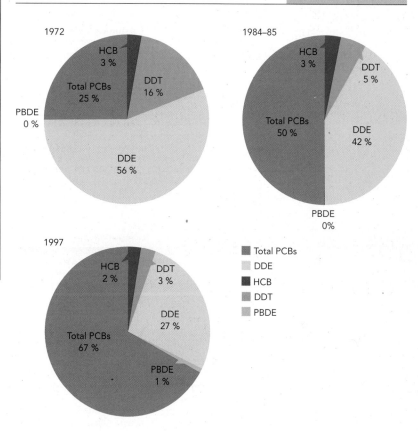

Amounts and distribution of organohalogen contaminants in human milk — Figure 6.6.

Notes: The area of the pie charts is proportional to the total sum of the contaminants in human milk from Sweden in the given years. Some metabolites e.g. DDE derived from DDT have much higher concentrations in milk than the original pollutant.

Source: Norén and Meironyté, 2000

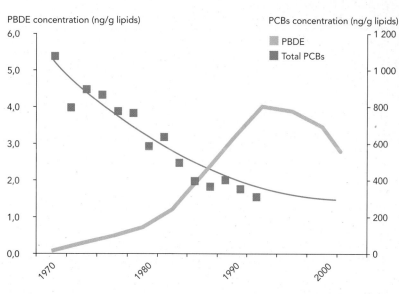

Concentrations and temporal trend of polybrominated diphenyl ethers (flame retardant substances) and polychlorinated biphenyls in human milk, 1972–2000 — Figure 6.7.

Sources: Swedish human milk data: Norén and Meironyté, 2000; Peltola and Ylä-Mononen, 2001

Table 6.3.	Estimated stockpiles of obsolete pesticides in central and eastern Europe and EECCA countries		

Notes: The quantities shown are based on estimated data in 1990s. New estimates will be reviewed and the inventory updated by IHPA in June 2003.

Source: IHPA, 2001

Country	Production and estimated waste in tonnes	Related problems in soil and water
Albania	Former lindane production sites	
Azerbaijan	20 000	
Armenia	Incomplete information but known to possess considerable stocks of obsolete pesticides	
Belarus	6 000	
Bosnia-Herzegovina	Data not available	
Bulgaria	4 000	
Croatia	Some estimates exist	
Czech Republic	The main stocks of obsolete pesticides were destroyed in early 1990s. Inventory and control is done by new Waste Act and new Chemical Act	
Estonia	700	
Eastern Germany (former)	Several 100 000s	Large-scale soil pollution with HCH and DDT
Georgia	2 000 (1999 report)	
Hungary	Ideas for inventory presented and start-up of pilot project	49 000 tonnes soil?
Kazakhstan	Production sites in west Kazakhstan, east Kazakhstan in Akmolinsk	Large diffuse soil pollution. Former agricultural aerodromes
Kyrgyzstan	171	Large-scale diffuse soil pollution? In former agricultural aerodromes in the southern regions (Osh), groundwaters are polluted by pesticides and fertilisers
Latvia	2 000	
Lithuania	3 280	3 500 tonnes polluted soils
FYR of Macedonia	33 000–38 000. Former lindane production	
Republic of Moldova	6 600	
Poland	50 000–60 000. Large numbers of time-bombs (bunkers) stored in the former producer's area	Direct spread from bunkers to surrounding soils and threat to groundwater
Romania	1 030	Big chemical plants at Bacau, Râmnicu, Vâlcea, Craiova, Pitesti and Turda historically produced large quantities of pesticides
Russian Federation	17 000–20 000. Former production at 23 factories	
Slovenia	350–400	
Slovak Republic	Ideas for inventory presented and start-up of pilot project	
Tajikistan		Large areas of soil pollution in the Amu-Darya and Syr-Darya basins
Turkmenistan	1 671	
Ukraine	15 000	Large regional soil pollution
Uzbekistan	10 000–12 000	Large diffuse soil pollution in Fergana, Andijan and Khorezm regions. Agricultural aerodromes

Sound Management of Chemicals, World Health Organization (WHO), United Nations Industrial Development Organization (UNIDO), industry and various non-governmental organisations. Signatory developed countries to the Stockholm POPs convention (UNEP, 2001) are also obliged to cooperate with countries requiring assistance in identifying POPs stockpiles, and ensure that they are managed or disposed of in an environmentally sound manner, which it is hoped will improve the existing situation in many countries.

6.4. Exposures and impacts of chemicals: selected illustrations

Human exposure to toxic chemicals can occur through a number of routes with diet and exposure via consumer products being two significant pathways. Recent examples of such exposures include elevated dioxin concentrations in UK fish oil supplements (where 12 of 33 products exceeded the new EU food safety limit) (FSA, 2002), and high concentrations of phthalates in children's toys in Denmark (Figure 6.8).

However, any adverse impacts of such exposures on human health or wildlife remain unclear. This is due to the large number of confounding factors, e.g. diet, exposure pathways, exposure to degradation products, and delays between exposure and observation of effects that hinder the establishment of causal relationships. Some of the issues are illustrated in the case of chemicals suspected of interfering with the hormonal systems of animals — the endocrine disrupting chemicals (see Box 6.4). Issues concerning trends in health impacts from chemicals are discussed further in Chapter 12.

Table 6.1 listed several chemicals known to persist in the environment together with examples of their uses and emission sources. Ecological impacts documented for wildlife which are associated with the presence of such chemicals are shown in Table 6.4, together with an assessment of the strength of the evidence for the association.

6.5. Progress in risk management?

Despite more than 25 years of chemical regulation in Europe and elsewhere, there remains a serious lack of public information on the amounts of hazardous chemicals

---

Box 6.3. Polybrominated flame retardants

PBDEs (polybrominated diphenyl ethers) are a family of structurally related flame retardant chemicals widely used in polyurethane foams and electronic goods. Some of these substances have high potential for uptake and accumulation by fish and other aquatic and terrestrial organisms. Concern has also recently been expressed that the octa-and deca- members of the PBDE suite of chemicals may break down in the environment to form more harmful compounds. The main non-workplace exposure pathway for humans is thought to be via the food chain.

In contrast to other organohalogen compounds, PBDE concentrations increased rapidly in breast milk from Swedish mothers during the period 1972–97 (see Figure 6.6) although recent levels appear to be decreasing due to due to substitution of one main substance (penta-BDE) in products.

PBDEs can migrate from flame-retardant materials in which they are contained and are therefore now widely dispersed in the environment. In December 2002, the European Union decided to ban the use of penta- and octa-BDE. The ban does not cover a third main controversial flame retardant (deca-BDE), with the law instead calling for the drafting of an 'immediate' risk reduction strategy for this chemical. Brominated flame retardants are also included in the list of chemicals for priority action under the OSPAR hazardous substances strategy.

Number of Danish toys and other articles for children found to contain phthalates above the maximum concentration limit (0.05 %) specified in Danish law	Figure 6.8.

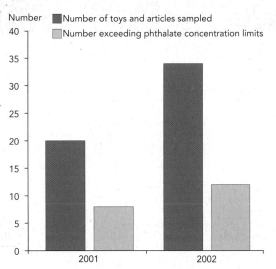

Source: Rastogi and Worsoe, 2001; Rastogi et al., 2002

Box 6.4. Endocrine disruptors in the environment

For more than 30 years, concern has been expressed over the potential adverse effects that may result from exposure to the group of chemicals known as endocrine disruptors which affect the functioning of the endocrine systems in wildlife and humans. For example, recent UK research on hormone disruption in fish performed for the Environment Agency of England and Wales revealed changes in the sexual characteristics of two coarse fish species in 10 river catchments and confirmed the presence of feminised male fish of both species (Environment Agency, 2002). The reproductive capability of the fish was also affected with up to half of the male fish at several sites failing to produce sperm. Steroid oestrogens which are released in small quantities from sewage works are thought to be the most important endocrine disruptors in British rivers (CEH, 2000).

The World Health Organization (WHO) has published a global assessment of the state of the science with respect to endocrine disruption in humans, experimental studies and wildlife species (WHO, 2002).

Table 6.4. | Some ecological impacts and possible associations with chemicals

Notes: The strength of the association is assessed on the scale: 1 = no observed association, 2 = suspected association, 3 = weak association, 4 = clear association, 5 = significant association.

Sources: EEA, 1998 (large-scale effects); Swedish EPA, 1998b (impairments in wildlife in relation to EDCs)

Observation/impact	Species	Substance	Association
Large-scale effects			
Eggshell thinning	Guillemot, eagle, osprey, peregrine falcon	DDT/DDE	5
Reproduction	Seal, otter	PCB	4
Skeletal malformation	Grey seal	DDT, PCB	4
Pathological changes	Seal	PCB, DDT, metabolites	3
Reproduction	Mink	PCB	5
Reproductive disturbances	Osprey	DDT, PCB	5
Reproductive disturbances	Eagle	DDT, PCB	2-3
Reproduction (M74 syndrome)	Salmon	Chlorinated substances	2
Imposex	Molluscs e.g. dogwhelk	TBT	5
Impairments in wildlife in relation to endocrine disrupting chemicals (EDCs)			
Sperm quality, cryptorchidism	Panther		2-3 (effects observed in inbred population)
Population decrease	Mink, otter		2-3
Female reproductive disorders, adrenocortical hyperplasia	Seal		4-5 4-5
Eggshell thinning Embryotoxicity and malformations Malformation of reproductive tract Reproductive behaviour	Birds		4-5 4-5 2-3 2-3
Microphalli and lowered testosterone levels	Alligators		3-4 (effects seen in connection with accidental contamination)
Vitellogenin	Fish		4-5
Masculinisation Lowered testosterone levels Reduced testis size M74 and early mortality syndromes			3-4 2-3 2-3 1-2
Imposex	Molluscs		5

produced, the uses of such chemicals in downstream products and processes, the amounts released to the various environmental media, and the effects of environmental and human exposures. Such information has either never been established, or else is not publicly available because of 'commercial confidentiality' issues. For example, there are insufficient data to conduct a basic risk assessment for 86 % of EU high production volume chemicals (ECB, 1999). The threat that chemical releases may pose to humans and the environment cannot, in many cases, be assessed. It must be remembered too, that absence of evidence (of ill effects) is not the same as evidence for the absence of such effects (EEA, 2001 — see Box 6.5.). A number of wider questions remain that Wallström (2002) and others have raised, for example:

- How can risks be combined to reflect different types of exposures and cumulative impacts?
- How can we account for interactions between host and exposure factors (including genetic, lifestyle, host susceptibility)?
- What options are there for developing policies that address mixtures of chemicals and the 'cocktail effect'?

- What are the current research priorities: exposure pathways and low dose impacts, or mechanisms of action?

Releases or use of some chemicals have resulted in significant environmental damage (EEA, 2001 — see Box 6.5.). Unlike products such as pharmaceuticals, no pre-market toxicity testing was required for most of these and so knowledge about their adverse effects was not available before they were used in large quantities e.g. DDT.

Evidence of dioxins and PCBs in food and livestock feedstuffs (in Belgium in 1999, 2000), phthalates exceeding permitted concentrations in children's toys (in Denmark in 2001, 2002), and flame retardants in human milk (in Sweden in 2000) illustrate the potential for accumulation from low exposures and possible risks.

Clearly, a top priority should be to get basic data on the properties of such substances that are produced and used, and especially those where emissions during production, use or disposal are significant (compared to their hazard potential). Currently industry has to submit notification dossiers for 'new chemicals' e.g. chemicals that were not identified on the European market in 1981. About 300 to 350 new substances are notified every year. The notification dossier should provide information on the substance, e.g. production process, proposed uses, results from analysis of physical and chemical properties, and test reports from toxicological and eco-toxicological assays.

However, even having such basic data cannot exclude the possibility that effects will occur at low doses and/or over a lifelong exposure. The precautionary principle may guide in the direction of reacting on early warnings, but data are still needed to provide a basis for applying the precautionary principle in practice. Having publicly available data and information on the substances in use may allow both the manufacturers, the industrial users (downstream users) and even consumers to take informed decisions on the risk associated with the use of a substance (see Box 6.6.) — little information is currently available about which substances can be safely used.

The European Commission acknowledges that current policies for risk assessment and control of chemicals take too long to implement. It also recognises that the

current risk assessment process used for 'existing' substances (those declared to be on the market before 1981) is 'slow and resource-intensive and does not allow the system to work efficiently and effectively' (European Commission, 2001). In addition to the proposals contained within the recent EU chemicals policy White Paper (see below), a number of other initiatives have been agreed in recent years that aim to reduce the environmental levels of chemicals (see Table 6.5).

6.6. Three recent initiatives: the EU chemicals policy White Paper, the Stockholm convention on POPs and the globally harmonised system of classification and labelling of chemicals (GHS)

The proposals outlined in the EU chemicals policy White Paper (European Commission, 2001) are among the most significant

---

Box 6.5. Association and causality

It is sometimes relatively easy to show that a measure of ill health, e.g. the number of hospital admissions per day, is associated with a possible cause such as the day-to-day variation in levels of air pollutants. To show that a causal relationship exists, a number of guideline tests have been developed. These include the consistency of results between different studies, the way in which the results of different studies fit together (coherence), whether there is a 'dose-response' relationship between the proposed causal factor and the effect, and whether the sequence of events makes sense i.e. the cause always precedes the effect.

Proof of causality is often very difficult to establish, but by the application of these and other criteria, an expert judgement as to whether an association is likely to be causal can often be made. Where effects are likely to be serious and/or irreversible, then a low level of proof as in the 'precautionary principle' may be sufficient to justify the removal or reduction of the probable causes.

Sources: WHO; EEA

Box 6.6. Voluntary phase-out of perfluorooctanyl sulphonate production

The oil and water repellent chemical perfluorooctanyl sulphonate (PFOS) was developed in the 1950s and has been used worldwide in a variety of specialist fire-fighting foams and oil and grease-resistant coatings for textiles and paper packaging.

Concerns over the potential health and environmental risks of this and similar chemicals were raised after its recent discovery at low concentrations in human and animal tissues from around the world. Despite there being no unambiguous evidence of toxicity, in a rare precautionary initiative to stop the use of the substance its principal manufacturer announced a voluntary phase-out of production. The move led other makers of similar compounds to launch their own investigations into the environmental fate, transport and effects of perfluorinated substances. A number of manufacturers have since agreed to phase-out these compounds and a subsequent 2002 Danish Environmental Protection Agency study found only three of 21 samples contained PFOS-like compounds. Danish environment minister Hans Christian Schmidt commended the phase-out as a good example of producer responsibility, noting that 'A number of companies have made a conscious choice not to use these problematic chemicals even though they are free to do so' (ENDS, 2002).

Table 6.5.	Some initiatives for reducing chemicals in the environment

Instrument	Year	Objectives
Montreal protocol	1987	Phase out certain ozone-depleting substances
Responsible care	1989	Industry initiative to promote environmental responsibility via concepts such as: • Sustainable development • Product stewardship • Implementation of good practice • Take-back schemes • Integrated product placement • Development of company pollutant release and transfer registers (PRTRs)
HELCOM convention	1992	Prevent and eliminate pollution to the Baltic Sea
Basel Convention on the Control of Transboundary Movements of Hazardous Wastes and their Disposal	Text concluded in 1989, and convention entered into force in 1992	Reduce/minimise hazardous wastes at source
OSPAR and HELCOM conventions	1998	Reduce discharges, emissions and losses of hazardous substances to the North Sea to near-zero or background levels by 2020
Rotterdam Convention on Prior Informed Consent	1998	Exporters of hazardous chemicals to get consent of receiving country before delivery
International Council of Chemical Associations (ICCA)	1998	Compiling hazard assessment information on 1 154 HPV chemicals by 2004
UNECE POPs protocol	1998	Reduce air emissions of POPs
UNECE heavy metals protocol	1998	Reduce emissions of cadmium, mercury and lead to 1990 levels
EU water framework directive	2000	An integrated approach to protecting water resources. Defines emission reduction/elimination targets for a limited number of priority hazardous substances. No comparable legislation currently exists for soils
Stockholm convention on POPs	2001	Elimination of POPs (production and use)
UNEP Global Assessment of Mercury	2001	Review health and environmental impacts of mercury and compile information on control and prevention strategies to potentially form a basis for international action
Globally harmonised system of classification and labelling of chemicals	2002	1. To enhance the protection of human health and the environment by providing an internationally comprehensible system for hazard communication 2. To provide a recognised framework for those countries without an existing system 3. To reduce the need for testing and evaluation of chemicals 4. To facilitate international trade in chemicals whose hazards have been properly assessed and identified on an international basis
Johannesburg summit	2002	Minimise adverse effects of chemicals on health and the environment by 2020. Implement the new globally harmonised classification and labelling system for chemicals by 2008

potential developments for risk assessment and management processes in the European region. The White Paper recognises that the public has a right of access information about the chemicals to which they are exposed (see Box 6.7). It reassesses existing EU directives and amendments and advocates a high level of protection for human health and the environment based on the precautionary principle. The Commission proposes to shift responsibility for generating and assessing data concerning the risks of use of substances onto industry. Downstream users would also be responsible for all aspects of the safety of their products and would have to provide information on use and exposure.

The White Paper sets out a timetable under which 'existing' substances (for which very little risk assessment data exist) would have to undergo assessment. 'Existing' and 'new' substances would be subject to the same risk assessment procedures using a single REACH (registration, evaluation, and authorisation of chemicals) system. The requirements that manufacturers/users of chemicals have to follow will depend on the proven or suspected hazardous properties, uses and exposures of the chemical concerned. The costs of implementing the REACH system have been estimated at between EUR 1.4 billion and EUR 7 billion over 10 years (most probably EUR 3.6 billion (RPA, 2002)). In comparison, EU chemical production in 2001 was valued at EUR 518 billion (CEFIC, 2002). No estimates have yet been made of the external health and environmental costs of chemicals (EEA, 1999), although such estimates are available for the energy and transport sectors (EEA, 2000).

Even though the proposed regime is a substantial improvement over that which currently exists, the new proposals do not go as far as some environmental organisations would like. For example, it has been recommended that: an EU chemicals policy should ensure that transparency of information is guaranteed; persistent and bioaccumulative chemicals should be phased out; the strength of evidence for regulation should be such that 'reasonable doubt' over safety is sufficient to lead to regulatory measures; endocrine disrupting substances should be included in the 'authorisation' procedure; and new non-animal testing techniques awaiting approval are reviewed as a matter of priority (FoE, 2002). Furthermore, the new system operates on

higher volume boundaries to trigger the need for testing than currently in force. There is therefore likely to be a need to check in future regulations that this compromise with industry is not under-protective for new chemicals.

The Stockholm convention on POPs (2001) aims to protect health and the environment through controlling POPs production and emissions. Like the EU chemicals policy White Paper, the concept of precaution as an important element in chemical risk management is acknowledged within the convention (Willis, 2001). For example, whether chemicals proposed as meeting POPs criteria are accepted under the convention is to be decided 'in a precautionary manner'.

Further progress in the protection of the public against chemical hazards and the risk associated with their exposure necessitates that better information on chemicals be made available. The new globally harmonised system of classification and labelling of chemicals (GHS) that was adopted in December 2002 (UNECE, 2002) will dramatically increase the level of information and access to it. Chemicals will be classified according to their potential hazards to humans and the environment. Related information will be communicated and displayed to the public so that appropriate protective measures can be

---

Box 6.7. Information for policy-makers and the public: pollutant release inventory initiatives

Pollutant release and transfer registers (PRTRs) are inventories of pollutant releases and transfers to the environment detailed by source. They provide an important means for members of the public to obtain information about the chemicals to which they are exposed, and governments to assess the relative contributions of different emission sources. They therefore enable prioritisation of sources in terms of developing strategies to eliminate or reduce the releases of pollutants, and measurement of progress towards the goal of minimising their emissions.

Increasing numbers of European countries now operate pollutant release inventories, although they often differ both with respect to media covered (air, water, land, waste, etc.) and the threshold and types of chemicals for which reporting is mandatory (OECD, 2000). Regional and international PRTR initiatives have also been developed e.g. OSPAR for emissions to the North Sea, and the pan-European EMEP/Corinair atmospheric emissions inventory.

Recognising both the utility of registers and the need to encourage their development on a national scale, a number of initiatives have been taken to facilitate their introduction in countries currently without release inventories. For example, the UNECE Aarhus convention on access to information, public participation in decision-making and access to justice in environmental matters was adopted in 1998. Under the convention, a working group on pollutant release and transfer registers was established to assist in the implementation of Article 5, establishing public access to information dealing with the environmental release or transfer of pollutants through the provision of national pollutant release and transfer registers. A protocol concerning implementation of this aspect of the convention has been prepared for the fifth 'Environment for Europe' ministerial conference, Kiev, 2003.

taken. Through the different steps from production, handling and transport to use, chemical products will be marked with universally understandable pictograms. The GHS also includes safety data sheets, presenting standardised content and extended information. The system, called for by the Rio summit in 1992, is now ready to be implemented, as requested at the Johannesburg summit (Article 22(c) of the plan of implementation).

Implementing EU environmental legislation will help the accession countries to meet the challenges in environmental protection. They need to include around 300 pieces of EU environmental law (some of them relevant to chemicals) into their national legislation, as well as to implement and enforce these laws. Most of these countries need to strengthen the environmental administration of ministries and agencies but especially also of local and regional offices.

In order to help the countries, the EU is assisting financially, for example with the LIFE programme, the Phare programme and the instrument for structural policies for pre-accession (ISPA); as well as with technical support through the twinning system. Furthermore, the EU has acknowledged

some specific problems for which transitional periods are necessary. Table 6.6 shows transitional periods of relevance to chemicals (European Commission, 2003).

Chemicals policy-making is undergoing a period of unprecedented change. It offers the prospect of reducing the risks to human health and the environment from chemicals in Europe and beyond. It can also lay the foundation for a more sustainable approach to the safety of chemicals throughout their entire life cycle and for stimulating innovation through 'greener' chemistry (European Commission, 2001) and other improvements in eco-efficiency. Future generations may therefore avoid paying the price of current deficiencies in chemical policies whilst retaining the benefits of chemical products.

6.7. References

AMAP (Arctic Monitoring and Assessment Programme), 2002. *Arctic Pollution 2002.* AMAP, Oslo.

Breiter, M., 1997. *Overview of the chemical industry in Russia*, 1990–1997. US and Foreign Commercial Service and US Department of State. Washington.

CEFIC, 2000. *Basic economic statistics of the European chemical industry: 'Production and employment' 2000.* European Chemical Industry Council. www.cefic.be/activities/eco/basic/tc.htm

CEFIC, 2002. *Facts and figures. The European chemical industry in a worldwide perspective.* June 2002. European Chemical Industry Council. www.cefic.org/factsandfigures

CEH (Centre for Ecology and Hydrology), 2000. *Annual report 1999–2000.* CEH, Monks Wood, UK.

ECB (European Chemicals Bureau), 1999. *Public availability of data on EU high production volume chemicals.* ECB, European Commission Joint Research Centre Ispra, Italy.

EEA (European Environment Agency), 1998. *Europe's environment: The second assessment.* EEA, Copenhagen.

EEA (European Environment Agency), 1999. *Chemicals in the European environment: Low doses, high stakes?* EEA and United Nations Environment Programme, Copenhagen.

Table 6.6.	EU accession countries: transitional periods for compliance to chemicals-related legislation

Country	Transitional agreement
Estonia	Emissions of volatile organic compounds from petrol storage (until 2006)
Latvia	Emissions of volatile organic compounds from petrol storage (until 2008) Prevention and reduction of environmental pollution by asbestos (until 2004) Health protection of individuals against ionising radiation in relation to medical exposure (until 2005)
Lithuania	Emissions of volatile organic compounds from petrol storage (until 2007)
Poland	Emissions of volatile organic compounds from petrol storage (until 2005) Discharge of dangerous substances into surface water (until 2007) Integrated pollution prevention and control (until 2010) Health protection of individuals against ionising radiation in relation to medical exposure (until 2006)
Slovakia	Emissions of volatile organic compounds from petrol storage (until 2007) Discharge of dangerous substances into surface water (until 2006) Integrated pollution prevention and control (until 2011)
Slovenia	Integrated pollution prevention and control (until 2011)

Source: European Commission, 2003

EEA (European Environment Agency), 2000. *Environmental taxes: Recent developments in tools for integration.* Environmental issue report No 18. EEA, Copenhagen.

EEA (European Environment Agency), 2001. *Late lessons from early warnings: The precautionary principle 1896–2000.* Environmental issue report No 22. EEA, Copenhagen.

EEA (European Environment Agency), 2003. *Chemicals in the European environment: A survey of monitoring and exposure information.* (In preparation.)

EMEP, 2002. *Reporting under UNECE Convention on Long-Range Transboundary Air Pollution.* http://www.emep.int/

ENDS, 2002. *ENDS Daily, 13 May 2002.* ENDS Environment Daily. Published by Environmental Data Services (ENDS). http://www.environmentdaily.com

Environment Agency, 2002. *Male fish fertility affected by endocrine disrupting substances.* Press release 26 March 2002. Environment Agency for England and Wales. http://www.environment-agency.gov.uk

European Commission, 2001. *Strategy for a future chemicals policy.* White Paper COM(2001) 88 final. Brussels.

European Commission, 2003. *Enlargement and environment: Questions and answers.* http://www.europa.eu.int/comm/environment/enlarg/faq_en.htm

Eurostat, 2001a. *Indicator: Production of toxic chemicals.* From Indicators on use of chemicals (Christian Heidorn, Eurostat). Meeting document ENV/01/4.4, Joint Eurostat/EFTA group, 19-21 September 2001.

Eurostat 2001b. *Eurostat yearbook 2001: The statistical guide to Europe data 1989–1999.* European Commission, Luxembourg. http://europa.eu.int/comm/eurostat/

FoE (Friends of the Earth), 2002. *Safety testing of chemicals and the new EU chemicals policy.* FoE, London.

FSA (Food Standards Agency), 2002. *Dioxins and dioxin-like PCBs in fish oil supplements.* FSA food surveillance information sheet 26/2002. www.food.gov.uk/science/surveillance/fsis-2002/26diox

Herve, S., Heinonen, P. and Paasivirta, J., 2002. *Survey of organochlorines in Finnish watercourses by caged mussel method.* Resources, Conservation and Recycling 35(1–2) (April): 105–115.

IHPA (International HCH and Pesticides Association), 2001. Technical summary of sessions. *Proceedings of 6th International HCH and Pesticides Forum, 20–22 March 2001, Pozna, Poland.*

Jensen, J. K., 2000. *Initiatives to collect and dispose of pesticides in developing countries.* Office of Pesticide Programs, US EPA. *Proceedings of the First National Conference on Pesticide Stewardship.* National Pesticide Stewardship Alliance.

Klint, M., 2001. *Disposal of obsolete pesticides in central and eastern Europe: Transfer of Danish experiences.* Danish EPA. *Proceedings of 6th International HCH and Pesticides Forum, 20-22 March 2001, Pozna, Poland.*

Lassen, C., *et al.*, 2003. *Survey of dioxin sources in the Baltic region.* Environment Science & Pollution Research 10(1): 49–56.

Longnecker, M. P., *et al.*, 2003. *Comparison of polychlorinated biphenyl levels across studies of human neurodevelopment.* Environmental Health Perspectives 111(1) (January 2003).

Münch, J. and Axenfeld, F., 1999. *Historic emission database of selected persistent organic pollutants (POPs) in Europe (1970–95).* Report from European Commission (DG Research), Environment and Climate Project ENV-CT96-0214. Brussels.

Norén, K. and Meironyté, D., 2000. *Certain organochlorine and organobromine contaminants in Swedish human milk in perspective of past 20-30 years.* Chemosphere 40: 1111–1123.

OECD (Organisation for Economic Co-operation and Development), 2000. *PRTR implementation: Member country progress.* Environment Policy Committee, OECD ENV/EPOC(2000)8/FINAL. Paris

Peltola, J. and Ylä-Mononen, L., 2001. *Pentabromodiphenyl ether as a global POP.* TemaNord 2001: 579. Nordic Council of Ministers, Copenhagen.

Rastogi, S. C. and Worsøe, I .M., 2001. *Analytical chemical control of phthalates in toys. Analytical chemical control of chemical substances and products.* NERI Technical Report No.

373. National Environmental Research Institute, Denmark.

Rastogi, S. C. Jensen G. H. and Worsøe, I. M., 2002. *Analytical chemical control of phthalates in toys. Analytical chemical control of chemical substances and products.* NERI Technical Report No. 404. National Environmental Research Institute, Denmark.

RPA (Risk and Policy Analysts Ltd), 2002. *Assessment of the impact of new regulations in the chemical sector.* RPA and Statistics Sweden. Report prepared for DG Enterprise, European Commission. Brussels

Swedish EPA, 1993. *Persistent organic pollutants and the environment. The environment in Sweden: Status and trends.* Solna, Sweden.

Swedish EPA, 1998a. *Persistent organic pollutants — a Swedish view of an international problem.* Swedish Environmental Protection Agency Monitor 16. ISBN: 91-620-1189-8.

Swedish EPA, 1998b. *Endocrine disrupting substances.* Swedish Environmental Protection Agency Report 4859. Stockholm.

TemaNord, 2002. *Mercury — a global pollutant requiring global initiatives.* TemaNord 2002: 516. Nordic Council of Ministers, Copenhagen.

UNECE, 1998. Convention on Long-Range Transboundary Air Pollution - POPs protocol. United nations Economic Commission for Europe, Geneva. http://www.unece.org/env/lrtap/pops_h1.htm

UNECE, 2002. Sub-committee on the globally harmonised system of classification and labelling of chemicals. United nations Economic Commission for Europe, Geneva. www.unece.org/trans/danger/danger.htm

UNEP, 2001. *Final act of the Conference of Plenipotentiaries on the Stockholm convention on persistent organic pollutants, Stockholm, 22–23 May.* UNEP/POPS/CONF/4. United Nations Environment Programme, Geneva.

UNEP, 2002. Meeting of the Global Mercury Assessment Working Group, Geneva, 9–13 September. United Nations Environment Programme, Geneva

Wallström, M., 2002. 'A new chemicals system is needed'. Presentation of M. Wallström, European Commissioner for Environment, 27 May. European Commission, Brussels

WHO (World Health Organization), 2002. *Global assessment of the state-of-the-science of endocrine disruptors.* Prepared by the UN International Programme on Chemical Safety (IPCS) on behalf of WHO, the International Labour Organisation and the United Nations Environment Programme.

Willis, J., 2001. Precaution and the Stockholm convention. (UNEP Chemicals). In: *The role of precaution in chemicals policy.* Freyberg *et al.* (eds). Favorita Papers, Diplomatic Academy of Vienna.

7. Waste generation and management

Total waste quantities continue to increase in most European countries. Municipal waste arisings are large and continue to grow. The quantities of hazardous waste generated have decreased in many countries but increased in others in some cases due to changes in definitions. In western Europe and the 12 countries of eastern Europe, the Caucasus and central Asia (EECCA) manufacturing waste arisings have increased since the mid-1990s in most countries for which data are available, while in central and eastern Europe, the picture is less clear. Mining and quarrying waste is the largest single category of waste in Europe; data on quantities available from only a few countries indicate a general decrease, which is in line with a reduction in mining and quarrying activity. The quantity of waste from energy production depends on the fuel used, but some indication of quantities can be derived from the amount of electricity generated.

Total waste generation has been decoupled from economic growth in a limited number of countries. Agreed objectives to stabilise the generation of municipal waste in the European Union have not yet been met. Quantities are increasing in most western European countries and to a lesser extent in most central and eastern European countries and the countries of EECCA.

Landfilling remains the dominant waste disposal method. Recycling is increasing in western Europe, while the countries of central and eastern Europe and EECCA still have relatively low recycling rates. Initiatives to promote waste prevention and recycling and raise the safety standards for final disposal are considered to be the most effective options for minimising the environmental risks and costs associated with waste generation, treatment and disposal.

7.1. Introduction

Waste is an issue in every European country, and waste quantities are generally growing. Unfortunately, the lack of available and comparable data for many countries does not always allow reliable comprehensive assessment of waste-related issues.

Waste is generated by activities in all economic sectors and is generally regarded as an unavoidable by-product of economic activity (waste generated from inefficient production processes, low durability of goods and unsustainable consumption patterns). The generation of waste reflects a loss of materials and energy (see Figure 7.1 and Chapter 2.0), and imposes economic and environmental costs on society for its collection, treatment and disposal. Waste forms an increasing part of the total material flow through the economy and, particularly in western Europe (WE), is increasingly being considered in the context of material flows as a whole.

The impact of waste on the environment, resources and human health depends on its quantity and nature. Environmental pressures from the generation and management of waste include emissions to air (including greenhouse gases), water and soil, all with potential impacts on human health and nature. Most of the municipal waste in Europe is landfilled, leading to significant pressures on the environment, while too little is recycled.

7.2. Trends in waste generation

7.2.1. Total waste quantities

It is estimated that more than 3 000 million tonnes of waste are generated in Europe every year. This equals 3.8 tonnes/capita in

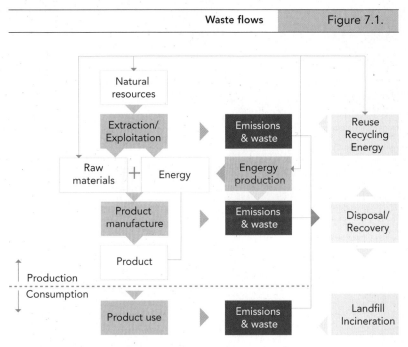

| Waste flows | Figure 7.1. |

Source: Irish Environmental Protection Agency

WE, 4.4 tonnes in central and eastern Europe (CEE) and 6.3 tonnes in the countries of eastern Europe, the Caucasus and central Asia (EECCA) (Figure 7.2). Total waste quantities are continuing to increase in most WE and EECCA countries for which data are available. In CEE, the picture is more mixed: quantities are increasing in some countries (Czech Republic, Hungary, Poland) and decreasing in others (Estonia and the Slovak Republic). In general, limited data sets preclude an accurate assessment.

Waste per gross domestic product (GDP) per capita expresses the link between waste generation and economic activity per capita: high values mean more waste generated per unit of economic output per capita. Data for a limited number of WE countries (Denmark, the Netherlands and Switzerland) show a decoupling of waste from GDP (Figure 7.3). Of the four CEE countries for which adequate data exist, there are signs of decoupling in the Slovak Republic and Estonia (Figure 7.4). Of the four EECCA countries for which data exist, only Belarus and Tajikistan show an indication of decoupling (Figure 7.5). In some cases, the apparent decoupling may be associated with significant structural changes and industrial decline. However, without detailed knowledge of specific economies, the uncertainty associated with such an aggregated indicator precludes more reliable conclusions.

Manufacturing industry, construction and demolition, mining and quarrying, and agriculture are the main sectors that contribute to waste generation (see Figure 7.6. and Sections 7.2.4, 7.2.7 and 7.2.5). Other important waste streams are municipal

| Figure 7.2. | Total waste generation per capita in countries in Europe, 1990–2000 |

Notes: Some WE and CEE countries and EECCA were not included due to lack of consistent time series. The figure for total waste generation for groups of countries is a highly aggregated indicator that can hide the waste generation profile of each country and consequently of Europe as a whole. Total waste includes all wastes generated and also includes materials which, in some countries, are not defined as wastes at all. Therefore interpreting total waste generation is difficult and policy decisions, especially for individual countries, should not be based on this indicator alone.

Source: Eurostat, 2000; EEA questionnaire (2002 — see Chapter 14)

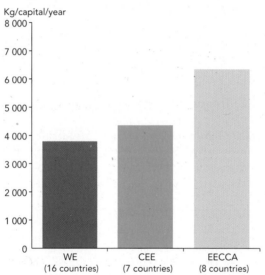

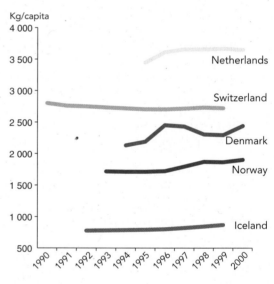

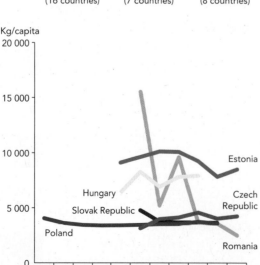

waste (see Section 7.2.2), hazardous waste (see Section 7.2.3), waste from end-of-life vehicles (see Box 7.1), sewage sludge, packaging waste and waste from energy generation (see Section 7.2.6). Different definitions in different countries can make comparisons of total amounts of waste extremely difficult. Changing definitions within individual countries can make time-series analysis equally difficult except where detailed information is available.

Box 7.1. End-of-life vehicles

The number of end-of-life vehicles in western Europe is increasing as the number of cars increases. In EU accession countries, a total increase of 124 % in the number of scrapped cars is projected between 2000 and 2015. Reasons include the ageing and growing car stock.

Cars contain materials such as lead, mercury, cadmium, hexavalent chromium and other environmentally harmful substances. About three quarters of a car by weight is steel and aluminium which is recycled. The rest, mainly plastics, is disposed of to landfills or by incineration. Cars also contain dangerous liquids (e.g. anti-freeze, brake fluid, oils) that are harmful to the environment if not disposed of properly.

The EU directive on end-of-life vehicles (Directive 2000/53/EC) has a strong focus on recovery, reuse and recycling. As a consequence, Member States will need to focus on improvements in the dismantling and shredder industry. By 2006, 80 % of an end-of-life vehicle is to be reused or recycled, with a projected 85 % by 2015. For recovery (including reuse and recycling) the targets are 85 % for 2006 and 95 % after 2015.

Illegal export of used cars from western Europe to central and eastern Europe is likely to cause major end-of-life vehicle waste problems in central and eastern European countries in the future.

Source: EEA, 2002a

7.2.2. Municipal waste

Municipal waste arisings in Europe are large, and continue to increase (Figure 7.7). More than 306 million tonnes are estimated to be collected each year, an average of 415 kg/capita. The collection of municipal waste varies considerably between countries and lies in the range of 685 kg/capita (Iceland) to 105 kg/capita (Uzbekistan). Municipal waste accounts for approximately 14 % of total waste arisings in WE and 5 % in CEE. Landfilling is still the predominant treatment option in most countries throughout Europe.

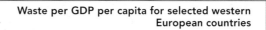

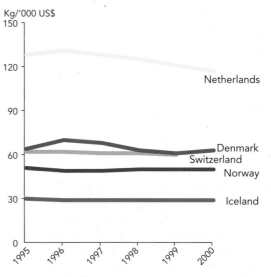

Waste per GDP per capita for selected western European countries

Figure 7.3.

Note: The definition of waste for the Netherlands includes wastes that are not included in other countries.

Source: Eurostat, 2002a

Waste per GDP per capita for selected central and eastern European countries

Figure 7.4.

Source: Eurostat, 2002a and information from Ministry of the Environment of the Slovak Republic, 2002; World Bank indicators on GDP in 1995 values from EEA data service

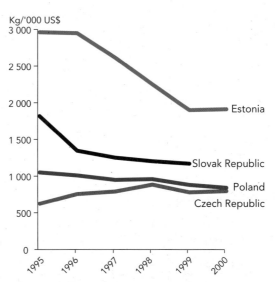

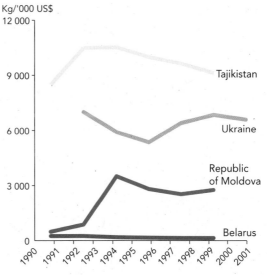

Waste per GDP per capita in selected eastern European, Caucasus and central Asian countries

Figure 7.5.

Source: EEA questionnaire (2002 — see Chapter 14); World Bank indicators on GDP in 1995 values from EEA data service

Figure 7.6.	Total waste generation by sector in WE and CEE

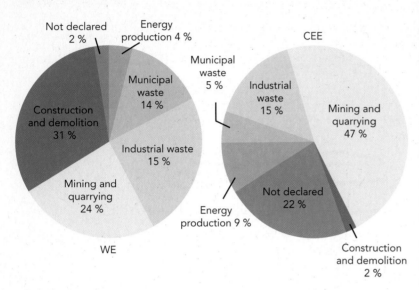

WE

CEE

Notes: Figure for WE does not include Belgium, Iceland, Luxemburg, Norway, Sweden, Spain, Switzerland. Figure for CEE does not include Bulgaria, Czech Republic, Estonia, Hungary, Poland, Slovak Republic and Slovenia.
Source: Eurostat, 2002a

Figure 7.7.	Municipal waste collected in selected countries

Notes: WE: Austria, Belgium, Denmark, France, Italy, Luxemburg, Netherlands, Portugal, Spain, Iceland, Norway and Switzerland. CEE: Bulgaria, Czech Republic, Estonia, Hungary, Latvia, Lithuania, Poland, Romania and Croatia. EECCA: Belarus, Republic of Moldavia, Tajikistan, Turkmenistan, Ukraine and Uzbekistan.

Source: Eurostat, 2000; EEA questionnaire (2002 — see Chapter 14)

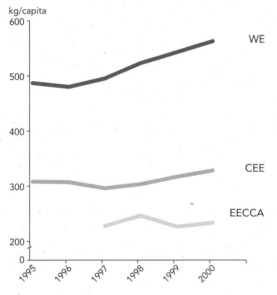

The fifth environment action programme (5EAP) of the European Community had set a target of stabilising municipal waste generation in the European Union (EU) at 1985 levels (300 kg/capita) by 2000. This target has been significantly exceeded in almost all countries, by 75–100 %. In the sixth environment action programme (6EAP) agreed in 2002, no quantitative waste targets have been included. The landfilling of municipal waste has decreased from 67 % in 1995 to 57 % in 1999 in EU countries, while composting and recycling rates have increased. Biodegradable municipal waste makes up approximately 60 % of the municipal waste stream in WE (see Box 7.2).

In CEE, municipal waste collection rates are lower than in WE, a result of different levels of economic resources and different consumption patterns and municipal waste disposal systems.

Many parts of CEE and EECCA, particularly rural areas, are not served by municipal waste collection systems. In CEE countries with available data, municipal waste generation, though currently lower than in other parts of Europe, is increasing. By comparison, the collection rates in EECCA appear to have been stable in recent years. In the Caucasus, it is reported that municipal waste landfills are often overloaded, improperly operated and maintained, and do not meet environmental and human health requirements (UNEP, 2002a). A similar situation is reported to a greater or lesser extent in several other CEE countries and EECCA (UNECE, 1995–2002). Illegal dumping of municipal waste, in particular in rural areas, is also common in many countries (UNEP, 2002a).

Box 7.2. Biodegradable municipal waste

In 1995, about 107 million tonnes of biodegradable municipal waste were generated in the EU and Norway, of which 66 % was landfilled.

Biodegradable municipal waste is generated by households and commercial activities and covers waste such as food, garden waste, paper and cardboard. Biodegradable municipal waste is a major contributor to the generation of leachate, landfill gas, odour and other nuisances in landfills. Alternative treatment methods such as composting or anaerobic digestion, if properly controlled, can eliminate or significantly reduce the polluting and emission potential of biodegradable waste.

The EU landfill directive imposes strict targets for the reduction of biodegradable municipal waste that may be disposed of to landfill, namely a reduction to 35 % by 2016 of the amounts going to landfill, taking 1995 as the starting point. Source separation, separate collection, more incineration, more composting and limits and bans on landfilling are among the key instruments needed to reach this target.

Source: EEA, 2001a

7.2.3. Hazardous waste

Hazardous waste is broadly defined as any waste that possesses one or more of 15 hazardous characteristics e.g. flammable, corrosive, infectious, eco-toxic. However, the definition of hazardous waste is not uniform in all countries. Consequently, direct comparison between countries may be questionable since total amounts can be made up of different waste types.

Hazardous waste generally makes up less than 1 % of all waste generated in Europe. However, due to the dangerous substances it contains, it presents a serious risk to the environment and human health if not managed and treated safely. Several EU countries report hazardous waste recovery rates (generally by separate collection and recovery as by-products) in excess of 40 %. In other regions, the situation is less clear but several countries report unsatisfactory disposal of hazardous waste.

Since the mid-1990s, overall quantities of hazardous waste generated per capita have dramatically changed in some WE countries (e.g. 62 % increase in Austria; 57 % decrease in Denmark); changes in definitions of hazardous waste might explain these trends (Figure 7.8). In Ukraine, hazardous waste generation decreased by 38 % between 1996 and 2000; in the Russian Federation, quantities increased by 32 % between 1996 and 1999. By contrast, in some CEE countries, overall quantities generated per capita have decreased substantially since the mid-1990s.

A limited number of economic sectors contribute substantially to hazardous waste generation, manufacturing industry being the main source. Hazardous waste is generally the subject of special legislation. It requires special management arrangements which require hazardous and non-hazardous waste to be kept separate and treated differently. Studies (EEA, 1999a; EEA, 2001b) have shown that a large proportion of hazardous waste in most WE countries consists of a relatively small number of waste types (typically 75 % of hazardous waste generated consists of 20 principal types — based on the EU hazardous waste list containing 236 codes for hazardous waste types). The major types differ from one country to another; examples include slag and fly ash from waste incineration, spent solvents and lead batteries. Similarly, in many CEE countries and EECCA, hazardous waste generation is often dominated by a relatively

small number of sources. This means that hazardous waste management, prevention or recycling programmes can be focused on the sources responsible for the generation of the majority of hazardous waste, thus allowing the maximum return on investment and effort.

In several WE countries, recovery has become the dominant hazardous waste management option, while in most other countries disposal by landfilling and incineration without energy recovery are widely used. In many countries, hazardous waste has to be stabilised before disposal, for example by physico-chemical treatment in order to meet the acceptance criteria for landfills. However, treatment methods are often poorly defined, or sometimes undeclared, and this leads to difficulties in comparing practices in different countries (Figure 7.9). For example, defining recovery operations such as 'incineration with energy recovery' and 'recovery of materials' in one group of countries does not allow an accurate comparison with hazardous waste treatment in other countries.

A relatively minor hazardous waste stream in most countries, healthcare waste is a cause of concern in terms of its potential to cause infection, injury and pollution (see Chapter

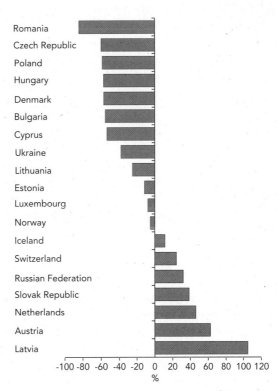

Percentage change in hazardous waste generation in 19 European countries in the period 1995–2000 or latest year available — Figure 7.8.

Notes: Includes only countries with at least four years of data. The graph is based on per capita estimates and the population changes 1995-2000 should be taken in to account.

Sources: Eurostat, 2002a; EEA questionnaire (2002 — see Chapter 14)

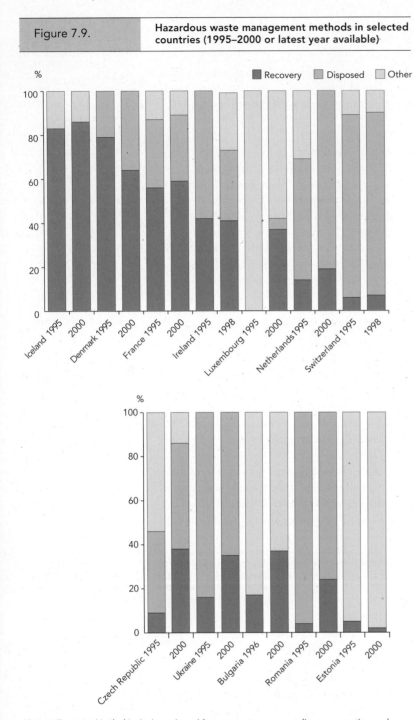

| Figure 7.9. | Hazardous waste management methods in selected countries (1995–2000 or latest year available) |

Notes: 'Recovery' includes: incineration with energy recovery, recycling, composting and other recovery methods. 'Other' treatment methods include: physico-chemical or biological treatment, permanent storage, release into water bodies and unspecified or not declared.

Sources: Eurostat, 2002a; EEA questionnaire (2002 — see Chapter 14)

12, section 12.3.4). In many countries, hazardous healthcare waste (needles, used dressings etc.) is not separated from municipal waste, and this can present an increased environmental risk in the proximity of landfills and other disposal facilities. As with other categories of waste, and hazardous waste in general, the establishment of a national policy, a legal framework, the training of personnel and the raising of public awareness are essential

elements of successful healthcare waste management (WHO, 1999).

In the Caucasus, it is reported that known hazardous waste disposal sites are overloaded and not adequately isolated from the environment, posing risks to the environment and human health. Because of the lack of sound law enforcement and monitoring systems there is a risk of the area becoming a 'haven' for international trading in hazardous waste (UNEP, 2002a). Although all the EECCA countries (except Kazahkstan and Tajikistan) are parties to the Basel convention (1989), many lack the national capacity as well as finances to fulfil commitments made under the convention. International assistance and regional cooperation are key to achieving effective waste management and environmental protection. Several CEE and EECCA countries report improved information on or definition of hazardous waste as a result of implementing the provisions of the Basel convention.

7.2.4. Waste from manufacturing industries

Approximately 740 million tonnes of waste are generated by the manufacturing industry in Europe every year. In WE and EECCA, manufacturing waste arisings have increased since the mid-1990s in most countries for which data are available. In EECCA, the increase followed a period in the early 1990s of drastic decline in industrial activity, and therefore in industrial wastes, after the disintegration of the USSR. In CEE, the picture is less clear, and some countries, including the Czech Republic, Hungary, Romania and the Slovak Republic, have produced decreasing quantities of such waste. As with many other waste categories, manufacturing waste is not defined consistently in different countries, making comparisons difficult (Figure 7.10).

The range of industrial wastes generated is as broad as the manufacturing industries that generate them, and as the waste management options used — which combine recycling, recovery and disposal techniques. Small and medium-sized enterprises, as well as some large enterprises, do not always have the expertise or the resources to ensure that the management of their waste does not have environmental impacts.

Manufacturing waste consists of food, wood, paper, chemical, non-metallic mineral, basic metal and other waste. A comparison of WE and CEE countries shows that WE generates most food, wood, paper, non-metallic and other manufacturing waste. The differences in the composition of manufacturing waste are probably influenced by the strong representation of paper industries in some reporting countries. CEE countries generate most manufacturing waste from chemical, iron and steel industries. In 1998, the main contributor to manufacturing waste in five CEE countries was the basic metals industry (contributing about 50 %). In WE, no dominant industry can be identified, but in five reporting countries the food, wood and paper industry each accounted for about 20 % in 1998. A comparison of manufacturing waste generated in selected CEE countries from 1995 to 1998 (Figure 7.11) shows that the contribution to the generation of manufacturing waste increased from 50 % to 59 %.

In EECCA, the oil industry and mineral resources extraction are major generators of industrial waste (UNEP, 2002a).

Manufacturing industry can play a central role in reducing the amount of waste generated by:

- incorporating life-cycle analysis in the design and manufacture of goods and services;
- promoting sustainable use of materials and energy;
- eliminating or reducing the use of substances or materials hazardous to health or to the environment.

7.2.5. Waste from mining and quarrying

Mining and quarrying waste is the largest single category of waste in Europe, accounting for more than 20 % of all waste generated. Quantities are generally decreasing in the United Kingdom, Poland and Romania. It is assumed that decreasing waste generation in these countries has resulted from a reduction in the level of mining and quarrying activity.

The disposal of mining waste can take up large areas of land and, unless properly managed, can result in detrimental impacts on air, water and soil quality. Recent uncontrolled releases from mining and tailings waste management facilities highlight the potential risks associated with poor waste management in this sector. In response, the EU has proposed initiatives that are designed to improve mining waste management, including a proposed directive

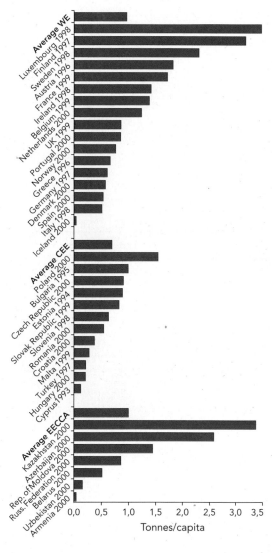

| Manufacturing waste generation per capita in European countries | Figure 7.10. |

Note: Consistent use of a standardised statistical classification of economic activity in defining manufacturing activities would help to eliminate differences in national definitions of manufacturing waste. For example: International Standard Industrial Classification of All Economic Activities, Third Revision, (ISIC, Rev.3), UNSD Statistical Classifications Section, http://unstats.un.org/unsd/class/family/famlist1.htm

Sources: Eurostat, 2002a; EEA questionnaire (2002 — see Chapter 14); updated data for Estonia

on the management of waste from the extractive industry (quarrying and mining) and a reference document on best available techniques in the management of tailings and waste rock from mining.

In many European countries, waste from mining and quarrying is not subject to environmental or waste management legislation. Consequently, information on waste quantities and management is scarce and the quality of data poor. A surrogate indicator (domestic extraction of fossil fuels and construction materials) is proposed to illustrate the scale of waste generation by mining and quarrying. Most mining and quarrying results in the extraction of material that is not used directly but is stored for later use, landfilled or otherwise disposed of. For example, fossil fuel extraction results

Figure 7.11.	Manufacturing waste profiles in selected countries in western Europe and central and eastern Europe

Notes: The figure for western Europe only contains data from Ireland, the Netherlands, Portugal, Sweden and Finland. The figure for CEE only contains data from Czech Republic, Hungary, Poland, Romania and Slovak Republic.

Source: Eurostat, 2000

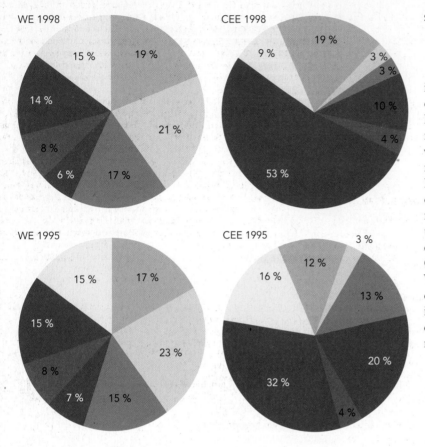

in up to 80 % of unused material. In contrast construction minerals extraction results in less than 20 % of unused material. Different mining and quarrying activities result in varying but significant quantities of unused material, of varying nature and potential hazard. Data for the EU show that domestic extraction of fossil fuels and construction materials (Figure 7.12) is decreasing and so, therefore, is the amount of unused material extracted (i.e. hidden flows). As illustrated in Chapter 2.0, the natural resources used in WE are increasingly being imported from countries outside the EU, e.g. increasing import of fossil fuels from EECCA, with consequent increased arisings of unused material in those countries.

- Food products, beveragen and tobacco products
- Wood and wood products
- Paper and paper products
- Chemicals and chemical product
- Non-metallic mineral products
- Basic metals
- Other manufacturing industries

Figure 7.12.	Domestic extraction of fossil fuels and construction minerals, EU

Source: Eurostat, 2002b

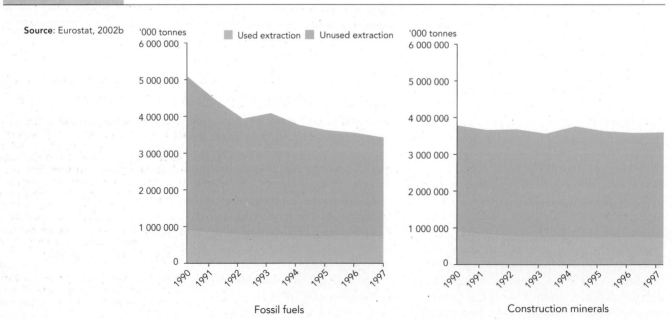

7.2.6. Waste from electricity production

The quantity of waste from energy transformation depends on the fuel used, but some indication of quantities can be derived from the amount of electricity generated (see Chapter 2.1).

Hydroelectric and gas-fired power stations generate no solid waste. Coal-fired power stations generate large quantities of bottom ash and fly ash. During the 1990s, the EU generated 50 million tonnes/year of coal ash of which, in those countries which reported, about 75 % was recycled (varying from 70 % to 98 %) (EEA, 2002b). Nuclear power generation results in waste that requires specialised and expensive management (see Box 7.3). A shift to cleaner (e.g. natural gas) and renewable sources of energy will result in reduced waste quantities. However, there is very little information on waste generation from power stations in Europe. Instead, for illustrative purposes, the relative use of various energy sources can be used as a surrogate indicator for waste types and quantities: coal and other fossil fuels produce the largest amounts of waste residues (e.g. fly ash).

7.2.7. Waste from construction and demolition

Waste generated from construction and demolition activities, including the renovation of old buildings, accounts for about 32 % of all waste generated in WE and a declared share of 2 % in CEE (the reasons for the difference are unclear — poor reporting in CEE may be a factor). Construction and demolition waste may contain dangerous substances, such as asbestos, which may be present in significant proportions when old buildings are demolished or renovated.

The generation of construction and demolition waste in WE generally increased during the 1990s: per capita generation increased in seven countries, remained constant in four and decreased in four (EEA, 2002b). In CEE, quantities have increased since 1995 in four of the five countries for which there are data. Time series are not available for EECCA.

In many countries, construction and demolition waste is mainly disposed of to landfill, despite its suitability for recycling. Some WE countries such as Germany, Denmark and the Netherlands, have achieved up to 90 % recycling of construction and demolition waste. Special initiatives were needed in each of these countries to drive up

the recycling rate: in Denmark, the introduction of landfill tax in the late 1980s and its enforcement in the 1990s motivated the recycling of demolition waste.

Many components of construction and demolition waste are readily recyclable and have the potential to replace up to 10 % of virgin raw materials. In order to promote the sustainable use of raw materials, the possibilities for recycling the components of construction and demolition waste should be exploited.

7.3. Waste management

7.3.1. Trends in waste management

One of the barriers to the establishment of improved waste management planning, monitoring and enforcement in many parts of Europe, including WE, is the lack of sound, reliable, comparable and available data. Reliable data are essential for the long-term prevention of illegal and polluting disposals

---

Box 7. 3. Waste from nuclear electricity generation

In general, the quantities of radioactive waste generated annually are very small compared with the quantities of hazardous waste and other non-radioactive waste. Due to its special nature, however, the management of nuclear waste is normally considered separately from other wastes.

Various wastes arise at each stage in the nuclear fuel cycle, classified in terms of their radioactivity content and, for the most highly radioactive wastes, their rate of heat generation. Some wastes which have low to medium levels of radioactivity and which lose their radioactivity relatively rapidly as a result of natural decay are generally disposed of, following studies of long-term safety, in engineered repositories constructed at or near the surface, for example in Finland, France, Sweden and the United Kingdom. Other wastes that are not suitable for disposal at or near the surface are normally held in specially built interim storage facilities that provide containment consistent with the hazard presented by the radioactive content.

In most European countries the favoured long-term solution for the wastes with the longest-lived radioactivity is deep geological disposal. Progress towards this objective has been slow, mainly because of societal concerns: the one deep disposal facility licensed to date, in Germany, will not operate in the foreseeable future. Site identification, characterisation and safety assessment programmes for the disposal of long-lived and heat-generating wastes are well advanced in a number of European countries. A site has been chosen in Finland, underground investigations are under way at a site in France, and the programme in Sweden is on track to select and develop a site in 2008.

In the case of decommissioning of nuclear reactors and installations, there are two main strategies. Immediate dismantling involves the cleaning and/or dismantling of all contaminated and radioactive components and structures, which are then packaged and transported to a waste disposal or storage site. This may take five or more years. Deferred dismantling involves making the plant structure safe for protective storage for an extended period of time (from 10 up to 150 years), including securing the part of the plant containing radioactive materials. The aim of deferred dismantling is that the radioactivity will decay so that the total radioactivity will be approximately 1 000 times less than its original level after 50 years of storage. When the radioactivity has decayed sufficiently the reactor will be decontaminated and dismantled as for immediate dismantling.

Sources: IAEA, 1994, 1996 and 1999; NEA, 2000

and the use of unreliable data can lead to poor policy-making decisions and the establishment of inappropriate waste management infrastructure. The data in this chapter are often of poor quality, reliability, comparability and availability. Consequently, it is difficult to establish a full picture of waste generation and management in Europe.

The preceding sections have shown that, with waste arisings growing in almost all regions of Europe, there is significant scope for improvement. Waste prevention should be the primary initiative since reducing the generation of waste at source reduces the need for collection and treatment and the associated costs and environmental impacts. Furthermore, natural resources and materials are saved, bearing in mind that waste is 'wasted' raw material.

A study (EEA, 2000) concluded that three principal impacts of landfill and incineration were significant at the global level because of their potential for transboundary migration: organic micro-pollutants (dioxins and furans), greenhouse gases (methane) and volatile heavy metals. Other emissions from incinerators (hydrogen chloride, heavy metals and salts) and landfill sites (nitrogen, ammonia, organic compounds and heavy metals), if uncontrolled, have the potential to cause severe contamination problems due to the dangerous substances contained and emitted. Minimisation of waste generation, reduction in the hazardous constituents of waste, especially those with the potential to cause adverse impacts on environmental quality and health, and adequate management of residual wastes are therefore the major challenges to be tackled in future years if these impacts are to be avoided.

Prevention
Waste prevention translates into a need to design materials, goods and services in such a way that their manufacture, use, reuse, recycling and end-of-life disposal results in the least possible generation of waste. Particularly in growing economies, waste prevention is a heavy challenge in order to achieve decoupling of waste generation from economic growth. However, waste prevention is only one element in the broader concept of cleaner production which has been promoted by the United Nations Environment Programme (UNEP) for some 15 years (UNEP, 2002b). As an additional approach, cleaner consumption has recently been promoted in tandem with cleaner production as a key to achieving

sustainable development (WSSD, 2002) through the adoption of a preventive approach to the entire product life cycle, incorporating design, manufacture, use and disposal. Cleaner production and consumption policies and initiatives are supported and coordinated worldwide by national cleaner production centres and international and regional conferences and roundtables. Many policies, tools, instruments and activities are available to governments for the promotion and implementation of cleaner production and consumption policies.

Recycling
Figures for recycling are rather discouraging. The rate of recycling in many countries throughout Europe is minimal. In relatively few WE countries, recycling of some waste streams has increased considerably during the past decade. In the EU, recycling (including composting) of municipal waste was 11 % during 1985-90 (EEA, 1999b), increasing to 21 % in 1995 and 29 % in 2000 (Eurostat, 2002). By comparison, in the eight EU accession countries where data exist, an average municipal waste recycling rate of 8.6 % was reported during the period 1998-2001. Among the EECCA countries, Ukraine has a total recycling rate of 10–12 %, Belarus 14–15 % (industrial waste only) and Uzbekistan 6–15 % (UNECE, 1995–2002).

There is thus plenty of scope for increasing the level of recycling in almost all European countries. A major challenge is to establish new and, to some extent, more comprehensive collection and recycling schemes. For some waste streams (e.g. construction and demolition waste) solutions may be fairly straightforward, while others (e.g. waste from electrical and electronic equipment) may demand a more complex system. There is a large potential for cooperation between countries especially in CEE and EECCA. Perhaps a greater challenge will be the development of sound and sustainable markets for recycled materials and products that will ensure the long-term viability of recycling systems. Technical and economic restrictions will need to be overcome in order to further stimulate the recycling of waste streams such as municipal and plastic waste. The creation of market opportunities and increased public acceptance is expected to dramatically increase the composting of separately collected green or biodegradable municipal waste in WE.

Incineration

Incineration with energy recovery is another option to avoid landfilling. In WE, 17 % of municipal waste was incinerated in 1995 and 18 % in 1999 (EEA, 1999b; Eurostat, 2002a), and in CEE 2.3 % and 6 % (Figure 7.13). No quantitative information is available for the EECCA countries. The operation of sub-standard incinerators is widely reported in CEE and EECCA. Three Balkan countries report the incineration of hospital waste though not all with flue-gas cleaning. In one case, a second-hand incinerator for hospital waste was obtained under 'bilateral cooperation', but without any pollution abatement. Obviously, in such a case, a balance must be struck between the need to separate hazardous hospital waste from municipal waste and the need to avoid environmental pollution in the incineration of hospital waste.

Landfilling

Landfilling is the lowest ranking waste management option in the waste hierarchy, but remains the dominant method used in Europe. One of the reasons could be the reluctance of public opinion to accept incineration as a safe treatment/disposal option, as well as local conditions which eventually prohibit the sustainability of operation of incineration plants (i.e. geographical constraints, long transport routes). Some 57 % of municipal waste in WE and 83.7 % in CEE was landfilled in 1999 (DHV CR, 2001). Little quantitative information on landfilling is available for EECCA, but it is clear that it is by far the most-used option. In the environmental outlook for the Caucasus (UNEP, 2002a), the situation is described as: 'overloaded, improperly managed and maintained municipal waste landfills that do not meet minimum health and environmental standards'.

Thus, to meet the waste hierarchy, wastes should be diverted away from landfill to higher-ranking management options. It should however be noted that in many CEE and EECCA countries, landfill capacity is unavailable and waste, including hazardous waste, is accumulating pending the availability of treatment or disposal options. In many instances, hazardous waste is stored under unsatisfactory conditions resulting in increased risks of industrial accidents, health impacts and environmental contamination. Estonia and Latvia have, however, demonstrated some success in this regard by establishing safe storage for large quantities of obsolete pesticides, although the question of disposal remains.

Another challenge for the future is to raise the standards of landfills and close improperly managed and maintained sites. In the EU Member States and accession countries, compliance with the EU directive on the landfill of waste (Directive 1999/31/EC) is expected to significantly reduce the potential for environmental pollution from landfills. The directive imposes stringent operational and technical requirements on landfilling and requires a reduction in the quantity of various waste streams entering landfills as well as treatment of all waste

Municipal waste management in selected countries of western Europe and central and eastern Europe, 1995 and latest year available   Figure 7.13.

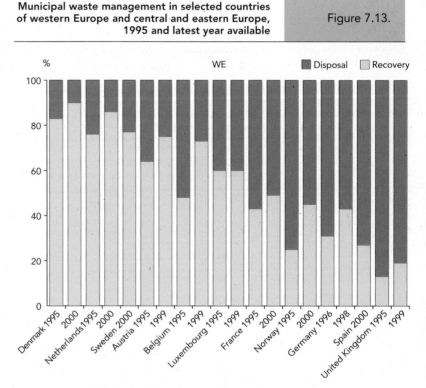
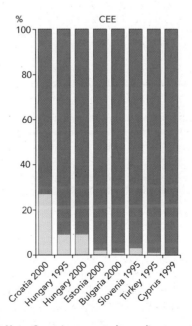

Note: Countries are sorted according to recovery rate obtained in year 2000 or latest year with information available.
Source: Eurostat, 2002a

| Figure 7.14. | Number of landfill sites in Europe, 1990–99 |

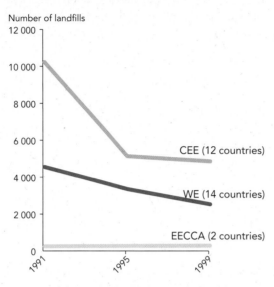

Notes: Due to lack of data reference years are partly combined (1990/91, 1997, 1998/99). If data for both combined years are available, the data of the later year are used. Data for the Slovak Republic on all landfills and registered dumps are included for the years 1993 to 1995, after which the dumps were closed or redefined as landfills. In the Slovak Republic, the number of dumps and landfills decreased from 8 372 in 1993 to 6 068 in 1995 to 568 landfills in 1998 to 156 landfills in 2002. Countries: WE: Austria, Belgium, Finland, France, Ireland, Italy, Luxembourg, Portugal, Spain, Sweden, the Netherlands, Iceland, Norway, Switzerland. CEE: Croatia, Cyprus, Czech Republic, Estonia, Hungary, Latvia, Lithuania, Malta, Poland, Romania, Slovak Republic, Turkey. EECCA: Belarus, Tajikistan.

Sources: Eurostat, 2002a; EEA, 1995; EEA, 1998; Austrian Federal Waste Management Plans 1992, 1995, 1998, 2001; EEA questionnaire (2002 — see Chapter 14); Ministry of Environment of the Slovak Republic

---

Box 7.4. Levies on the landfill of waste

A tax on the landfill of waste has become a widely used instrument and is now in use in nine western Europe countries. The tax has been applied for several reasons, including the stimulation of waste reduction, reuse and recycling; to raise revenue; and to internalise landfill costs. More than EUR 1.7 billion is raised each year in western Europe (Kirk McClure Morton, 2001). While the influence of landfill taxes on reducing the generation of some waste streams (e.g. municipal waste) is questionable, landfill taxes do provide price signals which should stimulate the adoption of more sustainable waste management practices.

The purpose of the tax, its design and its level vary from country to country.
• The general purpose is to internalise the environmental costs of final disposal of waste. In some countries, environmental tax revenues are used to offset revenues from other, distorting, taxes, for example on labour, in the framework of ecological fiscal reform (e.g. the Netherlands and Denmark); others use the revenue to support the remediation of contaminated sites (Austria and Switzerland).
• The level of the tax varies greatly, from EUR 79 per tonne in the Netherlands to EUR 15 per tonne in Finland.
• The tax may depend on the kind of waste being landfilled (e.g. United Kingdom and Italy) or may apply to all waste consigned to landfill (e.g. Sweden and Norway).
• Only two countries introduced the tax before 1990, the rest in the period 1993-2000.

Sources: OECD/EU, 2002; EEA-ETC/WMF

---

prior to landfill. Data for WE and CEE show that the number of landfills decreased significantly up to 1999 (Figure 7.14).

7.3.2. Review of policies
According to EU legislation (Directive 75/442/EEC), all Member States are required to produce one or more waste management plans. These must relate in particular to the type, quantity and origin of waste; its recovery or disposal; general technical requirements; special arrangements for particular wastes; and suitable disposal sites or installations.

Twelve EU countries have national waste management plans or strategies and three countries have prepared regional plans. The elements of national waste management plans have been provided for by many CEE countries, generally as part of the accession process (DHV CR, 2001). Several other CEE and EECCA countries have formulated waste management plans and programmes; however, the general lack of resources is commonly quoted as a significant barrier to their satisfactory and timely implementation (UNECE, 1995–2002).

The EU directive on waste (Directive 75/442/EEC) requires Member States to establish an integrated and adequate network of disposal installations. This may be done in cooperation with other Member States. The network must enable the Community as a whole to become self-sufficient in waste disposal, and must reflect the fact that certain wastes, particularly hazardous waste, may not be generated in one country in sufficient quantities to warrant the establishment of a dedicated disposal facility in that country.

Command-and-control measures are widely used in all European countries especially for hazardous waste management. For non-hazardous waste, the use of economic or market-based instruments is on the increase in WE and CEE countries. An important aspect is to make the polluters (i.e. the enterprises or households generating the waste) aware of the costs of their actions and to provide opportunities for alternative options. The costs are usually recovered through user charges that reflect the cost of collection and treatment of wastes, and through taxes. 'Pay-as-you-throw' schemes are gaining ground in several countries.

In WE countries, producer responsibility has been implemented for various waste streams such as packaging, batteries, waste from electrical and electronic equipment, paper and tyres. Voluntary agreements between authorities and industry have also been set up to some extent (e.g. end-of-life vehicles, construction and demolition waste).

The most commonly used instruments in CEE are user charges for the collection, transportation and treatment of municipal waste, and waste disposal charges (DHV CR, 2001; REC, 2001). Several countries have introduced deposit-refund systems on beverage containers and product charges on batteries. Many of the instruments have been relatively recently introduced due to the EU accession process and any assessment of their efficacy at this stage would be speculative.

Most EECCA countries operate various waste management and user taxes; however, the effectiveness of these instruments is generally limited (OECD, 2000). A centrally controlled deposit-refund system which used to exist for the collection and reuse of glass bottles has been abandoned in all the EECCA countries except Belarus, although privately operated systems have emerged in several other EECCA countries. Resistance from industry stifled attempts to introduce user charges on packaging in Georgia and Ukraine. In overall terms, the Organisation for Economic Co-operation and Development (OECD) recommended a 'comprehensive reform of economic instruments for environmental protection in the EECCA in the context of achieving priority objectives and targets of environmental policies.'

Economic instruments should serve not only to indicate and penalise undesirable waste management practices, but also to complement, encourage or reward desirable practices, namely waste prevention, minimisation, reuse, recycling and recovery (see Box 7.4.). However, the possible adverse impacts of incentives should also be taken into account when designing economic instruments. If the user charge or tax is too high, or an increase too abrupt, the risk of illegal dumping will increase.

Perhaps the greater challenge is the development of sound and sustainable markets for recycled materials and products that will ensure the long-term viability of recycling systems. Technical and economic restrictions will need to be overcome in order to further stimulate the recycling of

waste streams such as municipal and plastic waste. For compostable municipal wastes, a major step forward would be the creation of market opportunities and increased public acceptance of the use of compost.

7.4. References

Austrian Federal Waste Management Plans, 1992. Bundesministerium für Umwelt, Jugend und Familie, *Bundesabfallwirtschaftsplan.* Vienna.

Austrian Federal Waste Management Plans, 1995. Bundesministerium für Umwelt, *Bundes-Abfallwirtschaftsplan, Bundesabfallbericht.* Vienna.

Austrian Federal Waste Management Plans, 1998. Federal Ministry of Environment, Youth and Family Affairs. *Federal Waste Management Plan, Federal Waste Management Report.* Vienna.

Austrian Federal Waste Management Plans, 2001. Federal Ministry of Agriculture and Forestry, Environment and Water Management. *Federal Waste Management Plan, Federal Waste Management Report.* Vienna.

Basel convention, 1989. *Basel Convention on the Control of Transboundary Movements of Hazardous Wastes and their Disposal.* Adopted by the Conference of the Plenipotentiaries on 22 March 1989, as amended by Decisions of the Conference of the Parties. www.basel.int

DHV CR, 2001. *Waste management policies in central and eastern European countries: Current policies and trends.* DHV CR Ltd., Prague.

EEA (European Environment Agency), 1995. *Europe's environment: The Dobris assessment.* EEA, Copenhagen.

EEA (European Environment Agency), 1998. *Europe's environment: The second assessment.* EEA, Copenhagen.

EEA (European Environment Agency), 1999a. *Hazardous waste generation in selected European countries — comparability of classification systems and quantities.* Topic report No 14/1999. EEA, Copenhagen.

EEA (European Environment Agency), 1999b. *Environment in the European Union at the turn of the century.* EEA, Copenhagen.

EEA (European Environment Agency), 2000. *Dangerous substances in waste.* Technical report No 38. EEA, Copenhagen.

EEA (European Environment Agency), 2001a. *Biodegradable municipal waste management in Europe.* Topic report No 15/2001. EEA, Copenhagen.

EEA (European Environment Agency), 2001b. *Hazardous waste generation in EEA member countries — comparability of classification systems and quantities.* Topic report No 14/2001. EEA, Copenhagen.

EEA (European Environment Agency), 2002a. *Paving the way for EU enlargement. Indicators of transport and environment integration,* Environmental issue report No. 32, TERM 2002. EEA, Copenhagen.

EEA (European Environment Agency), 2002b. *Review of selected waste streams: Sewage sludge, construction and demolition waste, waste oils, waste from coal-fired power plants and biodegradable municipal waste.* Technical report No 69. EEA, Copenhagen.

Eurostat, 2000. New Cronos database.

Eurostat, 2002a. New Cronos database.

Eurostat, 2002b. *Material use in the European Union 1980–2000:* Indicators and analysis. Working paper and studies series. Eurostat, Luxembourg.

IAEA (International Atomic Energy Agency), 1994. *Classification of radioactive waste.* Safety Series No 111-G-1. IAEA, Vienna.

IAEA (International Atomic Energy Agency), 1996. *Issues in radioactive waste disposal.* IAEA-TECDOC-909. IAEA, Vienna.

IAEA (International Atomic Energy Agency), 1999. *World wide overview of inventories of radioactive waste.* IAEA, Vienna.

IEA (International Energy Agency), 2001. Basic energy statistics of OECD countries and non-OECD countries.

Kirk McClure Morton, 2001. *Introduction of a landfill levy.* Report prepared for Department of the Environment and Local Government, Dublin. http://www.environ.ie/environ/envindex.html

NEA, 2000. *Regulatory Reviews of Assessments of Deep Geologic Repositories.* Organisation for Economic Co-operation and Development — Nuclear Energy Agency, Paris

OECD (Organisation for Economic Co-operation and Development), 2000. S*urvey on the use of economic instruments for pollution control and natural resource management in the NIS: Preliminary conclusions and recommendations.* CCNM/ENV/EAP(2000)85.

OECD (Organisation for Economic Co-operation and Development), 2002. OECD/EU database on environmentally related taxes.(Forthcoming on line: http://www.oecd.org/EN/home/0,,EN-home-471-nodirectorate-no-no-no-8-log127588,00.html)

REC (Regional Environmental Centre for Central and Eastern Europe), 2001. *Environmental taxes in an enlarged Europe.* REC, Szentendre, Hungary.

UNECE, 1995–2002. *Environmental performance reviews programme.* Environmental Performance reviews of Estonia, Romania, Uzbekistan, Armenia, Bulgaria, Kazakhstan, Republic of Moldova, Latvia, Lithuania and Slovenia. www.unece.org/env/epr/

UNEP (United Nations Environment Programme), 2002a. *Caucasus environment outlook (CEO) 2002.* Tbilisi.

UNEP (United Nations Environment Programme), 2002b. *Global status 2002: Sustainable consumption and cleaner production.* UNEP Division of Technology, Industry and Economics, Paris.

WHO (World Health Organization), 1999. *Safe management of wastes from healthcare activities.* Prüss, Giroult and Rushbrook (eds). WHO, Geneva. http://www.who.int/water_sanitation_health/Environmental_sanit/MHCWHanbook.htm

WSSD, 2002. *World Summit on Sustainable Development: Plan of implementation.* Advance unedited text, 5 September 2002.

8. Water

Only a few European citizens suffer from the devastating shortages of water and poor water quality experienced by people in many other parts of the world. However, water resources in many areas of Europe are under threat from a range of human activities. About 31 % of Europe's population lives in countries that use more than 20 % of their annual water resource, this being indicative of high water stress. Drinking water quality is still of concern throughout Europe, with significant microbiological contamination of drinking water supplies in eastern Europe, the Caucasus and central Asia (EECCA), contamination by salts in central Europe and more than 10 % of European Union citizens potentially exposed to microbiological and other contaminants that exceed the maximum allowable concentrations.

Problems are generally highest near pollution 'hot spots' resulting from a range of industrial and other activities. The situation is generally of greatest concern in some EECCA countries, especially as regards the quality of drinking water in terms of microbiology and toxic substances. This reflects the relatively poor economic conditions in this region, and in several countries the deterioration or lack of infrastructure for providing clean drinking water.

The health of humans and ecosystems is also threatened in other parts of Europe. One example is water contaminated by organic and inorganic pollutants such as pesticides and heavy metals at concentrations greater than those laid down in standards by the EU and other international organisations.

Total fresh water abstractions fell during the last decade in most regions. However, 31 % of Europe's population lives in countries that experience high water stress, particularly during droughts or periods of low river flow. Water shortages also continue to occur in parts of southern Europe where there is a combination of low water availability and high demand, particularly from agriculture.

Although there has been significant progress in management of water resources and quality across Europe, problems still persist. This is especially so where there is a lack of capacity and financial resources for monitoring and for implementing essential measures and technical improvements.

In western Europe and the accession countries, river, lake and coastal water quality, in terms of phosphorus and organic matter, is generally improving, reflecting decreases in discharges, resulting mainly from improved wastewater treatment. Nitrate levels have remained relatively constant — but significantly lower in accession countries reflecting less intensive agricultural production than in the EU. Concentrations of nutrients are much higher than natural or background levels. Eutrophication, as indicated by high phytoplankton levels in coastal areas, is highest near river mouths or big cities.

Heavy metal concentrations in western European rivers, and their direct discharges and atmospheric deposition into the North East Atlantic Ocean and the Baltic Sea, have all fallen as a result of emission reduction policies. Existing information on the state of waters in EECCA shows that many rivers, lakes, groundwater and coastal waters are polluted, often with hazardous substances including heavy metals and oil. The pollution tends be concentrated in localised hot spots downstream of cities, industrialised and agricultural areas and mining regions. Away from these hot spots, river and lake water quality appears to be relatively good.

Oil pollution caused by discharges from coastal refineries and offshore installations is decreasing in western Europe. However, illegal discharges, mainly from ships, are still a problem, especially in the North Sea and Baltic Sea. Oil pollution in general, from several sources, is of major concern in the Black Sea, the Caspian Sea and the Mediterranean. The recent disaster involving the oil tanker Prestige, off the coast of northern Spain, highlighted the need to reduce risks from similar accidents in the future.

8.1. Introduction

Few European citizens suffer from the devastating water shortages and poor water quality experienced by people in so many areas of the world. However, water resources in Europe are, in many locations, under threat from a range of human activities leading in some areas to significant problems of overexploitation and of quality of inland and marine waters.

Pressures result from economic growth and economic recovery in some countries of central and eastern Europe, the Caucasus and central Asia (EECCA). In these countries, demands for agriculture, particularly for irrigation, growing urbanisation, continuing inadequacies in wastewater treatment and increasing leisure activities create high stresses on water. This arises both from natural changes and from disasters such as floods and droughts.

The environmental consequences of over-stressed water resources, improper irrigation practices, pollution discharges and poor water quality include salinisation, eutrophication, erosion and, in extreme cases desertification (see Chapter 9, Box 9.1). Problems are often greatest near 'hot spots' that result from a range of industrial and other activities. The situation is generally of greatest concern in some of the EECCA countries, with the disastrous changes in the Aral Sea being an extreme example, but the environment and the health of humans and ecosystems are also threatened in other parts of Europe. Of particular significance is water contamination by organic and inorganic pollutants such as pesticides and heavy metals at concentrations greater than those laid down in directives, recommendations and target levels from the European Union (EU) and other international organisations.

Although problems remain, there has been significant progress in the management of water resources and quality as a result of a number of policies and measures implemented in recent years following international and regional agreements and conventions. But some indicators of water quality show a slowing or even levelling out of the rate of improvement and, particularly in some eastern European countries, there is a lack of capacity and financial resources for monitoring and for implementing essential measures and technical improvements.

8.2. Water abstraction and use

8.2.1. Rates of water abstraction and their impacts

Overall, Europe abstracts a relatively small portion of its total renewable water resources each year. Total water abstraction in the region is about 595 km^3/year, only 7 % of the total freshwater resource. Resources are unevenly distributed across the region, and even if a country has sufficient resources at the national level there may be problems at regional or local levels. Kazakhstan, Turkmenistan, Cyprus, Tajikistan, Malta and Kyrgyzstan have the least available water, with an annual runoff of less than 160 mm, and as little as 37 mm for Kazakhstan. The countries with the highest runoff, more than 1 700 mm, are the ones most dependent on external resources, such as Bulgaria, Serbia and Montenegro, Croatia and the Netherlands.

For this assessment the following threshold values/ranges for the ratio of abstraction against renewable resources have been used to indicate levels of water stress:

- non-stressed countries — less than 10 %;
- low stress — 10 % to less than 20 %;
- stressed — 20 % to less than 40 %;
- severe water stress — 40 % or more.

The thresholds above are averages and it would be expected that areas for which the ratio is above 20 % would also experience severe water stress during drought or low river flow periods. In 33 countries this ratio is less than 10 % while in 14 countries it is more than 20 %.

Figure 8.1.	Changes in water abstraction in European regions (index 1990 = 100)

Notes: Western central: Austria, Belgium, Denmark, Germany, France, Luxembourg, Netherlands, England and Wales; western southern: Spain, France, Greece, Italy, Portugal; AC-10 (central accession countries): Bulgaria, Czech Republic, Estonia, Hungary, Lithuania, Latvia, Poland, Romania, Slovakia, Slovenia; EECCA: Armenia, Azerbaijan, Belarus, Georgia, Kazakhstan, Kyrgyzstan, Republic of Moldova, Russian Federation, Turkmenistan, Tajikistan, Ukraine, Uzbekistan.

Sources: Eurostat New Cronos; EEA questionnaire (2002)

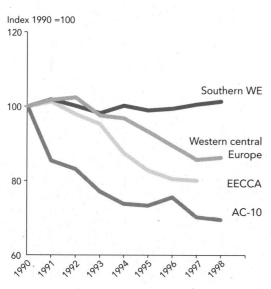

The region abstracts only 7 % of its freshwater resources. A total of 33 countries can be considered as non-stressed or low-stressed. However, there are 14 countries that abstract more than 20 % of their freshwater resources.

As a consequence, the most highly stressed countries have problems with overexploitation of groundwater resources and consequent water table depletion and salt-water intrusion into coastal aquifers. Basins with higher exploitation indices suffer the impacts of over-abstraction in many of their rivers or aquifers. The Mediterranean area is particularly affected by saline intrusion due to groundwater overexploitation. The drying-up of the Aral Sea and Lake Sevan (see Box 8.1) are examples of the consequences of very intensive abstraction.

High rates of direct river abstraction and the rapid expansion of groundwater abstraction over the past 30–40 years have supported new agricultural and socio-economic development in regions where alternative surface water resources are insufficient, uncertain or too costly (EU, 2000). Many originally perennial streams (particularly in arid regions) have become intermittent due to various abstractions (Smakhtin, 2001).

However there are examples of how water resources can recover once overexploitation has ceased. In Hungary (OECD, 2000a) the intensity of groundwater use has fallen by one third since the mid-1980s. In Transdanubia, after overexploitation of karstic groundwater by mining operations was stopped in the early 1990s, the water table, which had fallen by 30 m, recovered. In Latvia, intensive and non-balanced use of groundwater had caused large underground depression fields in Liepaja (1 000 km²) and Riga (7 000 km²) catchments but a decrease in water consumption during the 1990s, due to the implementation of water consumption accounting and economic instruments, has led to a gradual rise in the water level (Latvian Environment Agency, 2002) (Figure 8.2). In the Amsterdam dunes, a large-scale artificial recharge scheme made possible a substantial restoration of the freshwater store (EUCC, 2000). In the late 1980s the Spanish La Mancha Occidental in the upper Guadiana basin was declared overexploited with abstractions of 600 million m³/year. Since then abstractions have been reduced to 300 million m³/year and there has been a marked recovery of the water stored in the aquifer, which also means a recovery of the valuable associated ecosystems (Figure 8.3). This decrease in agricultural water use in the area was to a large degree the result of implementing an EU-funded agri-environment scheme.

Changes in the underground water level and water abstraction in Riga and Liepaja, 1980–2000 — Figure 8.2.

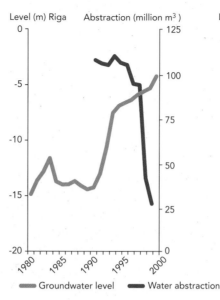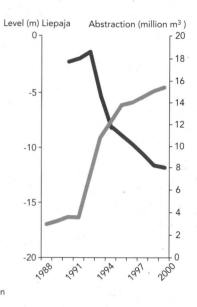

Source: Latvian Environment Agency, 2002.

Annual abstractions from the aquifer and water-level recovery at representative borehole in La Mancha Occidental — Figure 8.3.

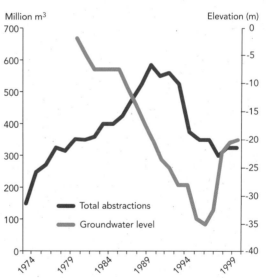

Source: MMA, 2000

Total fresh water abstractions have decreased over the past decade in most regions.

However, in southwestern European countries, some of which have high water stress, water abstraction has remained constant.

Box 8.1. Impact of water exploitation on major water bodies: examples of the Aral Sea and Lake Sevan

Figure 8.4.	Water consumption in Aral Sea basin

Aral Sea coastline

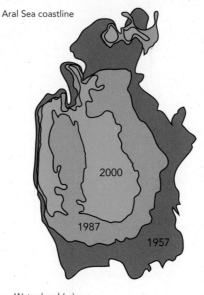

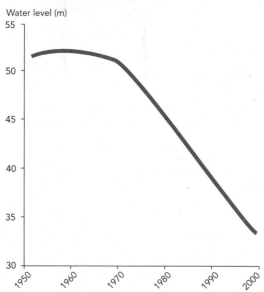

The Aral Sea was the fourth largest inland water body in the world before 1960 but the sea has been drying up since then. Central Asia uses almost 67 % of its freshwater resources and almost 100 % in the Aral Sea basin, largely for irrigation of cotton and rice. This has caused the sea level to fall by 17 m and the surface area to diminish by 75 %. As a consequence water salinity increased from 10 g/l in 1965 to 40–50 g/l in 2000 and the sea lost its fishery importance. In the late 1970s, several species of fish failed to reproduce. Marshes and wetlands which covered around 550 000 ha in 1960 have almost disappeared (only 20 000 ha were left in 1990). More than 50 lakes have dried up.

Most of the catchment is salinised because of irrigation, the salt content of soils and pastures being 0.5–1.5 %. It has been estimated that at least 73 km³/year of water would have to be discharged to the Aral Sea for a period of at least 20 years to recover the 1960 level (53 m above the sea level).

Lake Sevan in Armenia (1 256 km²) is another lake affected by the overexploitation of water resources. It is one of the oldest lakes in the world and has an important endemic flora and fauna. The surface of the lake has shrunk by 11 % over the past 60 years because of water overexploitation. Since 1981, there has been a tunnel transferring water from the Arpa River, which is in another catchment, to compensate for the loss of water.

The lake's water has traditionally been used for irrigating crops on the Ararat plain. The reduction in water levels and surface area has had detrimental consequences on the ecology of the lake: fish populations have decreased and the aquatic habitat has deteriorated. Fishing, tourism, irrigation, hydropower production and drinking-water supply have all been badly hit. In response, the Armenian Government initiated the Lake Sevan Environmental Action Programme in 1995 to solve or mitigate the problems.

Sources: UNEP/GRID-Arendal; Saving Aral Sea Fund (Aral Sea web page); Armenia, 1998

8.2.2. Water use by sectors

On average, 42 % of total water abstraction in Europe is used for agriculture, 23 % for industry, 18 % for urban use and 18 % for energy production (Figures 8.5 and 8.6).

> 😐 Agriculture accounts for 50–70 % of total water abstraction in southwestern European countries and EECCA. Cooling for electricity production is the dominant use in the central European countries.

In western central Europe, during the past decade, water abstraction for public water supply has fallen by about 9 %, for agriculture by 10 %, for energy production by 14 %, and for industry by a dramatic 28 %.

In southwestern countries, where water abstraction for agriculture is the dominant (70 %) water use, abstraction for irrigation increased by 5 % in the past decade. Abstraction for urban use and industry was relatively constant, and abstraction for cooling for energy production fell by 15 %.

In the EECCA and central accession countries, the decrease in industrial and agricultural activities (see Chapters 2.2 and 2.3) during economic transition led to a marked decrease in water abstraction for these uses. In the central accession countries water use by industry and agriculture both fell by 70 %, in EECCA; industrial use fell by 50 % and agricultural use by 74 %.

There was a 30 % decrease in abstraction for public water supply in the past decade in central accession countries. In EECCA there was also a 10 % reduction in urban water use. In most countries, the new economic conditions made companies increase the price of water and install water meters in houses. This contributed to a reduction in the amount of water used. Industries connected to the public supply system also had decreasing production. Nevertheless in most countries the supply network is still obsolete and losses in distribution still lead to high abstractions to meet demand.

Among the southern accession countries, there has been a recent 35 % increase in irrigation water demand in Turkey because of new irrigation projects (Table 8.1). In Malta, water abstraction for urban use has fallen and in Croatia there has been a 10 % reduction in water demand mainly because of the decline in industrial production (MZOPU, 2002).

Sectoral abstraction of water per region | **Figure 8.5.**

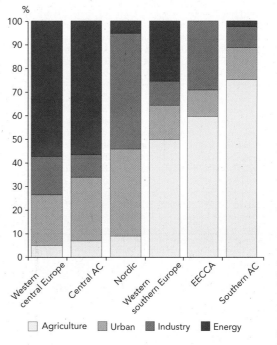

Notes: Western central: Denmark, Germany, Belgium, United Kingdom, Ireland, Austria, Luxembourg, Switzerland, the Netherlands, Liechtenstein; central accession countries: Poland, Czech Republic, Estonia, Lithuania, Latvia, Romania, Slovakia, Hungary, Slovenia, Bulgaria; Nordic: Finland, Sweden, Norway, Iceland; western southern: Spain, France, Greece, Italy, Andorra, Portugal, San Marino, Monaco; EECCA: Kazakhstan, Turkmenistan, Tajikistan, Kyrgyzstan, Ukraine, Russian Federation, Belarus, Uzbekistan, Republic of Moldova, Armenia, Azerbaijan, Georgia; southern accession countries: Cyprus, Malta, Turkey. Industry in EECCA may include water use for cooling.

Sources: Eurostat New Cronos; EEA questionnaire (2002); Aquastat (FAO), 2002 for EECCA countries

Agricultural water use
The major part (85 %) of irrigated land in western Europe (WE) is in the Mediterranean area (France, Spain, Italy, Portugal, Greece). In the accession countries the major part (93 %) is in Romania and Turkey. In EECCA, the Aral Sea basin accounts for 51 % of the total.

Traditionally, much of the irrigation in Europe has consisted of gravity-fed systems, where water is transported from surface sources through small channels and used to flood or furrow-feed agricultural land. However, in an increasing number of regions in the north and south, irrigation by sprinklers using pressure, often drawing water from subterranean aquifers, is the most common practice. It is often in these areas that the quantities of water used, and thus the impact on the environment, are the largest.

Irrigation is the main cause of groundwater overexploitation in agricultural areas. Examples include the Greek Argolid plain of eastern Peloponnesus, where it is common to find boreholes 400 m deep contaminated by sea-water intrusion. Irrigation in the area between the Danube and Tisza in Hungary,

Table 8.1.	Planned water supply projects in Europe
Greece	The Acheloos river diversion project aims to irrigate 380 000 ha in the plain of Thessalia, on the eastern side of the Mount Pindos watershed.
Portugal	The Alqueva water development project in the Guadiana basin (to be completed in 2024) is expected to have a strong irrigation component, expanding Portugal's current total 632 000 ha of irrigated land by some 110 000-200 000 ha, largely by converting traditional extensive agroforestry systems (*mentador*) to intensive irrigated cropping.
Spain	The old infrastructure of most irrigation projects and their poor maintenance was the basis for the Spanish national plan for irrigation, approved in 1996, which affects 1.1 million ha. The measures are intended to improve the efficiency of water use, adapt crops to production and avoid aquifer overexploitation and pollution. The Spanish national hydrological plan (SNHP) from 2001 proposes to meet the country's water demands by transferring water from areas where it is in excess to other areas with a water deficit. Water transfer was envisaged as the most feasible solution for satisfying water demands across the country, after a cost-benefit analysis which took account of the environmental, socio-economic and technical variables. The National SNHP Act does not allow the use of the transferred resources either for new irrigation projects or for broadening existing ones. The main water transfer is planned from the Ebro basin to the southeast, where water resources shortage has been identified as 'structural'.
Turkey	The southeastern Anatolia project (GAP) aims to develop an area of more than 7 million ha within the basins of the Dicle (Tigris) and Firat (Euphrates). It includes 13 sub-projects, to be completed over a period of 10 years and an extra 1.7 million ha will be irrigated.

Source: OECD, 1999–2001; national state of the environment reports

Box 8.2. Examples of the impacts of tourism on water resources

Greece
The most serious shortages occur in the Aegean islands. Tourism's heavy water demand sometimes leads to over-pumping of groundwater and salt intrusion into aquifers. Water use for tourism activities, which averages 450 l/day per tourist in deluxe hotels, is several times higher than average water use by Greek residents, placing a strain on water resources. The popularity of golf courses and swimming pools is a major factor in the high water intensity of the tourism sector. During the peak tourist season, tankers are used to transport drinking water to 14 islands in the Aegean, at an annual cost of EUR 1.5 million (OECD, 2000b).

Turkey
In many tourist areas (and nearby residential areas) adequate drinking water, sewerage and water treatment services are still sorely lacking. Tourism's heavy seasonal and geographical concentration results in over-pumping of groundwater and the discharge of large volumes of untreated wastewater to lakes, rivers and coastal waters. The development of golfing (land acquisition, high water use for sprinkling, fertiliser and pesticide use) also increases environmental pressures (OECD, 1999).

Croatia
Due to the concentration of tourists in space and time, there is often a shortage of freshwater, particularly on the islands and in the driest coastal regions. Existing sources of water are sufficient for most of the year but problems arise in the summer months, when water consumption is four to five times higher than in winter. The resulting shortage is resolved by bringing in water from the mainland (UNECE, 1999a).

Balearic Islands, Spain
Water demand per inhabitant is estimated to be around 279 l/day. Most of the water (89.5 %) is taken from groundwater, 2.5 % from surface water (reservoirs), 6.8 % is reused water and 1.2 % comes from desalination plants. Most of the available water is used for agriculture and urban purposes, but irrigation of golf courses is becoming more important. Different measures have been implemented to reduce the increasing demand for water created by tourism. These include the diversification of supply (e.g. desalination plants and wastewater reuse), water-saving campaigns and economic instruments such as an eco-tourist tax. (BIRHP, 1999).

and the aquifers of the upper Guadiana River basin in Spain, have both led to a lowering of the shallow groundwater table, threatening some natural wetlands.

In the 1990s there was a slight increase (1 %) in irrigated area in southwestern countries, mainly due to increased cropping and irrigation of maize. In the central accession countries and EECCA, the area under irrigation only decreased slightly during the 1990s, however, water use for irrigation dropped markedly (Figure 8.6). In many accession countries only a minor part of the area equipped with irrigation structures is actually irrigated, for example only 10-15 % in Romania. In many eastern countries and in EECCA, the water distribution networks, pumps, and sprinklers are badly maintained, leaks have increased and the pumping systems are highly energy intensive. In Armenia, for example, the cost of electricity for irrigation represents 65 % of the total operating cost of the irrigation system and is barely affordable.

Several new water supply projects are planned in Europe (see Table 8.1) and rehabilitation of the badly maintained irrigation structures in eastern Europe and EECCA may increase the demand for irrigation water.

Urban water use
Increased urbanisation, population growth and higher living standards have been major drivers of the increase of urban water use in the past century. In WE and the accession countries, urban use (households and industries connected to public water supply) of water per capita is around 100 m³/year. In some western countries, water use fell during the 1990s as a result of a focus on water saving, increased metering and the use of economic instruments (water charges and tariffs). In others, urban water use has continued to increase as a result of more people being connected to water supply systems, more households and changes to more water-consuming lifestyles (more washing machines, baths, swimming pools, etc.)

In the accession countries and EECCA, urban water use around 1990 was in general very high. However, in some countries there was a large rural population not connected to the public water supply. In the central accession countries and EECCA there was a 30 % and 10 % decrease, respectively, in urban water use during the 1990s (Figure 8.6).

Tourism water use

Tourism places severe, often seasonal, pressures on water resources at the regional and/or local level across parts of Europe, and is one of the fastest increasing socio-economic activities in Europe. The increase in water demand is often associated with recreational uses such as swimming pools, golf courses and aquatic parks as well as consumption by a much-increased population during holiday seasons (see Box 8.2.).

8.2.3. Measures to reduce water use

While there has been a general trend towards higher water prices throughout Europe, water prices still vary considerably. Milan and major cities in Turkey have the lowest prices, about 75 % below the average of approximately EUR 1/m³ in the late 1990s. Many of the capitals and major cities in Mediterranean countries also have below-average prices, as do those in countries with abundant water supplies. In contrast, water prices are highest in northern and western European cities (about 75–100 % more than the average). Charging consumers for water is an economic instrument used by some countries to help to reduce water use. Other factors that influence water-use patterns include climate variations, information campaigns, use of water-saving technologies and improved performance of distribution networks (reduction of leakages and mains pressures).

In many eastern European countries, water prices were heavily subsidised before 1990 but there was a marked increase in prices during transition, resulting in lower water use. In Hungary, for example, water prices increased 15-fold after subsidies were removed which led to a reduction in water use during the 1990s of about 50 % (Figure 8.7).

In many of the eastern European countries and EECCA the water supply networks are in a poor condition due to faulty design and construction, as well as lack of maintenance and ineffective operation as a consequence of the decline of the economic situation in the past decade. Leakages are generally high and in many cases 30–50 % of the water is lost. Some cities only have water for part of the day (UNECE, 1998–2000).

8.3. Drinking water quality

8.3.1. Overall trends

Drinking water quality in still of concern throughout Europe (Figure 8.8). All of the

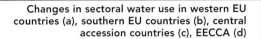
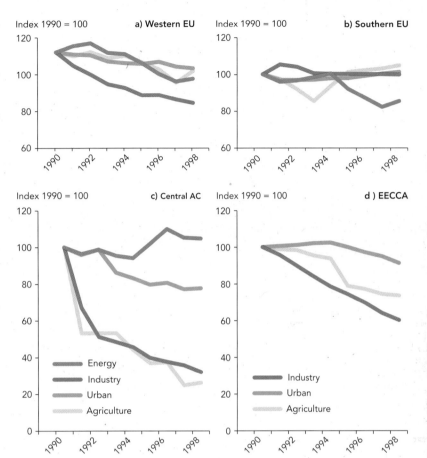

Figure 8.6. Changes in sectoral water use in western EU countries (a), southern EU countries (b), central accession countries (c), EECCA (d)

Notes: Western EU: Austria, Belgium, Denmark, Germany, France, Luxembourg, Netherlands, England and Wales; southern EU: Spain, France, Greece, Italy, Portugal; central accession countries: Bulgaria, Czech Republic, Estonia, Hungary, Lithuania, Latvia, Poland, Romania, Slovakia, Slovenia; EECCA: Armenia, Azerbaijan, Belarus, Georgia, Kazakhstan, Kyrgyzstan, Moldova, Romania, Turkmenistan, Tajikistan, Ukraine, Uzbekistan.

Sources: Eurostat New Cronos; EEA questionnaire (2002)

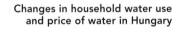
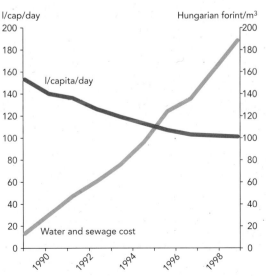

Figure 8.7. Changes in household water use and price of water in Hungary

Source: Hungarian Central Statistical Office, 2001

EECCA countries for which information was available (eight out of twelve countries) have major problems with microbiological contamination of drinking water supplies (Figure 8.9). The percentage of samples exceeding microbiological standards in EECCA is between about 5 % and 30 %. Exceedances are higher in non-centralised drinking water sources, primarily in rural areas. At least half the population of the Russian Federation is thought to be at risk from unclean water (OECD, 2000c) as a result of ageing infrastructures and the prohibitive cost of disinfectants. These countries also have problems with contamination from toxic chemicals and metals and there are also some reports of nitrate pollution.

EU countries also have problems with their drinking water. The most common problem identified from national reports is nitrate contamination (Figure 8.8). In addition, at least 12 % of citizens in nine EU countries were potentially exposed to microbiological and some other undesirable contaminants that exceeded the maximum allowable

concentrations laid down in the drinking water directive, in the years reported.

In the accession countries and southeastern European countries, the physico-chemical criteria for drinking water quality are the ones most commonly failed, often because of contamination by salts. The percentage of samples failed on the basis of other criteria implies that populations are also significantly exposed to other contaminants but the data are not available to calculate the proportion of the population affected.

8.3.2. The main source of drinking water: groundwater

Groundwater is a major source of drinking water all over Europe, and thus the state of groundwater in terms of quality and quantity is of vital importance (see Box 8.3). Groundwater is affected by human activities such as the use of nitrogen fertilisers and pesticides, water abstraction, and interventions in the hydrological cycle such as land sealing.

Nitrate in groundwater

Agriculture is the main source of nitrogen input to water bodies. The current usage of nitrogenous fertiliser per unit of arable land is highest in WE and lowest in EECCA (except for Uzbekistan). The agricultural use of commercial nitrogen fertilisers fell in nearly all of Europe in the 1990s (see Chapter 2.3). This decrease has been most marked in central and southeastern Europe (accession countries and others). However, average consumption per hectare remains lowest in EECCA.

Assessment of comparable time series for nitrate in groundwater shows relatively high mean values without any significant changes (Figure 8.10). Exceedances of the nitrate limit value (50 mg/l, defined in the EU drinking water directive) were found in around a third of the groundwater bodies for which information is currently available.

> In general, there has been no substantial improvement in the nitrate situation in European groundwater and hence nitrate pollution of groundwater remains a significant problem.

Pesticides in groundwater

Pesticides in groundwater (and surface waters) arise from diffuse and point sources. They are used in agriculture, horticulture,

Box 8.3. General groundwater quality in eastern Europe, the Caucasus and central Asia

For several countries, there is a substantial lack of comparable groundwater quality data. However, an assessment of national state of environment reports and other sources has provided some information.

In Armenia and Azerbaijan the groundwater resources are reported to be of high quality. However, Armenia has some local problems with high natural mineral content and also the threat of heavy-metal pollution from mine tailings. Belarus reports that its groundwater is generally of good quality with an improvement in overall quality over recent years. However, shallow wells in rural areas of Belarus are seriously affected by nitrates. In Georgia there are around 500 sites where groundwater pollution is found and in Kazakhstan there is extensive contamination with a number of toxic substances, and most areas do not comply with drinking water standards. In Kyrgyzstan increased nitrate concentrations have been observed at depths of 150 m in aquifers and serious groundwater contamination was reported in a region which provides 60 % of the drinking water for the capital. Approximately 75 % of deep aquifers in the Republic of Moldova have high natural mineralisation and so the water requires pre-treatment, and about 61 % of shallow rural wells have severe nitrate pollution. In the Russian Federation one of the main pollutants of groundwater is nitrate and in Ukraine there is major pollution from industry, mining and agriculture. Uzbekistan has a number of contaminated aquifers, particularly where the use of agricultural chemicals is high and close to large industrial enterprises.

Main drinking water problems identified by national reports	Figure 8.8.

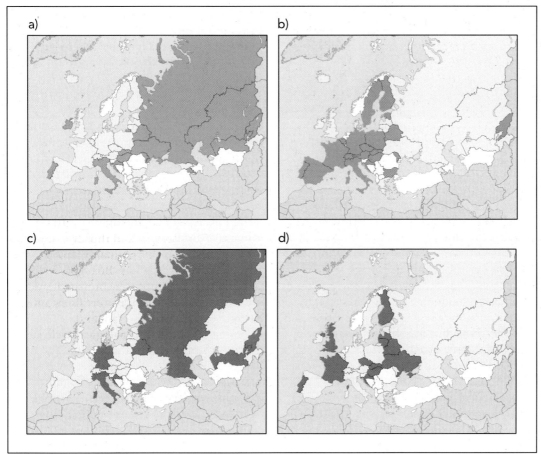

a) Microbiology
b) Nitrates
c) Toxics
d) Metals
No problems reported
No data
Outside data coverage

Notes: Data year is not the same for each country. Range of years 1997 to 2001.

Source: UNECE, 1998–2000; national state of environment reports

fruit growing, viticulture and forestry, for public and private pest-control purposes, manufacturing and industrial activities. As groundwater is a major source of drinking water and also forms the base flow of many rivers, the presence of pesticides in groundwater is of concern from the point of view of human health and the protection of aquatic ecosystems. The monitoring of pesticides is a challenging task due to the high number of registered pesticide substances, but the data suggest that pesticide pollution of groundwater is a problem in parts of Europe.

Pesticides are causing groundwater quality problems in many European countries. Six EU countries, six accession countries and eight of the twelve EECCA countries have indicated that there is a danger of pesticide pollution in their groundwater.

Samples exceeding microbiological parameters in the countries of eastern Europe, the Caucasus and central Asia	Figure 8.9.

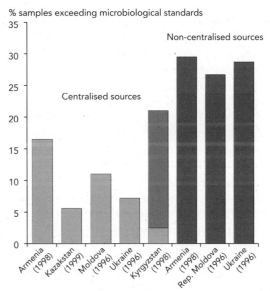

% samples exceeding microbiological standards

Non-centralised sources

Centralised sources

Note: Data for Kyrgyzstan show the range of percentage exceedances since the only regional data that were available could be not aggregated.

Source: UNECE, 1998-2000

Figure 8.10.	Temporal development of nitrate mean values in groundwater bodies

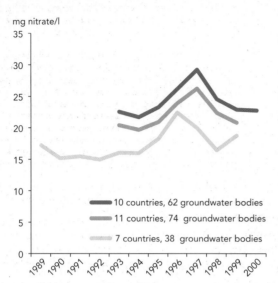

Notes: For each time series the annual mean values of sampling sites were aggregated on the level of groundwater bodies and, furthermore, the groundwater body means were aggregated at the European level (arithmetic mean). Elevated NO_3 mean concentrations in 1996, 1997 are mostly caused by single, very high nitrate concentrations. Data from Austria, Belgium, Bulgaria, Denmark, Estonia, Spain, Hungary, Lithuania, Latvia, Netherlands, Slovenia, Slovakia.

Source: Eurowaternet-Groundwater (2002)

8.4. Nutrient and organic pollution of inland and coastal waters

High organic matter concentration (measured as biological oxygen demand or BOD) has several effects on the aquatic environment including reducing the chemical and biological quality of river water, the biodiversity of aquatic communities and the microbiological quality of waters. High biological oxygen demand is usually a result of organic pollution, caused by discharges of untreated or poorly treated sewage, industrial effluents and agricultural runoff. A decrease in biological oxygen demand in rivers illustrates general improvements in river water quality in terms of the chemical and microbiological properties of the river.

Large inputs of nitrogen and phosphorus to water bodies (including rivers) can lead to eutrophication causing ecological changes. These result in a loss of plant and animal species, and have negative impacts on the use of water for human consumption and other purposes. Eutrophication contributes to a number of water quality problems such as phytoplankton blooms, reduced recreational aesthetics, oxygen depletion, and reduced transparency and fish kills. Some algal blooms produce toxins and also tastes and odours that make the water unsuitable for water supply.

In many catchments the main source of nitrogen pollution is runoff from agricultural land, though discharges from

wastewater treatment works can also be significant. For phosphorus, industry and households are often the most important sources though in some countries and agricultural catchments, and particularly where point sources have been reduced, agriculture can be the most important source.

8.4.1. In rivers

Organic matter concentrations (measured as biological oxygen demand at five days or BOD5) have fallen in rivers in accession countries and WE countries during the 1990s, with concentrations in accession country rivers being generally higher than those in WE rivers (Figure 8.11). The average orthophosphate concentrations are similar in rivers in WE countries and accession countries and have fallen during the 1990s. Concentrations are much lower in northern rivers and are around background levels.

Nitrate concentrations are considerably higher in WE rivers than in those in the accession countries, reflecting the more intensive agricultural practices in the WE countries. Concentrations in northern countries are much lower and are around background levels. Nitrate concentrations have remained fairly constant during the 1990s in northern accession countries and WE rivers.

In the central accession countries and Balkan countries, industrial production and pollution discharges decreased in the 1990s and there was a drastic reduction in pesticide and fertiliser use in agriculture. Consequently, pollution pressures on waters have eased considerably and in many places

☺ Levels of phosphorus and organic matter have generally been decreasing in rivers in WE countries and accession countries over the past decade. This reflects the general improvement of sewage treatment and, in the EU, the success of policies such as the urban wastewater treatment directive in reducing pollution of rivers.

☹ In contrast, levels of nitrate have remained relatively unchanged and above background levels in WE countries and accession countries. Levels of orthophosphate are also above background levels.

river quality has improved. However, there are still many polluted river stretches, in particular downstream of cities and industrial regions and in mining areas.

There are limited comparable data available from the EECCA countries. They indicate that phosphorus and nitrate levels in rivers are low compared to WE countries, and orthophosphate levels lower than those in the accession countries. Biological oxygen demand at five days is also generally low. Eight of the twelve EECCA countries identified nitrate levels as being of major concern in their rivers. Five countries reported ammonium and four countries reported microbiological quality as being a major concern. The latter is consistent with the reported high levels of microbiological contamination in drinking water in these countries.

8.4.2. Water quality in lakes and reservoirs

It has been recognised since the 1970s that anthropogenic discharges of nutrients were causing eutrophication in many European lakes. Since then, the proportion of lakes and reservoirs with low phosphorus concentrations (less than 25 (μ/l) has increased and the proportion with high concentrations (more than 50 (μ/l) has decreased. This indicates that eutrophication in European lakes is decreasing.

In the past, urban wastewater has been a major source of nutrient pollution but recently treatment has improved and outlets have been diverted away from many lakes. Diffuse pollution, particularly from agriculture, continues to be a problem.

Phosphorus enrichment of lakes is a bigger problem in the accession countries and WE than in the Nordic countries (Figure 8.12). This is because the Nordic countries (Iceland, Norway, Sweden and Finland) have lower population densities and lower agricultural intensities.

☺ Eutrophication of European lakes, reflected as phosphorus concentration, is generally decreasing.

☹ However, there are still many lakes and reservoirs with high concentrations of phosphorus due to human influence. Phosphorus concentrations are highest in the eastern European countries and lowest in the Nordic countries.

Biological oxygen demand at five days (a), orthophosphate (b), and nitrate (c) concentrations in rivers of western and northern part of western Europe and accession countries, 1990–2000	Figure 8.11.

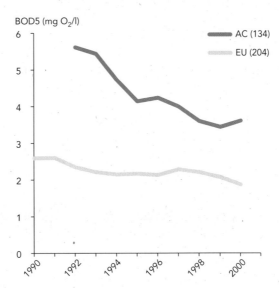

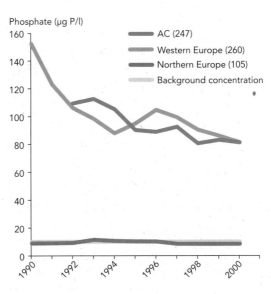

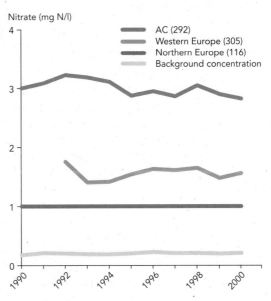

Notes: Number of stations in brackets and dotted line upper limit of the range of background concentrations.

Source: EEA European Topic Centre on Water (ETC/WTR), based on Waterbase

Figure 8.12.	Average summer total phosphorus concentrations in lakes: changes 1981–2001 (a) and in parts of Europe (b)

Source: EEA European Topic Centre on Water based on Waterbase

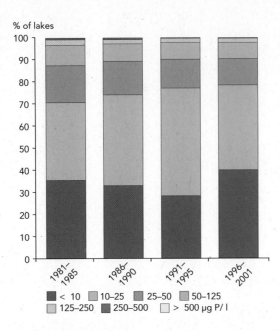

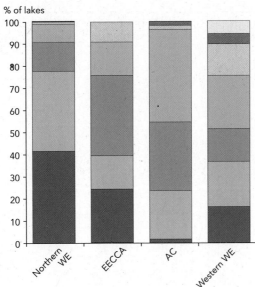

In many lakes, which were previously highly polluted by phosphorus, the phosphorus concentration has steadily decreased in recent decades in response to control of point sources such as urban wastewater treatment with phosphorus removal (e.g. Lake Constance and Ijsselmeer) (Figure 8.13).

In other lakes e.g. Loughs Neagh and Erne, concentrations have steadily increased. This is the result of a steady build-up of a surplus of phosphorus (arising from fertilisers) in the soils in the catchments draining into these lakes.

On many large European rivers, cascades of reservoirs have been constructed during the past century. The rivers Volga and Dnepr, for example, have six major reservoirs, each located on their main course, mostly downstream of large cities such as Moscow and Kiev. The reservoirs are heavily affected by nutrients and other pollutants discharged in the catchment.

8.4.3. Wastewater treatment

Wastewater from households and industry represents a significant pressure on the water environment. As well as containing organic matter and nutrients, it can also contain hazardous substances. The level of treatment of the wastewater before discharge and the sensitivity of the receiving waters will affect the impact it has on the aquatic ecosystem. EU countries have to implement directives such as the urban wastewater treatment directive, which prescribes the level of treatment required before discharge.

There has been marked improvement in the level of treatment (see Box 8.4 for definitions) and proportion of the population connected to treatment plants in WE countries since the 1970s. In the northern and central WE countries most of the population is now connected to wastewater treatment plants, many to tertiary plants which efficiently remove nutrients and organic matter.

In Belgium, Ireland and southwestern Europe only about half of the population is connected to wastewater treatment plants, with 30–40 % of the population connected to secondary or tertiary treatment plants.

In CEE countries on average 25 % of the population is connected to wastewater treatment plants, with most of the wastewater receiving secondary treatment. In some countries like Estonia around 70 % are

---

Box 8.4. Wastewater treatment — definitions

Primary treatment: removal of floating and suspended solids, both fine and coarse, from raw sewage.

Secondary treatment: following primary treatment by sedimentation, the second step in most wastewater systems in which biological organisms decompose most of the organic matter into an innocuous, stable form.

Tertiary treatment: the process which removes pollutants not adequately removed by secondary treatment, particularly nitrogen and phosphorus.

connected, while in countries like Hungary and Turkey only 32 % and 23 % are connected. There are still many large cities that discharge their wastewater nearly untreated (e.g. Bucharest).

There is no comparable or recent information for EECCA but the available information indicates that generally the level of wastewater treatment is low. At present only a small part of the population is connected to operating wastewater treatment plants and the existing plants are generally in a bad condition. There are high leakage levels in the networks, which leads to direct releases of raw wastewater to the environment (see Chapter 12). Many plants often operate only primary treatment, for technical reasons or because of economic conditions and the high price of electricity. However, in Belarus more than 70 % of the population is connected to operational urban wastewater treatment plants, the majority of which are in good operational condition. In addition, all cities have plants with biological treatment.

Though the percentage of the western European population that is connected to wastewater treatment plants increased between 1970 and 1990 and then remained fairly constant to 1999 (Figure 8.14), levels of biological oxygen demand have declined due to improvements in wastewater treatment. Organic matter discharged from urban wastewater treatment plants has decreased in Denmark, Finland, the Netherlands and the United Kingdom (Figure 8.15).

The levels of wastewater treatment in western Europe and in central and eastern Europe have improved significantly since the 1970s.

However the percentage of the population connected to wastewater treatment is still relatively low in central and eastern Europe, although increasing.

In eastern Europe, the Caucasus and central Asia there is a very low level of treatment of wastewater in terms of population connected to treatment works, treatment levels applied and the operational efficiency of those treatment plants that do exist.

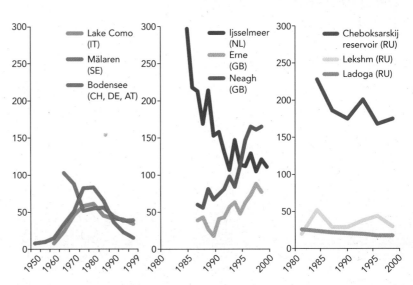

Trends in total phosphorus concentrations in some large European lakes — Figure 8.13.

Source: Information from national state of the environment reports

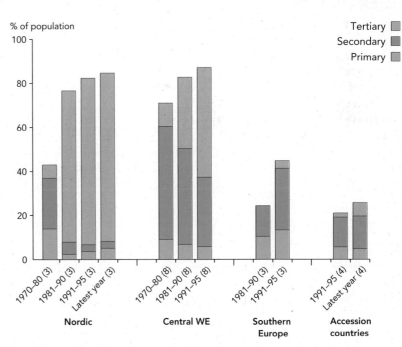

Changes in wastewater treatment in regions of Europe between 1980 and late 1990s — Figure 8.14.

Notes: Only countries with data from all periods included, the number of countries in parentheses; Nordic: Norway, Sweden, Finland; western central: Austria, Denmark, Germany, Ireland, the Netherlands, Luxembourg, Switzerland, United Kingdom; southern: Greece, Spain and Portugal; accession: Estonia , Hungary, Poland ,Turkey.

Source: Eurostat /OECD joint questionnaire (2000)

| Figure 8.15. | Discharge of organic matter (BOD) from urban wastewater treatment plants in Denmark, Finland, the Netherlands, and England and Wales |

Source: Information from national state of the environment reports and Eurostat /OECD joint questionnaire (2000)

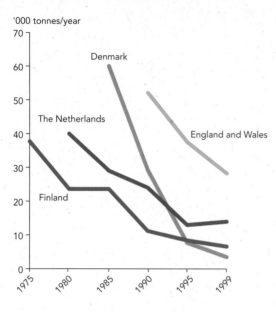

| Figure 8.16. | Discharge of organic matter (BOD) from point sources in five EU accession countries |

Note: Czech Republic, Estonia, Latvia, Lithuania and Slovakia.

Source: Information from national state of the environment reports

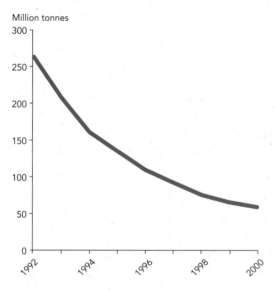

Organic matter discharged from point sources in the accession countries decreased dramatically during the 1990s (Figure 8.16). This may be due partly to the deep economic recession in the first half of the decade and the consequent decline in highly polluting heavy industry. Although economies have since improved and industrial output has increased, there has been a shift towards less-polluting industries.

Several industrial sectors, which in the 1970s and 1980s had large emissions of organic matter, have now markedly reduced their discharges by the introduction of cleaner technology and improved wastewater treatment (Figure 8.17).

The move towards cleaner technologies is driven partly by EU directives such as the integrated pollution prevention and control directive, which requires large facilities to use the best available technology to make radical environmental improvements.

In several countries in the northwestern part of Europe there was a marked increase in the percentage of the population connected to tertiary wastewater treatment (removal of nutrients) during the 1990s. In the countries included in Figure 8.18 the percentage of the population connected to tertiary treatment increased from 40 % to 80 %. In the same period the discharge of phosphorus and nitrogen from wastewater treatment decreased by 30 % and 60 % respectively, reflecting that nearly all the tertiary treatment plants have phosphorus removal while only some of the plants, in particular the large plants, have nitrogen removal.

8.4.4. Discharge of nutrients to the seas

There is a direct relationship between riverine and direct discharges of nitrogen and phosphorus and the concentration of nutrients in coastal waters, estuaries, fjords and lagoons, which in turn affects their biological state. Measures to reduce the input of anthropogenic nutrients and protect the marine environment are being taken as a result of various initiatives at all levels (global, regional conventions and ministerial conferences, European and national). The EU nitrate directive and urban waste water treatment directive aim at reduction of nitrate discharges mainly from washout from agricultural soils and nutrient discharges from point sources, respectively. Also, the recent EU water framework directive aims, among other things, at achieving good ecological quality of coastal waters.

There were significant reductions in phosphorus discharges to the North Sea from urban wastewater treatment works, industry and other sources between 1985 and 2000 (Figure 8.19.). The reduction from agriculture has been less and this source was the largest in 2000. Nitrogen discharges to the North Sea decreased significantly from all four sources between 1985 and 2000 with agriculture being the major source in 2000. However some countries such as Norway, Sweden and the United Kingdom reported higher riverine discharges (and direct discharges for the United Kingdom) of nitrogen to the North Sea in 2002 than in

🙂 Discharges of both phosphorus and nitrogen from all quantified sources to the North Sea and Baltic Sea have decreased since the 1980s.

😐 Agriculture is now the major source of nitrogen and phosphorus discharges into the North Sea. For the Baltic Sea agriculture is the main source of nitrogen pollution and urban wastewater treatment the main source of phosphorus pollution.

😐 Data for the Black Sea and Caspian Sea is less comprehensive than for the Baltic and North Seas, but indicates that riverine discharges are the largest sources of nitrogen and phosphorus for both seas.

😐 Comprehensive data are also not available for the Mediterranean, but all coastal cities discharge their (treated or untreated) sewage to the sea and only 4 % have tertiary treatment, indicating that the nutrient input from this source may be high.

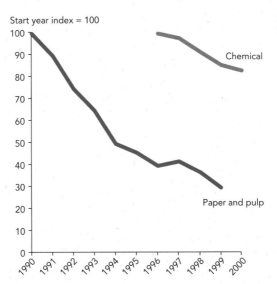

Discharge of organic matter (BOD) from selected industries

Figure 8.17.

Sources: CEPI Environment Report, 2000; CEFIC, 2001

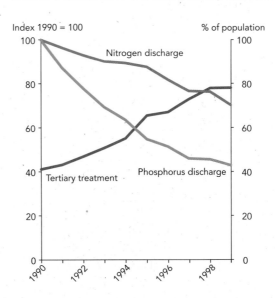

Changes in discharge of phosphorus and nitrogen from urban wastewater treatment plants and percentage of population connected to tertiary treatment

Figure 8.18.

Source: Information from national state of the environment reports and Eurostat/OECD joint questionnaire (2000)

1985, whereas the other states reported reductions (North Sea progress report, 2002). The high values in 2000 for Norway and Sweden could to a large extent be explained by unusually high precipitation levels during the autumn of that year causing high levels of non-anthropogenic runoff to rivers.

Even though the data for the Baltic Sea are less recent (late 1980s to 1995) they give a similar picture to the North Sea, with significant reductions in discharges of nitrogen and phosphorus from agriculture (partly due to the reduction in agriculture in some southern Baltic states), urban wastewater treatment works, industry and aquaculture (Figure 8.19). In 1995 the major sources of phosphorus and nitrogen to the Baltic Sea were urban wastewater treatment works and agriculture, respectively. Regarding point sources, the 50 % HELCOM (the governing body of the Convention on the Protection of the Marine Environment of the Baltic Sea Area) reduction target was achieved for phosphorus by almost all the Baltic Sea countries, while most countries did not reach the target for nitrogen (HELCOM, 2000).

The information from the Black and Caspian Seas is less comprehensive in terms of source apportionment and how discharges have changed with time (Figure 8.19.). In 1996 the most significant sources of phosphorus and nitrogen to the Black Sea were riverine inputs. The major rivers in the Black Sea catchment are the Danube, Dnepr, Don, southern Bug and Kuban, draining an area of around 2 million km² and receiving wastewater from more than 100 million people, heavy industries and agricultural areas. The Danube contributes about 65 % of the total nitrogen and phosphorus

Figure 8.19.

Source apportionment of nitrogen and phosphorus discharges to Europe's Seas and percentage reductions

Sources: North Sea progress report, 2002; Finnish Environment Institute, 2002; Black Sea Commission, 2002; Caspian Environment Programme, no date.

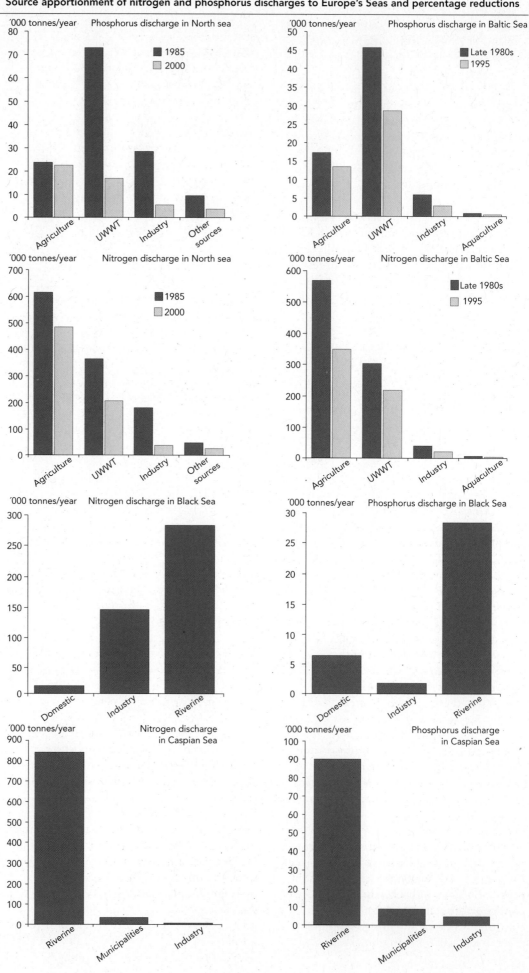

Winter surface nitrate concentrations in the greater North Sea are not changing. Concentrations are generally not changing in the Baltic Sea area, except for a fall at a few Danish, Finnish and Swedish stations. In the Black Sea, there is a slight decrease of nitrogen concentrations in Romanian coastal waters and a steady decline in Turkish waters at the entrance of the Bosphorus.

Decreases are observed in winter surface phosphate concentrations at a number of stations in the Belgian, Dutch, Norwegian and Swedish coastal waters of the North Sea and Skagerrak, and in the Danish, German, Lithuanian and Swedish waters of the Baltic Sea.

No general changes of total nutrient concentrations are observed at the majority of the coastal and marine stations in the Black Sea. A slow decrease in Turkish waters at the entrance of the Bosphorus is reported.

discharges from all sources. The information for the Caspian also shows riverine inputs contributing to the greatest proportion of nutrient loads. The Volga, Ural, Kura and Araks are the main rivers discharging into the Caspian Sea. The Volga's contribution to pollution discharges is more than 80 %.

Comprehensive data are also not available for the Mediterranean Sea, but all coastal cities discharge their (treated or untreated) sewage to the sea and only 4 % have tertiary treatment, indicating that the nutrient input from this source may be high. Agriculture is also intensive in the region and 80 rivers have been identified as contributing significantly to the pollution of the Mediterranean (EEA, 1999).

Quality of coastal waters
Maps 8.1 and 8.2 illustrate the mean winter surface concentrations (January to February/March, 0–10 m) of nitrate and phosphate, based on data from the Baltic Sea area, greater North Sea, Celtic, Mediterranean and Black Seas. In winter biological uptake and turnover of nutrients is lowest and the concentration of nutrients highest. There is a relationship between riverine discharges of nitrogen and phosphorus and the winter concentration of nutrients in lagoons, fjords, estuaries and coastal waters. Generally the nutrient concentrations decrease from fjords and estuaries through coastal waters to the open sea. Background nitrate concentrations in river water are between 0.1 and 1 mg N/l (7–70 μmol/l) and background phosphate concentrations are around 10 μg P/l (0.3 μmol/l).

The nutrient concentrations illustrated should be assessed against what is considered to be background levels of nutrients, which are quite different for the European seas (Table 8.2). The Mediterranean Sea is naturally oligotrophic and background nutrient levels would be expected to be lower than in the North or Baltic Seas. Due to the differences in nutrient regimes, no Europe-wide classification of nutrient concentrations is possible.

Nutrient concentrations at most stations have not significantly increased or decreased and levels at most stations in the Baltic, Mediterranean and Black seas are generally low. Some high nitrate and phosphate concentrations occur in the greater North and Celtic seas, particularly in estuaries, and there are some high phosphate concentrations on Italy's west coast.

At most of the stations for which there are enough data, no changes in nutrient concentrations are apparent. However, nitrate and phosphate concentrations are decreasing at a number of Danish and Swedish stations and decreases have also been reported in Turkish waters at the entrance of the Bosphorus (Black Sea Commission, 2002). Decreases in phosphate concentrations were also seen at some Belgian, Dutch, German and Lithuanian stations. However some Belgian and German North Sea stations showed increases. In two Finnish stations, increasing concentrations were also observed due to hypoxia and upwelling of phosphate-rich bottom water in the late 1990s.

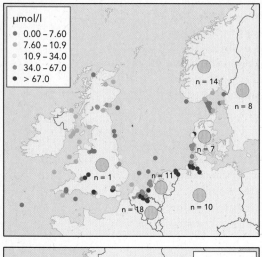

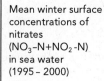

Mean winter surface concentrations of nitrates (NO$_3$–N+NO$_2$–N) in sea water (1995 – 2000)

Trend analysis 1985 – 2000 (stations with at least three years data 1995 – 2000 and at least five years in total)

■ Increase

▨ No trend

□ Decrease

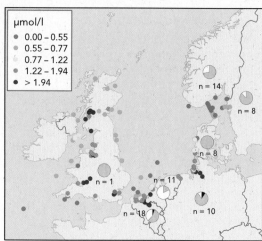

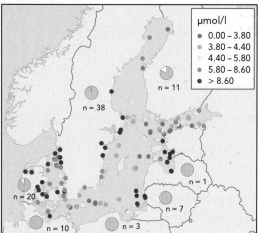

Map 8.1.

Notes: Classification not related to background values. In addition, the results of trend analyses of time series 1985–2000 (with at least three years data in the period 1995–2000) are shown for each country by a pie diagram. Pie diagrams are based on statistical trend assessments of nutrient concentrations at individual stations and show the percentage of stations with increasing, decreasing or no trend respectively.

Source: OSPAR, HELCOM, ICES, BSC and EEA member countries compiled by EEA European Topic Centre on Water

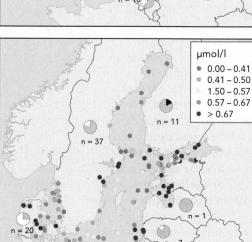

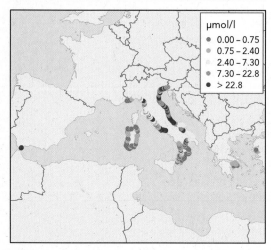

Map 8.2.

Mean winter surface concentrations of phosphate (PO$_4$ –P) in sea water (1995–2000)

Trend analysis 1985–2000 (stations with at least three years data 1995–2000 and at least five years in total)

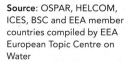

■ Increase

▨ No trend

□ Decrease

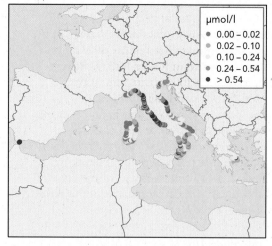

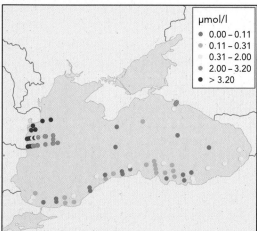

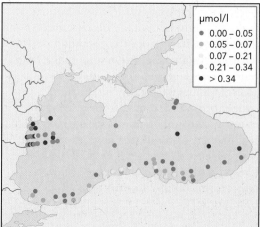

Eutrophication effects

In summer, phytoplankton primary production and chlorophyll-a concentration is nutrient-limited in most areas, and dependent on the general availability of nutrients (eutrophic level) in the specific area. The phytoplankton biomass expressed as chlorophyll-a determines the light conditions in the water column and the depth distribution of bottom vegetation, as chlorophyll-a might shadow the light necessary for growth of bottom vegetation. Secondary production of bottom fauna is most often food limited and related to the input of phytoplankton settling at the bottom, which in turn is related to the chlorophyll-a concentration (Borum, 1996). Adverse effects of eutrophication include low oxygen and hypoxic/anoxic conditions caused by the bacterial degradation of dead phytoplankton. Oxygen consumption is therefore high when the biomass of dead phytoplankton is high due to excessive growth of phytoplankton caused by enhanced nutrient availability. Bottom-dwelling animals and fish die if oxygen concentrations fall below 2 mg O_2/l. Eutrophication often leads to the disappearance of bottom vegetation in deeper coastal waters and the occurrence of harmful algal blooms.

Comparing seas on the basis of measurements from ships, mean summer surface chlorophyll-a concentrations are lowest (less than 0.4 µg/l) in Mediterranean open waters, low in the open North Sea (less than 3 µg/l) and high in the open waters of the Baltic Sea (more than 3 µg/l), probably due to summer blooms of cyano-bacteria. Some European coastal areas show higher chlorophyll concentrations, which reflect the land-based nutrient discharges to seas. These measurements are supported by satellite images.

Map 8.3 shows clear differences in the geographical distribution of concentration levels of chlorophyll-like pigments, especially in the eastern and southern North Sea and in the Baltic Sea. There are also relatively high concentrations seen in the Black Sea, particularly in the northwestern parts where hypoxia and hydrogen sulphide formation have gradually developed over the past 30 years leading to severe adverse effects on the ecological system. Thus, the area with hypoxic water in 2000 reached approximately 14 000 km², or 38 % of that part of the Black Sea. Table 8.3 summarises the areas where enhanced chlorophyll levels were observed from the satellite imagery.

Background concentrations of nutrients in µmol/l				Table 8.2.
	Rivers	North Sea	Baltic Sea	Mediterranean Sea	Black Sea
Nitrate + nitrite	7–70	9.2	4.6	0.5	0.1
Phosphate	0.3	1.3	0.68	0.03	0.29

Sources: EEA, 2001 (North and Baltic Sea); GESAMP (1990) (Mediterranean Sea)

Eutrophication is also a problem in the Caspian Sea, which is currently facing increasing anthropogenic pressures. However, chlorophyll-a is not routinely measured and so the extent of the problem is difficult to assess. It appears to be greatest in the shallow waters off the Volga delta (Caspian Environment Programme, no date).

In the Arctic Ocean, eutrophication is not a great problem since human population densities in the area are low and the duration of seasonal phytoplankton production is short due to the physical conditions (low temperatures and limited light during the winter).

Generally no changes have been observed in summer surface chlorophyll-a concentrations in the Baltic Sea, greater North Sea or Greek coastal waters during the past decade. Reductions have been observed at a few stations in Danish estuaries, and increases at a few stations in Belgian, Finnish, Lithuanian and Swedish coastal waters. The chlorophyll-a concentration is generally highest in estuaries and close to river mouths or big cities, and lowest in open marine waters.

Map 8.3.	Mean spring-summer concentrations of chlorophyll-like pigments in European seas determined from satellite observations

Source: Joint Research Centre, compiled by EEA

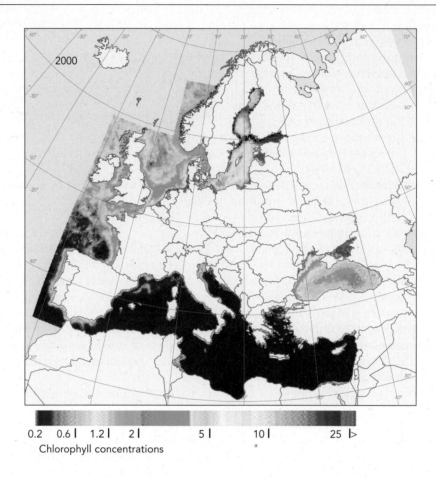

2000

0.2   0.6 | 1.2 | 2 | 5 | 10 | 25 |>

Chlorophyll concentrations

Table 8.3.	Coastal areas with apparently enhanced chlorophyll levels compared to neighbouring seas from the satellite spring-summer mean chlorophyll images

Source: EEA, 2001

Baltic Sea	Northeastern part and eastern coast of Bothnian Bay; the Quark area; coastal areas of Bothnian Sea; Gulf of Finland; Gulf of Riga; coastal areas off Kaliningrad and Lithuania; Gulf of Gdansk; Pomeranian Bight; Swedish Baltic coast proper
Belt Sea and Kattegat	Especially coastal and shallow areas of the Belt Sea and Kattegat
Skagerrak	Northeastern and southwestern parts and coastal areas of Skagerrak
North Sea	Eastern North Sea; German Bight; Wadden Sea; Southern Bight; UK coast and estuaries
English Channel	Coastal areas, especially Baie de Somme, Baie de Seine and Baie du Mont St Michel
Celtic Seas	Bristol Channel; Liverpool Bay with associated estuaries; Solway Firth; Firth of Clyde; Ireland's coast to the Irish Sea
Bay of Biscay and Iberian Coast	French coastal areas and estuaries in Bay of Biscay, especially in the vicinity of the Loire and Gironde estuaries; Spanish and Portuguese Atlantic coasts
Mediterranean Sea	Costa del Sol; vicinity of the Ebro delta; Gulf of Lyon; Italian west coast, especially Gulf of Gaeta, Napoli Bay and in the vicinity of the rivers Tiber and Arno; northern Adriatic Sea, especially Gulf of Venice and the areas influenced by the River Po; northern Aegean Sea, especially Bights of Thessaloniki and Thermaikos and in the Limnos area with inflow from the Black Sea through the Marmara Sea. Outside EU countries enhanced chlorophyll concentrations are found along the southeast coast of Tunisia and the Egyptian coast from Alexandria to Gaza
Black Sea, Marmara Sea and Sea of Azov	Marmara Sea, especially close to Istanbul and southern coastal areas; the northwestern Black Sea, especially along the Ukrainian and Romanian coasts influenced by the large rivers Danube, Dnieper, Dniester and Southern Bug, and less along the Bulgarian and Turkish coasts; the Sea of Azov

8.4.5. Bathing water quality

EU Directive 76/160 on bathing water quality was designed to protect the public from accidental and chronic pollution discharged in or near European bathing areas. The directive requires Member States to designate coastal and inland bathing waters and monitor the quality of these waters throughout the bathing season (May-September in most European countries). The directive sets both minimum standards (mandatory) and optimum standards (guideline). The designated beaches, for which data are reported by countries, are not the same each year, and compliance with the directive standards might be better than shown in Figure 8.20 if data from the same beaches were reported each year. However, studies have shown that meeting guide values does not necessarily protect public health. The European Commission proposed a new bathing water directive in October 2002.

Other European countries do not yet have to comply with the EU directive, although the accession countries have started its transposition into national law. In Romania there was an improvement of bathing water quality between 1996 and 2000. In Turkey in 1993, three of the 28 beaches along the Black Sea coast were unsuitable for bathing because the World Health Organization (WHO) standard for faecal streptococci was exceeded (OECD, 1999).

Within EECCA there are frequent closures of beaches on the Black Sea coast of the Ukraine, mainly because of the poor bacterial state of the water (UNECE, 1999b). One of the major causes of increased microbiological pollution in Ukrainian bathing waters is the lack of adequate systems for treatment of storm waters. River beaches in the Ukraine suffer from considerably higher bacterial pollution than sea beaches. In Georgia some beaches were closed in 1997 because of bacteriological pollution but since then there have been no closures despite the inadequate sanitary and epidemiological conditions of the beaches in summer seasons. In Azerbaijan, 95 % of the 140 km of Caspian Sea beaches and of the 10 km of lake and reservoir beaches meet national standards (Azerbaijan NCP, 2002).

☺ The quality of water at designated bathing beaches in the EU (coastal and inland) improved throughout the 1990s. In 2001, 97 % of coastal bathing waters and 93 % of inland bathing waters complied with the mandatory standards.

☹ Despite this improvement, 10 % of the EU's coastal bathing waters and 28 % of inland bathing beaches still do not meet (non-mandatory) guide values even though the bathing water directive was adopted almost 25 years ago.

☹ There are frequent problems with the quality of bathing waters reported for eastern Europe, the Caucasus and central Asia.

Compliance of EU coastal (a) and inland (b) bathing waters with the bathing water directive	Figure 8.20.

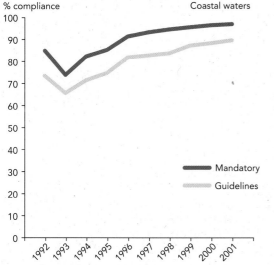

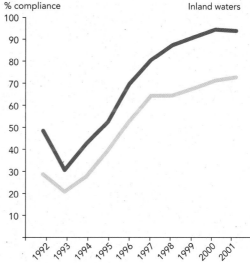

Notes: The directive sets both minimum standards (mandatory) and optimum standards (guide). For compliance with the directive, 95 % of the samples must comply with the mandatory standards. To be classified as achieving guide values, 80 % of the samples must comply with the total and faecal coliform standards and 90 % with the standards for the other parameters. The data set does not include France for 1999, 2000 and 2001.

Source: European Commission from annual reports by EU Member States

8.5. Pollution of water bodies by hazardous substances

The new EU water framework directive defines hazardous substances as 'substances or groups of substances that are toxic, persistent and liable to bio-accumulate; and other substances or groups of substances which give rise to an equivalent level of concern'. Hazardous substances include heavy metals, pesticides and other organic micro-pollutants (see Chapter 6) (see also EU, 2001a).

There is generally little comparable information at the European level on the presence and concentrations of hazardous substances in surface waters and groundwaters.

The quality of rivers in EECCA is hard to quantify because of the lack of comparable information. However, it is clear that many water bodies are heavily contaminated by hazardous substances. These hot spots are often downstream of major cities and/or major installations (e.g. industry or military) and/or mines.

Table 8.4 summarises information on the general status, main pressures and hot spots in rivers in EECCA, obtained from examination of national state of the environment reports and other sources. Some of the EECCA countries, such as Kyrgyzstan, Republic of Moldova and Tajikistan, reported that their surface waters are generally of good quality away from identified hot spots whilst others, such as Azerbaijan, Belarus, the Russian Federation and Ukraine, indicated higher levels of pollution. Two countries (Ukraine and Republic of Moldova) indicated that smaller rivers were more polluted than larger ones. Limited monitoring is also reported to be a problem in Armenia and Kyrgyzstan though it is likely that this is a problem in all EECCA. A common theme is the decline in economies leading to some industries closing but also to poor levels of treatment of effluents for those that remain. Also some countries have low levels of sewage treatment and connection to sewerage systems. The main sectors that affect water quality are reported to be industry, urban populations, mining, agriculture (particularly livestock), oil refining and military bases (including nuclear weapons testing sites).

8.5.1. Hazardous substances in rivers

Environmental quality standards are set for some hazardous substances for application at the EU level (List I substances — Figure 8.21) under the dangerous substances directive, and others are set nationally (e.g. List II substances). There are also standards for the levels of these substances in drinking water. These are to be complied with at the point of supply to the consumer (e.g. less than 0.1 µg/l for individual pesticides) but they are also useful for assessing concentrations in untreated water. For example Figure 8.22a shows the trends in occurrence of some commonly found pesticides in surface waters in England and Wales — the data show no definite trends but indicate that some pesticides occur at concentrations that would be of concern if the water were drunk untreated. Figure 8.22b shows the number of monitoring sites failing standards for the dangerous substances directive in England and Wales between 1994 and 2000. In terms of List I substances, compliance has improved over this period whilst there is no clear trend in terms of List II substances.

🙂 The concentrations of cadmium and mercury in selected EU rivers have decreased since the late 1970s, reflecting the success of measures to eliminate pollution by these two substances under the dangerous substances directive.

☹ Though there is evidence that the concentrations of some hazardous substances have been decreasing in some EU rivers, pesticides and other hazardous substances still occur at levels that are of potential concern in terms of supplies for drinking water and adverse effects on aquatic organisms.

☹ Though there is very limited information on the presence and levels of hazardous substances in their rivers, most of the EECCA countries identify the presence of hazardous substances as a major concern.

Summary of main hot spots and pressures in rivers in EECCA	Table 8.4.

Armenia	The main pollution problems in rivers originate from agriculture and municipal waste generation. Monitoring of water pollution is not well developed and will have to be extended as water management is improved.
	Water quality has improved in recent years as a result of the economic crisis and the reduction in industrial and agricultural activity. Regions with mines have high concentrations of heavy metals.
Azerbaijan	The estimates show that the total transit and flow of Azerbaijan's rivers on average (50% of provision) with only 30% of river flow resources formed within the country. Subsequently a large part of the pollution is of transboundary character. More than half of the larger rivers are considered contaminated. Many lakes are in a critical state.
Belarus	Most rivers in Belarus are moderately polluted. The most polluted tributary of the Dnieper is the Svisloch, which carries discharges from the Minsk sewerage system.
	With the decline in industrial production, the pollution load of water bodies has dropped significantly in recent years. In southern Belarus groundwater is considered to be relatively polluted.
Georgia	There are several polluted rivers in Georgia, where concentrations of phenols, hydrocarbons, copper, manganese, zinc and nitrogen are considerably higher than the national and international standards. Most water treatment plants are not operating or work at a very low level of efficiency; pollution by fertilisers and pesticides is also important.
Kazakhstan	Most water bodies suffer from serious environmental problems. Some of the most seriously polluted rivers are the Ural (phenols, petroleum by-products, boron), the Irtysch (copper, zinc, and petroleum by-products), Syr-Darya (sulphates and copper), Ilek (boron and chromium) and the Nura (mercury). The main polluters are industrial, mining, metal and refinery enterprises, and farms.
Kyrgyzstan	It is difficult to have a clear picture of the quality of surface waters, as monitoring is scarce and increasingly unreliable. In general it is said that the water bodies suffer only low levels of pollution. However, the quality of river water deteriorates near urban, agricultural and industrial centres. Pollution from mine tailing dumps also occurs in several places, for example contamination with radioactive materials, cadmium and other heavy metals (copper, zinc and lead).
Republic of Moldova	The water quality of the Dniester and Prut rivers, as well as of the lakes and reservoirs, is generally satisfactory. In comparison with the 1950s, the mineralisation of Dniester water has increased by 50 %. During the past two decades, concentrations of nitrogen and phosphorus have increased to 10 mg/l and 0.2 mg/l, respectively. The water of most small rivers falls between 'polluted' and 'strongly polluted'.
Russian Federation	Some of the major rivers in the Russian Federation (e.g. the Volga, Obj, Yenisej, Northern Dvina and the Don) and their tributaries are highly polluted. The main reservoirs are also highly polluted, especially the Volga cascade.
	The main sources of pollution are wastewaters discharged by industrial and agricultural enterprises, communal services, and also surface runoff. The most common surface water contaminants include oil, phenol, easily oxidised organic substances, metal compounds, nitrates and nitrites.
Tajikistan	The quality of surface water and groundwater in Tajikistan is high and only in separate regions does it tend to deteriorate. Huge pollution comes from housing and municipal sectors. Mining enterprises greatly influence the state of surface water and groundwater reservoirs. Sometimes, unexpected industrial water discharges result in fivefold to tenfold increases in the concentrations of toxic substances such as mercury, zinc or phosphorus in watercourses.
Turkmenistan	The Amu-Darya River is one of the most polluted water bodies of the central Asian region. The salt content of the river has increased markedly as a result of drainage from irrigated areas, which are for a significant part of transboundary character.
Ukraine	The main water-quality problems are related to municipal waste, diffuse sources of pollution and eutrophication. Almost all river basins in the Ukraine are classified as polluted or very polluted. The large rivers (Dnieper, Dniester, Southern Bug) are all polluted with oxygen-consuming substances, nutrients, heavy metals, oil and phenols. The smaller tributaries are more heavily polluted than the main rivers. However, there are also many unspoiled water bodies, particularly in the mountainous areas.
Uzbekistan	The majority of waterways are moderately polluted.
	The principal sources of water pollution are industry, agriculture and human settlements.

Sources: UNECE, 1998-2000; OECD, 1999-2001; national state of the environment reports

| Figure 8.21. | Annual average concentration of cadmium and mercury in EU rivers between late 1970s and 1996 |

Note: The EU environmental quality standards for cadmium and mercury in inland waters are 5 µg/l and 1 µg/l as annual averages, respectively.

Source: EU Member State returns under the exchange of information decision (European Council, 1977)

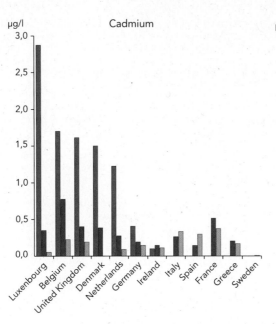

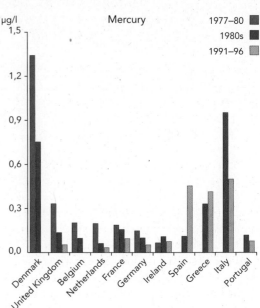

Ten of the twelve countries in EECCA identified heavy metals as a major problem in their rivers in their most recent state of the environment reports, with zinc, copper and cadmium being the metals most often reported as being of concern. In terms of organic micro-pollutants, oil and oil products were identified as a major concern by eight of the twelve countries, followed by phenol (seven) and pesticides (three) (see Box 8.5). Radioactivity was also reported to be a major concern in three countries. Ukraine and Kazakhstan reported the most 'major concerns'. More detailed information can be found in Table 8.4.

8.5.2. Input of hazardous substances to the seas

Inputs of hazardous substances to the seas result from direct discharges into marine waters, riverine inputs and atmospheric deposition, which follow emission of these substances into rivers and to air. There is specific legislation tackling these issues (see Box 8.6).

☺ Direct and riverine inputs of cadmium, mercury, lead and zinc into the North East Atlantic fell between 1990 and 1999, which shows the effects of emission reduction target setting in OSPAR.

☺ Atmospheric inputs of cadmium, lead and mercury into the North Sea fell between 1987 and 1995, showing the effect of air pollution abatement policies in the countries surrounding the North Sea.

☺ Discharges of many hazardous substances to the Baltic Sea have been reduced by at least 50 % since the late 1980s.

☹ There is very limited information on discharges to the Mediterranean, Black and Caspian Seas, and how these have changed over recent years.

Box 8.5. Pressures caused by cotton production in Europe

Cotton is an economically important crop for a few southern European and several central Asian countries. Cotton growers use large and increasing amounts of fertilisers, dangerous pesticides and large quantities of irrigation water, all of which give rise to a range of health and environmental problems. Cotton production has become increasingly associated with severe negative environmental impacts which include reduced soil fertility, salinisation, loss of biodiversity, water pollution, adverse changes in water balance, and pesticide-related problems including pollution and resistance.

Cotton production has played a big role in the degradation and drying-up of the Aral Sea (see Box 8.1). Cotton receives more pesticide (insecticides, herbicides, fungicides, defoliants) applications per season than any other crop, and accounts for at least one quarter of all agricultural insecticides used in the world. Banned pesticides (DDT, forms of HCH, aldrin and dieldrin) are associated with cotton-growing areas in several countries. For example, in Uzbekistan (the largest producer in central Asia), there are reported to be 1 500 tonnes of banned pesticides, including DDT and the HCH group, in various places (see also Chapter 2.3, Box 2.3.1).

North Sea states have met the 50 % reduction target for a large number of the 37 priority substances of the North Sea Conference, and most also achieved the 70 % reduction target for mercury, cadmium, lead and dioxins (Figure 8.23). However, targets were not consistently met for some other substances such as copper, tributyltin and some pesticides. For mercury and cadmium the largest sources in 1985 were industrial activities. In 1999 the importance of these sources had been reduced with waste disposal now the most important source for both metals (Figure 8.24).

Discharges of many hazardous substances to the Baltic Sea have been reduced by at least 50 % since the late 1980s — mainly as a result of the effective implementation of environmental legislation, the substitution of hazardous substances with harmless or less hazardous substances, and technological improvements. In Estonia, Lithuania, Poland and the Russian Federation, reductions have been due mainly to fundamental socio-economic changes (HELCOM web page). The reductions in Latvia have been due to construction of wastewater treatment facilities, and the implementation of new technologies and environmental legislation.

Occurrences of some commonly found pesticides in surface freshwaters in England and Wales, 1993–2000 — Figure 8.22a

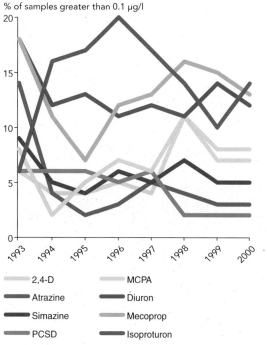

Source: Environment Agency of England and Wales web page

Non-compliance with List I and List II dangerous substances directive on environmental quality standards in England and Wales, 1994–2000 — Figure 8.22b

Box 8.6. Marine conventions legislation on reduction of emissions of hazardous substances and their inputs to seas

- The North Sea Conferences had set a target of a 50–70 % reduction in releases (discharges, emissions and losses) of several hazardous substances to water and air between 1985 and 1995. An action arising out of the Fourth North Sea Conference in 1995 was to continue to aim to achieve by 2000 the reduction targets set by the previous conference. It further agreed on the one-generation target for total cessation of discharges by 2020, which has also been adopted by the OSPAR Commission for the Protection of the North-East Atlantic. The ministers at the Fifth North Sea Conference in March 2002 recognised that increased efforts were necessary in order to meet the one-generation target.
- The Helsinki Commission for the Protection of the Baltic Sea adopted Recommendation 19/5 in May 2001 for cessation of hazardous substance discharge/emissions by 2020, with the ultimate aim of achieving concentrations in the environment near to background levels for naturally occurring substances and close to zero for man-made synthetic substances.
- The Mediterranean action plan (MAP) has three protocols which control pollution to the sea, including the input of hazardous substances. The dumping protocol lists a number of hazardous substances for which dumping is prohibited and sets out what must be considered before a dumping permit is issued for other substances. The emergency protocol details what national states must do when a harmful substance accidentally gets discharged, and the land-based sources protocol requires parties to eliminate pollution from certain hazardous substances and strictly limit pollution from others.
- Article VI of the Bucharest convention aims to prevent pollution of the Black Sea by hazardous substances and organic matters. The convention contains three protocols: the control of land-based sources of pollution, dumping of waste and joint action in the case of accidents.
- The Caspian Environment Programme is developing a strategic action plan to control pollution of the Caspian Sea, which should be adopted by the five states bordering the Caspian Sea.

Some marine conventions have monitoring programmes to measure the annual riverine inputs and direct discharges of hazardous substances as well as atmospheric deposition to seas.

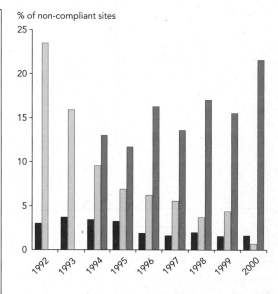

Source: Environment Agency of England and Wales web page

Figure 8.23.	Direct and riverine inputs into the North East Atlantic (a) and atmospheric inputs of some heavy metals into the North East Atlantic (b)

Source: OSPAR data, compiled by ETC/WTR

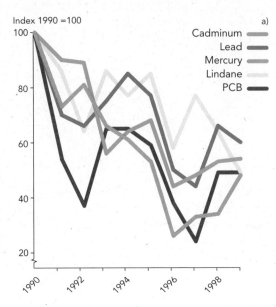

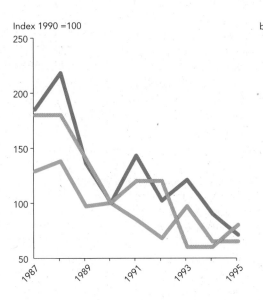

In the Mediterranean there is no available information on how discharges of hazardous substances have changed over time. MAP (UNEP/MAP, 1996) has estimated that riverine discharges are the largest source of mercury (92 %), lead (66 %), chromium (57 %) and zinc (72 %) although direct industrial discharges from the coastal zone are also significant (around 30 % of the total) for chromium and lead.

The Caspian Regional Thematic Centre for Pollution Control has estimated that 17 tonnes of mercury and 149 tonnes of cadmium are discharged into the Caspian Sea each year (Caspian Environment Programme, no date). The largest source of both metals is rivers although there are also

contributions from industry and municipalities.

The Arctic Ocean also receives considerable quantities of hazardous substances from rivers. For example, Eurasian rivers transport 10 tonnes of mercury each year to the Arctic Ocean although the main source of mercury is atmospheric deposition (AMAP, 2002). Atmospheric deposition and riverine inputs contribute equally to cadmium pollution. Persistent organic pollutants (POPs) also reach the Arctic Ocean via the atmospheric and riverine pathways with the Russian rivers, the Ob, Yenisej and Pyasina, having the largest inputs (AMAP, 2000a).

Effects of hazardous substances in seas
Hazardous substances may affect human health through consumption of marine organisms and have deleterious effects on marine ecosystem function. Lethal and sub-lethal effects on aquatic biota are known to occur. The long-term effects of these persistent substances in the European marine environment are not adequately known.

Contaminant concentrations above the limits for human consumption set by the EU for fish and shellfish (EU, 2001b; EU, 2002) are found mainly in mussels and fish from estuaries of major rivers. Examples are cadmium and PCB (polychlorinated biphenyls and their degradation products) in the Seine, northern France; lead in the Elbe; PCB in the Scheldt and the Rhine on the Belgium-Dutch border area and the Ems in northern Germany; cadmium (possibly from the River Rhone) near some industrial point discharges (e.g. cadmium and DDT in the Sørfjord, western Norway); and, lead in some harbours (e.g. lead and PCB in the inner Oslo Fjord) — see Map 8.4. Some areas remote from point sources may, however, have elevated concentrations of some hazardous substances (e.g. cadmium in northern Iceland, mercury in northern Norway).

The aggregated results on time trends in concentrations per sea area during the past 15 years (Figure 8.25) indicate falling concentrations of cadmium, mercury, lead, DDT, lindane and PCB in mussels and fish from both the North East Atlantic and the Mediterranean Sea. For each sampling site, the time trend was statistically analysed as well: of the 178 (DDT) to 286 (cadmium) time series analysed for mussels, 8–15 % showed significant trends, mostly of concentrations decreasing. Only 25 time series for lindane were available. All of these concerned mussels from the Mediterranean and seven showed significant decreases.

Analysis of time trends per sampling point indicates few significant trends in the coastal regions of the North East Atlantic but most of these show decreasing concentrations of cadmium, mercury, lead, DDT and PCB. In the Baltic the levels of cadmium, mercury and lead in herring muscle appear to be low and generally no trends were detected. The one area where mercury increased in this species was at the estuary of the river Oder (near Stettin). Concentrations of DDT and PCB in fish generally decreased although PCB concentrations in North East Atlantic cod increased. In the Mediterranean (only French and Greek data) concentrations of cadmium, mercury and lead are generally above background levels but below levels of potential concern. The results also suggest that concentrations are generally decreasing. The results for lindane (only French data) indicate low and decreasing concentrations.

Analysis of the concentrations of hazardous substances in water, sediment and biota in the Caspian Sea is so far inadequate to provide a comprehensive overview. It is, however, known that the greatest concentrations are found close to major coastal industries (e.g. the Absheron peninsular in Azerbaijan) and the mouths of rivers with industrialised catchments (Caspian Environment Programme, no date).

Hazardous substances also affect wildlife in the Arctic. Much of the pollution is from the long-range transport of persistent chemicals and is a legacy from previous emissions, although significant pollution is still occurring. Biomagnification of persistent organic pollutants up the food chain is particularly evident in the Arctic food web as the top predators, e.g. seals and polar bears, have large fat reserves where lipid-soluble compounds accumulate. There is also some evidence that mercury concentrations in marine mammals are increasing (AMAP, 2000b). Local metal pollution is very severe in some areas, for example in the Russian Federation on the Kola Peninsula and near Norilsk due to copper-nickel smelting (AMAP, 2002).

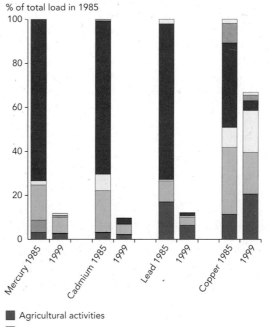

Main sources of some metal discharges to water in North Sea countries in 1999

Figure 8.24.

% of total load in 1985

Note: Waste disposal includes municipal wastewater. Discharges to water based on: mercury (Denmark, Germany, Norway, Netherlands, Sweden); cadmium (Denmark, Germany, Norway, Netherlands, Sweden)

Source: North Sea progress report, 2002

- ■ Agricultural activities
- ■ Small and medium enterprises
- ■ Waste disposal
- □ Transport and infrastructure
- ■ Households
- ■ Industrial activities (covered by IPPC directive)
- ■ Contaminated land and sediments
- □ Building materials

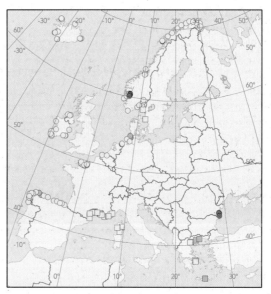

Median cadmium (Cd) concentrations in mussels, 1995–99

Map 8.4.

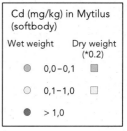

Cd (mg/kg) in Mytilus (softbody)

	Wet weight	Dry weight (*0.2)
	0,0–0,1	
	0,1–1,0	
	> 1,0	

Notes: Mussels: Mytilus edulis - North East Atlantic; M. galloprovincialis — Mediterranean and Black Sea. Classification uses background level for lower class and EU limit value for foodstuff for higher class. EU-legislation limit for cadmium in foodstuffs 'bivalve molluscs' is 1 mg/kg wet weight (EU, 2001b). Larger symbols may obscure other symbols. 2001 for Black Sea.

Sources: Compiled by ETC/ WTR based on data from OSPAR and EEA member countries (Mediterranean), and data reported by Romania

Figure 8.25.	**Concentrations of selected metals and synthetic organic substances in marine organisms in the Mediterranean and Baltic Seas, and in the North East Atlantic Ocean**

Sources: Complied by ETC/WTR from OSPAR, HELCOM and EEA Mediterranean member countries data

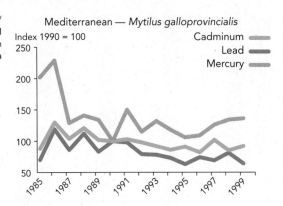

Mediterranean — *Mytilus galloprovincialis*
Index 1990 = 100
Cadminum
Lead
Mercury

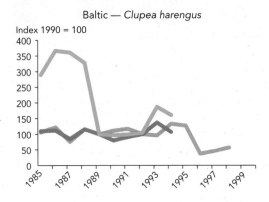

Baltic — *Clupea harengus*
Index 1990 = 100

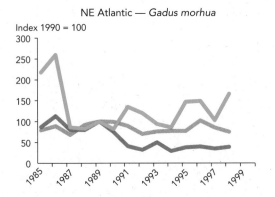

NE Atlantic — *Gadus morhua*
Index 1990 = 100

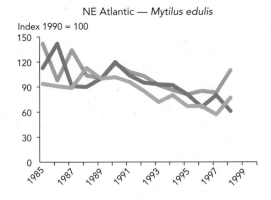

NE Atlantic — *Mytilus edulis*
Index 1990 = 100

☺ The levels of some hazardous substances in marine organisms are decreasing at some monitoring stations in the Mediterranean and Baltic Seas and the North East Atlantic Ocean in response to measures to reduce the inputs of these substances to these seas.

☹ However, contaminant concentrations above limits for human consumption are still found in mussels and fish, mainly from estuaries of major rivers, near some industrial point discharges and in some harbours.

Oil pollution
The main sources of oil pollution in the marine environment include maritime transport, coastal refineries and offshore oil and gas installations, land-based activities (either discharging directly or through riverine inputs) and atmospheric deposition. No reliable data sources exist at present for marine oil pollution from land-based activities and atmospheric deposition. Within the EU, the dangerous substances directive (Directive 76/464/EEC) includes targets for oil pollution discharges with reference to persistent and non-persistent mineral oils and hydrocarbons of petroleum origin. The OSPAR and HELCOM conventions set targets for oil pollution from land-based sources and offshore oil and gas installations. In accordance with the MARPOL 73/78 convention established by the International Maritime Organization (IMO) for the prevention of pollution from ships, aerial surveillance continues, allowing a control of observed slicks, in 'special areas' (e.g. Baltic, North Sea, Mediterranean Sea and Black Sea) where discharges are prohibited.

There is a large number of oil and gas installations over marine oil fields (Map 8.5). For instance, OSPAR has published a database of offshore installations including more than 900 different installations producing from a few tonnes to 800 000 tonnes per year (Figure 8.26). However, an assessment of discharges from refineries and offshore installations in the Mediterranean and Black Seas is lacking. There are extensive oil refining and petrochemical industries operating in the Mediterranean region (EEA, 1999) with 40 major refineries in 1997. The amount of oil discharged into the sea from 13 of these refineries was estimated in 1995 to be 782 tonnes (UNEP/MAP, 1996).

There is also a large seaborne trade of oil in the Mediterranean Sea. The risk of shipping accidents in the Mediterranean is very high and some of these cause oil pollution. Between 1987 and 1996 an estimated 22 000 tonnes of oil were spilled as the result of shipping incidents. The figures for individual years vary from some 12 tonnes in 1995 to 13 000 tonnes in 1991 (EEA, 1999).

Oil spills from accidents at sea in the Black Sea are relatively small compared with the inputs of oil from domestic and industrial land-based sources and from the River Danube.

Commercial oil and gas exploration took place in Azerbaijan's Caspian Sea shelf in 1950, and intensive exploration and production has been taking place in the Caspian coastal waters of Kazakhstan, the Russian Federation and Turkmenistan since the mid-1990s. In 1978–92, as the result of a critical rise in the water level, many oil wells and production enterprises on the Caspian coast and its shallow waters were flooded. The result was pollution of the coastal waters

☺ Despite increased oil production, oil discharges from offshore installations and coastal refineries in the EU are decreasing as a result of the OSPAR ban on discharges of oil-contaminated cuttings and an increased application of cleaning technologies and improved wastewater treatment before discharge. Additional improvements are expected in North Sea/Atlantic as a result of new (OSPAR) regulations, which entered in force in 2000.

☹ However, the level of discharges associated with the release of 'production water' on offshore installations is steadily increasing in the North Sea.

😐 Illegal oil discharges from ships and offshore platforms are regularly observed at sea. The number of illegal oil spills is slowly decreasing in the North Sea, but remains constant in the Baltic Sea.

☹ Despite pollution from oil spills on a worldwide scale being reduced by 60 % since the 1970s, major accidental oil tanker spills (i.e. greater than 20 000 tonnes) still occur at irregular intervals in European seas.

Location of offshore oil installations   Map 8.5.

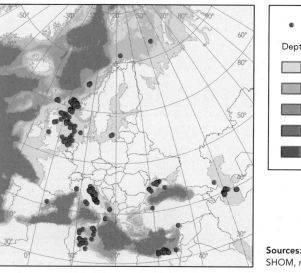
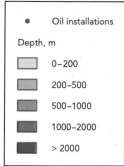

Sources: UKHO, no date; SHOM, no date

Total discharges of oil from refineries and offshore installations in EU (a) and annual number of observed oil slicks discharged mainly from ships in the North and Baltic Seas from aerial surveillance (b)   Figure 8.26.

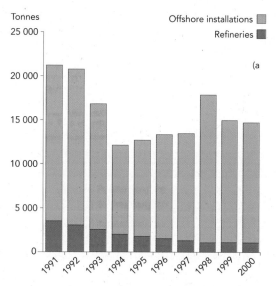

Source: OSPAR (1999; 2001); Eurostat (2001); DHI based on data from Eurostat (1999), OSPAR (1997) and CONCAVE (1999); Bonn agreement and HELCOM, 2001

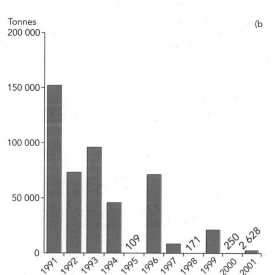

| Map 8.6. | Large accidental oil spills from tankers, 1970–2001 |

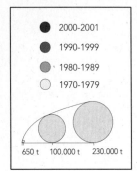

2000-2001
1990-1999
1980-1989
1970-1979

650 t   100.000 t   230.000 t

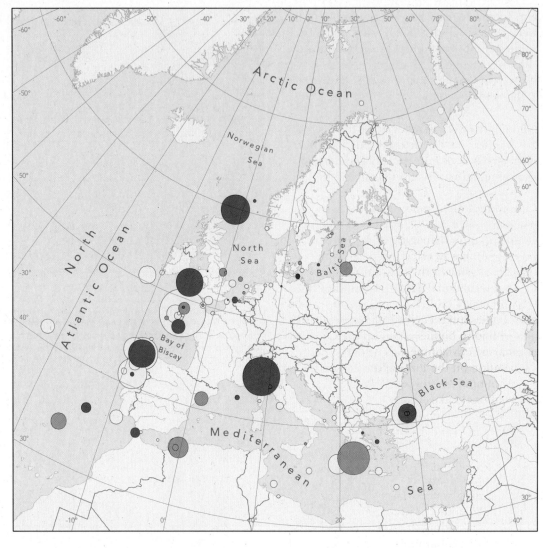

Source: EEA based on data
from.ITOPF

of all Caspian states by oil and oil products. The Caspian Regional Thematic Centre for Pollution Control estimated in 2001 that 160 000 tonnes were discharged each year into the Caspian Sea, with rivers being the most important source (47 %). Oil industry activities contributed only 5 % of the total with natural seepage contributing 13 % and erosion and other industry 21 %.

Oil exploration and production is also significant in the Arctic and is a major source of oil pollution. For example, produced water from drilling operations accounted for 76 % of oil pollution of the sea on the Norwegian shelf between 1990 and 1995 (AMAP, 2002). Oil pollution is also evident in a number of Russian rivers. For example, the lower part of the Ob is severely contaminated. Oil pollution from accidents in the region has also occurred, for example in the Komi Republic in 1994 when a dike containing oil from a leaking pipeline collapsed. The spill reached

the Kolva River, a tributary of the Pechora River and tar balls from the spill were found at the mouth of the Pechora.

Despite an increase in the marine transport of oil, the worldwide average number of accidental oil spills of more than 7 tonnes has been estimated at 24.1 per year for 1970–79, 8.8 per year for 1980–89 and 7.3 per year for 1990–99 (see Chapter 10, Section 10.2.3). In 2000 there was one spill of 250 tonnes (Germany) and in 2001 three spills totalling 2 628 tonnes including one spill (Denmark) of 2 400 tonnes. The Prestige accident in 2002 (Spain) spilled more than 20 000 tonnes. A few very large accidents are responsible for a high percentage of the oil spilt from maritime transport. For example, during the period 1990–99, from all the 346 accidental spills of more than 7 tonnes from tankers, combined carriers and barges, totalling 830 000 tonnes, just over 1 % of the accidents produced 75 % of the spilt oil volume.

Oil production and consumption are increasing, as are net imports of oil to the EU, which increases the risk of oil spills. More rapid introduction of double hulls for tankers will help to reduce this risk.

8.6. International cooperation on water management

8.6.1. Transboundary inland water courses

There are 150 major transboundary rivers in Europe that form or cross borders between two or more countries, some 25 major transboundary lakes, and some 100 transboundary aquifers.

Cooperation in managing transboundary waters requires an effective institutional structure such as a river commission based on an international agreement or other arrangement (Table 8.5). It is important that joint bodies interact closely with each other and with joint bodies established to protect the marine environment. The UNECE Convention on the Protection and Use of Transboundary Watercourses and International Lakes (http://www.unece.org/env/water/), which was adopted in Helsinki in 1992, supported by soft-law recommendations, guidelines and specific action plans, has proved to be a useful tool for institutional cooperation on transboundary waters. The convention has been signed and/or ratified by 32 countries of Europe including the Russian Federation and Azerbaijan, Kazakhstan, the Republic of Moldova and Ukraine from EECCA. The remaining EECCA countries have not signed the convention.

8.6.2. Marine conventions

Table 8.6 summarises the marine conventions covering Europe's seas. The future role of the marine conventions is currently under review as part of the process of developing and implementing the European Commission's strategy to protect and conserve the marine environment (European Commission, 2002). All regional marine conventions have established monitoring and assessment programmes. However, when seen in a European context, the programmes are not coherent in terms of scope, content, approach and detail. In addition there are problems, including inadequate spatial coverage and/or sampling frequency, which lead to lack of harmonisation between datasets, making their scientific analysis and comparability nearly impossible. The view of the European

Selected examples of international cooperation on inland surface waters	Table 8.5.

River, lake, basin	Commission
Danube	International Commission for the Protection of the Danube River (ICPDR) http://www.icpdr.org/pls/danubis/DANUBIS.navigator
Rhine	Internationale Kommission zum Schutz des Rheins (IKSR) http://www.iksr.org/
Elbe	Internationale Kommission zum Schutz der Elbe http://www.ikse-mkol.de/html/ikse/ikse/deutsch/index_d.htm
Oder	International Commission for the Protection of the River Oder (signed by Germany, Czech Republic and Poland on 11 April 1996)
Dnieper	International DNIPRO Fund (IDF) — National Program of Environmental Sanitation of River Dnipro Basin and Drinking Water Quality Improvement http://greenfield.fortunecity.com/hunters/228/toppage1.htm
Bodensee/ Lake Constance	Internationale Gewässerschutzkommission für den Bodensee http://www.igkb.de
Lake Geneva/ Lac Leman	Commission Internationale pour la Protection des Eaux du Léman contre la pollution (CIPEL) http://www.cipel.org
Lake Peipsi	A bilateral agreement between Estonia and the Russian Federation has been established regarding Lake Peipsi and its outlet, the Narva River. Regular exchanges of monitoring data, scientific information and information of public interest now take place through the subgroups that were established under the joint commission
Ohrid	On the basis of the UNECE convention on transboundary watercourses, Albania and the former Yugoslav Republic of Macedonia have an agreement on the common management of Lake Ohrid. There are several projects which aim at establishing sound environmental management of the lake and monitoring its quality
Kura-Araks rivers	There are no common management systems or environmental agreements on these rivers. Negotiations have started between Armenia, Azerbaijan and Georgia on a joint river management project
Aral Sea basin	Inter-State Commission for Water Coordination (ICWC) Water ministers of the five states in the basin, Kazakhstan, Kyrgyzstan, Turkmenistan, Tajikistan and Uzbekistan, signed the Agreement on Water Resources Management in the Aral Sea basin on 18 February 1992 and the ICWC was established with joint responsibility for water management with the two river basin agencies (Amu-Darya and Syr-Darya). The main functions of the ICWC include allocation of annual abstraction for each country, definition of regional water management policy and coordination of large projects

Note: See IWAC (www.iwac-riza.org) for complete list of transboundary cooperations.
Source: Compiled from various sources by ETC/WTR

Commission is that activities carried out for the implementation of the water framework directive could act as a stimulus for integration of the activities of the regional marine conventions. The inter regional forum set up by the EEA could possibly be the framework under which integration takes place.

Table 8.6.	Summary of marine conventions in Europe
OSPAR — The Convention for the Protection of the Marine Environment of the North-East Atlantic — Paris 1992, entered into force 1998 http://www.ospar.org/	The convention has been signed and ratified by all the contracting Parties to the former Oslo or Paris conventions (Belgium, Denmark, the Commission of the European Communities, Finland, France, Germany, Iceland, Ireland, the Netherlands, Norway, Portugal, Spain, Sweden and the United Kingdom) and by Luxembourg and Switzerland
HELCOM is the governing body of the Convention on the Protection of the Marine Environment of the Baltic Sea Area, more usually known as the Helsinki Convention http://www.helcom.fi/	Signatory or contracting Parties are: Denmark, Estonia, the European Community, Finland, Germany, Latvia, Lithuania, Poland, Russian Federation and Sweden
Convention for the Protection of the Mediterranean Sea against Pollution — Barcelona 1976 and protocols (1980, 1982) entered into force 1978	Signatory or contracting Parties are: Albania, Algeria, Bosnia-Herzegovina, Croatia, Cyprus, Egypt, France, Greece, Israel, Italy, Lebanon, Libyan Arab Jamahiriya, Malta, Monaco, Morocco, Slovenia, Spain, Syrian Arab Republic, Tunisia, Turkey
Convention on the Protection of the Black Sea against Pollution (Bucharest Convention); adopted 1992, in force 1994 and protocols (1992) http://www.blacksea-commission.net or http://www.blacksea-environment.org/	Signatory Parties are the Black Sea states: Bulgaria, Georgia, Romania, Russian Federation, Turkey and Ukraine.
AMAP — Arctic Monitoring and Assessment Programme — is an international programme established in 1991 to implement components of the Arctic environmental protection strategy (AEPS) of the Arctic Council for the Protection of the Arctic Marine Environment http://amap.no/	Member countries (the eight Arctic rim countries): Canada, Denmark/ Greenland, Finland, Iceland, Norway, Russian Federation, Sweden, United States

Source: Compiled from various sources by ETC/WTR

8.7. References

AMAP (Arctic Monitoring and Environment Programme), 2000a. *Persistent organic pollutants (POPs)*. Fact sheet No 1. Produced for the Arctic Council by AMAP. http://amap.no/

AMAP (Arctic Monitoring and Environment Programme), 2000b. *Heavy metals*. Fact sheet No 3. Produced for the Arctic Council by AMAP. http://amap.no/

AMAP, 2002. *Arctic pollution 2002*. AMAP's new state of the Arctic environment report describing the pollution status of the Arctic, updating the 1997 AMAP assessment. http://amap.no/

Aquastat (FAO), 2002. http://www.fao.org/ag/agl/aglw/aquastat/main/index.stm

Aral Sea homepage. http://www.grida.no/aral/aralsea/english/arsea/arsea.htm

Armenia, 1998. *State of the environment report 1998: Armenia*. http://www.grida.no/enrin/htmls/armenia/soe_armenia/soeeng.htm

Azerbaijan NCP (national contact point), 2002. Communication by the Azerbaijan national contact point to European Environment Agency (Review of draft Kiev report).

BIRHP (Balearic Islands regional hydrological plan), 1999. General Directorate of Water Resources, Conselleria de Medi Ambient.

Black Sea Commission, 2002. *State of the environment of the Black Sea: Pressures and trends 1996–2000*. Preprint copy, August.

Borum, J., 1996. Shallow waters and land/sea boundaries. In: *Eutrophication in coastal marine ecosystems*. Jørgensen, B. B. and Richardson, K. (eds). American Geophysical Union. pp. 179–205.

Caspian Environment Programme, no date. http://www.caspianenvironment.org/pollution/levels.htm

CEFIC, 2001. *Responsible care status report Europe 2001*. Europe Chemical Industry Council. http://www.cefic.be/Files/Publications/ceficrc.pdf

CEPI, Environment report 2000. Confederation of European Paper Industry. http://www.paperonline.org/images/pdfs/environment/env_rep_2000.pdf

EEA (European Environment Agency), 1999. *State and pressure of the marine and coastal Mediterranean environment*. Environmental assessment No 5. EEA and UNEP/Mediterranean Action Plan, Copenhagen

EEA (European Environment Agency), 2001. *Eutrophication in Europe's coastal waters*. Topic report No 7/2001. EEA, Copenhagen

Environment Agency of England and Wales web page. www.environment-agency.gov.uk/

EU, 2000. *Groundwater river resources programme on a European scale (GRAPES)*. Technical Report to the EU ENV4. CEH, Wallingford, UK.

EUCC, 2000. *Coastal guide on dune management*. European Union for Coastal Conservation International Secretariat. http://www.coastalguide.org/

EU, 2001a. *Decision No 2455/2001/EC of the European Parliament and the Council of 20 November 2001 establishing the list of priority substances in the field of water policy and amending Directive 2000(60EC*. Brussels.

EU, 2001b. *Commission Regulation (EC) No 466/ 2001 of 8 March 2001 setting maximum levels for certain contaminants in foodstuffs.* Brussels.

EU, 2002. *Commission Regulation (EC) No 221/ 2002 of 6 February 2002 amending Regulation (EC) No 466/2001 setting maximum levels for certain contaminants in foodstuffs.* Brussels.

European Commission, 2002. Communication from the Commission to the Council and the European Parliament. *Towards a strategy to protect and conserve the marine environment.* COM (2002) 539(01). Brussels

European Council, 1977. *Council Decision of 12 December 1977 establishing a common procedure for the exchange of information on the quality of surface fresh water in the Community.* Decision 77/795/EEC.

Finnish Environment Institute, 2002. *Evaluation of the implementation of the 1988 ministerial declaration regarding nutrient load reductions in the Baltic Sea catchment area.* Lääne A., Pitkänen, H., Arheimer, B., *et al.* The Finnish Environment 524. http:// www.vyh.fi/eng/orginfo/publica/electro/ fe524/fe524.htm

HELCOM web page. http://www.helcom.fi/

HELCOM, 2000. http://www.vyh.fi/eng/ orginfo/publica/electro/fe524/fe524.htm

HELCOM, 2001. *Environment of the Baltic Sea area 1994–1998.* Baltic Sea Environment Proc. No. 82 A. 23 pages.

Hungarian Central Statistical Office, 2001. Towards the application of the international water related environmental indicators in Hungary (Hungary, CSO). Doc. 4 in: *UNECE work session on methodological issues of environment statistics.* http://www.unece.org/ stats/documents/2001.10.env.htm

MMA, 2000. *Libro Blanco del Agua en Espana.* Spanish Ministry of Environment, Madrid.

MZOPU, 2002. *National environmental strategy.* Croatian Ministry for Environmental Protection and Physical Planning. Zagreb.

North Sea progress report, 2002. http:// www.dep.no/md/html/nsc/ progressreport2002/hoved.html

Latvian Environment Agency, 2002. *Environmental indicators in Latvia* 2002. http://www.vdc.lv/soe/2001_eng/

OECD (Organisation for Economic Co-operation and Development), 1999. *Environmental performance review Turkey.*

OECD (Organisation for Economic Co-operation and Development), 2000a. *Environmental performance review Hungary.*

OECD (Organisation for Economic Co-operation and Development), 2000b. *Environmental performance review Greece.*

OECD (Organisation for Economic Co-operation and Development), 2000c. *Environmental performance review Russia.*

OECD (Organisation for Economic Co-operation and Development), 2001. *Environmental performance review Portugal.*

SHOM (Service hydrographique et océanographique de la marine, France), no date. *Groupes d'avis aux navigateurs.* http:// www.shom.fr/

Smakhtin, V. U., 2001. Low flow hydrology: A review. *Journal of Hydrology* 240: 147–186.

UKHO (United Kingdom Hydrography Office), no date. Notices to mariners. http:/ /www.hydro.gov.uk/

UNECE, 1998. *Environmental performance review Moldova.* http://www.unece.org/env/ epr/countriesreviewed.htm

UNECE, 1999a. *Environmental performance review Croatia.* http://www.unece.org/env/ epr/countriesreviewed.htm

UNECE, 1999b. *Environmental performance review Ukraine.* http://www.unece.org/env/ epr/countriesreviewed.htm

UNECE, 2000a. *Environmental performance reviews Armenia.* http://www.unece.org/env/ epr/countriesreviewed.htm

UNECE, 2000b. *Environmental performance reviews Kazakhstan.* http://www.unece.org/ env/epr/countriesreviewed.htm

UNECE, 2000c. *Environmental performance reviews Kyrgyzstan.* http://www.unece.org/ env/epr/countriesreviewed.htm

UNEP/MAP, 1996. *The state of the marine and coastal environment in the Mediterranean region.* MAP Technical Reports Series No 100. Athens.

9. Soil degradation

In many areas of Europe, soil is being irreversibly lost and degraded as a result of increasing and often conflicting demands from nearly all economic sectors. Pressures result from the concentration of population and activities in localised areas, economic activities and changes in climate and land use. Cultivation systems are among the most important influences on the quality of soils in agricultural areas. Consumer behaviour and the industrial sector are contributing to the increase in the number of potential sources of contamination such as municipal waste disposal, energy production and transport, mainly in urban areas. Tourism is a further cause of soil degradation especially along the coasts of the Mediterranean. Many of the problems stem from past activities and poor management practices in eastern Europe, Caucasus and Central Asia.

The combined action of these activities affects quality and limits many soil functions including the capacity to remove contaminants from the environment by filtration and adsorption. This capacity and the resilience of soil mean that damage is not perceived until it is far advanced. This partly explains the low priority given to soil protection in Europe until recently. Moreover, since soil is a limited and non-renewable resource, when it is damaged, unlike air and water, it is not easily recoverable.

Major problems in Europe are irreversible losses due to soil sealing and erosion, continuing contamination from local and diffuse sources, acidification, salinisation and compaction.

The geographical distribution of soil degradation depends on several factors. Soil problems are influenced by the diversity, distribution and specific vulnerability of soils across Europe. They also depend on geology, topography and climate and on the distribution of driving forces. Better integration of soil protection into sectoral policies and better harmonisation of information across Europe are needed to move to more sustainable use of soil resources and promotion of sustainable models of its use.

9.1. Introduction

Soil has many ecological and socio-economic functions including the capacity to remove contaminants from the environment by filtration and adsorption. This capacity and

soil resilience mean that damage to soil is often not perceived until it is far advanced. Following the precautionary principle and taking account of the slow rate of soil formation, soil can be considered as a limited and non-renewable resource on a 50–100 year timescale.

The quality of Europe's soils is a result of natural factors, such as climate, the material out of which the soil was formed, vegetation, biota and topography, and human activities. As a consequence, there is a wide diversity of soil types, and soil degradation differs markedly across Europe.

9.1.1. Policy challenges
In many areas of Europe, soil is being degraded as a result of pressures coming from nearly all economic sectors. Among the most important influences on the quality of soil are the cultivation systems used in agriculture. Loss of organic matter, soil biodiversity and consequently soil fertility are often driven by unsustainable practices such as deep ploughing on fragile soils and cultivation of erosion-facilitating crops such as maize, and the continuous use of heavy machinery destroys soil structure through compaction (German Advisory Council on Global Change, 1994; EEA, 1999). In addition, overgrazing and the intensification of agriculture, some of which is linked in the European Union (EU) to the implementation of the common agricultural policy, may accelerate loss of soil through erosion.

In addition to agriculture, consumer behaviour is contributing to increases of sources of soil pollution: municipal waste, energy consumption, transport and emissions of exhaust gases (EEA, 2002a). The major impact of these is a reduction in soil buffering capacity, that is the capacity of soil to adsorb contaminants. The extent of this reduction is difficult to measure although there are signs that such capacity is near to exhaustion in many areas in Europe.

Many of these degradation processes have a direct impact on the global carbon cycle, particularly through the decrease in soil organic matter and the release of carbon dioxide to the atmosphere.

Soil erosion affects large areas of Europe — about 17 % of the total land area in Europe is affected to some degree, with around 27 million ha in the EU (Oldeman *et al.*, 1991). Climatic conditions make the Mediterranean region one of the areas most severely affected. Changes in land use, such as abandonment of marginal land with very low vegetation cover and increases in the frequency and extension of forest fires, have had a strong impact on soil resources since historical times. In the most extreme cases, soil erosion, coupled with other forms of land degradation, has led to desertification in some areas of the Mediterranean and eastern Europe (see Box 9.1). Soil erosion is also an increasing concern in northern

Europe, although to a lesser degree (EEA-UNEP, 2000; EEA, 2002a, b).

Despite the fact that a wide range of activities use and contribute to the depletion of soil resources, soil protection has not generally been the subject of specific policy objectives and targets, unlike water and air. Soil protection has rather been addressed indirectly through measures aimed at the protection of air and water or developed within sectoral policies. An important recent advance has been the inclusion of plans for a thematic strategy on soil protection in the sixth environment action programme (6EAP) in 2001 and the adoption of a Commission communication on soil protection, endorsed

---

Box 9.1. Implementation of the UN Convention to Combat Desertification

The UN Convention to Combat Desertification (UNCCD) was adopted in 1994 and came into force in 1997. Its provisions include a reporting obligation and the preparation of national, subregional or regional action programmes for its implementation. As of December 2002, 185 countries worldwide had ratified the convention.

The European Community and all but four countries in the area covered by this report have ratified the convention, although not all signatory Parties are affected by desertification. The area comprises three regional annexes of the convention: Asia (Annex II), northern Mediterranean (Annex IV) and central and eastern Europe (Annex V). Since its entry into force there has been some progress in implementing the convention in these regions, but it is still too early to register substantial progress and improvement in the state of environment.

Northern Mediterranean
In the northern Mediterranean, of ten affected countries, eight report regularly on progress in implementation; six are at different stages of preparing national action programmes and three (Portugal, Italy and Greece) are currently implementing them. Preparation of a subregional action programme is under way and a joint report has been presented. The development of these programmes and cooperation and exchange of information is supported by a number of projects. Interregional cooperation with northern African countries has started.

In general, countries report difficulties in establishing good cooperation and communication among stakeholders, with some exceptions. This could be crucial since desertification is a cross-cutting issue and combating it requires close integration of several policy sectors. Combating desertification often has a low priority so there is some difficulty in mobilising national funds. Even the three adopted national action programmes have no legal frameworks, and no independent budgets are assigned to the implementation of the convention.

Central and eastern Europe
In central and eastern Europe, nine countries have submitted national reports, three have adopted national action programmes (Armenia, the Republic of Moldova and Romania) and three have started preparing them (Bulgaria, Georgia and Hungary).

A common feature of the region is that most countries are only slightly affected by actual desertification, although large-scale land degradation is often reported. Countries use the convention as a tool for framing and fostering activities to combat land degradation.

In general, no specific budgets are allocated to combat desertification and measures are developed within sectoral policies. Limited resources are available at the national level to implement actions, as the countries of the region have economies in transition and most urgent basic needs get higher priority. However, some pilot projects are being implemented and trans-national cooperation is under way.

Caucasus and central Asia
The five Caucasus and central Asian countries have all adopted national action programmes and all report regularly to the convention.

Strategies to combat desertification are integrated within the national strategies for sustainable development. Strong links have been established with strategies to combat poverty and support socio-economic development.

Most of these countries are largely dry land (80 % of Uzbekistan, 90 % of Turkmenistan) and land degradation, drought and desertification occur on a large scale with dramatic effects on livelihood (e.g. the Aral Sea disaster). Combating desertification therefore has a high priority. However, lack of funds hinders the implementation of specific measures. Nevertheless, national institutional infrastructures have been established, monitoring and assessment activities have been set up and a number of pilot projects are being developed. Regional cooperation is well under way through the development of transboundary projects such as those being implemented in the Aral Sea basin and Caspian Sea.

Sources: UNCCD, 2002a; 2002b

by the European Council in 2002. The communication calls for the development of a European soil monitoring system capable of providing reliable, comparable and regular information on soil conditions in Europe (European Commission, 2002). Most international programmes also emphasise the need to improve soil monitoring in Europe (EEA-UNEP, 2000). However, the key to progress towards sustainable use of soil resources remains better integration of soil protection into sectoral, local and regional policies.

9.1.2. A regional overview

The occurrence and distribution of soil problems are influenced by the diversity, distribution and specific vulnerability of soils across Europe, coupled with physical aspects such as geology, relief and climate. A further factor is the distribution of driving forces across the continent (EEA-UNEP, 2000).

Western Europe
Soil contamination remains a problem in western Europe (WE) despite several national and international initiatives that have been set up during the past 10 years to reduce air emissions and control, for example, the application of sewage sludge and the use of landfill for waste disposal. WE is highly urbanised (built-up areas occupy 15 % of its territory) and competition for the limited land available results in the loss or degradation of soil resources and in particular the sealing of the soil surface at unsustainable rates, for example through urban development and the construction of transport infrastructures. Soil erosion greatly affects Mediterranean countries, where in the most extreme cases (arid and sub-humid climate) it leads to desertification. In addition, frequently repeated forest fires contribute to the desertification of marginal lands. Unsustainable irrigation systems contribute significantly to the salinisation and erosion of cultivated lands.

Central and eastern Europe
Soil degradation problems in the central and eastern European (CEE) countries are similar to those in WE, although there is less soil sealing. Most of the problems are inherited from the time of the former USSR, when environmental issues were of minor concern. Erosion is the most widespread form of soil degradation, linked to agricultural mismanagement and deforestation (van Lynden, 2000). Past agricultural policies that focused on increasing productivity led to incorrect use

of mineral fertilisers, pesticides and heavy machinery. The combined effects of these resulted in increased rates of soil loss by erosion, pollution of groundwater and reduction of soil fertility. Increased awareness of environmental issues, the obligation to implement EU legislation upon accession and declining economies are reducing the pressures from agriculture (decreases in fertiliser and pesticide consumption).

Soil contamination is, to a great extent, a result of the legacy of inefficient technologies and uncontrolled emissions. Problem areas include some 3 000 former military sites, abandoned industrial facilities and storage sites which may still be releasing pollutants to the environment (DANCEE, 2000). One of the major impacts is groundwater contamination and related health problems. Major concerns are the long time needed to regenerate contaminated soil and the considerable investment required for remedial measures.

Conflicts in the Balkans have had impacts, not only in the countries directly involved, but also in neighbouring areas as a consequence of the migration of refugees and increased demand for basic resources (food and firewood). In Bosnia-Herzegovina it has been estimated that the war damaged soil resources in an area of about 6 000 ha through deforestation, erosion, compaction, waste disposal and damage to industrial facilities (REC, 2001). A specific post-conflict situation in Bosnia-Herzegovina and Kosovo concerns land mines and unexploded ordinances. It is estimated that in Bosnia-Herzegovina there are between 3 and 6 million land mines disseminated in more than 16 000 minefields and that 27 % of the total arable land is mined. Until land mines are cleared, opportunities for reconstruction and agriculture work will be severely limited.

Eastern Europe, the Caucasus and central Asia
Over the past 50 years, the priority given to increasing the productivity of agriculture, combined with climatic factors, has resulted in soil and water pollution from the overuse of pesticides and fertilisers. Large areas have experienced salinisation as a consequence of unsustainable irrigation schemes and cultivation practices (the best-known case is the environmental disaster of the drying-up of the Aral Sea — see Section 9.5., Box 9.2.).

The most extreme forms of degradation have resulted in the desertification of large areas.

In Kazakhstan an estimated 60 % of the territory is at risk of desertification (UNECE, 2000a). The process is accelerated by the large-scale collective farms and the abandonment of marginal land, which cannot naturally recover because of the harsh climate.

During the past decade, the relatively high extent of soil degradation has been increasing in Azerbaijan. In 2000, between 3.7 and 8.6 million hectares of land were degraded through erosion and 30 000 hectares were degraded through soil contamination by a number of substances, including oil products (14 000 ha).

In central Asia, a wide transboundary region — which includes Kazakhstan, Kyrgyzstan, Tajikistan, Turkmenistan and Uzbekistan and is characterised by an arid and semi-arid climate — presents acute problems of desertification. For example, in Turkmenistan, livestock breeding is the most profitable and at the same time the least labour-intensive branch of the economy. About 90 % of the territory is covered by a desert landscape and serves as year-round pasture for sheep and camels. As a result, vast areas of pasture are degraded and have low productivity. Out of 39.5 million hectares of pasture, 70 % is degraded, 40 % receives poor water supply and 5 % has been transformed into bare moving sand, according to the report on the implementation of the UN Convention to Combat Desertification (UNCCD) in Turkmenistan (summarised in UNCCD, 2002c).

Heavy-metal contamination is common around major industrial areas (van Lynden, 2000). The problem is especially acute in the mining and metallurgical complexes of Kazhakstan (Rekacewicz et al., 2000) and in the Caspian area, where oil spills are also a major source of contamination (UNDP and GEF, 1998). Existing and planned oil and gas pipelines in the area are leading, or are expected to lead, to pressures on soil and, among other impacts, to the fragmentation of habitats. Contamination with radioactivity is also important as a result of nuclear weapons tests, improper radioactive waste disposal and the Chernobyl accident (UNEP, 1998 — see also Chapter 10).

The recent economic decline has reduced pressures on the soil and resulted in a decrease in fertiliser, pesticide and water consumption, and a general slowing of

industrial activity (UNEP, 2002). However, pressures on the soil are increasing at the local level mainly in urban areas and around rural settlements.

9.2. Soil sealing

Soil sealing is the covering of the soil surface with an impervious material or the changing of its nature so that the soil becomes impermeable. The greatest impacts are in urban and metropolitan areas where large portions of the land are covered with constructions. The development of transport infrastructures is another important cause. Built-up land is lost to other uses such as agriculture and forestry, and the ecological functions of soil, such as storage of carbon and habitat for unique biota, are limited or impeded. Soil sealing can also result in the fragmentation of habitats and disruption of migration corridors for wildlife species.

Soil sealing can have a major impact on water flows. Runoff water from housing and traffic areas is normally unfiltered and may be contaminated with harmful chemicals. Surface runoff can increase significantly in amount and velocity, causing problems of local flood control. Although floods are natural phenomena, they may be intensified by human alteration, as has been observed in Europe in recent years (PIK, 2000). The increasing demand for land for new residential areas or industrial facilities has resulted in development in areas at high risk of flooding (UNECE, 2000b).

Over the past 20 years, built-up areas have been steadily increasing all over Europe (Figure 9.1). Although geographical coverage is not complete and estimation methods may vary slightly from country to country, socio-economic factors appear to be the main driving forces for this growth. The most dramatic changes have been in WE, where the area of built-up land is increasing more rapidly than the population (EEA, 2002a). This is the result of the steady

> Soil sealing continues to increase especially in western Europe where the area of built-up land is increasing more rapidly than the population. This is a result of the steady increase in the number of households and average residential space per capita since 1980.

Figure 9.1.	Built-up areas in Europe as percent of total land

Notes: EU: data for Austria, Belgium, Denmark, France, Germany, Luxembourg, Netherlands and Spain. Accession countries: data for Czech Republic, Latvia, Lithuania, Poland, Romania and Slovakia. EECCA: data for Armenia, Azerbaijan, Belarus, Georgia, Republic of Moldova, Tajikistan, Ukraine and Uzbekistan.

Sources: For EU and accession countries: Eurostat New Cronos (2001); for EECCA countries: EEA 2002 questionnaire

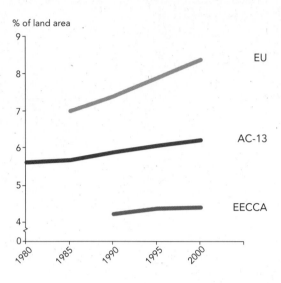

The extent of built-up area in the CEE countries was more or less constant during the late 1970s and the first half of the 1980s. Political and economic changes during the late 1980s resulted in the development of new infrastructures, the migration of rural populations to the cities and the development of new settlements (Baltic Environmental Forum, 2001). Slovakia and the Czech Republic have the highest percentage of built-up area (about 8 % of the total land area). Pressure is also increasing in some coastal zones, for example along the German, Latvian and Russian coasts on the Baltic Sea (Coalition Clean Baltic, 2002).

Soil sealing is still a minor problem in eastern Europe, the Caucasus and central Asia (EECCA) compared to other forms of soil degradation, such as erosion, salinisation and contamination. However, pressure is increasing around industrial and urban settlements and in tourist areas along the coasts of the Black Sea.

In the EU, policy measures explicitly related to land-use issues, such as spatial planning, have generally been the responsibilities of Member States, following the application of the principle of subsidiarity. Although mentioned in the fifth and sixth environment action programmes, spatial planning has only recently been specifically addressed, within the European spatial development perspective (1999) and the forthcoming European urban strategy. Although the communication on soil protection (2002) does not address the issue of spatial planning, it recognises sealing as a threat to soil.

The inclusion of environmental concerns and objectives in spatial planning is now widely recognised as a major tool for reducing the effects of uncontrolled urban expansion. This has led, for example, to the adoption of measures such as the reuse of underdeveloped or derelict urban areas (brownfields) and the adoption of specific targets in some countries (including Denmark, Germany and the United Kingdom) (EEA-UNEP, 2000). In 2003 the Commission will present a communication on 'Planning and environment: the territorial dimension'. This will address the need for rational land-use planning to enable the sustainable management of soil resources, limiting the sealing of greenfields and promoting the reuse of brownfields.

increase in the number of households and average residential space per capita since 1980, a trend that has accelerated since 1990 (EEA, 2001). At the same time, travelling distances to services increased with travelling mainly by private transport (EEA, 2000). As a consequence, the demand for new buildings and better transport infrastructures continues to rise. In addition, increasing prosperity has led to a higher demand for second homes, inevitably resulting in more soil sealing.

The countries with the highest share of built-up area (between 16 % and 20 % of total land area) are Belgium, Denmark and the Netherlands. In most cases, built-up areas have increased at expense of agricultural land, and to a lesser extent forests (EEA, 1999; 2002a) The effects of these changes can be observed, for example, in Spain, where highly productive agricultural land in the floodplains has been transformed into residential areas, transferring agricultural activities to less productive land. At the same time, intensive cultivation has been introduced to maintain productivity (MMA et al., 2002). In the Mediterranean countries, urbanisation has been growing in the coastal zones of southern France, Italy, southern Spain and the Mediterranean islands, where tourism is the main driving force (EEA-UNEP, 2000; see also Chapter 2.7).

9.3. Soil erosion

Soil erosion is a natural process linked to other processes such as seashore sedimentation. However, soil erosion has been exacerbated by human activities, leading to one of the major and most widespread forms of land degradation. About 17 % of the total land area in Europe is affected to some degree (Oldeman *et al.*, 1991; EEA, 2002b). Major causes are unsustainable agricultural practices, large-scale farming and overgrazing in WE and CEE, and poor water and irrigation management especially in EECCA (UNECE, 2001). In the Caucasus, the energy crisis and fuel shortages have resulted in an increase in woodcutting to obtain firewood for heating since the late 1980s, which has been one of the main drivers of soil erosion in this area (UNEP, 2002). In the past few years, the increase in frequency and extent of forest fires in the Mediterranean region has also had a significant impact on soil erosion. Tourism and transport may be important driving forces in localised areas (EEA, 2002b).

Soil erosion in Europe is due mainly to water (about 92 % of the total affected area) and less to wind. Wind erosion is localized in some parts of western Europe and CEE (EEA, 2002b). There is an increasing awareness that erosion, which is primarily responsible for the severe degradation occurring in topographically complex landscapes, is caused not only by wind and water but also by tillage, mainly due to the use of heavy powerful tillage machinery.

As the topsoil is eroded and washed away, the fertility and productivity of the remaining soil is reduced. Farmers have to apply more fertilisers to compensate for yield losses. Erosion is most serious in central Europe, the Caucasus and the Mediterranean region, where 50–70 % of agricultural land is at moderate to high risk of erosion (UNECE, 2001). Figure 9.2. and Figure 9.3 illustrate respectively the areas affected and the current rates of erosion in the various countries. The data show that the problem is

> Unsustainable agricultural practices, coupled with adverse natural and other factors, are increasing the loss of soil through erosion, some of which may be irreversible. About 17 % of the total land area in Europe is affected to some degree.

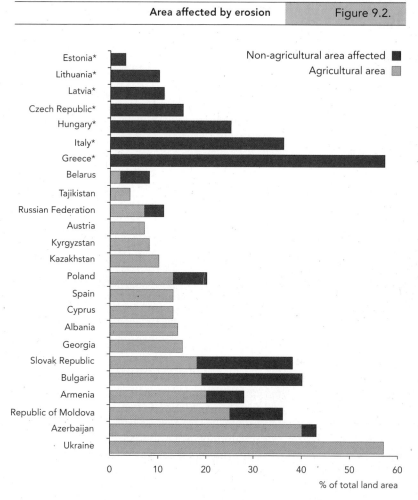

Area affected by erosion — Figure 9.2.

Non-agricultural area affected ■
Agricultural area ■

% of total land area

Notes: Asterisks indicate that data for agricultural area are not available. Ukraine: data includes area at risk of erosion. Data refer to 1990–99, except for Austria, Greece, Hungary, Italy, Poland, Slovak Republic and Spain where the data cover 1990–95.

Sources: EU: OECD-Eurostat (1997); eastern Europe: SOVEUR assessment (FAO and ISRIC, 2000) and EEA 2002 questionnaire; EECCA: EEA 2002 questionnaire; Azerbaijan (communication by EEA national contact point). Ukraine: State of the environment report (2002)

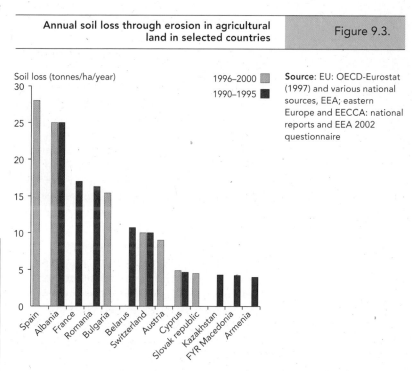

Annual soil loss through erosion in agricultural land in selected countries — Figure 9.3.

Soil loss (tonnes/ha/year)

1996–2000 ■
1990–1995 ■

Source: EU: OECD-Eurostat (1997) and various national sources, EEA; eastern Europe and EECCA: national reports and EEA 2002 questionnaire

mainly localised in agricultural areas. Olive plantations and vineyards, when intensively ploughed, are among the crops more susceptible to erosion because a high percentage of the soil surface remains uncovered by vegetation all the year round. Olive groves with minimum or no tillage are very effective agricultural systems in preventing erosion and desertification in the Mediterranean.

Since the rate of soil formation is so slow, any soil loss of more than 1 tonne/ha/year can be considered as irreversible within a time span of 50–100 years (EEA, 1999). Current rates of erosion in the Mediterranean countries, if confirmed, would mean that irreversible processes of soil degradation (and desertification in the most extreme cases) are already occurring in that region. In some areas, the situation is so extreme that there is no more soil left to erode.

Soil erosion has a major economic impact. Yearly economic losses in agricultural areas in Europe are estimated at around EUR 53/ha, while the costs of off-site effects on the surrounding civil public infrastructures, such as destruction of roads and siltation of dams, reach EUR 32/ha (García-Torres et al., 2001). In Armenia, for example, the costs of the damage from soil erosion in the past 20 years amounted to 7.5 % of national gross agricultural product (UNECE, 2000c).

The effects of soil erosion are expected to get worse, since climate change is expected to influence the characteristics of rainfall in ways which might increase soil erosion in central Europe (Sauerborn et al., 1999).

Policies to combat soil erosion comprise a wide range of actions: adoption of sustainable farming practices (including minimum tillage systems, contouring, terracing or strip cultivation); land planning to determine the most suitable crops for each area; ending set-aside of arable land; reclamation of highly degraded lands or areas affected by desertification; reforestation of watersheds; and incentives to promote more sustainable activities.

The common agricultural policy has undergone a substantial reform since 1992 and the adoption of Agenda 2000 in 1999. There has been a gradual elimination of many subsidies and a reinforcement of incentives to promote environmentally sensitive agriculture (see Chapter 2.4.). Soil protection measures have been reinforced

and expanded to encourage organic farming, the maintenance of terraces, safer pesticide use, the use of certified composts and afforestation, among others. However, farmers' participation in agri-environment schemes is still very low in areas of high erosion risk. Implementation of agri-environment measures can have positive effects in the enlarged EU, but considerable effort is required to support the widespread adoption of these instruments in the accession countries.

9.4. Soil contamination

Soil contamination from diffuse and localised sources can result in the damage of several soil functions and the contamination of surface water and groundwater.

9.4.1. Diffuse sources
The main diffuse sources of soil contamination are atmospheric deposition of acidifying and eutrophying compounds or potentially harmful chemicals, deposition of contaminants from flowing water or eroded soil itself, and the direct application of substances such as pesticides, sewage sludge, fertilisers and manure which may contain heavy metals. The soil functions most affected by contamination are its buffering, filtering and transforming capacities. Currently, the most important soil contamination problems from diffuse sources are acidification, contamination by heavy metals and the effects of a surplus of nutrients.

Acidification is the most widespread type of soil contamination in WE and CEE, where vast areas have been affected, especially in Poland (10 million ha including natural acidification) and Ukraine (about 11 million ha of agricultural land). High content of heavy metals in soils is reported in Ukraine at the local level (about 5 million ha, mostly in human settlements and around the industrial factories) and in Lithuania (nearly 3 million ha) (van Lynden, 2000). However, the relatively high heavy metal concentrations in Lithuania can be partly explained by high natural background levels. Contamination by pesticides is common in Ukraine (more than 5 million ha) and Romania (more than 4 million ha), where the estimated degree of contamination is light to moderate (van Lynden, 2000). The Chernobyl accident (1986) is still a major cause of contamination by radionuclides in Ukraine and some areas of the Russian

Federation. Nuclear tests performed in the past, uranium mining and processing, and the manufacture of nuclear fuel affected some areas in EECCA. Radioactive waste from uranium plants, mainly from former Soviet nuclear test sites, is still stored without protection in Kyrgysztan and Kazakhstan (UNECE, 1999; 2000d; 2000c).

9.4.2. Localised sources

Soil contamination from localised sources is often related to industrial plants no longer in operation, past industrial accidents and improper municipal and industrial waste disposals. In addition, at industrial plants still operating, soil contamination often has its origin in the past, and current activities still have significant impacts (EEA-UNEP, 2000). Effects of industrial activity (either historical or currently in operation) that pose a risk to soils and groundwater, and the spectrum of the various polluting activities, vary between countries. These variations may result in different classification systems and in incomplete information being available in some countries (Figure 9.4).

Sites contaminated in these ways can pose serious threats to health and to the local environment as a result of releases of harmful substances to groundwater or surface waters, uptake by plants and direct contact by people, and following explosion of landfill gases.

The largest and probably most heavily affected areas are concentrated around the most industrialised regions in northwest Europe, from Nord-Pas de Calais in France to the Rhein-Ruhr region in Germany, across Belgium and the Netherlands and the south of the United Kingdom (EEA-UNEP, 2000). Other areas where the probability of occurrence of local soil contamination is high include the Saar region in Germany, the Po area in northern Italy, and the so-called Black Triangle region located at the corner of Poland, the Czech Republic and the Slovak Republic. However, contaminated areas exist around most major cities and

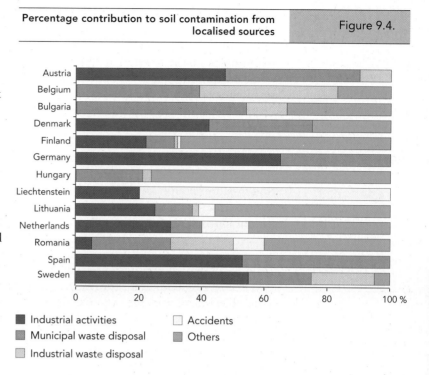

Percentage contribution to soil contamination from localised sources — Figure 9.4.

Legend:
- ■ Industrial activities
- ■ Municipal waste disposal
- □ Industrial waste disposal
- □ Accidents
- ■ Others

Notes: Belgium: data refer to Flanders. Germany: industrial activities also includes accidents and other, and municipal waste disposal also includes industrial waste disposal. Germany and Sweden: the percentage share refers to the total number of identified, suspected sites; data refer exclusively to abandoned sites (not in operation). Bulgaria: others include storage of pesticides, contaminated soils by mining and industry activities. Liechtenstein: minor accidents are not included. Denmark and Spain: municipal waste includes industrial waste.

Source: EEA

there are some individual contaminated sites in sparsely populated areas (EEA-UNEP, 2000).

A wide range of potentially harmful elements and chemical compounds is used in industry. Handling losses, defects, industrial accidents and leaching of hazardous substances at waste disposal sites can cause soil and groundwater contamination. Major pollutants include organic contaminants such as chlorinated hydrocarbons, mineral oil and heavy metals. In some parts of Europe, soil is contaminated by artificial radionuclides.

In the mining industry, which is a major driver of soil degradation in CEE countries, the risk of contamination is associated with sulphur and heavy metal-bearing tailings stored on mining sites, and the use of certain chemical reagents such as cyanide in the refining process. Acid mine drainage is a common long-term problem, as for example in the case of the serious incident at the Aznalcollar mine in Spain in 1998. The disaster affected a watercourse nearby for 63 km downstream and the adjacent land (Sol et al., 1999). Another recent accident was the cyanide spill in Romania from the

> 😞 Soil contamination from local sources, mainly waste disposal from municipal and industrial sources and industrial activities, is widespread in western Europe as well as in central and eastern Europe, the Caucasus and central Asia.

Aurul tailings re-treatment plant at Baia Mare in 2000. This disaster affected plankton and fish in the upper reaches of the Tisza River in Romania and Hungary. The spill occurred in an area already contaminated by heavy metals from a long history of mining and metal processing. Upstream locations unaffected by this particular spill also contained high levels of some heavy metals. The accident occurred in a region with a number of poorly maintained and operated plants and flotation ponds containing cyanide and/or heavy metals, many of which are leaking continuously (European Commission, 2000a).

Waste landfilling is another important potentially contaminating activity. On average, 57 % of municipal waste generated in the EU is landfilled, 84 % in CEE (see Chapter 7). Leachate from waste landfills can enter soil, groundwater and surface water. Particular concerns are related to landfills that operate or have operated in the past and that do not comply with the minimum requirements set by the landfill directive (Directive 1999/31/EC) (European Commission, 1999).

Contaminated land in CEE is the result of former military sites as well as industrial activities and waste management. Inefficient technologies and production systems, in

terms of raw material and energy consumption as well as waste production, were common in the past. Heavily contaminated sites covering several thousand square metres (e.g. in traditional large-scale industrial areas) may still represent a considerable risk to human health and the environment. However, the extent of the contribution of the military sector to soil contamination is not known, as data on contamination of military sites are not usually publicly available.

New legislative and regulatory frameworks at the national and EU level (landfill directive, integrated pollution and prevention control directive, water framework directive, environmental liability directive) are based on the precautionary principle. Their application should result in fewer inputs of contaminants, as a result of fewer handling losses and accidents at industrial sites, and in better control of soil contamination (EEA, 2001). Nevertheless, much effort is still needed to characterise and remediate old contaminated sites.

The management of contaminated sites is designed to remediate any adverse effects where impairment of the environment has been proved and to minimise potential threats. The whole process is carried out in several steps. Preliminary surveys provide a list of potentially contaminated sites and verify, or not, the existence of contamination and potential harmful effects to human health or the environment. The main site investigation focuses on the determination of the extent of the contamination. One of the next phases is the remediation plan, which includes a specific remediation investigation and measures to reduce adverse effects on human health or the environment. Targets for remediation and/or safety measures can vary according to the proposed land use. The management scheme must take into account the risk of secondary contamination due to further retention of contaminants by the soil.

Figure 9.5 summarises progress in the management of contaminated sites in 14 European countries. Preliminary surveys are far advanced in most of the surveyed countries. Further stages are proceeding slowly. However, data availability and data access have improved compared to earlier assessments.

In general, all countries apply the 'polluter pays' principle, to differing extents. However, a considerable share of total remediation costs has been provided from

| Figure 9.5. | Progress in the management of contaminated sites |

■ Preliminary survey   ▨ Main site investigation
▨ Preliminary investigation   ▨ Remediation activities implemented

Notes: France: mean value of estimated total number of sites according to preliminary survey; Romania: minimum value of estimated total number of sites according to preliminary survey. Spain: methods to estimate the total number have been revised therefore data are under consideration. All: information on completed remediation has not been included; missing information in the graph indicates that no data have been reported for the particular country.

Sources: EEA, 1999; 2001

The first step in the management of contaminated sites (preliminary survey/investigation) is well advanced in most of the surveyed countries, but subsequent phases are progressing slowly.

public money. Many countries have developed special funding tools for the clean-up of contaminated sites. For example, in some countries there are voluntary agreements with the petrochemical and oil industries to fund the remediation of abandoned petrol stations, financed by a fee included in the petrol price. Estimates of public expenditure are available from many countries, but information on private expenditure is scarce and depends on approximate estimates.

Annual remediation expenditure varies from EUR 35 to less than EUR 2 per capita in the reporting countries. The average cost for the countries surveyed was less than 1 % of GDP (Figure 9.6).

In the EU, implementation of new regulations that reflect the precautionary principle should help to avoid local soil contamination in the future. In the EU countries where data are available, expenditures on clean-up have remained constant over recent years (1997–2000). In future, expenditure will probably remain at a constant rate, except in countries that have only recently begun to address the problem, where an increase is expected. Many accession countries have started investigations, and the setting up of specific funding tools and cooperation with the EU are increasing.

Although the 'polluter pays' principle is generally applied, a huge sum of public money has to be provided to fund necessary remediation activities, which is a common factor across Europe. Even though a considerable amount of money has already been spent on remediation activities, the share of the total estimated remediation costs is relatively low (up to 8 %).

In CEE, most countries (e.g. Bulgaria) still do not have strategies and national policies for the management of contaminated sites or specific legislation regulating investigation and clean-up of contaminated land; others (e.g. Poland) have only recently introduced

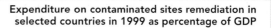

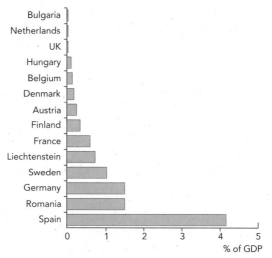

Figure 9.6. Expenditure on contaminated sites remediation in selected countries in 1999 as percentage of GDP

Notes: Belgium: data on remediation expenditures refer to Flanders; data on GDP refer to Belgium. France: data from 2001. Germany: projection from estimates of expenditures from some of the Länder.

Sources: For EU countries and Liechtenstein, data request EEA (2002); for accession countries: data request new EEA member countries (2002); World Bank, 2001

new laws on environmental protection. However, requirements for soil protection are generally included in several legislative acts (e.g. environment protection legislation and water, waste and mining legislation).

9.5. Salinisation

Salinisation, the accumulation of salts on or near the surface of the soil, results in completely unproductive soils, which are currently found mainly in the Mediterranean region, eastern CEE and EECCA. It is caused by improper irrigation methods and evaporation of saline groundwater, groundwater extraction and industrial activities (European Commission, 2000b).

Irrigated soils, particularly in arid regions, are affected to larger or lesser extent (Figure 9.7). For example, about half the irrigated land in Uzbekistan (State Committee of the Republic of Uzbekistan, 2000) and some 16 million ha (25 % of total irrigated cropland) in the Mediterranean countries (FAO, 1996) are affected.

Salinisation has major impacts on the economy. It has been estimated that in the central Asian republics, salinisation reduced cotton yields from 280 to 230 tonnes/km^2 between the late 1970s and the late 1980s, despite an increased use of fertilisers (Gardner, 1997). Salinisation may also have important off-site effects because salt that has moved to the upper layer of the soil can be carried by the wind to other areas.

Figure 9.7.	**Area of land affected by salinisation in selected countries**

Notes: Light: some signs of degradation are present, but the process is still at an initial phase. Moderate: salinisation is apparent, but control and full remediation to its current function is still possible with considerable efforts. High: evident signs of degradation — changes in soil qualities are significant and very difficult, if not impossible, to restore within reasonable limits. Spain: area with light salinisation not available. Figures at the top of the graph bars refer to the total area of land affected by salinisation in million ha.

Sources: For Hungary, Ukraine, Estonia, the Republic of Moldova, Bulgaria, the Russian Federation and Slovakia: FAO and ISRIC, 2000; for Turkmenistan, Uzbekistan and Ukraine: state of environment reports; for Spain: 2000 plan to combat desertification.

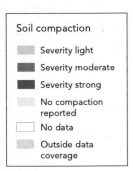

Moderate to high salinisation is affecting agricultural soils in the Mediterranean region and in eastern Europe, the Caucasus and central Asia mainly as a result of inappropriate irrigation systems. For example, salinisation affects 16 million ha or 25 % of irrigated cropland in the Mediterranean.

Salinisation has a major impact on soil quality and, above certain thresholds, restoration is very expensive if not impossible. Most remediation projects focus on improving soil condition and recovering the land for crop production by improving irrigation systems and the efficiency of water use, and by maintaining drainage systems. However, most of the severely affected areas are abandoned without any attempt at rehabilitation; for example, this applies to about 300 000 ha of affected soil in the Russian Federation (Stolbovoi and Fischer, 1997). Privatisation in EECCA and the lack of economic resources of private owners are making the implementation of improvements to irrigation systems and the maintenance of drainage systems difficult. Where drainage is too expensive, planting salt-resistant plants has helped to stabilise the soil and reduce erosion (Mainguet and Létolle, 2000). In most countries, rehabilitation projects are linked directly to programmes to combat desertification.

9.6. Soil compaction

Soil compaction is potentially a major threat to agricultural productivity (EEA, 1995a; Nolte and Fausey, 2000). The repetitive and

Map 9.1.	**Degree and extent of soil compaction in Europe**

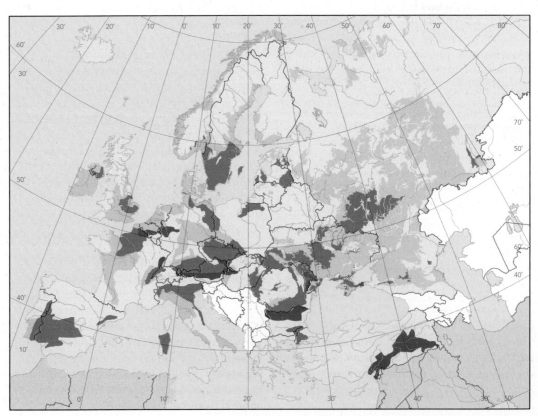

Sources: van Lynden, 1995; FAO and ISRIC, 2000

Box 9.2. Aral Sea: follow-up problems

In the 1960s, central Asia became the major producer of raw cotton in the former USSR. Cotton crops require extensive irrigation and the Aral Sea and its tributaries seemed a limitless source of water at the time. The local population grew from 14 million to about 27 million and the extent of irrigated land from about 4.5 million to almost 7 million ha between 1960 and 1980. The demand for water almost doubled (Figure 9.8) with more than 90 % of the water withdrawal used for agriculture. The water balance in the basin collapsed and, by the mid-1960s, the Aral sea level began to drop, reaching a critical point in 1980 (mean level decreased by 90 cm a year) (Islamov, 1999). By that time, the excessive use of agrochemicals together with industrial and municipal sources of pollution had already seriously degraded the quality of the water. As the sea shrank, enormous quantities of salts accumulated on its bed, leaving nothing more than a salty desert.

Figure 9.9 shows the increase of this new salty desert to its maximum by the mid-1970s. Because of the concentration of toxic salts in the upper soil layer, lack of nutrients and shortage of fresh water, the resulting desert land has been proving extremely resistant to natural and artificial revegetation (Micklin, 1988). However, the most serious problem is the blowing of salt and dust from the dried seabed, the impact of which will last for decades. The area affected by the spread of salt and dust is increasing every year. The disaster has also affected the deltaic ecosystems and biological productivity, in particular fisheries, the basic economy of surrounding communities. Moreover, the population faces appalling health problems. A negative effect on climate has also been observed, which has reduced the crops significantly (Hiltunen, 1998).

In the catchments of the Aral Sea, mismanagement of irrigation and drainage infrastructures have resulted in increased river water salinity, soil salinisation and water-logging. In addition, catchment areas have lost about half of their forest cover and soil erosion has intensified. As well as creating considerable environmental problems in the upper watersheds, all these factors have a negative impact on downstream areas.

In the past decade, the countries affected have taken various initiatives to tackle the problem, with the support of international institutions. The Aral Sea Basin Programme was launched in 1994 with the main objectives of rehabilitating the degraded area around the sea, improving management of land and water resources in the basin, and building the capacity of institutions at all levels in order to plan and implement the programme. The programme had to confront many problems, especially limited economic resources in relation to the scale of the disaster. Demand for water has

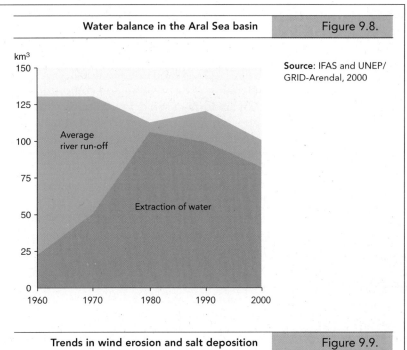

Water balance in the Aral Sea basin — **Figure 9.8.**

Source: IFAS and UNEP/GRID-Arendal, 2000

km³

Average river run-off

Extraction of water

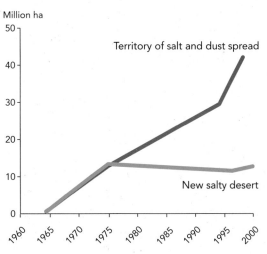

Trends in wind erosion and salt deposition — **Figure 9.9.**

Note: 'New salty desert' refers to the territory that appeared as a result of the sea drying out.

Source: IFAS

Million ha

Territory of salt and dust spread

New salty desert

levelled off to some extent, but the cultivation of many crops remains inefficient because insolvency of the water users has precluded the use of advanced irrigation techniques. As a result the water balance remains very precarious. Some pilot projects are focusing on integrated management of the land to prevent erosion and rehabilitate the most degraded areas (Aslov, 2000). However, these projects are still at a preliminary stage and extensive action is needed to avoid irreversible losses (Dukhovny and Sokolov, 2000).

cumulative effect of heavy machinery on the same piece of agricultural land causes soil compaction — soil particles are pressed together and the pore spaces between them reduced. Soil compaction slows infiltration and increases the volume of surface runoff, thus accelerating water erosion and the loss of topsoil and nutrients. Compaction also changes the quantity and quality of

biochemical and microbiological activity in the soil.

While compaction of topsoil can easily be countered by reworking the soil and can eventually be reversed if the biological processes in the soil remain undisturbed, deep compaction of subsoil is persistent and cannot easily be reversed (EEA, 1995b).

Deep soils with less than 25 % clay content are the most sensitive to subsoil compaction (Hébert, 2002). Sensitive soils are common in Belgium, northwest France, Germany, the Netherlands, Poland and the Russian Federation (EEA, 1995b). Soil compaction is the main form of soil degradation in CEE, where it has affected over 62 million ha or 11 % of the total land area in the surveyed countries (see Map 9.1). Particularly during the time of the former USSR, heavy machinery was used on soils sensitive to compaction. The degree of compaction is mostly light to moderate, but negative impacts on agricultural productivity have nevertheless been reported in more than half of all areas affected (van Lynden, 2000).

9.7. References

Aslov, S., 2000. Integrated land and water management in the upper watersheds in the Aral Sea basin: The case of Tajikistan. In: *Land-water linkages in rural watersheds: Electronic workshop, 18 September-27 October 2000.* Case Study 23. FAO.

Baltic Environmental Forum, 2001. *2nd Baltic state of the environment report: The Baltic environmental indicators set.* Baltic Environmental Forum, Riga. http://www.bef.lv/baltic/baltic2/content.htm

Coalition Clean Baltic (CCB), 2002. *Baltic Sea Hot Spots — Hazards and Possibilities for the Baltic Sea Region.* http://www.sll.fi/tiedotus/pressreleases/CCBHotSpots.html

DANCEE, 2000. *Management of contaminated sites and land in central and eastern Europe. Ad hoc international working group on contaminated land.* Ministry of Environment and Energy, Danish Environment Protection Agency, Danish Cooperation for Environment in Eastern Europe, Copenhagen.

Dukhovny, V. and Sokolov, V., 2000. *Integrated water resources management in the Aral Sea basin.* World Bank, Washington, DC.

EEA (European Environment Agency), 1995a. *Corine soil erosion risk and important land resources in the southern regions of the European Community.* Office for Official Publications of the European Communities, Luxembourg.

EEA (European Environment Agency), 1995b. *Europe's environment: The Dobris assessment.* Office for Official Publications of the European Communities, Luxembourg.

EEA (European Environment Agency), 1999. *Environment in the European Union at the turn of the century.* Environmental assessment report No 2. Office for Official Publications of the European Communities, Luxembourg.

EEA (European Environment Agency), 2000. *Are we moving in the right direction?* Environmental Issues Series No 12. Office for Official Publications of the European Communities, Luxembourg.

EEA (European Environment Agency), 2001. *Environmental signals 2001.* Environmental assessment report No 8. Office for Official Publications of the European Communities, Luxembourg.

EEA (European Environment Agency), 2002a. *Environmental signals 2002. Benchmarking the millennium.* Environmental assessment report No 9. Office for Official Publications of the European Communities, Luxembourg.

EEA (European Environment Agency), 2002b. *Assessment and reporting on soil erosion.* Technical report No 94. EEA.

EEA-UNEP, 2000. *Down to earth: Soil degradation and sustainable development in Europe. A challenge for the 21st century.* Environmental issues Series No 6. EEA, UNEP, Luxembourg.

European Commission, 1999. *Council Directive 1999/31/EC of 26 April 1999 on the landfill of waste.* Official Journal L 182. 16/07/1999. Brussels

European Commission, 2000a. *Safe operation of mining activities: A follow-up to recent mining accidents.* COM(2000) 664 final. Commission of the European Communities, Brussels.

European Commission, 2000b. *The environmental impacts of irrigation in the European Union.* Report to DG Environment prepared by Institute for European Environmental Policy, London, Polytechnical University of Madrid, University of Athens. EC, Brussels.

European Commission, 2002. *Towards a strategy for soil protection.* COM (2002) 179 final. http://europa.eu.int/comm/environment/agriculture/soil_protection.htm

FAO (Food and Agriculture Organization of the United Nations), 1996. *Report of the FAO*

Regional Conference for Europe. 20th Session, Tel Aviv, 29 April–3 May 1996. ERC/96/REP. FAO, Rome.

FAO and ISRIC (International Soil Reference and Information Centre), 2000. *Soil and terrain database, land degradation status and soil vulnerability assessment for central and eastern Europe (SOVEUR).* Version 1.0 (1:2.5 million scale). FAO Land and Water Digital Media Series 10. FAO, Rome.

García-Torres, L. *et al.*, 2001. Conservation agriculture in Europe: Current status and perspectives. In: *Conservation agriculture, a worldwide challenge. I World Congress on Conservation Agriculture. Madrid, 1–5 October 2001.* ECAF, FAO, Córdoba, Spain.

Gardner, G., 1997. Preserving global cropland. In: *State of the World 1997* (Brown, L. *et al.*, ed.). W. W. Norton, New York.

German Advisory Council on Global Change, 1994. *World in transition: The threat to soils. 1994 Annual Report.* Economica, Bonn.

Hébert, J., 2002. About the problems of structure in relation to soil degradation. In: *Soil degradation* (Boels, D., Davies, D. and Johnston, A. E., eds). A. A. Balkema, Rotterdam.

Hiltunen, M., 1998. *Environmental development co-ooperation opportunities — Kazakstan, Kyrgyz Republic, Turkmenistan, Uzbekistan.* Finnish Environment Institute. http://global.finland.fi/english/publications/discussion/envalku.html

IFAS and UNEP/GRID-Arendal, 2000. *State of environment of the Aral Sea basin. Regional report of the central Asian States 2000.* http://www.grida.no/aral/aralsea/index.htm

Islamov, B., 1999. Doubling freshwater inflow is key to curbing the Aral Sea crisis. In: *Slavic Research Center International Symposium 'Russian Regions: Economic Growth and Environment'. Sapporo, 21–24 July 1999.* Slavic Research Center, Hokkaido University, Sapporo, Japan.

Mainguet, M. and Létolle, R., 2000. Water problems in central Asia. Gigantomania should be replaced by small projects. In: *Proceedings of the workshop: New approaches to water management in central Asia. Aleppo, Syria, 6–11 November 2000.* UNESCO, ICARDA.

Micklin, P. P., 1988. Dessication of the Aral Sea: A water management disaster in the Soviet Union. *Science* 241: 1170–1176.

Nolte, B. H. and Fausey, N. R., 2000. Soil compaction and drainage. *Extension Bulletin AEX-301.* Ohio State University.

Oldeman, L. R. *et al.*, 1991. *GLASOD world map of the status of human-induced soil degradation.* ISRIC, Wageningen and UNEP, Nairobi.

PIK (Potsdam Institute for Climate Impact Research), 2000. *Proceedings of the European conference on advances in flood research.* Potsdam, November 2000. PIK Report 65. PIK.

REC (Regional Environmental Centre for Eastern and central Europe), 2001. *Final country report Bosnia and Hercegovina within strategic environmental analysis of Albania, Bosnia and Hercegovina, Kosovo and Macedonia.* http://www.rec.org/REC/Publications/CountryReports/Bosnia.PDF

Rekacewicz, P. *et al.*, 2000. *Environmental disaster in eastern Europe.* Le Monde Diplomatique 7 (July). Paris

Sauerborn, P. *et al.*, 1999. *Future rainfall erosivity derived from large-scale climate models — methods and scenarios for a humid region.* Geoderma 93: 269–276.

Sol, V. M., Peters, S. W. M. and Aiking, H., 1999. *Toxic waste storage sites in EU countries. A preliminary risk inventory.* R-99/04. WWF, Institute for Environmental Studies of the Vrije University, Amsterdam.

State Committee of the Republic of Uzbekistan, 2000. *State of environment in Uzbekistan.* State Committee of the Republic of Uzbekistan, Department for managing of ecological information and prognostification. http://www.grida.no/enrin/htmls/uzbek/soe2/english/index.htm

Stolbovoi, V. and Fischer, G., 1997. *A new digital georeferenced database of soil degradation in Russia.* Interim Report IR-97-084/November. IIASA, Laxenburg, Austria.

UNCCD (United Nations Convention to Combat Desertification), 2002a. *Synthesis and preliminary analysis of information contained in reports submitted by northern Mediterranean, central and eastern European and other affected* country Parties. ICCD/CRIC(1)/5/Add.1. Report presented by the UNCCD secretariat at the first session of the Committee for the Review of the Implementation on the Convention (CRIC1, Rome, November). http://www.unccd.int/cop/officialdocs/cric1/pdf/5add1eng.pdf

UNCCD (United Nations Convention to Combat Desertification), 2002b. *Synthesis and preliminary analysis of information contained in reports submitted by affected Asian country Parties.* ICCD/CRIC(1)/3/Add.1. Report presented by the UNCCD secretariat at the first session of the Committee for the Review of the Implementation on the Convention (CRIC1, Rome, November). http://www.unccd.int/php/document.php?ref=ICCD/CRIC(1)/3/Add.1

UNCCD (United Nations Convention to Combat Desertification), 2002c. *Compilation of summary of reports submitted by Asian country Parties prepared for the First Committee on the Revision of the Implementation of the United Nations Convention to Combat Desertification.* UNCCD secretariat. http://www.unccd.int/cop/officialdocs/cric1/pdf/3add2eng.pdf

UNDP and GEF (United Nations Development Programme and Global Environment Facility), 1998. *Environmental problems of the Caspian region. National report of the Russian Federation.* State Committee of the Russian Federation for Environmental Protection and Hydrometeorology, Moscow.

UNECE (United Nations Economic Commission for Europe) 1999. *Environmental performance review of Ukraine.* UNECE, Geneva.

UNECE (United Nations Economic Commission for Europe), 2000a. *Environmental performance review of Kazakhstan.* UNECE, Geneva.

UNECE (United Nations Economic Commission for Europe), 2000b. *Meeting of the Parties to the Convention on the Protection and Use of Transboundary Watercourses and International Lakes.* The Hague, Netherlands, 23-25 March 2000.

UNECE (United Nations Economic Commission for Europe), 2000c. *Environmental Performance Review of Armenia.* UNECE, Geneva.

UNECE (United Nations Economic Commission for Europe), 2000d. *Environmental performance review of Kyrgyzstan.* UNECE, Geneva.

UNECE (United Nations Economic Commission for Europe), 2001. *Assessment of progress in sustainable development since Rio 1992 for member states of the United Nations Economic Commission for Europe.* CEP/AC.12/3. UNECE, Geneva.

UNEP (United Nations Environment Programme), 1998. *National report on the state of the environment in the Russian Federation.* http://ceeri.ecoinfo.ru/state_report_98/eng/introduction.htm

UNEP (United Nations Environment Programme), 2002. *Caucasus environment outlook (CEO) 2002.* New Media, Tbilisi.

van Lynden, G. W. J., 1995. *The European soil resource: Current status of soil degradation causes, impacts and need for action.* Council of Europe, Strasbourg.

van Lynden, G. W. J., 2000. *Soil degradation in central and eastern Europe. The assessment of the status of human-induced degradation.* FAO Report 2000/05. FAO and ISRIC.

World Bank, 2001. *World development indicators.* http://www.worldbank.org/data/countrydata/countrydata.html

10. Technological and natural hazards

Technological accidents continue to occur in Europe, but those that involve large numbers of fatalities have decreased during the past decade, with the exception of mining disasters in Ukraine. The apparent increase in the total number of major accidents in the European Union since 1985 may be due to improved reporting as well as increases in industrial and other economic activities.

Natural disasters continue to have a far greater impact than technological accidents. Both the probability of occurrence and the consequences of natural disasters can be increased as a result of technological advances and human activities such as agriculture and forestry.

A holistic approach to hazard management, based on lessons learned from past accidents and natural disasters, recognition of the need for better emergency planning, and implementation of a number of EU directives, should help to reduce the numbers and consequences of technological accidents and reduce the impacts of some natural disasters.

10.1. Introduction

Major technological accidents continue to occur, even with advances in the safety management of hazards. Technological accidents claim only a fraction of the lives lost as a result of natural hazards (approximately 5 % of the total in the period 1985–96 in Europe). For both technological accidents and natural hazards, the risk depends on where people live. The explosion in the outskirts of Toulouse in September 2001 tragically illustrated the capacity of technological accidents to claim many lives.

The catastrophic earthquake in Turkey in 1999 demonstrated that human life remains vulnerable to the violent effects of nature. Natural catastrophes continue to have a far greater effect, in terms of fatalities, injuries and overall cost, than technological accidents. Flooding, landslides, avalanches and violent storms are all capable of causing multiple fatalities in one event, although none can match earthquakes for sheer numbers of fatalities. The costs of storms and flooding incidents can run into billions of euros.

The risk of fatality from natural hazards depends, to a large extent, on where people live. The seismically active areas in Europe are well documented, the location of volcanoes is known and the areas susceptible to flooding, landslides and avalanches can generally be predicted. However, there is still an element of unpredictability about when and exactly where such events will happen. All these can take people by surprise, as their onset may be very rapid.

Technological advances and human activities may be exacerbating the impacts of natural hazards, both at a chronic and an acute level. The apparent increase in flooding incidents seen across Europe in the past decade may be linked to chronic changes to the environment caused by human activities, such as global warming. Activities such as land clearing for agricultural purposes have been a cause of catastrophic landslides following periods of heavy rain.

For technological hazards and those activities that may exacerbate the effects of natural hazards, design evolution and operational experience have reduced the risk levels over the years. 'Holistic' approaches, which take an integrated perspective, are becoming more prevalent, with increasing attention to the reduction of risk of long-term environmental impact as well as acute health and property damage from accidents. However, there remains a residual risk that must be well managed at all times. This is particularly the case for those hazards that may have devastating consequences for a large number of people, such as serious nuclear accidents. Large-scale preparations are being considered for the various natural hazards so that the response is rapid and well coordinated to minimise the harmful effects.

10.2. Technological hazards

10.2.1. Industrial accidents

Between 1971 and 1992 there was, on average, one technological accident every year in Europe that resulted in 25 or more fatalities (Table 10.1). Thereafter, there were no accidents resulting in 25 or more fatalities until 1998 (although no data were available

| Table 10.1. | Industrial accidents resulting in more than 25 fatalities (since 1971) | | | |

Notes: Other events may have occurred that have not been widely documented. * Number of fatalities related directly to the explosion of the reactor; see Section 10.3.3 on fatalities from the effects of the accident.

Sources: UNEP, 2002a, 2002b; BBC, 2002a

Year	Location	Products involved	Type of accident	Fatalities
1971	Czechowice, Poland	Oil	Explosion	33
1971	English Channel	Petrochemicals	Ship collision	29
1973	Czechoslovakia	Gas	Explosion	47
1974	Flixborough, UK	Cyclohexane	Explosion	28
1976	Lapua, Finland	Gunpowder	Explosion	43
1978	San Carlos, Spain	Propylene	Fireball (road transport)	216
1979	Bantry Bay, Ireland	Oil, gas	Explosion (marine transport)	50
1979	Warsaw, Poland	Gas	Explosion	49
1979	Novosibirsk, USSR	Chemicals	Unknown	300
1980	Ortuella, Spain	Propane	Explosion	51
1980	Rome, Italy	Oil	Ship collision	25
1980	Danaciobasi, Turkey	Butane	Unknown	107
1982	Todi, Italy	Gas	Explosion	34
1983	Istanbul, Turkey	Unknown	Explosion	42
1984	Romania	Chemicals	Unknown	100
1985	Algeciras, Spain	Oil	Transhipment	33
1986	Chernobyl, USSR	Nuclear	Reactor explosion	31*
1988	Arzamas, USSR	Explosives	Explosion (rail transport)	73
1988	North Sea, UK	Oil, gas	Fire	167
1989	Acha Ufa, USSR	Gas	Explosion (pipeline)	575
1991	Livorno, Italy	Naphtha	Transport accident	141
1992	Corlu, Turkey	Methane	Explosion	32
1998	Donetsk, Ukraine	Methane	Explosion (mine)	63
1999	Zasyadko, Ukraine	Methane	Explosion (mine)	50
2000	Donetsk, Ukraine	Methane	Explosion (mine)	81
2001	Donetsk, Ukraine	Coal dust/methane	Explosion (mine)	36
2001	Toulouse, France	Ammonium nitrate	Explosion	31
2002	Donetsk, Ukraine	Methane	Explosion (mine)	35

for 1998 and 1999 on the UNEP database (UNEP, 2002a; 2002b) and the data were derived from isolated sources). It would appear that, in general, accidents involving large numbers of fatalities have decreased in the past decade, with the exception of methane explosions in Ukrainian mines.

There is generally an equal spread between those events that occurred in the European Union (EU) and those in eastern Europe, although before the fall of the 'Iron Curtain' there may have been a number that were not widely reported. In recent years, however, there have been disproportionate numbers of multiple-fatality accidents in Ukrainian mines (see Box 10.1). One of the major reasons for this is a lack of investment, compounded by poor safety and environmental management. This is a common theme that runs through many technological industries in eastern European countries, certainly when compared to western Europe.

Many countries in Europe have used the EU Seveso II directive as a model and this should help to decrease the number of major accidents. It is anticipated that this will bring consistent standards and an improvement in safety performance throughout Europe.

The total number of major accidents reported each year in the EU from 1985 to 1999 shows a steady increase, with the maximum number reported during 1998 (Figure 10.1). This may be due to a number of factors, including increased industrial and other economic activity and increased population densities around potentially hazardous sites, only partly compensated for by increased awareness and safety measures (see Box 10.2). The rapid rise in the number of accidents in the first few years of the MARS (major accident reporting system) database may have been due to better reporting. Many companies are now using the data from accidents to help understand their underlying causes, such as management failure. This learning exercise is one element of an improved approach to safety and environmental management that is being used by organisations in general, following the advent of the Seveso II directive.

When analysing the causes of major accidents, by far the biggest immediate cause is mechanical failure. Operator error is also a significant contributor (Figure 10.2). Both these are likely to be due to some kind of management failure, which is thus the underlying cause. For example, a failure due to corrosion may have been caused by a lack of monitoring. In fact, for 67 % of the accidents reported in the MARS database, the dominant underlying causes were poor safety and environmental management (Drogaris, 1993; Rasmussen, 1996). The Seveso II directive puts emphasis on mechanisms for the prevention of accidents, such as good safety management; this is a major improvement from the earlier Seveso directive.

10.2.2. Pipeline accidents

The impacts of pipeline accidents are usually only environmental, i.e. release of hydrocarbon liquid to surface waters and groundwater and release of gas to the atmosphere. There have been no recorded fatal accidents following gas releases from transmission pipelines over the period 1970–2000 in those countries included in the EGIG (European Gas pipeline Incident data Group) database (all within western Europe, see Figure 10.3). However, fatal accidents can certainly occur, as illustrated by an

Box 10.1. Ukraine's troubled mines

Ukraine has the world's highest coal industry death rate, with an average of about 300 deaths per year. In recent years, there have been several multiple-fatality accidents. Funding cuts since the break-up of the USSR in 1991 have forced the industry to struggle for survival and have led to a neglect of safety. Even in Soviet times, working practices were shoddy and safety standards low.

Underground explosions are common and are the main cause of fatalities, usually caused by methane that builds up in poorly ventilated shafts. Other deaths have been caused by roof collapses or the breakdown of ventilation systems. Equipment is outdated and often faulty; exposed wires can set off explosions, gas sensors and oxygen tanks do not work, and pit props are broken.

The majority of the mines are uneconomic, only 50 of more than 200 are viable. This, combined with very poor safety management, has led to the multitude of tragic accidents.

Source: BBC, 2000

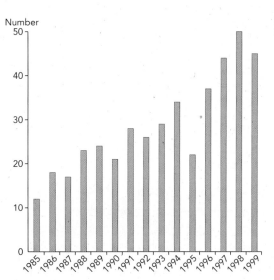

Number of major accidents reported on the MARS database (EU)
Figure 10.1.

Source: MARS database, 2002

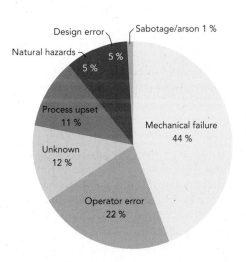

Causes of major accidents in the process industries
Figure 10.2.

Source: J&H Marsh & McLennan, 1998

Box 10.2. Ammonium nitrate explosion in Toulouse, France, 2001

On 21 September 2001, a huge explosion ripped through the AZF fertiliser factory in an industrial zone on the outskirts of Toulouse, France, leaving a 50 m diameter crater more than 10 m deep. Thirty-one people were reported dead, including some outside the plant, and 2 442 were injured. More than 500 homes were made uninhabitable and almost 11 000 pupils were kept at home after some 85 schools and colleges were damaged. Windows in the city centre 3 km away were blown out.

The explosion occurred in a warehouse in which granular ammonium nitrate was stored. Ammonium nitrate can explode under certain conditions. These must include added energy (heat, shock), especially under conditions of confinement or in the presence of contaminants. Although ammonium nitrate is generally used safely and is normally stable and unlikely to explode accidentally, accidental explosions of ammonium nitrate have resulted in loss of life and destruction of property.

The AZF plant was opened in 1924 in what was then countryside, but the urban sprawl from Toulouse (population 700 000) led to homes being built closer and closer to the plant. The AZF site is one of 1 250 factories in France classified as high risk. The site falls under the rules of the Seveso II directive.

Source: UNEP, 2002c

Figure 10.3. **Pipeline accidents and average amount spilt in western Europe**

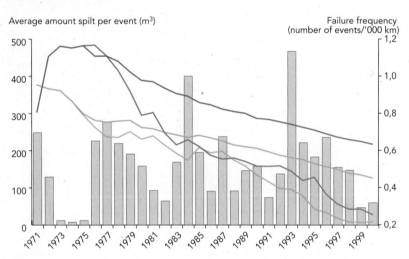

Average amount spilt per event (m³)

Failure frequency (number of events/'000 km)

Legend:
- Average amount spilt per event (m³)
- Overall failure frequency average up to the year (liquids)
- Moving 5-year average (liquids)
- Overall failure frequency avewrage up to the year (gas)
- Moving 5-year average (gas)

Sources: CONCAWE, 2002; EGIG, 2002

accident near Ufa, Russia, on 4 June 1989, when two trains, each carrying more than 500 passengers, passed each other within a cloud of natural gas arising from a pipeline leak (see Table 10.1). The gas exploded and most of the passengers in one train were killed outright; hundreds of passengers in the other (many of them children) suffered severe burns. This was not an isolated incident. The *Oil and Gas Journal* in 1993 reported that Russian oil and gas pipelines are plagued by accidents, citing an example

of a major pipeline break in western Siberia in 1993 when more than 2 000 m³ of crude were lost. More and more new pipelines are being constructed to transport oil and gas to the west from the new frontiers in the east, such as the Caspian region and Siberia.

The failure rate of liquid and gas pipelines in the EU since 1971 shows a significant downward trend, which is a reflection not just of better design and construction, but also of the improved safety management of existing pipelines, for example with improved corrosion protection and monitoring systems. In particular, there has been a marked improvement in the five-year moving average failure rate in both types of pipeline, with a four to fivefold decrease in the rate since records began. However, there has been no general decrease in the average amount spilt per event.

10.2.3. Oil spills

Another major hazard where the impact is predominantly environmental is marine oil spills. Worldwide, the annual number of oil spills and the total oil spilt from tankers shows a downward trend despite increasing maritime transport of oil, although the rate of improvement has decreased since about 1980 (Figure 10.4). European figures generally reflect the world situation; for the EU, for instance, tanker oil spills continue, although both the frequency and the amounts involved have fallen over the past decade. The erratic occurrence of such accidents, however, is illustrated by the recent Prestige disaster off the west coast of Spain.

Tanker safety is a major issue on the International Maritime Organisation's (IMO) protection agenda. In 1992, the IMO mandated the phasing out of conventional, single-hulled tankers. By 2010, all tankers and super tankers carrying crude oil must have double hulls; this will reduce the likelihood of spills. For spills greater than 700 tonnes, about 77 % are due to collisions, groundings and hull failures (Figure 10.5). Double hulls should reduce the frequency of such spills, so a further decrease in large spills worldwide, including in European waters, is expected.

However, the *Prestige* accident on 13 November 2002 has highlighted the potential environmental impact that oil transportation still poses. The *Prestige* suffered hull damage in heavy seas off northern Spain and developed a severe list.

She was taken in tow and moved away from the coast, but eventually broke in two and sank in just over 3 km of water. She was carrying a cargo of some 77 000 tonnes of heavy fuel oil, some of which was lost at the time of the initial damage and more subsequently (ITOPF, 2002b).

Oil released before the vessel broke in two came ashore intermittently along the predominantly rocky coastline between Cabo de la Nave and Punta Langosteira in northwest Spain, a distance of 100–150 km and reached French coasts later on. The affected area supports a rich and diverse fishing and aquaculture industry, including the cultivation of mussels, oysters, turbot and several other species, and the harvesting of various 'wild' species of fish and shellfish. The adverse social and economic effects may be felt for many years.

Since this disaster, the European Commission has accelerated tanker safety measures. It has published a blacklist of 66 ships deemed too dangerous for European waters, 16 of which are oil and chemical tankers. France and Spain agreed to check all ageing single-hulled vessels in their waters and force them out if necessary. They have adopted the emergency measures introduced by the EC without waiting for the rest of the EU to endorse them (BBC, 2002b).

10.2.4. Tailings dam failures

A number of tailings dam failures that have led to pollution of surface waters and widespread fish kills have occurred in recent years (Table 10.2.). As with industrial accidents, these have occurred with almost equal frequency in EU and eastern European countries. The incident at Stava, Italy, in 1985 claimed the lives of 268 people. The most devastating incident environmentally was that in Baia Mare, Romania, in 2000, where the release of highly toxic cyanide resulted in the killing of tonnes of fish and the poisoning of potable water for more than 2 million people in Hungary. Such an incident could occur in many areas across the whole of Europe, since the use of cyanide is still the preferred method for processing gold ores.

Another major cause of surface water pollution is firewater runoff following major incidents involving toxic substances. This is best illustrated by the warehouse fire at the Sandoz plant near Basel, when many toxic substances in the firewater flowed into the

| Number of oil spills worldwide and total oil spilt, 1970–2000 | Figure 10.4. |

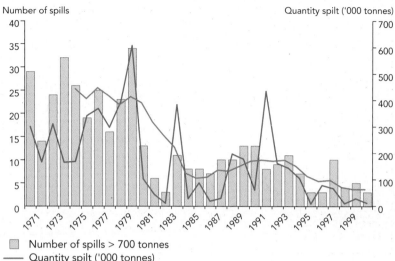

Source: ITOPF, 2002a

| Causes of oil spills 1974-2000 (spills greater than 700 tonnes) | Figure 10.5. |

Source: ITOPF, 2002a

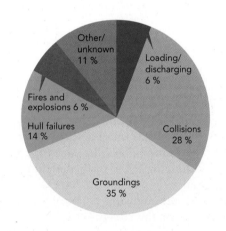

Rhine and caused the death of almost all aquatic life as far as 100 km downstream. Similar incidents could occur across the whole of Europe unless precautions are taken to contain and treat firewater onsite.

Directive 2000/60/EU of the European Parliament and the Council, establishing a framework for Community action in the field of water policy, entered into force on 22 December 2000. Among its central aspects was an obligation to progressively reduce discharges, emissions and losses of hazardous substances, including those due to accidents.

Table 10.2.	Tailings dam failures since 1980		

Source: UNEP, 2001

Date	Location	Release	Impacts
20 Jan 1981	Lebedinsky, USSR	3.5 million m³	Tailings travelled distance of 1.3 km
15 Sep 1983	Stebnik, Ukraine	1.2 million m³ of brine	Dnestr river polluted for hundreds of km, damaging the fish resources and biodiversity of the river
19 Jul 1985	Stava, Trento, Italy	200 000 m³	268 people killed
1 Mar 1992	Stara Zagora, Bulgaria	500 000 m³	Not known
1 May 1996	Sgurigrad, Bulgaria	220 000 m³	The tailings wave travelled 6 km and destroyed half of a village 1 km downstream, with 107 victims
25 Apr 1998	Aznalcóllar, Spain	4-5 million m³ of toxic water and slurry	Thousands of hectares of farmland covered with slurry and water contamination in national park of Doñana
31 Dec 1998	Huelva, Spain	50 000 m³ of acidic and toxic water	The liquid spilled into Ría de Huelva, a tributary of Río Tinto
30 Jan 2000	Baia Mare, Romania	100 000 m³ of cyanide-contaminated liquid (105-110 tonnes equivalent of cyanide)	Contamination of the Somes/Szamos stream, tributary of the Tisza River
10 Mar 2000	Borsa, Romania	22 000 tonnes equivalent of heavy-metal contaminated tailings (70-100 tonnes equivalent of copper)	Contamination of the Vaser stream, tributary of the Tisza river
8 Sep 2000	Gällivare, Sweden	1.5 million m³ of water carrying some residual slurry	The bed of the Vassara river was covered over a length of at least 7–8 km with a white slurry

10.3. Nuclear hazards

10.3.1. Nuclear power stations
Apart from the 1986 Chernobyl accident (see Section 10.3.3) other accidents have occurred in Europe over the past 40 years. Some of these have had environmental consequences and a handful have resulted in loss of life, although all have been minor compared with the effects of Chernobyl. A review of nuclear accidents up to 1996 has shown a highly disproportionate number of accidents in the former Soviet countries.

Figure 10.6 shows the number of nuclear power reactors currently operating (research reactors are not included). France, which has the most reactors of any one nation, has had only a small number of minor incidents. The Russian Federation, which has half the number of reactors, has had a multitude of incidents. This distinction between eastern and western Europe is mirrored by the other nations, suggesting a lower level of safety standards in the east.

Since 1970, the number of nuclear installations in Europe has increased and many European countries now have nuclear reactors at or towards the end of their working lives, as shown in Figure 10.7. It can be seen that there will be an increasing number of old reactors operating in Europe. At present, the United Kingdom is the only nation with a number of operational reactors above 36 years old and thus the United Kingdom has a significantly disproportionate number of old reactors at the end of their working lives.

It should be noted that in recent years, the safety of Soviet-designed reactors has improved. This is due largely to the development of a culture of safety encouraged by increased collaboration with western Europe countries, and substantial investment in improving the reactors. Since 1989, more than 1 000 nuclear engineers from the former USSR have visited western nuclear power plants and there have been many reciprocal visits, with more than 50 twinning arrangements put in place (UIC, 2001).

However, accidents at a number of nuclear plants have led to low public confidence in

---

Box 10.3. Hazards linked to armed conflicts

Recent evidence suggests that military activities are among the world's most environmentally destructive activities. The environmental impacts of war begin with disturbance and destruction of natural habitats, and progress to contamination of land, air and water with the wastes of people and machines. In most war zones, the impacts on the environment are long term or permanent.

Preparation
Military bases require large areas of land and often lead to the permanent destruction of flora and fauna. Large sectors of most countries are reserved for military exercises, which may include some related to chemical and biological warfare. In countries that manufacture weapons, areas may be used for testing missiles, chemical and biological warfare products, and nuclear weapons. All of these activities severely degrade natural ecosystems and tend to be treated as exceptions to any environmental regulations.

Conflict
As seen in the recent conflicts in the Balkans, human deaths and the destruction of 'military targets' are not the only immediate consequences of war. Modern weapons rely on toxic chemicals for much of their explosive force and propulsion. Hence they create negative environmental impacts through their own composition as well as their destructive power. When a heavy bomb goes off, it creates temperatures of approximately 3 000 °C; this not only annihilates all flora and fauna but also destroys the lower layers of soil, which can take anywhere between 1 000 and 10 000 years to regenerate.

Although the weapons constitute the most obvious threat to the environment, the targets that they destroy are also a highly significant contributor to the environmental devastation of war. Hazardous materials such as fuels, chemicals and radioactive substances may be targeted and thereby leak into surface waters and groundwater. During the recent war in the Balkans, NATO bombed petrochemical plants in the suburbs of Belgrade. Toxins such as chlorine and vinyl chloride monomer were released into the atmosphere.

Associated fuel combustion contributes to ozone depletion. The energy demands of military activities

have been estimated at 6 % of the global total, which is more than that of many countries.

Combatants may plunder natural resources to finance military operations. Furthermore, combatants may deliberately or indiscriminately target the environment, seeking to deprive opposing troops of shelter, food, water and fuel. The oil slicks and burning oil wells of Kuwait demonstrated that natural fuel resources can also be caught up in armed conflict, with catastrophic impacts on the environment.

The aftermath
Discarded weapons, including chemical and biological, are potential sources of contamination and injury to plant and animal species, including humans. Military wastes have created major remediation challenges throughout the world. When Soviet troops withdrew from the former East Germany in 1992, 1.5 million tonnes of ammunition were destroyed, with the release of nitrogen oxides, highly toxic chemical dioxides and heavy metals to the atmosphere. Abandoned garrison towns around Berlin have hidden waste tips with millions of gallons of spent tank and truck oil, and chemical wastes, as well as ammunition. Officials have estimated that the 4 % of East German territory that was occupied by former Soviet bases and facilities is severely polluted.

In addition to the machinery of war, the movement, accommodation and wastes of millions of humans creates major impacts on natural systems. By far the majority are refugees displaced from their homes by military activities. As recent events have demonstrated, the tens of thousands of ethnic Albanian refugees pouring out of Kosovo into neighbouring countries quickly exceeded the capacity of those countries to support them. Food, water, sanitation and even land space were simply unavailable in some locations.

According to the International Committee of the Red Cross, landmines kill or maim between 1 000 and 2 000 people every month. A hundred million landmines now lie in wait around the world. Most victims are civilians in peacetime, with children being especially vulnerable.

Sources: Bruch, 2002; Heathcote, 2002; Eco-compass, 2002; The History Guy, 2001

---

the nuclear industry, and even minor incidents now accentuate the problem of diminishing public trust. Reports of increased numbers of leukaemia cases in areas surrounding some nuclear installations provoke great concern amongst the general public, in spite of independent investigations which conclude that there is no proof of a link between reports of higher doses of radiation in these areas and the incidence of leukaemia (European Commission, 1999).

By means of comparison, atmospheric nuclear testing of nuclear weapons resulted in the largest release of radionuclides into the environment and by far the largest

collective dose from man-made sources, as shown in Table 10.3. By contrast, nuclear power production, nuclear weapons fabrication and radioisotope production result in comparatively small collective doses to the population. Accidents may have significant local impact, but only Chernobyl gave rise to a substantial population dose.

10.3.2. Radioactive waste management
Accidents and incidents involving the management of radioactive waste materials are not common occurrences. Between 1993 and February 1997, no incident or accident of radiological significance was observed in radioactive waste management operations. It

| Figure 10.6. | Number of operational nuclear power reactors in Europe (research reactors not included) |

Source: IAEA, 2002a

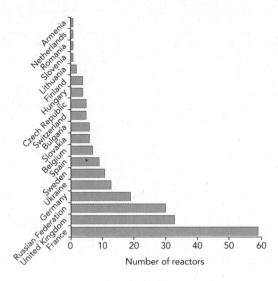

| Figure 10.7. | Age profile of operational nuclear reactors in Europe |

Source: IAEA, 2002a

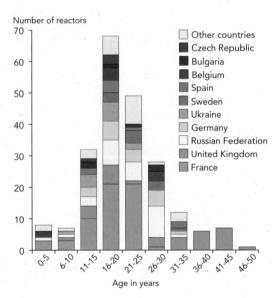

| Figure 10.8. | The international nuclear event scale |

Source: IAEA, 2002b

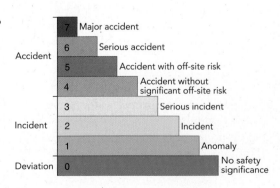

is particularly noteworthy that in the area of transport of radioactive waste, which comes under close scrutiny by non-governmental organisations and the public, not a single entry is to be found in the INES (international nuclear event scale) database maintained by the International Atomic Energy Agency (IAEA) (Figure 10.8). The Chernobyl accident is so far the only nuclear accident to be assigned a 7 on the INES scale.

Fleets of nuclear power vessels also pose the problem of managing decommissioned material. Of the countries covered by this report which have fleets of nuclear powered vessels (France, the Russian Federation and the United Kingdom), the Russian Federation has built a massive 248 submarines, of which only 77 were in service in 1998 (NATO, 1998). Approximately 110 submarines have been taken out of operation in the Northern Fleet. It is anticipated that 18–20 submarines can be dismantled per year. As of beginning of 2002, 94 decommissioned nuclear submarines were stored afloat and have spent fuel in their nuclear reactors (Shishkin et al., 2002).

10.3.3. Environmental and health effects of the Chernobyl accident

The explosion at the Chernobyl plant, Ukraine, exposed the reactor core and released radioactive fission and neutron activation products, including transuranics, from the reactor to the atmosphere. Most of refractory radionuclides in the form of hot fuel particles were deposited in the vicinity of the destroyed reactor. For some volatile radionuclides the release rate and transportation distance were exacerbated by heat from the fire that lasted 10 days. Estimated releases of the most radiologically important volatile radionuclides I-131, Cs-137 and Cs-134 were about 1 500, 85 and 46 PBq. The altitude which radioactive cloud reached (up to 3 km) and the prevailing winds meant that most of Europe was affected by the fallout. More than 140 000 km² of the territory of the three most affected countries, Ukraine, Belarus and the Russian Federation, and more than 45 000 km² of other European countries were contaminated with Cs-137 over 40 kBq/m² (see Map 10.1).

Several organisations have reported on the impacts of the Chernobyl accident, but all have had problems assessing the significance of their observations because of the lack of reliable public health information before

1986. In 1989 the World Health Organization (WHO) first raised concerns that local medical scientists had incorrectly attributed various biological and health effects to radiation exposure (UIC, 2001).

An IAEA study involving more than 200 experts from 22 countries published in 1991 was more substantial. In the absence of pre-1986 data it compared a control population with those exposed to radiation. Significant health disorders were evident in both control and exposed groups but, at that stage, none was radiation related.

Subsequent studies in the Ukraine, the Russian Federation and Belarus were based on national registers of over 1 million people possibly affected by radiation. These confirmed a rising incidence of thyroid cancer among exposed children. Late in 1995, WHO linked nearly 700 cases of thyroid cancer among children and adolescents to the Chernobyl accident, and among these some 10 deaths are attributed to radiation (see Chapter 12, Section 12.2.4).

Doses from man-made sources		Table 10.3.
Source	**Collective effective dose (man Sievert)**	
Atmospheric nuclear testing	30 000 000	
Chernobyl accident	600 000	
Nuclear power production	400 000	
Radioisotope production and use	80 000	
Nuclear weapons fabrication	60 000	
Kyshtym accident	2 500	
Satellite re-entries	2 100	
Windscale accident	2 000	
Other accidents	300	
Underground nuclear testing	200	

Source: Bennett, 1995

Deposition from Chernobyl in Europe	Map 10.1.

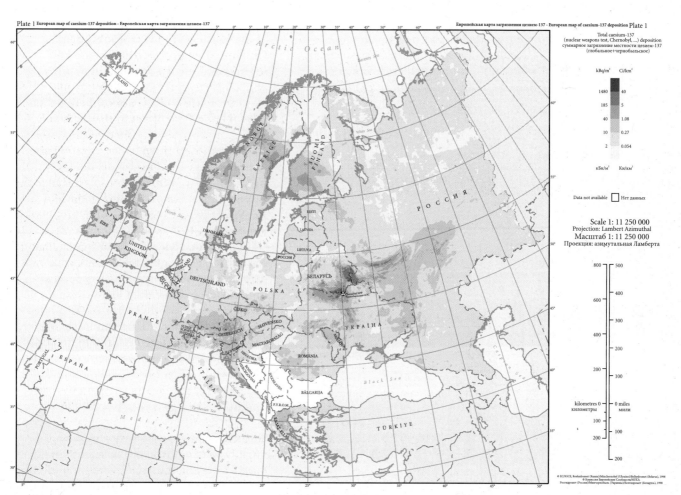

Source: European Commission, 1998

Despite the decay of most deposited radionuclides and applied countermeasures, a few tens of thousands of square kilometres in Belarus, the Russian Federation and the Ukraine will remain substantially contaminated with long-lived radionuclides, i.e. Cs-137, Sr-90, plutonium and Am-241 for decades. The levels of human external exposure and enhanced radionuclide concentrations in agricultural animal and natural food products (e.g. mushrooms, berries, lake fish and game) will also remain elevated over a long period (see also UN, 2002). These abnormal human exposure levels still require regular monitoring and, in some areas, remediation actions. Up to now approximately 100 000 inhabitants of contaminated areas receive additional annual doses above 1 mSv caused by the Chernobyl fallout (around 50 % less than the yearly dose from natural sources).

Psychosocial effects among those affected by the accident are emerging as a major problem, and are similar to those arising from other major disasters such as earthquakes, floods and fires.

10.4. Natural disasters

Natural disasters, such as earthquakes and landslides, are often more devastating, in terms of loss of life and environmental damage, than technological accidents, which they can also precipitate. The cost of natural disasters may run into billions of euros, rather than the millions associated with most technological accidents (with the exception of some worst cases such the Chernobyl accident). As with technological accidents, the consequences depend both on the magnitude of the event and factors such as population density, disaster-prevention measures and emergency planning.

10.4.1. Events associated with natural disasters

Figure 10.9 illustrates, for the whole of Europe, the number of events associated with natural disasters and the associated number of fatalities between 1980 and 2000. Several types of natural hazards are included and it is clear that they have the potential to cause large numbers of fatalities. The hazard that causes by far the largest numbers of fatalities in one event during this 20-year period is an earthquake. On 17 August 1999, a major earthquake in northwest Turkey, measuring 7.4 on the Richter scale, caused the deaths of more than 17 000 people, most of whom were crushed in the rubble of their collapsed homes. The earthquake also precipitated technological accidents, when fires broke out in oil refineries and explosions rocked the rubble as leaking gas ignited. On 7 December 1988, a massive earthquake rocked northwest Armenia, killing some 25 000 people (EQE Engineering, 1989). The recent earthquake at the southern Italian village of San Giuliano di Puglia on 31 October 2002 highlighted the traumatic effects caused by all fatal earthquakes. Of the 29 people killed, 26 were young children, buried after their school building collapsed (BBC, 2002c).

In Europe, as worldwide, storms and floods are the most common natural disaster and, in terms of economic and insured losses, the most costly, as illustrated in Table 10.4 (Swiss Re, 2002a).

Winter storms in Europe represent a major hazard to people and a major economic loss. Two of the worst storms hit Europe at the end of December 1999. On 26 December, Lothar crossed northern France, southern Germany and Switzerland within a few hours, leaving a path of destruction. The next day, Martin passed through further to the south, also causing heavy losses in central and southern France, northern Spain, Corsica and northern Italy (Swiss Re, 2002b).

The high speeds of both storms were attributable to unusually heavy westerly winds. Lothar attained its maximum intensity on the French Atlantic coast, maintaining its force far inland. Peak gust velocities reached

Figure 10.9.	Events involving natural hazards and the associated number of fatalities in Europe, 1980–2000

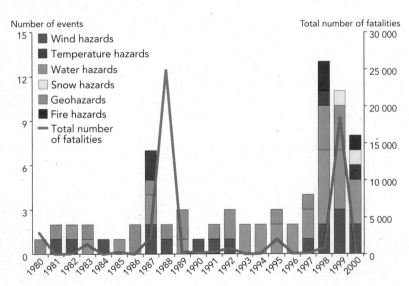

Source: Munich Re, 2001

Date	Countries	Event	Victims	Insured loss (US$ billion, 2001 levels)
25 Jan 1990	Western Europe	Winter storm Daria	95	6.2
26 Dec 1999	Western Europe	Winter storm Lothar	80	6.2
15 Oct 1987	Western Europe	Storms and floods in Europe	22	4.7
25 Feb 1990	Western/central Europe	Winter storm Vivian	64	4.3
27 Dec 1999	France, Spain, Switzerland	Winter storm Martin	45	2.6
3 Dec 1999	Western/northern Europe	Winter storm Anatol	20	1.6

Most costly natural hazard insurance losses in Europe — Table 10.4.

Source: Swiss Re, 2002a

170 km/hour in the heart of Paris and more than 180 km/hour at Orly airport, or 20 % above the maximum wind speed previously on record. Even before Lothar died out over eastern Europe, another powerful storm, Martin, reached the west coast of France at the latitude of La Rochelle. While Martin crossed the country about 200 km south of Lothar's track and registered weaker peak gusts, wind speeds of some 160 km/hour and 140 km/hour were registered in Vichy and Carcassonne, respectively.

Particularly in France, but also in southern Germany and Switzerland, losses triggered by Lothar and Martin were paralleled only by the storms of 1990. Casualties exceeded 80, not counting the lives claimed in the course of clean-up work. Some 44 of these fatalities occurred in France alone, while 17 were reported in Germany and 13 in Switzerland. The storms ravaged some 60 % of the roofs in the Paris region and damaged more than 80 % of the buildings in surrounding towns, some of them substantially.

Forests also sustained tremendous damage: in France, Germany and Switzerland, for example, the storms toppled several times the average annual timber yield. Power supply was also affected more seriously than ever before: in France alone, Lothar blew over more than 120 large power supply pylons (the combined total with Martin exceeded 200), leaving more than 3 million households without power for days.

Lothar and Martin generated economic losses of some USD 12 billion and USD 6 billion, respectively. Of these amounts, USD 6.2 billion (Lothar) and USD 2.6 billion

(Martin) were insured. Overall, more than 3 million claims were filed with insurance companies in France, leading to claims settlements which exceeded the capacity of some insurers. These sums are in the top range of losses caused by winter storms in Europe to date and can be compared only with those triggered by the series of winter storms in 1990 (Swiss Re, 2002b).

Flood damage depends on the duration and height of water levels, topography and use of the flood plain, flood defence measures, and the awareness of the population likely to be affected by flooding. The frequency of major flooding events in Europe has increased in recent years. As an example, at Kehl on the German-French border, between 1900 and 1977 the Rhine's floodwaters rose more than 7 m above flood level only four times. From 1977 to 1996, that level was reached 10 times, an average of once every other year (UWIN, 1996)

During the period 1978–2000, including natural variations, the level of the Caspian Sea rose by about 2.3 m. Flooding in coastal zones inundated residential areas, transport, telecommunications and energy infrastructure, chemical and petrochemical industries, croplands and hatcheries, forcing thousands of residents to be evacuated from flooded homes. In Turkmenistan, the town of Dervish, which is detached from the western part of the mainland, is turning into an island due to the rise in sea level (EIA, 2000).

In July 1997, floodwaters killed at least 52 people in Poland and 39 in the Czech Republic (ESA, 2001). A year later, again in

Figure 10.10.	Flooding along the Danube River, Hungary, Croatia, and Serbia and Montenegro in April 2002

Source: NASA, 2002a

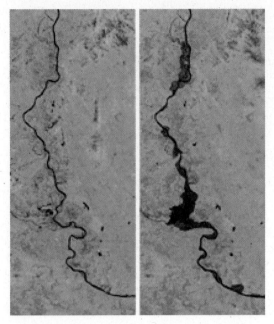

March 17, 2002   April 2, 2002

July, at least 46 died during flooding in the Slovak Republic, during a 'supercell storm'.

However, the catastrophic flooding in central Europe and the Black Sea region of the Russian Federation in August 2002 has surpassed these in terms of impact. At least 111 people died, with hundreds of thousands evacuated (BBC, 2002d). Many homes were completely destroyed. In Hungary, the River Danube broke high-water marks along 170 km of its length (Figure 10.10). The water reached a record of 8.49 m, breaking the previous record of 8.45 m set in 1965. In Dresden, Germany, the River Elbe reached 9.39 m, the highest since records began in the 16th century. Floods in Prague were the worst for 175 years. Economic losses have been estimated at more than EUR 15 billion (Swiss Re, 2002c).

Potentially dangerous acute and chronic impacts on industry were also apparent. A cloud of chlorine gas (several hundreds of kilograms) escaped from a flood-damaged chemical plant in Neratovice, about 20 km north of Prague. Considerably larger amounts (some 80 tonnes equivalent) were released into the water. Releases of some persistent organic substances could not be excluded. The impact of these releases is being evaluated. A dam burst near the town of Bitterfeld in southeast Germany, resulting in the evacuation of 16 000 people, and the emergency was heightened by the flooding

of the adjacent chemical complex, where a military operation was launched to stop chemicals flowing into the River Mulde (BBC, 2002e). Most sewage plants along the Rivers Elbe and Vltava in the Czech Republic were put out of action, raising the prospect of environmental damage. The overall cost to industry and the general population is likely to run into many billions of euros.

Heavy rain and flooding can also precipitate landslides, which may be more catastrophic in terms of fatalities. In October 2000, Gondo, a Swiss alpine village, was 'sliced in two' by a fatal 40 m wide landslide, following three days of incessant rain (SAEFL, 2002).

Fatal avalanches have also hit alpine regions in recent years. In Europe, the winter of 1998/99 was one of the 'snowiest' in 50 years. Major snow storms created a number of avalanches in populated mountain areas across the Alps. Three separate incidents in February 1999 at Galtür (Austria), Evolene (Switzerland) and Chamonix (France) claimed the lives of 51 people (OFEFP, 2002).

10.4.2. Natural disasters exacerbated by human activities

From the available data (Figure 10.1 and Figure 10.6) it appears that the trend for the annual number of natural disasters is more obviously upward than that for major technological accidents. This is particularly apparent for those precipitated by human activities. For example, drainage of wetlands and straightening of rivers can influence both the probability and the magnitude of flooding, by increasing peak water flows. There is also an increased probability of occurrence of certain natural disasters, such as flooding and droughts, due to climate change, in many temperate regions (see Chapter 3). Climate change may be a contributor to the recent increase in flooding incidents.

Landslides are likely to increase unless there is better management of land to reduce soil erosion. Land clearing for agricultural reasons combined with the increased frequency of heavy storms and flooding will increase the risk. The landslide at Campania, Italy tragically illustrated this in May 1998 when, after two days of incessant rain, a torrent of mud engulfed hundreds of homes in the towns of Sarno and Quindici and surrounding villages. Almost 300 people were killed and about 2 000 made homeless. The clearing of trees and burning of scrubland to create pastures had led to massive erosion and in some areas chestnut trees had been replaced by hazelnut trees, which are much weaker and produce a smaller root system (EEA, 1999).

Land clearing by deliberately starting forest fires has led to direct hazard from the fire itself. Arson is a major cause of forest fires, although such fires have also occurred through natural processes. Forest fires, which occur every year across Europe, can cause fatalities and create vast clouds of smog over the surrounding area, in addition to the environmental disaster of the loss of extensive areas of forest. However, planned fires (if managed properly) clear away dead and dying vegetation to help rejuvenate forests and reduce the risk of larger, uncontrolled wildfires. Fire is also used to help clear forests for human developments. Around the world, every year, from 750 000 to 8.2 million square km of forest and grassland is burnt (NASA, 2002b).

10.5. Risk management

Disasters will continue to occur throughout Europe — some due to technology, some to the forces of nature, some to the combined effects of the two. Inevitably, there will be loss of life and environmental damage.

However, better management of hazards can reduce the risks. Although it is not possible to predict when disasters will occur it may be possible to identify the general areas where they are more likely, so that responses can be pre-planned and loss of life and environmental impacts minimised.

10.5.1. Technological hazards

For many technological hazards, holistic approaches are becoming more prevalent, with increasing attention to reducing the risks of long-term environmental impacts as well as acute health and property damage. For the process industries, the Seveso II directive in the EU requires industrial operators to demonstrate that they have taken all necessary measures to prevent major accidents and limit their consequences for humans and the environment.

There is an improved culture with regard to reporting accidents and sharing the lessons learnt. Experience of accidents to cross-country pipelines and oil tankers has guided design, construction and operation, with a substantial reduction in incidents.

However, catastrophic events that are difficult to predict because of lack of specific experience are likely to remain a difficult problem. Although technological disasters account for only a fraction of the number of fatalities of natural disasters, there remains a perception that technological hazards pose a considerable risk, particularly to people living nearby. This is particularly true for nuclear hazards. There are many reasons for this, including lack of knowledge and dread, but also acceptability. An additional factor is a common aversion to technologies that could cause multiple fatalities. This is taken into account in the Dutch societal risk criteria where (for fatalities of 10 or more), a decrease in frequency of two orders of magnitude is required for an order of magnitude increase in fatalities (Figure 10.11).

Planners and policy-makers take such issues into account. Following the Toulouse accident, one of the points of the European Parliament Resolution of 3 October 2001 was that the current approach to 'risk management' had been overtaken by events and that it was now necessary and urgent to adopt an approach based on 'risk removal'.

Pre-planning for technological disasters is now common, through emergency response plans. In particular, since 1986, many countries and organisations in the EU have developed sophisticated computerised systems for gathering, managing, assessing and disseminating information about possible future nuclear accidents. For the

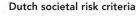

Dutch societal risk criteria	Figure 10.11.

Source: VROM (the Netherlands Ministry of Housing, Spatial Planning and the Environment)

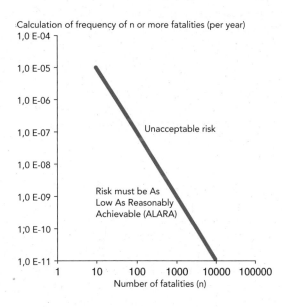

process industries, the Seveso II directive has prescribed that onsite and offsite emergency plans must be in place and practised at regular intervals. EU countries are generally better prepared for technological disasters than those in eastern Europe.

Major transportation accidents pose a particular problem because it is difficult to predict their location. Many railways cross densely populated cities, and although the capacity of a standard tank car is limited to about 50 tonnes, this may be sufficient to cause a major catastrophe if a hazardous material is released in or close to an inner-city area. The consequences of a pipeline rupture could be severe, as a large amount of material could be released before isolation. With an ever-increasing pipeline network throughout eastern Europe and the Caspian region, there is an increasing likelihood of such events unless the risks are better managed.

For the non-EU states, the use of the Seveso II directive and other relevant directives, such as the water framework directive (Directive 2000/60/EU), appears appropriate and some are already using these, including some non-accession countries. The comprehensive nature of such directives, with their power to prohibit unacceptable activities, provides a valuable model for the more effective management of safety.

Increasingly, the management of technological risks must include the threat of international terrorism. The recent attack on the French oil tanker Limburg off the coast of Yemen on 6 October 2002 has highlighted this. There has been speculation that the Toulouse incident of 21 September 2002 was an act of sabotage. Whilst security of such sites has been increased over the last few decades, particularly those sites with nuclear installations, there are many softer targets at risk. Transportation routes are particularly vulnerable, and the example of oil pipelines attacks in Africa has demonstrated the potential for major accidents, disruption and environmental damage.

10.5.2. Natural hazards
For natural hazards, particularly earthquakes, the problem of predicting exactly when and where they may occur is a major difficulty for risk management. This is compounded by the fact that there are no means of preventing some natural events,

such as earthquakes and volcanic eruptions, although for some events, mitigation measures that could be used are not adequately applied in land-use planning. The management of these hazards could benefit from the application of some of the control, mitigation and response approaches developed for technological hazards.

Adequate land management is essential. 'Inherent safety' is a term often used in the process industries to avoid the hazard in the first place. The corresponding approach would be to discourage settlement growth and reduce urban sprawl in areas that are susceptible to natural hazards. Where susceptible areas are populated, societal risk criteria, such as those shown in Figure 10.11 could be a useful tool in land-use management to limit settlement growth.

For regions under development, a holistic approach should ensure that all hazards are identified and that the risks from these are balanced against each other. The interactions between humans and the natural environment should be taken into account, as recent accidents have shown that this is an increasing causal mechanism. For example, while shrub clearing for agriculture may increase the likelihood and consequences of flooding, soil erosion and landslides in areas susceptible to heavy rainfall, it may help to prevent fires in susceptible areas.

For some natural hazards, some control measures may prevent the full potential of the hazard from being realised, even if they cannot prevent it. For example, the catastrophic effects of an avalanche can be reduced by initiating controlled avalanches to avoid a large build-up of unstable snow. Flood warning systems may provide sufficient time to remove people from the source of danger. For a number of years, the Thames Barrier has protected London from flooding due to a high tide. The huge cost of an accident, including that associated with loss of life and injury, generally far outweighs the cost of such risk reduction measures. Increasingly, in seismically active regions, new buildings, chemical plants and pipelines are designed to withstand the stresses of earth movement. Shoddily built housing was the main factor cited for the high death toll in the 1999 Turkey earthquake.

Some EU Member States have procedures in place for taking account of the risks of flooding, avalanches, landslides and earthquakes in their planning and development processes. However, these procedures have resulted in haphazard responses to natural disasters and, in many cases, the impacts on humans, the environment and the local economy have not been mitigated. According to experts, poor planning, fragmented warning and defence systems, and deforestation may have all worsened the consequences of the flooding in central Europe during 2002 (BBC, 2002f). The 1999 Turkey earthquake is a tragic reminder of how a lack of comprehensive disaster management can increase the consequences. In the weeks after the earthquake, health workers battled to prevent the spread of typhoid fever, cholera and dysentery. According to the International Red Cross, even one year after the disaster, the survivors were the victims of psychological trauma and physical deprivation (CNN, 2000). Even 10 years after the 1988 Armenia earthquake, some 350 families were still waiting for homes to be constructed for them and were living in containers, wagons or shacks (Naegele, 1998).

10.6. References

BBC, 2000. *Ukraine's troubled mines.* 12 March 2000. http://news.bbc.co.uk/hi/english/world/europe/newsid_674000/674542.stm

BBC, 2002a. *Dozens killed in Ukraine mine fire.* 7 July 2002. http://news.bbc.co.uk/hi/english/world/europe/newsid_2109000/2109140.stm

BBC, 2002b. *Europe names its 'fleet of shame'.* 3 December 2002. http://news.bbc.co.uk/hi/english/world/europe/2538987.stm

BBC, 2002c. *Italian earthquake.* 1 November 2002. http://news.bbc.co.uk/1/hi/world/europe/2385687.stm

BBC, 2002d. *Flood safety enquiry pledged.* 20 August 2002. http://news.bbc.co.uk/1/hi/world/europe/2206349.stm

BBC, 2002e. *Budapest braves flood menace.* 19 August 2002. http://news.bbc.co.uk/1/hi/world/europe/2202220.stm

BBC, 2002f. *Europe's flood lessons.* 19 August 2002. http://news.bbc.co.uk/1/hi/world/europe/2203152.stm

Bennett, B. G., 1995. Exposures from worldwide releases of radionuclides. In:

Proceedings of a symposium on environmental impact of radioactive releases. Vienna, 8–12 May 1995. IAEA-SM-339/185.

Bruch, C., 2002. *Legal mechanisms for addressing the environmental consequences of armed conflicts.* http://www.globesa.org/bruch.htm, accessed 20 June 2002.

CNN, 2000. *Turks mourn on anniversary of earthquake.* 17 August 2000. http://www.cnn.com/2000/WORLD/europe/08/17/turkey.quakeanni/index.html

CONCAWE, 2002. *Western European cross-country oil pipelines thirty year performance statistics.* Prepared by D. Lyons. Brussels.

Drogaris, G., 1993. *Major accident reporting system — lessons learned from accidents notified.* EUR 15060 EN. Elsevier, Amsterdam.

Eco-compass, 2002. *The environmental impacts of war.* http://www.islandpress.org/eco-compass/war/war.html, accessed 20 June 2002.

EEA (European Environment Agency), 1999. *Environment in the European Union at the turn of the century.* EEA, Copenhagen. p. 233.

EGIG (European Gas pipeline Incident data Group), 2002. *Overview and Conclusions.* http://www.gastransportservices.nl/egig/nav/overview.htm, accessed 12 June 2002.

EIA (Energy Information Administration, US Department of Energy), 2000. *Caspian Sea region: Environmental issues.* April 2000. http://www.eia.doe.gov/emeu/cabs/caspenv.html

EQE Engineering, 1989. *December 7, 1988 Armenia, USSR Earthquake: An EQE summary report.* SEL TA654.6.E677. EQE Engineering, San Francisco.

ESA (European Space Agency), 2001. *Austria, Czech Republic, Poland and Germany flooding July-August 1997.* http://earth.esa.int/ew/floods/au_pl_de_97/

European Commission, 1998. *European Chernobyl atlas.* http://www.ec-gis.org/atlas.htm

European Commission, 1999. *Communication and fourth report from the Commission on the present situation and prospects for radioactive waste management in the European Union.* Brussels.

Heathcote, I., 2002. *The Environmental consequences of war.* http://cwx.prenhall.com/

bookbind/pubbooks/nebel2/medialib/update25.html

IAEA (International Energy Atomic Agency), 2002a. *Latest news related to PRIS and the status of nuclear power plants.* Paris. http://www.iaea.org/programmes/a2/index.html, accessed 30 July 2002.

IAEA (International Energy Atomic Agency), 2002b. *The IAEA emergency response system.* http://www.iaea.org/worldatom/Periodicals/Factsheets/English/emergency.html, accessed 20 December 2002.

ITOPF (International Tanker Owners Pollution Federation Ltd), 2002a. *Accidental tanker oil spill statistics.* http://www.itopf.com/stats.html

ITOPF (International Tanker Owners Pollution Federation Ltd), 2002b. *News.* http://www.itopf.com/news.html#prestige

J&H Marsh & McLennan, 1998. *Large property damage losses in the hydrocarbon-chemical industries: A thirty-year review.* 18th edition. New York.

MARS data base, 2002. 'Major accident reporting system'. European Commission, Joint Research Centre, Ispra. http://natural-hazards.jrc.it/

Munich Re, 2001. *Annual review: Natural catastrophes 2000.* http://www.munichre.com

Naegele, J., 1998. *Armenia: Eyewitnesses recall earthquake of 1988.* 17 March 1998. http://www.rferl.org/nca/features/1998/03/F.RU.980317131055.html

NASA, 2002a. *Flooding along the Danube River.* Earth Observatory, Natural Hazards. http://earthobservatory.nasa.gov/NaturalHazards/natural_hazards_v2.php3?img_id=2641, accessed 26 June 2002.

NASA, 2002b. *Fire.* Earth Observatory, Natural Hazards. http://earthobservatory.nasa.gov/NaturalHazards/natural_hazards_v2.php3?topic=fire, accessed 26 June 2002.

NATO (North Atlantic Treaty Organisation), 1998. *Cross border environmental problems emanating from defence-related installations and activities, phase II: 1995-1998. Final report. Volume 3: Management of defence-related radioactive waste.* NATO, Norway.

OFEFP (Office fédéral de l'environnement, des forêts et du paysage), 2002. *Avalanches de l'hiver 1998/1999.* Cahiers de l'environnement No 323. Bern. p. 93.

Rasmussen, K., 1996. *The experience with the major accident reporting system from 1984 to 1993.* EUR 16341.

SAEFL, 2002. *Environment Switzerland 2002 - policies and outlook.* Swiss Agency for the Environment, Forests and Landscape, Bern. p. 356.

Shishkin,V. A. *et al.*, 2002. 'Transportation-technological flowsheets of the SNF handling from the utilized submarines in the northwest and far east regions of Russia. Problems and solutions'. Presented at NATO Advanced Research Workshop, Moscow, 22-24 April 2002.

Swiss Re, 2002a. The 40 most costly insurance losses 1970–2002. *Sigma.* January. http://www.swissre.com/

Swiss Re, 2002b. *Winter storms Lothar and Martin.* http://www.swissre.com/

Swiss Re, 2002c. *Torrential rains cause major flooding across Europe.* 21 November 2002. http://www.swissre.com/

The History Guy, 2001. *New and recent conflicts of the world.* http://www.historyguy.com/new_and_recent_conflicts.html, updated 30 December 2001.

UIC (Uranium Information Centre Ltd), 2001. *Chernobyl accident.* Nuclear Issues Briefing Paper No 22. March 2001. http://www.uic.com.au/nip22.htm

UN (United Nations), 2002. *Chernobyl disaster, 15 years* (1986–2001). New York. http://www.un.org/ha/chernobyl/chernob.htm

UNEP (United Nations Environment Programme), 2001. *Chronology of major tailings dam failures.* http://www.antenna.nl/wise/uranium/mdaf.html, last updated 22 December 2001.

UNEP (United Nations Environment Programme), 2002a. APELL — awareness and preparedness for emergencies on a local level. *Disasters by category.* http://www.uneptie.org/pc/apell/disasters/lists/disastercat.html, accessed 13 June 2002.

UNEP (United Nations Environment Programme), 2002b. APELL — awareness and preparedness for emergencies on a local level. *Recent disasters.* http://www.uneptie.org/pc/apell/disasters/lists/recent.html, accessed 13 June 2002.

UNEP (United Nations Environment Programme), 2002c. APELL — awareness and preparedness for emergencies on a local level. *Ammonium nitrate explosion in Toulouse.* http://www.uneptie.org/pc/apell/disasters/toulouse/home.html accessed 13 June 2002.

UWIN, 1996. *Worldwide paper on river and wetland development.* Universities Water Information Network, Southern Illinois University, Carbondale.

11. Biological diversity

In addition to a responsibility to reduce its ecological footprint on the rest of the world, Europe has a global responsibility to preserve the character of its varied ecosystems and landscapes, and to conserve the migratory species that cross the continent and the threatened species that it hosts. This includes responsibility for controlling the collection and trade in wildlife specimens that is occurring on a global scale.

Some areas, like the Mediterranean and Caucasus, stand out for their species and genetic richness. The continent is also home to a large proportion of the world's domestic animal diversity, and nearly half of Europe's breeds are at risk of extinction. Important ecosystems continue to be at risk including forests, wetlands, species-rich agricultural habitats, several dry and arid areas and some marine areas.

Species population trends are mixed — some previously highly threatened species are starting to recover, others continue to decline at alarming rates, generally as a result of the disappearance or degradation of their habitats. Decline is now also perceptible in previously common species. As in other continents, the spread of invasive alien species is an increasing threat.

In applying global, European, regional or national commitments, countries are implementing plans to halt the further degradation of biodiversity. Designated areas continue to be a major instrument for such conservation strategies and constitute core elements for the establishment of a pan-European ecological network. Meanwhile, integration of biodiversity concerns into sectors is progressively becoming a reality. While at global level the Johannesburg summit agreed on 'the achievement by 2010 of a significant reduction in the current loss of biological diversity', governments at pan-European level are considering a stronger commitment, i.e. 'to halt the loss of Europe's biodiversity by 2010'. Monitoring of biodiversity trends as well as of policy effectiveness is still largely insufficient. However, promising pan-European coordinated initiatives are on the way.

11.1. Introduction

Europe's biodiversity in its widest sense — from wild to cultivated species, with all their genetic variability, and from little utilised to highly cultivated ecosystems — is mainly embedded in a complex network of rural landscapes, fragmented by transport and urban infrastructures (EEA, 1995; 1998; 1999). Although largely rural, Europe is the most urbanised and, together with Asia, the most densely populated continent in the world. Northern and central Asia, however, still have extensive barely utilised areas. The diversity of the continent's landscapes, which results from a marriage of nature and human settlements, is a significant part of the European heritage.

Biodiversity has its own intrinsic value, but is also increasingly recognised for the goods and services it provides. Agriculture, forestry, fisheries, hunting and the production of other biological products, including many pharmaceuticals, depend directly on biodiversity. It is also important for nutrient cycling and soil fertility, flood and storm protection, erosion prevention, air and climate regulation, etc.

Biodiversity is affected by major changes in land use, large-scale impacts of air and water pollution, such as eutrophication, and invasive species; the effects depend strongly on the biogeographic and cultural context. The consequences of climate change, while still difficult to predict, are likely to lead to considerable changes in species distribution, physiology and migration behaviour (Green *et al.* 2001; Parry, 2000). Furthermore, we can expect functional ecosystem responses. Desertification as a result of land use, combined with climate change, is occurring in, or threatening a large part of the biodiversity and landscapes in Mediterranean area and the dry areas of central and eastern Europe as well as central Asia.

Threats to biodiversity are different in each of the 11 biogeographic regions recognised at pan-European level by the Council of Europe and the European Union (EU) (see Map 11.1) (EEA, 2002a).

11.2. Europe's responsibility for biodiversity: wild species

11.2.1. Species richness, only one side of the coin
Biodiversity is not evenly distributed in Europe and some areas harbour greater

	Biogeographic region	Main threats to biodiversity
	Arctic region	Climate change may change conditions for plant and animal communities Ozone depletion
	Boreal region	Intensive forestry practices Exploitation for hydroelectric power Freshwater acidification
	Atlantic region	High degree of habitat fragmentation by transport and urban infrastructures Intensive agriculture Eutrophication with massive algal blooms Invasive alien species
	Continental	High degree of habitat fragmentation by transport and urban infrastructures Industry and mining Atmospheric pollution Intensive agriculture Intensive use of rivers
	Alpine (Alps, Pyrenees, Carpathians, Dinaric Alps, Balkans and Rhodopes, Scandes, Urals and Caucasia).	Climate change may change conditions for plant and animal communities Transport infrastructures Tourism Dams
	Pannonian	Intensification of agriculture Drainage of wetlands Irrigation combined with evaporation leads to salinisation and alkalisation Eutrophication of large lakes Mining industry with heavy metals pollution of some rivers
	Mediterranean	The world's most important tourism destination High pressures from urbanisation in coastal areas Intensification of agriculture in plains, land-abandonment in mid-mountains Desertification in some areas Invasive alien species
	Macaronesian (Includes Azores, Madeira, Canaries islands)	Invasive alien species Tourism Forest fires and uncontrolled tree-felling Intensification of agriculture with large greenhouses
	Steppic	Intensification of agriculture, e.g. abandonment of nomadic pastoral activities Desertification Large mining and industrial settlements, with pollution problems
	Black Sea	Intensification of agriculture: irrigation, salinisation Waterlogging Tourism
	Anatolian	Intensification of agriculture : conversion of steppes into arable lands, irrigation, drainage of wetlands, overgrazing Building of dams

Map 11.1.

Main threats to biodiversity by European biogeographic context (terrestrial part)

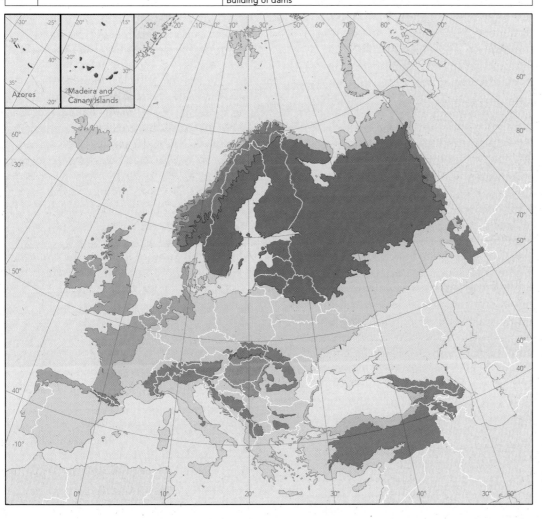

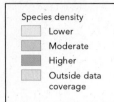

| Map 11.2. | Species richness in Europe (vertebrates and vascular plants) in proportion to countries' surface area |

Species density
Lower
Moderate
Higher
Outside data coverage

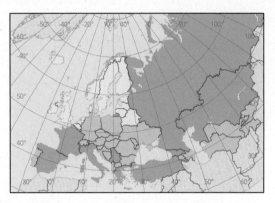

Notes: It is not possible to discriminate between data from the European and the Asian part of the Russian Federation. Macaronesia is not taken into account. An analysis by biogeographic region would be more relevant. However, lack of harmonised geo-referenced data on species distribution, particularly plants, does not yet allow such analysis. Despite their essential role in ecosystem functions, invertebrates and lower plants are not taken into account due to knowledge deficiency.

Source: ETC/NPB EUNIS database on Species (from various sources, including national biodiversity reports)

concentrations of species, as reflected in Map 11.2.

Species richness is not the only measure of a country's responsibility for conservation. At the global level, the notion of 'biodiversity hot spots', as defined by Conservation International (Myers *et al*, 2000), also includes richness in endemic species, i.e. species which are not found elsewhere, genetic resources and threats to habitats. Among the 25 identified 'hot spots' in the world, only two are partly in Europe — the Mediterranean basin and the Caucasus. These areas are of global concern for biodiversity (UNEP-WCMC, 2001; 2002).

Conservation International stresses that the identification of hot spots does not mean that 'focus should only be on these hot spots, ignoring everything else. ...Every nation's biodiversity is critically important to its future.' Thus species-poorer areas may have important key species; for example in the Arctic region there are often large and exceptionally productive populations of diptera and moths. Similarly, in any biogeographic region, some habitat types can be highly valuable because of their very specific ecological conditions and functions or their scarce distribution.

11.2.2. Europe as a crossroads for migratory species

Europe is the seasonal home and an important crossroads for huge populations of migratory species, sharing these species with

other regions including Africa, the Near East and North America. This responsibility is ensured through the Convention on Migratory Species (Bonn convention) and its underlying agreements. This has provided a global framework for, in particular, EU nature-protection directives. Success or failure in providing sufficient resting, feeding and breeding grounds in Europe (including hunting bans) will influence biodiversity in other continents, just as successes and failures there will influence biodiversity in Europe.

11.2.3. Globally threatened species present in Europe

Among the 3 948 globally-threatened vertebrate species (IUCN categories Vulnerable, Endangered and Critically endangered) assessed by IUCN-The World Conservation Union, 335 occur in European and central Asian countries; of these 37 % are mammals, 15 % birds, 4 % amphibians, 10 % reptiles and 34 % freshwater fish. Figure 11.1 shows their occurrence in different regions and therefore the shares of responsibility for their conservation.

For the flora, analysis of threats is more difficult because of taxonomic problems. However, it is estimated that of about 32 000 globally threatened plant species, about 800 occur in Europe (excluding the Caucasus).

Figure 11.2 shows the level of protection of globally threatened species by European legal instruments e.g. the Bern convention and the EU birds and habitats directives. The EU directives include provisions from other global instruments such as the Bonn, Ramsar and CITES conventions.

Except for fish, globally threatened vertebrates are generally well covered by legal instruments, especially in EU countries with a combination of EU directives and the Bern convention. In non-EU countries, where only the Bern convention applies, gaps in protection remain. With the EU

8.5 % of the globally threatened species of vertebrates occur in Europe and central Asia. The countries of eastern Europe, the Caucasus and central Asia have a particular responsibility for the conservation of the threatened mammals and birds, western Europe and central and eastern European countries for threatened freshwater fish.

enlargement process new species, some of which are globally threatened, will be added to the habitats directive. It is important to stress, however, that both the EU habitats directive and the Bern convention (through the Emerald process) will protect a wide range of species in an indirect way by protecting their habitats.

For invertebrates, major gaps in knowledge remain and the level of protection is probably quite insufficient.

11.2.4 Trade issues

Trade has considerable impacts on biodiversity, both within Europe and at the global level. It is often linked to other sectors such as agriculture, forestry, fisheries and energy as well as hunting and tourism/recreation. Trade has a direct impact on wild species and on natural habitats (conversion into productive land for marketable goods and services, for crops, timber, resource mining and so on).

Europe is known as a supplying, consuming and re-exporting region for wildlife and wildlife products. The EU Member States constitute one of the three largest wildlife consumer markets in the world, alongside the United States and Japan.

Europe is a net importer of wildlife specimen, but is also a significant supplier of wildlife and wildlife products, for example caviar, swordfish, Saiga antelope horn, hunting trophies, dried medicinal plants and plant bulbs. Eastern European countries have wildlife resources and biological diversity of global significance, but are confronted with enormous problems in monitoring and controlling the exploitation of their wild fauna and flora. Although there are signs that it is now beginning to change, exploitation of wildlife has been at levels sufficient to endanger native species in the Russian Federation and central Asian countries (TRAFFIC Europe, 1998).

The world market for threatened wild plants and animals is regulated by the Convention on International Trade in Endangered Species of Wild Fauna and Fauna (CITES). While all western European (WE) countries are contracting parties to CITES, 2 out of 18 countries in central and eastern Europe (CEE) (Berkhoudt, 2002) and 5 out of 12 countries in eastern Europe, the Caucasus and central Asia (EECCA) are still not. However, even if awareness and regulation of wildlife trade are much improved, illegal trade remains high.

European responsibility for conservation of globally threatened vertebrates within European regions	Figure 11.1.

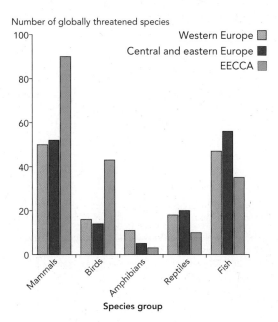

Source: Hilton Taylor, 2000; IUCN Red List of threatened species (database); ETC/NPB-EUNIS database

Level of protection of world threatened taxa occurring in Europe, protected by EU directives and Bern convention	Figure 11.2.

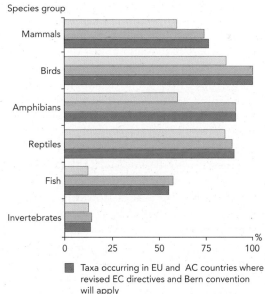

Notes: The EU birds directive calls for the protection of all bird species. The Bern convention applies to all countries of the 'Environment for Europe' process except Armenia, Bosnia-Herzegovina, Belarus, Georgia, Kazakhstan, Kyrgyzstan, the Russian Federation, Tajikistan, Turkmenistan, Uzbekistan, and Serbia and Montenegro.

Sources: 2000 IUCN Red List of threatened species (database); ETC/NPB- EUNIS database; (EU Habitats Directive Annex II & IV, EU Bird Directive, Bern Convention Annex I & II)

☺ Except for fish, globally threatened vertebrates are generally well covered by legal instruments, especially in EU countries with a combination of EU directives and the Bern convention.

☹ Although progress is noticeable, exploitation of wildlife for trade is endangering native species, particularly in the Russian Federation and central Asian countries. This is partly due to demands by western European citizens.

have been set up as part of the FAO Global Plan of Action for the Conservation and Sustainable Utilization of Plant Genetic Resources for Food and Agriculture. Although central Asian countries host rich genetic resources, conservation programmes are generally not yet well developed.

11.3. Europe's responsibility for biodiversity: domestic animals and crops

In relation to its size, Europe is home to a large proportion of the world's domestic animal diversity with 2 576 breeds registered in the Food and Agriculture Organization of the United Nations (FAO) breeds database (FAO, 2000). This represents almost half of the world's recorded breed diversity. Of the European breeds, almost half are categorised as being at risk of extinction. Two successive updatings of the database (1995 and 1999) show critical trends: the percentage of mammalian breeds in Europe at risk of extinction increased from 33 % to 49 %, and of bird breeds from 65 % to 79 %.

The declining genetic diversity of livestock is due to large-scale industrialisation of farming and globalisation of world trade in agricultural products and breeding stocks. The consequences include the destruction of the traditional farming systems associated with livestock breeds, the development of genetically uniform breeds, and changing farmer and/or consumer preferences for certain varieties and breeds.

However, Europe is the region where the highest proportion of breeds is under active conservation programmes, covering about 26 % of the mammalian and 24 % of the bird breeds.

Although not often thought of as a major centre of crop diversity, the continent also harbours wild relatives of many crop and tree species which form a gene pool to breed and cross with species currently used in agriculture. These include cereals, food legumes, fruit crops, vegetables, pot herbs, condiments and aromatic plants. It also harbours a very large number of ornamentals, many of which have been taken into cultivation in Europe.

Although difficult to quantify, genetic erosion of such resources has been globally recognised and a number of coordinated in-situ and ex-situ conservation programmes

11.4. State and trends of some vulnerable European ecosystems

The need to monitor the state of ecosystems is now widely recognised, as reflected, for example, in the global Millennium Ecosystem Assessment programme: 'The capacity of ecosystems to produce goods and services ranging from food to clean water is fundamentally important for meeting human needs and ultimately influence the development prospects of nations. But while policymakers have ready access to information on the condition of their nation's economy, educational programs, or health care system, comparable information on the condition of ecosystems is unavailable despite the important role that they play.' This general statement is also valid for Europe. However, most European countries are making some progress in monitoring their main ecosystems. The data currently reflects mainly the quantity (area) of the ecosystems — information about their quality is scarce.

11.4.1. Wetlands
Wetlands provide multiple social, economic and environmental benefits, for example water flows regulation. They cover about 9.9 % of the whole of Europe, about 4.4 % of the EU, 4.4 % of non-EU Europe excluding the Russian Federation and 12.7 % of the Russian Federation. In southern European countries, wetlands are now scarce (0.3–2.1 % of the land area).

Wetlands have been generally declining for decades — both in area and quality — but this is still difficult to quantify with wetlands inventories in Europe developing only slowly. The intensity and the effects of pressures depend largely on the type of wetlands concerned (marshlands, bogs, floodplains and so on). An indication of the main threats to wetlands can be derived from the Ramsar database (Figure 11.3).

Ramsar sites relate mainly to wetlands that are important for waterbirds and do not fully reflect the general situation of wetlands. In boreal countries with large areas of wet forests and upland wetlands, the main

There are multiple threats to Ramsar sites and the surrounding areas. In all countries, agriculture is perceived as the main threat, followed by pollution and water regulation — both probably partly due to agriculture.

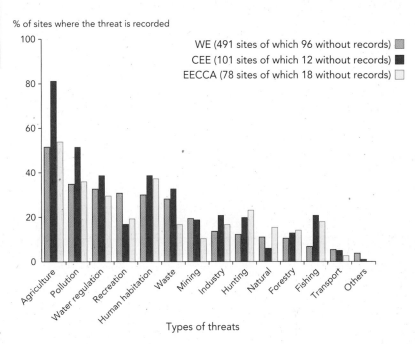

Threats to wetlands in European Ramsar sites, as reported by countries — Figure 11.3.

% of sites where the threat is recorded

WE (491 sites of which 96 without records)
CEE (101 sites of which 12 without records)
EECCA (78 sites of which 18 without records)

Types of threats

Source: Ramsar database managed by Wetlands International (2002a)

threats to these ecosystems are forestry, with draining and clear-felling, and peat extraction. The presence of human habitations within Ramsar sites is perceived as a greater source of threat in CEE countries and EECCA than in WE countries, possibly due, among other reasons, to less well developed contractual agreements with local residents.

Estimates of loss of wetland habitats are available from a pilot project led by Wetlands International and from national reports on biodiversity (Table 11.1). Only Denmark provides recent indication of trends, showing no further loss since the 1990s.

At the EU level, the water framework directive, which sets provisions for the protection of water resources at the catchment level, will help in developing wetland conservation strategies. The European Charter on Water Resources, adopted by the environment ministers in October 2001, provides a framework at the European level.

As agreed in the Ramsar convention, many countries have implemented policies or national action plans to halt the decline of wetlands. These, combined with increasing wetlands restoration programmes, may be stabilising the very negative trend perceptible up to the late 1980s, at least in the EU countries. Rates of wetland loss resulting from the different economic

conditions in eastern Europe are likely to be higher now than in the mid-1980s (Moser, 2000).

Figure 11.4 shows the level of implementation of wetlands conservation-related policies in European countries, as reported in their second national reports under the Convention on Biological Diversity (CBD). Countries in their national reports have recently made more specific and complete information available to the Ramsar convention.

11.4.2. Low-intensity farming systems and semi-natural grasslands

The importance of semi-natural grasslands and low-intensity farming for biodiversity is discussed in Chapter 2.3. Establishing

Trends in wetlands loss as compiled in the European review of national wetland inventories — Table 11.1.

Country	Armenia	Bulgaria	Belarus	Denmark	France	Lithuania	Switzerland	Turkey
Estimated surface area loss	20 000 ha drained	90 %	50 % wet meadows 80 % floodplains	60 % shallow wetlands	75 % wetlands	70 % wetlands	90 % of all Swiss wetlands	1 300 000 ha
Reference period	Over last 50 years	Since beginning 20th century	Meadows: since 1930–45 Floodplains: 1950-90	Since 1870 No further loss recorded for last 10-15 years	Between 1900 and 1993	Over last 30 years	Since 1800	Since 1900s, mainly since 1960

Source: Wetlands International, 2002b

Figure 11.4.

Implementation of national and/or sectoral plans for the conservation and sustainable use of inland water ecosystems

Note: WE countries: 9 responses missing; accession countries: 5 responses missing; Russian Federation and western EECCA: 3 responses missing; Caucasian countries: 2 responses missing; central Asian countries: no response. This diagram refers only to inland water ecosystems.

Source: CBD secretariat, 2002

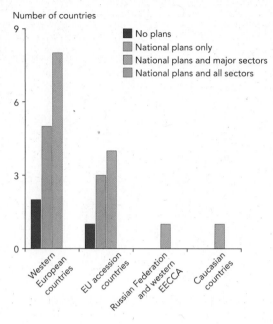

Figure 11.5.

Share of intensive and extensive agricultural habitats within proposed sites of community interest, EU

Note: Extensive agricultural habitats include salt marshes, salt pastures, salt steppes, heath, scrub, maquis and garrigue, phygrana, dry grassland, steppes, humid grassland, mesophile grassland, alpine and sub-alpine grassland, extensive cereal cultures (including rotation cultures with regular fallowing), non-forest areas cultivated with woody plants (including orchards, olive groves, vineyards, dehesas). Intensive agricultural habitats include ricefields, improved grassland, other arable land.

Source: ETC/NPB, 2002a; NATURA 2000 database

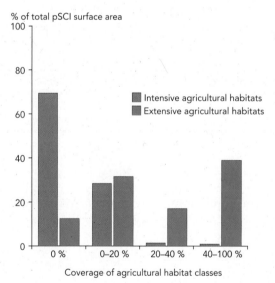

😐 Extensive agricultural habitats contribute significantly to the high nature value of sites proposed under the EU habitats directive.

🙂 A significant number of European countries are implementing national or sectoral plans for conservation and sustainable use of inland water ecosystems.

biodiversity trends for such ecosystems in Europe is even harder than for wetlands. An analysis made by the European Topic Centre on Nature Protection and Biodiversity (ETC/NPB) on proposed sites of Community interest (pSCI) under the EU habitats directive shows that extensive agricultural habitats occur much more frequently in the pSCIs than do intensive agricultural habitats. Analysis shows that 39 % of the total surface area of pSCIs relate to sites where extensive agricultural habitats occupy more than 40 % of the site and that up to 70 % of the total area of pSCIs relate to sites that have no intensive agricultural habitats at all. Extensive agricultural habitats in pSCIs are to be found mostly in the alpine, Mediterranean and Atlantic regions.

Bignal *et al.* (1996) provide an estimate of the proportion of low-intensity farming systems in various European countries on the basis of national expert judgement (see Table 11.2). Mediterranean countries and those with large upland or mountain areas show the highest proportion of low-intensity farming systems since physical conditions in these areas put strong constraints on the intensity of agricultural land use. The relatively low scores for CEE countries may result from different standards being applied by national experts in Hungary and Poland than in western countries. Data on semi-natural grasslands (see Chapter 2.3) show that CEE countries often still contain large areas of species-rich agricultural habitats that depend on low-input farming (Balazy and Ryszkowski, 1999). Time series are not available for any of these datasets, but the trends in farm structure, farm management and farmland species leave little doubt that species-rich agricultural habitats in Europe have declined considerably during recent decades.

In the European part of the Russian Federation, pastures and hayfields represent 4.6 % of the territory. The trend during recent decades has been for these areas to be converted into forest land; about 30 % of previous pastures and hayfields had become forests or other wooded land by the late 1990s (RCMC, 2000).

Large old world natural steppe areas remain in central Asia (mainly Kazakhstan, Mongolia and the Russian Federation) despite the conversion of huge areas to intensive agriculture between 1954 and 1965 when the USSR administration promoted the so-called 'upturn of virgin lands'. With the liberalization of the economy, agriculture in Kazakhstan has rapidly decreased since 1992, and more than 50 % of ploughed steppes have returned to natural steppes (Sánchez-Zapata *et al*, 2003).

At the European level, the Bern convention and its Emerald network recognise the importance of extensive farming systems and semi-natural grasslands. So, at EU level, does Annex I of the habitats directive. Extensification of farming practices is part of the agri-environmental measures implemented in the EU (European Commission, 1998a) as well as in some accession countries.

11.4.3. Marine and coastal biodiversity

Marine biodiversity, including phytoplankton and microbes, is important for the healthy functioning of ecosystems. Marine and coastal areas provide a huge number of goods and services, including fisheries, aquaculture, recreation and bathing, oil and gas, shipping, wind energy, sand and gravel extraction. Some of these involve the exploitation of marine and coastal resources (e.g. fish, mammals, molluscs, crustaceans), for example for eco-tourism, hunting, angling or food, and depend on the good functioning of the whole ecosystem. Chapter 2.5 provides data on fish stocks. Marine

ecosystems also play a significant role in global carbon exchange.

Biodiversity in seas and oceans suffers from a number of pressures of varying intensity depending on the environmental pressures as shown in Table 11.3. These threats result in loss or degradation of biodiversity and changes in its structure, loss of habitats, contamination by dangerous substances and

Table 11.2. Proportion of low-intensity farming systems as percentage of the total utilised agricultural area

Source: Bignal et al., 1996

Country	%
Spain	82
Greece	61
Portugal	60
Ireland	35
Italy	31
France	25
United Kingdom	25
Hungary	23
Poland	14

Table 11.3. Main pressures affecting biodiversity in the different seas around Europe

Pressure	Arctic	Azov Sea	Baltic Sea	Black Sea	Caspian Sea	Mediterranean	North Sea	Wider Atlantic
Eutrophication (fertilisation, sewage, combustion)		XX	XX	XX	XX	XX (locally)	XX	XX (locally)
Contamination (pesticides, waste, sewage, oil and gas, other industries)	X	XX	XX (locally)	XX	XX	XX (locally)	XX	XX (locally)
Construction (dredging, dumping of dredged material)			XX	XX	XX	XX	X	X
Recreational activities and tourist infrastructures			X	XX (locally)		XX		
Fishing (overfishing, bottom trawling, mariculture) or whaling	XX	XX	XX	XX	XX	XX	XX	XX
Exotic species	X	?	X	XX	X	XX	X	X
Climate change	XX	X	X	X	X	X	X	X

Note: XX: major impact. X: serious impact. ?: unknown.
Sources: EEA, 1998; EEA, in preparation; ETC/TE and comments by countries through EIONET

nutrients, and possible future effects of climate change.

The conservation and sustainable use of marine and coastal biodiversity are covered by regulatory frameworks at the international and regional level. These include the Convention on Biological Diversity, the OSPAR Commission for the Protection of the Marine Environment of the North-East Atlantic, the Helsinki convention (Baltic Sea), the Barcelona convention (Mediterranean) and the Black Sea convention.

At the EU level, the sixth environment action programme (6EAP) stipulates the development of a thematic strategy for the protection and conservation of the marine environment with the overall aim 'to promote sustainable use of the seas and conserve marine ecosystems'. It will be supported by a revision of the common fisheries policy, the general principles of which are reflected in the EU Biodiversity Action Plan on Fisheries.

Coastal biodiversity is quite well covered by the birds and habitats directives, as well as the Bern convention, but the marine compartment is far less well covered. However, following a recent interpretation by the Commission — now accepted by Member States — the EU birds and habitats directives apply to offshore waters, beyond the territorial waters to the 200-mile limit of exclusive economic zones. The European strategy also enhances nature protection in coastal areas by integrated coastal zone management, adopted in September 2000 (European Commission, 2002).

Under the pan-European biological landscape diversity strategy (PEBLDS) process, the Council of Europe ministers adopted a European code of conduct for the coastal zone in April 1999 (Council of Europe, 1999a).

At the national level, all 19 countries with a coastal interface covered by this report say that they promote the conservation and sustainable use of marine and coastal biodiversity in their national strategy and action plan, 13 to a significant extent and six to a limited extent (CBD secretariat, 2002).

11.4.4. Mountain ecosystems

Most European mountain ranges from the western Mediterranean to the borders of Siberia are included in the definition of the alpine biogeographic region (see Map 11.1). These are: the Alps, Pyrenees, Carpathians, Dinaric Alps, Balkans and Rhodopes, Scandes, Urals and Caucasus. They represent some of the oldest and the newest mountains to be found in the world. However, other major mountain chains are to be found in other biogeographic regions, for example the Mediterranean and the Anatolian regions.

Natural and semi-natural habitats cover more than 90 % of the alpine region: forests more than 40 % and grasslands more than 25 %. Mountain ranges represent some of the largest reservoirs of flora and fauna in Europe and central Asia (see Box 11.1.), including endemic species as well as large predators: large carnivores and raptors.

The mountain ranges also host an exceptional gene bank and are a natural laboratory where evolutionary processes can be studied. As a whole, mountain flora is estimated at over 7 000 species, with a maximum number in the Caucasian mountains (one of the 25 hot spots of

Figure 11.6.	Flora richness in some main European mountain ranges

Source: Davis et al., 1994-97

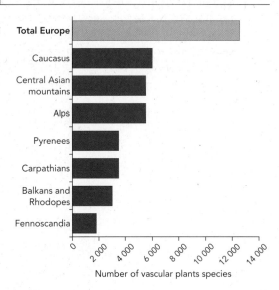

Number of vascular plants species

Box 11.1. Kyrgyzstan: leading nature conservation and enhancement of cultural values in central Asia

With a large part of its territory as mountains, Kyrgyzstan has chosen a sustainable development strategy based on natural and cultural values and excluding mining and hydroelectric developments. Thus the Issyk-Kul biosphere reserve covers almost a quarter of the country's territory. Furthermore, a transboundary biosphere reserve is being created in the western Tien Shan, at the border between Kyrgyzstan, Kazakhstan and Uzbekistan. This is part of the IUCN project 'Transboundary protected areas for peace and cooperation', which aims at protecting biodiversity while moderating potential tensions linked to national borders.

biodiversity in the world) (Figure 11.6). This represents more than half of the total number of European vascular plants.

The extreme physical conditions make mountains a fragile environment. Key issues, which are being addressed within different research, administrative and non-governmental organisation fora and in the context of the 2002 United Nations International Year of Mountains, include:

- international and regional agreements for cooperation on sustainable mountain development, such as the Alpine and the forthcoming Carpathian convention;
- national policies and institutions for sustainable mountain development;
- legal, economic and compensation mechanisms in support of sustainable mountain development;
- sustainable livelihoods and poverty alleviation;
- tourism and the conservation and maintenance of biological and cultural diversity;
- institutions for democratic and decentralised sustainable mountain development;
- conflicts and peace in mountain areas;
- mountain infrastructure: access, communications, energy;
- promotion and integration of education, science and culture in mountain protection and development;
- water, natural resources, hazards, desertification and the implications of climate change.

11.5. Ups and downs in species populations

The implementation of policies for the protection of species and habitats, combined with restoration programmes and moves towards more sustainable management practices are all helping to counteract major negative impacts on Europe's biodiversity. But such measures have not yet reversed the general decline.

Red Lists are often used for assessing biodiversity status at a particular time. There are national Red Lists in almost all European countries (ETC/NPB, 2002b) while regional Red Lists have been established under regional conventions such as the marine conventions. However, Red Lists are poor at measuring changes in biodiversity over time. No European overview is yet available, despite on-going joint efforts between the Council of

Europe, the European Environment Agency (EEA) and IUCN to establish European lists of threatened vertebrates and plants; the latter also in collaboration with the Planta Europa network.

The trends in biodiversity vary between species, ecosystems and regions: some previously highly threatened species are starting to recover, with stabilised or even increasing populations. Others continue to decline at an alarming rate. Some species have been monitored for a long time, because they are particularly rare, endemic or flagship species (Table 11.4.). For these, data on remaining populations, threats and requirements for conservation provide a sound basis for the design of specific, adapted action plans. This has been done, for example, for some of the most threatened birds in Europe (Gallo-Ursi, 2001; Tucker and Heath, 1994) and the large European predatory mammals (Boitani, 2000; Brettenmoser, 2000; Delibes et al, 2000; European Commission, 1997; Landa, 2000).

Rare or flagship species are not alone in providing a picture of biodiversity trends. Results from surveys on common breeding bird species, based on long time series, are beginning to be available for a number of European countries. They show the serious decline in some previously widespread species towards very unstable populations and reduced distribution ranges.

A recent survey from comparable monitoring data in France, the United Kingdom and the Netherlands shows the trends in the populations of common bird species, covering the 20 most declining species and the 10 most increasing ones (Table 11.5).

While some common birds have shown an important increase in their populations over the past decade, significant numbers are facing severe decline. Some of the trends can be related directly to changes in habitats and the ways they are managed. For example, the skylark and the grey partridge which breed and winter in arable lands seem to face an overall decline at European level (for instance up to 95 % since 1960 for the grey partridge in Hungary) due to intensification of agriculture. Other trends are more difficult to relate to one single type of pressure. It is recognised that the more a bird species is dependent on a habitat, the more significant is its current decline, because such birds are less able to adapt to other habitat types when their favourite one is degraded.

Changes in habitat can be beneficial to some species during part of their life cycle. For instance several waterbird species that winter in Europe (some ducks and geese) benefit from grasslands that are richer in nutrients as a result of the intensification of agriculture. This, combined with hunting bans, has resulted in significant increases in populations as recorded by the International Waterbird Census (Wetlands International, 2002c), one of the very few coordinated long-term monitoring programmes in Europe. Figure 11.7. shows the population trend of the wigeon (Anas penelope) in northwest Europe since 1974.

In general, European time series data are still lacking. They are scarcely available for birds though that is the best covered species

☹ Focus has long been on the most threatened and flagship species, such as large carnivores, and the population trends for these vary considerably. However, some previously common species are now facing serious decline towards very unstable populations and reduced distribution ranges, for example the skylark (as a result of agricultural intensification).

Table 11.4.	State and trends of large European carnivores

Species	Previous distribution in Europe	Remaining population	Current trends	Main threats
Iberian lynx	Endemic in the Iberian peninsula	No more than 150–200 Only two areas in Spain	↓↓ and may disappear in the first half of the 21st century	- Decline in prey (rabbit) - Habitat deterioration (dams, afforestation, road building) - Accidental catches in traps and snares
Eurasian lynx	Originally throughout Europe, except large islands and Iberian peninsula Exterminated in western Europe in the 1950s	7 000 Reintroduced in certain areas in the 1970s	↑ in northern and eastern Europe	- Deforestation - Loss of prey species - Expansion of agriculture - Unsustainable hunting and poaching - Traffic accidents
Brown bear	Throughout Europe except large islands	50 000 (14 000 outside Russia)	↓ for small, isolated populations (France) ↓ for larger populations	- Logging and forest clearance - Habitat fragmentation (high-speed roads and rail networks) - Poaching
Wolf	At the end of 18th century, in all European countries In 1960s, numerous populations in southern and eastern Europe	Around 16 000 Largest populations in southern and eastern countries Only small remnants in Portugal, Spain, Italy, Greece, Sweden and Finland	↓ or ↑ but many small, vulnerable populations	- Persecution - Poaching - Habitat fragmentation - Poisoning - Lack of prey availability
Wolverine	European Russia, Norway, Finland, Sweden, Baltic states, northeast Poland During the 19th century, disappeared from the southernmost of these areas	2 000	↑ and remain in high altitude alpine habitats	- Too small and fragmented distribution - Conflicts with semi-domestic reindeer and livestock owners - Increased human access to the habitat

Decline :
Less than 30 %: ↓
Between 30–55 %: ↓↓
More than 55 %: ↓↓↓

Increase:
Between 30–55 %: ↑
Between 55 % and 100 %: ↑↑
More than 100 %: ↑↑↑

Source: WWF, 2002

Comparative trends in selected common bird species populations in three western European countries (France, the Netherlands and United Kingdom) between 1989 and 2001					Table 11.5.

Bird species		Population trends in			Average population trends	
Common name	Scientific name	Netherlands	France	United Kingdom	average	
Wood warbler	*Phylloscopus sibilatrix*	-72 %	-73 %	-76 %	-74 %	↓↓↓
Whinchat	*Saxicola rubetra*	-83 %	-69 %	-20 %	-65 %	↓↓↓
Grey partridge	*Perdix perdix*	-63 %	-49 %	-59 %	-57 %	↓↓↓
House martin	*Delichon urbica*	-39 %	-84 %	17 %	-51 %	↓↓
Tree pipit	*Anthus trivialis*	8 %	-41 %	-75 %	-45 %	↓↓
Tree sparrow	*Passer montanus*	-35 %	-24 %	-65 %	-44 %	↓↓
Willow tit	*Parus montanus*	0 %	-47 %	-63 %	-42 %	↓↓
Turtle dove	*Streptopelia turtur*	-65 %	9 %	-45 %	-41 %	↓↓
Linnet	*Carduelis cannabina*	-20 %	-62 %	-30 %	-40 %	↓↓
Magpie	*Pica pica*	-39 %	-61 %	1 %	-38 %	↓↓
Willow warbler	*Phylloscopus trochilus*	-15 %	-56 %	-33 %	-37 %	↓↓
House sparrow	*Passer domesticus*	-41 %	-21 %	-33 %	-32 %	↓↓
Starling	*Sturnus vulgaris*	-11 %	-27 %	-51 %	-32 %	↓↓
Lapwing	*Vanellus vanellus*	-39 %	-24 %	-25 %	-30 %	↓↓
Marsh tit	*Parus palustris*	26 %	-59 %	-29 %	-29 %	↓
Reed bunting	*Emberiza schoeniclus*	29 %	-58 %	-27 %	-26 %	↓
Meadow pipit	*Anthus pratensis*	14 %	-58 %	-14 %	-26 %	↓
Cuckoo	*Cuculus canorus*	-21 %	-28 %	-26 %	-25 %	↓
Skylark	*Alauda arvensis*	-31 %	-18 %	-17 %	-22 %	↓
Bullfinch	*Pyrrhula pyrrhula*	+8 %	-47 %	-15 %	-21 %	↓
Great spotted woodpecker	*Dendrocopos major*	+62 %	+9 %	+26 %	+30 %	↑
Song thrush	*Turdus philomelos*	+ 78 %	+65 %	-12 %	+37 %	↑
Blackcap	*Sylvia atricapilla*	+80 %	+2 %	+55 %	+42 %	↑
Whitethroat	*Sylvia communis*	+75 %	+8 %	+51 %	+42 %	↑
Robin	*Erithacus rubecula*	+31 %	+79 %	+31 %	+45 %	↑
Sedge warbler	*Acrocephalus schoenobaenus*	+82 %	+117 %	+10 %	+63 %	↑↑
Collared dove	*Streptopelia decaocto*	+16 %	+188 %	+71 %	+78 %	↑↑
Goldfinch	*Carduelis carduelis*	+188 %	+31 %	+61 %	+82 %	↑↑
Stonechat	*Saxicola torquata*	+170 %	+59 %	+103 %	+105 %	↑↑↑
Buzzard	*Buteo buteo*	+212 %	+18 %	+237 %	+132 %	↑↑↑

Decline:
Less than 30 %: ↓
Between 30–55 %: ↓↓
More than 55 %: ↓↓↓

Increase:
Between 30–55 %: ↑
Between 55 % and 100 %: ↑↑
More than 100 %: ↑↑↑

Sources: Baillie *et al*, 2001, Van Dijk *et al*, 2001, Julliard *et al*, 2002

| Figure 11.7. | Northwest European population trends of the wigeon (Anas penelope) as recorded at wintering sites |

Source: Wetlands International database, 2002c

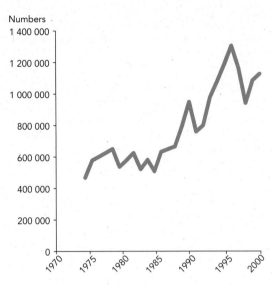

Numbers

group. However, within the pan-European bird monitoring strategy, led by European Bird Census Council and Bird International, promising indicator-based results may be expected in the short term for important sites and for rare and common birds (Gregory *et al*, 2003).

As for plants, the recently launched European plant conservation strategy, jointly led by the Council of Europe and Planta Europa (2002) as a contribution to the global plant conservation strategy under the CBD, should enhance monitoring efforts and contribute to a better knowledge of the conservation status of Europe's flora.

The recently launched European biodiversity monitoring and indicator framework (EBMI-F) (ECNC and EEA, 2002) under the pan-European biological and landscape diversity strategy should support improved coordination and ensure that the monitoring of biodiversity is better targeted.

Box 11.2. Invasive alien species: the case of the western corn rootworm

A recent invasive American pest on arable land in Europe is the western corn rootworm (*Diabrotica virgifera virgifera*). It is likely to have arrived in Yugoslavia in the early to mid-1980s. By the end of 2001 it had spread over 182 000 km² in Europe (Bulgaria, Bosnia-Herzegovina, Croatia, Hungary, Romania, Slovakia, and Serbia and Montenegro). Western corn rootworm beetles were trapped in 1998 and 1999 in Italy, near Venice airport and in 2000 in Switzerland, near Lugano. The spread of western corn rootworm has continued in all directions from the original infestation point (Figure11.8). It has become an economic pest of maize fields in Serbia and Montenegro (yield losses of up to 70 %). Several research projects focus on the possibility of biological control of such pests.

11.6. Invasive alien species — a serious threat to biodiversity

Alien species have been introduced intentionally or unintentionally for centuries (see Box 11.2.). The process has accelerated during recent decades with the growth in transport and the use of alien species for aquaculture, fisheries, game, crops, forestry and horticulture. For instance, freshwater fish have been introduced for aquaculture, angling/sport, aquaria and weed control.

In general, only some introduced species survive in their new environment and eventually become naturalised without creating any problems. However, others are highly successful competitors for space and food and become a threat to indigenous species or to a whole ecosystem by disrupting the food chain or altering the habitat. Other problems relate to mixing with original gene pools (for example wild salmon, wild boar, many plant species including trees, and recent concerns regarding genetically

| Figure 11.8. | Spread of the western corn rootworm (Diabrotica virgifera virgifera) in Europe |

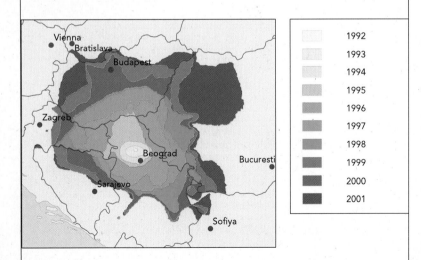

Source: Prepared by FAO Network (Edwards, Kiss (2001)), based on data from Bertossa, Boriani, Festic, Furlan, Gogu, Igrc-Barcic, Ivanova, Omelyuta, Princzinger, Rosca, Sivcev and Sivicek. Government of Hungary and of United Kingdom, 2002

😐 There is a general consensus that the intentional introduction of species should be avoided unless detailed assessments show that the benefits of an introduction are much greater than the associated risks.

modified organisms) or the introduction of diseases. This is happening both within and outside protected areas. There is growing concern about how some of these alien species may benefit from newly created conditions resulting from climate change and become even more competitive to other species.

The planning of more effective strategies to deal with biological invasions has become a global conservation priority.

The loss of biodiversity caused by invasive alien species is given high priority in the Convention on Biological Diversity and the Ramsar, Bern and Bonn conventions. A global invasive species programme has been set up under the CBD, and the sixth CBD Conference of Parties in 2002 urged Parties to implement strategies and action plans to control alien species. This is reflected at the European level in the European strategy on invasive alien species developed by the Council of Europe (Council of Europe, 2002a). The Cartagena protocol on biosafety adopted in 2000 under the CBD seeks to protect biological diversity from the potential risks posed by living modified organisms resulting from modern biotechnology.

In the marine area, the International Council for the Exploration of the Sea set up in 1994 a code of practice for the introduction and transfer of marine organisms.

At the EU level, the EU regulation for the implementation of CITES provides a basis for controlling imports of certain species that may become invasive. The recent EU biodiversity strategy (European Commission, 1998b) calls for the application of the precautionary principle to avoid detrimental effects of invasive alien species.

11.7. A constantly evolving policy framework in relation to biodiversity and its sustainable use

The policy framework has evolved considerably, at the international, EU, regional and national level, towards better consideration of all biodiversity aspects well beyond — but complementary to — the initial instruments targeted on nature protection (Table 11.6). These instruments should benefit from more and more synergy, with increasing cooperation between

convention secretariats, leading to a more integrated and transboundary approach. As a contracting Party to most international conventions, the EU aims at integrating the provisions of such global instruments within EU policies, while also applying its specific policy objectives.

Most of these instruments call for monitoring in order to assess effective implementation. Progress in this direction remains insufficient. In addition to these legal frameworks, many initiatives are undertaken by non-governmental organisations.

11.7.1. Designated areas, a tool for biodiversity conservation

Sites of high nature value have been protected from adverse human activities for more than 100 years, the earliest protected areas being in central and eastern Europe. Each country developed its own system of designation types, ranging from very strict nature reserves and national parks to more flexible protection such as landscape parks and areas under specific conservation management. There are nearly 600 different types of designation and more than 65 000 designated sites in western, central and eastern Europe. There has been a huge increase in national designations since the 1970s (Figure 11.9) when most countries started to implement national laws on nature protection.

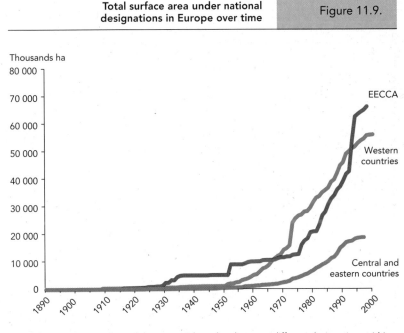

| Total surface area under national designations in Europe over time | Figure 11.9. |

Thousands ha

Note: Areas are overestimated due to partial overlaps between different designations within a country.

Source: Common database on designated areas (CDDA) (EEA, Council of Europe, WCMC)

Table 11.6.	Conventions and major instruments

Global

Conventions

Convention on Wetlands of International Importance — Ramsar — (1971) (http://www.ramsar.org)

Convention concerning the Protection of the World Cultural and Natural Heritage (1972) (http://whc.unesco.org/)

Convention on International Trade in Endangered Species of Wild Fauna and Flora, CITES (1973) (http://www.cites.org/)

Convention on the Conservation of Migratory Species of Wild Animals, Bonn (1979) (http://www.wcmc.org.uk/cms/), including agreements and memoranda of understanding on: *Conservation of Seals in the Wadden Sea (1990), Conservation of Small Cetaceans of the Baltic and North Seas (1991) (ASCOBANS), Conservation of Bats in Europe (1991) (EUROBATS), Conservation Measures for the Slender-billed Curlew (1994), Conservation of African-Eurasian Migratory Waterbirds (1995), Conservation of Cetaceans of the Black Sea and Contiguous Atlantic Area (1996) (ACCOBAMS), Conservation and Management of the Middle-European Population of the Great Bustard (Otis tarda) (2001)*

Convention on Long-Range Transboundary Air Pollution (1979)

Convention on the Law of the Sea (1982) (http://www.un.org/Depts/los/convention_agreements/convention_overview_convention.htm)

Convention on Biological Diversity (1992) (http://www.biodiv.org)

Convention to Combat Desertification (1992) (http://www.unccd.int/)

Convention on Climate Change (1992) (http://unfccc.int/)

Other initiatives
Man and Biosphere Programme (http://www.unesco.org/mab/)
Global Plan of Action for the Conservation and Sustainable Utilization of Plant Genetic Resources for Food and Agriculture (http://www.fao.org/waicent/FaoInfo/Agricult/AGP/AGPS/)
International Treaty on Plant Genetic Resources (2001) (http://www.ukabc.org/iu2.htm)

Regional

Conventions

Convention on Fishing and Conservation of the Living Resources in the Baltic Sea and the Belts (1973)

Convention on the Protection of the Marine Environment of the Baltic Sea Area (1974)

Convention for the Protection of the Mediterranean Sea against Pollution, Barcelona (1976) (http://eelink.net/~asilwildlife/barcelona.html)

Convention on the Conservation of European Wildlife and Natural Habitats, Bern (1979) (http://www.nature.coe.int/)

Convention concerning the Protection of the Alps (1991) (http://www.mtnforum.org/resources/library/cpalp02a.htm)

Convention on the Protection of the Marine Environment of the Baltic Sea Area, HELCOM (1992) (http://www.helcom.fi/)

Convention for the Protection of the Marine Environment of the North-East Atlantic, OSPAR (1992) (http://www.ospar.org/)

Convention on Cooperation for the Protection and Sustainable Use of the Danube River (1994) (http://www.defyu.org.yu/E-catchment/catchment2-2-1.htm)

Convention on the International Commission for the Protection of the Oder (1998)

Convention on the Protection of the Rhine (1998) (http://www.internationalwaterlaw.org/RegionalDocs/Rhine_River.htm)

European Landscape Convention (2000) (http://www.nature.coe.int/english/main/landscape/conv.htm)

Other initiatives
Environment for Europe process (http://www.unece.org/env/europe/)

Pan-European biological diversity and landscape strategy (http://www.nature.coe.int/)

Ministerial Conference for the Protection of Forests in Europe (http://www.minconf-forests.net/)

Arctic environment protection strategy (http://www.arctic-council.org/files/pdf/artic_environment.PDF)

Strategic action plan for the conservation of biological diversity (SAP BIO) in the Mediterranean region (http://www.sapbio.net/)

European Union

Sixth environment action programme (6EAP) and seven related thematic strategies (http://europa.eu.int/comm/environment/newprg/index.htm)

EU sustainable development strategy (http://europa.eu.int/comm/environment/eussd/)

EU biodiversity strategy and associated plans (http://europa.eu.int/comm/environment/docum/9842en.pdf)

EU birds directive (http://europa.eu.int/comm/environment/nature/legis.htm)

EU habitats directive (http://europa.eu.int/comm/environment/nature/legis.htm)

Water framework directive (http://europa.eu.int/comm/environment/water/water-framework/index_en.html)

Common agricultural policy including agri-environmental measures and rural development regulation (http://europa.eu.int/comm/environment/agriculture/links.htm)

Common transport policy
Environmental impact assessment

Other international and EU instruments such as the Ramsar convention (1971) and the EU birds directive (1979) made it compulsory for countries to designate sites for protection, which probably influenced the rate at which new sites were designated under national systems.

Thus, by developing their own system of nationally designated areas, countries set their own priorities for protecting local biodiversity values, while contributing to the implementation of international and Community legal frameworks.

The extent of surface area designated is likely to level off for a number of reasons, at least in WE. Increasing land-use conflicts from transport, urbanisation and intensive agriculture are diminishing the remaining semi-natural remote areas. On the other hand, concern for biodiversity is becoming more and more integrated into sectoral policies, for instance with agri-environmental measures or sustainable forestry policies, but these do not necessarily lead to new designations of sites.

In the EU, the implementation of the Natura 2000 network demonstrates a huge effort by countries to ensure the coordinated conservation of a selection of species and habitats of European concern. The first 10 accession countries are preparing to join this process. The Natura 2000 network is a key, compulsory instrument for halting the loss of biodiversity (European Commission, undated); the Natura barometer assesses progress periodically (European Commission, 1996 to 2002). By April 2002 in the EU, 2 827 sites, covering 222 480 km², had been designated as special protection areas under the birds directive and 14 901 sites, covering 436 756 km², had been proposed as sites of community interest under the habitats directive. This represents up to 16 % of the EU territory.

At the European level, the Emerald network aims to establish a network of areas of special conservation interest for the threatened and endemic species listed in the appendices of the Bern convention and for the endangered habitat types that have been identified by the Standing Committee as 'requiring specific conservation measures' (Council of Europe, 1999b). The contribution of EU countries to the Emerald network is Natura 2000. A number of non-EU countries have shown great interest in joining the Emerald process, starting with a pilot phase (Figure 11.10).

> 😐 15 % of the total area of western Europe is under national designation for nature protection, 9 % of central and eastern Europe and 3 % of the 12 countries of eastern Europe, the Caucasus and central Asia.

Progress in non-EU European countries joining the Emerald process

Figure 11.10.

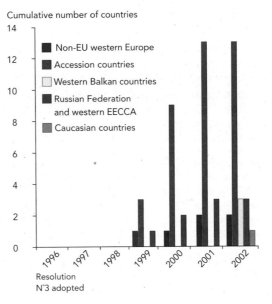

Note: In 1996, by adopting Resolution N° 3, the Standing Committee to the Bern Convention resolved to „set up a network (EMERALD Network) which would include Areas of Special Conservation Interest".

Source: Council of Europe, 2002b

In addition to the national and European designations, countries also designate sites under international and regional conventions and programmes (Delbaere and Beltran, 1999): World Heritage (51 sites), biosphere reserves (163 sites), Ramsar sites (736 sites), biogenetic reserves (343 sites), European diploma (61 sites), Barcelona convention (208 sites) and Helsinki convention (62 sites). Most of the international and European designations overlap with national designations and sometimes among themselves, which, in principle ensures stronger protection. Since each designation is made with a specific purpose, a site of particularly high nature value can benefit from several international

> 🙂 The Natura 2000 network is progressively taking shape at the EU level, with up to 16 % of the EU territory covered. The corresponding initiative for non-EU countries, the Emerald network, under the Bern convention, is at an encouraging pilot stage.

designations. For instance Doñana in Spain and the Camargue in France each enjoy six overlapping international and European designations.

Designated areas are not only of critical importance for protecting sites of high nature value from the impacts of large infrastructures and intensive agriculture, forestry or fishery, they are also areas where it is easier to implement coordinated biodiversity monitoring and public awareness campaigns. More and more, designated areas are recognised as areas where sustainable management practices and the ecosystem approach can be tested through collaboration between different actors (Council of Europe, 1998).

Most of these designated areas are core elements in the establishment of a pan-European ecological network (Bouwma *et al*, 2002; Council of Europe, 2000), one of the key objectives of the pan-European biological and landscape diversity strategy. Several national initiatives aim at establishing ecological corridors to link these core elements, in particular for large carnivores. There is also increasing interest in developing marine ecological corridors.

11.7.2. Integrating biodiversity into sectors
Traditional nature protection instruments ensure a broader perspective for the sustainable management of species and ecosystems, and therefore remain vital. However, increasing demand for land from various sectors, and the uncertainties related to large-scale changes, demand a more integrated approach to biodiversity in all the main sectors of concern.

The main sectors that impact on biodiversity — and therefore where integration of biodiversity concerns is needed — differ from region to region, as shown in Figure 11.11.

WE countries consistently highlight the same sectors, in particular agriculture, forestry, fisheries and transport. In comparison, the CEE countries emphasise forestry and to a lesser extent agriculture and tourism. The EECCA countries emphasise agriculture and forestry. This picture may change significantly with EU enlargement, and therefore implementation of the common agricultural policy in the accession countries (Donald *et al*, 2002), and also as a result of the likely development of transport infrastructures (EEA, 2002b). Other sectors, such as spatial planning and finance, although not directly addressed by countries, have an obvious influence on biodiversity.

There has been some progress in integration in some sectors, for example through the introduction of agri-environment schemes, the EU sustainable development strategy and the EU biodiversity strategy (European Commission, 1998b). At the European level, the outcomes of the high-level Conference on Agriculture and Biodiversity, held in Paris in November 2002 (Council of Europe, 2002c) and the proposal for a ministerial conference in 2005 should help by better identifying problems and areas for actions.

In the transport sector, despite the continuing development of the code of practice for the introduction of biological landscape considerations into transport sector, the absence of a strong policy framework and the inexorable growth in demand are likely to lead to increasing impacts on biodiversity.

During the World Summit on Sustainable Development in Johannesburg, the heads of state and government agreed to '...the

| Figure 11.11. | **Regional European differences highlighting sectoral pressures on biodiversity** |

Source: National reports to CBD secretariat, analysed by Drucker and Damarad, 2000 (amended)

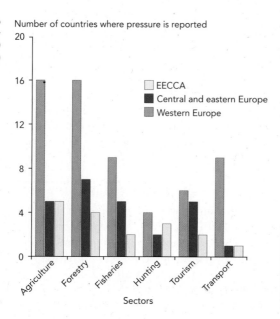

Number of countries where pressure is reported

Legend:
☐ EECCA
■ Central and eastern Europe
▨ Western Europe

Sectors

> 😐 All major sectors influence and possibly impact on biodiversity, though with regional differences. Agriculture and forestry are the sectors reported as having such impacts in the largest number of countries.

achievement by 2010 of a significant reduction in the current loss of biological diversity.... and to actions at all levels to (a) integrate the objectives of the Convention on Biological Diversity into global, regional and national sectoral and cross-sectoral programmes and policies, in particular in the programmes and policies of the economic sectors of countries and international financial institutions'.

At the European level, the pan-European biological and landscape diversity strategy provides a coordinated framework for implementing these objectives and even suggests a stronger commitment, i.e. 'to halt the loss of Europe's biodiversity by 2010'.

11.8. References

Baillie, S. R. *et al.*, 2001. *Breeding birds in the wider countryside: Their conservation status 2000.* BTO Research Report No 252. BTO, Thetford. http://www.bto.org/birdtrends

Balazy, S., Ryszkowski L., 1999. *Protection of biological and landscape diversity in agricultural landscapes of central and eastern Europe.* Nature and Environment series No 94. Council of Europe, Strasbourg.

Berkhoudt, K., 2002. *Focus on EU Enlargement and Wildlife Trade: Review of CITES Implementation in Candidate Countries.* TRAFFIC Europe report. Brussels

Bignal, E. M., McCracken, D. I. and Curtis, D. J. (eds), 1996. *Nature conservation and pastoralism in Europe.* European Forum on Nature Conservation and Pastoralism. Bridgend.

Boitani, L. 2000. *Action plan for the conservation of the wolves (Canislupus) in Europe.* Council of Europe. Nature and Environment series No. 113. Council of Europe, Strasbourg.

Bouwma, I. M., Jongman, R. H. G. and Butovsky, R. O. (eds), (2002). *The indicative map of the pan-European ecological network - technical background document.* ECNC technical report series. European Centre for Nature Conservation, Tilburg, the Netherlands and Budapest.

Brettenmoser, U., 2000. *Action plan for the conservation of the Eurasian lynx (Lynx lynx) in Europe.* Council of Europe. Nature and Environment series No. 112. Council of Europe, Strasbourg.

CBD (Convention on Biological Diversity) secretariat, 2002. *First and second national reports on biodiversity.* http://www.biodiv.org/world/reports.asp

Council of Europe, 1998. *Protected areas: Centres for propagating a general nature conservation policy* (1998) (Abruzzi National Park, Italy, 8-10 June 1997). Environmental Encounters. Strasbourg.

Council of Europe, 1999a. *Model law on sustainable management of coastal zones and European code of conduct for coastal zones.* Nature and Environment series No. 101. Strasbourg.

Council of Europe, 1999b. *'The Emerald Network — a network of Areas of Special Conservation Interest for Europe'.* Document T-PVS (99) 36. Strasbourg.

Council of Europe, 2000. *First International symposium of the Pan-European Ecological Network — 'Nature does not have any borders: towards transfrontier ecological networks'.* Proceedings of the symposium held in Paris (France) on 2–3 September 1999. Environmental Encounters No. 44. Council of Europe, Strasbourg,

Council of Europe, 2002a. *European Strategy on Invasive Alien Species* T-PVS (2002) 8. Strasbourg.

Council of Europe, 2002b. Emerald Network Bulletin, n°3. Strasbourg. http://www.nature.coe.int/english/main/econets/emerald/EmNB3.htm

Council of Europe, 2002c. *Proceedings of the High-level Pan-European Conference on Agriculture and Biodiversity: towards integrating biological and landscape diversity for sustainable agriculture in Europe* (Paris, France, 5–7 June 2002). Strasbourg

Davis, S., Heywood, V. H. and Hamilton, A. C. (eds), 1994-97. *Centres of plant diversity.* Three vols. World Wide Fund for Nature and IUCN-The World Conservation Union, Gland, Switzerland.

Delibes, A., Rodriguez, A. & Ferreras, P. 2000. *Action plan for the conservation of the Iberian lynx (Lynx pardinus) in Europe.* Nature and Environment series No 111. Council of Europe, Strasbourg.

Delbaere, B., J. Beltran, 1999. *Nature conservation sites designated in application of* international instruments at pan-European level. Nature and Environment series No. 95. Council of Europe, Strasbourg.

Donald P.F, Pisano G., Rayment M.D and Pain D.J. 2002. *The Common Agricultural Policy, EU enlargement and the conservation of Europe's farmland birds.* Agriculture, Ecosystems & Environment, Volume 89, Issue 3, May 2002, Pages 167–182. Elsevier science.

European Centre for Nature Conservation (ECNC) & European Environment Agency (EEA), 2002. The European Biodiversity Monitoring and Indicators Framework (EBMI-F). http://www.strategyguide.org/ebmf.html

European Commission (undated). *Natura 2000 managing our heritage.* Luxembourg.. http://europa.eu.int/en/comm/dg11/dg11home.html.

European Commission, 1996 to 2002. *Natura 2000.* European Commission DG Environment Nature newsletter. Issues 1 to 15. Luxembourg.

European Commission, 1997. *Conservation of the Brown Bear in the European Union*, Co-financed actions within LIFE-Nature. Prepared by O. Patrimonio (Ecosphère). Brussels, 44pp.

European Commission, 1998a. *State of Application of Regulation (EEC) n° 2078/92, Evaluation of agri-environmental programmes.* Report to the Parliament.

European Commission, 1998b. Integrating biodiversity. A European Community strategy for action. Luxembourg: Office for Official Publications of the European Communities. 20 pp

European Commission, 2002. *Council Recommendation of the European Parliament and the Council of 30 May 2002 concerning the Implementation of Integrated Coastal Zone Management in Europe (2002/413/EC).* Brussels.

EEA (European Environment Agency), 1995. *Europe's Environment. The Dobris Assessment.* Copenhagen.

EEA (European Environment Agency), 1998. *Europe's environment: The second assessment.* EEA, Copenhagen.

EEA (European Environment Agency), 1999. *Environment in the European Union at the turn of the century.* Copenhagen.

EEA (European Environment Agency), 2001. TERM 2001 — *Indicators tracking transport and environment integration in the European Union.* Copenhagen.

EEA (European Environment Agency), 2002a . *Map of Biogeographical Regions with documentation.* http://dataservice.eea.eu.int/dataservice/metadetails.asp?table=Biogeo01&i=1

EEA (European Environment Agency), 2002b. *Paving the way for EU enlargement. Indicators of transport and environment integration. TERM 2002.* Copenhagen.

EEA (European Environment Agency), in preparation. Report on Europe's Biodiversity.

European Topic Centre on Nature Protection and Biodiversity (EEA-ETC/NPB), 2002a. *NATURA 2000 database.* (On behalf of the European Commission). Paris

European Topic Centre on Nature Protection and Biodiversity (EEA-ETC/NPB), 2002b. *Checklist of Red Books on Species and Habitats in Europe.* http://nature.eionet.eu.int/activities/products/redbooks/index_html

FAO (Food and Agriculture Organization), 2000. *World watch list for domestic animal diversity (3rd Edition).* Roma.

Gallo-Orsi, U. 2001. *Saving Europe's most threatened birds: progress in implementing European Species Action Plans.* BirdLife International, Wageningen, the Netherlands.

Government of Hungary in co-operation with the Government of the United Kingdom and the Bern Convention, 2002. *Report on Invasive Alien species.* Prepared for the Sixth meeting of the Council for the Pan-European Biological and Landscape Diversity Strategy. Budapest, 24–28 February 200. Document STRA-CO (2002) 42. Council of Europe, UNEP.

Drucker, G., Damarad, T., 2000. *Integrating Biodiversity in Europe — A review of Convention of Biological Diversity General measures and Sectoral policies.* ECNC Technical report series. European Centre on Nature Conservation, Tilburg, the Netherlands.

Green, R.E., Harley. M., Spalding. M. and Zöckler, C. (Ed). 2001. *Impacts of climate change on wildlife.* RSPB, UNEP-WCMC. English Nature, World Wild Fund for nature (WWF).

Gregory *et al*, 2003. *From bird monitoring to policy-relevant indicators: exploring the potential of a Pan-European common breeding bird monitoring programme to deliver bio-indicators in a changing European environment.* Internal report to Wetlands International, member of the EEA-European Topic Centre on Nature Protection and Biodiversity. Paris.

Hilton-Taylor, C. (Compiler), 2000. *2000 IUCN Red List of Threatened Species,* IUCN, Gland, Switzerland and Cambridge, United Kingdom.

Julliard, R., Jiguet, F. and Weltz, M., 2002. *Devenir de 89 espèces d'oiseaux communs en France entre 1989 et 2001.* Muséum d'histoire naturelle, Paris. www.mnhn.fr/mnhn/meo/crbpo

Landa, A., 2000. *Action plan for the conservation of wolverines (Gulo gulo) in Europe.* Nature and Environment series No. 114. Council of Europe, Strasbourg.

Moser, M., 2000. *Wetlands status and trends in Europe: The case for rehabilitating and restoration of naturally functioning wetlands.* In Proceedings of the WWF/EU seminar: 'The role of wetlands in river basin management', Brussels 9–10 November 2000.

Myers, N., Mittermeier, R.A., Mittermeier, C.G., da Fonseca, G.B., & Kents, J., 2000. *Biodiversity hotspots for conservation priorities.* In: Nature 403, 853–858 (2000).

Parry, M.L. (Ed), 2000. *Assessment of potential effects and adaptation for climate change in Europe: the Europe Acacia project.* Jackson Environment Institute, University of East Anglia, Norwich, United Kingdom.

Planta Europa, 2002. *A European plant Conservation Strategy.* Council of Europe, Strasbourg. http://www.plantaeuropa.org/html/plant_conservation_strategy.htm

RCMC (Russian Conservation Monitoring Centre), 2000. Russian contribution to 'Report on Europe's Biodiversity (EEA, in preparation)'. Irina Merzliakova (ed.). State Committee of the Russian Federation on Environment.

Sánchez-Zapata, J-A., Carrete, M., Gravilov, A., Sklyarenko, S., Ceballos, O, José Donázar, A. and Hiraldo, F., 2003. *Land use changes and raptor conservation in steppe habitats of eastern Kazakhstan.* Biological Conservation, Volume 111, Issue 1, pages 71–77.

TRAFFIC Europe, 1998. *Overview of wildlife trade in the central Asian countries.* World Wild Fund for nature and International Union for Nature Conservation. http://www.traffic.org/publications/summaries/wildlifetrade-centralasia.html

Tucker, G.M., Heath, M.F., 1994. *Birds in Europe, their conservation status.* Birdlife International. Cambridge, UK.

UNEP - WCMC (World Conservation Monitoring Centre), 2001. *Global Biodiversity. Earth's living resources in the 21st century.* Our Planet. http://www.ourplanet.com/imgversn/105/global.html

UNEP-WCMC (World Conservation Centre), 2002. *World Atlas of Biodiversity.* http://www.unep-wcmc.org/

Van Dijk, A. J., Dijksen, L., Hustings, F., Zoetebier, D. and Plate, C., 2001. *Broedvogel Monitoring Project jaarverslag 1998-1999.* SOVON-monitoring rapport 2001/03. SOVON, Beek-Ubbergen. http://www.sovon.nl/eng/engindex

Wetlands International, 2002a. *A directory of Wetlands of International Importance.* http://www.wetlands.org/RDB/Directory.html

Wetlands International, 2002b. *Pan-European review of (national) wetland inventory.* http://www.wetlands.org/inventory&/pewi.htm

Wetlands International, 2002c. *The International Waterbird Census (IWC) in the Western Palearctic and Southwest Asia.* http://www.wetlands.org/IWC/wpal&swa/wpal.htm

WWF (World Wide Fund for Nature), 2002. *Large carnivores initiative.* http://large-carnivores-lcie.org/

12. Environment and human health

There is growing concern about the links between the environment and health. Worldwide, and probably also in Europe, one quarter to one third of the burden of disease appears to be attributable to environmental factors. Vulnerability and exposure, however, vary markedly between different groups and areas, with children and the elderly being particularly at risk.

There is reasonable understanding of cause-and-effect relationships between water, air pollution and human health. However, the health consequences of other environmental factors and exposures, such as those resulting from climate change and chemicals in the environment, are a result of complex interactions between the environment and humans that are far less understood. For some chemicals, such as endocrine-disrupting substances, the effects on humans are particularly difficult to unravel but the impacts on wildlife have been substantial, with implications for human health. Other chemicals in the environment, the disposal of wastes and noise continue to cause worry.

There are several diseases that are of concern, as expressed in the European Union research agenda. Examples include: allergy and asthma, neurotoxic effects of environmental contaminants, environmental factors influencing the onset of puberty, food and fertility; and cancer, heart disease and obesity associated with risk correlated to environment, diet and genetic factors.

Outdoor air pollution plays a role in the causation and aggravation of asthma and allergic responses, which are increasingly prevalent diseases, especially in children. Much outdoor air penetrates indoors, and as people breathe both, an integrated approach to both outdoor and indoor air pollution is needed.

While there have been considerable improvements in European levels of air and water pollution in recent decades some of the traditional, environmentally related diseases such as cholera, typhoid, malaria etc. persist, and in some parts of eastern Europe, the Caucasus and central Asia have increased. Transport continues to be a significant contributor to health effects throughout the European region from accidents, air pollution and noise.

Pharmaceuticals and consumer care products and electromagnetic fields are emerging issues. Many
types of chemical classes, ranging from endocrine disruptors, anti-microbials and antidepressants to lipid regulators and synthetic musk fragrances have been identified in sewage and domestic wastes. While exposures are very low, the increasing presence of such biologically active substances is of concern.

12.1. Introduction

While the past decade has seen various achievements that give grounds for optimism about improvements in Europe's environment and health in the 21st century, understanding the complexities of what environmental factors cause ill health is clearly going to remain difficult and, very often, the more we know the more we realise what we do not know. It does not come as a surprise, therefore, that scientific and public controversies over environment and health have been (e.g. over leaded petrol and brain damage in children), or are currently (e.g. over antibiotic growth promoters in animal feed and increased human resistance to antibiotics) common within scientific and public circles.

Public policy decisions on 'real' or 'perceived' environmental hazards (potential damage) and risks (probability of damage) are thus difficult to make and evaluate. However, understanding the types of information needed for environmental health decision-making, as well as its use and limitations (see Box 12.1), will contribute to a wider appreciation of the reasons for public 'concerns', differences in expert opinions, and the actions, or inactions, of governments.

People indeed feel very concerned about the links between their environment and their health, more so now than in the early 1990s when environmental issues were much higher on their and the media's agenda (EEA, 1999). A recent study (WHO, 2002a) confirms that the region still faces many urgent and serious challenges. This rising concern was clearly reflected in the 1999 London Declaration in which European ministers of environment and health committed themselves to taking action on a number of issues, based on the precautionary principle (WHO, 1999a), to be appraised at their next meeting in 2004, in Budapest.

The EU fifth framework research programme, while gathering facts on this matter, concluded that:

'The most common diseases affecting Europeans today are the result of a combination of factors occurring at various timescales, and for different periods, on people whose vulnerability is determined by their genetic make-up, age, state of health, diet and well-being. Consequently, it is difficult to disentangle the exact causes of ill health. ... Cancers have been linked to tobacco smoke, asbestos, some pesticides, diet, sunlight, pollutants in diesel fumes, heavy metals, and many other carcinogens. Cardiovascular diseases have been blamed on inhalable particles, tobacco smoke, carbon monoxide, and a high-cholesterol diet. Exposure to lead, cadmium, (methyl), mercury, tobacco smoke, and pesticides are all being associated with delayed or abnormal pre- and postnatal development. Noise can also have serious health effects. Some facts and figures illustrate these problems:

- occupational exposure to certain pesticides may increase the risk of Parkinson's disease (or Parkinsonism) by 15 to 20 %;
- some 10 million people in Europe are exposed to environmental noise levels that can result in hearing loss;
- worldwide, it has been estimated that 3 million people die prematurely because of air pollution;
- in Europe, asthma affects one child in seven. Allergies, notably asthma, have continued to increase dramatically over the past 30 years;
- environmental tobacco smoke increases the risk of lung cancer in non-smokers by 20 to 30 %;
- in the United Kingdom alone, the total annual cost of asthma is estimated at over EUR 3.9 billion; and
- in some European countries, testicular cancer is increasing in prevalence and an increasing number of young men have low sperm counts; similar symptoms can be produced in rats by exposure to specific chemicals, but there is so far no clear evidence that environmental exposure to these chemicals affects male reproductive health in humans.' (European Commission, 2002)

Bearing these findings in mind, new environment and health priority areas were set for the sixth framework research programme (European Commission, 2003):

- human health implications of exposure to chemical residues in the environment;
- allergy and asthma;
- neurotoxic effects of environmental contaminants;
- effects of environmental exposure to complex chemical mixtures;
- environmental factors influencing puberty onset;
- cancer risk correlated to environment, diet and genetic factors;
- food and fertility.

Taking this background into consideration, the chapter aims to:

- give an overview of monitored and emerging environmental health issues in Europe;
- describe the health effects of some air

Box 12.1. Environmental health indicators

Background
The Third Ministerial Conference on Environment and Health (London, 1999) acknowledged the need for further development of information and assessment systems as a basis for implementing and monitoring policies and also for communication with the public.

Data systems on environment and health are spread among different agencies and the links between environmental impacts and health effects are not sufficiently considered. It is also difficult to compare the environmental health situation across Europe since the methods of data collection, reporting, analysis and communication are not harmonised.

Objective
Recognising these problems, WHO Europe (World Health Organization), supported by a large group of Member States, and in collaboration with the European Environment Agency (EEA), is developing and testing a European system of environmental health indicators covering all main environmental issues of health relevance.

The process
A set of 'core' indicators has been selected for pilot implementation on the basis of a feasibility study in 14 Member States. The set includes indicators that are feasible, relevant for policy and that enable comparative assessments across Europe. Selected countries of the WHO European Region have volunteered to pilot test the proposed indicator system.

Outcomes
When established, the system should:
• enable tracking of progress in environmental health across Europe;
• provide countries with appropriate environmental health information to make comparisons and support their national policies;
• contribute to the broader objective of reporting on sustainable development.

A proposal for a comprehensive system of environmental health indicators linked with assessment and reporting mechanisms will be prepared for endorsement by ministers of environment and health at the Fourth Ministerial Conference on Environment and Health in Budapest, 2004, for implementation in the WHO European Region.

Source: http://www.euro.who.int/EHindicators

and water pollutants where the cause-and-effect relationships are quite well established;

- increase awareness of the multi-causality of many diseases, where multi-exposures of pollutants and lifestyles also play an important role;
- inform on the multiple impacts of large-scale environmental problems, e.g. climate change and wastes, where the impacts on health are complex, often delayed, and are the product of many, perhaps small, environmental factors acting together;
- describe the environment/health risks of one vulnerable group: children.

12.2. Environmental health problems — an overview

Childhood and maternal underweight, unsafe sex, high blood pressure, high cholesterol, unsafe water sanitation and hygiene, indoor smoke from solid fuels, tobacco and alcohol are the leading causes of the global burden of disease. It is estimated that 25–33 % of such disease is attributable to environmental factors (WHO, 2002) though this varies considerably between regions of the world (Lancet, 2002), with 'lifestyle' factors such as tobacco, high blood pressure alcohol, high cholesterol and physical inactivity dominating the developed regions. Europe is predominantly developed but with some parts, particularly in some areas of EECCA, having features common to developing countries.

Attributing environmental risk factors to the total disease and lack of well being burden in Europe is extremely difficult because of scientific uncertainty and poor data, but it could be between 2–20 % or more, varying from 100 % for some diseases such as lead poisoning to 2 % for waterborne diseases.

Everyone is vulnerable to environmental impacts but the ability of people and societies to adapt and cope is very varied. Vulnerability is not equally spread, and some groups (e.g. poor people, children, women, old people) are at greatest risk.

This section is limited to a selection of those environmental stressors which people may be exposed to indoors or outside. It does not cover occupational impacts on health in any detail, for reasons of space, focus and time. A more comprehensive and integrated environment and human health paper will be prepared for the World Health Organization (WHO) Ministerial Conference on Environment and Health 2004. Reflecting, in this context, the important contribution of transport to environmental health issues, the Transport, Health and Environment Pan-European Programme was launched three years ago to streamline existing activities and make progress towards transport patterns that are sustainable for both health and the environment (see Box 12.2).

12.2.1. Health effects of pollutants
Three major groups of air pollutants are of primary health importance in relation to outdoor air quality: particulate matter (PM), ozone and heavy metals (see Chapters 4 and 5).

Particulate matter
There have been several studies on morbidity and mortality from respiratory or cardiovascular diseases resulting from exposure to PM.

PM covers a highly correlated mixture of primary pollutants such as black smoke, nitrogen oxides (NO_x), sulphur dioxide (SO_2) and carbon monoxide (CO). Association of health outcomes with concentration of suspended PM is best established for respirable or inhalable particles (PM_{10} or PM_{25}). However, data from routine monitoring of PM_{10} is available from a limited proportion of cities, and even fewer regularly collect data on PM_{25} (see Chapter 5, Section 5.3.2). Therefore, data for total suspended matter or black smoke were alternatively used for estimation of health impacts, using the risk coefficients obtained in studies based on the same exposure matrix to calculate an annual average PM_{10}. The resulting population exposure is presented in Figure 12.2, which shows that more than half of the population of cities participating in the latest WHO survey are exposed to PM_{10} levels higher than the target limit value of 40 µg/m³ in the EU accession countries, while the exceedance is estimated at only 14 % of the population in EU cities.

An estimate of mortality due to long-term exposure, assuming that the risk of mortality increases linearly with annual concentrations of PM, showed (WHO, 2001a) that around 60 000 deaths per year may be associated with the long-term exposure to particulate air pollution exceeding the level equivalent to PM_{10} = 5 µg/m³ in the 124 cities with PM data. If this number is extrapolated to the whole urban population of Europe, the number of deaths is four times greater (i.e. about 240 000), and since life is shortened, on average, by at least a year in each of the cases, this contributes significantly to the burden of disease in Europe.

The proportion of mortality associated with PM is greater in cities in the accession countries than in the EU cities. Exceedances of the 2001 target limit value of 40 µg/m³ account for about 1 % of mortality due to natural causes in EU cities, and 5 % in the EU accession countries (WHO, 2002a).

For example in 2000 the monthly average concentration of particulate matter in the air exceeded the environmental safety standard in 23 Ukrainian cities. Only 15.3 % of the population in Ukraine lives in settlements with low air pollution. 52.8 % with considerable air pollution, 24.3 % with high air pollution and 7.6 % with very high air pollution.

Studies have also been performed on the relationship between exposure to PM and respiratory or cardiovascular diseases leading to admission to a hospital. In the 91 cities with daily average PM_{10} data included in the analysis, the daily variations in PM levels above 10 µg/m³ were associated with nearly 6 700 admissions for respiratory diseases and 2 600 admissions for cardiovascular diseases per year. If the PM pollution is assumed to be similar in other cities of the EU, then the number of hospitalisations associated with the daily increases of PM levels would amount to 47 000 per year, the incidence rate being markedly higher in the accession countries than in the EU.

There are no air quality monitoring data from EECCA that allow reliable health impact assessment for these countries. However, the scarce and not very precise information available indicates that urban air pollution levels in large cities of the region are higher than in the western parts of Europe (see Chapter 5, Box 5.3), so the health impacts may be expected to be significant. The situation highlights the need for improvement of assessment capacities, as a necessary part of air quality improvement programmes.

There is an uncertainty factor of at least two in these estimates and calculations, which also take no account of whether the sources are local or long range. In many populated areas, particularly where there are no heavily

Box 12.2. Transport, environment and health

Transport is the dominant source of air pollution in urban areas, with a large part of the urban population still being exposed to excesses of ambient quality levels for one or more pollutants (particulate matter — PM, nitrogen dioxide, benzene and ozone) (EEA, 2002). Current levels of air pollutants, including PM, in Europe have a major impact on mortality (see Section 12.2.1). Traffic-related air pollution is estimated to account, each year, for more than 25 000 new cases of chronic bronchitis in adults, more than 290 000 episodes of bronchitis in children, more than 0.5 million asthma attacks, and more than 16 million person-days of restricted activity (Dora and Racioppi, 2001).

Despite some improvements in recent years, traffic accidents still cause approximately 120 000 deaths and 2.5 million injuries per year in Europe (Dora and Racioppi, 2001; ECMT, 2002). Figure 12.1 generally shows a decrease in mortality caused by road traffic accidents, probably due to a reduction in their severity, resulting from improvements in the safety of vehicles and road infrastructures and progress in the treatment of trauma. Although the death rate in the 12 countries of eastern Europe, the Caucasus and central Asia (EECCA) has fallen considerably since 1991, it is still about 1.5 times higher than in the EU. In the EU, the death rate in the worst-performing country (Greece) is about four times that in the best-performing one (Sweden).

Deaths caused by road traffic accidents	Figure 12.1.

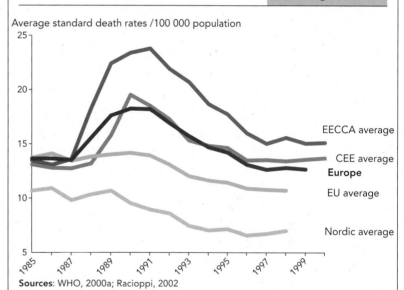

Average standard death rates /100 000 population

Sources: WHO, 2000a; Racioppi, 2002

The annual number of accidents causing injuries has been more constant, with a slightly increasing trend since 1993, possibly as a result of a reduction in the severity of accidents, consistent with the reduction in death rates (WHO, 2000a; Racioppi, 2002).

Speed and alcohol are the two major causes of road traffic accidents. A 1.6 km/hour reduction in average speed is linked with approximately a 5 % reduction in accidents and injuries of all severities. Alcohol is involved in about 15–20 % of traffic accidents in Europe. One in four deaths of young men in the age group 15–29 is related to alcohol, with crashes accounting for a large portion of these premature deaths. In parts of eastern Europe the figure is as high as one in three, as highlighted at the WHO European Ministerial Conference on Young People and Alcohol (Stockholm, 19 February 2001).

Pedestrians and cyclists are particularly vulnerable, accounting for about 20 % of those involved in serious road accidents in the European Region. This appears to play a major role in discouraging cycling and walking as a transport mode, which is most regrettable since these modes are good for the health. This stresses the desirability of providing appropriate and safe conditions for walking and cycling.

Road traffic is the predominant source of human exposure to noise, except for people living near airports and railway lines. Around 65 % of the people in Europe, about 450 million, are exposed to noise levels leading to serious annoyance, speech interference and sleep disturbance (Dora and Racioppi, 2001).

Other effects of traffic that may impact on human health include aggression and nervousness, reduced community contacts and constraints on child development.

Sources: WHO, 2000a; Racioppi, 2002

Figure 12.2.	Population exposure to estimated PM₁₀ levels in 124 European cities

Source: WHO, 2001a

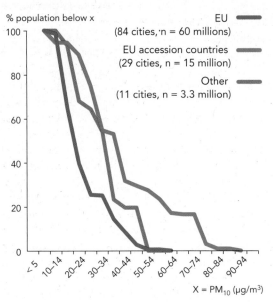

polluting local sources of particulate matter, as much as 40–60 % of PM₁₀ levels may be attributable to long-range transport, which is therefore a substantial contributor to the total exposure of the European population to airborne particulates (WHO, 2002a).

Ozone
Ground-level ozone and other photochemical oxidants are formed in the lower atmosphere by reactions of volatile organic compounds and nitrogen oxides in the presence of sunlight. Ozone can be transported over long distances and is therefore a regional air pollution problem causing damage to crops, etc. (see Chapter 5). High concentrations of ozone in the troposphere, typical for the summer months, lead to an increase in the frequency of respiratory symptoms; nearly 1 000 emergency hospital admissions and more than 2 000 premature deaths per year can be attributed to this pollution in the EU countries (WHO, 2002a).

Heavy metals
Heavy metals such as cadmium, lead and mercury are common air pollutants and are emitted predominantly into air as result of various industrial activities (see Chapters 5 and 6). Their long-range transboundary effects have been assessed in a number of studies (WHO, 2002b).

Lead and its compounds may enter the environment at any point during its mining, smelting, processing, use, recycling or disposal. Children are the critical population for environmental lead exposure which may influence cognitive functions as well as the central nervous system. The influence may occur when living in close proximity to point sources of emission, by exposure to lead paint flakes or lead-contaminated soil; long-range transport of lead is assumed to contribute about 0.03 % to the actual lead content in the topsoil layer and therefore does not influence the lead content of food to any significant degree. A persisting, local problem is exposure to lead from its continued use in transport fuels in several countries in the eastern part of the region, in spite of commitments made by ministers of transport and environment at the Vienna Regional Conference on Transport and Environment (Vienna, November 1997) to phase out leaded gasoline.

12.2.2. Water and sanitation
Worldwide, insufficient water quality and supply, sanitation and hygiene are believed to be the second biggest cause, after malnutrition, of loss of potentially healthy years of life due to death and illness. The measure used is disability adjusted life years (DALY).

Drinking-water related infections
A number of serious infectious diseases, such as hepatitis A, cholera and typhoid fever, can be spread via contaminated drinking water, as can more common intestinal diseases such as gastroenteritis. It is estimated that there are about 4 billion cases worldwide of diarrhoea per year, resulting in 2.2 million deaths (WHO, 2002a).

Table 12.1 provides the latest information available from 17 European countries on possible waterborne diseases in the period 1986–96. Only 2 % of the cases caused by bacteria, viruses and parasites are reported as being linked to drinking water (WHO, 2002c). However, a number of confounding factors (e.g. social conditions, immunity, reporting and assessments) make the estimates unreliable. Flooding also contribute to waterborne diseases; in Ukraine, in 1998, during the floods in Trans-Carpathian region the rate of the typhoid fever sickness exceeded the average indicator (0.28 cases per 100 000 inhabitants) in the country with 6.83 cases per 100 000 inhabitants (Ukraine NCP, 2002).

A recent study compared the under-five mortality rate from diarrhoeal diseases per

100 000 in European countries with the United National Development Programme (UNDP) human development index (HDI) and World Bank income groupings. It reported markedly higher mortality in people with lower middle/low income in countries with medium level of development than in other population groups (Figure 12.3). The relationship seems to be applicable for the whole decade 1991–2000, but there has been considerable improvement for the two groups since 1993.

A similar relationship between European countries with a medium HDI and people with a lower middle/low income was found with regard to incidences of viral hepatitis A per 100 000, but with less improvement during the 1990s (Figure 12.4). Lower middle income was also a strong determinant of the incidence in countries with high HDI until 1998.

Compliance with drinking-water standards
WHO guidelines for drinking-water quality recommend that indicators of faecal contamination (Escherichia coli (E. coli) or thermo-tolerant coliform bacteria) should not be detectable in any 100 ml sample of water intended for drinking, water entering the distribution system, or water within the distribution system. An overview of results is given in Figure 12.5.

It is not possible from the material available to establish a direct relation between exceedances of standards and occurrence of drinking-water related diseases, but, generally speaking, the higher the exceedance, in each case and relatively (i.e. percentage of all samples exceeding standards), the higher the risk of drinking-water related diseases.

Chemicals and drinking-water quality
WHO has established guideline values for more than 100 chemicals in drinking water, all being of health concern. However, in European countries only a few are important for routine monitoring purposes: lead, arsenic, fluoride, nitrate/nitrite and pesticides. Only nitrate/nitrite and pesticides will be dealt with here since they are the ones that most frequently give rise to health concerns.

High concentrations of nitrate in drinking water are of concern because nitrate can be reduced to nitrite, which can cause methaemoglobinaemia, a disease especially dangerous in babies (blue baby syndrome).

Reported cases of gastrointestinal or other possibly waterborne diseases and cases of these diseases linked to drinking water in 17 European countries, 1986–96		Table 12.1.

Causative agent diseases	Total number of cases reported	Number of cases and linked to drinking water
Bacteria: bacterial dysentery, cholera, typhoid fever and others	534 732 (20.8 %)	15 167 (2.8 %)
Viruses: hepatitis A and Norwalk-like virus	343 305 (13.4 %)	6 869 (2.0 %)
Parasites: amoebic dysentery, amoebic meningoencephalitis, cryptosporidiosis and giardiasis	220 581 (8.6 %)	4 568 (2.1 %)
Chemicals: dental/skeletal flourosis and methaemoglobinaemia	7 421 (0.3 %)	2 802 (37.8 %)
Unspecified cause: gastroenteritis and severe diarrhoea	1 461 171 (56.9 %)	22 898 (1.6 %)
Total	**2 576 210 (100 %)**	**52 304 (2.0 %)**

Notes: Countries included are Andorra, Austria, Croatia, Czech Republic, England and Wales, Estonia, Germany, Hungary, Latvia, Lithuania, Malta, Norway, Republic of Moldova, Romania, Slovakia, Slovenia and Sweden. On average, the countries had data available for 7 of the 12 diseases (range 3–10). Other bacterial agents include: Aeromonas, Campylobacter and Salmonella spp.

Source: WHO, 2002b

Under five mortality rate from diarrhoeal diseases per 100 000	Figure 12.3.

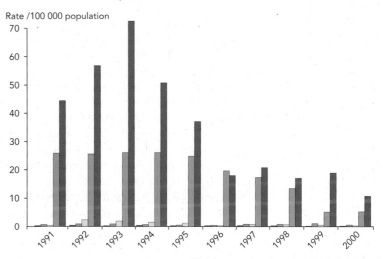

Rate /100 000 population

High human development & High income ■
High human development & Upper middle income ■
High human development & Lower middle income □
Medium human development & Lower middle income ■
Medium human development & Low income ■

Source: WHO, 2002a

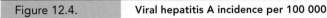

Figure 12.4. | Viral hepatitis A incidence per 100 000

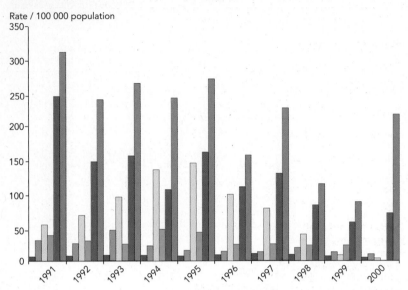

Rate / 100 000 population

■ High human development & High income
■ High human development & Upper middle income
□ High human development & Lower middle income
■ Medium human development & Upper middle income
■ Medium human development & Lower middle income
■ Medium human development & Low income

Source: WHO, 2002a

guidelines for pesticides and the general incidence of morbidity or mortality has been established, possibly because the safety margin built into EU standards/WHO guidelines is considerable, and because of the scarcity of appropriate studies.

However, over the past 10 years UK industry has spent more than USD 1.5 billion on capital expenditure, and an additional USD 150 million per year on running costs, to remove residues from drinking water. This is not sustainable over the long term as pesticide removal is an energy and resource-intensive process. It would be better if the money spent on removing pesticides from drinking water were diverted to developing non-chemical alternatives, where that is feasible (Pesticide Action Network (UK), 2002).

Water supply, coverage, discontinuity
The percentage of the total population served by piped water supply in Europe mostly varies between 50 % and 100 %, with over or well over 90 % in many countries. The proportion of the population connected can vary significantly between different areas of the same country. For example, 78 % of the population in the northeastern part of Italy is connected to a public supply, compared with only 27 % in the Italian islands. The rural population, which in many countries accounts for around 50 % of the total population, is the worst supplied. Only in a few countries (e.g. Iceland, Norway, Denmark) is all of the rural population connected to a home water supply, while in Republic of Moldova and Ukraine 18 % and 25 % respectively enjoy the same facility (see Box 12.3). The situation in EECCA has not improved over the past decade. On the contrary, many of the supply systems, especially in rural areas, broke down during the first half of the 1990s due to lack of economic resources for repair and maintenance, and are now beyond rehabilitation. In these areas people rely on local, often individual, water sources and latrines, a situation which frequently causes a health hazard because of the short distance between drinking-water intake and a possible source of faecal contamination.

Discontinuity of supply, especially when combined with severe leaks in supply pipelines, also affects drinking-water quality and thus health. Problems in providing the population with continuous supply vary from non-existent in some countries to being of major importance in some eastern European

Progressive symptoms are stupor, coma and, in some cases, death.

Analysis of methaemoglobinaemia-related data has been made in several countries (Figure 12.6). For instance, in Romania between 1985 and 1996, 2 913 cases were recorded of which 102 were fatal. The severest conditions prevail when drinking water is contaminated microbially and with high concentrations of nitrate (maybe up to 1 000 mg/l) at the same time.

Water resources located in intensively farmed agricultural land are liable to be contaminated by nitrate (see Chapter 8). Consequently the rural population is at highest risk. Some countries in Europe consider contamination by pesticides to be among their major problems with drinking-water quality. A number of reports on exceedances of standards (for EU countries) and/or WHO guidelines exist, some of the exceedances being quite severe and frequent. For example, 12.3 % of drinking-water samples tested in 1995 in England and Wales exceeded the national standard for isoproturon of 0.1 µg/l. Nevertheless, the significance of concentrations exceeding EU standards or WHO guidelines for human health is unclear. No association between exceedances of EU standards or WHO

countries and EECCA, mostly due to economic difficulties, lack of maintenance, or interruptions in power supplies. In many towns in these countries, the population only has water supply during a few hours per day and water pressure is often only sufficient to reach the lowest two to four floors of apartment buildings. People are often tempted to leave their taps open in order to collect a few buckets of water when it comes, which, although understandable from an individual point of view, causes much water loss.

Consumption and leaks
The big differences in drinking-water consumption patterns between western and eastern Europe are probably the result of discontinuity of supply and leaks. Other reasons for low water use efficiency may be low water prices and lack of awareness-raising campaigns. While 150–300 l/person/day seems to be the norm in western Europe (WE), 400–600 l/person/day is found quite frequently in some towns of eastern Europe and EECCA. In addition to the waste of resources, this also adds to the economic difficulties of public utilities in these countries. Water abstraction, treatment and pumping are quite expensive. From a health point of view this money could be better used to repair leaks and ensure continuity of supply. This should be considered a priority area of effort for most eastern European and all EECCA countries.

Leaks are not only a question of waste of resources; they also affect health as they serve as entry points for contaminants. The more leaks, the more the health hazard, especially if leaks are associated with discontinuity of supply as vacuum in the pipes will then easily occur. Losses vary from country to country and within the same country (Table 12.2). Leaks cannot be totally avoided, and poor metering and monitoring in some countries make accurate estimates difficult. However, 10 % or less loss through leaks would be a good benchmark.

Sanitation, coverage
The global coverage of sanitation by world region in 2000 has been estimated in WHO, 2001b. The sanitation situation in European urban areas is comparable to those in North America and Oceania (nearly 100 % coverage), while the situation in European rural areas (about 70 % coverage) is worse than in North America and Oceania (80 % upwards). The percentage coverage is barely increasing with time. In this estimate

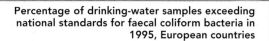

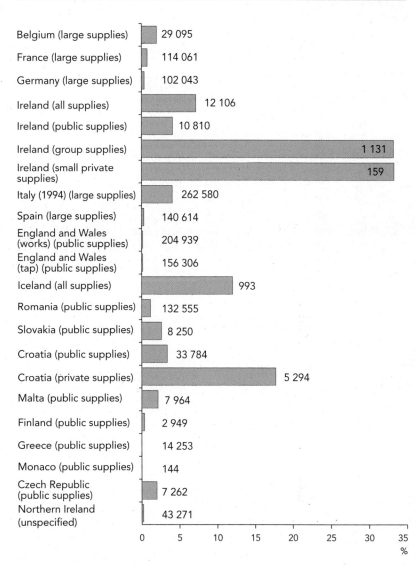

Note: Numbers give the number of samplings
Source: WHO, 2002a

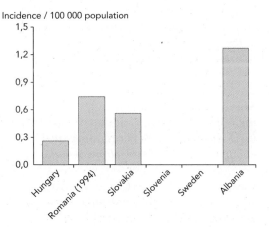

Note: Records for methaemoglobinaemia in Romania are for cases related to well water only.

Source: WHO, 2002b

Box 12.3. Health water-related issues in the Republic of Moldova

In the Republic of Moldova the most commonly reported infectious diseases are viral hepatitis A and acute intestinal diseases, 15-18 % of which are transmitted via drinking water. From the non-infectious diseases the most commonly reported is fluorosis, which is directly related to the use of water with high concentration of fluorine; 100 000 cases of fluorosis were reported among the population from around 70 settlements in the country.

The centralised water supply serves 55 % of the population. The rural population (54 % of the total population) uses 90–95 % of well water and only 5–10 % of tap water, though 18 % are connected to the centralised water supply while 82 % and 18 % of the urban population is served with centralized water supply and wells respectively. The water is supplied with breaks from 8 to 16 hours per day, with the exception of Chisinau. In the country, the average water consumption does not exceed 30 l/person/day in rural settlements and 50–70 l/person/day in urban settlements. In Chisinau and Balti the water consumption is 130–140 l/person/day. At present 42 % of the population is connected to a sewage system (68 % and 9 % of the urban and rural population respectively).

According to the State Sanitary Service drinking water is extracted for 70 % from groundwater and for 30 % from surface water. More than 50 % of the population do not have access to drinking water of good quality; the worst situation is in the southern part of the country. 49 % of the centralized reservoirs of drinking water, 83 % of the non-centralized reservoirs and 39 % of the surface reservoirs used by population show a non-compliance with the health standards. For wells the major problem is due to high nitrate concentrations — 74 % of the samples.

Another major problem is the microbial pollution of the water sources. Among the samples showing a non-compliance with the health standards, 14 % are from groundwater, 32.3 % from wells and for surface water 62 % from the Dniester river and 23 % from the Prut river.

Regarding bathing waters, an intensive bacteriological pollution is reported. Coliform lacto-positive bacteria was reported for more than 240 000 cases. From 37 recreational places only 2 correspond to the sanitation and hygiene standards.

Source: Republic of Moldova NCP, 2002

'sanitation' is understood as any kind of disposal facility, on or off site. It does not necessarily mean that a sewerage system is available. No assessment of sanitation coverage in European subregions is available.

The linkage between water supply, sanitation, hygiene and health is important. In a household without tap water it is difficult to make a flushing toilet work properly, if at all, and it is a demanding exercise to keep personal hygiene, the cleanliness of the dwelling and clothes at a satisfactory level. Hygiene, well-being, and consequently health, are at serious risk

Recreational water
Recreational water environments have a diverse range of hazards to human health. These include factors associated with microbial pollution, accidents, exposure to toxic algae products, occasional exposure to chemical pollution and sunburn.

Clear evidence indicates that exposure to faecal pollution when bathing leads to health effects. Gastroenteritis is the most

frequently reported adverse health outcome investigated, and evidence suggests a causal relationship between increasing recreational exposure to faecal contamination and frequency of gastroenteritis. There is also reason to believe that other severe infectious diseases such as typhoid fever and viral diseases such as hepatitis A and E may be transmitted to susceptible bathers who make recreational use of polluted water.

Monitoring for compliance with EU and national standards or WHO guidelines has been used for a number of decades as a tool to ensure bathing water quality that is not likely to cause harm to health (see Chapter 8). Compliance in EU countries is increasing slightly for seawater bathing points, while a considerable improvement has been noted for freshwater bathing points in the period 1993 (30 % of sites complying) to 1997 (80 % of sites) (WHO, 1999b). Results in five non-EU countries are similar (WHO, 2002c), but data are too few and sporadic for a comprehensive assessment of the situation in non-EU countries.

Like any kind of compliance monitoring, bathing water quality monitoring always gives a retrospective picture of the situation. Efforts are therefore being made to develop another approach to classifying beaches for health risk by combining a measure of faecal contamination with an inspection-based assessment of the susceptibility of an area to direct influence from human faecal contamination (WHO, 2002c).

An overview of mortality rates from accidental drowning and submersion per 10 000 population in 38 European countries in 1994 is given in WHO, 2002a. Data suggest that males are more likely to drown (range: 0.08 per 10 000 population for the United Kingdom to 3.77 for Latvia) than females (range: 0.02 for the United Kingdom to 0.55 for Lithuania), but it is not clear whether this is because more males swim. Greater alcohol consumption by men is also a contributing factor, as are heart attacks, sea currents and surf.

In terms of all accidental deaths in the European Region, drowning accounts for less than 10 % of the 280 000 deaths due to accidents.

While discussions of the health hazards associated with recreational use of bathing water and beaches have concentrated on compliance with bathing water quality standards and the data on drowning/ submersion), other health hazards like incidental cuts (sharp stones, metal and glass pieces, needles, urchins) and sunburn that can lead or contribute to development of skin cancer may be more important in terms of morbidity and mortality.

12.2.3. Food-borne diseases

Food-borne diseases caused by microbial hazards are a growing public health problem. The WHO Programme for Surveillance of Food-borne Diseases in Europe has been collecting official information from the Member States of the WHO European Region for the past 20 years. Most countries with systems for reporting food-borne diseases have documented significant increase during that period in the incidence of diseases caused by micro-organisms in food including *Salmonella* (Figure 12.7) and *Campylobacter*. New hazards have emerged in the food chain such as enterohaemorrhagic *E. coli*, multi-drug-resistant *Salmonella typhimurium* DT-104 and bovine spongiform encephalopathy (BSE). Variant Creutzfeldt-Jacob disease, with 105 deaths reported in Europe, is strongly linked to exposure to BSE.

The possible hazards to human health from genetically modified foods (see for example Advisory Committee on Novel Foods and Processes, 1994; Royal Society, 1998) include: new allergens being formed through the inclusion of novel proteins which trigger allergic reactions at some stage; antibiotic resistance genes used as 'markers' in the genetically modified (GM) food being transferred to gut micro-organisms and intensifying problems with antibiotic-resistant pathogens; and the creation of new toxins through unexpected interactions between the product of the GM and other constituents.

Estimated losses from water networks in selected European countries, mid-1990s	Table 12.2.

Country	Comments/observations
Albania	Up to 75 %
Armenia	50–55 %
Bulgaria	Sofia 30–40 % Other than Sofia — more than 60 %
Croatia	30–60 %
Czech Republic	33 %
France	National average (1990) 30 % Paris 15 % Highly rural areas 32 %
Germany (former West Germany)	3 700 l/km of mains pipe per day 112 litres per property per day
Hungary	30–40 %
Italy	National average 15 % Rome 31 % Bari 30 %
Kyrgyzstan	20–35 %
Republic of Moldova	40–60 %
Romania	21–40 %
Slovakia	27 %
Spain	20 % Bilbao 40 % Madrid
Ukraine	30–50 %
United Kingdom (England and Wales)	8 400 l/km/day of mains pipe 243 litres per property per day

Sources: Mountain Unlimited, 1995 and 1997; Water Research Centre, 1997; Istituto di Ricerca sulle Acque, 1996; WHO, 2002a

Incidence of salmonellosis in selected European countries, 1995–98	Figure 12.7.

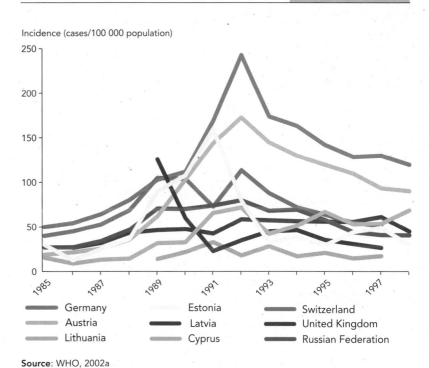

Incidence (cases/100 000 population)

Germany — Austria — Lithuania — Estonia — Latvia — Cyprus — Switzerland — United Kingdom — Russian Federation

Source: WHO, 2002a

12.2.4. Ionising radiation

It is generally (and cautiously) assumed that the effect of radiation on health is proportional to the dose received. Exposure of the European population to ionising radiation, as in the rest of the world, is almost entirely from natural sources (about 94 % on average), with about 6 % from medical exposures and about 0.1 % from man-made sources. Nuclear power accounts for about 0.02 % of the total (see also Chapter 10, Table 10.3, which, however, excludes natural sources).

Exposure to radiation from natural sources can be quite significant in terms of the health burden in some populations. For example, radon in the domestic environment can give rise to annual doses that exceed the International Commission on Radiological Protection (ICRP) dose limit for occupational exposure. A small proportion of the population in countries such as Finland, Sweden and the United Kingdom receive considerably higher than average doses, causing several thousands lung cancers in Europe.

Routine releases of radioactive material from nuclear installations to the marine environment have fallen significantly since the 1970s. In 1996 atmospheric discharges accounted for 88 % of the total collective dose from nuclear installations, with power stations contributing half the collective dose. The reprocessing plants at Cap la Hague and Sellafield have provided the largest

contribution to collective dose. Individual doses near nuclear sites were all below the relevant dose limit set by ICRP. Improvements to the transparency and availability of radiation exposures and doses have recently been proposed (Spira et al, 2002).

Few releases of ionising radiation have been reported as a result of accidents at nuclear power plants or the testing and disposal of weapons (see Chapter 10, Section 10.3.1). The Chernobyl accident is so far the only nuclear accident to be assigned a 7 on the INES (international nuclear event scale) scale (see Chapter 10, Figure 10.8), with significant health consequences, besides its psychological effects.

Almost immediately, serious health effects were seen from the Chernobyl accident. Of the 600 workers present at the plant when the accident took place, 134 received high doses (0.7–13.4 Gy) and suffered from radiation illness. Among those, 28 died during the first three months following the accident and 2 more soon after. About 200 000 recovery operation workers received doses of between 0.01 and 0.5 Gy between 1986 and 1987. This group is at potential risk for late consequences and is being followed closely (UNSCEAR, 2000).

The population in the affected territories has since 1986 been subjected to both external and internal exposure to radiation from the deposited radionuclides, which has gradually decreased with time. Bioaccumulation in the food chain has contributed significantly to the internal exposures. Contaminated vegetation led to contamination of dairy and meat products of animals that were grazing in areas affected by atmospheric fallout. There are still a number of indigenous populations in northern Europe and the Arctic, many of which subsist on a diet that includes natural food products (reindeer meat, fish, berries and mushrooms), which were all found to have high radio-caesium contents post-Chernobyl.

Among the individuals exposed in childhood, especially in the most severely contaminated areas in Ukraine, Belarus and the Russian Federation, about 1 800 cases of thyroid cancer had been found by 1999. This is an increase in the numbers found by WHO in 1995 (see Chapter 10), and additional cases are to be expected, especially among those exposed at a young age. In Ukraine, on the basis of yearly checking, the number of healthy children is decreasing. Among the

| Figure 12.8. | Thyroid gland cancer of population from different regions in Ukraine |

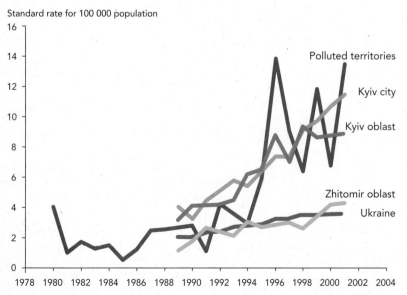

Standard rate for 100 000 population

Source: Anon, 2002

children reported as affected by the Chernobyl accident, 59.3 % were reported as being healthy in 1987 and 23.9 % in 2000. The number of children (among the children affected by the accident) with malignant new growths in 1993–2000 has increased by 55 %, and in particular the number of children with malignant tumours of the thyroid gland has increased by 28 %. The increase in thyroid cancer now appears to affect the general population of the Ukraine, though increases in general tumour rates are usually due to a combination of factors (see Figure 12.8) (Anon, 2002).

However, the conclusions of the Third International Conference on the Health Effects of the Chernobyl Accident, held in Kiev in June 2001 (UNSCEAR, 2001) on these issues were:

- 'There is no doubt that the incidence of thyroid cancer has substantially increased in children who were 0-18 years old at the time of the accident and that this is related to radiation from the accident. An increased number of cases of thyroid cancer among liquidators who worked in 1986 is expected to occur.
- There is no significant increase in leukaemia in adults or children living on contaminated territories of the three affected countries.
- While there has been increased incidence of solid tumours, there is little significant and/or consistent evidence of a radiation-related increase in clean-up workers, evacuees, or residents of contaminated areas in the three affected countries.'

On other health effects, UNSCEAR, 2001 concluded:

'At 15 years after the accident other types of health effects seem to have emerged. These are primarily neuropsychiatric and cardiovascular diseases, but also include: deteriorating health of liquidators, increased invalidity among liquidators, decreasing birth rate, diminishing health of new-borns, increased pregnancy complications, impaired health of children.

A number of factors inherent to the Chernobyl accident, including worsening socio-economic conditions, continuing residence in contaminated territories, diminishing food supply, vitamin deficiency, relocation, and psychological stress, may contribute to these effects.'

The conference made a number of recommendations for further collaborative studies.

Better monitoring and preparedness was another consequence of the accident. A large number of monitoring stations and automated alarm networks were established throughout Europe. For example, 92 stations were established in the United Kingdom as part of the RIMNET, the radioactive incident monitoring network, which was set up by the UK Government in response to the accident, to enable the country to be better prepared should a similar event occur in the future.

12.2.5. Electromagnetic fields

Electromagnetic fields (EMF) can be broadly divided into static and low-frequency electric and magnetic fields (ELF), where the common sources include power lines, household electrical appliances and computers, and high-frequency or radio-frequency fields (RF), for which the main sources are radar, radio and television broadcast facilities, mobile telephones and their base stations, induction heaters and anti-theft devices. Exposure to the public to EMF is large and increasing, so even small health impacts could be of significant public health interest.

Complying with exposure limits recommended in national and international guidelines helps to control risks from exposures to EMFs that may be harmful to human health. However, long-term, low-level exposure below the exposure limits may cause adverse health effects via 'chronic' impacts, or otherwise influence people's well-being.

Scientific knowledge about the health effects of ELF is substantial and is based on a large number of epidemiological, animal and in-vitro studies (WHO, 2002d). Many health outcomes ranging from reproductive defects to cardiovascular and neuro-degenerative diseases have been examined, but the most consistent evidence to date concerns childhood leukaemia.

In 2001, an expert scientific working group of WHO's International Agency for Research on Cancer (IARC) reviewed studies related to the carcinogenicity of static and extremely low frequency (ELF) electric and magnetic fields. Using the standard IARC classification that weighs human, animal and laboratory evidence, ELF magnetic fields were classified as 'possibly carcinogenic to humans' on the basis of epidemiological studies of childhood leukaemia, which showed, on average, a 2 fold excess of leukaemia associated with living near power lines.

The IARC 'strength of evidence' for this risk is half way between the strongest categories ('a human carcinogen', or a 'probable carcinogen') and the weakest ('insufficient evidence' and 'probably not a carcinogen') in their 5 categories. It is possible that there are other explanations for the observed association between exposure to ELF and childhood leukaemia, and the extent of the hazard, if true, appears to be small. Sweden, for example, estimates less than one extra leukaemia case in children per year from overhead power lines (Socialstyrelsen, 2002). Options for reducing exposures to ELF from power lines varies from low to very high cost options (California Dept of Health, 2002).

Currently, research efforts are concentrated on whether long-term, low level radio-frequency exposure, even at levels too low to cause significant temperature rise, can cause adverse health effects. Several recent epidemiological studies of mobile phone users found no convincing evidence of increased brain cancer risk. However, the technology is too recent to rule out possible long-term effects. Mobile phone handsets and base stations present quite different exposure situations. Radio-frequency exposure is far higher for mobile phone users than for those living near cellular base stations. Apart from the infrequent signals used to maintain links with nearby base stations, handsets transmit radio-frequency energy only while a call is being made. However, base stations are continuously transmitting signals, although the levels to which the public are exposed are extremely small, even if they live nearby. Given the widespread use of the technology, the degree of scientific uncertainty and the levels of public apprehension, more research, clear communications with the public and exposure reductions in line with the precautionary principle, especially for children (Stewart, 2000), are needed. Some European countries have taken exposure reduction steps e.g. Italy, Switzerland, Belgium and parts of Austria. Exposure reduction measures need to address total exposures to RF from base stations mobile phones and other RF sources. Network infrastructure sharing by phone operators is one of the Stewart Report recommendations that could reduce both exposures and public concern.

12.3. Multi-causality and multi-exposure, and the importance of timing

Fully integrated approaches to health would include, among all stressors, environment-related stressors. This is not only because human lungs and livers do not discriminate between pollutants that come from the factory or the street. Exposures to stressors from all sources may be additive, synergistic (more than the sum of the parts) or antagonistic (less than the sum of the parts), and therefore need to be included in any integrated assessment of environmental health risks.

12.3.1. Chemicals, with a focus on endocrine-disrupting substances

Chemicals, whether anthropogenic, from different points along the life cycle of a product or in foods, or naturally present in the environment at high concentrations, can have many different health effects. The trends in health effects from chemicals are difficult to gauge, although many scientific papers on their potential hazards to human health have been published during recent decades. Knowledge of causal factors and the chemical pollutants that may contribute to human health effects, including the sensitive groups, is summarised in Table 12.3.

Increased incidences of testicular cancer and breast cancer, as well as a decline in the quality of sperm, have been observed in several countries. The causes of these trends are largely unknown; exposure to chemicals may be responsible (the endocrine-disrupter hypothesis), but so may changes in lifestyle.

Pesticides are the most common cause of acute and sub-chronic poisoning. The main reason for this is not only the amount of pesticides used in comparison with other chemicals, but also their high toxicity, their use by non-professionals, and inappropriate storage.

Scientific evidence and information concerning actual exposures to chemical substances and their possible health effects is lacking in most European countries. Lack of data for health impact assessment poses a big problem. Indeed, there has been little progress since Europe's environment: *The second assessment* (EEA, 1998).

The past two decades have witnessed growing scientific concern and public debate over the potential adverse effects that may result from exposure to a group of chemicals that are able to alter the normal functioning of the endocrine system in humans and wildlife, endocrine-disrupting substances (EDS). These concerns emanate primarily from adverse effects in certain wildlife, fish and ecosystems, the increased incidence of certain endocrine-related human diseases, and endocrine disruption resulting from exposure to certain environmental chemicals observed in laboratory experimental animals.

The International Programme on Chemical Safety has performed a global assessment of the current state of the science relative to environmental endocrine disruption in humans and wildlife (Table 12.4). Generally, studies examining EDS-induced effects in humans have yielded inconsistent and inconclusive results, which is the reason for the overall data being classified as 'weak'. This highlights the need for more rigorous studies. Most evidence showing that humans are susceptible to EDS is provided by studies of high exposure levels. The effects of chronic, low levels of EDS are much more obscure. In particular, the relationship between early-life exposures to EDS in humans and functioning in adult life is poorly understood.

Compared with humans, the evidence that wildlife has been adversely affected by exposures to EDS is extensive. In part, this may reflect the fact that many studies on wildlife have been conducted in areas where the levels of environmental chemicals are known to be high (e.g. point source discharges in the Baltic and the Great Lakes). These studies have focused predominantly on animals inhabiting aquatic ecosystems, which bioaccumulate certain EDS, and represent one of the largest sinks of environmental chemicals that may act as EDS.

Given the dynamic nature of the endocrine system, future efforts in the study of EDS need more focus on the timing, frequency and duration of exposure to these chemicals.

12.3.2. Allergies and asthma

Outdoor air pollution plays a role in the aggravation, and possible the causation of asthma and allergic responses, which are increasingly prevalent diseases, especially in children. Outdoor air pollution penetrates indoors, which makes it necessary to have an integrated approach to both outdoor and indoor air pollution. Other key components of indoor pollution which have been associated with respiratory and allergic

Major health impacts and some associations with environmental exposures to chemicals	Table 12.3.

Health impact	Associations with some environmental exposures
Infectious diseases	• water, air and food contamination • climate change
Cancer	• smoking and environmental tobacco smoke (ETS) • some pesticides e.g. phenoxy herbicides • asbestos • natural toxins • food, e.g. low fibre, high fat • polycyclic aromatic hydrocarbons, e.g. in diesel fumes • some metals e.g. cadmium, chromium • radiation (incl. sunlight) • several hundred other animal carcinogens
Cardiovascular diseases	• smoking and ETS • carbon monoxide (CO) • lead • inhalable particles • food, e.g. high cholesterol • stress
Respiratory diseases, including asthma	• smoking and ETS • sulphur dioxide • nitrogen dioxide • inhalable particles • fungal spores • dust mites • pollen • pet hair, skin and excreta • damp
Skin diseases	• some metals, e.g. nickel • some pesticides, e.g. pentachlorophenol • some foods (allergies)
Diabetes, obesity	• food, e.g. high fat • poor exercise
Reproductive dysfunctions	• polychlorinated biphenyls (PCBs) • DDT • cadmium • pthalates and other plasticisers • endocrine disruptors
Developmental (foetal and childhood) disorders	• lead • mercury • smoking and ETS • cadmium • some pesticides • endocrine disruptors
Nervous system disorders	• lead • PCBs • methyl mercury • manganese • aluminium • some solvents • organophosphates
Immune response	• UVB radiation • some pesticides
Chemical sensitivity?	• trace amounts of many chemicals?

Source: EEA

Table 12.4.	Some key points from the executive summary of the WHO/IPCS scientific assessment of endocrine disrupting substances, 2002

Source: IPCS, 2002

Species/impact	Evidence	Knowledge gaps
Humans		
Sex ratios declining (fewer males)	'Associated with unidentified external influences'	'Stressors and mechanisms of action unknown'
Infertility and spontaneous abortions	'Associated with high exposures to certain chemicals'	'EDS relationship is speculative'
Birth defects in males	'Increases reported and animal data shows EDS damage to male reproductive tract'	'Role of EDS is unclear'
Falling sperm counts	'Declines observed in several, but not all countries/regions'	'No firm data addressing link to EDS'
Early puberty	'Concerns about EDS'	'Mechanisms of action and other causes e.g. nutrition need clarifying. In most instances EDS mechanisms not demonstrated'
Neurological development	'Human and animal studies clearly indicate that prenatal PCBs can have adverse effects'	
Immune function	'Exposure to EDS in humans and animals has altered immune function'	'Not clear that is due to endocrine medicated mechanisms'
Cancer - breast	'Evidence does not support a direct association with EDS: Mid-century exposures to organochlorines were higher than today'	'Exposure data from critical periods of development are lacking'
Cancer - testes	'Increases in some countries from 1910 and earlier cannot be attributed solely to chemicals introduced later. Some evidence of increases e.g. similar geographic variations links to birth defects'	'EDS exposure data are lacking'
Cancer - thyroid	'Direct association between exposure to EDS not demonstrated'	
Cancer - endometrial	'Limited data do not support causal role for EDS'	
Endometriosis	'Associated with some EDS'	'Studies remain equivocal'

Overall assessment: 'Biological plausibility is strong for possible damage to some functions, particularly reproductive and developmental. Some health trends warrant concern and more research. Non-EDS causes need exploring'.

responses are dust mites, spores from pets, damp, environmental tobacco smoke and nitrogen oxides from gas ovens. Other lifestyle factors of importance are family size, vaccinations, day care, illnesses and medication, and diet.

The prevalence of asthma in children of school age varies in different locations of Europe. Wide geographical variation in prevalence is noted also in adults. There is an indication that prevalence has increased over the past decade. The frequency of asthma attacks, sometimes requiring medical assistance or hospitalisation, has been shown to be associated with air pollution levels. Also indoor air pollution, notably biological aerosols, such as house mite dust, has been found to be associated with asthma symptoms. However it is not certain if the environmental conditions cause the onset of the disease, or only increase the chance of exacerbation of the symptoms, and it is not known to what extent the geographical variations in asthma level and trends are related to environmental factors. Some factors that may contribute to the observed rise in asthma include increased loads of aero-allergens in indoor spaces (linked with the reduction of ventilation and increased moisture build-up in 'energy efficient' houses), changes in diet (less omega-3 fatty acids and antioxidants) and less-developed immune systems in 'highly civilised' societies. However the present data raise more questions than answers (Strachan, 1995). Figure 12.9 illustrates the multi-causal chain of factors implicated in childhood asthma.

12.3.3. Climate change, ozone depletion and health effects

Some characteristics of global environmental issues are their multi-causality and their extensive and delayed direct and indirect effects (Figure 12.10).

The potential consequences of climate change include increases in sea level, more frequent and intensive storms, floods and droughts, changes in biota and food productivity (see Chapter 3). Changes in ecosystems may affect the growth, transmission and activity of vector-borne or infectious diseases, such as malaria and dengue fever. Human health is likely to be adversely affected, either directly or indirectly, through complex interactions of ecological systems (McMichael, 1998; WHO, 1999c). The direct effects may result from changes in exposure to thermal extremes, and be expressed by an increase in heat-related disease and death, but also by a decrease in cold-related disease.

Although it is difficult to attribute recent floods or periods of excessive heat to climate change (see Chapters 3 and 6), experience from past events demonstrates their relevance to human health. Physical health effects from floods do not only occur immediately during or after the incidents (e.g. drowning), they also arise as a consequence of living in damp or dusty conditions, or they appear as communicable diseases, chest infections, coughs and colds, during the weeks or months following flooding. Drought and desertification can also affect human health directly and indirectly, for example through changes in the areas of occurrence of infectious and respiratory diseases (UNCCD secretariat, 2000). Other extreme weather events can lead to psychological disorders, disease or death, indirectly causing an increase in morbidity. Although there are some signs of these climate effects already beginning to happen, (shifting geographical range and longer seasons of some vector-borne diseases (WHO, 1999c), much of the burden of ill

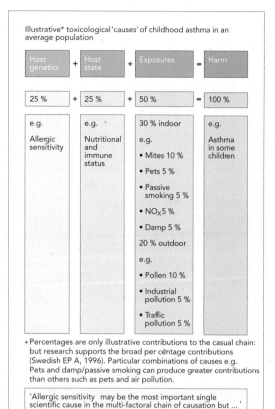

Scientific causes and social intervention causes for childhood asthma   **Figure 12.9.**

Source: EEA

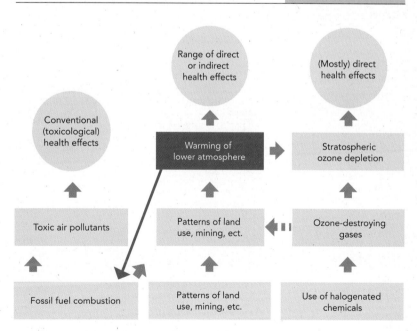

Interactions between climate change, stratospheric ozone depletion, air pollution and health effects   **Figure 12.10.**

Sources: McMichael, 1998; WHO, 1998

health from climate change will be on our children and theirs. Climate change policies based on avoiding these health impacts will also have considerable secondary benefits of avoiding shorter-term health impacts from fossil fuel combustion. Very few countries have addressed human health effects within their national climate change impact assessments (Figure 12.11) and comparisons between countries or regions are difficult, as assessment methods differ from country to country (WHO, 2001c).

An increase in ultraviolet solar radiation as a result of stratospheric ozone depletion (see Chapter 4) is associated with a number of health effects (WHO, 2000b). A 10 % decrease in stratospheric ozone is projected to cause an additional 300 000 non-melanoma skin cancers and 4 500 melanoma cases per year, worldwide (UNEP, 1994). For each 1 % decrease in stratospheric ozone, the average annual percentage increase in the incidence of non-melanoma skin cancer ranges from 1 % to 6 %, and for squamous cell carcinoma and basal cell carcinoma from 1.5 % to 2.5 %. Over the past two decades it has become clear that UVB exposure can impair specific and non-specific immune responses. Children are particularly vulnerable to the adverse health effects of stratospheric ozone depletion because of the long time-period of exposure, and the length of time available for an adverse health effect to appear.

12.3.4. Waste

Efficient disposal of wastes is one of the basic requirements for people's well-being. Waste disposal (including collection, transport, treatment and final disposal) is therefore an important environmental health issue (see Box 12.4).

Generally speaking, waste disposal sites that are within 1 km of residential areas, gardening, agricultural activities, hospitals, schools, kindergartens or playgrounds may have an impact on human well-being and/or health. Groundwater abstraction within a radius of 2 km may also be considered a risk. Direct health consequences of waste disposal are, however, difficult to prove and therefore poorly illustrated.

In spite of many and extensive studies, a plausible link between chemical waste deposits and measurable illness has only been found at a minority of locations. The results of these epidemiological studies are seriously affected by many confounding factors, e.g. different lifestyles, smoking, diet, housing quality, and susceptibility of ethnic, gender or age-specific groups to particular medical conditions (Rushbrook, 2001a).

Reported health effects from hazardous waste sites range from non-specific symptoms, such as headache, nausea, vomiting, stomach ache, fatigue and irritative symptoms, to specific conditions such as low birth weight, congenital defects and a

| Figure 12.11. | Pathways by which climate change affects health |

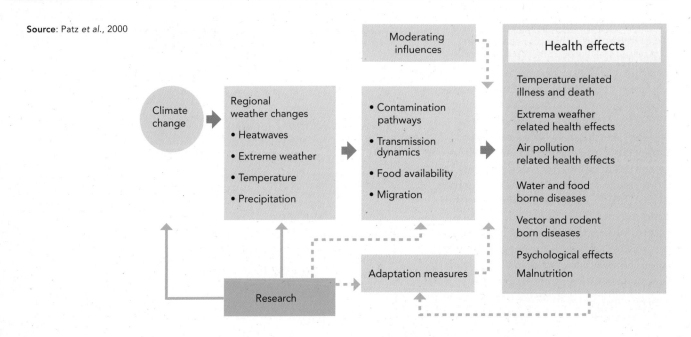

Source: Patz et al., 2000

constellation of neurobehavioural deficits (EEA/WHO, 2002). A study on the risk of congenital anomalies near hazardous waste sites in Europe showed a 33 % increase in the risk of non-chromosomal anomalies (Dolk *et al.*, 1998), and another study (Vrijheid, 2002) suggests a similar risk of increased chromosomal anomalies.

Healthcare waste, i.e. wastes from hospitals and medical practices, is composed of two fractions of which 'non-risk' healthcare waste typically represents 75–90 %. This fraction is comparable to municipal waste, while the remaining fraction, 'hazardous' or 'risk' healthcare waste includes all items that may have an elevated chemical, biological or physical risk to health. This fraction which is divided into a number of categories (potentially infectious waste, pathological

waste, used sharps, pharmaceutical waste, chemical waste, pressurised cylinders and radioactive waste) is believed to have a much higher potential to cause ill health (Rushbrook, 2001b).

There is very little quantitative data on the probability of pathogen transmission from most healthcare waste to medical and waste workers and none that demonstrates transmission to the general public.

12.4. Children — a vulnerable group

European children (at least those in western Europe) today benefit from better food, cleaner water, more preventive health measures, such as vaccination, and a higher standard of housing and living than ever

---

Box 12.4. Pharmaceuticals and personal care products in sewage and water

While the point source emissions of pollutants from manufacturing waste streams have long been monitored and subject to controls, the environmental impact of the public's activities regarding the use of chemicals is more difficult to assess. Of particular concern is the widespread release to sewage and surface waters or groundwaters of pharmaceuticals and personal care products (PPCP) after their ingestion, external application, or disposal. Certain pharmaceutically active compounds (e.g. caffeine, nicotine and aspirin) have been known for more than 20 years to enter the environment, by a variety of routes — primarily via treated and untreated sewage effluent. A larger picture, however, has emerged only more recently, where it is evident that numerous personal care products (such as fragrances and sunscreens) and drugs from a wide spectrum of therapeutic classes can occur in the environment and drinking water (albeit at very low concentrations), especially in natural waters that receive sewage.

During the past three decades, the impact of chemical pollution has focused almost exclusively on conventional 'priority pollutants' especially on those collectively referred to as 'persistent, bioaccumulative and toxic' (PBT) pollutants or persistent organic pollutants (POPs). This diverse 'historical' group of persistent chemicals (comprising mainly agricultural and industrial chemicals and synthesis by-products, heavily represented by highly halogenated organics) may however be only one piece of a larger puzzle. This bigger picture, if it does exist, has been largely unattainable with respect to risk assessments. Many other chemical classes (those that can be loosely referred to as 'unregulated bioactive pollutants' or 'unassessed pollutants') must also be better considered as part of a larger puzzle. Pharmaceuticals can be viewed simply as an example of one set of environmental pollutants that have received little attention with respect to potential impact on either ecological or human health.

Sewage and domestic wastes are the primary sources of pharmaceuticals and personal care products in the environment. These bioactive compounds are continually introduced to the environment (primarily via surface waters and groundwaters) from human and animal use largely through sewage treatment works systems, either directly by bathing/washing/swimming or indirectly by excretion in the faeces or urine of un-metabolised parent compounds.

Whether pharmaceuticals and personal care products survive in natural waters sufficiently long to be taken up in untreated drinking water, or whether they survive drinking water treatment, creating the potential for long-term exposure of humans, has received even less investigation than has their environmental occurrence. Certain drugs/metabolites, however, have been documented in potable waters in Europe (Daughton and Ternes, 1999). The extremely low concentrations (parts per trillion, ng/l), orders of magnitude below therapeutic threshold levels, might be expected to have minuscule (but still unknown) health consequences for humans, even for those who continually consume these waters over the course of decades; the primary concern, if any, would focus on those with heightened drug responses or the health-impaired (e.g., foetuses, infants and children, or aged or diseased individuals).

A myriad of chemical classes, ranging from endocrine disruptors, anti-microbials and antidepressants to lipid regulators and synthetic musk fragrances have been identified in sewage and domestic wastes. Excluding the anti-microbials and steroids (which include many members), over 50 individual pharmaceuticals and personal care products or metabolites (from more than 10 broad classes of therapeutic agents or personal care products) had been identified as of 1999 in environmental samples (mainly surface and ground waters). Concentrations generally range from the low ppt- to ppb-levels. It is important to note that these only comprise a subset of substances in wide use.

Sources: Daughton and Ternes, 1999; Daughton, 2001

before. Globally, however, about 1 in 10 children will not live to see their fifth birthday, although this global average conceals wide variations. This is due chiefly to infectious diseases, which still kill many children in the less developed world. There are also parts of Europe, such as areas in EECCA, where, following social and economic breakdown, the classic infectious diseases, such as diphtheria, malaria, TB, cholera and typhoid, are re-emerging. The life expectancy of people in some areas of some EECCA countries has fallen dramatically within the last decade, to an average of less than 50 years in several of the more polluted and impoverished zones, such as in Kazakhstan and Tajikistan. Infant mortality rates in Europe vary enormously, reflecting the large differences in social, economic and environmental conditions, as well as the healthcare systems across the region.

While most children in WE are no longer dying of infectious diseases, they are at increased risk from some cancers and birth defects, as well as asthma, allergies, brain damage and behavioural disorders. This has been called the 'new paediatric morbidity' (EEA, 1999). The causes of these diseases are not as obvious as the causes of infections but, as they have grown to prominence fairly recently, changes in the environment and other factors of modern life are likely to be playing a significant role.

Children today are routinely exposed to a number of 'hidden hazards' from micro-pollutants in air, water, food, on soils and surfaces, and in consumer products. These include newly created synthetic chemicals, which did not exist 50 years ago. For 84 % of the high production volume chemicals on the European market, there is insufficient toxicity information available for even the most basic risk assessments recommended by the Organisation for Economic Co-operation and Development (OECD). Children are not 'little adults' but are particularly vulnerable to pollutants because of their immature biological development, behaviour, metabolism, greater exposure to pollutants, relative to body weight, and longer life at risk than adults. 'It's the timing of the dose that can make the poison.'

Children are therefore potentially more vulnerable to environmental hazards than adults, and require special protection. However, this is not generally provided for since most safety standards for chemicals are based on adult data, although improvements to standards are developing continuously. Some pesticide residues in food and water, because they can accumulate in the particular diets of children, are of concern, especially for possible impacts on the brain and on behaviour. Environmental causes of autism, attention deficit/hyperactivity disorder (ADHD) and lowered IQ are being investigated and seem to be involved in some of the increases in these disorders.

Some other chemicals that can damage the brain and affect behaviour are lead, mercury, polychlorinated biphenyls (PCB) and dioxins which can be absorbed via food, water, air, surfaces and consumer products. Some chemicals (PCB, dioxins) accumulate in body fat and are passed on to the foetus and infant. Although more dose is passed on through breast milk, the lower, pre-natal dose via the mother appears to be more hazardous because of the greater vulnerability of the foetal brain. Hormones in meat may cause brain damage and cancer.

Other environmental pollutants include some radionuclides, which are especially dangerous for children, because they penetrate into children's bodies in the process of growth and serve as 'building material'. Primarily, this has an impact on the genetic code and disruption of the immune system leading to malignant new growths (formations) (see Section 12.2.4).

Environmental health impacts on children (some of which only become apparent in adult live) in Europe could include: reproductive disorders (cancers and defects of the testes, breast cancer, falling sperm counts); asthma; other respiratory diseases and allergies; some other cancers, such as leukaemias and nervous system tumours; and injuries. The possible environmental causes of these health impacts include passive smoking, pesticides and other chemicals, traffic, alcohol, diet and poverty (EEA/WHO, 2002).

The contribution of environmental pollutants to some diseases of US children has recently been estimated. The environmental attributions to the diseases were: lead poisoning (100 %), asthma (30 %), cancer (5 %) and neurobehavioral disorders (10 %). The corresponding estimates of annual costs were: lead poisoning (USD 43.4 billion), asthma (USD 2.0 billion), cancer (USD 0.3 billion) and neurobehavioral disorders (USD 9.2 billion). The total annual costs were USD 54.9 billion,

	Perinatal disease	Respiratory illness	Diarrhoeal disease	Insect-borne disease	Physical injuries
Housing and shelter	xxx	xxx	xx	xxx	xxx
Water supply and quality	x	x	xxx	xxx	xx
Food safety and supply security	xx	xx	xxx	xx	xxx
Sanitation and hygiene	x	x	xxx	xxx	xx
Solid waste	xx	xx	xxx	xxx	xx
Outdoor air pollution	xx	xx	x	x	x
Indoor air pollution	xxx	xxx	x	x	x
Hazardous chemicals	xxx	x	x	x	xxx
Technological accidents	xx	xx	x	x	xxx
Natural hazards	xx	xx	xx	xxx	xxx
Disease carrying factors	xx	xx	xx	xxx	xxx
Social/work environment	xxx	xx	xxx	xxx	xxx

Environmental risk factors for children's health   Figure 12.12.

Source: WHO, 2003

XXX High risk source   XX Moderate risk source   X Low risk source

2.8 % of total US healthcare costs (Landrigan *et al.*, 2002).

Children's environmental health is now receiving special attention, especially in North America, and increasingly in Europe (International Conference, Ukraine 2002). Priorities for action include better exposure monitoring, research, exposure standards designed for children, reduced exposures, information to consumers and citizens about residues and emissions, and awareness-raising, education and training of health professionals and child carers, including parents. Table 12.5 shows an approach to the development of children and environmental health indicators which will provide the basis for the first pan-European report on this issue to be presented at the Budapest Ministerial Conference on Health and Environment, 2004.

12.5. References

Advisory Committee on Novel Foods and Processes, 1994. *Report on the use of antibiotic resistance markers in genetically modified food organisms.* July. MAFF, London.

Anon, 2002. *National report on the state of the environment in Ukraine.* Kiev.

California Dept of Health, 2002. *An Evaluation of possible risks from EMFs from powerlines (etc.).*

Daughton, C. G. and Ternes, T. A., 1999. Pharmaceuticals and personal care products in the environment; Agents of subtle change? *Environmental Health Perspectives* 107 (suppl. 6): 907-938. http://www.epa.gov/nerlesd1/chemistry/pharma/index.htm

Daughton, C. G., 2001. Pharmaceuticals in the environment: Overarching issues and overview. In: Daughton, C. G. and Jones-Lepp, T. (eds). *Pharmaceuticals and personal care products in the environment: Scientific and regulatory issues.* Symposium Series 791. American Chemical Society, Washington, DC. pp. 2–38.

Dolk, H., Vrijheid, M., Armstrong, B. et al., 1998. Risk of congenital anomalies near hazardous waste landfill sites in Europe: The EUROHAZCON study. *Lancet* 352: 423–427.

Dora, C. and Racioppi, F., 2001. *Transport, environment and health in Europe: Knowledge of impacts and policy implications.* Rome.

ECMT (European Conference of Ministers of Transport), 2002. *Statistical trends in transport 1970–2002.* Paris.

EEA (European Environment Agency), 1998. *Europe's environment: The second assessment.* EEA, Copenhagen.

EEA (European Environment Agency), 1999. *Environment in the European Union at the turn of the century.* EEA, Copenhagen.

EEA (European Environment Agency), 2002. *Environmental signals 2002 — Benchmarking the millennium.* EEA, Copenhagen

EEA/WHO (European Environment Agency/WHO Regional Office for Europe), 2002. *Children's health and environment. A review of evidence.* EEA, Copenhagen.

European Commission, 2002. *Fifth framework programme: Quality of life.* http://europa.eu.int/comm/research/quality-of-life/ka4/index_en.html

European Commission, 2003. *Sixth framework programme: Food and safety.* http://europa.eu.int/comm/research/fp6/p5/index_en.html
http://www.cordis.lu/fp6/food.htm

International Conference, Ukraine 2002 (Report from). *Healthy children: growth, development and recent standards.* BSMA Department of Developmental Paediatrics Bukovinian State Academy, Chernivtsy, October 10–11, 2002.

IPCS (International Programme on Chemical Safety), 2002. *Global assessment of the state-of-the-science of endocrine disruptors.* WHO/IPCS/EDS/02.2.

Istituto di Ricerca sulle Acque, 1996. *Evoluzione dei fabbisogni idrici civili ed industriali* (Development of human and industrial water requirements). Cosenza.

Lancet, 2002. Vol 360 November 2.

Landrigan, P. J. *et al.*, 2002. Environmental pollutants and disease in American children: Estimates of morbidity, mortality, and costs for lead poisoning, asthma, cancer, and developmental disabilities. *Environmental Health Perspectives* 110(7).

McMichael, A., 1998. Personal communication.

Mountain Unlimited, 1995. *Water supply and sanitation in central and east European countries, new independent states and Mongolia.* Hall, Tirol.

Mountain Unlimited, 1997. *Water supply and sanitation in central and east European countries, new independent states and Mongolia.* Vol. II, draft version. Hall, Tirol.

Patz, J. A. *et al*, 2000. The potential health impacts of climate variability and change for the United States. Executive summary of the report of the health sector of the US national assessment. *Environmental Health Perspectives* 108: 367–376.

Pesticide Action Network (UK), 2002. UK Minister pledges pesticide reform. *Pesticides News* No 58.

Racioppi, F., 2002. Personal communication.

Republic of Moldova NCP, 2002. Communication to European Environment Agency from national contact point.

Royal Society, 1998. *Genetically modified plants for food use.* London.

Rushbrook, P., 2001a. The health effects from wastes — overplayed or underestimated? *Workshop: Health Impact of Waste Management Activities.* IWM Annual Conference. Paignton, UK.

Rushbrook, P., 2001b. Public health perspective of clinical waste management. *Waste Management 2001 — Asia. Solid & Hazardous Waste Management Conference.* Kuala Lumpur.

Smith, K. R., Corvalán, C. F. and Kjellström, T., 1999. How much global ill health is attributable to environmental factors? *Journal of Epidemiology* 10(5): 573–584.

Socialstyrelsen, 2002. *Environmental health report, 2001.* The National Board of Health and Wellfare, Stockholm

Strachan, D. P, 1995. Editorial: Time trends in asthma and allergy: Ten questions, fewer answers. *Clin Exper Allergy* 25: 791–794.

Stewart, 2000. Independent expert group on mobile phones, National Radiological Protection board (NRPB), United Kingdom.

Ukraine NCP, 2002. Communication to European Environment Agency from national contact point.

UNCCD (UN Convention to Combat Desertification) secretariat, 2000. *Down to Earth.* Newsletter, December 2000. Bonn.

UNEP (United Nations Environment Programme), 1994. *Environmental effects of ozone depletion.* Nairobi.

UNSCEAR (UN Scientific Committee on the Effects of Atomic Radiation), 2000. *Sources and effects of ionizing radiation. Volume 1: Sources.* Report to the General Assembly with scientific annexes. United Nations Publication, New York.

UNSCEAR (UN Scientific Committee on the Effects of Atomic Radiation), 2001. www.unscear.org/chernobyl.html

Vrijheid, M. *et al.*, 2002. Chromosomal congenital anomalies and residence near hazardous waste landfill sites. Lancet 259: 320–322.

Water Research Centre, 1997. *International comparison of the demand for water: A comparison of the demand for water in three European countries: England and Wales, France and Germany.* London.

WHO (WHO Regional Office for Europe), 1998. *Report of a WHO/EURO international workshop on the early human health effects of climate change, 21–23 May 1998.* Copenhagen.

WHO (WHO Regional Office for Europe,) 1999a. *Declaration of the Third Ministerial Conference on Environment and Health.*

WHO (WHO Regional Office for Europe), 1999b. *Overview of the environment and health in Europe in the 1990s.* Copenhagen.

WHO (WHO Regional Office for Europe), 1999c. 'Early human health effects of climate change'. Background document for 1999 London conference. Copenhagen.

WHO (WHO Regional Office for Europe), 2000a. *Transport, environment and health.* Copenhagen.

WHO (WHO Regional Office for Europe), 2000b. *Climate change and stratospheric ozone depletion. Early effects on our health in Europe.* Copenhagen.

WHO (WHO Regional Office for Europe, European Centre for Environment and Health), 2001a. *Health impact assessment of air pollution in the WHO European Region.* Bonn.

WHO (World Health Organization), 2001b. *Water quality, guidelines, standards and health.* IWA Publishing.

WHO (WHO Regional Office for Europe), 2001c. 'First Meeting on Guidelines to Assess the Health Impacts of Climate Change'. Meeting report. Victoria.

WHO (WHO Regional Office for Europe), 2002a. *European health report* 2002. http://www.euro.who.int/europeanhealthreport/20020903_2

WHO (WHO Regional Office for Europe, European Centre for Environment and Health), 2002b. *Health risk of heavy metals from long-range transboundary air pollution. Preliminary assessment.* WHO and UNECE, Bonn.

WHO (WHO Regional Office for Europe), 2002c. *Water and health in Europe.* A joint report from the European Environment Agency and the WHO Regional Office for Europe, Copenhagen.

WHO (World Health Organization), 2002d. *Establishing a dialogue on risks from electromagnetic fields.* Geneva.

WHO, 2003. *Making a difference: indicators for children's environmental health.* WHO Geneva (in print).

13. Progress in managing the environment

The concept of integration is well known, but the degree to which it is incorporated into strategic policy-making varies. At European Union level, the Cardiff integration process has led to an increased awareness among policy-makers of the importance of harmonisation and integration, but the process has lacked urgency and has yet to have a significant impact on sectoral policy-making, let alone on improvements on the ground.

Within countries, integration is generally approached through the concept of sustainable development, via national sustainable development strategies, but the stage of development of these varies. Integration of the environment into other policy areas is far from comprehensive, and implementation in particular causes problems. The 12 countries of eastern Europe, the Caucasus and central Asia are aware of the requirements of integration but do not generally have the capacity to carry forward initiatives for drafting strategies and plans, or to implement them.

The concept of integrated coastal zone management has been spreading during the past 10 years. However, this has not kept up with growing pressures, especially on the Black Sea, southeast Mediterranean and Caspian Sea coasts.

Urban planning is a major area for integration, but innovative policies including stronger linkages to other policy areas are needed to overcome the many pressures towards unsustainable spatial development. There has therefore been a growing emphasis on integration of planning with sectoral policies, an ecosystems approach, and better institutional support mechanisms including procedures to improve public and stakeholder participation.

Market mechanisms are increasingly seen as tools of integration policy alongside more traditional regulatory mechanisms. Some accession countries and countries in transition economies have a history of using market mechanisms, but others do not. Overall, only very limited steps have been taken towards ecological tax reform.

Integration cannot be achieved solely by governments and other public sector bodies: a commitment from industrial and commercial sectors is also needed. There was a significant increase in interest in voluntary 'green' business initiatives in Europe in the 1990s, mostly by

companies in EU countries and multinational organisations. These include negotiated agreements and self-commitments, eco-labelling, and environmental management and reporting.

Useful sector-specific strategic environmental assessment experience has developed in some countries, but this cannot necessarily be duplicated for other sectors or countries because of the different issues, institutions, legal frameworks and stakeholders involved. Strategic environmental assessments need to be integrated with other requirements, such as sustainability appraisals.

13.1. Introduction

The 1995 Environmental Programme for Europe recommended that participants should integrate environmental considerations into all decision-making processes, taking into account environmental costs, benefits and risks, applying the precautionary and 'polluter pays' principles, and promoting partnerships between government, parliaments, businesses and non-governmental organisations (NGOs).

A first step is to adopt adequate strategies and policies both in the international arena and at the national level to ensure that environmental considerations are integrated into all policy sectors. Progress towards this end is described in Section 13.2, giving some subregional examples, which often provide a context for efforts at the national level. The focus, however, is on the wide array of new approaches and tools to reach harmonisation and integration at the national level.

But adopting integrated strategies and policies alone is not enough. The next step is to ensure that such integrated plans are indeed implemented, that actual results can be seen on the ground. Considering the complexity of ecosystems and societies, specific approaches to integration may be required in the management of specific sectors, regions or types of region. Section 13.3 gives two examples of progress in the development of integrated planning and management instruments in specific types of area (coastal zone management) and sector (urban development).

In general, integration requires an ability to deal with complexity in a flexible way, addressing all segments of society. Hence traditional legislative instruments are not really sufficient to achieve integrated development. A growing pool of policy measures is being applied, which reflects the realisation that full integration cannot be achieved by government action alone. Partnerships between government institutions, economic actors and civil society at large are needed, as well as initiatives by specific stakeholders. Such partnerships often reach across national boundaries, requiring intensive transboundary cooperation between different governments and institutions. Harmonised approaches, data and information will facilitate mutual understanding and communication, and thus cooperation, among the wide variety of actors involved in integrated development. Section 13.3 illustrates the range of policy instruments currently being applied in both public and private sectors.

13.2. Integration of environmental considerations into strategies and policies

Most national efforts towards integration are not isolated actions but take place in the context of international processes. These range from the global level (such as the global conventions dealing with climate change and with biodiversity, the Rio conference on environment and development and the Johannesburg summit on sustainable development) to the subregional level (for instance for a particular river basin). Section 13.2.1 outlines the key regional or subregional processes and initiatives which aim to stimulate or achieve harmonisation and integration. Section 13.2.2 summarises progress in harmonisation and integration at the national level.

13.2.1. Integration at the subregional and regional level

At European level, the 'Environment for Europe' process has been very important in facilitating regional cooperation by promoting harmonisation and integration of the environment into other policies. Chapter 6 of a recent UN publication (UNECE/UNEP, 2002) summarises the achievements of the Environment for Europe process and progress in the development of regional conventions as tools for harmonisation and integration. Box 13.1 lists key regional and

---

Box 13.1. Key European initiatives promoting integration

Regional conventions (excluding the many subsequent protocols)
1979 Convention on Long-Range Transboundary Air Pollution (CLRTAP)
1991 Convention on Environmental Impact Assessment in a Transboundary Context (Espoo)
1992 Convention on the Protection and Use of Transboundary Watercourses and International Lakes
1992 Convention on the Transboundary Effects of Industrial Accidents
1998 Convention on Access to Information, Public Participation in Decision-making and Access to Justice in Environmental Matters (Aarhus)

Other regional initiatives
1995 Environmental Programme for Europe (UNECE)
1998 The Pan-European Biodiversity and Landscape Diversity Strategy (PEBLDS)
1999 London Charter on Transport, Environment and Health

Subregional conventions
1992 Convention on the Protection of the Marine Environment of the North-East Atlantic (OSPAR)
1992 Convention on the Protection of the Marine Environment of the Baltic Sea Area (HELCOM)
1992 Bucharest Convention on the Protection of the Black Sea against Pollution
1995 Revision of the Convention on the Protection of the Mediterranean Sea against Pollution; implemented through the Mediterranean action plan (1979 Barcelona convention)
1995 Convention on the Protection of the Alps
1998 Danube River Protection Convention
2001 (adopted) New Convention for the Protection of the Rhine

Other subregional initiatives
1993 Environmental Action Programme for Central and Eastern Europe (EAP)
1994 Environmental Performance Review programme of UNECE for countries in transition
1994 MED 21 (Mediterranean)
1995 Regional Environmental Centre for Central and Eastern Europe (REC); followed by RECs for the Russian Federation, Ukraine, Republic of Moldova, the Caucasus and central Asia
1997 Vienna Programme of Joint Action on Transport and the Environment
1998 Baltic 21
1998 Caspian Environment Programme
1998 EU Cardiff process (see details below)
1998 Nordic Strategy on Sustainable Development
1998 Central Asian Interstate Council on Sustainable Development
1999 Stability Pact for South Eastern Europe

---

subregional conventions and other initiatives relevant to harmonisation and integration of environmental considerations into other policies, which are detailed in the UN report.

The report states that in Europe 'a great deal of harmonisation and integration has got its start through consideration of transboundary environmental issues, such as industrial accidents and air pollution. Significantly, there has been a shift in the region during the last few years towards improving compliance with multilateral environmental agreements, especially with respect to UNECE conventions. Also ratification of significant global agreements is high in the region, and fairly balanced among the subregions. However, ratification and implementation are affected by both environmental and economic problems within states' (UNECE/UNEP, 2002). In another recent UN report on lessons learned through the Environmental Performance Review programme, interesting details are given on progress in harmonisation and integration in central and eastern Europe (CEE) and the 12 countries of eastern Europe, the Caucasus and central Asia (EECCA) (UNECE, 2002). Some details are given below for the European Union (EU).

At the EU level, the requirement to integrate environmental concerns into other policy areas has been incorporated into the Treaty that forms the basis of the Union, thus making it one of the guiding principles of the EU. Article 6 of the Treaty establishing the European Community states that: 'Environmental protection requirements must be integrated into the definition and implementation of the Community policies and activities'.

As a contribution to implementing this requirement, the Cardiff process was initiated at the European Council in Cardiff under the UK presidency in June 1998. This called on key meetings of the Council of Ministers (e.g. for transport, agriculture, fisheries) to develop their own strategies for integrating environmental concerns into their respective policy areas. EU heads of state and government, to whom regular reports are made, oversees the Cardiff process. Nine strategies are currently in place or under development, and these are at various stages of elaboration (presented in waves in Table 13.1).

Evaluations of the Cardiff strategies (IEEP, 2001a; 2001b) have revealed that:

- none contained all of the elements that one might expect a 'strategy' to comprise (such as objectives, measures, indicators, timeframes and review mechanisms);
- some aspects of strategy formulation were more fully developed, or at least under development (e.g. indicators), than others (e.g. specific targets);
- the strategies did not contain many new measures.

On balance, the transport strategy is the most developed strategy, and has two notable integration mechanisms, which play an important role in its development. A joint expert group on transport and environment, which is chaired by the Commission and incorporates national transport and environment officials, oversees the transport integration process. Additionally, the

transport and environment reporting mechanism (TERM) has been developed by the European Environment Agency (EEA) and the Commission to monitor the impact of the strategy.

Further indicators are being developed to monitor other sectoral strategies, with targets and timetables for instance now elaborated for fisheries integration policy (CEC, 2002). In addition a set of 'headline indicators' to cover all aspects of sustainability is under development. These indicators are meant to be used by heads of state and government to monitor the EU's progress.

The development of the Cardiff strategies has been accompanied by a number of other integration mechanisms within the European Commission, such as the creation of special units dedicated to environmental matters in several of the Commission's directorates general. There is also a system of undertaking ex ante environmental appraisals of Commission proposals, which was introduced in 1993, but which the Commission itself acknowledges has not yet worked well.

Overall, the Cardiff process and other Community initiatives have been useful, despite the relatively modest progress. In particular, the Cardiff process has raised awareness of Article 6 and its requirements among a broader range of decision-makers. However, integration initiatives have as yet had a relatively minor impact on the political agenda, as they have not commanded sufficient political will to address some of the fundamental problems that still exist. Where integration has progressed, it has been largely as a result of more pressing political problems, such as the Kyoto protocol or the Millennium Round of the World Trade Organisation (WTO). Establishment of minimum requirements for implementation and follow-up of integration strategies has yet to be taken forward (Ecologic and IEEP, 2002).

> In the EU, the Cardiff and other integration processes have raised awareness of environmental issues, but have not yet had a decisive effect on sectoral policies.

Criteria for strategy analysis	First wave councils			Second wave councils			Third wave councils		
	Agriculture	Energy	Transport	Development	Industry	Internal market	Economic and finance	General affairs	Fisheries
Strategy content									
Scientific/research basis for formulating problem	-	-	-	-	-	-	-	-	-
Problem formulation	•	/	/	•	●	/	•	•	•
Risk assessment and option appraisal	-	-	•	-	-	•	-	-	-
Aims/objectives/guiding principles	/	/	●	/	/	/	•	•	/
Targets	•	-	/	-	-	-	-	-	•
Measures/actions — including beyond existing commitments	/	/	/	/	/	/	•	/	/
Recognition of the extra-Community/global dimension	•	•	/	/	/	•	/	/	/
Reference to other relevant EU/international policy agendas	/	/	/	/	●	•	•	/	/
Resource implications	-	-	•	/	/	•	•	-	-
Timetables	/	/	/	•	•	•	•	•	-
Procedural characteristics									
Roles and responsibilities for ensuring implementation	/	•	•	/	/	/	/	/	•
Monitoring and review arrangements	/	/	•	/	•	•	●	•	-
Indicators — extent and nature	/	/	•	•	/	/	/	•	•
Reporting mechanisms/requirements	•	/	/	/	•	•	•	-	-
Future milestones	•	•	/	•	•	•	/	•	•

An evaluation of the Cardiff strategies — Table 13.1.

Note: •: little attention to this aspect   /: some effort to address this aspect, but incomplete   ●: relatively full treatment of this aspect

Source: IEEP, 2001 b

13.2.2. Integration at the national level

Transboundary initiatives are often put in place as a result of the initiatives of a few countries with societies that are developing in an innovative way. At the same time countries are stimulated by such international action to take up the cause of harmonisation and integration within their own boundaries. Indeed, countries all over Europe have adopted or are in the process of adopting specific approaches (usually a mixture of different approaches) to better coordinate and integrate sectoral policies and relevant governmental decisions with the principles of sustainability. Box 13.2 describes three such approaches to sectoral integration. Neither geographic nor economic characteristics can fully explain the variations in approaches. For example, among western European (WE) countries, Austria, Finland, Italy, Norway and Switzerland have established sustainable development coordination structures, but Denmark, Germany, Spain and Sweden have not. Among EU accession countries, the Czech Republic, Estonia, Hungary, Poland and Slovakia have, but Latvia, Lithuania, Romania and Slovenia have not. In EECCA, such bodies have been established in Belarus and Uzbekistan but not, for instance, in Armenia or Tajikistan. In a very few countries, an implementing agency has been established, such as the National Environmental Centre for Sustainable Development in Kazakhstan.

Box 13.2. National approaches to integration

A *coordination approach*, based on the creation of broad inter-ministerial committees, commissions, working groups and task forces. For example, the United Kingdom has established a Cabinet committee of 'green' ministers, supported by civil servants in each department. Poland set up the National Commission for Sustainable Development in late 1994 to coordinate and facilitate governmental activities towards integration of economic, environmental and social aspects. France has created an inter-ministerial steering group to coordinate 'greening of government' activities.

A *strategic approach*, based on the development of a shared agenda with the government through sustainable development strategies, policies and executive programmes. This approach is common throughout the region, particularly after the Lucerne ministerial conference 'Environment for Europe', and very often connected to 'coordination' and 'structural' approaches.

A *structural approach*, based on integration of sectoral policies into 'mega-ministries'. Examples of this approach include, in the United Kingdom, the Department of the Environment, Transport and Regions; in Poland, the Ministry of Environmental Protection, Natural Resources and Forestry; in Belgium, the Ministry of Social Affairs, Public Health and the Environment; and, in the Netherlands, the Ministry of Housing, Physical Planning and the Environment.

Source: UNECE/UNEP, 2002

At western European national level, the strategic framework for integrating environmental considerations into other sectoral policy areas has been primarily through national sustainable development strategies (SDSs) (see also Box 13.2), which have either been finalised or are in draft form. These strategies seek to integrate sustainable development concerns, i.e. including the environment alongside economic and social considerations in policy-making, and often focus on sectors such as agriculture, industry, transport and energy. Most are of quite a high standard, in that they address the main requirements of a policy strategy, i.e. objectives, measures, indicators, timetables and follow-up.

In most countries, a cross-departmental committee of some description has been set up to contribute to the development of the SDS, while in others, a commission or council has been established to monitor progress towards sustainable development.

In western Europe, national SDSs are accompanied by various sectoral policy

documents which have been developed to steer more detailed policy action. These are also at varying stages of development and address particular sectors, e.g. transport and energy, or particular environmental problems, e.g. waste or water.

The Nordic countries in particular have good experiences with the integration approach. Norway, for example, considers the integration of environmental concerns into sectoral policies as vital in order to achieve overarching environmental policy goals. To this end, the government plans to 'clarify the sector's responsibility for achieving environmental policy goals through sectoral environmental action plans' and to set up a national monitoring system (Ministry of Environment, Norway, 1997). The Netherlands and Denmark also follow this approach, but such coherent strategies are not universal.

In the CEE countries, the integration process is still at a relatively early stage. Environmental policy is set out in national environmental strategies that sometimes take the form of national environmental action plans (NEAPs) or national environmental and health action plans (NEHAPs). Beyond this, attention in many countries is now turning towards the development of national SDSs, which, again, may be accompanied by the formation of a national sustainable development commission. In Poland, for instance, such a commission was already set up in 1994.

Integration in the CEE countries is addressed mainly in a rather fragmented way. Implementation, monitoring and follow-up are difficult to ensure. The Croatian Government, for example, has recognised that there are no legal obligations that call for the environment to be addressed in the preparation of sectoral policies. Nevertheless, sectoral strategies and plans are developing. These typically cover industry, energy, agriculture, transport and tourism.

Some instances of good cooperation between environmental and other ministries are reported, but the practical impacts of integrated sectoral strategies and policies are still not materialising. Coordination is often lacking, as a result of limited organisational and administrative resources (von Homeyer, 2001). Such resource constraints also weaken integration at the regional and local levels (von Homeyer, 2002). Nevertheless, awareness of the need for integration and a willingness to pursue it is quite high

At western European national level, integrative processes have raised awareness of environmental issues and integrated strategies are often in place, but they have not yet had a decisive effect on sectoral policies, let alone on actual implementation.

throughout CEE. The EU accession process reinforces this requirement. Accession countries are already adopting the environmental and other requirements of the body of EU law, and will be bound by the integration requirements of the Treaty when they join the EU in 2004 (see for example Box 13.3).

For EECCA, the integration of environmental considerations into other policy areas is happening at a significantly slower pace than elsewhere in Europe, as a result of the difficult transition process away from centrally planned economies. Priorities are for the time being on economic development. There has, however, been some progress, for example in Kazakhstan (Box 13.4). Georgia has launched a programme on socio-economic restructuring and economic growth, which consists of various pre-existing strategies, focusing for example on industrial development. The programme is geared towards the introduction of an integrated and effective economic system, but although it includes measures concerning the environment, these are not a central priority.

The regulatory and enforcement structures in EECCA are still very weak as a result of a lack of financial resources or of capacity to utilise effectively those resources that are available. Even where institutions have a real commitment to achieving environmental objectives, as in the case of Kazakhstan's NEAP and NEHAP, their weak position within government and their resource constraints hinder effective integration.

13.3. Implementation of integrated development strategies and policy

As is clear from the above, the intentions and strategic actions taken in most parts of Europe to achieve integration of environmental considerations into other policy are certainly moving in the right direction. However, truly integrated development is only beginning to be

Integration is advancing in the countries of central and eastern Europe and those of eastern Europe, the Caucasus and central Asia, but more slowly, particularly in the latter, than in western Europe, owing to resource limitations and competing priorities.

Box 13.3. Sectoral integration in the Baltic countries

Of the EU accession countries, Estonia is among the front-runners in integrating environmental considerations into agricultural policy. National agri-environment measures were implemented in pilot areas in 2001 with state funds. Payments to subsidise conversion to organic agriculture have been available since 2000, and now nearly 2 % of the agricultural area is certified as organic. Training programmes on environmental issues for farmers and farm inspectors have been taking place since 2000.

A code of good agricultural practice for Latvia was prepared by the Ministry for Environmental Protection and Regional Development and the Ministry of Agriculture, following EU requirements and HELCOM recommendations. Most of the aspects of the code will be obligatory for farmers operating in ecologically sensitive zones and for farmers using assistance within the framework of special accession programmes for agriculture and rural development (SAPARD). The law on pollution will regulate big farms, since they fall under integrated pollution prevention and control requirements.

The national energy strategy of Lithuania, approved in 1999, reflects the requirements and guidelines of the European Association Treaty, the Energy Charter Treaty and other international agreements in the field of energy such as the principles of the energy policy of the European Union and its Member States. One of the main priorities in the strategy is the reduction of the negative impact of the energy sector on the environment, including nuclear safety requirements.

Source: Laansalu, 2001; Mikk, 2001; UNECE, 2000a and 2000b

Box 13.4. Environment and health plan in Kazakhstan

National environment action plans (NEAP) and national environment and health action plans (NEHAPs) provide an opportunity for looking at environmental and health issues from a cross-sectoral perspective, and for identifying priorities and areas for action on the basis of a broad consensus of stakeholders. Some interesting experiences are evolving in Kazakhstan.

There are health risks in the country from past and present man-made environmental causes, such as radiation, the Aral Sea disaster and traffic-related air pollution. However, environmental mortality and morbidity seem to be related more to such issues as drinking-water quality, food quality and nutrition.

While the NEAP deals with environmental issues related to past and present industrialisation and pollution prevention, the NEHAP deals more specifically with sanitary-hygiene environmental issues related to current human health problems. Taking both plans together, the most important topics in environmental health in Kazakhstan are drinking-water quality, sewage disposal and personal hygiene; food quality and nutrition; radiation safety; and ambient air quality in large cities.

Source: UNECE, 2000c

implemented, for example in integrated coastal zone management (Section 13.3.1) and urban planning and development (Section 13.3.2). Section 13.3.3 gives other examples of integration policy instruments that are beginning to work.

13.3.1. Integrated coastal zone management
Europe's coastal zones are of great economic, environmental, social, cultural and recreational importance. For example, after tropical forests, the areas on Earth with the highest biodiversity are coastal zones. However, a range of pressures, including population growth, and increased shipping,

industrial and tourist activity, threatens Europe's coasts. The effects of climate change, in particular rising sea levels and increased storm frequency, have increased coastal erosion and flooding. Meanwhile, the decline in fish stocks and fishing activity, and oil transport and spill accidents, have also made many fisheries-dependent areas particularly vulnerable (see Chapters 2.7 and 8).

Integrated coastal zone management (ICZM) seeks to manage such multiple pressures in a way that is environmentally sustainable, economically equitable and sensitive to local cultures. ICZM is an iterative, proactive and adaptive process to plan and manage coastal areas with a view to sustainable development. It encompasses a range of approaches, which together demonstrate:

- the need for authorities at different levels of administration to cooperate amongst themselves and with stakeholders;
- the establishment of a participation process with all the actors from the beginning of the project;
- implementation of transparent procedures, from an environmental audit to the design of an action plan with local communities involved;
- an agreed work programme with an agenda, concrete objectives and a balanced budget.

From the mid-1980s, significant efforts have been made in Europe to develop and apply ICZM principles. Organisations for the regional seas have played a key role in this development. Often there is a mixture of international strategies and agreements and more local level management and implementation. Interestingly, in such programmes countries are grouped using the natural boundaries of shorelines (eco-zoning) rather than applying administrative boundaries and political groupings. For Europe this means:

Regional sea	Subregional groupings
Atlantic	EU
North Sea	EU
Baltic	EU, northern CEE, EECCA
Mediterranean	EU, southern CEE, northern Africa
Black Sea	Southeastern CEE, EECCA
Caspian Sea	EECCA

Within the EU, a May 2002 recommendation on ICZM calls upon Member States to produce their own national ICZM strategies on the basis of a stocktaking of the pressures and administrative structures influencing the evolution of their coastal zones. This followed an EU ICZM demonstration programme involving 35 pilot projects around western Europe's coastline. Box 13.5 summarises some applications of ICZM tools in the EU.

The following are the key regional sea initiatives in Europe; Table 13.2 shows the extent to which these have used ICZM-related development tools.

The Mediterranean action plan (UNEP/MAP) was the first programme to formulate its own subregional Agenda 21, which emphasised the need for integration and partnerships. A key feature of the Mediterranean is the large number of bordering countries (more than 20) from three continents (Europe, Asia and Africa), with different cultures, religions, political organisations and socio-economic situations. Since 1989 the Programme of Integrated Coastal Area Management has developed management projects on the Albanian and Syrian coasts, in Croatia (Kastela Bay), Greece (Rhode Island), Tunisia (Sfax) and Turkey (Izmir Bay), Egypt and Israel. Projects in Algeria, Lebanon, Malta, Morocco and Slovenia have followed. However, the impressive ICZM efforts have not yet been sufficient to stop major environmental problems arising from highly concentrated pressures such as urbanisation and tourism.

The North-East Atlantic and Baltic Sea conventions, OSPAR and HELCOM of 1992, have promoted strategic and integrated planning, using management tools such as Local Agenda 21, in addition to specific ICZM projects. Under both conventions, strong commissions have been vested with powers to make recommendations for the adoption of specific legislative measures to be taken by the Party states. Both initiatives have been successful in developing dynamic networks between the countries and civil society. In addition, HELCOM has achieved much in balancing the environmental differences between West and East. Financial assistance from the wealthier EU states around the Baltic to the others is an important key to this, and to the anticipated future success of the programme. At least partly as a result of these efforts, there have been improvements in several aspects of water quality in North Sea coastal waters. For the Baltic region, it is estimated that the environmental quality that prevailed in 1950 will be regained in 2050, if the current pace of improvements is maintained.

In the Black Sea, the Black Sea Commission secretariat has coordinated ICZM actions at the subregional level. Due to well-developed landscape research and the long tradition of centralised planning, ICZM development has a strong territorial planning component. It is, however, intended to build on experience and results from other regional seas, including strengthening bottom-up participation involving local communities and NGOs. Unfortunately, the Black Sea countries do not have the same kind of financial support as their counterparts around the Baltic. The lack of economic capacity to manage the pressures on the Black Sea coasts remains a major obstacle to success.

In the Caspian Sea, the Caspian Environment Programme was launched in 1998, supported by the littoral states

---

Box 13.5. Application of integrated coastal zone management tools in the EU

- Germany, the Netherlands and Denmark have developed joint, cross-border management plans to protect specific natural areas in the Wadden Sea.
- Some of Spain's Local Agenda 21 activities focus on coastal municipalities and coastal regions. Examples are Costa de Janda in Andalucia, and the Maresme coast in Catalonia, where the Diputacion of Barcelona has created a municipality network for sustainable development.
- The French Conservatoire du Littoral et des Rivages Lacustres has acquired large stretches of coastal natural areas, to be managed by local and regional bodies applying ICZM principles.

(Azerbaijan, Iran, Kazakhstan, the Russian Federation and Turkmenistan), the Global Environment Facility, UNEP, the World Bank, the EU and growing participation of the private sector. One of the tasks of the Caspian Environment Programme was to prepare the Framework Convention for the Protection of the Marine Environment of the Caspian Sea. A major stumbling block in the implementation of the programme has been differences between the littoral states over ownership and development rights in the sea. The potential oil and natural gas wealth, along with the associated environmental risks of resource development, have heightened the stakes for each country. And,

---

Development of tools related to integrated coastal zone management by regional seas						Table 13.2.

	Atlantic	North Sea	Baltic Sea	Mediterranean Sea	Black Sea	Caspian Sea
National legal and juridical instruments	XXX	XXX	XX	XXX	X	-
Development of management plans (dunes, beaches, estuaries, islands, denominated areas, etc.)	XXX	XXX	XX	XXX	X	-
Protected coastal areas (e.g. natural parks) linked with local development programmes	XXX	X	XX	XX	X	X
Local Agenda 21	XX	XX	XXX	XXX	X	-
Strategic/regional coastal planning involving cooperation between stakeholders, authorities and sectors	XX	XX	XXX	XX	X	-
Concerted actions with sectors and populations (to lower emissions, or pressures on land)	XXX	XX	XXX	XX	X	-
Coastal land acquisition managed by different local bodies	XXX	XX	X	XX	-	-
ICZM demonstration projects	XXX	XXX	XX	XXX	X	X
Integrating science and information	XXX	XXX	XXX	XXX	XX	-
ICZM formation and training	XX	XX	XX	XXX	-	-
ICZM evaluation	XX	XX	XX	XXX	-	-

Note:
XXX: fully implemented.
XX: partially implemented.
X: partially used.
-: not used.

Source: EEA

> 🙁 The concept of integrated coastal zone management has been spreading around European coastlines for 10 years, but implementation has failed to keep up with growing environmental, financial and political pressures.

as with the Black Sea convention, lack of economic capacity will hamper implementation even further.

13.3.2. Urban planning and development

At a more local level than ICZM, there have been interesting developments towards harmonisation and integration in urban planning. Urban planning is a vital tool for intervention to shape a sustainable future, protect and enhance the environment, and improve the quality of life. Indeed, policies and plans for urban development commonly make explicit commitment to the principles of sustainable development. Implementation of environmentally sustainable spatial planning, however, is clearly more difficult.

The reasons lie in the planning systems themselves and in continued pressures for unsustainable development, especially between and at the peripheries of urban areas. Substantive urban planning actions, such as innovative urban renewal and transformation, and ecosystem approaches to the use and management of land, remain fragmented and partial, without full political support at all levels of government. Market forces (both corporate and individual private interests) are still powerful determinants of spatial patterns. Currently, policies focus less on the direct implementation of plans by the public sector, and more on spatial frameworks to ensure that the private sector delivers sustainable outcomes. Even in countries with well-established planning institutions, these frameworks do not determine all development: national interests (especially for economic development) sometimes over-ride local controls. Where planning institutions are weak or unsupported, unregulated development can occur. In some countries, these issues are compounded by the shift from highly regulated economies to more market-based systems, with the consequent pressures of privatised land use, newly privatised mobility, and the need to attract inward investment. Despite the difficulties, examples from cities and regions all over Europe reveal many innovative policies and

practices, and newly designed spatial planning systems that integrate urban land-use management and environmental issues. Distinctive national systems of planning are changing and inter-mixing, and experiences, including the approaches discussed below, are being shared across the continent. City leaders talk to each other even without waiting for clearance from national or regional governments. Cities like Lyon, Geneva and Turin get together to see how their Alpine corner of Europe can keep its wealth while protecting its common mountain environment.

*Integration of urban planning
with other sectors and policy areas*
A significant change in spatial planning during the 1990s was the recognition that isolated physical planning responses to urban problems are insufficient. Urban planning needs to be integrated with other interventions, and with social and economic policy. Large-scale projects and smaller-scale public interventions to refurbish public spaces, open up waterfronts and reclaim road space for pedestrians or cyclists have acted as catalysts for wider urban regeneration, investment and cultural renaissance. Positive planning policies to direct development and investment to damaged or derelict urban land are also important in urban transformation, especially where they operate in tandem with other regulatory, development and financial agencies: Tallinn, for instance, is recovering its Hanseatic glory as a Baltic trading centre. Places like Marseilles, Barcelona and Liverpool are converting their once run-down red-light port districts into new hubs linking people to the sea.

There has been a shift of focus from central areas to the relatively marginalised or peripheral communities. Successful projects such as that in Vienna (Box 13.6) show the benefits of integration with social and economic interventions, such as in the housing market and in community capacity-building, with clear political commitment and integration across different institutions.

Another incentive for integrated planning is the need to address closely related urban problems (such as traffic volumes, community severance and air pollution), which together diminish urban quality of life and endanger health. Members of the World Health Organization (WHO) Healthy Cities Network adopt a combination of key objectives and planning actions as a solution. Examples include urban planning for safe and convenient environments that encourage walking and cycling to work, shops, school and other facilities to promote health and exercise, and that ensure provision for market gardens, allotments, local markets and diverse retail facilities to meet the objectives of local, low-input food production.

There is some evidence that such policies have been successful in revitalising cities, generating increased investment, and stemming urban decline. However, the problems of displacement of certain groups by higher land values, and of unequal access to the benefits of new investment, remain serious.

Ecosystems approaches

Spatial planning decisions also need to respect biophysical and environmental resources essential to sustain human quality of life. There are many indications that the urban planning system is adopting a broader, more holistic view, and is paying regard to resource flows (such as energy, materials and water). But there are very few examples of a fully eco-centric plan, using concepts of critical natural capital or carrying capacity, being implemented. However, many urban plans do now require that developments meet standards for biodiversity protection and enhancement, flood risk avoidance, and water, energy and materials efficiency (see, for example, Box 13.7 on Hanover).

Another example is of a more holistic approach that pursues a greater degree of food self-reliance by producing more food locally, especially fruits and vegetables. Traditional horticultural food production in urban areas has largely disappeared in WE, apart from some recreational gardening, but in CEE and EECCA subsistence food production in and around cities has increased as the output from the large old collective farms has decreased. Such urban vegetable and fruit production has positive impacts on local employment and local economic growth, and results in lower cost of local foods, enhanced access to healthier food, closer links between consumers and producers, and greener, healthier cities.

There are similar developments in WE. In Sweden, for example, new buildings are planned with composting facilities, and municipally owned city farms use this compost, so contributing both to a reduction of the environmental impact of waste and to social cohesion and local economic growth.

Box 13.6. Urban renewal scheme in Vienna, Austria

In Vienna, an urban renewal scheme was aimed at social renewal. It did so through the use of criteria such as avoiding segregation or forced change of ownership, renewal of occupied stock with the tenants' participation, the use of targeted subsidies (to avoid displacement of local occupants), and using a city block approach to ensure cohesiveness and participation. This has enabled the scheme to combine improvements to the flats and other buildings with improvements to the wider living environment, through provision of green space, traffic calming, preservation of small businesses and the provision of social services.

Source: Dubai awards, 2000

Box 13.7. The integrated urban water policy of Hanover, Germany

In Hanover, water policy is guided by the principles of sustainable development, and the aims of a secure water supply, permanent protection of groundwater and surface water reserves, and water conservation. This is done through:

- rainwater absorption: since 1994, every development plan submitted for approval must address the feasibility of absorbing rainwater on site rather than channelling it into the drains;
- rainwater exploitation: the use of rainwater rather than the municipal water supply, and therefore the installation of rainwater collection systems, is encouraged through financial incentives;
- ecological restoration of waterways;
- tertiary water treatment.

Source: ICLEI

Institutional planning frameworks

Local Agenda 21 has emphasised the importance of community participation (such as two-way community and stakeholder participation and active involvement) leading to new approaches in those countries where planning lacked such a tradition, and new techniques elsewhere (such as visioning exercises). Most of the examples given above rely heavily on community participation in one form or another. In the 10 years since the Rio summit, many urban planning initiatives have drawn on the Local Agenda 21 visions or strategies adopted by local communities, which have generated greater political support. This is especially the case in WE and the accession countries. In Majorca, for example, these principles are being used to change the whole direction of spatial policy (Box 13.8).

In many EECCA countries, the responsibility for preparing and adopting plans for urban development, within the framework of a national plan, falls to federal authorities. However, there are overlapping jurisdictions, and vertical and horizontal integration is difficult. Municipalities are often small and numerous (in the Russian Federation, for example, there are more than 13 000 municipalities), with little planning expertise. And these countries in transition

Box 13.8. Local Agenda 21 and spatial planning in Calvia, Spain

In the early 1990s, the town council of Majorca began a series of programmes which resulted in 1995 in a decision to promote a new, long-term strategy aimed at retargeting tourist and local development in accordance with sustainability principles, with the environment seen as a key for the future.

This process initiated Calvia's Local Agenda 21, which in turn has led to the adoption of its new general plan, which breaks with the previous model in:

* reducing the expected population and hence the amount of building land allowed;
* fostering the protection of rural areas and promoting urban regeneration;
* adopting new eco-responsibility regulations (on bio-climatic adaptation, separation of waste and building materials, etc.).

Implementation is through clearing of buildings and rationalising land use and infrastructures, and linking the tourist eco-tax at regional level to local and regional funding to support land purchase.

Source: Ajuntament de Calvia, 2000

Box 13.9. The national plan of spatial development in Belarus

In Belarus, a national plan of spatial development was approved by the Council of Ministers in February 2000, and work on regional level plans is progressing. Master plans for half the urban settlements have been approved since 1990 (with a plan date of 2010). However, many problems remain:

* lack of legal and normative bases for public participation in plan making or development control;
* poor integration of planning programmes with mechanisms for providing compensation or amelioration arising from planning decisions;
* shortage of funds for urban planning documentation, causing delays and poor implementation.

Source: VASAB, 2000

from centrally planned economic and political systems have little history of community autonomy or public participation in the physical planning process. In the Russian Federation, these problems are compounded by the pressures of internal migration from the east to the western cities of the country (Traynor, 2002; Artobolevskiy, 2000).

Nevertheless, there is enthusiasm for change, recognising the importance of integrating environmental protection into democratically approved plans, and for sharing of experiences with other countries of WE and countries in transition. For example, VASAB 2010 (Vision and strategies around the Baltic) is a project to promote urban systems and urban networking in the Baltic Sea region, ultimately to promote a joint spatial development perspective. Working with other international initiatives such as Baltic 21 (a Regional Agenda 21), and the EU's Interreg II, Phare and Tacis programmes, VASAB links spatial (urban settlements, infrastructure and non-urban areas) and institutional elements (planning systems and procedures). Box 13.9 describes such a development in Belarus.

Experience shows clearly that urban planning polices that do not have the support or approval of local communities risk ineffective implementation and loss of trust in planning decisions. However, bottom-up involvement is not likely to be sufficient to achieve sustainable development (Naess, 2001). All stakeholders need to be involved, ranging from various government levels to the business community and the local public. Ecologically defensible land use and resource consumption require a real break with business-as-usual lifestyles. A good example of urban development where the three approaches singled out above are combined (integration of different sectors, an eco-system approach and Local Agenda 21 with strong local level partnerships) is described in Box 13.10 for the city of Malmö.

In the EU, many of the good practices identified above are being networked and shared among planning authorities at various levels and in many countries.

Although there have been substantial obstacles in the EU accession countries to moving towards more integrated and environmentally sound urban planning systems, a number of towns and cities are pursuing good practice. Many are networking and adopting measures to integrate physical, social and economic planning, to take on board ecological principles, and to make use of appraisal tools and participative processes. A survey of 12 towns in the Slovak Republic, for example, revealed that a variety of different approaches to planning were being applied (author's data).

In EECCA, it has proved difficult to shift from a physical planning tradition to a more holistic spatial planning approach, integrated with other economic sectors and policy regimes, and working within environmental constraints. However, countries such as Belarus, Ukraine and the Russian Federation are setting up new legal frameworks and systems for urban plan preparation and adoption, and for land privatisation and reform. The strengths of these new systems lie in their familiarity with setting strategic aims, a firm policy framework, technical expertise, a high degree of education and a learning culture. The weaknesses remain a static approach to plan documentation, with little attention to implementation, and a tradition of monitoring without evaluation (Wernstedt, 2002).

13.3.3. Other integration policy instruments

Since the early 1970s, when environmental issues began to appear on political agendas, many regulatory instruments have been put in place, mainly following command-and-control rules (polluters have to pay and governments have to monitor enforcement and impacts). Technological progress played a major role in the development of such instruments. It has facilitated reduced consumption of energy, water and minerals, and the increased application of recycling, material substitution and use of renewable resources. This section, however, focuses on newer policy instruments that have been introduced in more recent years in the fight against environmental degradation: economic instruments and economic integration, voluntary approaches and environmental assessments.

Economic instruments and economic integration

In the past decade, market-based (economic) instruments such as taxes, charges and emission-permit trading systems have increasingly been applied to offer greater flexibility, and sometimes more cost-effective solutions, than traditional instruments such as individual environmental licences or generic rules and standards. Subsidies, sometimes financed from the revenues of charges, can also be used to encourage environmentally beneficial behaviour or reduce environmental damage.

Environmental taxes and charges

Environmental taxes and charges have become mature instruments in the instrument mix available to policy-makers, and have been increasingly implemented since the1980s. (Table 13.3.) The use of these instruments has been tied to the polluter pays principle as they internalise the external costs (see Box 13.11) of the pollution that results from production or consumption activities. These external costs can be significant and environmental taxation can help to correctly internalise these costs in market prices of goods and services.

Taxes and charges have historically been applied on a one-by-one basis — as a choice for meeting particular objectives. However, in many countries they are increasingly being applied within a general strategy of environmental tax reform (ETR) and more recently of ecological fiscal reform. The

former only addresses taxes and charges, whereas the latter also includes the reduction of environmentally harmful subsidies. Since the first ETR in the early 1990s in the Nordic countries and the Netherlands, more countries (e.g. Germany and the United Kingdom) are looking at a broad strategy of shifting the tax base, lowering labour taxes and increasing environmental and natural resource-use taxes. The aim is to improve the functioning of markets and shift the tax burden from 'goods' (e.g. employment) to 'bads' (e.g. environmental damage).

Box 13.10. Sustainable urban development in the city of Malmö, Sweden

The municipality of Malmö launched two integrated projects to transform the western harbour of Malmö from a polluted wasteland to an ecologically leading-edge example of sustainable urban development. In doing so, it took into account its Local Agenda 21 action plan, the comprehensive plan for Malmö 2000, its environmental programme and its 2001 gender equality plan. Key characteristics of the projects were:

- partnerships between local authorities, local housing companies and the local community;
- new and rehabilitated housing, including for people with special needs (such as the elderly and students);
- cleaning polluted soil and better maintaining green spaces;
- better infrastructure for traffic, energy, waste and water (affordable shared transport through an electric car pool, locally produced renewable energy, recycling projects, local treatment of surface water runoff so decreasing the risk of flooded basements during heavy rain).

As a result of these projects, the city of Malmö has noted a change in people's attitudes and behaviour with increased recycling of household waste and increased popularity of the bicycle as a means of transport. A wide range of innovative 'green' products and services has resulted from the projects e.g. green roofs, low energy villas and renewable energy solutions. This concerted effort and commitment of the local authorities and its partners demonstrates that Local Agenda 21 is a viable concept for sustainable urban development. The projects meet the basic criteria of impact, partnership and sustainability as well as additional considerations of leadership and community empowerment, gender equality and social inclusion, innovation within a local context and transferability.

Source: Dubai awards, 2002

Box 13.11. Estimates of external costs

Estimates of the external costs of fossil fuel-based electricity production in the EU range from EUR 0.1 to EUR 0.4/kWh for natural gas-based electricity and EUR 0.02 to EUR 0.15 for coal-based electricity (EEA, 2002b). The external costs of transport in the EU amount to around 8 % of GDP, with road transport accounting for more than 90 % of these costs (EEA, 2001).

Ecological taxation and 'green' charges are now established, but they have as yet had limited practical effect.

Internalisation in market prices of external costs is incomplete in many areas.

While the principle of ETR has gained favour throughout much of Europe, in aggregate such changes are not proceeding very quickly. Since 1995, labour taxes in the EU have decreased from 23.8 % to 23.0 % of GDP, and environmental taxes increased from 2.77 % to 2.84 % (EEA, 2002a).

Taxes relating to energy and transport remain a key indicator. In most of northwest Europe, taxes on the five main energy products are already equal to or higher than those that were proposed by the European Commission for 2002 in the 'Monti proposal' (CEC, 1997). However, taxation levels are significantly lower in the cohesion countries — Spain, Portugal, Greece and Ireland — and in Luxembourg and Switzerland. Most western European states also now have a road vehicle tax system which is differentiated to one extent or another according to environmental criteria or to some proxy for these (e.g. fuel consumption, engine power) (see, for example, Box 13.12).

Road use and congestion charging is also gaining political momentum in many western European countries. The European Commission is currently developing a framework proposal for infrastructure charging which would agree a common methodology to enable countries to charge for the external costs of using transport infrastructure. A number of Member States, including Germany and the United Kingdom, are planning to introduce their own systems of distance charges for lorries. In Switzerland, such a system already exists whereby lorries are charged for their use of the entire road network. Congestion charging for urban areas is also gaining political support, with London the largest city in Europe to implement such a system.

Taxes and charges on products are relatively scarce, but include a few good examples of effective economic instruments. The recently introduced levy on plastic shopping bags in Ireland has had a dramatic impact (see Box 13.13).

In some CEE countries (e.g. Hungary), efforts have been made to increase taxation on energy products. Some accession countries will need to raise duties on mineral oils further to comply with the EU's current minimum requirements; and all would need to make increases across the range of energy products to reach the levels proposed in the 'Monti proposal'. Environmental differentiation of vehicle taxes is found in some states (e.g. Bosnia-Herzegovina, Hungary, Romania and the Slovak Republic) but is not the norm.

Box 13.12. Annual taxation of passenger cars in the United Kingdom

In the United Kingdom, annual taxation of passenger cars was until recently undifferentiated, but now falls into one of five bands directly related to carbon dioxide (CO_2) emissions. It is proposed that a new energy and CO_2 labelling system will reflect the same bands. The company car taxation system has also been restructured to encourage take-up of cars with lower CO_2 emissions. These changes were welcomed in a recent communication from the European Commission (CEC, 2002b).

Box 13.13. Levy on plastic shopping bags in Ireland

Since 4 March 2002, retailers in Ireland are obliged to charge a EUR 0.15 levy on each plastic bag they provide to their customers. Revenues go to an Environment Fund. In the first three months of its existence, the tax had achieved a reduction in the provision of plastic bags of more than 90 %. More than 1 billion plastic bags per year are expected to be removed from circulation as a result of the tax.

Source: Department of the Environment and Local Government, 2002

☺ An increasing number of environmental taxation systems are being introduced throughout the EU with the aim of improving environmental quality in an efficient way and reducing the burden of taxation on labour and other production costs.

😐 There are some indications of the effectiveness of environmental taxes, but evaluative studies are generally lacking.

😐 Taxes and charges on emissions to air and water and on natural resources are quite widespread in CEE and EECCA, but their effectiveness is uncertain.

 Energy, waste and product taxes still lag behind.

Environmental taxes and charges in western Europe, central and eastern Europe and the 12 countries of eastern Europe, the Caucasus and central Asia

Table 13.3.

Country	Natural resources				Waste			Emissions		Selected products					Other	
	a	b	c	d	e	f	g	h	i	j	k	l	m	n	o	p
Albania	✔															
Armenia	✔	✔		✔	✔			✔	✔		✔	✔				
Austria				✔	✔				✔		✔	✔				
Belarus								✔								
Belgium	○	○							○	✔	✔	✔				
Bosnia & Herzegovina	✔															
Bulgaria	✔		✔	✔				+	+							
Croatia	✔	✔		✔				+	✔					✔		
Czech Republic	✔	✔					✔	✔	✔	✔					✈	✔
Denmark	✔		✔		✔	✔			✔	✔	✔	✔	✔	✔		
Estonia	✔	✔	✔		✔			✔	✔		✔					
Finland	✔		✔		✔				✔		✔		✔			
France		✔				✔			✔							
Germany		○				✔			✔							
Greece		✔	✔						✔							
Hungary	✔	✔	✔	✔			✔	+	✔		✔	✔			✈	
Iceland			✔					✔			✔			✔		
Ireland									✔					✔		
Italy					✔			✔	✔					✔	✈	
Kazakhstan	✔	✔	✔	✔	✔			✔	✔							
Kyrgyzstan	✔	✔	✔					✔	✔							
Latvia	✔	✔	✔	✔	✔			✔	✔	✔	✔	✔				
Lithuania	✔	✔	✔	✔				✔	✔							
Moldova, Rep. of	✔	✔						✔	✔							
Netherlands		✔		✔	✔			✔	✔						✈	
Norway		✔		✔	✔	✔		✔	✔	✔	✔				✈	
Poland	✔	✔	✔	✔			✔	✔	✔	✔	✔					✔
Portugal			✔													
Romania		✔				+			✔							
Russian Fed.	✔	✔		✔				✔	✔							
Slovak Rep.	✔	✔			✔			✔	✔	✔	✔			✔		✔
Slovenia			✔				✔									
Spain								○	✔							
Sweden	✔		✔		✔			✔	○			✔	✔			
Switzerland								✔					✈			
Turkey								✈	○						✈	
United Kingdom	✔				✔											
Ukraine	✔		✔		✔			✔	✔							
Uzbekistan	✔	✔	✔	✔	✔			✔	✔							

Note: Charges which only cover the costs of production or public services (e.g. waste collection fees, waste water treatment) are not included.

Key: ✛ = Non Compliance Fees (fees/penalties which only apply to emissions above limits).
○ At the regional (sub-national) level.
✈ Aircraft only

a	Mining, minerals, gravel, sand, etc	i	To water
b	Groundwater, surface water	j	Chemical substances
c	Hunting, Fishing	k	Packaging
d	Forest use, tree cutting	l	Batteries
e	Landflling	m	Pesticides
f	Incineration	n	Plastic bags
g	Hazardous waste	o	Noise
h	To air	p	Land use change

Source: EEA, 2000; OECD 2000, 2002a; REC, 1999; UNECE Environment Performance Review reports

Taxes and charges on energy products remain quite low in EECCA, and there appears as yet to be little attention to improving vehicle fleet performance through differentiated taxation. In the 1990s, many of the EECCA countries introduced charging systems to raise revenues for environmental investments, create incentives for pollution control and reduction, enforce permit requirements, and implement the polluter pays principle (UNECE, 2002). These charges have generally been introduced in conjunction with a permit system: a base charge is applied for permitted emissions and a penalty rate encourages compliance with the permitted standard.

Subsidies
There are many examples of subsidies across Europe. For example, most forms of public transport are subsidised in most countries, in recognition of the fact that public transport serves important social goals and provides an alternative to (generally more damaging) private transport, particularly private cars. Some western European countries and most CEE countries and EECCA have historically subsidised spending to a high level, but in many countries, these subsidies are under pressure from national and local authority budgetary limits. Particularly in the countries in transition, budgets for public transport have been cut back severely, and service levels and quality have suffered as a result.

To combat carbon dioxide (CO_2) emissions and other forms of pollution from fossil-fuelled power stations, most western European countries in particular offer direct or indirect subsidies for renewable energy plants. Indirect subsidies tend to be mechanisms that operate within the framework of electricity supply pricing, such as the German 'feed-in' law or the United Kingdom's renewables obligation. The Community also collectively supports renewables investments through the second ALTENER programme, while the parallel SAVE II programme encourages energy efficiency investments.

In recent years, there has been an increase in some countries in support for environmentally sensitive farming. It is increasingly recognised that farmers, foresters and others supplying environmental or social benefits may need direct economic incentives. Such incentives are playing a bigger role in agriculture policy and at the same time there is a growing emphasis on attaching

environmental conditions to support payments, as proposed on an increased scale by the Commission in the mid-term review of the common agricultural policy (CAP).

The EU has increased the level of resources devoted to agri-environment schemes dramatically since 1992. They now cover around 20 % of the total agricultural area and include measures to support organic farming and reduce pollution pressures, and the management of cultural landscapes. Several CEE countries have also adopted this approach.

Environmental funds (usually funded by receipts from pollution charges) have been important in securing environmental investments in some CEE countries and EECCA which have undergone the most rapid reform, as capital is otherwise in short supply. In many other countries, industrial output is at about half its pre-transition levels; here environmental policies rarely provide sufficient incentives for action, while environmental funds have been more limited and less effective (UNECE, 2002).

Environmentally damaging subsidies and tax exemptions
Financial support to industries, activities and products may also have significant negative impacts on the quality of the environment. Such subsidies, which may be either direct (visible) or indirect (invisible), are widespread both in Europe and in the rest of the world. Direct subsidies include financial support for production, e.g. in agriculture (price and income support for farmers) and energy (coal subsidies, or tax exemptions for aviation, commercial fishing or certain industrial sectors). Indirect subsidies occur where markets are protected (e.g. at the EU's outer borders), and where governments provide products and services for prices that do not cover the costs, e.g. in waste and wastewater collection and treatment, and the provision of clean water and of infrastructure for transport. In the EU, the European Commission has the role of policing subsidies, particularly in areas where either direct or hidden subsidies could distort the Single Market. However, the Community's influence in national energy policy is very limited; but the Commission oversees the CAP, which incorporates a large and elaborate system of subsidies, compensation payments, tariffs and price supports, and which accounts for 45 % of the Community's entire budget.

Figure 13.1. shows the development of total support to agriculture in a number of countries during the 1990s. In most countries for which data are available, subsidies to agriculture show a decreasing trend. OECD countries, like others, are committed to reducing support to agriculture. However, the pace of such reductions has generally been slow and some aspects of support are excluded from the reduction commitment as they are classified by the WTO as 'green box' or 'blue box' support. The recent proposals from the Commission for the mid-term review of the CAP would result in a very significant 'decoupling' of support from production.

In the energy area, subsidies to coal production dominate in the EU. These subsidies are stable or show a decreasing trend but especially in Germany, coal subsidies are still a substantial share of GDP.

Total support estimates (TSE) to agriculture in EU and selected countries	Figure 13.1.

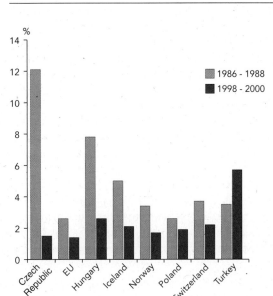

Note: The TSE is the total share of GDP in agricultural support (three-year averages in %). It includes both transfers from consumers (through domestic market price support) and from taxpayers (through budgetary or tax expenditures).

Source: OECD

Tax reductions and exemptions for energy use in European countries	Table 13.4.

Country	Coal VAT	Coal Energy tax	Natural gas Vat	Natural gas Energy tax	Electricity VAT	Electricity Energt tax
Austria		E		RL		RL
Belgium	R	E				
Bulgaria		–		–		–
Cyprus		–		–		–
Czech Republic	R	–	R	–	R	–
Denmark		RL		RL		
Estonia		–		–		–
Finland			(R)	R		RL
France		–		–		–
Germany	E	–	RL	–		RL
Greece		–		–	R	–
Hungary	(E)	–	(R)	–		R
Iceland		–		–	RH	–
Ireland	RH	–	RH	–	RH	–
Italy	R	(E)	R	RHL	R	RHL
Latvia		–		–		–
Lithuania		–		–		–
Luxembourg	R	–	RH	–	R	–
Netherlands				RHL		RHL
Norway					R*	
Poland		–		–		–
Portugal		–	(R)	–		R
Romania	EH	–	EH	–	EH	–
Russian Fed.		–		–		–
Slovak Rep.	R	–	R	–	R	–
Slovenia		E		E	(R)	E
Spain		–		–		
Sweden		RL		RL		EL
Switzerland		–				–
Turkey		–	R	–		–
United Kingdom	RH	EH	RH	EH	RH	EH

Notes: R denotes a tax reduction; E an exemption. L indicates tax reductions/exemptions for large energy users (and/or specific sectors, such as greenhouse horticulture). H indicates tax reductions/exemptions for households. Tax reductions/exemptions for renewable energy are not considered to be environmentally harmful subsidies and therefore not included. Brackets indicate arrangements that have recently been abolished. — indicates the absence of any specific energy/CO_2 taxes. * indicates only in certain regions.

Source: Oosterhuis, 2001

In many European countries, the use of energy is further subsidised (usually for social or competitiveness reasons) by means of tax reductions (see Table 13.4).

Unlike agriculture and energy, the size of subsidies to transport is not currently estimated on an internationally comparable basis. These subsidies mainly consist of below-cost provision of infrastructure, the failure to tax the external cost of pollution, congestion and accidents, and tax reductions and exemptions for specific modes of transport. Again this is often done for reasons of social inclusion or commercial competitiveness. Among the latter, however, the absence of taxes on aircraft fuel is the most obvious example. The European Commission recommended in 2000 that the EU Member States should intensify their work within the International Civil Aviation Organisation's framework for the introduction of taxation on aviation fuel (CEC, 2000), but relatively little progress has been made. Work continues on a possible European aviation charge.

In the CEE countries and EECCA, artificial price levels and other forms of subsidy were common under the former centrally planned economies. Through the 1990s, however, economic dislocation and restructuring severely reduced the funds available to national governments. In addition, international financing institutions have insisted on far-reaching reforms as preconditions of loans and grants. These two effects have combined to bring about substantial reductions in the level of subsidies in most sectors.

> Environmentally damaging subsidies and tax exemptions remain substantial. Subsidies are generally falling, but favourable tax treatment remains common.

Emissions trading
The newest economic regulatory instrument in the EU is emissions trading. While there has historically been reluctance to use emissions trading in the EU, this changed with the incorporation of 'flexible mechanisms', which include emissions trading, in the 1997 Kyoto protocol. Ever since, there has been a rapidly growing interest in tradable permits or emissions trading, both at the EU and Member State level. An EU-wide greenhouse gas emissions trading programme for a list of industrial sectors is planned to be operational in 2005.

Discussions on the design and implementation of domestic greenhouse gas emissions trading schemes are taking place in a number of Member States, including the Netherlands, Sweden, Germany, France and Switzerland. Denmark and the United Kingdom have already launched domestic emissions trading schemes, which became operational in 2001 and 2002 respectively (OECD, 2002b).

Although major tradable permit schemes deal with greenhouse gases, the instrument in general seems to be attracting more interest. The Netherlands have been seriously considering a nitrogen oxide (NO_x) tradable permit scheme, and in the United Kingdom a quasi-trading scheme for sulphur dioxide (SO_2) was implemented though company 'bubbles' for the then National Power and PowerGen. Several countries are introducing tradable renewable energy certificates (e.g. Belgium, Denmark, Italy and the Netherlands) and the United Kingdom has developed tradable certificates for waste (OECD, 2002b).

> Emissions trading has been launched in the EU as a new regulatory instrument that promises to offer new opportunities for further cost-effective reductions in pollution.

Voluntary approaches
In addition to governmental action, some initiatives have been taken, which emphasise the private sector's own responsibility for a better environment. As well as regulators and firms entering into negotiated agreements (NAs) and self-commitments that specify targets to be achieved, companies are discovering the value of a 'clean' image and of selling 'green' products and services. However, vested interests, ingrained habits and institutional barriers may obstruct the 'greening' of industry. Generally speaking, the number of voluntary actions has increased substantially in the past decade. Negotiated agreements are also increasingly seen as instruments within a portfolio of instruments, and the approach of 'which instrument is best' has changed to one of 'which package of instruments forms an optimal instrument mix'.

Business participation in negotiated agreements
Under negotiated agreements, governments and industrial sectors or a group of individual companies agree to reach certain environmental objectives in a certain timeframe (Box 13.14). Many negotiated

agreements are based on civil law, i.e. bilateral agreements between contracting partners, while others are more 'gentlemen's agreements' that are not legally binding. The choice depends on the particular legal structures of the country.

The number of negotiated agreements increased during the 1990s and spread to most EU Member States, but they are as yet very limited in CEE countries and EECCA (EEA, 1997; OECD, 1998 and 1999; ten Brink, 2002). Today, several hundred negotiated agreements operate in the EU, most of them at national level, but with many local negotiated agreements in some countries and only a handful of Community-wide agreements focusing on products widely traded in the internal market. Based on a strong tradition of consensual politics, the Netherlands leads with more than 100 negotiated agreements, though there is significant growth in the use of these instruments in many other Member States.

Crucial for effective NAs are credibility of agreements, strong commitment of the parties involved, transparency of monitoring and quantitative targets. A 'big stick' of regulatory threat improves effectiveness, but sometimes such a stick does not appear necessary (de Clercq *et al.*, 2000). It is important to stress that NAs can be seen as a process and that with due government interest and pressure, sometimes facilitated by NGO initiatives, an agreement can be improved over time.

> The use of negotiated agreements grew significantly during the 1990s, particularly in western Europe, but scepticism still remains regarding their effectiveness.

Certified environmental management systems (EMS)
Since the 1980s, large companies have developed environmental management systems (EMS) in response to pressure to demonstrate environmental performance. In 1996, developments culminated in the introduction of two EMS standards: ISO 14001 (under the auspices of the International Organization for Standardization) for all types of organisations worldwide and EMAS (eco-management and audit scheme) for industry in the EU. In 2001, a renovated EMAS-2 was closely dovetailed with ISO 14001 and is now also available for non-industrial sites. Companies can certify their EMS according to ISO and EMAS. EMS targets are

> **Box 13.14. Key areas addressed by negotiated agreements**
>
> Over the past few years the key area of growth in the use of negotiated agreements (NAs) is climate change. NAs have also been increasingly linked to environmental taxes (e.g. UK climate change agreements are linked to the climate change levy). The EU also fosters the further development of NAs where these offer particular added value (CEC, 1996; 2002b).
>
> NAs have been launched to address a wide range of environmental challenges, covering pollution from process activities (e.g. SO_2 and NO_x emissions in the Netherlands, emissions to water in Portugal, CO_2 emissions in the United Kingdom and Switzerland), process activity efficiency (e.g. energy use and efficiency in Finland, Germany, the Netherlands), product use (e.g. batteries in Germany and Belgium), wastes related to products (e.g. packaging waste in Sweden, transport packaging in Denmark).

prescribed as legal compliance and a continuous improvement of environmental performance. These wordings give businesses flexibility in implementation.

In five years, ISO 14001 and, to a lesser extent, EMAS have become popular with businesses. As Table 13.5 shows, several thousand companies have certified their EMS. Geographically, there is an emphasis on northwest Europe. Accession EU countries are catching up on ISO 14001. EMAS has become popular in a few countries, notably Germany, Austria, Denmark and Sweden. In business sectors, emphasis is on multinational corporations, with the chemicals industry as the prime example.

A caveat is that a certified EMS does not automatically improve environmental performance. A recent research project found no relation between certification and performance (Berkhout et al., 2001). Moreover, companies have substantial freedom to choose their own priorities in EMAS/ISO 14001. Chain management and green procurement are options, but are not compulsory. Most companies focus their effort on internal production processes, but electronics and car manufacturers have started to look at procurement policies as a means for environmental improvements through chain management.

Business environmental reporting
The 1990s saw the inception of business environmental reporting (Figure 13.2.). Developments run five years behind EMS, showing that a well-functioning EMS is a prerequisite for serious reporting. EMAS obliges a company to publish a certified statement, but ISO 14001 does not.

So far, uniform reporting formats are missing. This brings much confusion and makes comparisons between companies

Table 13.5.	Number of ISO 14001 and EMAS certificates in selected European countries as of January 2002

Note: Number of certificates in countries not listed is less than 20. – : not applied

Sources: www.ecology.or.jp/ isoworld; www.europa.eu.int/comm/ environment/emas

Country	ISO 14001	EMAS	Country	ISO 14001	EMAS
Germany	3 380	2 692	Norway	297	64
United Kingdom	2 500	78	Poland	294	–
Sweden	2 070	211	Austria	224	360
Spain	2 064	154	Ireland	200	8
Italy	1 108	68	Czech Rep.	197	6
France	1 092	35	Slovenia	138	–
Netherlands	942	25	Belgium	130	14
Denmark	919	174	Turkey	91	–
Switzerland	762	–	Slovak Rep.	73	–
Finland	678	36	Greece	66	6
Hungary	300	–	Portugal	47	2

Figure 13.2.	Corporate reporting by country in 2002, top 100 companies

Source: KPMG, 2002

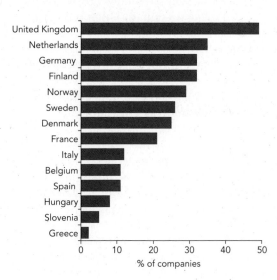

% of companies

The number of companies that report on environmental performance is still increasing. A central register of environmental reports does not exist, but of the biggest corporations in the Fortune Top 250 list, 45 % now publish an environmental report (KPMG, 2002). Companies in the chemicals, gas, oil, electronics, automotive and utilities sectors are front-runners. A 2002 UNEP study lists 'the magnificent seven' as best in class: Cooperative Bank (UK), Novo Nordisk (pharmaceutics; Denmark), BAA (airports; UK), British Telecom (UK), Rio Tinto (minerals; UK), Royal Dutch/Shell (oil; UK/Netherlands) and BP (oil; UK). These companies combine good governance with transparency (UNEP/SustainAbility, 2002).

As with EMS certification, the smaller the size of a company, the smaller is the probability of an environmental report.

International business organisations for sustainable development
Since 1995, the World Business Council for Sustainable Development (WBCSD) has become a leading platform for business cooperation in the field of sustainable development. In 2002, WBCSD had about 150 member companies, of which 50 % are based in Europe. In WBCSD projects, corporate representatives develop know-how on topics such as eco-efficiency, innovation and corporate social responsibility. On sustainability reporting, WBCSD cooperates

difficult. In 1997 the Global Reporting Initiative (GRI), an NGO backed by UNEP, started the development of sustainability reporting guidelines (GRI, 2001).

Some EU countries oblige certain sectors of industry to publish environmental reports: Denmark (since 1996; several thousand sites), the Netherlands (since 1999; 250 companies), Sweden (since 1999; paragraph in financial report) and France (to start in 2002; for publicly quoted companies).

closely with GRI. The 111 corporations that use the GRI guidelines are almost all WBCSD members. In January 2003 WBCSD released a report intended to increase the standing of corporate sustainability reporting as a business tool. It has also produced guidance to help companies produce reports and make the information contained more relevant to stakeholders.

The chemical industry initiated the Responsible Care programme in 1984 aimed at improving performance, open communication with the public and the diffusion of best practice. Responsible Care is a voluntary programme that is continually upgraded and adapted to meet new demands on environmental management.

Most trade associations, national and international, have developed schemes to assist member companies in environmental management. Some of these provide codes of conduct and environmental manuals for their members. However, they do not have such a demanding scheme as the chemical industry and, in the absence of monitoring, the likelihood of compliance to codes of conduct is rather low.

Product eco-labelling
The oldest national eco-labelling scheme, the German *Blauer Engel*, started 25 years ago. The German system emphasises a few product criteria deemed most important for environmental performance. Later schemes use a cradle-to-grave approach by making a product life cycle assessment (LCA). Developed in parallel with many national schemes, the EU introduced its eco-label 'flower' in 1993. This scheme now covers 18 product groups, and another eight are under development. National eco-labelling schemes operate in Germany, Finland, Sweden, Denmark, Norway, Iceland, Spain and Catalonia, France, Austria, the Netherlands, Croatia, the Czech Republic, Hungary, Poland and Slovakia.

In addition to EU and national eco-labels, there are many private and specialised labels. Private labels, covering several product groups, play a role in only a few countries. Examples are TCO (Sweden) and Good Environmental Choice (United Kingdom, Sweden). Specialised labels cover one product group only. They are relatively well developed for products from agriculture and forestry. The EKO-label, upheld by an NGO called SKAL, certifies products from organic farming in about 30 countries (Bushmovich

et al., 2001). Emphasis is on food products, but non-food products such as cotton textiles are also included.

In forestry, the Forest Stewardship Council (FSC) has become the dominant initiator of sustainable forest management worldwide. Initiated in 1993 and based in Mexico, FSC-certified forests cover 27 million hectares. In 2002, 23 European countries had FSC-certified forests, of which Poland, Sweden, United Kingdom, Estonia and Latvia are most prominent (with over 0.5 million ha each). In several transition countries, environmental labels have been created for promoting the use of environmentally acceptable products and manufacturing procedures. They are modelled on similar labels in WE. A number of products have received these labels, but as yet there is little information on their commercial effect. Probably the main effect of eco-labels has been to recognise the environmental efforts and motivate the producers, and to establish a dialogue between industry and environmental authorities. International eco-labels have also had an impact in transition countries. Several international networks of organic food certification are present in the region through their local NGO counterparts, along with many domestic organic and quality labels for food products. In a few cases, forests and wood processing companies are obtaining Forest Stewardship Council certification in order to be able to sell wood and wood products to western markets (UNECE, 2002).

> The use and coverage of eco-labels continues to spread across Europe, but still for few product groups and in few countries.

Environmental impact assessment
Environmental impact assessment (EIA) is an important tool both for harmonisation of policies and for integration of environmental considerations into economic and other sectoral decisions. It combines the precautionary principle with principles of public participation and of preventing environmental damage.

In western Europe, the situation regarding implementation of EIA at the project level is positive, with only Monaco reporting a lack of legislation. In general the practice of EIA is also good. Progress has been driven, to a significant extent, by the EU's environmental impact assessment directive (Directive 85/337/EEC as amended by 97/11/EC) and by the Espoo convention (EIA in a transboundary context) that entered into force in 1997. In terms of continuing issues with EIA, while procedural compliance with the directive is generally very good, responses to questionnaires indicate that there are areas for improvement. These particularly regard public participation at the scoping stage, rather than involving the public too late in the process, when project options have already been selected. There has been progress in some countries with the weight given to an EIA in decision-making, with incorrect predictions made in the EIA being subject to variations in permissions granted. However, the norm is still for incomplete implementation of mitigation measures to go both unmonitored and unpunished. More attention is therefore needed on monitoring impacts and finding ways of dealing with unpredicted outcomes.

The Netherlands' EIA system relies on an independent EIA commission to assist in identifying the scope of the assessment (where it includes a wider audience than just the authorities involved) and reviewing the environmental impact statement. This is an accepted way of dealing with bias and quality issues.

The new Portuguese EIA system has novel post-evaluation procedures. These include a requirement for an 'impact assessment compliance report' indicating how mitigation measures outlined in the environmental impact statement were incorporated into the design of the project. The EIA authority may impose project or management adjustments or additional mitigation measures where unforeseen impacts occur. Interested parties, including the public, can raise complaints on the environmental impacts of projects which must be dealt with by the relevant authorities.

In CEE countries, progress with implementing EIA and the practice of EIA is also good. There has been a series of capacity-building programmes which have helped to achieve compliance with the requirements of EU directives; however, not all countries have been through this process. Other problems cited are that, having been through capacity-building programmes and having new legislation in place, there remain operational problems through a lack of training of responsible officers, or a lack of organisations with suitable experience to be able to carry out EIA. Other issues cited are that the quality of environmental statements

is poor and that specific guidance needs to be developed; that the EIAs take too long under the administrative procedures adopted (over a year in some cases); and lack of baseline environmental data. Some countries need time to build experience, which could be helped with more emphasis on training, ideally ensuring that long-term measures are in place, such as courses available at universities. Other countries still need capacity-building in terms of changes to legislation and building the administrative framework to allow the process to work successfully.

In EECCA, EIA systems are primarily based on the state ecological review (SER) and assessment of ecological impacts (OVOS) systems inherited from the former USSR. There are commonly cited problems in the operation of these systems. These include citizens being unaware of their rights and duties and so not participating properly in EIA; financial constraints preventing the operation of the EIA framework; quality of environmental impact statements being poor; guidance being inadequate; there being no consideration of transboundary impacts; there being no, or few, EIA specialists; and penalties for non-compliance being inadequate. Another common problem is that the transition of legislation from the former SER/OVOS system to a more 'western' style of EIA in some countries is leading to a situation where two systems are operating in parallel, thus causing confusion.

Strategic environmental assessment
Progress with strategic environmental assessment (SEA) in western Europe is far more patchy. The European Union has adopted a directive on SEA (Directive 2001/42/EC) which must be implemented in Member States by July 2004. In western European countries, there is a lot of experience with application of SEA, and some countries have working systems. However, SEA is far more commonly carried out in an ad hoc way, and is largely confined to specific sectors (particularly land-use plans and transport plans). Many countries cite their only experience of SEA being through the assessment of regional plans as

> The implementation and use of environmental impact assessment is now widespread across Europe, but its effectiveness is limited.

required by the European Council regulation for structural funds (2081/93, now superseded by 1260/1999) and indicate a lack of guidance as a key barrier to successful implementation of legal or administrative requirements.

In some CEE countries, it is too early to say whether new SEA provisions are working well, in others new legislation is still in the process of development. Yet other countries cite a number of problems with the implementation of SEA. Principal among these are a lack of systematic coverage of content requirements, a lack of enforcement provisions and a lack of application of SEA to any sector other than land use. Accession countries will however soon be subject to the requirements of the EU's SEA directive, and this may have a beneficial effect.

In EECCA, the SER and OVOS systems theoretically also cover SEA, and so the problems for SEA are similar to those for EIA, as detailed above. It is also likely that progress in many EECCA countries will be slow because of the financial situation in those countries — capacity-building assistance should be considered here as it has proved successful in many accession countries.

> The application of strategic environmental assessment is patchy, and clear guidelines for its coverage and use are lacking.

Recent initiatives
A recurring theme across all of Europe, especially in CEE and EECCA, is the quality of the public involvement in the EIA and SEA processes. In this context, the first meeting of the Parties to the Aarhus convention took place from 21 to 23 October 2002 in Lucca, Italy and confirmed a compliance mechanism that is open to communications from the public and whose committee members may be nominated by NGOs. This approach was strongly defended by several groups, including the European Union. The mechanism may set a precedent for more effective conventions in the future and could help to foster more open decision-making through example.

There are other examples of recent efforts to improve the integration of policies and ensure realistic implementation. These include the EU initiative on impact assessment (see Box 13.15) and the draft UNECE protocol on strategic environmental

---

Box 13.15. A new EU initiative towards more integration: impact assessment

The May 2002 communication from the Commission (CEC, 2002c) formally launched the EU's initiative to use 'impact assessment' (IA) to improve the quality and coherence of the policy development process. The intention is that an IA will be carried out for all major initiatives, whether strategies and policies, programmes or legislation. There is now pressure for the application of IA to various policies, building on previous analysis of trade policy (called sustainability impact assessment or SIA).

Impact assessment is intended to help analyse the impacts of such initiatives in terms of the three pillars of sustainable development — economic, social and environmental. It should also highlight who is affected and what the trade-offs are, both across the three pillars and between stakeholder groups. The IA tool is also intended to simplify the process of assessing major initiatives, by incorporating the key elements of several existing evaluation methodologies and superseding them. These include business impact assessment (BIA), regulatory impact assessment (RIA), health impact assessment (HIA) and even SEA. However, a key question is how far these aims can be fully translated into practice and whether key issues previously highlighted under existing techniques will lose some of their prominence.

At the national level, there is as yet no requirement to use IA. National approaches using RIA, SIA, BIA, SD (sustainable development) assessment, etc., will continue, although it is likely that broader IAs will develop. Currently Finland carries out SIA through the use of adapted SEAs. The Netherlands applies a range of coordinated tests, including inter alia the environment test (E-test) and business test (B-test), and feasibility and enforceability tests. The United Kingdom is piloting its own tool — integrated policy appraisal (IPA) — as well as having adopted RIA as a standard and integrated approach to policy-making.

The requirement to use IA should help to ensure that the sustainability impacts of major initiatives and stakeholders' concerns are noted early enough for the proposals to be improved in advance of being launched. Similarly, by requiring others' interests to be taken into account at an early stage, the use of the IA promises to facilitate a greater integration of sustainability concerns into policies and to ensure greater policy coherence across policy actors and domains.

IA offers the potential to support sustainable development and encourage more effective and efficient policy-making.

---

assessment. This latter is on course for signing at the ministerial conference 'Environment for Europe' in Kiev in May 2003, and may bring benefits in extending SEA practice across the region.

13.4. References

Ajuntament de Calvia, 2000. *Plan general de ordenacion urbana de 2000 de Calvia.*

Artobolevskiy, 2000. New principles for Russian regional policy. *European Spatial Research and Policy* 7(2): 21–33.

Berkhout, F. *et al.*, 2001. MEPI: *Measuring the environmental performance of industry.* SPRU, University of Sussex, Brighton.

Bushmovich, A. *et. al.*, 2001. *Towards sustainable production and consumption of textile products.* EPCEM, Vrije Universiteit, Amsterdam.

CEC, 1996. *Communication from the Commission to the Council and the European Parliament on environmental agreements.* COM (96) 561 final. Brussels.

CEC, 1997. *Proposal for a Council directive restructuring the Community framework for the taxation of energy products.* COM(1997)30 final. Brussels.

CEC, 2000. *Communication from the Commission to the Council, the European Parliament, the Economic and Social Committee and the Committee of the Regions: Taxation of aircraft fuel.* COM(2000)110 final. Brussels.

CEC, 2002a. *Communication from the Commission setting out a Community Action Plan to integrate environmental protection requirements into the Common Fisheries Policy.* COM(2002)186. Brussels.

CEC, 2002b. *Communication from the Commission to the Council and the European Parliament: Taxation of passengers cars in the European Union — options for action at national and Community levels.* COM(2002)431. Brussels.

CEC, 2002c. *Communication from the Commission on impact assessment.* COM(2002)276. Brussels.

de Clercq, M. *et. al.*, 2000. *A comparative study of environmental negotiated agreements.* Universiteit van Gent, Ghent.

Department of the Environment and Local Government, 2002. Press release dated 26 August 2002. Ireland.

Dubai awards, 2000 and 2002. Dubai international awards for best practices in improving the living environment. http://www.sustainabledevelopment.org/blp/awards/awardsmain.html

Ecologic and IEEP, 2002. *EU environmental governance: A benchmark of policy instruments with a focus on agriculture, energy and transport.* IEEP and Ecologic, London.

EEA (European Environment Agency), 1997. *Environmental agreements: Environmental effectiveness.* EEA, Copenhagen.

EEA (European Environment Agency), 2000. *Environmental taxes: Recent developments in tools for integration.* Environmental Issues Series No 18. EEA, Copenhagen.

EEA (European Environment Agency), 2001. TERM 2001. *Indicators tracking transport and environment integration in the European Union.* EEA, Copenhagen.

EEA (European Environment Agency), 2002a. *Environmental signals 2002.* EEA, Copenhagen.

EEA (European Environment Agency), 2002b. *Energy and environment in the European Union.* Environmental issues report No 31. EEA, Copenhagen.

GRI (Global Reporting Initiative), 2001. *Sustainability reporting guidelines.* Boston.

IEEP, 2001a. *The effectiveness of EU Council integration strategies and options for carrying forward the Cardiff process.* IEEP and Ecologic, London.

IEEP, 2001b. *Review of progress made under the 2001 Swedish presidency of the EU on Council integration strategies for carrying forward the Cardiff process.* IEEP, London.

KPMG (KPMG Global Sustainability Services), 2002. *International survey of corporate sustainability reporting 2002.* De Meern.

Laansalu, A., 2001. *Agriculture and rural development — an overview 2000/2001.* Ministry of Agriculture, Tallinn.

Mikk, M., 2001. *Organic agriculture in Estonia.* SOEL, Duerkheim.

Ministry of Environment, Norway, 1997. *Environmental policy for sustainable development. Joint efforts for the future.* Report to the Storting No 58. Oslo.

Naess, P., 2001. Urban planning and sustainable development. *European Planning Studies* 9(4): 503–524.

OECD (Organisation for Economic Co-operation and Development), 1998. *The use of voluntary initiatives in the European Union: An initial survey.* ENV/EPOC/GEEI (98)29/Final. OECD, Paris.

OECD (Organisation for Economic Co-operation and Development), 1999. *Voluntary approaches for environmental policy: An assessment.* OECD, Paris.

OECD (Organisation for Economic Co-operation and Development), 2000. *Survey* on the use of economic instruments for pollution control and natural resource management in the NIS: Preliminary conclusions and recommendations. CCNM/ENV/EAP(2000)85.

OECD (Organisation for Economic Co-operation and Development), 2002a. OECD/EU database on environmentally related taxes.(Forthcoming on line: http://www.oecd.org/EN/home/0,,EN-home-471-nodirectorate-no-no-no-8-log127588,00.html)

OECD (Organisation for Economic Co-operation and Development), 2002b. *Implementing domestic tradeable permits: Recent developments and future challenges.* OECD, Paris.

Oosterhuis, F. H., 2001. *Energy subsidies in the European Union.* Final report. W-01/21. Institute for Environmental Studies, Vrije Universiteit, Amsterdam.

REC (Regional Environmental Centre for Central and Eastern Europe), 1999. *Sourcebook on economic instruments for environmental policy.* REC, Szentendre.

ten Brink, P., 2002. *Voluntary environmental agreements: Process, practice and future use.* Greenleaf Publishing, United Kingdom.

Traynor, I., 2002. For Siberia, a return to wasteland. *The Guardian* newspaper. 12 June. London.

UNECE, 2000a. *Environmental Performance Review of Lithuania: Report on Follow-up.* UNECE, Geneva.

UNECE, 2000b. *Environmental Performance Review of Latvia: Report on Follow-up.* UNECE, Geneva.

UNECE, 2000c. E*nvironmental Performance Review of Kazakhstan.* UNECE. Geneva

UNECE, 2002. 'Environmental policy in transition: Lessons learned from ten years of UNECE environmental performance reviews'. CEP/2002/3 — Draft for discussion. UNECE, Geneva.

UNECE/UNEP, 2002. *Sustainable development in Europe, North America and Central Asia: Progress since Rio.* ECE/CEP/84. UN, Geneva.

UNEP/SustainAbility, 2002. *Trust us: The 2002 global reporters survey of corporate sustainability reporting.* UNEP, Paris.

VASAB (Vision and strategies around the Baltic), 2000. *Compendium of spatial planning systems in the Baltic Sea countries.*

von Homeyer, I., 2001. *EU environmental policy on the eve of enlargement.* EUI.

von Homeyer, I., 2002. 'The impact of enlargement on EU environmental policy: A historical-institutionalist perspective'. Paper presented at the conference EU Enlargement and Environmental Quality in Central and Eastern Europe and Beyond.

Wernstedt, K., 2002. Environmental protection in the Russian Federation. *Journal of Environmental Planning and Management* 45(4): 493–516.

14. Information gaps and needs

14.1. Introduction

The preceding chapters of this report describe the past and current state of the pan-European environment, as required of the European Environment Agency (EEA) by the European ministers for the environment. Although the information on trends shows clearly the areas which still face environmental problems, limitations of data availability and comparability continue to pose difficulties in the development and systematic use of indicators (see Chapter 1). This chapter reviews these limitations and gives examples of some of the most important needs and gaps in the provision of information for reporting and policy-making, and of current and proposed initiatives to improve information systems.

In this context, the report helps to show that:

- much more data and additional information are available in most countries than generally perceived, but a lack of structuring and accessibility hinders their use;
- awareness of the 'Environment for Europe' process and the preparation of indicator-based reports can help to harmonise monitoring and reporting activities in the long term;
- the more structured and systematic involvement of public authorities and public participation in countries that are not members of the EEA would allow a longer-term vision of improved and relevant data flows;
- the framework for cooperation between countries provided by the United Nations Economic Commission for Europe (UNECE) working group on environmental monitoring (WGEM) was very appropriate for experience-sharing and common implementation of monitoring methods and reporting techniques;
- the progress and steps taken over the past few years to streamline data flows in Europe, for example on greenhouse gas emissions and water quantity and use, are examples to be analysed for application to less-developed areas.

14.1.1. Main gaps in information and the role of monitoring

Information on the interlinkages within the environmental causality chain is indispensable (see Chapter 1, Figure 1.1 on the DPSIR assessment framework). It is no coincidence that it is in this area that the report most lacks complete and consistent information on trends, since many of the needs have only been identified relatively recently and the related data collection processes are either not in place or have yet to be identified and implemented. Even in areas where monitoring activities have been in place for the past 25 years or so, such as for aspects of air quality and water quality, the required information on past trends, for example on the effects of urban air pollution on the population, is not always available.

This potential for inefficiencies in monitoring, together with the need for new information to address new environmental paradigms, was recognised at the 'Bridging the gap' conference (UK EA, 1998), which concluded that:

'At present some of the systems for monitoring and gathering information about the environment in European countries are inefficient and wasteful. They generate excessive amounts of data on subjects which do not need it; and they fail to provide timely and relevant information on other subjects where there is an urgent policy need for better focused information, and for consistent environmental assessment and reporting.'

The conference has since generated many discussions which all recognised the need for a concerted European movement involving the EEA, the European Commission, countries and international organisations with the view to:

- streamlining environmental monitoring and practices;
- focusing new information gathering on key issues and perspectives;
- developing indicators, which would need to be widely agreed, that illuminate the significance of environmental change and measure progress towards sustainability.

In tackling this issue, the EEA Management Board later concluded, at the 'Streamlining

Box 14.1. Towards a shared European environment information system

Countries in Europe report a huge amount of environmental data and information to the international organisations every year. It is now widely accepted that a revision is necessary in order to increase efficiency (EEA, 2002). For a concerted European movement involving 'the environmental reporting community' (EEA, European Commission, countries and international organisations), products and services need to be developed with an integrated, comprehensive and systematic approach within an information system, such as the European environment information system (EEIS) illustrated in Figure 14.1. This system comprises the people and organisations in the network, their networking activities within the reporting system, and the supporting infrastructure and electronic tools referred to as ReportNET. The collective pool of validated and quality-assured data, information, assessments, reports and expertise made available within the system is referred to as the reference centre. The EEA is supporting and working towards such a shared information system expanding on the systematic approach of EEA and EEA's European environment information and observation network (EIONET).

Under the umbrella of the EEIS, the development of a shared environmental information structure should allow better use and reuse of the reported information, leading to a reduction in the reporting burden at the national level, while providing the international reporting community with better, faster and more policy-relevant information. The international environmental reporting networks that are currently operating, such as the EEA EIONET, and those of the European Commission, the countries and the various international conventions, should define and share a common understanding and goals. These should be largely in the form of an information structure, which each organisation can use for its own purposes as well as to support the overall goals. A wider use of the ReportNET tools will help to achieve this objective.

ReportNET is built on the basis of the key principles of a shared European environment information system: harmonised collection, providing the data once and using it for many purposes, proceeding with a common validation and aggregation, and delivering policy-relevant assessments. To satisfy these principles, ReportNET includes components for reporting obligations, metadata, directory services, data repositories, indicator management and process monitoring and is built using and contributing to IDA (the European Commission initiative on interchange of data between administrators) common tools and techniques. ReportNET covers the functions that are needed by the input part of the EEIS. The components described in Figure 14.2 do not include databases and other systems at the national level, because these are different for each country. The country links are through harmonised collection of data and based on data exchange modules.

The European environment information system   Figure 14.1.

EEA — Networking — Eionet

Community institutions — International institutions — The reference centre — Shared area — Scientific/research community — National institutions

Components of ReportNET   Figure 14.2.

ReportNET — Indicator management — Reporting obligations — Data dictionary — European data warehouses — Data exchange modules — Content registry — Directory — National repositories

reporting' seminar (EEA, 2001a) that 'the current situation in environmental monitoring is chaotic'. A vision of a shared environmental reporting system in Europe was set out. It was based on the conclusion that the need to improve the quality and timeliness of information and prevent double, overlapping and confusing requests for information from international organisations remained, despite progress being made in national attitudes to the development of information systems (see Box 14.1).

In addition, seen in the context of *Europe's environment: The third assessment*, even where there is collection of data, complete data appear not to be available. For example, significant gaps in country coverage are revealed by the submission of data from international databases, as stated in a report (ECE/EEA, 2003) prepared by the EEA in consultation with the UNECE secretariat for the Kiev ministerial conference. A number of UNECE countries, although members of relevant international organisations and conventions, do not submit data, or their submissions are either incomplete or do not cover the agreed time intervals. The biggest gaps in data availability throughout the region are related to urban air pollution, soil contamination, soil remediation, waste management systems including hazardous waste, water quality, wastewater treatment, discharges to water, hazardous substances and long-term series on biodiversity (see Section 14.2 for further details).

14.1.2. The data collection process for Europe's environment: the third assessment

The most important principle for the collection of data for this report has been to avoid any unnecessary burden on the countries. The EEA has therefore used data from international databases as much as possible and *Guidelines for the data collection of the Kiev report* (EEA, 2001b) were produced to make the data collection as transparent and coherent as possible.

Where data were not available from international databases, as was the case for a number of environmental variables, they were collected by the EEA European topic centres (EEA/ETCs). Three questionnaires were developed, on soil, waste and water topics, to extend the data from international organisations and EEA/ETCs. These covered key topics such as soil sealing, degradation and contamination, waste generation and treatment, waste treatment facilities, water resources and water quality including marine waters. Twenty-two countries that are not

members of EEA completed the questionnaires: the non-EEA western European (WE) countries, the new Mediterranean EEA countries, the western Balkan countries and the 12 countries of eastern Europe, the Caucasus and central Asia (EECCA).

All the data collected were stored in the EEA data warehouse (see Figure 14.3).

Support for data collection to the non-EEA member countries was part of European Union (EU) CARDS (regional environment reconstruction programme for Balkans) funding for the western Balkan countries (Albania; Serbia and Montenegro not included at that time). It was part of EU Tacis (technical assistance programme for countries in transition) funding for the 12 countries of EECCA. Support was provided for activities such as:

- collecting data and assisting in the completion of the questionnaires;
- providing helpdesk support, progress control and follow-up;
- building and strengthening networks, and promoting coordination and links between institutions by organising meetings on specific topics;
- processing data (validation, quality control) and making these available by translating and summarising them;
- making collected data available to the relevant EEA/ETCs.

The UNECE ad hoc WGEM was established in order to operationalise national contributions to information gathering at the UNECE level (see Chapter 1 for more details). WGEM was, with the UNECE working group of senior officials preparing the Kiev conference, the main group involved in the preparation of the Kiev report.

14.2. Existing information and new needs

The EEA reports *Europe's environment: The Dobris assessment* (EEA, 1995) and *Europe's environment: The second assessment* (EEA, 1998) included overviews of the strengths and weaknesses of environmental and related information. There has been some progress since these reviews but much remains to be done to allow comprehensive and relevant indicator-based reporting for Europe. Nevertheless, the present report, the Organisation for Economic Co-operation and Development (OECD) and UNECE

Figure 14.3.	Data flows for the Kiev report

country environmental performance reviews, and the report *Environment in the European Union at the turn of the century* (EEA, 1999), show that more use is being made of the information currently available to highlight the state of knowledge and the remaining gaps and inconsistencies.

The following sections review, for each economic sector and environmental issue covered in this report, the main information strengths, weaknesses and gaps and what is being done to address some of the major deficiencies. They are not intended to be exhaustive, but highlight the main areas where action is either under way or needed.

14.2.1. Developments in economic sectors

The following subsections present the information situation for each sector regarding environmental assessment, eco-efficiency, market integration and management integration. All the main economic sectors are addressed except the household sector, which is not analysed per se in the report because of too large gaps in information. However, households are an important part of the economy and as a source of environmental pressure and resource use. Households, as a target group, are still often overlooked in integration policies, compared with other groups such as producers. The importance of the sector lies in its demand for resources, the waste generated through the consumption of those resources and its capacity to influence industrial and commercial activities through its spending power. Several factors determine the overall impact of the sector on the environment, including population growth, the ageing population, the number of households and household size, the growth in disposable income and consumer spending, and the greater availability, affordability and sophistication of items available for purchase. A corresponding information provision process is necessary to improve assessment of these pressures on the environment and of the related policies.

Material flows

The flows of materials are systematically described and monitored through material flow accounting, which includes the production of indicators on the 'metabolic performance' of national economies. For the analysis of material flows, there are substantial data gaps that prevent the presentation of a comprehensive cycle of 'industrial metabolism' (changes in the natural environment brought about by

human activities and the corresponding flows of materials) in all the countries covered by this report. The situation is best in the EU, for which full, comprehensive, reliable and long time-series datasets are available. This also includes comprehensive data on foreign trade, which allow calculation of domestic material input (DMI) and domestic material consumption with a high degree of accuracy. For the accession countries, the statistics on foreign trade and imports of commodities are incomplete, so DMI is the only indicator that can readily be derived. Using DMI, indicators of the efficiency of resource use (see Chapter 2.0., Box 2.0.1) have been developed for the countries of the EU and the accession countries. For the EECCA countries, data were not available to derive a reliable set of material flow indicators.

Moreover, it has not been possible to measure the global consequences of a country's materials flows. Total material requirement, which accounts not only for domestic environmental burdens but also for the environmental pressures exerted during the production of imported goods, is still only available for a limited number of countries. Despite the lack of robust indicators for all the countries covered, all countries should be aware of the impact that they are having on the rest of the world by using — and especially importing — raw materials. This underlines that sustainability assessments are most meaningful when carried out in a global, rather than a regional or national, context. However, such a global perspective has not been possible in this report as many of the required data are lacking.

Energy

Relatively good information is available in most areas to support a comprehensive *environmental assessment* of the sector; the main area of weakness is waste generation. *Eco-efficiency* indicators have been developed for many years by the OECD International Energy Agency and in various countries. A selection is to be included in the EU project on indicators for the integration of the environment in energy policies, and data availability is generally good. To improve the use of market-based instruments, studies have been done on the external costs of the energy sector, but no country comparisons are readily available. For energy use by the transport sector, information will also be needed on the contributions to overall external costs of the different types of externality — climate change, air pollution, waste. Some information is available on the use of taxes, subsidies and voluntary agreements, but little is known about the effectiveness of such instruments for alleviating the environmental impacts of energy use for transport. For *management integration*, little is known about the extent and effectiveness of environmental impact assessments of energy projects.

Industry
Data for air, waste and water pollution are available only for some countries. The main areas of weakness are waste generation and soil contamination. Data on industrial pollution, water and energy use are limited to some countries. For these few countries, *eco-efficiency* indicators are well developed, in particular for comparing output with air emissions and also with contaminant discharges to freshwater bodies and the sea. Some data on recycling rates by key industries are also available. For *market integration*, there are no data available on external costs. As for other sectors, data will be needed on the contributions made to overall external costs of the different types of externality — air pollution, water pollution, waste generation, soil contamination. There is some information available on expenditure by industry on environmental compliance. Current deficiencies include incomplete coverage of countries and expenditure categories, and lack of time series. The European Commission has a work programme in place to develop this important area further. Some information is available on the extent of use of instruments such as taxes, subsidies and voluntary agreements, but little is known about the effectiveness of such instruments for alleviating the environmental impacts of the sector. An exception is water discharges where there are assessments available showing the impact of charging on minimising effluent discharges. For *management integration*, relatively good information is available on the extent of use of tools such as environmental impact assessments, environmental management systems and green procurement policies. However, little is known about their effectiveness in minimising environmental impacts. Corporate environmental reporting becomes increasingly available but so far uniform reporting parameters and formats are missing.

Agriculture
The available data on impacts (positive or negative) are gradually being extended. It is often difficult to distinguish the specific contributions of agriculture to changes in the environment, such as water stress or changes in breeding birds. The OECD has been working on a set of agri-environmental indicators since the mid-1990s. At the EU level, corresponding indicators on agri-environmental policy integration (IRENA operation) are being developed within the framework of the Cardiff process. In the meantime, *eco-efficiency* indicators that compare agricultural outputs with inputs such as fertilisers and pesticides are available at the European level. But time series for important inputs to the sector (e.g. pesticide and fertilisers) are incomplete. Data on agricultural land use are often too limited to enable inferences on the distribution of semi-natural habitats, a key issue for biodiversity on farmland. Similarly, data on actual *management* practices on farms are nearly completely lacking. In terms of policy response, information is available on the implementation of agricultural policy instruments, such as agri-environment schemes, but little is known about the effectiveness of these instruments. These information gaps can only be filled through targeted surveys that collect key data for a representative sample of farms.

Forestry
There is a relatively large amount of information available in most areas to support a comprehensive environmental assessment of the sector. *Eco-efficiency* indicators have been developed in various countries. As a result of the decline in natural forests during the 1980s, monitoring programmes have been established on forest resources, ownership and the management status of forest and other wooded land, biological biodiversity and environmental protection (e.g. UNECE/FAO (Food and Agriculture Organization of the United Nations), IUCN-The World Conservation Union). Good country coverage in international databases should be maintained, in particular data submission of UNECE regions to the UNECE/FAO database on forests. The European project 'Forest reserves research (COST E4)'aims at harmonising definitions and data collection on protected areas at the EU and the pan-European level.

Fisheries and aquaculture
Data are available for environmental assessment of the sector. *Eco-efficiency* indicators have been developed, but the data availability is very poor, even in western Europe, and needs urgent improvement.

Progress in taking measures as well as in the current situation is now reported with regard to overfishing of several species in several seas. But only a limited number of fish stocks are being addressed. Better assessment is needed for the Mediterranean, Black Sea and Caspian Sea and deep-sea fish stocks. Other environmental problems that may affect the sector, such as the effects of climate change, pollution and habitat destruction on fish stocks, are poorly understood. Countries should continue to submit data to the international organisations (FAO, International Council for the exploration of the Sea (ICES), Eurostat, OECD) and to the international fisheries organisations (IFOs). There are gaps in datasets on fleet capacity, especially for CEE and EECCA. Data on the sale of fishing vessels or through fishing agreements with third-party countries is lacking, to address the export of overcapacity of the fishing fleet.

Marine aquaculture has grown dramatically in WE. The local effects of aquaculture practices on the aquatic environment are well understood, and highly regulated and monitored in the main producing countries but data are seldom available at the European level. The wider impacts on the nutrient status of receiving waters, and effects on wild populations via escapees and parasites are, however, less well understood and more difficult to monitor and manage. Further research is needed. In the EU, these concerns should be more effectively addressed under the water framework directive, the EU recommendations on integrated coastal zone management and strategic environmental assessment.

Transport
There is relatively good information available on transport supply in terms of vehicle fleet size or length of infrastructure, and fuel prices. Data on demand (passenger- and tonne-km) is of lesser quality, particularly for private transport. The main information weaknesses that hamper a comprehensive *environmental assessment* of the sector are in the areas of transport noise, land use for infrastructure, habitat fragmentation and access to basic services. *Eco-efficiency* indicators have been identified under the EU transport environment reporting mechanism (TERM). Data are available, for example for fuel efficiency and the proportion of the vehicle fleet that meets air emissions standards, but not always for all countries or on a comparable basis. Indicators of the eco-efficiency of transport

by mode with respect to air emissions are being developed by Eurostat and the EEA. For *market integration*, data on the external costs to the environment are available for most countries, but more information is needed on the contributions to overall costs of the different types of externalities — noise, air pollution, congestion, etc. More consistency is needed on the definitions and methodologies used by countries to compile estimates of external costs; also trend data are not yet available. Some information is available on instruments such as taxes, subsidies and voluntary agreements, but little is known about their effectiveness for alleviating environmental impacts; trend data are also needed. For *management integration*, little is known about the extent and effectiveness of environmental impact assessments for transport projects.

Tourism
Apart for the measurement of the economic performance of the sector, there has been no agreed framework either globally or in Europe to develop indicators across the DPSIR framework. There are no data which measure the positive and negative impacts of tourism on the environment and how these are being dealt with through policy responses, including the use of economic instruments. The main problem is measurement of tourism activity at the local level, where the bulk of tourism impacts occur. There are no agreed *eco-efficiency indicators* for tourism and data availability is likely to be a problem once such indicators have been defined. For *market integration*, there is no information available at the European level on the costs of the various externalities: water pollution, land and soil degradation, soil erosion, heritage loss, landscape loss. For *management integration*, there are no data available on environmental impact assessments for tourism projects or non-green procurement strategies. Policy awareness on the cross-cutting dimension of the tourism sector increased in 2002, both at the international and the European level, especially the need for a more integrated approach to developing tourism markets and activities, particularly when seeking to preserve a high-quality environment. The EEA is now developing a set of environmental indicators for tourism.

14.2.2. Prominent environmental problems

Climate change
There have been improvements in the completeness, consistency and comparability

of greenhouse gas inventories through improved reporting by many countries to the UN Framework Convention on Climate Change (UNFCCC) including the EECCA countries. Many countries now use the Intergovernmental Panel on Climate Change (IPCC) *Guidelines* and also increasingly the IPCC *Good practice guidance* for estimating greenhouse gas emissions. In the EU the continuing cooperation between the EEA and the European Commission (under the EU monitoring mechanism for greenhouse gases) has also helped to improve the quality of EU Member States' greenhouse gas inventories. However, the Kyoto protocol increases the demand for further improvement of quality, for reducing and managing the uncertainties of inventories and for improving estimates of removals through land-use change and forestry ('carbon sinks'), for which IPCC guidance is expected to be available in 2003. In addition, the increasing demand for high quality sectoral greenhouse gas emission indicators, showing eco-efficiency (e.g. emissions per vehicle-km/energy consumption) also provides a stimulus, in particular for data gathering of the required underlying statistics.

Stratospheric ozone depletion
Reporting emissions of ozone-depleting substances to the Ozone secretariat is well established under the terms of the Montreal protocol. Data on trading and smuggling of ozone-depleting substances are lacking.

Air pollution
There have been improvements in the consistency and comparability of air pollutant emission inventories through improved reporting by many countries to the UNECE Convention on Long Range Transboundary Air Pollution (CLRTAP). Countries increasingly use the new reporting format that is more consistent with the format used for reporting of greenhouse gas inventories. For the EU recent (2002) reporting under the national emission ceiling directive is also helping to improve emission data quality. However there still remains substantial scope for countries to report their emissions data in a more complete way in particular by including better sectoral emission data. Although all European countries have signed protocols under CLRTAP, air emissions are not properly inventoried in many countries in EECCA. This constrains the possibility of producing complete assessments in support of policy

developments. Emission data are best for acidifying pollutants and ozone precursors, but less well developed for the 'newer' pollutants: fine particulates, heavy metals and persistent organic pollutants. The increasing demand for high quality sectoral greenhouse gas emission indicators, showing eco-efficiency (e.g. emissions per vehicle-km/energy consumption) also provides a stimulus, in particular for data gathering of the required underlying statistics.

Coverage and data availability for urban air quality monitoring are still poor in some countries due to lack of data. The effect of air pollution on human health is among the most serious environmental problems faced by the cities of the 12 countries of EECCA and urban monitoring is not covered by EMEP (the CLRTAP programme). Therefore efforts should be made to improve urban air quality monitoring in the framework of the Environment for Europe process in general.

Chemicals
Much of the monitoring effort and work on risk assessment has been focused on the *toxicity* of chemicals in the environment. Overall, there are still inadequate toxicity data for about 75 % of the chemical substances in use in western Europe, and inadequate eco-toxicity data for 50-75 % of the 2 500 priority high production volume chemicals (HPVCs) — chemicals whose production exceeds 1 000 tonnes/year. In recent years, there has been increasing recognition of the need to shift towards monitoring and assessment of the risk of exposure of people and nature to chemicals. However, there is also a major lack of human health and exposure data for these HPVCs. Downstream users (e.g. industrial users, formulators and product manufacturers) do not have to provide any data. Information on the uses of specific substances is therefore difficult to obtain, and knowledge about subsequent environmental and human exposures from use of downstream products is scarce. Other information deficiencies for chemicals include: the pathways, fate and concentrations of many chemicals in the environment; the use of chemical substances and their presence in consumer products; and the costs of the impacts on people and nature of exposure to chemicals, including mixtures of chemicals (EEA/UNEP, 1999). Monitoring and reporting of chemicals in Europe is uncoordinated, with an imbalance between different substances.

Pharmaceuticals and their metabolites are monitored occasionally. A relatively few selected heavy metals, persistent organic pollutants and pesticides seem to be the only groups of substances that are frequently monitored in most environmental areas, food, consumer products and human tissues. An integrated monitoring and exposure assessment should ideally consider all relevant sources during the life cycle of a product, emphasise the complete sequence of direct and indirect routes of exposure, and especially consider the exposure of sensitive groups. Most of these data are currently lacking. Long-term and systematic monitoring of concentrations of hazardous substances in ecosystems, food and human tissues is scarce in all European countries.

Waste
There has been little progress in the quality of information. Detailed analysis is hampered by the lack of comparable statistical information across Europe. Even for municipal and household wastes, which are normally thought of as areas with good statistics, confusion prevails. Reliable time series of data can only be obtained with a great effort to collect supplementary information and interpret the definitions used in different countries. These problems can only be overcome by harmonising definitions and collection of data on a common platform. For life-cycle analysis of products, there is a lack of systematic knowledge of the connection between the composition of individual products and resulting emissions from different treatment types when they end up in the waste stream. There is also a need for better transfers of information between product developers and producers and the waste management sector in order to develop a system whereby products and waste management fit better together. Although data on the generation and management of different waste categories and total waste generated are generally accessible, data quality is not good enough for analysis in all countries. In several countries, hazardous waste data are unreliable because of inaccurate inventories and different classification systems. Waste classifications need to be harmonised to improve the situation.

Water
Information on regional freshwater resources and water abstraction has improved. Methodological differences make it difficult to produce comparable data at the European level on the uses of freshwater.

Relatively little is known about the diffuse discharges to freshwater bodies from agricultural activities and their impacts on the state and quality of European freshwater bodies. More data are available on the quality of European rivers than for lakes and groundwaters. In collaboration with member countries and western Balkan countries, EEA is also developing Eurowaternet/Waterbase to help improve data comparability and provide the information relevant to the proposed EU water framework directive. However, there are still few data on small rivers and lakes, organic micro-pollutants and metals. Water-quantity and water-use data were mostly available. There is a general lack of environmental monitoring and comparable data and information on the state of waters in EECCA (rivers, lakes, groundwater and coastal waters). National surface-water monitoring systems are not coherent, as neither the data reporting systems nor the methodologies are harmonised.

Information on riverine inputs and direct discharges from point sources to the marine environment remains limited especially for the Mediterranean Sea, Black Sea and Caspian Sea, as well as for atmospheric deposition of hazardous substances, oil and nutrients. Monitoring of illegal oil discharges is carried out only in the North Sea and Baltic Sea and should be extended into the Mediterranean and Black Sea. Data on water quality are only available for a few substances. The EEA has brought together the various marine conventions and programmes in an interregional marine forum to help improve the comparability and timeliness of information for future assessment and reporting.

Soil
Despite the efforts that have been made in recent years in implementing a monitoring and assessment framework for soil, important data gaps still remain. These gaps are a consequence of the lack of soil protection legislation at the EU level and the consequent absence of legal requirements for reporting. Moreover, little funding is available for monitoring. This situation is expected to improve in the future, as a thematic strategy on soil protection is being developed and a proposal for a soil monitoring directive is expected for mid-2004.

More data on some aspects of soil contamination have gradually become available through the establishment of European data flows, but analysis is hampered by lack of comparability. Aggregated information on driving forces and responses is available on contamination from localised sources, partly based on expert estimations, while little information is available on pressures and impacts (e.g. amount of hazardous substances released to soil or impacts of soil contamination on drinking-water supplies).

Monitoring of historic contamination is provided through national surveys, which have been established to serve management needs and therefore are not directly focused on environmental protection objectives. An adequate assessment of the current state of soil erosion in Europe is still missing. Information on the extent of area affected by soil erosion is available for most countries, but measurement approaches and reporting units used are not homogeneous, making comparisons across Europe difficult. The situation should improve in the future, as model-based regional assessments of soil erosion risk will become available, as a result of EU research efforts.

Information on the loss of soil resources through sealing is still patchy. Due to the lack of monitoring on the amount of soil actually sealed, a proxy indicator on built-up areas is used. Major sources of information are national land-use statistics. While time series on land-use changes exist in all countries, detailed surveys on built-up areas are only carried out in a few of them. Basic data, such as detailed European soil maps, are still unavailable for assessment, and problems with data access and data ownership remain.

Technological and natural hazards
There is an improved culture with regard to industrial accident reporting and sharing the lessons learnt. The European Commission's industrial accident database MARS (major accident reporting system), only for EU countries, is now complemented by SPIRS (Seveso plants information retrieval systems) which will cover information related to location and amount of substances handled in each 'Seveso plant' in the EU. For the non-EU states, the use of the Seveso II directive (and other relevant directives) appears appropriate and some are already using these, including some non-accession countries. The comprehensive nature of such directives provides a valuable model for more effective monitoring of risk

management measures and accidents. An enormous amount of accident monitoring and environmental radioactivity data are now being collected across Europe that now need to be better linked and used. Major transportation accidents are subject to improved reporting. Information about the risks and environmental impacts of natural hazards and interactions with human activities is not widely available. A holistic approach should ensure that all hazards are identified and that the risks from these are balanced against each other. Cooperation with insurance companies on accident-reporting data is to be developed.

14.2.3. Cross-cutting impacts

Biological diversity
In general, the natural biodiversity is better known and understood in Europe than in many other parts of the world. However, our knowledge is far from covering all the many elements of biodiversity (species, habitats, genetic resources). By 2000 most countries had or were planning a basic national nature or biodiversity monitoring programme with a data flow for the first very limited set of biodiversity indicators to suit national environmental reports as well as international reporting to conventions and directives. The best data exist for vertebrates and vascular plants; data for some invertebrate groups (butterflies) and lower plants are improving. Red Lists for the same species groups now exist in most countries.

In Europe the EU LIFE and Corine biotopes programmes, but also large-scale non-governmental organisation (NGO) programmes have enhanced inventories. The most comprehensive datasets are being collected on species, habitats and sites for Natura 2000 (the birds and habitats directives) for the EU countries and for non-EU European countries in the related Emerald network of the Bern convention. Many of the datasets are being used by the EEA through the European nature information system (EUNIS) in cooperation with the European Commission, the Council of Europe and international nature conservation organisations. However, the many activities in monitoring, indicator developments and assessments create problems of overlaps and unclear data flows and still need much effort in coordination and harmonisation, nationally, in Europe and globally.

The main challenges for the future therefore concern:

- Coordination across Europe on indicators and monitoring, relating this to European and global efforts. Ongoing, global: Convention on Biological Diversity indicators (gaining impetus), forest indicators (the Ministerial Conference on the Protection of Forests in Europe (MCPFE), finalised 2003), OECD and Eurostat indicators (ongoing since 1990s). Ongoing, pan-European: biodiversity monitoring and indicator framework (EBMI-F, agreed 2002) forum under the pan-European biological and landscape diversity strategy (PEBLDS), international working group on biodiversity monitoring and indicators (IWG Bio-MIN technical group, led by EEA, started 2002), EEA biodiversity indicators (started 2002), including biodiversity implementation indicators (Bio-IMPs, started 2003). Several NGO indicator initiatives are based on long-term monitoring such as on birds or wetlands.
- Using harmonised reference tools: geo-references such as biogeographical regions and regional seas, assessment criteria such as harmonised by IUCN (threats, management categories), species names, habitat classifications (such as the EUNIS habitat classification).
- Broadening the scope of biodiversity to include other important species groups and habitat types (the common ones) as well as genetic aspects.
- Developing more widely usable sets of general bio-indicators or biomarkers for environmental change (hormones in species, biomass, CO_2 functions etc.).
- Ensuring set-up and maintenance of a selection of long-term harmonised monitoring programmes to catch the generic trends of biodiversity conditions.
- Enhancing and maintaining open access to datasets and information held by countries and organisations, such as by using the national and EU internet-based clearing house mechanisms, related to the Convention on Biological Diversity.

Human heatlh

For human health issues, there are long-established monitoring systems, for example for quality of urban air and drinking water. Little progress has been made in relating these monitoring data to the consequences for human health. A study to relate water quality to human health has been jointly published by the EEA and WHO (WHO/EEA, 2002). Some progress has been seen for exposure assessment, in particular population exposure to air pollution (both indoor and outdoor). However, little is known about dose/response relationships and about the impacts on human health of exposure to mixtures of pollutants from multiple exposure routes. Some research and modelling has been undertaken in limited communities to understand better the relationships between human health and the low levels of chemicals and pollution that many people are exposed to on a daily basis. These studies have shown some indication of impacts on human health and behaviour e.g. lower sperm counts and neurotoxic effects, but the links between multiple, low-level exposures to chemicals (including pharmaceuticals) in food, water, air and consumer products and impacts on people remain largely unexplored. Data and information are particularly needed on cumulative chemical exposures, and related biologically effective doses, to sensitive subgroups, such as the foetus, children, the elderly, pregnant women, and those with depressed immune systems; on the antagonistic and synergistic interactions between these exposures; and on biomarkers of exposure, early effects and susceptibilities, which together can help identify potential threats to sensitive communities so that adverse impacts can be avoided or minimised.

Pharmaceuticals and consumer care products are emerging issues. Many types of chemical classes, ranging from endocrine disruptors, anti-microbials and antidepressants to lipid regulators and synthetic musk fragrances have been identified in sewage and domestic wastes. Food-borne diseases caused by microbial hazards are a growing public health problem. The WHO Programme for Surveillance of Food-borne Diseases in Europe has been collecting official information from the Member States of the WHO European Region for the past 20 years. Scientific knowledge about the health effects of electromagnetic fields is substantial, and is based on a large number of epidemiological, animal and in-vitro studies. Many health outcomes ranging from reproductive defects to cardiovascular and neuro-degenerative diseases have been examined, but the most consistent evidence to further monitor concerns childhood leukaemia.

14.3. Some ways forward: a better integration of environmental monitoring and reporting systems

Although the information on trends is incomplete, this report clearly shows the areas where achievement of environmental objectives is likely to present the greatest future challenge. The development of appropriate data flows in these areas is required so as to allow relevant and regular indicator-based reporting that enables progress to be assessed. An important part of such work still concerns harmonisation of definitions (e.g. air quality measuring methods), data collection methods and agreement on terminology for reporting (e.g. waste classifications). Having the right information, moreover, is important not only for helping to frame and monitor the policies required for improving the state of the environment, but also for changing societal behaviour and influencing in a positive way the impact that society as a whole has on the environment.

International legal instruments can play an important role in the implementation of environmental monitoring regimes. In this respect, the UNECE Convention on Access to Information, Public Participation in Decision-making and Access to Justice in Environmental Matters (the Aarhus convention) has made significant progress. It requires governments to provide the public with access to environmental data, thus enabling the public to hold data up to scrutiny and, in some cases, apply pressure on the governments to fill in gaps in information (see Box 14.2). Furthermore, Article 5, Paragraph 4 of the convention clearly conveys the legal obligation to 'publish and disseminate a national report on the state of the environment, including information on the quality of the environment and information on pressures on the environment'. The most significant development under the convention with respect to the generating and collecting of data has come in the form of the new protocol on pollutant release and transfer registers (PRTRs). Under this new instrument, negotiated under the auspices of the Aarhus convention, companies will be required to report annually on their releases and transfers of certain pollutants. The information will then be placed on a public register, known as a pollutant release and transfer register or PRTR. Each Party to the protocol will be required to establish a publicly accessible and user-friendly PRTR,

based on a mandatory scheme of annual reporting. The data generated will contribute to building up a picture on the movement of pollutants and how they enter the environment.

By providing the basis for a phase of 'learning from lessons', this report marks the start of a new phase of cooperation in environmental monitoring and reporting in Europe. This new phase is characterised by more systematic approaches, a policy focus and a clearer organisational structure for supporting long-term partnerships between countries and funding by international donors. From the start of its activities, the WGEM has been involved in articulating the contents of the report to make it relevant to policies and include proper analyses, and has remained involved in the necessary data flows and information processing. Such an activity has been important in establishing an effective bridge between a responsive monitoring system and a relevant reporting process in support of policy-making. For the future, it may be appropriate to formalise the role of this group and to extend its remit and coverage to take account of broader information needs and wider participation by international organisations other than the EEA.

At the international level, further development of an analogous framework for cooperation between countries, as provided by UNECE in past years and as demonstrated by the preparation process of this report, is required. The importance of this work should be adequately backed at the political level. A higher level of national investment, in particular in the 12 countries of EECCA, is required. Environmental monitoring investments are needed especially for raw data collection (networks), processing capacities (human resources) and equipment (computer hardware and software).

In the UNECE region, priority areas for improving environmental monitoring capacities are: air quality, water quality, waste management, biodiversity, and chemicals in ecosystems and foodstuffs. Substantial efforts are still needed to develop proper networks for providing environmental data and information. The experience of the EIONET network developed by the EEA should be taken fully into account for improving the capacity of the various national institutes in their task of providing environmental information.

The experience gained from the data collection for this report has proved that only some of the requested data were in fact publicly available (e.g. in state of the environment reports or from state statistical sources). To remedy to this situation, national implementation of the Aarhus convention on access to information and justice in environmental matters should be supported. Specific efforts are required under relevant international organisations and conventions to cover existing gaps. This would improve compliance and reporting systems and facilitate data collection for future pan-European environmental assessments. In this context, building on the upcoming proposal for an EU framework directive on reporting to take account of European needs could be considered appropriate.

Recommendations for future developments in order to improve the environmental monitoring capacities in Europe and allow for a real pan-European monitoring and reporting process are thus (ECE/EEA, 2003) to:

- develop indicators, which would need to be widely agreed, that illuminate the significance of environmental change and progress towards sustainability;
- focus on new information gathering on key issues and perspectives;
- maintain the framework for cooperation on environmental reporting and information management between countries at the pan-European level;
- ensure an appropriate level of investment in basic environmental monitoring infrastructure;
- establish mechanisms for the provision of environmental information by countries, in particular EECCA countries;
- encourage international collaboration to enhance cross-border and international comparability of information, in the priority areas of air emissions, urban air quality, transboundary inland water pollution, marine pollution, hazardous waste, waste management and biodiversity;
- encourage UNECE countries to submit data to international organisations and conventions according to their international commitments;
- strive towards the effective implementation of relevant legal instruments such as the Aarhus convention and its new protocol on PRTRs.

> **Box 14.2. Implementing the Aarhus convention**
>
> The United Nations Economic Commission for Europe (UNECE) Convention on Access to Information, Public Participation in Decision-making and Access to Justice in Environmental Matters (the Aarhus convention) was adopted in Aarhus (Denmark) on 25 June 1998 and entered into force on 30 October 2001. As of 1 February 2003 23 countries had ratified, approved, accepted or acceded to the convention. By recognising citizens' environmental rights to information, participation and justice, the Aarhus convention aims to promote greater transparency and accountability in environmental governance. While the convention is an instrument of international environmental law, by emphasising the responsibilities that governments have towards the citizens, it also promotes democracy and good governance. More specifically, the convention aims to:
>
> - allow members of the public adequate access to environmental information held by public authorities, thereby increasing the transparency and accountability of government;
> - provide an opportunity for people to actively participate in the decision-making process on environmental matters;
> - provide the public with access to review procedures when their rights to information and participation have been breached and with respect to general violations of environmental law.
>
> The first meeting of the Parties to the convention took place in Lucca, Italy on 21–23 October 2002. A number of significant results were achieved at the meeting, including the establishment of several new subsidiary bodies. The participants present at the meeting adopted the Lucca Declaration, which emphasised the importance of the convention and set out the direction of work for the nearer future. Furthermore, the meeting adopted 14 decisions on specific substantive issues (genetically modified organisms - GMOs, PRTRs, access to justice and electronic information tools), review of compliance, capacity-building, and other elements concerning the procedural and institutional architecture that will support the implementation and future development of the convention. Environmental NGOs played an active role during the negotiation of the convention to an extent unprecedented in the development of an international legal instrument. Their active involvement continues to be an important feature of the implementation processes.

Knowledge of developments that support policy processes with environmental information is needed for improving the state of the environment in Europe. This report and eventual follow-up studies may become a catalyst for improved information and data flows at the national and the pan-European level. These would form the legal background for improving and strengthening capacities in national environmental monitoring and reporting, and allow comprehensive and relevant indicator-based reporting for Europe.

14.4. References

ECE/EEA (Economic Commission for Europe/European Environment Agency), 2003. 'Conclusions on lessons learned from the preparation of the Kiev assessment'. Document for the fifth ministerial conference 'Environment for Europe'. ECE/EEA, Geneva.

EEA (European Environment Agency), 1995. *Europe's environment: The Dobris assessment.* Office for Official Publications of the European Communities, Luxembourg.

EEA (European Environment Agency), 1998. *Europe's environment: The second assessment.* Office for Official Publications of the European Communities, Luxembourg.

EEA (European Environment Agency), 1999. *Environment in the European Union at the turn of the century.* Office for Official Publications of the European Communities, Luxembourg.

EEA (European Environment Agency), 2001a. Chairman's conclusions, 'Streamlining reporting' seminar. EEA Management Board seminar. EEA, Copenhagen.

EEA (European Environment Agency), 2001b. *Guidelines for the data collection of the Kiev assessment report.* Technical report No 66. EEA, Copenhagen.

EEA (European Environment Agency), 2002. *Development of common tools and an information infrastructure for the shared European environment information system.* Technical report No 83. EEA, Copenhagen.

EEA/UNEP (European Environment Agency/United Nations Environment Programme), 1999. *Chemicals in the European environment: Low doses, high stakes?* EEA and UNEP, Copenhagen.

UK EA (UK Environment Agency), 1998. *Chairman's conclusions, 'Bridging the gap' conference.* UK EA, VROM (the Netherlands) and European Environment Agency, London.

WHO (WHO Regional Office for Europe), EEA (European Environment Agency), 2002. *Water and health in Europe.* A joint report from the European Environment Agency and the WHO Regional Office for Europe, Copenhagen.

Acronyms and abbreviations

AC	accession country
AC-10	accession countries minus Bulgaria, Romania, Turkey
AC-13	all 13 accession countries
ACEA	European automobile manufacturers association
AEPS	Arctic Environmental Protection Strategy
AF	annual felling (forestry)
AFIT	Agence française de l'ingénierie touristique
Airbase	European air quality information system (EEA)
Altener	EU programme for renewable energy
^{241}Am	americium 241
AMAP	Arctic Monitoring and Assessment Programme
BAT	best available technology
BIA	business impact assessment
bq	bequerel
bn	billion
BOD	biological oxygen demand
BOD5	idem at 5 days
CAFE	Clean air for Europe programme (EC)
CAP	common agricultural policy (EU)
CARDS	Community assistance for reconstruction, development and stabilisation (the Balkans)
CBD	Convention on Biological Diversity
CDM	clean development mechanism (UNFCCC)
CEE	central and eastern Europe (see box 1.1.)
CEFIC	European Chemical Industry Council
CFCs	chlorofluorocarbons
CFP	common fisheries policy (EU)
CH_4	methane
CHP	combined heat and power
CITES	Convention on International Trade in Endangered Species of Wild Fauna and Flora
CLRTAP	UNECE Convention on Long-Range Transboundary Air Pollution
CMR	carcinogenic, teratogenic, mutagenic and reprotoxic chemicals
CO_2	carbon dioxide
CONCAWE	The oil companies' European organisation for environment, health and safety
^{137}Cs	caesium 137
DALY	disability adjusted life years index (WHO)
DDE	dichloro diphenyl ethylene
DDT	dichloro diphenyl trichloroethane
DMI	direct material input
DPO	domestic processed outputs
EBRD	European Bank for Reconstruction and Development
EC	European Community
ECB	European Chemicals Bureau
ECCP	European climate change programme
ECMT	European Conference of Ministers of Transport
EDS	Endocrine disruptive substance
EEA	European Environment Agency
EEA/ETC	EEA European topic centre
EECCA	12 countries of eastern Europe, Caucasus and central Asia (see Box 1.1)
EfE	Environment for Europe (UNECE)
EFTA	European Free Trade Association
EGIG	European Gas pipeline Incident data Group
EIA	environmental impact assessment
EIB	European Investment Bank

EIFAC	European Inland Fisheries Advisory Commission
Einecs	European inventory of existing chemical substances
Eionet	European environment information and observation network
EMAS	eco-management and audit scheme
EMEP	UNECE Cooperative Programme for Monitoring and Evaluation of the Long-range Transmission of Air Pollutants in Europe
EMF	electromagnetic field
EMS	certified environmental management systems
ESA	European Space Agency
ET	emissions trading (UNFCCC)
ETC/ACC	European Topic Centre on Air and Climate Change
ETC/NPB	European Topic Centre on Nature Protection and Biodiversity
ETC/WMF	European Topic Centre on Waste and Material Flows
ETR	environmental tax reform
EU	European Union (see box 1.1.)
EUNIS	European Nature Information System
FAO	Food and Agriculture Organisation
FAR	fatal accident rate
FoE	Friends of the Earth
FSA	Food Standards Agency
FSC	Forest Stewardship Council
GDP	gross domestic product
GEO	UNEP's global environment outlook process
GFCM	General Fisheries Commission for the Mediterranean
GHS	globally harmonised system of classification and labelling of chemicals
GMO	genetically modified organism
GRI	Global Reporting Initiative
Gt C	gigatonne carbon
GWh	giga watt hours
GWP	global warming potential of gases
Gy	gray
HBFCs	hydrobromofluorocarbons
HC	hydrochlorides
HCB	hexachlorobenzene
HCFCs	hydrochlorofluorocarbons
HCl	hydrogen chloride
HDI	human development index (UN)
HELCOM	Helsinki Convention - Baltic Sea
HFC	hydrofluorocarbons
HGV	heavy goods vehicle
HIA	health impact assessment
IA	impact assessment
IAEA	International Atomic Energy Agency
IBSFC	International Baltic Sea Fishery Commission
ICCAT	International Convention for the Conservation of Atlantic Tuna
ICES	International Council for the Exploration of the Sea
ICLEI	International Council for Local Environmental Initiatives
ICM	integrated crop management
ICRP	International Commission on Radiological Protection
ICWC	Interstate Commission for Water Coordination
ICZM	integrated coastal zone management
IEA	International Energy Agency
IFAS	International Fund for Saving the Aral Sea
IFOs	international fisheries organisations
IHPA	International HCH and Pesticides Association
IIASA	International Institute for Applied Systems Analysis
IMO	International Maritime Organisation
INES	international nuclear event scale database
IPA	integrated policy appraisal
IPCC	Intergovernmental Panel on Climate Change (UN)
IPPC	integrated pollution prevention and control (EU Directive)

IQM	integrated quality management
ISO	International Standardisation Organisation
ITOPF	International Tanker Owners Association
IUCN	International Union for Nature Conservation
IWAC	International Water Assessment Centre
JI	joint implementation (Marrakech accords)
JRC	Joint Research Centre (European Commission)
kg	kilogramme
kgBq	kilogrammes bequerel
l	litre
L_{dn} dB(A)	day-Night Level, a descriptor of noise level which is based on the energy-equivalent noise level (Leq) over the whole day with a 10 dB(A) penalty to noise levels experienced during night time (22.00–07.00 hrs)
LA21	local agenda 21
LCA	product life cycle analysis
m^3/ha/year	cubic meter per hectare per year
MAP	Mediterranean action plan (UNEP)
MARS	major accident reporting system (JRC)
MFA	material flow accounting
MLS	minimum landing size (fishing)
mph	miles per hour
MSC-W	Meteorological Synthesising Centre — West
MSC-E	Meteorological Synthesising Centre — East
mSv	millisievert
Mt	million tonnes
N_2O	nitrous oxide
NAs	negotiated agreements
NAI	net annual increment (forestry)
NAS	net additions to stock
NASA	National Aeronautics and Space Administration (USA)
NASCO	North Atlantic Salmon Conservation Organisation
NATO	North Atlantic Treaty Organisation
NEAFC	North East Atlantic Fisheries Commission
NEHAPS	national environmental and health action plans
NECD	national emission ceilings directive (EU)
ng/g	nanogramme per gramme
Ng/l	nanogramme per litre
NGO	non-governmental organisation
NH_3	ammonia
NH_x	ammonium plus ammonia
NMVOC	non-methane volatile organic compounds
NO_2	nitrogen dioxide
NO_x	nitrogen oxides
O_2	oxygen
O_3	ozone
ODP	ozone-depleting potential
ODS	ozone-depleting substances
OECD	Organisation for Economic Cooperation and Development
OGJ	The oil and gas journal
OSPAR	joint Oslo and Paris Commissions — North Sea
OVOS	assessment of ecological impacts
P	phosphorus
PAHs	polyaromatic hydrogens
Pb	lead
PBDEs	polybrominated diphenyl ethers
PBq	penta bequerel
PBTs	persistent, bioaccumulative and toxic chemicals
PCB	polychlorinated biphenyl
PEBLDS	pan-European biological landscape diversity strategy
PEEN	Pan-European Ecological Network
PEMA	pollution emissions management areas

PFCs	perfluorocarbons
PFOs	persistent fluorinated compounds
PM	particulate matter
POPs	persistent organic pollutants
ppb	particle per billion
ppt	particle per tonne
PRTR	pollutant release and transfer register
pSCI	proposed sites of Community interest (EC habitat directive)
REACH	Registration, evaluation and authorisation of chemicals (EU)
REC	Regional Environmental Centre for Central and Eastern Europe
RIA	regulatory impact assessment
RPA	Risk and Policy Analysts Ltd, UK
Sapard	Special Accession Programme for Agriculture and Rural Development
SDS	sustainable development strategy
SEA	strategic environmental assessment
SF_6	sulphur hexafluoride
SIA	sustainability impact assessment
SMEs	small and medium sized enterprises
SO_2	sulphur dioxide
SoE	national state of environment report
^{90}Sr	strontium 90
SSB	spawning stock biomass
SSBblim	SSB safe biological limit
SSBpa	precautionary level of SSB
TACIS	technical assistance for the CIS countries (now EECCA countries) (EC programme)
te	tonnes equivalent
TEN-T	trans-European transport network
TERM	transport and environment reporting mechanism
TINA	transport infrastructure needs assessment
TMR	total material requirement
TSE	total support estimates (agriculture)
UAA	utilised agricultural area
µg/l	microgrammes per litre
µg/m^3	microgrammes per cubic metre
mol/l	micromoles per litre
UNCSD	UN Commission on Sustainable Development
UNDP	United Nations Development Programme
UNECE	United Nations Economic Commission for Europe
UNECE EPR	UNECE Environmental Performance Reviews
UNEP	United Nations Environment Programme
UNFCCC	UN Framework Convention on Climate Change
UNSCEAR	UN Scientific Commission on the Effects of Atomic Radiation
UV	ultraviolet
UWWT	urban wastewater treatment
UXOs	unexploded ordinances
VOCs	volatile organic compounds
WB	World Bank
WBCSD	World Business Council for Sustainable Development
WE	western Europe
WEI	water exploitation index
WFD	water framework directive
WGECO	ICES Working Group on the Ecosystem Effects of Fishing Activity
WGEM	UNECE Ad Hoc Working Group on Environmental Monitoring
WHO	World Health Organisation
WMO	World Meteorological Organisation
WSSD	World Summit on Sustainable Development (Johannesburg)
WTO	World Tourism Organisation
WWF	World Wildlife Fund
6EAP	Sixth environment action programme (EU)

Annex I: Country tables of key statistics

	Population	Population density	Total area	GDP	% change GDP 1990–2000	GDP per capita	GVA agriculture	GVA industry	GVA manufacturing
Year	2000	1999	1999	2000	1990–2000	2000	2000 (3)	2000 (3)	2000 (3)
Unit	'000	Person/km²	km²	Million US$	%	US$	Million US$	Million US$	Million US$
Albania	3 411	119	28 750	3 068	11	899	1 593	823	363
Andorra	67	149	450						
Armenia	3 803	128	29 800	3 711	-32	976	1 278	1 111	787
Austria	8 110	97	83 860	265 715	25	32 763	5 810	77 025	50 061
Azerbaijan	8 049	93	86 600	4 071	-43	506	769	800	542
Belarus	10 005	48	207 600	27 618	-11	2 760	1 575	5 421	4 673
Belgium	10 252	310	33 120	316 070	23	30 830	4 976	85 123	58 893
Bosnia-Herzegovina	3 977	78	51 130	6 068	293	1 526	733	1 379	937
Bulgaria	8 167	74	110 910	12 277	-18	1 503	1 872	3 757	
Croatia	4 380	77	56 540	22 538	-13	5 146	1 758	6 150	4 437
Cyprus	757	82	9 250	10 646	50	14 063			
Czech Republic	10 273	130	78 870	54 561	0	5 311	2 715	19 742	
Denmark	5 336	124	43 090	205 551	26	38 521	6 405	43 595	30 177
Estonia	1 369	30	45 100	6 066	-14	4 431	345	1 543	992
Finland	5 177	15	338 150	165 787	24	32 024	5 936	54 202	38 650
France	58 892	107	551 500	1755 614	19	29 811	52 163	415 443	296 111
Georgia	5 024	72	69 700	2 505	-77	499	955	404	238
Germany	82 150	230	357 030	2 680 002	18	32 623	33 277	759 134	533 377
Greece	10 560	80	131 960	138 386	25	13 105	10 847	28 110	15 264
Hungary	10 022	108	93 030	54 371	8	5 425	2 632	17 260	13 753
Iceland	281	3	103 000	8 796	29	31 304	711	1 828	
Ireland	3 794	54	70 270	105 248	99	27 741			
Italy	57 690	191	301 340	1 204 868	17	20 885	36 065	331 283	237 379
Kazakhstan	14 869	5	2724 900	22 487	-31	1 512	2 184	7 287	
Kyrgyzstan	4 915	25	199 900	4 350	-34	885	897	323	96
Latvia	2 372	37	64 600	6 160	-38	2 597	432	1 759	1 202
Liechtenstein	32	200	160						
Lithuania	3 695	57	65 200	7 597	-32	2 056	772	2 158	1552
Luxembourg	438			24 713	76	56 372	184	5 050	3 073
Macedonia, Former Yugoslav Republic of	2 031	79	25 710	5 138	-9	2 530	528	1 453	921
Malta	390	1 219	320	3 987	60	10 223			
Moldova, Republic of	4 282	383		2 722	-65	636	667	477	
Monaco	32	14							
Netherlands	15 919	120	41 530	492 956	32	30 966	14 222	116 700	75 884
Norway	4 491	109	323 880	170 452	39	37 954	3 732	49 052	18 618
Poland	38 650	94	323 250	163 236	43	4 223	7 842	58 511	
Portugal	10 008	9	91 980	128 039	30	12 794	4 981	35 625	22 781
Romania	22 435	450	238 390	32 748	-17	1 460	5 369	13 208	9 827
Russian Federation	145 555	110	17 075 400	357 322	-34	2 455	21 230	131 835	
San Marino	27	98	60						
Serbia and Montenegro	10 637		102 170	13 187	7	1 240			
Slovakia	5 402	78	49 010	22 471	5	4 160	1 107	7 065	5 471
Slovenia	1 988	20	20 250	23 177	20	11 659	724	7 798	5 841
Spain	39 465	174	505 990	702 395	29	17 798	29 853	204 820	118 877
Sweden	8 869	43	449 960	276 768	19	31 206	5 512	79 547	49 935
Switzerland	7 180		41 290	335 570	9	46 737			
Tajikistan	6 170	11	143 100	2 381	-62	386	1 143	551	755
Turkey	65 293	82	0	204 651	41	3 134	27 535	53 922	38 012
Turkmenistan	5 199	246	488 100	7 157	-24	1 377	1 011	4 976	
Ukraine	49 501	55	603 700	44 352	-57	896	5 444	19 735	16 835
United Kingdom	59 739	104	242 910	1 294 359	24	21 667	18 811	335 572	
Uzbekistan	24 752		447 400	12 007	-4	485	3 142	2 760	
Sources:	WB	WB/FAO	FAO (1)	WB	WB	WB	WB	WB	WB

	Socio-Economy					Nuclear waste production	Number of operational power reactors
	GVA services	Unemployment as % of total labour force	Number of households	Final households consumption expenditure	% change households consumption expenditure 1990–2000		
Year	2000 (3)	2000 (3)	2000 (4)	2000 (3)	1990–2000 (3)	2000	2000
Unit	Million US$	%		Million US$	%	Tonnes HM	Number
Albania	652	18		2 873	37		
Andorra							
Armenia	961	9,3		3 899	-11		1
Austria	147 910	4,7	3 264	145 399	23	0	
Azerbaijan	1 928	1,2		2 796			
Belarus	6 191	2		9 678	0		
Belgium	191 516	7	4 314	166 443	20	110	7
Bosnia-Herzegovina	4 134						
Bulgaria	5 845	16,3	2 789	8 854	-30		6
Croatia	10 250	16,1		13 715			
Cyprus		3,3	219				
Czech Republic	25 355	8,8	3 850	29 755	10	41	5
Denmark	127 799	5,4		99 579	23	0	
Estonia	3 449	14,8	551	3 647	-6		
Finland	85 226	9,8		80 944	15	74	4
France	1 102 720	10	24 411	953 667	15	1 141	59
Georgia	895	13,8		2 546			
Germany	1 640 434	8,1	37 478	1 510 900	21	420	19
Greece	78 825	10,8	3 886	95 922	22	0	
Hungary	26 822	6,5	3 740	33 011	-3	47	4
Iceland	3 991	2		5 217	31	0	
Ireland		4,7	2 963	48 082	56	0	
Italy	710 472	10,8	21 659	731 239	18	0	0
Kazakhstan	11 646	13,7		14 623			0
Kyrgyzstan	392			1 213	-45		
Latvia	3 160	8,4	956	4 190	-47		
Liechtenstein							
Lithuania	3 868	11,1		5 819			2
Luxembourg	16 354	2,4	164	10 451	34	0	
Macedonia, Former Yugoslav Republic of	2 425	34,5		4 069	28		
Malta		5,3					
Moldova, Republic of	1 247	11,1		2 448			
Monaco							
Netherlands	296 264	3,6	6 822	235 720	28	12	1
Norway	93 415	3,4		85 515	35	0	
Poland	76 578	16,7	12 264	111 957	79		
Portugal	69 478	3,8	3 389	83 126	38	0	
Romania	11 235	10,8	7 656	24 325	-9		1
Russian Federation	176 096	11,4		215 846	-1		29
San Marino		4,1					
Serbia and Montenegro							
Slovakia	14 298	18,9	1 577	10 998	-20	43	6
Slovenia	11 023	7,5	695	12 689	28		1
Spain	407 065	14,1	12 982	418 639	26	180	9
Sweden	161 402	5,1		138 193	13	250	11
Switzerland		2,7		197 884	10	64	5
Tajikistan	1 178	2,7		1 569	-61		
Turkey	100 305	8,3		145 672	43	0	
Turkmenistan	1 274						
Ukraine	16 199	11,9		25 116	-49		13
United Kingdom	797 010	5,3	25 491	870 546		650	33
Uzbekistan	4 388	0,4					
Sources:	WB	WB	Eurostat	WB	WB	OECD	IAEA

	Energy						
	Total primary energy supply	Total primary energy supply per capita	Total primary energy supply vs. GDP	Electricity generation	Total final electricity consumption	Final energy consumption per capita	Renewable final energy consumption per capita
Year	1999	1999	1999	1999	2000 (3)	1999	1999
Unit	toe	toe/capita	'000 toe/million US$	GWh	GWh	toe/capita	toe/capita
Albania	1052	0,31	0,37	5396	2649	0,21	0,02
Andorra							
Armenia	1845	0,49	0,53	5717	3639	0,26	
Austria	28432	3,51	0,11	59151	52370	2,99	0,32
Azerbaijan	12574	1,58	3,43	18177	13974	0,82	0,00
Belarus	23895	2,38	0,92	26516	27135	1,83	0,06
Belgium	58642	5,74	0,19	83373	77542	4,04	0,03
Bosnia-Herzegovina	2008	0,52	0,35	2615	2092	0,33	0,05
Bulgaria	18203	2,22	1,57	38019	23793	1,18	0,05
Croatia	8156	1,86	0,38	12239	11698	1,40	0,08
Cyprus	2305	3,06	0,23	3139	2768	2,24	0,06
Czech Republic	38584	3,75	0,73	64158	49381	2,42	0,03
Denmark	20070	3,77	0,10	38869	32462	2,94	0,10
Estonia	4557	3,29	0,80	8268	4763	1,82	0,30
Finland	33372	6,46	0,21	69433	75450	4,88	0,89
France	255043	4,35	0,15	519821	385111	2,90	0,17
Georgia	2573	0,51	1,05	8046	6593	0,44	0,01
Germany	337196	4,11	0,13	551315	490225	2,92	0,02
Greece	26894	2,55	0,20	49382	43151	1,80	0,10
Hungary	25289	2,51	0,49	37154	29441	1,70	0,04
Iceland	3173	11,43	0,38	7188	6938	7,73	1,85
Ireland	13979	3,73	0,15	21807	20201	2,82	0,04
Italy	169041	2,93	0,14	259245	272975	2,29	0,02
Kazakhstan	35439	2,37	1,73	47498	36545	1,34	0,01
Kyrgyzstan	2451	0,50	0,59	13160	7354	0,40	0,00
Latvia	3822	1,59	0,66	4110	4461	1,38	0,32
Liechtenstein							
Lithuania	7909	2,14	1,08	13088	6543	1,26	0,15
Luxembourg	3492	8,08	0,15	358	5716	7,95	0,04
Macedonia, Former Yugoslav Republic of	3058	1,52	0,62	6863	5121	0,84	0,09
Malta	987	2,54	0,26	1792	1460	1,47	
Moldova, Republic of	2813	0,66	1,05	3814	2659	0,45	0,01
Monaco							
Netherlands	74068	4,69	0,16	86680	97938	3,66	0,02
Norway	26606	5,97	0,16	121723	109678	4,56	0,30
Poland	93382	2,42	0,60	140001	97051	1,60	0,10
Portugal	23627	2,37	0,19	42930	38373	1,78	0,10
Romania	36432	1,62	1,13	50713	33926	1,06	0,13
Russian Federation	602952	4,12	1,83	845347	592617	2,81	0,03
San Marino							
Serbia and Montenegro	13375	1,26	1,07	33370	29746	0,80	0,02
Slovakia	17991	3,34	0,82	27501	22010	2,40	0,00
Slovenia	6506	3,28	0,29	13262	10361	2,33	0,11
Spain	118467	3,01	0,18	206317	188459	2,11	0,08
Sweden	51094	5,77	0,19	155169	128347	4,00	0,60
Switzerland	26689	3,74	0,08	68528	52373	3,00	0,12
Tajikistan	3344	0,54	1,52	15797	13317	0,48	
Turkey	70326	1,09	0,37	116440	95873	0,81	0,11
Turkmenistan	13644	2,68	2,24	8860	4812	1,68	
Ukraine	148389	2,97	3,54	172120	115073	1,77	0,01
United Kingdom	230324	3,87	0,18	363896	328919	2,69	0,02
Uzbekistan	49383	2,02	4,28	45300	40248	1,51	
Sources:	IEA	IEA/WB	IEA/WB	IEA	IEA	IEA	IEA

	Agriculture					
	Agricultural area	Fertiliser consumption per agricultural land area unit	% change fertiliser consumption 1990–99 per agricultural land area unit	Pesticide consumption per agricultural land area unit	Certified organic and in-conversion farming land area	Certified organic and in-conversion farming land area as % of area
Year	1999	1999	1990 (4)–1999	1999 (3)	2000	1999
Unit	km²	Tonne/km²	%	Tonne/km²	km²	%
Albania	11 280	0,98	-89	0,022		
Andorra	260					
Armenia	13 940	0,44	-78	0,002		
Austria	34 190	7,11	-18	0,102	2 670	8,482
Azerbaijan	44 620	0,31	-83			
Belarus	92 810	9,2	-38			
Belgium	15 210	19,66	-24	0,55	203	1,287
Bosnia-Herzegovina	18 500	2,27				
Bulgaria	62 030	1,98	-82		5	
Croatia	31 510	6,34	-17	0,106		
Cyprus	1 470	13,74	-2	1,534	1	0,02
Czech Republic	42 820	6,28	5	0,095	1 657	2,587
Denmark	26 440	14,79	-35	0,108	1 653	5,548
Estonia	14 340	1,90	-57	0,006	99	0,279
Finland	22 720	13,69	-26	0,05	1 474	6,015
France	299 000	15,90	-14	0,326	3 700	1,057
Georgia	29 990	1,33	-43			
Germany	170 130	17,83	-4	0,192	5460	2,658
Greece	90 200	5,20	-31	0,102	248	0,194
Hungary	61 860	6,26	-40	0,224	472	0,558
Iceland	22 810	0,96	-5		34	0,11
Ireland	44 180	15,84	29	0,051	324	0,735
Italy	162 680	10,89	-6	0,553	10 404	5,893
Kazakhstan	2 124 610	0,02	-93	0,004		
Kyrgyzstan	107 260	0,28	-11			
Latvia	24 860	2,19	-67	0,015	200	0,805
Liechtenstein	100				7	6,6
Lithuania	34 960	5,23	18	0,026	47	0,114
Luxembourg					10	
Macedonia, Former Yugoslav Republic of	12 910	3,37		0,041		
Malta	90	7,92	32	2,533		
Moldova, Republic of						
Monaco						
Netherlands	19 670	24,15	-14	0,438	278	1,094
Norway	10 270	19,38	-10	0,087	205	1,828
Poland	184 350	8,28	1	0,047	220	0,06
Portugal	41 420	6,20	-11	0,334	500	1,158
Romania	147 810	1,60	-81	0,095	10	0,007
Russian Federation	2167 900	0,66	-73			
San Marino	10					
Serbia and Montenegro	56 000	2,89	82	0,054		
Slovakia	24 420	3,65	10	0,126	600	2,457
Slovenia	5 000	15,72	40	0,223	52	0,6
Spain	299 800	7,72	19	0,11	3 809	1,175
Sweden	32 350	8,55	-11	0,046	3 717	9,482
Switzerland	15 800	7,45	-10	0,097	950	5,324
Tajikistan	43 600	0,92	-68	0,019		
Turkey					210	
Turkmenistan	323 950	0,21	-61			
Ukraine	414 530	1,01	-84			
United Kingdom	172 190	11,88	-9	0,202	5 273	2,27
Uzbekistan	276 500	3,01	14			
Sources:	FAO (1)	FAO (1)	FAO (1)	FAO (1)	N.Lampkin	FAO (1), N. Lampkin

	Agriculture	Forestry				Fisheries and aquaculture
	Number of certified organic and in-conversion farms	Total annual felling - forest available for wood supply (2)	Total net annual increment -forest available for wood supply (2)	Total fellings as percentage of annual increment (2)	Average annual change in forest area	Fish catches
Year	2000 (3)					2000
Unit	Number	1 000 m³ o.b	1 000 m³ ob	%	Hectares	Tonnes
Albania		677	895	70	-7 800	3 321
Andorra						1
Armenia		150	36	375	4 200	1 107
Austria	18 360	19 521	27 337	66	7 700	859
Azerbaijan		0	234	0	13 000	18 798
Belarus		9 450	24 560	28	256 200	553
Belgium	666	4 400	5 137	86	-1 264	29 800
Bosnia-Herzegovina		1 200			0	2 501
Bulgaria		4 852	10 236	39	20 380	6 999
Croatia	20	4 600	7 133	57	2 000	21 489
Cyprus	15	50	44	114	0	2 308
Czech Republic	563	16 200	20 355	69	500	4 655
Denmark	3 466	2194	3 200	69	982	1534 094
Estonia	231	4028	7 137	56	12 500	113 349
Finland	5 225	54 300	72 470	75	8 000	162 906
France	9 260	60 174	92 299	63	61 600	667 274
Georgia	5	500	800	63	0	2 450
Germany	12 740	48 584	88 998	55	22 000	205 690
Greece	5 270		3 520		30 000	99 292
Hungary	471	5 880	9 925	54	7 200	7 101
Iceland	30	0	37	0	600	2 000 026
Ireland	1 014	2 330	3 450	68	17 000	309 331
Italy	49 790	8 746	18 713	47	29 500	301 955
Kazakhstan		1 400	3 519	26	239 000	25 775
Kyrgyzstan					22 800	52
Latvia	225	6 570	11 050	50	12 700	136 404
Liechtenstein	33	16	18	89	80	1
Lithuania	230	5 240	8 504	47	4 800	78 988
Luxembourg	51		667		0	1
Macedonia, Former Yugoslav Republic of		999			0	208
Malta		0	0		0	1 045
Moldova, Republic of	5	483	580	49	650	151
Monaco						3
Netherlands	1 391	1 438	2 205	61	1 000	495 804
Norway	1 823	11 632	22 041	52	31 000	2895 844
Poland	1 419	30 532	39 436	54	11 000	218 355
Portugal	763	11 200	12 900	85	57 000	188 392
Romania	100				14 700	7 372
Russian Federation	15	125 500	742 000	16	-1 090 000	4027 371
San Marino						0
Serbia and Montenegro	30	3 082	6 145	50	-1 447	1 099
Slovakia	100	7 100	12 337	26	6 875	2 256
Slovenia	620	2 300	6 132	20	2 200	1 862
Spain	13 394	11 028	28 589	39	86 000	991 134
Sweden	14 329	66 115	85 431	74	600	338 535
Switzerland	5 852	7 076	8 155	84	4 300	1 660
Tajikistan		0	0		2 000	59
Turkey	10 000	17 380	32 519	48	46 000	503 352
Turkmenistan		10	119	8	0	12 229
Ukraine		8 500	21 270	34	31 000	392 732
United Kingdom	3 563	9 500	14 590	64	20 000	746 297
Uzbekistan					4 580	3 387
Sources:	N. Lampkin	UNECE/FAO	UNECE/FAO	UNECE/FAO	UNECE/FAO	FAO

	Fisheries and aquaculture			Transport							
	% change fish catches 1990–2000	Aquaculture production	% change aquaculture production 1990 (4)–2000	% change passenger transport 1990–99 (3), (4), (5), (6), (7)			% change freight transport 1990–99 (2000 for air) (3), (4), (8), (9)				
Year	1990 (4)–2000	2000	1990 (4)–2000	Rail	Road	Air	Water	Rail	Road	Air	Water
Unit	%	Tonnes	%	%	%	%	%	%	%	%	%
Albania	-67	308	-94	-84		75		-95	118	0	
Andorra	0	903									
Armenia	-59	2 848	-82	-97	-4	-14		-92	-80	-25	
Austria	61	120	-9	-7		250	0	33	218	724	419
Azerbaijan	-54	6 716	-90	-71	-48	-83		-88	-79	137	-55
Belarus	-81	1 641	-60	-21		-87		-60	-57	-33	-94
Belgium	-28		143	13	16	132	-32	-12	29	55	
Bosnia-Herzegovina	25	3 654		-94		5		-97	1 161	50	
Bulgaria	-86	6 674	-53	-51		-35		-63	-46	-28	-83
Croatia	-20	1 878	-2	-67	-21	1 144		-72	-7	136	-97
Cyprus	-11	19 475	1 385			44				25	
Czech Republic	46	43 609	-4	-48	24	41		-59	57	113	-32
Denmark	4	225	4	5	12	26	-1	23	95	61	
Estonia	-69	15 400	-76	-84		124		1	90	600	
Finland	15	267 769	-17	3	13	61	20	17	32	97	6 074
France	-4	86	4	4		92	13	5	33	31	12
Georgia	-98	59 891	-86	-60		5		66		11	
Germany	-37	79 880	-7	30		147	-6	4	17	78	12
Greece	-25	12 886	739	-22		7	48	-52	2	15	
Hungary	-56	3 624	-27	-17		90		-54	23	706	-93
Iceland	31	51 247	28			139				225	
Ireland	24	216 525	92	19		142	25	-21	60	31	
Italy	-19	1 154	41	-10		67	14	12	8	49	
Kazakhstan	-67	58	-88	-54		-85		-77		-63	-99
Kyrgyzstan	-84	325	-94	-85	-25	-6		-86	-80	443	-93
Latvia	-71		-85	-82		-1		-34	-29	-33	0
Liechtenstein	0	1 996									
Lithuania	-77		-57	-80		-64		-56	6	-63	-98
Luxembourg	0			44		192	0	-12	45	56	
Macedonia, Former Yugoslav Republic of	7	1 626	60	-58		105		-51	-62	8	
Malta	37	1 746	769			157				198	
Moldova, Republic of	-94	1 168	-84	-79	-32	-95		-92	-85	-92	
Monaco	50					100				0	
Netherlands	22	75 339	-25	35		141	-19		52	100	16
Norway	61	487 921	224	11	24	52		14	21	55	30
Poland	-51	35 795	36	-57		33		-34	75	55	-1
Portugal	-42	7 540	52	-23		46	16	51	67	34	
Romania	-92	9 727	-72	-60	-62	-4		-74	-54	-5	34
Russian Federation	-47	77 132	-70	-49		-40		-52	-69	23	1
San Marino											
Serbia and Montenegro	-79	2 843	24	-71	-37			-78	-25		-30
Slovakia	90	890	-44	-54	-24	1 070		-57	-30	200	-45
Slovenia	-52	1 182	36	-56		163		-39	-30	129	
Spain	-12	312 171	53	17	-2	83	18	13	23	15	
Sweden	35	4 834	-47	19	-12	16	11	-22	-3	51	9
Switzerland	-47	1 101	3	13		108		-2	15	109	-13
Tajikistan	-79	86	-98	-83	16	-90		-33		12	
Turkey	33	79 031	1 267	-4		162		3	132	270	4
Turkmenistan	-71	547	-77	-70		-59		-77	-56	417	-59
Ukraine	-60	30 971	-62	-37		-83		-67	-68	-66	-51
United Kingdom	-3	152 487	205	17	12	45	10	13	22	35	7
Uzbekistan	-29	5 142	-77	-64		-59		-45	-76	104	
Sources:	FAO	FAO	FAO	UNECE	UNECE	UNSD (ICAO)	Eurostat	UNECE	UNECE	WB (ICAO)	UNECE

	Transport			Tourism		
	Number of passengers cars per 1000 capita	% change passenger cars 1990–99 (3), (4)	% change road transport fuel prices: unleaded gasoline 1990–2001 (8), (10)	% change in number of tourist arrivals 1990–99 (3), (4)	Tourist expenditure on travel abroad per capita	% change tourist expenditure on travel abroad 1990–99 (3), (4)
Year	1999 (3)	1990–99	1990 (4)–2000	1990–99	1999 (3)	1990–99
Unit	Cars/'000 capita	%	%	%	US$/capita	%
Albania	29,3	75		30	1,5	25
Andorra	623,1	14				
Armenia	69,5	-9		356	8,9	3 300
Austria	495,5	34	0	-8	1 211,4	27
Azerbaijan	39	20		956	17,4	-5
Belarus	127	112		93	11,6	107
Belgium	448,2	19	12	22	943,6	84
Bosnia-Herzegovina	22,5	28		8 800		
Bulgaria	232,5	45		87	63,8	177
Croatia	242,1	33		-51	171,7	3
Cyprus	340,8	44		56	383,3	160
Czech Republic	334,7	13	7	-26	143,4	224
Denmark	346,5	16	-7	-5	955,8	38
Estonia	330,8	90		79	156,5	1 042
Finland	403,2	7	4	46	391,3	-28
France	468,8	17	4	39	317,8	50
Georgia	47,9	-46		352	53,7	193
Germany	515,6	17	29	0	590,8	44
Greece	254,5	54	4	37	378,5	266
Hungary	224,1	16	-4	-16	118,3	150
Iceland	545,6	26		85	1 549,5	50
Ireland	338,3	59	-19	75	698,3	125
Italy	555,8	17	-17	37	293,4	64
Kazakhstan	66,2	22			26,4	39
Kyrgyzstan	38,5	-4		92	0,6	50
Latvia	218,1	58		-21	111,2	1 962
Liechtenstein				-23		
Lithuania	294,5	121		82	92,2	2 742
Luxembourg	609,9	38	17	2		
Macedonia, Former Yugoslav Republic of	143,8	26		-68	15,9	45
Malta	470,7	67		39	518	47
Moldova, Republic of	54,1	11		-93		
Monaco				13		
Netherlands	401,3	22	13	71	719,1	54
Norway	406,6	12	26	129	1 065,2	29
Poland	240,2	76	53	58	93,1	751
Portugal	493,7	93	-13	45	226,8	161
Romania	132,7	131	160	4	17,6	283
Russian Federation	134,8	120	-33		50,8	5
San Marino						
Serbia and Montenegro	161,1	22		-87		
Slovakia	229,2	41	6	19	62,8	87
Slovenia	427,6	47		44	271,5	91
Spain	427,4	40	-18	37	140,1	30
Sweden	439,2	8	6	12	853,2	20
Switzerland	485,6	16	14	-19	958,3	16
Tajikistan	24,2	-35				
Turkey	60,5	133	15	44	22,9	183
Turkmenistan	48,8	25		500		
Ukraine	101,9	52		17	89,1	69
United Kingdom	413,9	15	61		598,8	103
Uzbekistan	43,4	4		504		
Sources:	UNECE	UNECE	IEA	WTO	WTO (1)	WTO (1)

	Tourism				Air pollution				
	% change tourism arrivals by transport mode 1990–99 (3), (4)				Carbon dioxide emission per capita	% change carbon dioxide emission 1990–2000	Nitrogen oxide emission per capita	% nitrogen oxide emission 1990–99	Sulphur dioxide-emission per capita
Year	rail	road	air	sea	2001 (3)	1990–2000 (3)	1999 (3)	1990–99 (3)	1999 (3)
Unit	%	%	%	%	kg/capita	%	kg/capita	%	kg/capita
Albania		-61	315	31					
Andorra									
Armenia							2,89	-76	0,26
Austria					8 150	6	22,61	-9	5,19
Azerbaijan									
Belarus									
Belgium		91			12 392	8	28,26	-10	17,7
Bosnia-Herzegovina									
Bulgaria	-4	-61	30	-1	5 902	-38	24,61	-44	114,77
Croatia	63	83	133	430			16,69	-17	20,8
Cyprus			56	44			27,85	17	67,64
Czech Republic	43	101	114		12 450	-22	38,14	-47	26,27
Denmark					9 905	0	41,36	-20	10,15
Estonia	-46	16	88	168	12 307	-56	28,84	-41	73,56
Finland					12 035	0	47,63	-18	16,84
France	-5	36	-1	106	6 825	2	25,83	-20	12,52
Georgia									
Germany		49			10 443	-15	19,94	-40	10,14
Greece	-86	4	58	-12	10 187	25	36,33	17	51,45
Hungary	-74	-18	205	-14	5 932	-17	19,87	-16	58,6
Iceland			89	14			102,2	65	98,54
Ireland		1	118	46	11 577	39	31,72	1	42,38
Italy	-45	-4	39	69	8 032	5	25,76	-23	16,01
Kazakhstan									
Kyrgyzstan							0,41	-80	0,82
Latvia	-84	43	9	-8	2 887	-71	14,94	-61	12,45
Liechtenstein									
Lithuania					4 508	-58	14,6	-66	18,92
Luxembourg		43			12 314		37,04	-27	9,26
Macedonia, Former Yugoslav Republic of		-32	73				8,44		31,76
Malta			38	58					
Moldova, Republic of							3,73	-84	2,56
Monaco									
Netherlands					10 901	9	26,76	-26	6,45
Norway					9 190	17	53,81	6	6,28
Poland	-18	478	141	754	8 529	-11	24,66	-34	44,47
Portugal	-31	45	60	13	6 310	43	37,02		37,72
Romania	-72	-1	153	-27	5 525		13,99		39,86
Russian Federation	598	240	17	58			17,05	-31	14,1
San Marino									
Serbia and Montenegro							4,32	-30	33,4
Slovakia	132	156	0	-91	7 678	-31	21,87	-45	31,88
Slovenia	-98	-98	-24	-97	7 904		29,21	-11	52,88
Spain	-83	-63	95	26	7 770	35	34,96	7,7	41,1
Sweden					6 298	0	30,14	-24	6,1
Switzerland							13,73	-36	3,36
Tajikistan									
Turkey	-68	-1	83	10			14,81	48	32,72
Turkmenistan		598	755						
Ukraine							7,56	-60	20,99
United Kingdom			36	-5	9 141	-8	26,96	-42	20,32
Uzbekistan									
Sources:	WTO	WTO	WTO	WTO	EEA	EEA	EEA	EEA	EEA

	Air pollution			Waste			Water
	% sulphur dioxide emission 1990–99	Methane emission	% change methane emission 1990–2000	Total waste generation per capita	Municipal waste generation per capita	Total hazardous waste production	Water consumption (supplied) per capita
Year	1990–99 (3)	2000 (3)	1990–2000 (3)	1999 (3)	2000 (3)	1999 (3)	1999
Unit		'000 tonnes	%	kg/capita	kg/capita	' 000 tonnes	m³_/capita
Albania							
Andorra							
Armenia	-99						
Austria	-54	447,7	-17	6 006	556	972	
Azerbaijan							
Belarus							
Belgium	-49	523,58	-5	3 438	534		
Bosnia-Herzegovina							
Bulgaria	-53	483,3	-66			853	717
Croatia	-49			1 453			
Cyprus	11				677	52	
Czech Republic	-86	510,21	-36	4 033	334	2 393	154
Denmark	-70	273,95	-2	2 300	665		
Estonia	-60	118,23	-43	7 823	462	5 860	
Finland	-66	187,14	-36			485	
France	-45	2871,23	-9	2 192	530		
Georgia							
Germany	-84	2 884,89	-45	923	537	11 372	
Greece	7	518,44	25	3 163	372	350	
Hungary	-42	553,01	2	7 908	454	914	536
Iceland	13			869	705	8	494
Ireland	-14	609,52	0	15 736	601	370	
Italy	-44	1 801,23	-4	1263	502	4 058	
Kazakhstan							
Kyrgyzstan	-92						
Latvia	-75	120,81	-38		242	96	171
Liechtenstein							
Lithuania	-69	176,75	-53		294	106	
Luxembourg	-71	22,76			643	201	118
Macedonia, Former Yugoslav Republic of				315			
Malta					481		
Moldova, Republic of	-96						
Monaco							
Netherlands	-50	982,75	-24	2 498	613	1 500	
Norway	-48	324,45	6	1 474	613	631	545
Poland	-48	2 250,19	-20	3 585		1 134	276
Portugal	4	625,41	2	2 243	453	595	
Romania		1 460,9		3 569	355	2 174	
Russian Federation	-56						
San Marino							
Serbia and Montenegro	-30						
Slovakia	-68	214,51	-34		316	1 420	505
Slovenia	-47	112,85		2 291	584	46	203
Spain	-25	1 826,83	29				
Sweden	-51	279,69	-14	9 896	428		339
Switzerland					663	1 043	
Tajikistan							
Turkey	175				394	71	
Turkmenistan							
Ukraine	-47						
United Kingdom	-68	2 426,68	-33	6 353	493		
Uzbekistan							
Sources:	EEA	EEA	EEA	Eurostat	Eurostat	Eurostat	Eurostat

	Water		Technological hazards
	Annual water abstraction	Water exploitation (2)	Number of notified industrial accidents over the period 1990–2000
Year	1999 (3)		1990–2000
Unit	Million m³	%	Number
Albania		0	
Andorra			
Armenia		28	
Austria	3 561	3	3
Azerbaijan		55	
Belarus		5	
Belgium	7 442	43	9
Bosnia-Herzegovina			
Bulgaria	6 818	65	
Croatia		1	
Cyprus	426	27	
Czech Republic	1 976	21	
Denmark	754	20	4
Estonia	1 527	1	
Finland	2 328	2	7
France	32 323	18	103
Georgia		5	
Germany	40 591	30	98
Greece	8 695	7	4
Hungary	5 540	7	
Iceland	156	0	
Ireland		2	1
Italy	56 200	29	17
Kazakhstan		31	
Kyrgyzstan		48	
Latvia	307	1	
Liechtenstein			
Lithuania	4 644	1	
Luxembourg	61		
Macedonia, Former Yugoslav Republic of			
Malta	19	109	
Moldova, Republic of		25	
Monaco			
Netherlands	4 655	9	15
Norway	2 420	1	
Poland	12 246	20	
Portugal	11 136	11	5
Romania	8 570	12	
Russian Federation		2	
San Marino			
Serbia and Montenegro			
Slovakia	1 162	4	
Slovenia	318	2	
Spain	28 552	28	17
Sweden	2 711	2	3
Switzerland	2 566	2	
Tajikistan		74	
Turkey	38 900	14	
Turkmenistan		96	
Ukraine		19	
United Kingdom		8	60
Uzbekistan		115	
Sources:	Eurostat	FAO (1)	MARS/JRC

Annex II:
Ratification of multilateral environmental agreements
(as per February 2003)

Convention/protocol columns:
C1 = Convention on Environmental Impact Assessment in a Transboundary Context (UNECE)
C2 = Convention on Long-Range Transboundary Air Pollution (CLRTAP) (UNECE)
C3 = Kyoto protocol to the United Nations Framework Convention on Climate Change (UNFCCC)
C4 = Montreal Protocol on Substances that Deplete the Ozone Layer to the Vienna Convention for the Protection of the Ozone Layer
C5 = Convention on the Control of Transboundary Movements of Hazardous Wastes and their Disposal (Basel convention)
C6 = Convention on the Transboundary Effects of Industrial Accidents (UNECE)
C7 = Convention on Biological Diversity
C8 = Convention on the Conservation of European Wildlife and Natural Habitats (Bern convention)
C9 = Cartagena Protocol on Biosafety to the Convention on Biological Diversity
C10 = Aarhus Convention on Access to Information, Public Participation in Decision-making and Access to Justice in Environmental Matters (UNECE)
C11 = Convention on the Protection and Use of Transboundary Watercourses and International Lakes (UNECE)
C12 = United Nations Convention to Combat Desertification (UNCCD)

Region	Countries	C1 S R I	C2 S R I	C3 S R I	C4 S R I	C5 S R I	C6 S R I	C7 S R I	C8 S R I	C9 S R I	C10 S R I	C11 S R I	C12 S R I
EU-15	EUROPEAN COMMUNITY	✓✓✓	✓✓✓	✓✓	✓✓✓	✓✓	✓✓	✓✓✓	✓✓✓	✓✓	✓	✓✓✓	✓✓✓
	Belgium	✓✓✓	✓✓✓✓	✓✓	✓✓✓	✓✓	✓	✓✓✓	✓✓✓	✓	✓✓✓	✓✓✓	✓✓
	Denmark	✓✓✓	✓✓✓	✓✓	✓✓✓	✓✓	✓✓✓	✓✓✓	✓✓✓	✓✓	✓✓✓	✓✓✓	✓✓✓
	Germany	✓✓✓	✓✓✓	✓✓	✓✓✓	✓✓	✓✓✓	✓✓✓	✓✓✓	✓	✓	✓✓✓	✓✓✓
	Greece	✓✓✓	✓✓✓	✓✓	✓✓✓	✓✓✓	✓✓✓	✓✓✓	✓✓✓	✓		✓✓✓	✓✓✓
	Spain	✓✓✓	✓✓✓	✓✓	✓✓✓	✓✓✓	✓✓✓	✓✓✓	✓✓✓	✓✓	✓	✓✓✓	✓✓✓
	France	✓✓✓	✓✓✓	✓✓	✓✓✓	✓✓	✓	✓✓✓	✓✓✓	✓	✓✓✓	✓✓✓	✓✓✓
	Ireland	✓✓✓	✓✓✓	✓✓	✓✓✓	✓✓✓		✓✓✓	✓✓✓	✓	✓		✓✓✓
	Italy	✓✓✓	✓✓✓	✓✓	✓✓✓	✓✓✓	✓✓✓	✓✓✓	✓✓✓	✓	✓✓✓	✓✓✓	✓✓✓
	Luxembourg	✓✓✓	✓✓✓	✓✓	✓✓✓	✓✓✓	✓✓✓	✓✓✓	✓✓✓	✓✓	✓	✓	✓✓
	Netherlands	✓✓✓	✓✓✓	✓✓	✓✓✓	✓✓	✓	✓✓✓	✓✓✓	✓✓	✓	✓✓✓	✓✓✓
	Austria	✓✓✓	✓✓✓	✓✓	✓✓✓	✓✓✓	✓✓✓	✓✓✓	✓✓✓	✓✓	✓	✓✓✓	✓✓✓
	Portugal	✓✓✓	✓✓✓	✓✓	✓✓✓	✓✓✓	✓	✓✓✓	✓✓✓✓	✓	✓	✓✓✓	✓✓✓
	Finland	✓✓✓	✓✓✓	✓✓	✓✓✓	✓✓	✓✓✓	✓✓✓	✓✓✓	✓✓	✓	✓✓✓	✓✓✓
	Sweden	✓✓✓	✓✓✓	✓✓	✓✓✓	✓✓✓	✓✓✓	✓✓✓	✓✓✓	✓✓	✓	✓✓✓	✓✓✓
	United Kingdom	✓✓✓	✓✓✓	✓✓	✓✓✓	✓✓✓	✓✓✓	✓✓✓	✓✓✓	✓	✓	✓	✓✓✓
EFTA-4	Iceland	✓	✓✓✓	✓	✓✓	✓✓		✓✓✓	✓✓✓	✓	✓		✓✓
	Liechtenstein	✓✓	✓✓✓	✓	✓✓	✓✓✓		✓✓✓	✓✓✓		✓	✓✓	✓✓
	Norway	✓✓✓	✓✓✓	✓✓	✓✓✓	✓✓✓	✓✓✓	✓✓✓	✓✓✓	✓✓	✓	✓✓✓	✓✓✓
	Switzerland	✓✓	✓✓✓	✓	✓✓✓	✓✓✓	✓✓✓	✓✓✓	✓✓✓	✓✓	✓	✓✓✓	✓✓✓
Others	Andorra					✓✓		✓✓✓					✓✓
	Monaco		✓✓	✓	✓✓	✓✓	✓✓	✓✓✓	✓✓	✓	✓		✓✓
	San Marino		✓					✓✓✓					✓✓
Accession countries	Bulgaria	✓✓✓	✓✓	✓✓	✓✓	✓✓	✓✓	✓✓✓	✓✓	✓✓	✓✓	✓	✓✓
	Czech Republic	✓✓✓	✓✓	✓✓	✓✓	✓✓	✓✓	✓✓✓	✓✓✓	✓✓	✓	✓✓	✓✓
	Estonia	✓✓	✓✓	✓✓	✓✓	✓✓	✓✓✓	✓✓✓	✓✓	✓	✓✓✓	✓✓✓	
	Hungary	✓✓✓	✓✓✓	✓	✓✓	✓✓	✓✓✓	✓✓✓	✓✓	✓	✓✓✓	✓✓✓	✓✓
	Latvia	✓✓	✓✓	✓✓	✓✓	✓✓	✓	✓✓✓	✓✓✓		✓✓✓	✓✓✓	✓✓
	Lithuania	✓✓	✓✓	✓✓	✓✓	✓✓	✓✓✓	✓✓✓	✓✓✓	✓	✓✓✓	✓✓✓	
	Poland	✓✓✓	✓✓✓	✓✓	✓✓	✓✓	✓✓✓	✓✓✓	✓✓✓	✓	✓✓✓	✓✓✓	✓✓
	Romania	✓✓✓	✓✓✓	✓✓	✓✓	✓✓		✓✓✓	✓✓✓	✓	✓✓✓	✓✓✓	✓✓
	Slovakia	✓✓✓	✓✓	✓✓	✓✓	✓✓		✓✓✓	✓✓✓	✓		✓✓	✓✓
	Slovenia	✓✓	✓✓	✓✓	✓✓	✓✓	✓✓	✓✓✓	✓✓✓	✓✓	✓	✓✓	✓✓
	Cyprus	✓✓	✓✓	✓	✓✓	✓✓✓		✓✓✓	✓✓✓		✓		✓✓
	Malta		✓✓	✓✓	✓✓✓	✓✓		✓✓✓	✓✓✓		✓✓✓		✓✓✓
	Turkey		✓✓✓		✓✓	✓✓✓		✓✓✓	✓✓✓				✓✓✓
Other central European countries	Albania	✓✓✓			✓✓	✓✓	✓✓✓	✓✓	✓✓✓		✓✓✓	✓✓✓	✓✓
	Bosnia-Herzegovina		✓✓		✓✓	✓✓		✓✓					✓✓
	Macedonia, Former Yugoslav Republic of	✓✓	✓✓		✓✓	✓✓		✓✓	✓✓✓	✓	✓✓		✓✓
	Croatia	✓✓	✓✓	✓	✓✓	✓✓	✓✓	✓✓✓	✓✓✓	✓✓	✓	✓✓	✓✓✓
	Serbia and Montenegro		✓✓		✓✓	✓✓		✓✓✓					
Eastern Europe, the Caucasus and central Asia	Armenia	✓✓			✓✓	✓✓	✓✓	✓✓✓			✓✓✓		✓✓✓
	Azerbaijan	✓✓		✓	✓✓	✓✓		✓✓✓	✓✓		✓✓	✓✓	✓✓
	Belarus	✓	✓✓✓		✓✓✓	✓✓		✓✓✓			✓	✓✓✓	✓✓
	Georgia		✓✓	✓	✓✓	✓✓		✓✓			✓✓✓		✓✓✓
	Moldova, Republic of	✓✓	✓✓		✓✓	✓✓	✓✓	✓✓✓	✓✓	✓	✓✓✓	✓✓	✓✓
	Russian Federation	✓	✓✓✓	✓	✓✓✓	✓✓✓	✓✓✓	✓✓✓				✓✓✓	
	Ukraine	✓✓✓	✓✓✓	✓	✓✓✓	✓✓	✓✓✓	✓✓✓	✓✓	✓	✓✓✓	✓✓	✓✓
	Kazakhstan	✓✓	✓✓		✓✓		✓✓	✓✓			✓✓✓	✓✓	✓✓✓
	Kyrgyzstan	✓✓	✓✓		✓✓	✓✓		✓✓			✓✓		✓✓
	Tajikistan				✓✓			✓✓			✓✓		✓✓
	Turkmenistan			✓✓	✓✓	✓✓		✓✓			✓✓		✓✓✓
	Uzbekistan			✓✓	✓✓	✓✓		✓✓					✓✓✓

Notes: S = signed   R = ratified   I = into force

Annex III:
Comparisons with other parts of the world

Selected international comparisons for the following themes:

- Energy

- Agriculture

- Forestry

- Fisheries

- Transport

- Tourism

- Climate change

- Stratospheric ozone depletion

- Air pollution

- Waste generation and management

- Water

- Biological diversity

Theme: Energy
Indicator title: Electricity consumption per capita

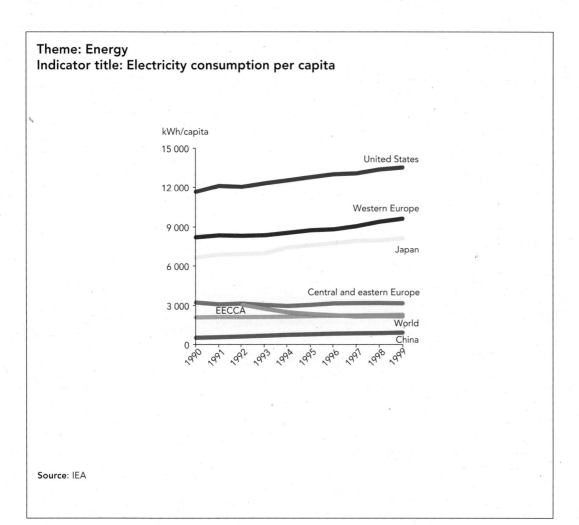

Source: IEA

All the regions and countries considered, with the exception of central and eastern Europe and eastern Europe, the Caucasus and central Asia (EECCA), show an increasing trend in electricity consumption, and all, with the exception of EECCA and China, consume above the world average. Globally, per capita consumption rose by 9 % over the period 1990–99. The United States has the highest per capita consumption of electricity, equal to more than six times the world average.

Per capita consumption in central and eastern Europe and EECCA decreased by 2 % and 29 %, respectively. Within EECCA, consumption in the Republic of Moldova and Kazakhstan dropped by about 50 %. China almost doubled its electricity consumption during the same period. Japan increased its per capita consumption by 22 %, while Western Europe and the United States increased theirs by 17 % and 16 %, respectively.

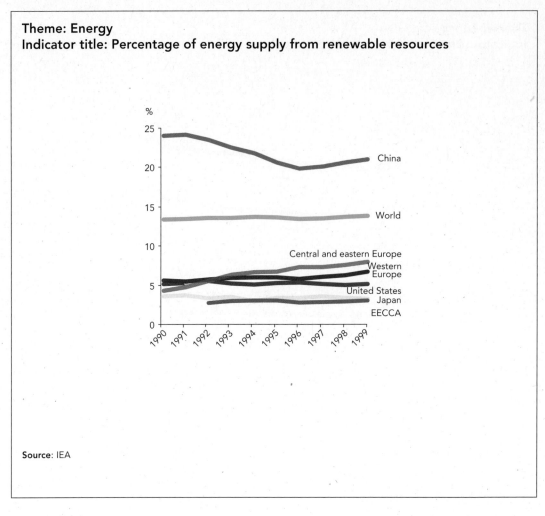

Theme: Energy
Indicator title: Percentage of energy supply from renewable resources

Source: IEA

China is the only country of those considered which has a percentage share of energy supply from renewable resources that is higher that the world average. It is also the only one showing a decreasing trend, from 31 % in 1980 to 21 % in 1999, although the production of energy from renewable resources grew by 25 % over the same period.

Globally, the production of energy from renewable sources increased by 16 % over the period 1990–99. A similar trend was observed in the United States (17 %), while western Europe and central and eastern Europe showed increases of 32 % and 84 %, respectively. Japan increased its production of renewable energy sources by 88 % during 1980–89 but by only 6 % between 1990 and 1999.

Eastern Europe, the Caucasus and central Asia (EECCA) was the only region showing a decrease, of 18 %, in the production of energy from renewable resources since 1992, although share of the total energy supply increased slightly, from 2.8 % to 3.1 %. In the United States the percentage of energy supply from renewable sources remained the same compared with 1990, in western Europe there was a limited increase (from 5.6 % to 6.8 %), while in central and eastern Europe the percentage almost doubled (from 4.3 % in 1990 to 8.1 % in 1999). Renewable sources contributed to 13.9 % of the average worldwide energy supply. The increase compared with 1990 was limited, mainly due to the increase in total energy production outweighing the small increase in energy production from renewable sources.

Theme: Agriculture
Indicator title: Arable land per capita

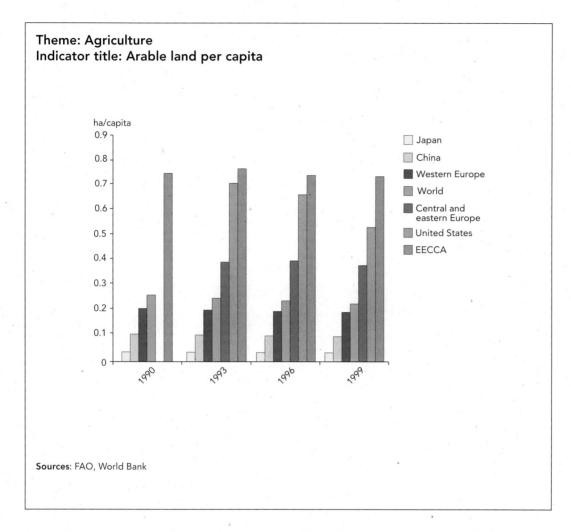

ha/capita

Legend:
- Japan
- China
- Western Europe
- World
- Central and eastern Europe
- United States
- EECCA

Sources: FAO, World Bank

Arable land per capita declined throughout the 1990s, for the world in general as well as for the selected regions and countries. This is the result of an increasing population combined with a slightly declining area of arable land. The only exception is China where the arable land remained almost unchanged throughout the reference period (0.5 % increase), although this was outweighed by a 10 % increase in population.

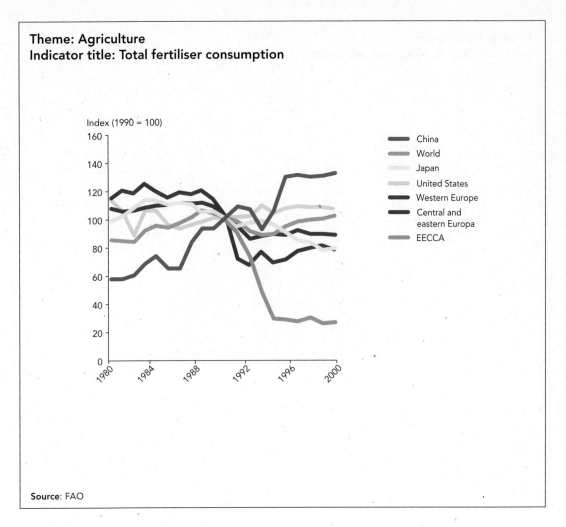

Theme: Agriculture
Indicator title: Total fertiliser consumption

Index (1990 = 100)

Legend:
- China
- World
- Japan
- United States
- Western Europe
- Central and eastern Europa
- EECCA

Source: FAO

Over the period 1980–99, world fertiliser consumption grew by 20 %. Fertiliser consumption in western Europe, central and eastern Europe, and Japan rose slowly up to 1987–88; it then started to decline regularly through the 1990s. The United States, although recording the highest consumption, reports a declining trend since the beginning of the 1980s. In China, the development has been the opposite as consumption has more than doubled during the period. In 1999 more than a quarter of the world's consumption was in China, and since 1987 its consumption has constantly exceeded that of western Europe. This development mirrors the fact that China is in the process of increasing its agricultural production and productivity, whereas western Europe, the United States and Japan are reducing the environmental impacts of a highly productive agricultural sector.

Theme: Forestry
Indicator title: Felling as a percentage of net annual increment

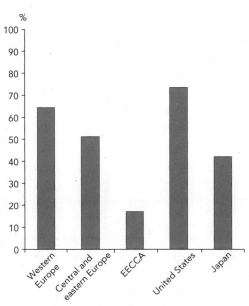

Notes: No data available for Greece, Luxembourg, Andorra, Monaco, San Marino, Romania, Malta, Bosnia-Herzegovina, Kyrgyzstan, Uzbekistan.

Definitions: Annual felling is the average annual standing volume of all trees, living or dead, felled during the given reference period, including the volume of trees or parts of trees that are not removed from the forest, other wooded land or other felling site. The net annual increment (NAI) is defined as the average annual volume over the given reference period of gross increment less that of natural losses on all trees.

Sources: UNECE/FAO, 2000

Annual felling is lower than the net annual increment in all the regions and countries considered. Eastern Europe, the Caucasus and central Asia (EECCA) has the lowest rate of utilisation of forest resources, with only 17 % of their net annual increment utilised, in line with the major contributor, the Russian Federation, while the United States presents a rate of utilisation of more than 70 %.

Theme: Fisheries
Indicator title: Total fish landings as share of world total

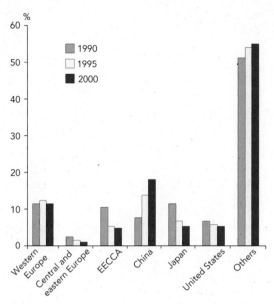

Notes: Description of data: nominal catch of fish, crustaceans and molluscs, the production of other aquatic animals, residues and plants and catches of aquatic mammals, taken for commercial, industrial, recreational and subsistence purposes from inland, brackish and marine waters. The harvest from mariculture, aquaculture and other kinds of fish farming is excluded. Data include all quantities caught and landed for both food and feed purposes but exclude discards. Catches of fish, crustaceans and molluscs are expressed in live weight, i.e. the nominal weight of the aquatic organisms at the time of capture. The harvest of aquatic plants is given in wet weight. Whales, seals and crocodiles are excluded.

Source: FAO

Since 1988 total world landings have increased by 7 %. The contribution to world landings of the groups and countries considered has, however, decreased by 4 % over the period 1990–2000, from 49 % in 1990 to 45 % in 2000. China, whose landings increased to almost three times their original figure over the period, has the highest share with 18 %. Landings remained constant in western Europe over the last decade, while they decreased by more than 60 % in central and eastern Europe and Japan, by 55 % in eastern Europe, the Caucasus and central Asia (EECCA) and by 16 % in the United States.

Theme: Transport
Indicator title: Passenger transport by mode

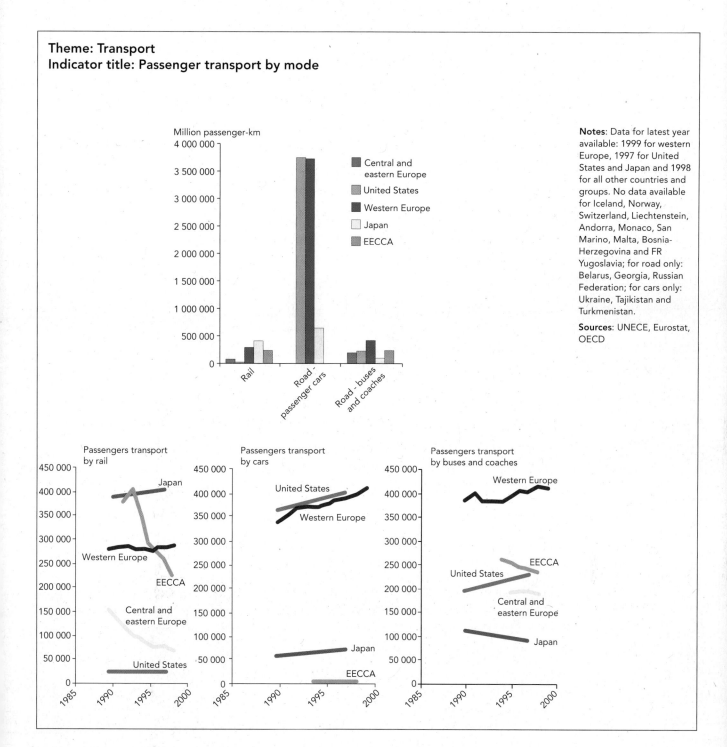

Million passenger-km

Central and eastern Europe
United States
Western Europe
Japan
EECCA

Passengers transport by rail

Passengers transport by cars

Passengers transport by buses and coaches

Notes: Data for latest year available: 1999 for western Europe, 1997 for United States and Japan and 1998 for all other countries and groups. No data available for Iceland, Norway, Switzerland, Liechtenstein, Andorra, Monaco, San Marino, Malta, Bosnia-Herzegovina and FR Yugoslavia; for road only: Belarus, Georgia, Russian Federation; for cars only: Ukraine, Tajikistan and Turkmenistan.

Sources: UNECE, Eurostat, OECD

In the last decade, in western Europe, the United States and, to a lesser degree, in Japan passenger transport by rail and road increased, while in central and eastern Europe, as well as in eastern Europe, the Caucasus and central Asia (EECCA), it decreased. Over the period 1990–98 (1997 for Japan and the United States) rail passenger transport grew by 3 %, 4 % and 5 % in western Europe, Japan and the United States, respectively. In EECCA (since 1992) it decreased by 39 %, and in central and eastern Europe by 52 %.

In EECCA a similar decrease, 42 %, was observed in passenger transport by car. Western Europe saw the highest increase in passenger transport by car since 1990, with 17 %, followed by Japan (15 %) and the United States (9 %). The trend in western Europe is partly explained by increased transport demand following urban sprawl, higher car ownership, prioritisation of investments in roads and low costs of using private transport compared with public transport. The United States has increased the share of public transport in total travel, with bus transport growing by 17 %, compared with only 7 % in western Europe. In Japan public transport use decreased by 16 %. In EECCA and central and eastern Europe transport by bus and coach decreased by 11 % and 2 %, respectively.

Theme: Transport
Indicator title: Passenger cars per 1 000 persons

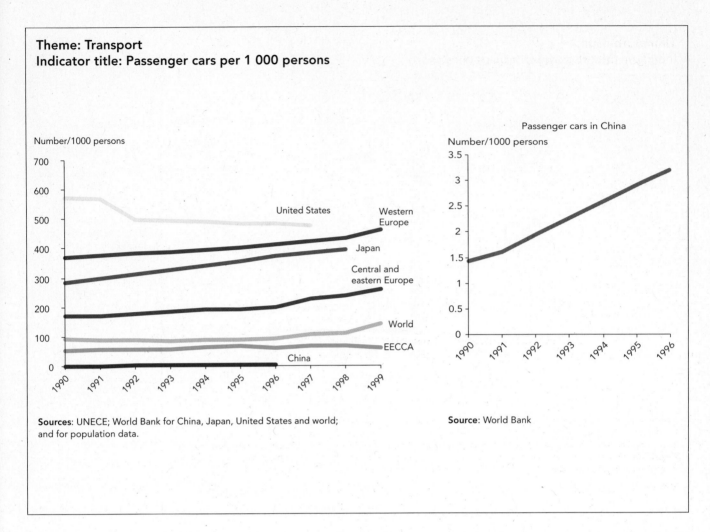

Number/1000 persons

Passenger cars in China
Number/1000 persons

Sources: UNECE; World Bank for China, Japan, United States and world; and for population data.

Source: World Bank

Starting from significantly different levels in 1990, western Europe, Japan and the United States are, in 1999, converging to a similar level of car ownership. During the period 1990–97, the number of cars per thousand people increased in western Europe and Japan by 14 % and 36 %, respectively, while it declined in the United States by 17 %. Although pickups, vans, sport utility vehicles and other light trucks are increasingly replacing ordinary passenger cars in the United States, the numbers of such vehicles were excluded in the total number of cars. Adding this group of trucks increases the total from 478 to 755 cars per thousand people in 1997. The figures for the United States could therefore be misleading.

An increasing trend is pronounced in central and eastern Europe with a growth of 53 % since 1990, at lower levels than Japan, western Europe and the United States, but higher than the world average. Below the world average are eastern Europe, the Caucasus and central Asia (EECCA) and China. EECCA saw an increase of 15 % throughout the 1990s.

World average car ownership was stable. In 1997, total car ownership worldwide represented approximately a quarter of the total for western Europe. And despite the more than doubling of car ownership in China between 1990 and 1996, the level is still less than 1 % of the total for western Europe in 1996. The trend is expected to continue as a result of increasing income levels.

Theme: Tourism
Indicator title: Number of tourist arrivals

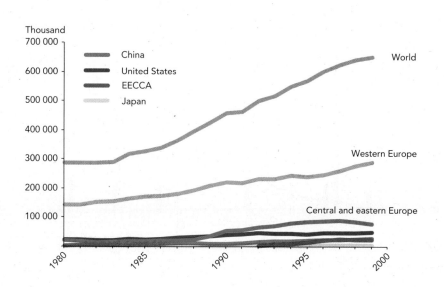

Thousand

- China
- United States
- EECCA
- Japan

World

Western Europe

Central and eastern Europe

700 000
600 000
500 000
400 000
300 000
200 000
100 000

1980   1985   1990   1995   2000

Notes: A tourist is an overnight visitor, i.e. a visitor who stays at least one night in a collective or private accommodation in the place visited. Arrivals refer to actual arrivals and not to the number of people travelling: one person visiting a country several times during the year is counted each time as a new arrival. The term 'visitor' describes 'any person travelling to a place other than that of his/her usual environment for less than 12 months and whose main purpose of visit is other than the exercise of an activity remunerated from within the place visited'.

Source: WTO

Western Europe contributed the largest share of the world's total tourist arrivals in 1999 (44 %), compared with12 % from central and eastern Europe and 4 % from eastern Europe, the Caucasus and central Asia (EECCA). The United States, China and Japan contributed 7 %, 4 % and 1 % of arrivals, respectively. Between 1985 and 1999, the number of tourist arrivals worldwide increased tremendously. In 1998 France, Italy and Spain were at the top of the list of the 40 most popular tourist destinations in terms of international arrivals. Also included in the list were the United States, China and Japan.

The trends in western Europe and the United States follow the worldwide growth pattern, with the number of tourist arrivals at least doubling between 1980 and 1999. Over the same period arrivals in China increased by almost eight times the original figure, and in Japan by four times. Compared with 1990, arrivals in central and eastern Europe increased by 45 % and, compared with 1992, arrivals in EECCA increased by more than four times the original figure.

International tourism was projected to grow at an annual average rate of 4.3 % through to the year 2020. However, growth in the normally buoyant tourism sector came to a halt in 2001 and international arrivals declined by 1.3 % (this may be attributed to the September 11 event).

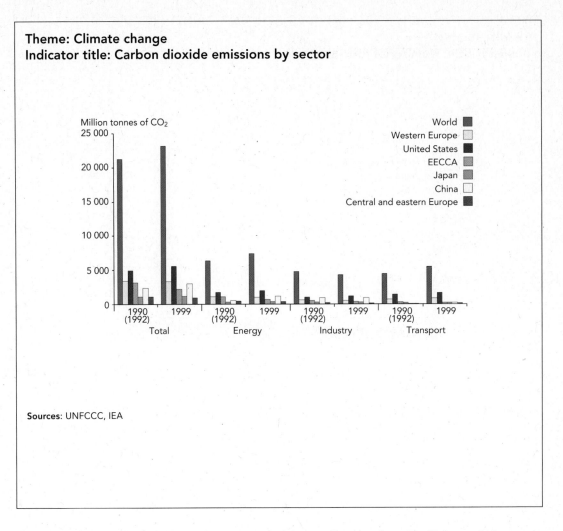

Theme: Climate change
Indicator title: Carbon dioxide emissions by sector

Sources: UNFCCC, IEA

Total carbon dioxide (CO_2) emissions decreased by 1.4 % in western Europe between 1990 and 1999; between 1992 and 1999 emissions decreased by 10 % in central and eastern Europe and by 29 % in eastern Europe, the Caucasus and central Asia (EECCA). Overall world emissions increased by 9 %. The United States, Japan and China increased their emissions by 13 %, 9 % and 25 %, respectively.

While CO_2 emissions from the industry and energy sectors in western, central and eastern Europe decreased, the emissions from transport increased by almost 23 % in western Europe and by 27 % in central and eastern Europe. EECCA was the only region where CO_2 emissions from the transport sector decreased (by 34 %). The transport sector accounted for the large increases in the United States, Japan and worldwide.

In China on the other hand, the biggest increase in emissions came from energy industries: 108 %. CO_2 emissions from transport in China increased by 75 %.

Theme: Air Pollution
Indicator title: Sulphur dioxide emissions

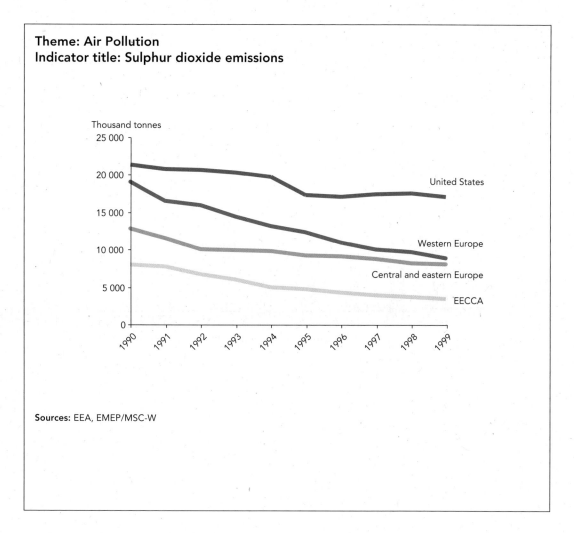

Thousand tonnes

United States

Western Europe

Central and eastern Europe

EECCA

Sources: EEA, EMEP/MSC-W

Taken as a whole, as well as individually, the 21 Parties to the 1985 Sulphur protocol have reached their target by reducing 1980 sulphur emissions by at least 30 %. The 1994 Oslo protocol sets differentiated emission reduction obligations for the Parties, by the years 2005 and 2010. In all groups and countries considered the trend is decreasing. In western Europe and in eastern Europe, the Caucasus and central Asia (EECCA) emissions decreased by 53 % and 56 %, respectively, over the period 1990–99. In central and eastern Europe they decreased by 37 %, and in the United States by only 20 %. In transition economies, the reduction of air pollutants is also a result of economic restructuring.

Theme: Air pollution
Indicator title: Emissions of nitrogen oxides

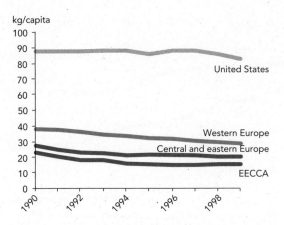

Sources: EEA, EMEP/MSC-W, World Bank

Although the per capita emissions of the United States decreased by 6 % over the period 1990–99, it has the highest emissions of nitrogen oxides (NO_x) in total as well as per capita. The United States is also the only country with a positive trend in total emissions, with an increase of 5 % over the period 1990–99.

Western Europe, central and eastern Europe, and eastern Europe, the Caucasus and central Asia (EECCA), all decreased their NO_x emissions. Per capita, the reductions of emissions were 26 %, 29 % and 37 %, respectively.

Theme: Stratospheric ozone depletion
Indicator title: Production and consumption of selected ozone-depleting substances

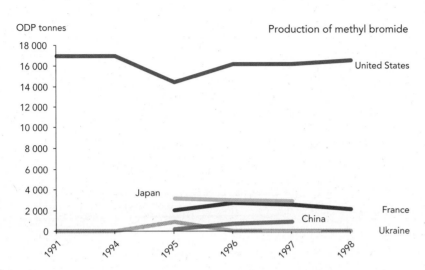

ODP tonnes   Production of methyl bromide

18 000
16 000   United States
14 000
12 000
10 000
8 000
6 000
4 000
2 000   Japan   France
0   China   Ukraine

1991   1994   1995   1996   1997   1998

Notes: Data available only for France, Romania, Ukraine, Japan, China, United States. Romania is not shown in the graph because of low values.

Source: UNEP Ozone Secretariat

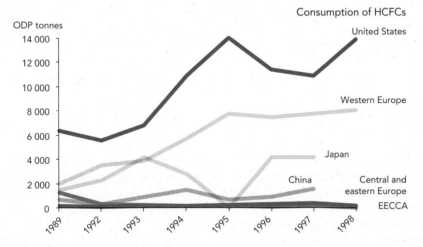

                                          Consumption of HCFCs
ODP tonnes   United States
14 000
12 000
10 000
8 000   Western Europe
6 000
4 000   Japan
2 000   China   Central and
                                                eastern Europe
0   EECCA

1989   1992   1993   1994   1995   1996   1997   1998

Notes: No data available for Andorra, San Marino, Albania, Armenia, Kazakhstan, Kyrgyzstan, Tajikistan.

Sources: UNEP Ozone Secretariat

In developed countries, the production of ozone-depleting substances (ODS) has been phased out in accordance with the requirements of the Montreal protocol, except for methyl bromide. Between 1991 and 1998, France and the United States reduced production of methyl bromide by 17 % and 3 %, respectively. Japan reduced production by 14 % between 1991 and 1997. On the other hand China increased its consumption by 265 % between 1995 and 1997.

Developing countries, which account for 83 % of the remaining global chlorofluorocarbon (CFC) consumption, are allowed to extend the period to phase out the production of ozone-depleting substances. China has seen a big increase in the production and consumption of halons in recent years.

Hydrochlorofluorocarbons (HCFCs) have replaced CFCs in most developed countries.

Theme: Waste generation and management
Indicator title: Municipal waste generation

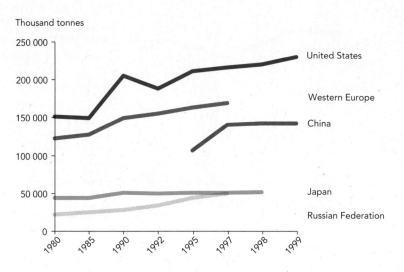

Thousand tonnes

Note: Western Europe includes EU-15 (aggregate value), Norway and Switzerland.

Sources: National sources, OECD

Western Europe, the United States and the Russian Federation show an increasing trend in the generation of municipal waste. For China and Japan a more stable trend is observed. Between 1980 and 1997 western Europe saw an increase of 38 % in generation of municipal waste, the United States 43 % and the Russian Federation 127 %. Over the same period Japan increased its municipal waste production by only 16 %.

One of the main driving forces for this trend in all countries is the general growth of consumption. The level of municipal waste production appears to be correlated with the level of industrialisation and the level of income. In western European countries and Japan the daily generation of municipal waste by one person is approximately of 1.1–1.2 kg, whereas in the United States it is almost equal to 2 kg.

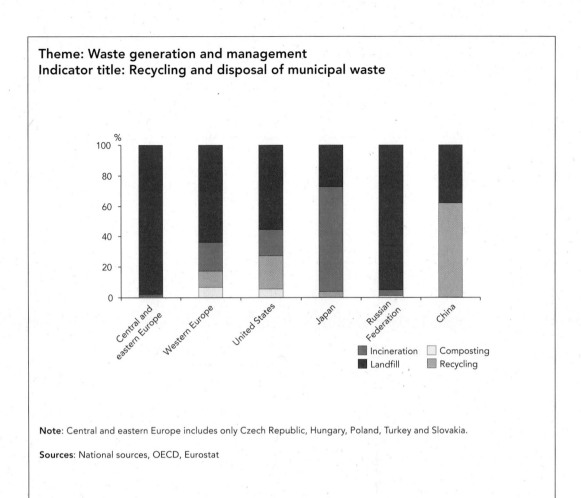

Theme: Waste generation and management
Indicator title: Recycling and disposal of municipal waste

Legend: Incineration · Landfill · Composting · Recycling

Note: Central and eastern Europe includes only Czech Republic, Hungary, Poland, Turkey and Slovakia.

Sources: National sources, OECD, Eurostat

The only method of waste disposal in central and eastern Europe, as well as in the Russian Federation, is landfill. In western Europe landfill still represents 63 % of waste management methods, followed by incineration (18 %).

Compared to the United States (which also relies predominantly on landfill in waste management), western Europe recycles and composts less (17 % in western Europe against 27 % in the United States). Though in many EU countries the rate of reuse of waste is higher than in the United States, the aggregated figure remains low because main waste generators (Italy, the United Kingdom and France — Germany is an exception) recycle and compost less than 10 % of the total amount of waste.

In Japan, the most common method of waste disposal is incineration (76 %). China has reported 62 % of its municipal solid waste treated in 1999, but ways of treatment have not been specified.

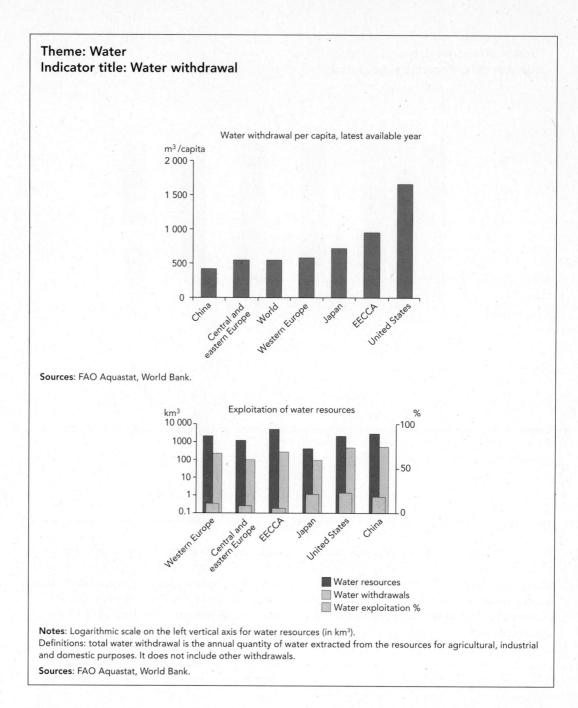

Theme: Water
Indicator title: Water withdrawal

Water withdrawal per capita, latest available year

Sources: FAO Aquastat, World Bank.

Exploitation of water resources

- Water resources
- Water withdrawals
- Water exploitation %

Notes: Logarithmic scale on the left vertical axis for water resources (in km³).
Definitions: total water withdrawal is the annual quantity of water extracted from the resources for agricultural, industrial and domestic purposes. It does not include other withdrawals.

Sources: FAO Aquastat, World Bank.

Water withdrawal per capita in western, central and eastern Europe is comparable to the world average. The United States has the highest level of water withdrawals per capita, equal to almost three times the global average.

Although eastern Europe, the Caucasus and central Asia (EECCA) has a high level of water withdrawals, it also has the lowest water exploitation percentage (5 %) of all regions and countries considered, due to the large water resources available. Western Europe and central and eastern Europe have comparable water exploitation levels (8 % and 11 %, respectively), while China, Japan and the United States have water exploitation percentages of 19 %, 21 % and 23 %, respectively.